A Reference Index to Twelve Thousand Spanish American Authors

Publications of the Inter-American Bibliographical and Library Association

SERIES I

Vol. 1. Rubio, D. & M. C. Sullivan. A Glossary of Technical Library and Allied Terms in Spanish and English.

Vol. 2. Wilgus, A. Curtis. Histories and Historians of Hispanic America.

Vol. 3. Gosnell, Charles F. Spanish Personal Names.

Vol. 4. Hill, Roscoe R. The National Archives of Latin America. (This volume will be distributed about July 1st for the year 1938-39).

Vol. 5. Boggs, Ralph S. Bibliography of Spanish American Folklore. (This volume will be distributed to members for the year 1939-40).

SERIES II

Vol. 1. Proceedings of the First Convention of the Inter-American Bibliographical and Library Association.

Vol. 2. Proceedings of the Second Convention of the Inter-American Bibliographical and Library Association. In progress.
(Series II is limited to the "Proceedings" of the annual convention).

SERIES III

Vol. 1. Grismer, Raymond L. A Reference Index to Twelve Thousand Spanish American Authors.
(Spanish ed.: Índice de Doce Mil Autores Hispanoamericanos)

INTER-AMERICAN BIBLIOGRAPHICAL AND LIBRARY
Series III   ASSOCIATION PUBLICATIONS   Volume 1

A Reference Index to Twelve Thousand Spanish American Authors

A Guide to the Literature of Spanish America

By

RAYMOND L. GRISMER, PH.D.
University of Minnesota

THE H. W. WILSON COMPANY
NEW YORK — NINETEEN HUNDRED THIRTY-NINE

Published July 1939

Printed in the United States of America

To "BUSTER"

an "A" student, a good musician
and a fine son.

FOREWORD

by

L. S. ROWE, PH.D., LL.D.
Director General of the Pan American Union

A sign of our times, which should be a source of gratification to everyone concerned with international relations, is the manifest desire of the peoples of the Western Hemisphere to do away with the spiritual isolation in which we have lived for so long. This barrier, which can keep nations apart in a more real sense than conflicting trade interests, or ancestral economic rivalries and language differences, is one that will easily give way when the people of the Americas are determined to know each other better and to profit by one another's experience and outlook on life. An exchange of material goods, essential though it is to inter-American relations, is not superior in value to an effective give and take in the realm of the spirit.

A tradition of friendship between the most representative of our men was, fortunately, established in the formative period of these republics. Among the links forged in those early years to unite North and South America it is inspiring to remember the friendships between the great Cuban poet José María de Heredia and our own William Cullen Bryant; the Argentine poet José Antonio Miralla and Henry Wadsworth Longfellow; José Martí, the Cuban liberator, and Charles A. Dana; Domingo Faustino Sarmiento, educator and President of Argentina, and our Horace Mann.

Poets, writers, artists and educators have slowly but surely laid down the cultural foundations on which our relations as peoples must ultimately rest. They traditionally make good neighbors, and so it seems logical to think that their work should be considered as one of the cornerstones of our fellowship of nations.

As this deep-felt conviction of our present leaders becomes more and more a feeling shared by the public in general, it is not too optimistic to expect that there will be increasing eagerness on the part of students, librarians, and university people in general to become acquainted with the work of Latin American writers. Anticipating this need, the present Index is a welcome addition to the collection of tools placed at the disposal of persons interested in the problem of gaining an insight into the psychology, customs, and ideals of our Latin American neighbors through the work of the finest exponents of their culture.

The work has been done by numerous paid and voluntary assistants under the direction of the compiler who has tried to check every item personally. This proved impossible in the case of certain books submitted by other libraries during his absence in South America inasmuch as these books had to be returned within a brief space of time.

We have listed the writers alphabetically by their one or several surnames and then by their given names. For instance, *Fernández, José* will precede *Fernández A., José* and *Fernández Coria, José* and *Fernández de Castro, José,* etc. Similarly, *Fernández y González, José* will precede *Fernández y González, Manuel.*

Whenever the author's pseudonym is known, he is listed under both his real name and his pseudonym. For instance, the entries "Gabriela Mistral" and "Mistral, Gabriela" both read "(*pseud.*) *see* Godoy Alcayaza, Lucila."

All available dates of birth and death have been carefully included. One or both dates have been given for more than three thousand writers.

A list of the works consulted has been placed at the end of the PREFACE. A similar list giving the abbreviations used and the works to which they refer has been placed, for the sake of greatest convenience, at the end of the book.

Arabic numerals refer to pages, large Roman numerals to volumes and small Roman numerals to introductory pages so numbered in the works consulted.

Spanish authors have been included if they were closely associated with Spanish America. For instance, Ercilla y Zúñiga is included because his *Araucana* is as closely associated with Chilean literature as with Spanish.

At the end of the reference to an author's life and works we have placed the name of the country either in which he was born or with which he was closely associated. Such identification has been found impossible when we had insufficient evidence regarding the author, and in the cases of authors who were born in one country and kept moving from one to another.

We wish to thank Dr. L. S. Rowe, Director General of the Pan American Union, for contributing the *Foreword* to this volume. We feel gratified that our *Index* has been found worthy of such recognition.

We have been particularly fortunate to enlist the active interest and generous aid of Mrs. Concha Romero James, Chief of the Division of Intellectual Cooperation of the Pan American Union, and Dr. Charles E. Babcock of the same institution. The library of the Pan American Union has been most helpful in lending us books which were not available in the University of Minnesota library. The compiler wishes to acknowledge also valuable suggestions which he received from Dr. Frank K. Walter, Head Librarian of the University of Minnesota.

The scope of this work easily indicates that a great deal of assistance was required to complete it. Much of the labor of collecting and filing items was done by workers on WPA Official Project 665-71-3-69, by Federal Aid students, and by friends. In the first group, supplied by WPA, are Miss Ruth E. Cox, forewoman, Miss Mary V. Andrews, and Miss Elsie Ziebarth. To all of these we express our appreciation for the many hours spent preparing this INDEX.

Not less valuable was the checking done by Miss Clara Ostrowsky, Miss Helen Hayward, Miss Dorothea Jabusch, Miss Helen Carlson, Mrs. Helyne Franklin, Miss Mary Lynn Austin, and Lloyd Goldich, students of the University, whose education is being partially financed by Federal Aid.

I am also deeply grateful to Miss Mary B. MacDonald, Miss Edith Grace Lawson, Miss Helen M. Williams, Mr. Irving Spiegel and others, who have voluntarily assisted me in this undertaking.

RAYMOND L. GRISMER

University of Minnesota
1939

Bibliography of Books on Spanish-American Literature
Consulted for This Index

Aita, Antonio
La literatura argentina contemporánea, (1900-1930). Buenos Aires, 1931. (LAC)

Alarcón, Abel
"La literatura boliviana, 1545-1916" in *Revue Hispanique* 41, 1917, pp. 563-633. (LB)

Amézaga, Carlos G.
Poetas mexicanos. Buenos Aires, P.E. Coní e hijos, 1896. (PoM)

Albir, Francisco José
"Writers of Honduras" in *Bulletin of the Pan American Union* 49, 1919, pp. 187-90. (WH)

Amunátegui Solar, Domingo
Historia de Chile. Santiago, Balcells y Cía., 1925. (HC)

Antología de poetas modernos de México. México, Tip. Murguía, 1920. (APMM)

Arias, Augusto
Panorama de la literatura ecuatoriana. Quito, Ecuador, 1936. (PLE)

Artigas, Miguel
Catálogo general de la librería española e hispanoamericana. Madrid-Barcelona, Cámaras Oficiales del Libro, 1932. 3 vols. (not finished.) (CG)

Artucio Ferreira, Antonia
Parnaso uruguayo, (1905-1922). Barcelona, Edit. Maucci, s. a. (PU)

Asenjo, Conrado
Quién es quién en Puerto Rico. San Juan, P.R., Real Hermanos Inc., 1st edit., 1933-1934; 2d edit., 1936-1937. (QPR 1, 2)

Avellaneda, Nicolás
Grandes escritores argentinos. Buenos Aires, El Ateneo, 1927-1928 (GEA)

Báez, Paulino G.
Poetas jóvenes cubanos. Barcelona, Edit. Maucci, 1922. (PJC)

Barbagaleta, Hugo D., and Ventura García Calderón
"La literatura uruguaya, 1757-1917" in *Revue Hispanique* 40, 1917, pp. 415-542. (LUr)

Bazil, Osvaldo
Parnaso antillano. Barcelona, Edit. Maucci, 1916. (PA)

Parnaso dominicano. Barcelona, Edit. Maucci, 1915. (PD)

Biografías de literatos nacionales. Guatemala, Tip. "La Unión", 1889. (BLN)

Blanco Meaño, Luis F.
Parnaso boliviano. Barcelona, Edit. Maucci, s.a. (PB)

Bolívar Coronado, Rafael
Parnaso costarricense. Barcelona, Edit. Maucci, 1921. (PC)

Brenes-Mesén, Roberto
Crítica americana. San José de Costa Rica, Ediciones del Convivio, 1936. (CrA)

Brissa, José
Parnaso ecuatoriano. Barcelona, Edit. Maucci, s.a. (PE)

Brughetti, Romualdo
18 Poetas del Uruguay. Montevideo-Buenos Aires, Sociedad Amigos del Libro Rioplatense, 1937. (PoU)

Caro Grau, Francisco
Parnaso colombiano. Barcelona, Edit. Maucci, 1920. (PCo)

Coester, Alfred
A Tentative Bibliography of the Belles-Lettres of the Argentine Republic. Cambridge, Harvard University Press, 1933. (A)

A Tentative Bibliography of the Belles-Lettres of Uruguayan Literature. Cambridge, Harvard University Press, 1931. (U)

Historia literaria de la América Española. Madrid, Lib. y Casa Edit. Hernando, 1929. (CHL)

Literary History of Spanish America. New York, Macmillan Co., 1916. (CLH)

Craig, G. Dundas
The Modernist Trend in Spanish-American Poetry. Berkeley, University of California Press, 1934. (MSAP)

Cuesta, Jorge
Antología de la poesía mexicana moderna. México, 1928. (PMM)

Daireaux, Max
Panorama de la littérature hispano-américaine. Paris, Editions KRA, 1930. (PLHA)

De Vitis, Michael Angelo
Florilegio del parnaso americano. Barcelona, Edit. Maucci, 1927. (FPA)
Parnaso paraguayo. Barcelona, Edit. Maucci, s.a. (PPa)

Díaz Arrieta, Hernán
Las cien mejores poesías chilenas. Santiago de Chile, Editorial Zig-Zag, s.a. (CMPC)

Dobles Segreda, Luis
Índice bibliográfico de Costa Rica. San José, Imp. Lehmann, 1930. Vol. 4. (IBCR)

Donoso, Armando
La otra América. Madrid, Talleres Calpe, 1925. (OA)
Los nuevos. La joven literatura chilena. Valencia, F. Sempere y Compañía, 1910. (N)

Doyle, Henry Grattan
A Tentative Bibliography of the Belles-Lettres of the Republics of Central America. Cambridge, Harvard University Press, 1935. (CA)
A Tentative Bibliography of the Belles-Lettres of Panama. Cambridge, Harvard University Press, 1934. (Pan)

Durón, Rómulo E.
Honduras literaria. Tegucigalpa, Tipografía Nacional, 1896-1899. 2 vols. (HL)

Erazo, Salvador L.
Parnaso salvadoreño. Barcelona, Edit. Maucci, s.a. (PS)

Esteva, Adalberto A. and José Pablo Rivas
Parnaso mexicano. Barcelona, Edit. Maucci, s.a. 2 vols. (PMe)

Estrada, Genaro
Poetas nuevos de México. México, Porrúa Hnos, 1916. (PNM)

Ford, Jeremiah D.M., and Maxwell I. Raphael
A Bibliography of Cuban Belles-Lettres. Cambridge, Harvard University Press, 1933. (Cu)

García Calderón, Ventura
"La literatura peruana, 1535-1914" in *Revue Hispanique* 31, 1914, pp. 305-91. (LP)
Parnaso peruano. Barcelona, Edit. Maucci, s.a. (PPe)
Semblanzas de América. Madrid, Cervantes, 1920? (SA)

García Godoy, Federico
La literatura americana de nuestros días. Madrid, Sociedad Española de Librería, s.a. (LAND)
"La literatura dominicana" in *Revue Hispanique* 37, 1916, pp. 61-104. (LD)

García Prada, Carlos
Antología de líricos colombianos. Bogotá, Imprenta Nacional, 1936. 2 vols. (ALC)

García Samudio, Nicolás
"Columbian Literature" in *Bulletin of the Pan American Union* 53, 1921, pp. 258-76. (CoL)

García Velloso, Enrique
Historia de la literatura argentina. Buenos Aires, Ángel Estrada y Cía., s.a. (HLA)

Ghiraldo, Alberto
Antología americana. Madrid, Renacimiento, Vol. II. 1923. (AA)

Goldberg, Isaac
Studies in Spanish-American Literature. New York, Brentano, 1920. (SAL)

Gómez Restrepo, Antonio
"La literatura colombiana" in *Revue Hispanique* 43, 1918, pp. 79-204. (LC)

González Peña, Carlos
Historia de la literatura mexicana. México, 1928. (HLM)

Grismer, Raymond L.
A Bibliography of Articles and Essays on the Literatures of Spain and Spanish America. Minneapolis, Perine Book Co., 1935. (G)

Grismer, Raymond L., Joseph E. Lepine, and Richard H. Olmsted
A Bibliography of Articles on Spanish Literature. Minneapolis, Burgess Publishing Co., 1933. (GLO)

Guillén, Alberto
Breve antología peruana. Santiago de Chile, Nascimiento, 1930. (BAP)

Hanke, Lewis
Handbook of Latin-American Studies. Cambridge, Harvard University Press, 1936. (LAS)

Holmes, Henry Alfred
Spanish America in Song and Story. New York, Henry Holt, 1932. (SASS)

Iguíñiz, Juan B.
Bibliografía de novelistas mexicanos. México, 1926. (Ig)

Isaza, Emiliano
Antología colombiana. Paris, Bouret, 1911. 2 vols. (AC)

James, Concha Romero
An Annotated Bibliography of Latin American Literature. Washington, Pan American Union. (AB)

Jiménez, Juan Ramón
La poesía cubana en 1936. La Habana, Institución Hispanocubana de Cultura, 1937. (PoC)

Jiménez Rueda, Julio
Historia de la literatura mexicana. México, Ediciones Botas, 1934. (HLMex)

Korsí, Demetrio
Antología de Panamá. Barcelona, Edit. Maucci, 1926. (AP)

Laverde Amaya, Isidoro
Bibliografía colombiana. Bogotá, Colombia, Imprenta y Librería de Medardo Rivas, 1895. (BC)

Leavitt, Sturgis E.
A Tentative Bibliography of Bolivian Literature. Cambridge, Harvard University Press, 1933. (B)
A Tentative Bibliography of Peruvian Literature. Cambridge, Harvard University Press, 1932. (P)
"Chilean Literature" in *Hispanic American Historical Review* 5, 1922, pp. 116-43, 274-97, 516-34, 760-76. (CL)
"Uruguayan Literature" in *Hispania* (Calif.) 5, 1922, pp. 121-32, 186-96. (UL)

Leavitt, Sturgis E., and Carlos García-Prada
A Tentative Bibliography of Colombian Literature. Cambridge, Harvard University Press, 1934. (Co)

Lee, Muna
"Contemporary Spanish-American Poetry" in *North American Review* 219, 1924, pp. 687-98. (CP)

Luisi, Luisa
"The Literature of Uruguay" in *Bulletin of the Pan American Union* 64, July-December 1930, pp. 655-95. (LU)

Marinello, Juan
Literatura hispanoamericana. México, Ediciones de la Universidad Nacional, 1937. (LH)

Martin, Percy A.
Who's Who in Latin America. Palo Alto, Stanford University Press, 1935. (WLA)

Medina, José Toribio
Biblioteca hispano-chilena. Santiago de Chile, Imp. de J. T. Medina, 1897-8-9. 3 vols. (BHC)

Menéndez y Pelayo, Marcelino
Historia de la poesía hispano-americana. Madrid, Librería General de Victoriano Suárez, 1911-1913. 2 vols. (HPHA)

Miranda S., Estela
Algunas poetisas de Chile y Uruguay. Santiago de Chile, Editorial Nascimiento, 1937. (PCU)

Monterde, Francisco
Bibliografía del teatro en México. México, Imp. de la Secretaría de Relaciones Exteriores, 1933. (TM)

Morales, Ernesto
El sentimiento popular en la literatura argentina. Buenos Aires, Pedro Garúa, 1926. (SPLA)

Moses, Bernard
Spanish Colonial Literature in South America. New York, Hispanic Society of America, 1922. (SCL)

Noé, Julio
Antología de la poesía argentina moderna, (1900-1925). Buenos Aires, "Nosotros," 1926. (APAM)

Onís y Sánchez, Federico de
Antología de la poesía española e hispanoamericana, 1882-1932. Madrid, Revista de Filología Española, 1934. (APEH)

Otero Muñoz, Gustavo
Resumen de historia de la literatura colombiana, 1538-1819. Bogotá, Editorial ABC, 1937. (RHLC)

Ortiz, Alberto
Parnaso nicaragüense. Barcelona, Edit. Maucci, s.a. (PN)

Oviedo Reyes, I. Augusto
Nicaragua lírica. Santiago de Chile, Editorial Nascimiento, 1937. (NL)

Parker, William B.
Argentines of Today. New York, Hispanic Society of America, 2d ed. 1920. (AT)
Bolivians of Today. New York, Hispanic Society of America, 2d ed. 1922. (BT)
Cubans of Today. New York, Putnam, 1919. (CT)
Paraguayans of Today. New York, Hispanic Society of America, 1921. (PT)
Uruguayans of Today. New York, Hispanic Society of America, 1921. (UT)

Pedreira, Antonio S.
Bibliografía puertorriqueña, 1493-1930. Madrid, Hernando, 1932. (BP)

Pedro, Valentín
Nuevo parnaso argentino. Barcelona, Edit. Maucci, s.a. (NPA)

Perrier, José Luis
Bibliografía dramática cubana. New York, Phos Press, 1926. (BDC)

Picón-Febres, Gonzalo
La literatura venezolana en el siglo diez y nueve. Caracas, Imp. "El Cojo", 1906. (LV)

Pimentel, Francisco
Historia crítica de la poesía en México. México, Secretaría de Fomento, 1892. (HPM)

Porta Mencos, H.
Parnaso guatemalteco. Barcelona, Edit. Maucci, 1931. (PG)

Puig, Juan de la C.
Antología de poetas argentinos. Buenos Aires, Martín Biedma é hijo, 1910. (APA)

Raphael, Maxwell I., and J. D. M. Ford
A Tentative Bibliography of Paraguayan Literature. Cambridge, Harvard University Press, 1934. (Par)

Ratcliff, Dillwyn Fritschel
Venezuelan Prose Fiction. New York, Instituto de las Españas, 1933. (VPF)

Remos y Rubio, Juan J.
Resumen de historia de la literatura cubana. Habana, Tipos Molina y Cía., 1930. (RLC)

Reyles, Carlos
Historia sintética de la literatura uruguaya. Montevideo, Edit. A. Vila, 1931. 3 vols. (HSLU)

Riva Abreu, Valentín
Parnaso cubano. Barcelona, Edit. Maucci, 1926. (PCu)

Rivera, Guillermo
A Tentative Bibliography of the Belles-Lettres of Ecuador. Cambridge, Harvard University Press, 1934. (E)
A Tentative Bibliography of the Belles-Lettres of Porto [sic] *Rico.* Cambridge, Harvard University Press, 1931. (PR)

Rojas, Ricardo
La literatura argentina. Buenos Aires, Juan Roldán y Cía., 1924-1925. 8 vols. (LA)

Rosenberg, S. L. Millard, and Ernest H. Templin
A Brief Anthology of Mexican Prose. Palo Alto, Stanford University Press, 1928. (BAMP)

Roxlo, Carlos
Historia crítica de la literatura uruguaya. Montevideo, Edit. Barreiro y Ramos, 1912. 2 vols. (HCLU)

Salazar y Roig, Salvador
Historia de la literatura cubana. Habana, Imp. Avisador Comercial, 1929. (HLC)

Sánchez, José Rogerio
Autores españoles e hispano-americanos. Madrid, Perlado, Páez y Ca., 1911. (AEHA)

Sánchez, Luis Alberto
  Breve historia de la literatura americana.
  Santiago de Chile, Ediciones Ercilla, 1937.
  (BHLA)

Silva Arriagada, L. Ignacio
  La novela en Chile. Santiago de Chile, Imp.
  "Barcelona", 1910. (NC)

Solar, Hernán del
  Índice de la poesía chilena contemporánea.
  Santiago de Chile, Ediciones Ercilla, 1937.
  (PCC)

Sotela, Rogelio
  Escritores y poetas de Costa Rica. San José,
  Costa Rica, Imp. Lehmann, 1923. (EPCR)

Torres-Ríoseco, Arturo
  Bibliografía de la novela mejicana. Cam-
  bridge, Harvard University Press, 1933.
  (NM)

Torres-Ríoseco, Arturo, and Raúl Silva-Castro
  *Ensayo de bibliografía de la literatura chi-
  lena.* Cambridge, Harvard University
  Press, 1935. (C)

Torres-Ríoseco, Arturo, and Ralph E. Warner
  Bibliografía de la poesía mexicana. Cam-
  bridge, Harvard University Press, 1934.
  (PM)

Torres Rivera, Enrique
  Parnaso portorriqueño. Barcelona, Edit.
  Maucci, s.a. (PP)

Trelles, Carlos M.
  "Bibliografía de autores de la raza de color,
  de Cuba" in *Cuba Contemporánea* 43, 1927,
  pp. 30-78. (ARC)

Underwood, Edna Worthley
  Anthology of Mexican Poets. Portland,
  Maine, Mosher Press, 1932. (AMP)

Urbina, Luis G., Pedro Henríquez Ureña, and
  Nicolás Rangel
  Antología del centenario. México, Imp.
  Manuel León Sánchez, 1910. 2 vols. (ACe)

Uriarte, Ramón
  Galería poética centro-americana. Guate-
  mala, Tipografía "La Unión", 1888. 3 vols.
  (GPCA)

Velázquez Bringas, Esperanza, and Rafael
  Heliodoro Valle
  Índice de escritores. México, Herrero Her-
  manos Sucesores, 1928. (IE)

Vera M., Tobías
  Parnaso chileno. Barcelona, Edit. Maucci,
  s.a. (PCh)

Vergara y Vergara, José María
  Historia de la literatura en Nueva Granada.
  Bogotá, Edit. Minerva, 1931. 2 vols.
  (HLNG)

Wagner, Max Leopold
  Die spanisch-amerikanische Literatur. Leipzig-Berlin, B. G. Teubner, 1924. (WSAL)

Waxman, Samuel Montefiore
  *A Bibliography of the Belles-Lettres of
  Santo Domingo.* Cambridge, Harvard
  University Press, 1931. (SD)
  *A Bibliography of the Belles-Lettres of
  Venezuela.* Cambridge, Harvard Univer-
  sity Press, 1935. (V)

Zum Felde, Alberto
  Proceso intelectual del Uruguay. Monte-
  video, Imp. Nacional Colorada, 1930. 3 vols.
  (PIU)

Abbreviations of Names of Countries

Arg. ....Argentina
Bol. ....Bolivia
Chil. ....Chile
Col. ....Colombia
C. R. ....Costa Rica
Cu. ....Cuba
Dom. ....Dominican Republic
Ecua. ....Ecuador
Guat. ....Guatemala
Hond. ....Honduras
Mex. ....Mexico
Nicar. ....Nicaragua
Pan. ....Panama
Para. ....Paraguay
Per. ....Peru
Port. ....Portugal
P. R. ....Puerto Rico
Salv. ....El Salvador
Sp. ....Spain
Uru. ....Uruguay
Venez. ....Venezuela

A Reference Index to Twelve Thousand Spanish American Authors

A. Cu 7 *Cu.*
A.A. TM 393 *Mex.*
A.B.C. UL 122 *Uru.*
A.F. A 1 *Arg.*
A., J. Cu 7 *Cu.*
A., J.J. E 1 *Ecua.*
A., M.M. E 1 *Ecua.*
A.M.V. Par 5 *Para.*
A.P.N. TM 74 *Mex.*
A., R. de Cu 7 *Cu.*
A. y L. UL 122 *Uru.*
Abad, Diego José (1727-1779) ACe 662;
HLM 180; HLMex 80; HPHA I, 87;
HPM 288; PM 17 *Mex.*
Abad, José Ramón SD 3 *Dom.*
Abad Jáuregui, Josefina E 1 *Ecua.*
Abad Ramos, J. PR 45 *P.R.*
Abad y Queipo, Manuel HLMex 103 *Mex.*
Abades, Ramiro J. A 1, 79 *Arg.*
Abadia Méndez, Miguel (1867-   ) CG I,
3; WLA 1 *Col.*
Abadiano y Jaso, José Blas ACe 666 *Mex.*
Abalos, Arturo A 1, 79 *Arg.*
Abarca, José Mariano (1720-   ) TM 9
Mex.
Abarca Valda y Velásquez, Joseph Mariano
de PM 17 *Mex.*
Abarzúa F., Bernardino C 1, 25; NC 403
Chil.
Abarzuza, Buenaventura de BDC 1 *Cu.*
Abarzuza, Francisco de Cu 7 *Cu.*
"Abate Benigno, El" (*pseud.*) see Gómez
Ugarte, José
Abbad y Lasierra, íñigo PR 48 *P.R.*
Abdías Deheza, J. see Deheza, José Abdías
Abdón Calderón E 1 *Ecua.*
Abecía, Valentín B 1 *Bol.*
Abeillera Torres, R. A 1 *Arg.*
Abeledo, Amaranto Antonio (1886-) WLA
1 *Arg.*
Abellá, Juan Carlos (1893-   ) HSLU III,
pt 8, 13; IE 7; PIU III, 189; U 1 *Uru.*
Abella Caprile, Margarita (1901-   ) A 1;
APAM 435; LAC 148; NPA 225; PLHA
181; WLA 1 *Arg.*
Abella M., Temístocles Co 1 *Col.*
Abente y Haedo, Luis Par 5; PPa 181
Para.
Abente y Lago, Victorino A 1; Par 5 *Para.*
Abogado, Rafael (-1828) ACe 667 *Mex.*
Abrams, F. de J. V 24 *Venez.*
"Abrego" (*pseud.*) see Abreu, Héctor
Abreu, Héctor ("Abrego") Cu 7 *Cu.*
Abreu, Manuel Cu 7 *Cu.*
Abreu, Raúl LD 101; SD 3 *Dom.*
Abreu Gómez, Ermilo (Ermilio) (1894-   )
CG I, 10; G 354; HLM 516; IE 7; Ig 11;
NM 1, 6; TM 10, 511, 593; WLA 2 *Mex.*

Abreu Licairac, Rafael SD 3 *Dom.*
Abril, Xavier BAP 99 *Per.*
Abril de Vivero, Pablo BAP 51 *Per.*
Abril y Ostaló, Mariano (1862-   ) BP
498, 569; CG I, 10; PR 15, 31, 41; QPR
(1) 17; WLA 2 *P.R.*
"Abul Bagí" (*pseud.*) see Babuglia, Antonio
"Acaico, Ipandro" (*pseud.*) see Montes de
Oca y Obregón, Ignacio
Acal Ilisaliturri, Jesús PM 17; TM 11 *Mex.*
Acebal, Francisco A 1, 79; CG I, 11 *Arg.*
Acebal, Sergio PCu 7; PJC 22 *Cu.*
Aceña Durán, Ramón CA 60; CG I, 12
Guat.
Aceña I., Ramón CA 60 *Guat.*
Acereto Cortés, A. PM 17 *Mex.*
Acero, Julio CG I, 12; NM 6; PM 17 *Mex.*
Acevedo, Alfonso Co 1 *Col.*
Acevedo, Eduardo (1858-   ) HCLU I,
380; UT 1 *Uru.*
Acevedo, Jesús T. (1892-1918) HLM 513
Mex.
Acevedo, José L. E 2 *Ecua.*
Acevedo, Martín TM 11 *Mex.*
Acevedo, Napoleón V 25 *Venez.*
Acevedo, Pedro Tadeo ("Hugo Aníbal")
A 1, 78 *Arg.*
Acevedo, Rafael Alberto PM 17 *Mex.*
Acevedo de Castillo, Olga C 25 *Chil.*
Acevedo de Gómez, Josefa (1803-1861) BC
5; CG I, 13; Co 1; LC 115 *Col.*
1. Acevedo Díaz, Eduardo (1851-1924)
BHLA 401; CG I, 13; CHL 224; CLH
187; HSLU I, pt 5, 5; LU 64, 670; LUr
466; PIU I, 275; SASS 474; U 1; UT 3
Uru.
2. Acevedo Díaz, Eduardo (hijo) CG I, 13;
U 1 *Uru.*
Acevedo Escobedo, Antonio (1909-)
WLA 3 *Mex.*
Acevedo Hernández, Antonio BHLA 513,
549; C 1, 43; CG I, 13 *Chil.*
Acevedo Vallarino, Arturo (1876-   ) Co 1
Col.
Acevedo Vallarino, Ricardo Co 1 *Col.*
Acevedo Yenro, C. TM 593 *Mex.*
"Aclea, Dámaso Gil" (*pseud.*) see Márquez,
Matías F.
Aconrado, H. PB 34 *Bol.*
Acosta, Alfredo A 1; CG I, 14 *Arg.*
Acosta, Antonio E 2 *Ecua.*
Acosta, Cecilio (1831-1881) AEHA 17;
BHLA 298, 370; CG I, 14; CHL 366;
CLH 315; FPA 550, 561; LV 29 *et passim;*
V 25 *Venez.*
Acosta, Francisco T. BDC 1; Cu 8 *Cu.*
Acosta, Ignacio María de ("íñigo") (1814-
1871) BDC 1; Cu 8, 85 *Cu.*
Acosta, Javier PCo 19 *Col.*

Acosta, Joaquín (1799-1852) BC 10; CHL 341; CLH 300; Co 1; RHLC 198 *Col.*

Acosta, José de (1539?-1600) BHLA 118; HLM 67; SCL 105, 585 *Per.*

Acosta, José Eusebio V 25 *Venez.*

Acosta, Joseph de TM 511 *Sp.*

Acosta, Juan Cu 8 *Cu.*

Acosta, Julio (1872-   ) CA 1; EPCR 247 *C.R.*

Acosta, Luiz Gonzalo (-1887) Cu 8 *Cu.*

Acosta, M. E. PM 17, 40 *Mex.*

Acosta, Manuel M. E 2 *Ecua.*

Acosta, Marciano CA 1 *C.R.*

Acosta, Mariano E 2 *Ecua.*

Acosta, Nicolás (1844-1893) B 1 *Bol.*

Acosta, Vicente (186.-   ) FPA 501, 508; GPCA III, 397; PS 146 *Salv.*

Acosta C., I. E 2 *Ecua.*

Acosta de Samper, Soledad (1833-1903) BC 11; CHL 337, 351; CLH 290, 300; Co 1; LC 155; RHLC 184 *Col.*

Acosta Delgado, Pedro V 25 *Venez.*

Acosta G., Raúl CA 1; IBCR IV, 193 *C.R.*

Acosta García, Julio CA 1 *C.R.*

Acosta García, Luis A 1 *Arg.*

Acosta Medina, Antonio V 25 *Venez.*

Acosta Quintero, Ángel PR 8 *P.R.*

Acosta Rubio, Raoul Cu 8 *Cu.*

Acosta y Bello, Agustín (1885-   ) APEH 673; Cu 8; G 335; GLO 242; HLC 206; LH 123; PA 7; PCu 9; PJC 15; PoC 3; RLC 364; SASS 289; WLA 3 *Cu.*

Acosta y Calvo, José Julián (1825-1892) PR 8, 15, 25, 45, 48 *P.R.*

Acosta y Casanova, Manuel Mariano Cu 8 *Cu.*

Acosta y Lara, Federico CG I, 14; PU 249; U 1 *Uru.*

Acosta y Lara, Manuel CG I, 15; G 386; HSLU II, pt 6, 23; LU 64, 677 *Uru.*

Acosta y Zenea, Francisco Mateo Cu 8 *Cu.*

Acuña, Ángel A 1 *Arg.*

Acuña, Ángela CA 1; EPCR 521 *C.R.*

Acuña, Carlos (1886-   ) C 1, 25; CG I, 17; PCC xv, 123 *Chil.*

Acuña, Cristóbal de CG I, 17; SCL 295, 358, 586 *Ecua.*

Acuña, José G. Par 5 *Para.*

Acuña, Luis Alberto Co 2 *Col.*

1. Acuña, Manuel Par 5 *Para.*

2. Acuña, Manuel (1849-1873) AEHA 21; AMP 291; BHLA 334; CHL 402; CLH 350; G 354; HLM 392; HLMex 194; HPHA I, 159; HPM 849; PM 17; PMe I, 5; PoM 191; SASS 357; TM 12, 393 *Mex.*

Acuña de Figueroa, Francisco ("Cid Fragueiro Fonseca") (1790-1862) AEHA 19; BHLA 170; CHL 205; CLH 169; HCLU I, 90; HPHA II, 480; HSLU I, pt 1, 32; LA IV, 919; LUr 426; PIU I, 99; PLHA 66; SASS 452; U 1 *Uru.*

Acuña Núñez, Carlos PCh 381 *Chil.*

Achá, Francisco X. de (1828-1888) BHLA 312; CHL 211; CLH 174; U 1 *Uru.*

Achá, Vicente (-1867) Cu 8 *Cu.*

Achá y Aguirre, Fernando PB 27 *Bol.*

"Adalid, Justo" (*pseud.*) see Monterde García Icazbalceta, Francisco

Adams, Manuel TM 12, 216 *Mex.*

"Adán Marset" (*pseud.*) see Mata, Andrés A.

"Adán, Martín" (*pseud.*) see La Fuente Benavides, Rafael de

Addesso, Miguel V. A 1 *Arg.*

Adler, Raquel A 1 *Arg.*

"Adolfo de la Azucena" (*pseud.*) see Zenea, Juan Clemente

Adriano, Juan HPM 95 *Mex.*

Adriazola Cruz, Hernando NC 405 *Chil.*

Adsuar, Jorge PR 15, 41 *P.R.*

"Aecio" (*pseud.*) see Alfonso, Juan

Aeguez, Felisa PB 30 *Bol.*

Aenlle, César Cu 8 *Cu.*

"Aerolito" (*pseud.*) see Bravo, Vicente M.

Afanador, José Pascual BC 14; Co 2 *Col.*

"Agapito Candileja" (*pseud.*) see Soiza Reilly, Juan José de

"Agapito Canelón" (*pseud.*) see Agostini, Rafael

"Agar" A 1; CG I, 21 *Arg.*

Ager, Alfonso María de E 2 *Ecua.*

Agorio, Adolfo (1888-   ) CG I, 22; HSLU III, pt 4, 45; LU 64, 683; PIU III, 296; U 1; UT 9; WLA 4 *Uru.*

Agostini, Rafael ("Asmodeo" or "Agapito Canelón" or "Inístoga") Co 14; V 26, 32, 84 *Venez.*

Agosto Méndez, José María LV 360; V 26 *Venez.*

Agramonte, Ignacio (1841-1873) RLC 227 *Cu.*

Agramonte y Pichardo, Roberto Daniel (1904-   ) BHLA 571; CG I, 23; LAS 198; WLA 5 *Cu.*

Agrelo, Pedro José (1776-1846) LA V, 214 *Arg.*

Aguado, Pedro de BHLA 62; Co 2; HLNG I, 117; RHLC 8; V 26 *Col.*

Aguayo, C. PR 15 *P.R.*

Aguayo y Sánchez, Alfredo Miguel (1866-   ) CT 285; WLA 5 *Cu.*

Agüero, Concepción BDC 1; Cu 8 *Cu.*

Agüero, Miguel C. A 1 *Arg.*

Agüero, Raúl CA 1 *C.R.*

Agüero Bueno, Federico BAP 45 *Per.*

Agüero de Costales, Corina Cu 8 *Cu.*

Agüero Vera, Nicolás A 1 *Arg.*

Agüero y Agüero, Brígida PCu 21 *Cu.*

Agüero y Agüero, Francisco (1832-1891) Cu 8 *Cu.*

Agüero y Sánchez, Pedro de (1821-   ) Cu 8 *Cu.*

Agüeros, Agustín TM 512 *Mex.*

Agüeros, Victoriano (1854-1911) CHL 410; CLH 357; HLM 497; HLMex 239; Ig 12; NM 1, 6; TM 512 *Mex.*

Aguerrevere, Felipe V 27 *Venez.*

Aguerrevere, Juan José V 27 *Venez.*

Aguerrevere, Santiago V 27 *Venez.*

Aguerrevere Pacanins, T. V 27 *Venez.*

Aguerri, Josefa Toledo de (1866-) WLA 5 *Nicar.*

Aguiar, Adriano M. U 1 *Uru.*

Aguiar, Enrique G 385; PD 23; SD 3 *Dom.*

Aguiar, Justo Manuel IE 9; U 1 *Uru.*

Aguiar, Mariano del R. Par 5 *Para.*

Aguiar Poveda, Luis ARC 42; PCu 23 *Cu.*

Aguilar, Alejandro CA 1 *C.R.*

Aguilar, Arturo CA 1 *C.R.*

Aguilar, Federico Cornelio (1834-1887) BC 14; Co 3 *Col.*
Aguilar, Felipe N. PM 18 *Mex.*
Aguilar, Gilberto F. (1888-) Ig 14; NM 6 *Mex.*
Aguilar, Gustavo F. (1884-) G 355; PM 18; TM 12 *Mex.*
Aguilar, Juan C. TM 393 *Mex.*
Aguilar, Luis Alejandro V 27 *Venez.*
Aguilar, Luis Antonio HPM 449 *Mex.*
Aguilar, Nicanor E 2 *Ecua.*
Aguilar, Pedro T. E 2 *Ecua.*
Aguilar, Sinforo *or* Sinforoso ("Xavier de Ximénez") (1891-) CA 60; FPA 292, 304; WLA 6 *Guat.*
1. Aguilar, Ventura A 1 *Arg.*
2. Aguilar, Ventura Cu 8 *Cu.*
Aguilar del Río, Juan Bautista SCL 289, 586 *Per.*
Aguilar H., Jerónimo NL 185 *Nicar.*
Aguilar Machado, Alejandro CA 1; EPCR 637; IBCR IV, 319 *C.R.*
Aguilar Mora, Teodoro (1872-) QPR (2) 19 *P.R.*
Aguilar N., María Esperanza TM 512 *Mex.*
Aguilar Paz, Jesús (1895-) WLA 6 *Hond.*
Aguilar Vázquez, C. E 2 *Ecua.*
Aguilar Vidal, Oscar C 59 *Chil.*
Aguilar y Córdoba, Diego de HPHA II, 141 *Per.*
Aguilar y Marocho, Ignacio (1813-1884) HLM 362 *Mex.*
Aguilera, Francisco C 59 *Chil.*
Aguilera, Gervasio B 1 *Bol.*
Aguilera, José CG I, 29; V 27 *Venez.*
Aguilera, José Miguel ACe 672 *Mex.*
Aguilera, Miguel RHLC 212 *Col.*
Aguilera, Rodolfo Co 3; Pan 1 *Pan.*
Aguilera Malta, Demetrio BHLA 594; E 2, 73; LAS 203 *Ecua.*
Aguiluz, Teodoro (1827-1883) HL II, 89 *Hond.*
Aguinagalde, I. R. V 27 *Venez.*
Aguinagalde, Martín María V 27 *Venez.*
Aguirre, J. T. E 2 *Ecua.*
Aguirre, Jacobo M. TM 13 *Mex.*
Aguirre, Jesús E. PM 18 *Mex.*
Aguirre, José M. (-1919) E 2 *Ecua.*
Aguirre, José María (1778-1852) ACe 673 *Mex.*
Aguirre, Juan ("Juan Negro") BHLA 626 *Chil.*
Aguirre, Juan Bautista de (1725-1786) BHLA 98; E 3; G 343; PE 269; PLE 24; SCL 545, 586 *Ecua.*
Aguirre, Juan Francisco de (1772-) LA IV, 1002 *Arg.*
Aguirre, Junio PIU III, 233; U 1 *Uru.*
Aguirre, Manuel Agustín PLE 142 *Ecua.*
Aguirre, Manuel Alberto LAS 207 *Per.*
Aguirre, Miguel E 3 *Ecua.*
Aguirre, Miguel de BHC I, 460; SCL 271, 586 *Per.*
Aguirre, Mirta (1912-) PoC 8 *Cu.*
Aguirre, Nataniel (1843-1888) B 1; G 320; LB 600, 606; SASS 105 *Bol.*
Aguirre, Pamón V 27 *Venez.*
Aguirre, Pedro Antonio de TM 13 *Mex.*
Aguirre, R. Cu 8 *Cu.*
Aguirre, Regino TM 14 *Mex.*

Aguirre Achá, José (1877-) B 1; BT 1; CG I, 31; PB 38; WLA 7 *Bol.*
Aguirre Bretón, N. C 43 *Chil.*
Aguirre Bretón, Nicolás E 3 *Ecua.*
Aguirre de Hornillos, Lino Cu 8 *Cu.*
Aguirre Fierro, Guillermo PM 18; TM 15 *Mex.*
Aguirre Gámez, Agustín TM 15 *Mex.*
Aguirre Morales, Augusto (1890-) BHLA 516; CrA 89; P 1 *Per.*
Aguirre Vargas, Carlos (1852-1886) CL 120; HC 251 *Chil.*
Aguirre Vargas, Vicente (1851-1912) CL 120; HC 251 *Chil.*
Aguirre Velázquez, Eduardo CA 60 *Guat.*
Aguirre y de la Torre, Manuel Cu 9 *Cu.*
Aguirre y Sánchez, Carlos Cu 9 *Cu.*
Aguirre y Tamayo, Virgilio E 3 *Ecua.*
Aguirrezábal, Pablo PU 9 *Uru.*
Agusti y Milá, Jaime PR 15 *P.R.*
Agustín, Gaspar de TM 15 *Mex.*
"Agustín Oteiza" (*pseud.*) *see* Oteiza y Dongo, Manuel José de
Agustini, Delmira (1886-1914) APEH 907; BHLA 533; CHL 233; FPA 528, 544; G 386; GLO 253; HSLU II, pt 3, 3; pt 8, 9; LU 64, 657; LUr 525; PCU 154; PIU II, 217; PLHA 178; PoU 27; PU 11; SASS 461; U 1 *Uru.*
Aita, Antonio A 1; G 309 *Arg.*
"Aitz-Gorri" (*pseud.*) CG I, 35; Cu 9 *Cu.*
Aizpuru, Aizpuru (1877-) AP 11; Pan 1 *Pan.*
"Akara" (*pseud.*) *see* Bigotte, Félix E.
A. L. P. B. C 59 *Chil.*
Alacán, Oscar P. ARC 42 *Cu.*
Alaín Acuña, Elías (1893-) AP 15; Pan 1 *Pan.*
Alamán, Lucas (1792-1853) BHLA 253; CG I, 36; CHL 410; CLH 356; HLM 348; HLMex 134 *Mex.*
Álamo, Ángel María V 27 *Venez.*
Álamo, Antonio V 27 *Venez.*
Álamo, Francisco V 27 *Venez.*
Alarcón, Abel (1881-) B 1; BHLA 513; BT 5; CG I, 37; CHL 311; LB 616; PB 31 *Bol.*
Alarcón, José C. Co 3 *Col.*
Alarcón, Juan Miguel V 27 *Venez.*
Alarcón, Pedro Nolasco TM 15 *Mex.*
Alarcón, Ruiz de *see* Ruiz de Alarcón y Mendoza, Juan
Alarcón Lobos, Roberto C 1; NC 11, 407 *Chil.*
"Alas, Claudio de" (*pseud.*) *see* Uribe, José Escobar
Alas, Domingo V 27 *Venez.*
Alava de Villareal, José HLNG I, 173 *Col.*
Alavés Pinelo, Alonso de PM 18 *Mex.*
Alayza Paz Soldán, Luis (1883-) LAS 203; P 1 *Per.*
Alba, Alberto G. de (1894-) Pan 1 *Pan.*
Alba, Amando J. de PM 18 *Mex.*
Alba, Francisco de PM 18 *Mex.*
Alba, Rafael de PoM 378 *Mex.*
Alba C., Manuel María Pan 1 *Pan.*
Alba y Monteagudo, José de (1761-1800) HLC 15; RLC 25 *Cu.*
Albaladejo, Mariano PCu 25; PJC 30 *Cu.*
Albán, Carlos (1844-1900?) Co 3 *Col.*

Albareda, Ramón P 1 *Per.*
Albarracín C., Jacinto Co 3 *Col.*
Albasio, Luigi E. A 1, 79 *Arg.*
Alberdi, Juan Bautista ("Figarillo") (1810-
  1884) A 1, 79; BHLA 270, 283, 357; CG I,
  42; CHL 143; CLH 121; G 309; GEA II,
  IV; HLA 369; HPHA II, 455; HSLU
  III, pt 4, 15; LA VI, 681, 899; PLHA
  247; SASS 79; SPLA 229 *Arg.*
Albert, Luis J. A 2 *Arg.*
Albert, Totila OA 241
Albertazzi Avendaño, José (1892-   ) CA
  2, 5; EPCR 529; FPA 123, 159; IBCR IV,
  145 *C.R.*
Alberti y Bosch, Narciso SD 3 *Dom.*
"Alberto, Jorje" (*pseud.*) A 37 *Arg.*
Albiñana Sanz, José María CG I, 46; NM 6
  Mex.
Albis, Manuel María Co 3 *Col.*
Albornoz, Miguel Ángel (1876-   ) E 3
  Ecua.
Albornoz Serantes, M. C 1 *Chil.*
Albornoz y Montoya, Z. Par 5 *Para.*
Albuja, José D. E 3 *Ecua.*
Alcácer, Pedro S. A 2 *Arg.*
Alcalde, Juan (1864-1925) Cu 9 *Cu.*
Alcántara, Francisco Linares V 27 *Venez.*
Alcántara, Manuel Cu 9 *Cu.*
Alcaraz, Ángela TM 16 *Mex.*
Alcaraz, Ramón Isaac (1823-1886) HLM
  303; HPM 904; PM 19; TM 17 *Mex.*
Alcázar, Ricardo de ("Florisel") G 355;
  PM 19, 44 *Mex.*
Alcedo, Antonio de (1735-   ) BHLA 140;
  PLE 17; SCL 473, 515, 586 *Ecua.*
Alcedo y Herrera, Dionisio de (1690-1777)
  CG I, 54; E 4; SCL 514, 586 *Ecua.*
"Alcestes" (*pseud.*) TM 480 *Mex.*
Alcobre, Manuel A 2 *Arg.*
Alcocer, Arturo G 355 *Mex.*
Alcocer Irigoyen, Fidel B 2; C 1
Alcover, Antonio Miguel (1875-1915) CG I,
  56; Cu 9 *Cu.*
Alcover y Jauna, Antonio Miguel BDC 1;
  Cu 9 *Cu.*
Aldana, Ramón (1832-1882) HPM 874; TM
  17, 513 *Mex.*
Aldana, Ruperto I. TM 18 *Mex.*
Aldana, Ruperto J. PM 19 *Mex.*
Aldao, Martín (hijo) A 2; G 309 *Arg.*
Aldao, Martín C. (1879-   ) A 2; CG I, 58;
  CLH 168; G 309; PLHA 195, 270 *Arg.*
Aldereguia, Ignacio Cu 9 *Cu.*
Aldrey, Fausto Teodoro V 27, 84 *Venez.*
Aldrey Jiménez, Teófilo V 27 *Venez.*
Aldunate, Roberto C 43 *Chil.*
Aldunate Phillips, Arturo C 25 *Chil.*
Alecio, Adriano de P 1 *Per.*
Alegre, Francisco Javier (1729-1788) HLM
  181, 209; HLMex 82; HPHA I, 87, 90;
  HPM 473; PM 19; TM 513 *Mex.*
Alegría, Adolfo Isaac Ig 15; NM 6 *Mex.*
Alegría, Alfredo NL 223 *Nicar.*
Alegría, Ciro BHLA 605, 609; LAS 203
  Per.
Alegría, José Manuel V 27 *Venez.*
Alegría, José S. PP 280 *P.R.*
Alejandro, Esteban NC 114 *Chil.*
"Alejandro García Nieto" (*pseud.*) *see*
  Urbaneja, Alejandro

Alem, Leandro N. (1844-1896) A 2; LA
  VII, 328 *Arg.*
Alemán, José María (1830-1887) AP 17;
  BC 21; Co 3; Pan 1, 2 *Pan.*
Alemán, Mateo V 27 *Venez.*
Alemán Bolaños, Gustavo (1884-   ) G
  375; IE 12 *Nicar.*
Alemany Villa A 2; CG I, 61 *Arg.*
Alemar, Luis E. SD 3 *Dom.*
"Alfa, Brigadier" (*pseud.*) *see* Velarde, César
  Augusto
Alfaro, Anastasio *see* Alfaro González,
  Anastasio
Alfaro, Anselmo (1852-   ) Ig 16; NM 6
  Mex.
Alfaro, Eloy (1842-   ) E 4 *Ecua.*
Alfaro, Gabriel TM 514 *Mex.*
Alfaro, Jesús NM 6 *Mex.*
Alfaro, Ricardo Joaquín (1882-) AP 21;
  Pan 2 *Pan.*
Alfaro Cooper, José María (1861-) CA
  2, 3; EPCR 47; GPCA III, 311; PC 167
  C.R.
Alfaro González, Anastasio (1865-) CA
  2, 3; CG I, 63; EPCR 51; IBCR IV, 129,
  220 *C.R.*
Alfau y Galván, Jesusa SD 3 *Dom.*
Alfau y Rojas, Ulises SD 3 *Dom.*
Alfonseca, José Dolores SD 3 *Dom.*
Alfonso, Eduardo CG I, 65; Cu 9 *Cu.*
Alfonso, Graciliano HPHA I, 336; PR 31
  P.R.
Alfonso, José B. Cu 9 *Cu.*
Alfonso, José R. Cu 9 *Cu.*
Alfonso, Juan ("Aecio") LV 367; V 26, 27
  Venez.
Alfonso, Luis Cu 9 *Cu.*
Alfonso, Luis Gerónimo V 27 *Venez.*
Alfonso, Luis Juan A 2 *Arg.*
Alfonso, Melitón A 2 *Arg.*
Alfonso, Paulino CL 120 *Chil.*
Alfonso, Ramón María CG I, 65; V 27
  Venez.
Alfonso, Salvador A 2, 40, 79 *Arg.*
Alfonso, Víctor R. Cu 9 *Cu.*
Alfonso Conzi de Duarte, María U 1 *Uru.*
Alfonso Roselló, Arturo (1897-   ) Cu 9
  Cu.
Alfonso y de la Torre, Francisco Cu 9 *Cu.*
Alfonso y García, José Luis, Marqués de
  Montelo (1810-1881) Cu 9; RLC 88 *Cu.*
Alfonzo, Aureliano V 28 *Venez.*
"Alfredo de Lery" (*pseud.*) *see* Franchi,
  Alfredo C.
Algara R. de Terreros, Ángel CG I, 66;
  TM 18 *Mex.*
Aliaga, A. Cu 9 *Cu.*
Aliaga Rueda, María A 2 *Arg.*
"Alidauro Zacintio" (*pseud.*) *see* Pérez
  Salazar y Osorio, Ignacio
Alio, Carolina Adelia A 2 *Arg.*
Alix, Juan Antonio SD 3 *Dom.*
"Alma" (*pseud.*) *see* Cergoglio Boero, Vio-
  leta Blanca
Almada, Amadeo CG I, 68; U 2; UL 122
  Uru.
Almada, Pedro J. NM 6 *Mex.*
"Almafuerte" (*pseud.*) *see* Palacios, Pedro
  Bonifacio
Almansa, José Mariano de ACe 676 *Mex.*
Almansa, Rafael (1843-1927) Co 3 *Col.*

"Almanzor" (*pseud.*) *see* Zamora, Antonio G.

Almasque, Juan Antonio Cu 10 *Cu.*

Almazán, Pascual ("Natal de Pomar") (1813-1886) Ig 17; NM 6, 43; PM 19, 69 *Mex.*

Almeida, Francisco E 4; PLE 15 *Ecua.*

Almeida, Pedro PM 19 *Mex.*

Almendaro, José Pablo ("Mauricio de Bracy") NM 6 *Mex.*

Almeyda, Luis Cu 10 *Cu.*

Aloisi, Enzo (1886-) A 2, 79; CG I, 74; WLA 14 *Arg.*

Alomia, Antonio (1867-) E 4 *Ecua.*

Alomia, Fidel E 4 *Ecua.*

Alomia de Guerrero, Pastora E 4 *Ecua.*

"Alone" (*pseud.*) *see* Díaz Arrieta, Hernán

Alonso, Aladro José Cu 10 *Cu.*

Alonso, Amado LAS 198

Alonso, Carmen P. de A 2 *Arg.*

Alonso, Dora (1912-) PoC 14 *Cu.*

Alonso, José TM 18 *Mex.*

Alonso, Longinos ARC 42 *Cu.*

Alonso, Manuel A. (1822-) BP 518, 570; CHL 499; CLH 440; PR 31, 55 *P.R.*

Alonso Criado, Emilio A 2; CG I, 77 *Arg.*

"Alonso de la Veracruz" (*pseud.*) *see* Gutiérrez, Alonso

Alonso Pizarro, Manuel BP 509; PR 10 *P.R.*

Alonso Ruiz de Conejares, Francisco PM 19 *Mex.*

Alonso V., Roberto CL 120 *Chil.*

Alonso y Trelles, José ("El viejo Pancho") (1867-1925) APEH 558, 1188; BHLA 532; CG I, 80; PIU III, 150; PU 227; U 2 *Uru.*

Alonzo Patiño, Felipe TM 18 *Mex.*

Alpízar, Raúl E. BDC 1 *Cu.*

Alpízar A., Emilio CA 3 *C.R.*

Alpízar A., Rafael CA 3 *C.R.*

Alpuche, Wenceslao (1804-1841) AMP 230; BHLA 171, 187; CHL 101; CLH 84; HLM 303; HPM 812; PMe I, 21 *Mex.*

Alsina, Adolfo (1829-1877) LA VII, 322 *Arg.*

Alsina, Valentín (1802-1869) LA VI, 887 *Arg.*

Altamirano, Ignacio Manuel (1834-1893) AEHA 55; AMP 253; BAMP 29; BHLA 334; CG I, 84; CHL 399; CLH 345; G 355; HLM 377, 436; HLMex 186; Ig 18; NM 1, 6; PM 19; PMe I, 23; PoM 78; SASS 355; TM 19, 514 *Mex.*

"Alter" (*pseud.*) *see* Frías, Valentín F.

1. Althaus, Clemente (1835-1881) AEHA 265; BHLA 319; CHL 296; CLH 250; HPHA II, 259; LP 360; PLHA 74; PPe 78 *Per.*

2. Althaus, Clemente (1862-1906) P 1 *Per.*

Altierry, Genaro BP 518 *P.R.*

Alú Fernández, José ("Fernando Jules Zea") (-c.1906) Cu 10, 182 *Cu.*

Alva, Bartolomé TM 394 *Mex.*

Alva, Juan de Cu 10 *Cu.*

Alva, Manuel M. (1833-1878) Ig 22; NM 7 *Mex.*

"Alva, Martín" (*pseud.*) *see* Martínez Álvarez, Rafael

Alvarado, Alejandro (hijo) *see* Alvarado Quirós, Alejandro

Alvarado, Francisco de HLM 22 *Mex.*

Alvarado, José María V 28 *Venez.*

Alvarado, Juan Crisóstomo V 28 *Venez.*

Alvarado, León (1819-1870) HL I, 199 *Hond.*

Alvarado, Lisandro CG I, 86; LV 10; PLHA 284; V 28 *Venez.*

Alvarado, María de ("Amarilis") BHLA 93; CLH 21; HPHA II, 156; LP 309; P 1 *Per.*

Alvarado, María J. (1888-) Pan 2 *Pan.*

Alvarado, Max TM 593 *Mex.*

Alvarado, Ramón CA 60 *Guat.*

Alvarado Fajardo, Federico CA 60; CG I, 87 *Guat.*

Alvarado Manzano, Rafael (1836-) HL I, 575 *Hond.*

Alvarado Quirós, Alejandro (1876-) CA 3; CG I, 87; EPCR 256; IBCR IV, 104 *et passim;* IE 17 *C.R.*

Álvarez, Agustín (1857-1914) A 2; G 309; LA VII, 121; SASS 82 *Arg.*

Álvarez, Alejandro O. (1868-) WLA 15 *Chil.*

Álvarez, Antonio Ramón V 28 *Venez.*

Álvarez, Carmen Olivo V 28 *Venez.*

Álvarez, Consuelo Cu 10 *Cu.*

Álvarez, Diego de (-1824) ACe 678 *Mex.*

Álvarez, Eduardo (hijo) A 3; CG I, 89 *Arg.*

Álvarez, Elena TM 19 *Mex.*

Álvarez, Emilio C 43 *Chil.*

Álvarez, Enrique (1847-) BC 23 *Col.*

Álvarez, Eudófilo (-1917) CG I, 89; E 4; PLE 88 *Ecua.*

Álvarez, Federico C. SD 3 *Dom.*

Álvarez, Francisco (1847-1881) BDC 1; BP 509, 519, 571; CHL 502; CLH 443; HPHA I, 348; PP 105; PR 10, 25, 31 *P.R.*

Álvarez, Gregorio A 3 *Arg.*

Álvarez, José Manuel Cu 10; PJC 26 *Cu.*

Álvarez, José Sixto ("Fray Mocho") (1858-1903) A 3, 78; BHLA 503; CG I, 89; CHL 196; G 309; LA VIII, 736; LAC 136; PLHA 225; SASS 60; SPLA 249 *Arg.*

Álvarez, Juan (1878-) AT II, 899; CG I, 90 *Arg.*

Álvarez, Manuel CG I, 90; Cu 10 *Cu.*

Álvarez, Ramón E 4 *Ecua.*

Álvarez, Ricardo E 5; PLE 114 *Ecua.*

Álvarez, Secundino M. (1830-1877) BC 22; Co 3 *Col.*

Álvarez, Urbano A 3 *Arg.*

Álvarez, Víctor M. V 28 *Venez.*

Álvarez Alvarado, Raúl Pan 2 *Pan.*

Álvarez Arteta, Segundo CG I, 91; E 5 *Ecua.*

Álvarez Berrocal, Rigoberto CA 4; EPCR 639 *C.R.*

Álvarez Bonilla, Enrique (1848-1913) CG I, 91; Co 3; LC 177; PCo 20 *Col.*

Álvarez Castro, Miguel GPCA I, 53 *Salv.*

Álvarez de Flórez, Mercedes (1859-) BC 25; CHL 350; CLH 299; Co 4 *Col.*

Álvarez de la Fuente, Ubaldo TM 19 *Mex.*

Álvarez de la Riva, Luis M. Cu 10 *Cu.*

Álvarez de Lugo, Eladio V 28 *Venez.*

Álvarez de Toledo, Fernando BHLA 73; C 25; CLH 12; HPHA II, 328; SCL 199, 587 *Chil.*

Álvarez de Velasco, Gabriel (1595-1658) Co 4; HLNG I, 177 *Col.*

Álvarez de Velasco, Mercedes *see* Álvarez de Flórez, Mercedes

Álvarez de Velasco y Zorrilla, Francisco BHLA 94; CHL 34; CLH 29; Co 4; CoL 264; HLNG I, 287; RHLC 25 *Col.*

Álvarez del Castillo, Graciana PM 19 *Mex.*

Álvarez del Castillo, Miguel (1890-) CG I, 92; G 355; PM 19 *Mex.*

Álvarez del Castillo, Santiago HLNG I, 138 *Col.*

Álvarez Henao, Enrique (1871-1914) Co 4; E 5; LC 193; PCo 22; RHLC 153 *Col.*

Álvarez Ibarra, H. V 28 *Venez.*

Álvarez Lozano, Rafael (1805-1845) BC 25; Co 4; RHLC 103, 160 *Col.*

Álvarez Lleras, Antonio (1892-) CG I, 94; Co 4; G 328; LC 197; RHLC 171 *Col.*

Álvarez Lleras, Jorge (1885-) Co 4 *Col.*

Álvarez Magaña, Manuel PS 195 *Salv.*

Álvarez Marrón, M. CG I, 95; Cu 10 *Cu.*

Álvarez Mercado, Martín P 1 *Per.*

Álvarez Núñez, Domingo Cu 10 *Cu.*

Álvarez Pérez, J. Cu 10 *Cu.*

Álvarez Piñeiro, Armando CP 688; PA 267; PD 13; SD 3 *Dom.*

Álvarez Prieto, Fernando NM 7 *Mex.*

Álvarez y Real, Eusebio Cu 10 *Cu.*

Alvear, Juan I. E 5 *Ecua.*

Alvear y Ponce de León, Diego de (1749-1830) LA IV, 1000 *Arg.*

Alvéstegui, David (1887-) BT 11 *Bol.*

Alvial, Gustavo C 25 *Chil.*

Alzate, José Antonio (1737-1799) ACe 664; HLMex 90; HPM 474 *Mex.*

Alzueta, Nemesio A 3 *Arg.*

Alzuro Espinosa, Emilio PE 78 *Ecua.*

Allende, Juan Rafael (1850-1909) C 1, 14, 25, 43; CHL 257; HC 224; NC 11, 353, 407; PCh 71 *Chil.*

Allende Iragorri, Tomás (1881-) A 2; APAM 129; CG I, 106; G 309 *Arg.*

Allende Lezama, Josefa A 2; CG I, 106 *Arg.*

Allende Ríos, Enrique C 1; NC 12, 14 *Chil.*

Allendes, Wáshington CL 120 *Chil.*

Aller, Ángel PoU 35 *Uru.*

Alloza, Juan de (1597-1666) CHL 25; P 1; SCL 449, 587 *Per.*

Amadeo y Antomarchi, Jesús María BDC 1; BP 501, 509; PR 11, 16, 26, 41 *P.R.*

Amador, Armando C. (1897-) IE 18; Ig 23; NM 7; PM 19 *Mex.*

Amador, Fernán Félix de (1889-) A 3; APAM 133; APEH 666; G 309; GLO 235; LAC 144; PLHA 147 *Arg.*

Amador, María Ester ("Diana Clara") CA 4, 13; IBCR IV, 314 *C.R.*

Amador, Severo Ig 24; NM 8; PM 20 *Mex.*

Amarante, P. J. C 53 *Chil.*

"Amarilis" (*pseud.*) *see* Alvarado, María de

"Amaro, Severino" (*pseud.*) *see* Molina, Gaspar

Amat, Joaquín TM 19 *Mex.*

Amat, Manuel de BHC III, 344 *et passim Chil.*

Amaya, Alberto TM 621 *Mex.*

Amaya, Alejo (1870-) Co 4 *Col.*

Amaya, Florencio J. A 3; CG I, 109 *Arg.*

Ambrosetti, Juan B. (1865-1917) A 3; CG I, 109; LA VII, 239 *Arg.*

Ambruzzi, Lucilo U 2 *Uru.*

Amechazurra de Pellerano, Isabel PD 15; SD 4 *Dom.*

Ameghino, Florentino (1854-1911) BHLA 392; CG I, 110; GEA XVI; LA VII, 77 *Arg.*

Amendolla, Luis NM 8 *Mex.*

Amengual, Vicente V 28 *Venez.*

América, Enrique TM 20 *Mex.*

"Américo Hispano" (*pseud.*) *see* Pozo, José Miguel

"Américo Llano" (*pseud.*) *see* Vasseur, Álvaro Armando

Amézaga, Carlos Germán (1862-1906) AEHA 393; BHLA 429; CHL 299; CLH 253; LP 368; P 1; PPe 152 *Per.*

Amezcua, José Luis NM 8 *Mex.*

Amézquita, Cándido Co 4 *Col.*

Amiama, Francisco Xavier SD 4 *Dom.*

Amiama Gómez, Francisco X. PD 17; SD 4 *Dom.*

Amieva, José BDC 2; Cu 10 *Cu.*

"Amores, Jacinto" (*pseud.*) *see* Ascasubi, Hilario

Amorim, Enrique M. (1900-) A 3; APAM 439; BHLA 641; HSLU II, pt 6, 9; PU 251 *Uru.*

Amórtegui, Octavio Co 4 *Col.*

Amunátegui Jordán, Gabriel C 60; CL 125 *Chil.*

Amunátegui Reyes, Miguel Luis C 60; CG I, 116; CL 125 *Chil.*

Amunátegui Solar, Domingo (1860-) BHLA 493, 618; C 60; CHL 272, 286; CL 126; NC 408; WLA 19 *Chil.*

Amunátegui y Aldunate, Gregorio Víctor (1830-1899) BHLA 347; C 59; CG I, 116; CHL 284; CL 121, 122; CLH 241; E 5; HC 96; SASS 185 *Chil.*

Amunátegui y Aldunate, Miguel Luis (1828-1888) BHLA 347; C 1, 59; CHL 284; CL 121; CLH 241; E 5; HC 96; LV 80; NC 407; SASS 185 *Chil.*

Amy, Francisco Javier (1837-1912) BP 519, 571; CHL 502; CLH 443; PP 77; PR 5, 16, 26, 31, 48 *P.R.*

Anabalón, Luisa V. ("Juana Inés de la Cruz") PCh 413 *Chil.*

"Anastasio el Pollo" (*pseud.*) *see* Campo, Estanislao del

Anaya, Jesús NM 8 *Mex.*

Anaya, José Lucas (1716-1771) HPM 464 *Mex.*

Ancell, Carlos F. A 4; CG I, 119 *Arg.*

Ancízar, Manuel (1820-1882) Co 4; LC 152; V 28 *Col.*

Ancona, Eligio (1836-1893) G 355; HLM 344, 492; Ig 24; NM 8; TM 20 *Mex.*

Ancona Albertos, Antonio (1883-) Ig 26; NM 8 *Mex.*

Anchieta, José (1533-1595) LA III, 394 *Arg.*

Anda, J. S. TM 20 *Mex.*

Andagoya, Pascual de SCL 55, 588 *Pan.*

Andara, José Ladislao V 28 *Venez.*

Andía, Ernesto Daniel A 4 *Arg.*

Andino, Marcelo PR 48 *P.R.*
Andonaegui y Altuna, José Cu 10 *Cu.*
Andrade, Agustina (1861-1891) A 4; LA VIII, 792 *Arg.*
Andrade, Crispino Co 4 *Col.*
Andrade, José Arturo (1891-   ) RHLC 198 *Col.*
Andrade, José E. V 28 *Venez.*
Andrade, José Julián E 5 *Ecua.*
Andrade, Luis CG I, 121; TM 20, 21 *Mex.*
Andrade, Manuel de Jesús CG I, 121; E 5 *Ecua.*
Andrade, Manuel Pardo de APA I, 279 *Arg.*
Andrade, Modesto N. E 5 *Ecua.*
Andrade, Olegario Víctor (1841-1882) A 4; AEHA 62; BHLA 309; CG I, 121; CHL 180; CLH 154; FPA 15, 32; G 309; HLA 439; HPHA II, 461; LA VII, 442; PLHA 72; SASS 36; SPLA 98; WSAL 32, 72 *Arg.*
Andrade, Pedro V 28 *Venez.*
Andrade, Raúl BHLA 597 *Ecua.*
Andrade, Roberto (1851-   ) E 5, 73; PLA 50; WLA 19 *Ecua.*
Andrade, Vicente de Paúl HLM 492; NM 1; TM 515 *Mex.*
Andrade, Víctor E 6 *Ecua.*
Andrade Berti, Josefa ("Hulda") V 28, 84 *Venez.*
Andrade Coello, Alejandro (1888-   ) CG I, 121; CHL 320; CLH 272; E 6, 7; IE 19; LAS 198; PE 44; WLA 20 *Ecua.*
Andrade Ch., Alfonso E 6 *Ecua.*
"Andrea, Sordello" (*pseud.*) *see* Nin Frías, Alberto
Andreoli, L. Enrique U 2 *Uru.*
Andreu de Aguilar, Isabel (1887-   ) QPR (1) 21 *P.R.*
Andreve, Guillermo (1879-   ) AP 31; CG I, 126; Pan 2 *Pan.*
Andueza, José María de BDC 2; Cu 10 *Cu.*
Aneiros Pazos, Luciano Cu 10 *Cu.*
"Anfibio" (*pseud.*) *see* Crespo y Borbón, Bartolomé José
Angarita Arvelo, Rafael V 28 *Venez.*
Ángel, José (1777-   ) HLNG II, 82 *Col.*
Ángel Gaitán, José María (1819-1851) BC 33; Co 4; LC 139; RHLC 178 *Col.*
Ángel Montoya, Alberto Co 5; LAS 206 *Col.*
"Ángel Pino" (*pseud.*) *see* Díaz Garcés, Joaquín
"Ángela" (*pseud.*) Ig 27; NM 8 *Mex.*
"Angélica Farfalla" (*pseud.*) *see* Bourguet, Lola S. B. de
Angelici, Pedro E 7 *Ecua.*
Angelis, María Luisa de PR 5, 8 *P.R.*
1. Angelis, Pedro de (1784-1859) CG I, 127; HLA 370; LA VI, 816, 826; Par 1 *Arg.*
2. Angelis, Pedro de PR 8, 16, 31, 48 *P.R.*
Anglería, Pedro Mártir de (1457-1526) HLM 29 *Mex.*
Anglés y Gortari, Matías de SCL 426, 588 *Para.*
Anguita, Bernabé F. C 1, 25; NC 408 *Chil.*
Ángulo, José Paul A 4, 79 *Arg.*

Ángulo, Lucas CA 60 *Guat.*
Ángulo Verdesi, Cruz ARC 42 *Cu.*
Ángulo y Guridi, Alejandro (1826-1906) Cu 11; LD 80; SD 4; V 28 *Dom.*
Ángulo y Guridi, Javier (1816-1884) BDC 2; BHLA 226, 244; CHL 493; CLH 433; Cu 11; LD 80; SD 4 *Dom.*
Ángulo y Heredia, Antonio (1837-1875) Cu 11 *Cu.*
Ángulo y Velasco, Hernando Co 5; HLNG I, 138 *Col.*
"Aníbal, Hugo" (*pseud.*) *see* Acevedo, Pedro Tadeo
"Aníbal Latino" (*pseud.*) *see* Ceppi, José
"Aniceto el Gallo" (*pseud.*) *see* Ascasubi, Hilario
Anievas, José Ignacio de HPM 831; TM 21 *Mex.*
Anillo, Alberto Cu 11 *Cu.*
Annel, José CA 4 *C.R.*
Anrique, Nicolás Reyes C 60; CG I, 130; E 7 *Chil.*
"Antaño, El Cronista de" (*pseud.*) *see* Urbina y Sánchez, Luis Gonzaga
"Antares" (*pseud.*) A 4 *Arg.*
Antepara, Luis TM 74 *Mex.*
"Antici Irene" (*pseud.*) A 36 *Arg.*
Antich é Izaguirre, Francisco CG I, 131; Cu 11 *Cu.*
"Antioco" (*pseud.*) *see* Gutiérrez González, Gregorio
Antomás, Domingo SCL 456, 588 *Chil.*
Anton, Enrique de A 4 *Arg.*
"Antón Martín Saavedra" (*pseud.*) *see* Salaverri, Vicente A.
Antonelli, Mauricio A 4 *Arg.*
Antúnez, Francisco ARC 42 *Cu.*
Antuña, José G. (1888-   ) HSLU III, pt 4, 46; IE 20; PLHA 269; PU 20; U 2; UL 122; WLA 23 *Uru.*
Antuña Elzear, José Luis (hijo) U 2 *Uru.*
Antuñano y Landa, Eulogio TM 489 *Mex.*
Anunciación, Juan de la HLM 23 *Mex.*
Anzola, Juvenal V 29 *Venez.*
Añez, Jacinto V 29 *Venez.*
Añez, Juana V 29 *Venez.*
Añez, Julio (1857-   ) BC 36; Co 5 *Col.*
Añez Casas, Víctor Reparado V 29 *Venez.*
Añez Gabaldón, Francisco V 29 *Venez.*
Añez Gabaldón, Julia V 29 *Venez.*
Añez Luengo, J. de J. ("Benito Blanco") V 29, 40 *Venez.*
Añon, Francisco A 4 *Arg.*
"Apaikán" (*pseud.*) *see* Fernández de Tinoco, María
Apello Corbulacho, Juan Carlos de PM 20 *Mex.*
Apenta, Fray C 60 *Chil.*
Aponte, Deudoro Co 5 *Col.*
Aponte, José Agustín BP 519; PR 31 *P.R.*
Aponte, José Manuel B 2 *Bol.*
Aponte, Rafael CG I, 148; TM 74 *Mex.*
Aprile, Bartolomé R. A 4 *Arg.*
Aquenza, Jacinto ("A. Pineda") PR 16, 20 *P.R.*
"Aquino, Hernando d'" (*pseud.*) *see* Hernández, Manuel H.
Aquino, Pedro Benjamín (1887-   ) A 4, 80 *Arg.*
Ara Carrió, Fernando G. A 4 *Arg.*

Aragón, Adolfo de (1864-) CT 111 *Cu.*
Aragón, Antonio (1835-) GPCA II, 161 *Nicar.*
Aragón, Arcesio (1872-) CG I, 154; Co 5 *Col.*
Aragón, Joaquín (1863-) CHL 507; CLH 448; GPCA III, 501; PS 89 *Salv.*
Aragón, Manuel G. TM 75 *Mex.*
Aragonés, Eutiquio Cu 12 *Cu.*
"Aragonés, Un" Cu 12 *Cu.*
Aramburo y Machado, Mariano (1870-) CG I, 156; CT 607; Cu 12; HLC 211; RLC 106, 347 *Cu.*
Aramburu, G. J. V 29 *Venez.*
Aramburu, Joaquín Nicolás (1855-) CG I, 156; CT 437; Cu 12 *Cu.*
Aramburu, Julio A 4; CG I, 156; LAC 137 *Arg.*
Arana, Belisario F. A 4 *Arg.*
Arana, Felipe N. PR 31 *P.R.*
Arana, Juan Pablo A 4, 80 *Arg.*
Arancibia Prado, Pedro C 2; NC 16 *Chil.*
Arancibia V., Aquilino C 2 *Chil.*
Aranda, Ángel PM 20 *Mex.*
Aranda, Francisco V 29 *Venez.*
Aranda de Aguirre, Felipe Cu 12 *Cu.*
Aranda y Ponte, Francisco V 29 *Venez.*
Araneda Mangelsdorff, Rosa C 25 *Chil.*
Arango, Rodolfo Cu 12; PCu 28; PJC 24 *Cu.*
Arango Acosta, Luis Co 5 *Col.*
Arango C., Luis CG I, 160; Co 5 *Col.*
Arango Vélez, Dionisio (1895-) Co 5; WLA 24 *Col.*
Arango Villegas, Rafael Co 5 *Col.*
Arango y Escandón, Alejandro (1821-1883) AEHA 89; CHL 393; CLH 341; HLM 295; HLMex 157; HPHA I, 151; HPM 908; PM 20; PMe I, 33; TM 423 *Mex.*
Arango y García, Juan Cu 12 *Cu.*
Arango y Parreño, Francisco de (1765-1837) RLC 39, 41 *Cu.*
Aranza, José Ignacio PM 20 *Mex.*
Aranzaes, Nicanor (1849-) B 2; BT 23 *Bol.*
Araña L., Rafael Pan 2 *Pan.*
Aráoz de Lamadrid, Gregorio (1795-1857) LA VI, 1062 *Arg.*
Araoz Ocampo, Aurora P 2 *Per.*
"Araucana" (*pseud.*) C 2 *Chil.*
Araucho, Francisco HCLU I, 73; PIU I, 89 *Uru.*
Araucho, Manuel de HCLU I, 73; PIU I, 90; U 2 *Uru.*
Araujo, Agustín M. PM 20 *Mex.*
Araújo, Bernardo I. BC 41 *Col.*
Araújo, Dionisio H. BC 41 *Col.*
Araujo, Gonzalo CG I, 163; E 7 *Ecua.*
Araujo, Joaquín Miguel de (1764-1841) E 8 *Ecua.*
Araujo, José de Jesús E 8 *Ecua.*
Araujo, José Joaquín (1762-1834?) HLA 95 *Arg.*
Araujo, L. F. E 8 *Ecua.*
Araujo, Miguel Joaquín E 8 *Ecua.*
Araujo, Orestes (1853-) CG I, 163; U 2 *Uru.*
Araujo Villagrán, Horacio CG I, 164; U 2 *Uru.*
Aravena González, Héctor C 2 *Chil.*
Aravena Mella, Manuel C 2 *Chil.*

Aray, Enrique A. E 8 *Ecua.*
Araya, Carlomagno CA 4; EPCR 640 *C.R.*
Araya, Juan Agustín ("O. Segura Castro") PCh 363 *Chil.*
Araya, Trinidad de Jesús CA 5; IBCR IV, 199 *C.R.*
Araya U., Juan Agustín C 25, 35, 68 *Chil.*
Arbeláez, Juan Clímaco (1844-) BC 41; Co 5 *Col.*
Arbieto, Ignacio de (1585-1676) SCL 339, 589 *Per.*
Arbo de Diego, Clarisa G. A 4 *Arg.*
Arboleda, Enrique Co 5 *Col.*
Arboleda, Gonzalo Co 5 *Col.*
Arboleda, Gustavo (1881-) CG I, 165; Co 5; RHLC 201 *Col.*
Arboleda, Julio ("Don Julio") (1817-1862) AC I, 133; AEHA 475; ALC I, 127; BC 41; BHLA 238; CHL 326; CLH 278; Co 5; CoL 269; FPA 81, 94; HPHA II, 54; LC 126; PCo 31; PLHA 75; RHLC 89; SASS 217 *Col.*
Arboleda, Manuel Esteban (1800-1871) Co 6 *Col.*
Arboleda, Sergio (1822-1888) BC 45; Co 6; LC 172; RHLC 210 *Col.*
Arboleda C., Enrique Co 6 *Col.*
Arboleda R., Gustavo E 8 *Ecua.*
Arboleda y Restrepo, Gustavo (1881-) CG I, 165; WLA 25 *Col.*
Arboleda Zavaleta, J. H. E 8 *Ecua.*
Arcadio Ugarte, Lucas BDC 3 *Cu.*
"Arcases" (*pseud.*) *see* Castro Esquível, Arturo
Arcaya, Pedro Manuel CG I, 166; V 29 *Venez.*
Arce, Enrique José (1871-) CG I, 166; Pan 2 *Pan.*
"Arce, José" (*pseud.*) *see* Martínez, Manuel
Arce, Julio César (1885-) Co 6 *Col.*
Arce, Miguel NM 8 *Mex.*
Arce, Milagros CG I, 167; Cu 12 *Cu.*
Arce, Napoleón (1885-) AP 37; Pan 2, 3 *Pan.*
Arce Lacaze, Luis B 2; CG I, 167 *Bol.*
Arce V., Alfonso María E 8 *Ecua.*
Arce Velarde, Enrique PB 21 *Bol.*
Arce y Sotomayor, Juan Manuel de BHC II, 382 *Chil.*
Arce y Valladares, Manuel José (1907-) CA 60; PG 475 *Guat.*
Arceo, Ernesto TM 594 *Mex.*
Arcía, Juan E. LV 360; V 30 *Venez.*
Arcila, Aníbal (1889?-1915) Co 6 *Col.*
Arciniega de la Torre, Rosa (1909-) WLA 27 *Per.*
Arciniegas, Germán (1900-) LAS 203; WLA 27 *Col.*
Arciniegas, Ismael Enrique (1865-) AC II, 353; ALC I, 303; APEH 123, 1179; Co 6; E 8; G 343; LC 183; PCo 33; RHLC 151; WLA 27 *Col.*
Arconada, César M. CG I, 169; NM 8 *Mex.*
"Arcos, Dr." (*pseud.*) *see* Delgado, Camilo S.
Arcos y Segovia, Luis de ("Fray Verdades") (1886-) A 4, 78, 80 *Arg.*
Archambault, Pedro María SD 4 *Dom.*
Archilla Cabrera, Ángel PR 31 *P.R.*
Ardila, Julio Pan 3 *Pan.*
Arecha, Waldemar A 4 *Arg.*

Arechederreta y Escalada, Juan Bautista ACe 682 *Mex.*
Arellano, Carlos HPM 118 *Mex.*
Arellano, Jerónimo M. PM 20 *Mex.*
Arellano Belloc, Francisco NM 8 *Mex.*
Arellano Lamota, Alfredo E 8 *Ecua.*
Arellano R., Abel Antonio C 25 *Chil.*
Arellano y Yecorat, Juan CL 127 *Chil.*
Arellano y Yecorat, Nicolás C 43 *Chil.*
Arenal, César del BDC 3; Cu 12 *Cu.*
Arenales, Alejandro CA 60 *Guat.*
Arenales, Alfonso C 2 *Chil.*
"Arenales, Ricardo" (*pseud.*) *see* Osorio, Miguel Ángel
Arenas, Antonio Vicente RHLC 212 *Col.*
Arenas, Jesús Co 6 *Col.*
Arenas Guzmán, Diego Ig 29; NM 8 *Mex.*
Arenas Lavín, Zulema C 2 *Chil.*
Arengo, Eduardo L. A 4 *Arg.*
Arengo, Juan B. A 4 *Arg.*
Arengo, L. Par 5 *Para.*
Arenzana, Manuel de TM 603 *Mex.*
"Areopagita, Dionisio" (*pseud.*) *see* Dávalos Mora, Rafael
Aréstegui, Narciso (1826-1869) BHLA 338; P 2 *Per.*
Arestigueta Montero, Rafael V 30 *Venez.*
Areta, Ricardo María E 8 *Ecua.*
Arévalo, Carlos NM 9 *Mex.*
Arévalo, José TM 423 *Mex.*
Arévalo González, Rafael (1866-) BHLA 526, 572; V 30; VPF 75; WLA 28 *Venez.*
Arévalo Martínez, Rafael (1884-) APEH 857, 1191; CA 60, 61; CG I, 175; FPA 291, 300; G 346; IE 21; PG 366; SASS 131; WLA 28 *Guat.*
Argáez, Enrique de (1858-) Co 6 *Col.*
Argáez, Jerónimo (1841-) BC 50 *Col.*
Argañarás, Héctor D. A 4 *Arg.*
Argañarás, Segundo M. A 4 *Arg.*
Argerich, Antonio CHL 191; CLH 164; LA VIII, 629 *Arg.*
Argerich, Juan Antonio (1862-1924) A 5; CG I, 176 *Arg.*
Argilagos, Rafael G. CG I, 177; PCu 29; PJC 28 *Cu.*
Argüedas, Alcides (1879-) B 2; BHLA 484; BT 27; CG I, 177; CHL 311; G 320; GLO 238; LB 627; PLHA 208, 285; SASS 109; WLA 28 *Bol.*
Argüedas Prada, Juan (1830-1869?) P 2 *Per.*
Argüelles, Agustín PR 55 *P.R.*
Argüelles Bringas, Roberto (1875-1915) AMP 109; APMM 1; HLM 519; PNM 1 *Mex.*
Argüello, Agenor NL 173 *Nicar.*
Argüello, Lino (188.-) FPA 358, 370; NL 158; PN 65 *Nicar.*
Argüello, Rodolfo NL 258 *Nicar.*
Argüello, Santiago (1872-) CG I, 177; CHL 504; CLH 499; FPA 357, 364; G 375; IE 21; LAS 198, 206; NL 38; PLHA 135; PN 199; SASS 128 *Nicar.*
Argüello, Solón PN 57, 223 *Nicar.*
Argüello Mora, Manuel (1834-1902) CA 5; EPCR 33; IBCR IV, 14 *et passim C.R.*
Argumosa, Domingo PM 20 *Mex.*
Arias, Ana Dolores GPCA III, 275; PS 134 *Salv.*
Arias, Céleo (1835-1890) HL I, 417 *Hond.*

Arias, Eduardo Co 6 *Col.*
Arias, Harmodio Pan 3 *Pan.*
Arias, Ignacio TM 75 *Mex.*
Arias, Juan de Dios HLM 490 *Mex.*
Arias, Luis SD 4 *Dom.*
Arias, Miguel E 8 *Ecua.*
Arias, Pedro BDC 3; Cu 13 *Cu.*
Arias Argáez, Daniel (1869-) Co 6; LC 195; RHLC 211 *Col.*
Arias Caballero, José PM 20 *Mex.*
Arias de Ugarte, Hernando (1561-1633) HLNG I, 235 *Col.*
Arias Robalino, Augusto (1903-) BHLA 593; CG I, 178; E 8; WLA 30 *Ecua.*
Arias Sánchez, Alberto E 9, 73 *Ecua.*
Arias Suárez, Eduardo ("Constantino Pla") (1896-) Co 6, 56; RHLC 193 *Col.*
Arias Vargas, Leopoldo (1832-1883) BC 51; Co 7; RHLC 165 *Col.*
Arié, Adriano CA 5 *C.R.*
Ariel, Jorge (Humberto Salvador G.) E 9 *Ecua.*
Ariel Rodríguez, Julio A 5 *Arg.*
"Ario" (*pseud.*) TM 343 *Mex.*
Arismendi, Pedro V 30 *Venez.*
Arismendi Brito, Pedro CG I, 180; LV 50; V 30 *Venez.*
Arista, Juan HPM 95 *Mex.*
Aristeguieta Grillet, Luis V 31 *Venez.*
Aristeguieta Rojas, F. de P. V 31 *Venez.*
Aristi, Manuel TM 76, 423 *Mex.*
Aristigueta, Joaquín Cu 13 *Cu.*
Aristimuño Coll, Carlos V 31 *Venez.*
Aristizabal, Miguel E 9 *Ecua.*
Aristondo, Ángel A 5 *Arg.*
Aristy, J. R. PD 19; SD 4 *Dom.*
Ariza, Juan de Cu 13 *Cu.*
Arizabalo, Lorenzo BHC II, 295 *Chil.*
Arizaga, José Rafael (1825-1899) E 9 *Ecua.*
Arízaga, Manuel Nicolás E 9; PE 215 *Ecua.*
Arjona, Pedro de PM 20 *Mex.*
Arjona Quintero, Julio (1878-) AP 39; CG I, 182; Pan 3 *Pan.*
Arlegui, José BHC II, 434 *Chil.*
Arlt, Roberto (1900-) A 5; LAC 135 *Arg.*
Armada, Selim Cu 13 *Cu.*
"Armando Duval" (*pseud.*) *see* Monteagudo Rodríguez, Joaquín
"Armando Ruido" (*pseud.*) *see* Martínez Nadal, Rafael
Armanini, José A 5 *Arg.*
Armas, Augusto de (1859-1893) Cu 13 *Cu.*
Armas, Blanca Angélica de V 31 *Venez.*
Armas y Cárdenas, José de ("Justo de Lara") (1866-1919) CG I, 183; Cu 13, 88; G 335; HLC 75; LAS 198; RLC 304 *Cu.*
Armas y Céspedes, Francisco ARC 75 *Cu.*
Armas y Céspedes, José de (1834-1900) Cu 13; RLC 141, 227 *Cu.*
Armas y Céspedes, Juan Ignacio de (1842-1889) Cu 13 *Cu.*
Armas y Colón, Ramón de Cu 13; PCu 31 *Cu.*
Armas y Martínez, Francisco Cu 14 *Cu.*
Armaza, Emilio BAP 101 *Per.*
Armenteros y Ovando, A. Cu 14 *Cu.*
Armenteros y Ovando, P. R. Cu 14 *Cu.*
Armentia, Nicolás (1845-) B 2 *Bol.*
Armida, José Q. PM 20 *Mex.*

Armín, Betina de E. Cu 14 *Cu.*
Armiño de Cuesta, Robustiana PR 31 *P.R.*
Armstrong, Emilia V. PA 147 *P.R.*
Arnáiz, Álvaro PB 53 *Bol.*
Arnaldo Meyners, José (1904-   ) QPR (1) 178 *P.R.*
Arnao, Nicolás Cu 14 *Cu.*
Arnau y Garavídez, José BDC 109; PR 11 *P.R.*
Arocena, Alfredo (1869-   ) UT 41 *Uru.*
Arocha, José PB 26 *Bol.*
Arocha, José Ignacio BC 52 *Col.*
Arocha, Pablo José ("Fausto") V 31, 70 *Venez.*
Arocha Moreno, Jesús V 31 *Venez.*
Arochena, Antonio CA 61 *Guat.*
"Arona, Juan de" (*pseud.*) *see* Paz Soldán y Unánue, Pedro
Aronowsky, Eliezer Cu 14 *Cu.*
Arosemena, Domingo (-1886) BC 52; Co 7; Pan 3 *Col.*
Arosemena, Juan Demóstenes Pan 3 *Pan.*
Arosemena, Justo (1817-1896) AP 41; BHLA 377; LC 156; Pan 3 *Pan.*
Arosemena, Mariano (1794-1868) Pan 3 *Pan.*
Arosemena, Pablo (1836-1920) Pan 3 *Pan.*
Aróstegui, Gonzalo Cu 14 *Cu.*
Arozteguy, Abdón (1853-   ) UT 43 *Uru.*
Arpesella, L. A. A 5; CG I, 192 *Arg.*
Arquellada Mendoza, Domingo José de BHC III, 97, 98 *Chil.*
"Arquitecto-poeta, El" (*pseud.*) *see* Seijas Cook, Rafael
Arraiz, Antonio V 31 *Venez.*
Arraiz, Juan V 31 *Venez.*
Arrangoiz, Francisco de Paula HLM 358 *Mex.*
Arrascaeta, Enrique de CHL 211; CLH 174; HCLU I, 321, 418 *et passim;* U 2 *Uru.*
Arrate, Félix de (1697-1766) RLC 30, 31, 43, 174 *Cu.*
Arrázola, Antonio María (1835-   ) BC 56; Co 7 *Col.*
Arrázola, Joseph de HPM 101 *Mex.*
Arreaza Calatrava, José Tadeo CG I, 199; V 31 *Venez.*
Arredondo, Marcos F. A 5; CG I, 199 *Arg.*
Arredondo, Vetilio SD 4 *Dom.*
Arredondo, Vicente TM 76, 313 *Mex.*
Arreguine, Víctor (1868-   ) CG I, 200; CHL 222; CLH 185; PLHA 236; U 2; UL 122 *Uru.*
Arriaga, Alberto F. Ig 29; NM 9; PM 21 *Mex.*
Arriaga, Cristóbal de BHLA 118 *Chil.*
Arriaga, José Joaquín (1831-1896) Ig 30 *Mex.*
Arriaga, Ponciano (1811-1865) HLM 361 *Mex.*
Arriaza, A. Pedroso de Cu 14 *Cu.*
Arriaza, Armando ("Hermes Nahuel") C 15 *Chil.*
Arriaza, Eugenio de (-1886) Cu 14 *Cu.*
Arriaza, Ignacio Gonzalo de TM 76 *Mex.*
Arricivita, Juan Domingo ACe 684 *Mex.*
Arrieta, Diógenes A. (1849-1897) BC 56; Co 7; PCo 42; RHLC 143 *Col.*
Arrieta, Emilio V 31 *Venez.*

Arrieta, Rafael Alberto (1889-   ) A 5; APAM 140; APEH 659, 1188; CG I, 201; G 309; LAC 82, 143; NPA 113; SASS 49; WLA 30 *Arg.*
Arrieta Canas, Luis C 60 *Chil.*
Arrigunaga y Gutiérrez, Joaquín de TM 76 *Mex.*
Arrioja, Manuel TM 77 *Mex.*
Arrioja, Manuel M. TM 76 *Mex.*
Arriola, Emilio de TM 77 *Mex.*
Arriola, Juan de PM 21 *Mex.*
Arriola, M. Y. CA 61; CG I, 201 *Guat.*
Arriola, Manuel N. A 5 *Arg.*
Arriola, Osmundo (1881-   ) CA 61, 62; FPA 292, 309; PG 424 *Guat.*
Arriola, Pedro Juan (1698-   ) HPM 453 *Mex.*
Arriola Adame, J. TM 423 *Mex.*
Arriola Ledesma, Abelardo LAS 207 *Per.*
Arriola P., Juan José TM 77 *Mex.*
Arrocha Graell, C. Pan 3, 4 *Pan.*
Arrondo, Matías Cu 14 *Cu.*
Arróniz, Joaquín HLM 492 *Mex.*
Arróniz, Marcos (-1858) HLM 318, 358; HLMex 151; HPM 828; NM 1; PoM 156; TM 526 *Mex.*
Arroyo, Carlos Alberto A 5; CG I, 202 *Arg.*
Arroyo, J. I. V 31 *Venez.*
Arroyo, José Manuel V 31 *Venez.*
Arroyo, Santiago Co 7 *Col.*
Arroyo Cordero, Américo BP 498 *P.R.*
Arroyo de Anda, Francisco TM 11, 78 *Mex.*
Arroyo de Anda, Jr., Andrés PM 21 *Mex.*
Arroyo de Llorente, María P 2 *Per.*
Arroyo del Río, C. A. PE 59 *Ecua.*
Arroyo Diez, Jaime (1815-1863) Co 7 *Col.*
Arroyo Lameda, Eduardo V 31 *Venez.*
Arroyo Pastor, César Emilio (1890-   ) BHLA 517; CG I, 202; E 9, 73; G 343; IE 23; PLE 122; WLA 31 *Ecua.*
Arrubla, Gerardo (1873-   ) CG I, 204; III, 20; Co 7, 33 *Col.*
Arrubla de Codazzi, María Teresa BC 59; Co 7 *Col.*
Arrué, María Teresa de PS 182 *Salv.*
Arrué de Miranda, Luz (1852-   ) CA 62; PS 131 *Salv.*
Arruebarrena, Miguel I. Cu 14 *Cu.*
Arrueta, Mariano Benjamín (1882-   ) BT 31 *Bol.*
Arrufat y Herrero, José (1843-1883) Cu 14 *Cu.*
"Arrugado, El Vate" (*pseud.*) *see* Roquero y Domínguez, Juan
Arsamasseva, Margarita E. A 5 *Arg.*
Arslan, Emir Emin A 5 *Arg.*
Artaza, Policarpo Par 5; PPa 261 *Para.*
Arteaga, Alfredo de A 5; CG I, 194; G 309 *Arg.*
Arteaga, José Joaquín (1878-1926) Co 7 *Col.*
Arteaga, Manuel Cu 14 *Cu.*
Arteaga, Ricardo (1843-1915) RLC 240, 242 *Cu.*
Arteaga Alemparte, Domingo (1835-1880) BHLA 347; C 25, 60; CHL 255; CL 127; CLH 215; HC 157, 175; HPHA II, 371; PCh 63 *Chil.*

Arteaga Alemparte, Justo (1834-1882) C 60; CG I, 194; CHL 255; CL 128; CLH 215; HC 172 *Chil.*

Artel, Jorge (1909-   ) BHLA 588 *Col.*

Artiga, Juan GLO 242 *Cu.*

Artigas, José Gervasio (1764-1850) AA II, 30, 300 *Uru.*

Artucio Ferreira, Antonia CG I, 197; PU 24; U 2 *Uru.*

Arvelo, Atilia de V 31 *Venez.*

Arvelo, Clotilde Crespo de (1887-   ) V 31; WLA 31 *Venez.*

Arvelo, José Antonio ("Joaner") V 32 *Venez.*

Arvelo, Martín Matos SD 4 *Dom.*

Arvelo, Rafael V 32 *Venez.*

Arvelo Larriva, Alfredo BHLA 522; V 32 *Venez.*

Arvelo Torrealba, Alberto V 32 *Venez.*

Arzarello de Fontana, Sofía HSLU II, pt 8, 18; PoU 49; U 2 *Uru.*

Arze, Elías C 2 *Chil.*

Arzeno, Julio V. SD 4 *Dom.*

Asanza, José ARC 42 *Cu.*

Asbaje y Ramírez de Cantillana, Juana Inés de ("Sor Juana Inés de la Cruz") (1651-1695) AB 21; AEHA 278; AMP 219; BHLA 93; CG I, 205, 725; CHL 30; CLH 26; FPA 339, 341; HLM 161; HLMex 70; HLNG I, 288; HPHA I, 73; HPM 235; PM 21, 31; PMe I, 247; PoM 19; SAL 17; SASS 348; TM 106; WSAL 10 *Mex.*

Ascanio, Efraín PM 21 *Mex.*

Ascarrunz, Moisés (1862-   ) B 2; BT 37; CG I, 205 *Bol.*

Ascasubi, Hilario ("Aniceto el Gallo" "Paulino Lucero" "Jacinto Amores" or "Simón Peñalva") (1807-1875) A 6; BHLA 280; CG I, 205; CHL 158; CLH 137; G 309; HLA 392; LA II, 621, 676, 686; PLHA 79; SASS 13; SPLA 62 *Arg.*

Asenjo, Federico ("Don Claro-Oscuro") PR 16, 18, 45 *P.R.*

Asenjo y del Valle, Conrado (1881-   ) PR 24, 48; QPR (1) 25; (2) 26 *P.R.*

Asensio, Esteban de CG I, 207; Co 7; HLNG I, 120; RHLC 21 *Col.*

Ashton, H. E. SD 4 *Dom.*

Asís, Francisco de HLNG I, 191 *Col.*

"Asmodeo" (*pseud.*) *see* Agostini, Rafael

Asorrey, José Manuel ACe 685 *Mex.*

Aspiazu, Agustín (1817-1897) B 3 *Bol.*

Astol Bussati, Eugenio (1872-   ) BP 498, 574; PR 11, 41, 48, 49, 55; QPR (2) 27 *P.R.*

Astorquiza, Eliodoro C 60; NC 491 *Chil.*

"Astrea, Barón de" (*pseud.*) *see* Guerra, Ramón Héctor

Astúa Aguilar, José (1859-   ) CA 5; EPCR 58 *C.R.*

Astudillo, D. R. E 9 *Ecua.*

Astudillo Morales, Efrén E 9 *Ecua.*

Astudillo Ortega, José María E 9 *Ecua.*

Asturias, Miguel Ángel CA 62; CG I, 213 *Guat.*

"Atbe" (*pseud.*) *see* Barrera, Ángel T.

"Athos" (*pseud.*) *see* Moncayo, Abelardo

Atiles García, G. PR 8, 16, 31 *P.R.*

"Atl, Doctor" (*pseud.*) *see* Murillo, Gerardo

Atria, Jorge Octavio CL 128 *Chil.*

Attwell de Veyga, José Eduardo A 6 *Arg.*

Auber, Virginia ("Felicia") Cu 14, 56 *Cu.*

Auclair, Marcelle C 2, 44 *Chil.*

Audivert, Santiago ARC 42 *Cu.*

Audivert Pérez, Francisco ARC 42 *Cu*

Audivert Tibeau, Francisco ARC 43 *Cu.*

Augier, Ángel I. (1910-   ) PoC 16 *Cu.*

"Augusto d'Halmar" (*pseud.*) *see* Thomson, Augusto

Aulino, Pedro A 6 *Arg.*

Auñon, Marqués de V 75 *Venez.*

"Aurora" (*pseud.*) *see* Riverol y Campos, Aurora

Austria, Guillermo V 32 *Venez.*

Austria, José de CG I, 220; V 32 *Venez.*

Autrajicilio V 32 *Venez.*

Auzón, Edgardo E. A 6 *Arg.*

Auzón, Eugenio A 6 *Arg.*

Ávalos Droguett, Gerardo C 2, 44; NC 16 *Chil.*

Ávalos y Figueroa, Diego de (fl. c. 1600) CHL 25; CLH 22; GLO 252; P 2 *Per.*

Aveledo, Antonio V 33 *Venez.*

Aveledo, J. M. V 33 *Venez.*

Aveledo Urbaneja, Agustín V 33 *Venez.*

Avelino, Andrés SD 4 *Dom.*

Avella Martínez (*or* Mendoza), Temístocles (1841-   ) BC 61; Co 7 *Col.*

Avellán Ferres, Enrique E 9 *Ecua.*

Avellaneda, Elena (1904-   ) A 6 *Arg.*

Avellaneda, Gertrudis Gómez de *see* Gómez de Avellaneda y Arteaga, Gertrudis

"Avellaneda, La Señorita de" TM 344 *Mex.*

Avellaneda, Luis NM 9 *Mex.*

Avellaneda, Marco Manuel de (1813-1841) CG I, 222; LA VI, 1095 *Arg.*

Avellaneda, Nicolás (1837-1885) A 6, 24; CG I, 222; G 309; GEA III, XVII; HLA 429; LA VI, 1132; VII, 385 *Arg.*

Avellanet, Juan C 44; CG I, 222 *Chil.*

Avellanet Mattei, Ernesto PR 31 *P.R.*

Avendaño, Francisco de BHC II, 276; CG I, 223 *Chil.*

Avendaño de Pérez de León, Jacoba Ig 33; NM 9 *Mex.*

Avendaño F., Onofre C 44 *Chil.*

Avendaño Losada, V. M. V 33 *Venez.*

Ávila, Domingo P 2 *Per.*

Ávila, Esteban TM 78 *Mex.*

Ávila, F. A. TM 78 *Mex.*

Ávila, Gaspar de SCL 210, 589 *Chil.*

Ávila, Julio Enrique (1892-   ) IE 25 *Salv.*

Ávila, Lorenzo E. Cu 15 *Cu.*

Ávila y Uribe, M. C. de TM 78 *Mex.*

Avilés, Juan Ramón (1886-   ) PN 81; WLA 34 *Nicar.*

Avilés, Luis PN 195 *Nicar.*

Avilés, Maximiliano PR 45 *P.R.*

Avilés M., Eleodoro E 9 *Ecua.*

Avilés P., Miguel C. (1892-   ) Pan 4 *Pan.*

Avilés Ramírez, Eduardo (188.-   ) FPA 358, 366 *Nicar.*

Avilés Ramírez, Luis (188.-   ) FPA 357, 365; NL 83; PN 195 *Nicar.*

"Ayala, Fernando de" (*pseud.*) *see* Ortega, Simón

Ayala, Francisco B 3 *Bol.*

Ayala, José Ramón V 33 *Venez.*
Ayala, Juan de la Cruz Par 5 *Para.*
Ayala, María Delfina E 9 *Ecua.*
Ayala, Martín V 33 *Venez.*
Ayala A., Ramón V 33 *Venez.*
Ayala de Larrondo, Cristina ARC 43; Cu 15 *Cu.*
Ayala Duarte, Crispín CG I, 226; E 9; LAS 198; PR 25; SD 5
Ayala Duarte, Miguel Ángel CG I, 226; V 33 *Venez.*
Ayala Michelena, Leopoldo V 33 *Venez.*
Ayala Moura, Eladio BP 502; PR 26 *P.R.*
Ayala y Aguilar, José de Cu 15 *Cu.*
Ayala y Lozano, Rafael de BC 63 *Col.*
Ayala y Rojas, Íñigo de BHC I, 192 *Chil.*
"Ayanque, Simón" (*pseud.*) *see* Terralla y Landa, Esteban de
Aybar, Andrejulio (1893-   ) FPA 228, 248; PA 257; PD 20; SD 5 *Dom.*
Aybar, Manuel Eudoro PD 25; SD 5 *Dom.*
Aycardo, Soledad TM 79 *Mex.*
Aycinena, Juan Fermín (1838-1898) CA 62; GPCA III, 21 *Guat.*
Ayerra y Santa María, Francisco (1630-1708) HLM 157; HPM 204; PR 31 *Mex.*
Ayllón, Joaquín (1712-   ) BHLA 119, 135; PLE 17 *Ecua.*
Ayllón, Juan de (1604 *or* 1605-   ) BHLA 91; CHL 25; LP 318; P 2 *Per.*
Aymerich, Juan A 6 *Arg.*
Ayora, Benjamín E 9 *Ecua.*
Ayora, Isidro R. CG I, 228; E 9 *Ecua.*
Ayora, José E 9 *Ecua.*
Azamor y Ramírez, Manuel (1733-1796) HLA 36; LA IV, 654 *Arg.*
Azara, Félix de LA IV, 991 *Arg.*
Azarola-Gil, Luis Enrique (1882-   ) CG I, 231; WLA 34 *Uru.*
Azcárate, Nicolás (1828-1894) BHLA 350, 389; CHL 465; CLH 406; Cu 15 *Cu.*
Azcárate y Lezama, José Ignacio de ACe 685 *Mex.*
Azcárate y Lezama, Juan Francisco (-1831) ACe 686; HLMex 118; HPM 497 *Mex.*
Azcuénaga, Domingo de APA I, xlvi, 183; HLA 93; SPLA 29 *Arg.*
Azevedo, Francisco de PM 21 *Mex.*
Azevedo Lúquez, Pastor A 6 *Arg.*
Azlor, Clementina I. A 6 *Arg.*
Aznar Barbachano, Luis TM 79 *Mex.*
Aznar Di-Bella, Eduardo V. PM 21 *Mex.*
Azócar, Rubén C 25, 60 *Chil.*
Azo-Cart, Rafael C 44 *Chil.*
Azpúrua, Francisco de CG I, 235; V 33 *Venez.*
Azpúrua, Ramón LV 8; V 33 *Venez.*
"Azucena, Adolfo de la" (*pseud.*) *see* Zenea, Juan Clemente
Azuela, Mariano (1873-   ) BHLA 557; CG I, 235; G 355; HLM 517; Ig 33; LAS 203; NM 9; WLA 35 *Mex.*
Azuero, Vicente (1787-1844) HLNG II, 522 *Col.*
Azuola, Eduardo CA 6 *C.R.*
Azuola y Lozano, José Luis de (1754?-1826) Co 8; HLNG II, 391 *Col.*
Azurdia, José CA 62 *Guat.*

B

"B. A., C." (*pseud.*) *see* Bethencourt Apolinaris, Cayetano
B., J. J. Cu 15 *Cu.*
B. O. F. C 44 *Chil.*
Bablot, Alfredo TM 424 *Mex.*
Babuglia, Antonio ("Abul Bagí") A 6, 78 *Arg.*
Baca, Francisco NL 210 *Nicar.*
Baca, Luis TM 603 *Mex.*
Bacardí Moreau, Emilio (1844-1922) BDC 109; CG I, 237; Cu 15; GLO 242; RLC 337 *Cu.*
"Bachiller Munguía" (*pseud.*) *see* Churión, Juan José
"Bachiller Sansón Carrasco" (*pseud.*) V 33 *Venez.*
"Bachiller Toribio Sánchez de Almodóvar" (*pseud.*) *see* Monte y Aponte, Domingo del
Bachiller y Morales, Antonio (1812-1889) ARC 76; BDC 3; BHLA 390; CHL 482; CLH 422; Cu 15; RLC 146, 172, 246 *Cu.*
Bachini, Antonio U 2; UL 123 *Uru.*
Badeau, Adam Cu 16 *Cu.*
Badilla, Eduardo Segundo C 44 *Chil.*
Badillo, José Enrique TM 79 *Mex.*
Badillo, Manuel Cu 16 *Cu.*
Baena, Fernando E. PCo 52 *Col.*
Báez, Buenaventura SD 5 *Dom.*
Báez, Cecilio (1862-   ) CG I, 239; Par 5; PPa 89; PT 11; WLA 35 *Para.*
Báez, Jorge Par 7 *Para.*
Báez, Paulino González CG I. 239; Cu 16; PCu 32; PJC 32 *Cu.*
Báez, Ramón SD 5 *Dom.*
Báez Camargo, Gonzalo PM 21 *Mex.*
Baeza, Alejandro CL 129 *Chil.*
Baeza Repetto, Letizia C 2 *Chil.*
"Bagí, Abul" (*pseud.*) *see* Babuglia, Antonio
Bagnat, Clemente A 6 *Arg.*
Bahamonde, Manuel A 6; LA VIII, 593 *Arg.*
Balach, José A 6 *Arg.*
Balagué, Juan B 19; CG I, 243 *Bol.*
Balaguer, Joaquín (hijo) CG I, 243; SD 5 *Dom.*
Balaguer de Salcedo, Pedro P 2 *Per.*
Balanzó, Miguel ARC 43 *Cu.*
Balarezo Pinillos, Ezequiel (1892-   ) P 2 *Per.*
Balbás, Casiano BDC 3; BP 509; PR 11 *P.R.*
Balbás Capó, Vicente CG I, 245; PR 16 *P.R.*
Balbín de Unquera, Antonio CG I, 245; V 33 *Venez.*
Balboa Troya y Quesada, Silvestre de HLC 14; HPHA I, 216; RLC 20 *Cu.*
Balbontín, Manuel (1824-1894) Ig 36; NM 10 *Mex.*
Balbuena, Bernardo de (1568-1627) CG I, 246; CHL 23, 498; CLH 20; HLM 93; HLMex 43; HPHA I, 52; HPM 112; PM 21; WSAL 6, 64 *Mex.*
Balcarce, Florencio (1818-1839) A 7; BHLA 215; CHL 124; CLH 107; HLA 260; LA VI, 1093; SPLA 73 *Arg.*
Balcázar Grijalba, Nicolás (1848-1873) Co 8 *Col.*

Balcazas, Emilia A 7 *Arg.*
Baldivieso, Enrique WLA 36 *Bol.*
Baldorioty de Castro, Román (1822-)
BHLA 391; CHL 501; CLH 441; PR 45
P.R.
Baliño, Carlos B. ARC 43 *Cu.*
Balmaceda Toro, Pedro C 60; CL 129;
NC 409 *Chil.*
Balmaceda Valdés, Gustavo C 2 *Chil.*
Balmaseda, Francisco Javier (1833-1907)
BDC 4; CG I, 247; Cu 16; RLC 223 *Cu.*
Balmes, Jaime CG I, 248; E 9 *Ecua.*
Balseiro, Benigno (1842-1895) BDC 109;
PR 11 *P.R.*
Balseiro, José A. (1900-) BP 502, 520,
576; CG I, 248; IE 25; PP 332; PR 16,
26, 32, 49; QPR (2) 28 *P.R.*
Balladares, Ángela CA 6 *C.R.*
Ballagas, Emilio (1910-) BHLA 569;
LAS 206; LH 131, 141; PoC 22 *Cu.*
Ballesteros, Antonio BDC 4; CG I, 254;
Cu 18 *Cu.*
Ballesteros, Fernando PB 186 *Bol.*
Ballesteros, Manuel Ejidio (1844-1914) HC
247 *Chil.*
Ballesteros y Larraín, Juan PCh 277 *Chil.*
Balleydier, Alfonso V 33 *Venez.*
Balliván Rocha, Rafael (1897-) BT 47
Bol.
Balliván, Adolfo (1831-1874) B 3 *Bol.*
Balliván, Manuel Vicente (1848-) BT
43; CG I, 256 *Bol.*
Balliván y Rojas, Vicente (1810-1891) B 3
Bol.
Bambill, Julio ("Falucho") Par 7 *Para.*
Banchs, Enrique (1888-) A 7; APAM
152; APEH 703; AT II, 871; BHLA 529;
CHL 186; CLH 160; FPA 16, 52; LAC
142; MSAP 174, 317; NPA 91; PLHA
149; SASS 50 *Arg.*
Bandera, Manuel BDC 5 *Cu.*
Bandera, Quintín ARC 43 *Cu.*
Bañados Espinosa, Julio C 60; CL 129;
NC 410 *Chil.*
Baños y Sotomayor, Diego de SCL 377,
589 *Venez.*
Baptista, Mariano (1832-1907) B 3 *Bol.*
Baptista Quevedo, I. V 33 *Venez.*
Baqué, Santiago (1889-) AT II, 673;
CG I, 259 *Arg.*
Baquerizas, José Manuel A 7 *Arg.*
Baquerizo Moreno, Alfredo (1859-)
BHLA 517; E 9; PE 5; PLE 56 *Ecua.*
Baquero L., Leónidas M. E 10 *Ecua.*
Baquijano y Carrillo, José BHLA 138 *Per.*
Barahona, José Antonio C 2; NC 409 *Chil.*
Barahona Vega, Clemente ("Cucalón")
(1863-) C 2, 25, 44, 60; CG I, 260; CL
130; NC 353, 410; PCh 293 *Chil.*
Barainca, José Ramón C 44 *Chil.*
Barajas Lozano, Ignacio (1899-) CG I,
261; PM 21 *Mex.*
Baralt, Blanche Zacharie de (1865-) CG
I, 261; CT 169; WLA 38 *Cu.*
Baralt, Rafael María (1810-1860) AEHA
131; BHLA 348; CG I, 261; CHL 357;
CLH 306; FPA 549, 558; HPHA I, 393;
LV 2, 87, 272; PLHA 278; SASS 543;
V 33, 64, 71 *Venez.*

Baralt y Peoli, Luis A. (1849-) CT 189;
Cu 18 *Cu.*
Baranda, Joaquín CG I, 261; TM 526 *Mex.*
Barasorda Larrazábal, Nicolás Javier (1688-
1753) Co 8; HLNG I, 361 *Col.*
Baraya, José María (1828-1878) Co 8 *Col.*
Barazábal, Mariano (1772-) ACe 714;
HLM 247; HPM 480; PM 21 *Mex.*
Barazarte, Alejandro V 34 *Venez.*
Barazarte, Amando V 34 *Venez.*
"Barba Jacob, Porfirio" (*pseud.*) *see* Osorio,
Miguel Ángel
Barbachano, Manuel TM 79, 527 *Mex.*
Barbagelata, Hugo David (1887-) CG I,
262; IE 26; PLHA 287; U 2; UT 47;
WLA 38 *Uru.*
Barbará, Federico A 7; CG I, 262 *Arg.*
Barbé Pérez, Luis Víctor G 386; U 2 *Uru.*
Barberá, José Domingo BDC 5; Cu 18 *Cu.*
Barberii, Ángel Félix V 34 *Venez.*
Barbero Torres, J. CA 6 *C.R.*
Barbosa, Tomás U 2 *Uru.*
Barbosa Terra, J. UL 123 *Uru.*
Barboza, Genaro E 10 *Ecua.*
Barceló, Simón CG I, 265; V 35 *Venez.*
Bárcena, Lucas AP 45; Pan 4 *Pan.*
Barcena, Serapio E. U 2 *Uru.*
Barcena Valmaceda, Miguel de PM 21
Mex.
Barco, Jesús María BC 66; Co 8 *Col.*
Barco, José Antonio Co 8 *Col.*
Barco Centenera, Martín del (1535-1605)
A 7; BHLA 62; CG I, 267; CLH 16; G
310; HPHA II, 374; LA III, 194; SCL
222, 590 *Arg.*
Barchetta, Arduino A 7 *Arg.*
Barea, Juan Bautista (1742-1789) Cu 18;
RLC 33 *Cu.*
Bareiro, Francisco L. Par 7; PPa 143
Para.
Barella, Carlos C 25; PCh 419 *Chil.*
Barés, Justo Fausto Cu 18 *Cu.*
Bari M., David C 25 *Chil.*
Barilli, Antonio TM 603 *Mex.*
Barinaga y Ponce de León, Graziella CG I,
270; Cu 18 *Cu.*
Barletta, Leónidas (1903-) A 7; BHLA
635; CG I, 271; LAC 61, 136 *Arg.*
Barnechea y Albiz, Juan de BHC I, 586
Chil.
"Baró, A. L." (*pseud.*) *see* Iglesia y Santos,
Álvaro de la
"Barón de Astrea" (*pseud.*) *see* Guerra,
Ramón Héctor
Barón de Gostkowski *see* Gosdawa, Gustavo
"Barón de Keef, El" (*pseud.*) *see* Elguera,
Federico
Barona, Miguel Ángel PE 239 *Ecua.*
Barona Pizarro, José María Co 8 *Col.*
Barquera, Juan María Wenceslao (1779-
1840) ACe 227; HLM 246, 253; HPM
491; TM 80, 587 *Mex.*
Barquero, Antonio NL 191; PN 177 *Nicar.*
Barra, Bernabé de la C 2; NC 16 *Chil.*
"Barra, Casimiro de la" (*pseud.*) *see* Soto
Borda, Clímaco
Barra, Ema de la ("César Duayén") A 7,
78; CHL 195; CLH 167; LA VIII, 623
Arg.
Barra, Federico de la A 7 *Arg.*

Barra Fontecilla, Tomás de la C 25 *Chil.*
Barra Lastarria, Eduardo de la ("Rubén Rubí") (1839-1900) BHLA 424; C 25, 26, 61; CHL 260; CL 131; CLH 221; HC 163; PCh 93; SAL 110 *Chil.*
Barra y Valenzuela, Pedro NM 10 *Mex.*
Barragán de Toscano, Refugio (1846-1916) Ig 38; NM 10; PM 22; TM 80 *Mex.*
Barrajón Cervantes, Germinal A 7 *Arg.*
Barranco, Francisco Salustiano Cu 18 *Cu.*
Barranco, Manuel IE 28 *Mex.*
Barrantes Molina, Luis CA 6; EPCR 387; IBCR IV, 129 *et passim C.R.*
Barrasa, Jacinto (-1704) SCL 340, 590 *Per.*
Barreda, Domingo ACe 723 *Mex.*
Barreda, Ernesto Mario (1883-) A 7, 71, 80; APAM 171; APEH 833; BHLA 529; CG I, 282; CHL 187; LAC 146; NPA 81 *Arg.*
Barreda, Francisco BHC I, 368 *Chil.*
Barreda, Gabino BHLA 389 *Mex.*
Barreda, Octavio G. TM 424 *Mex.*
Barreda, Rafael A 7, 80; CG I, 282 *Arg.*
Barreda y Laos, Felipe (1888-) P 2 *Per.*
Barreiro, Segundo PU 31 *Uru.*
Barrenechea, Andrés B 3 *Bol.*
Barrenechea, Julio (1906-) C 26; CMPC 156; LAS 206; PCC xxiii, 285 *Chil.*
Barrenechea, Mariano Antonio CG I, 283; LAC 156 *Arg.*
Barrenechea y Albis, Juan de (1669-) CHL 17; CLH 14; HPHA II, 336; SCL 331, 548, 590 *Chil.*
Barrera, Ángel T. ("Atbe") CG I, 213, 283; E 10, 73 *Ecua.*
Barrera, Carlos (1888-) AMP 129; APMM 5; HLM 524; Ig 39; NM 10; PM 22; TM 424, 527 *Mex.*
Barrera, Francisco O. (1827?-1861) BC 68 *Col.*
Barrera, H. J. E 10 *Ecua.*
Barrera, Isaac J. (1884-) CG I, 283; E 10; IE 29; LAS 198; PE 110; PLE 92 *Ecua.*
Barrera, José de la PM 22 *Mex.*
Barrera, Juan Manuel (1828-1888) BC 67; Co 8 *Col.*
Barrera, Manuel de Jesús (1836-) BC 68 *Col.*
Barrera, Pantaleón Ig 40; NM 10 *Mex.*
Barrera, Pedro A. de la C 26 *Chil.*
Barrera, Pedro María TM 81 *Mex.*
Barrera, Ramón Cu 18 *Cu.*
Barrera de León, Ignacio TM 81 *Mex.*
Barrera F., Diógenes (-1904) C 2; NC 16 *Chil.*
Barrera Parra, Jaime Co 8 *Col.*
Barrera Peniche, Alfonso (1864-1903) Ig 40; NM 10 *Mex.*
Barreras, Antonio Cu 18 *Cu.*
Barrero, José Co 8 *Col.*
Barret *see* Barrett
Barreto, Cimón CA 6 *C.R.*
Barreto, Federico (1872-) P 2 *Per.*
Barreto, José María ("Ramón Román") (1875-) CG I, 284; P 2 *Per.*
Barreto, Marino ARC 43 *Cu.*
Barreto Álvarez, Celestino CG I, 284; Co 8 *Col.*

Barreto Peña, Samuel V 35 *Venez.*
Barrett, Rafael CG I, 284; GLO 235; OA 99; Par 7; U 3; UL 123 *Uru.*
Barrientos Díaz, P. J. C 61; NC 411 *Chil.*
Barriga, Honorato Co 8 *Col.*
Barriga, Isidoro E 10 *Ecua.*
Barriga, José Elías P 2 *Per.*
Barriga, Juan Agustín C 61; CG I, 285; CL 131 *Chil.*
Barrio, Rafael del Cu 18 *Cu.*
Barrionuevo, Joaquín (1889-) CA 6; EPCR 391; IBCR IV, 65 *C.R.*
Barrios, Braulio V 35 *Venez.*
Barrios, Eduardo (1884-) BHLA 511; C 2, 44; CG I, 287; CHL 280; G 323; GLO 239; NC 354; OA 153; PLHA 208; SASS 171 *Chil.*
Barrios, Evaristo A 8 *Arg.*
Barrios, Héctor L. Par 7 *Para.*
Barrios, Roberto (189.-) FPA 358, 379 *Nicar.*
Barrios Cruz, Luis V 35 *Venez.*
Barrios de los Ríos, José María ("Duralis Estars") (1864-1903) CG I, 288; II, 194; NM 10; PM 22, 41 *Mex.*
Barrios F., Ciriaco ("Gil Guero") C 26; CG I, 287 *Chil.*
Barrios Hudtwalcker, Eduardo (1884-) WLA 40 *Chil.*
Barrios Vallejo, Francisco A 8 *Arg.*
Barrón R., Alberto TM 424 *Mex.*
Barros, Claudio C 26 *Chil.*
Barros, José P. A 8 *Arg.*
Barros, Juan C 2 *Chil.*
Barros Arana, Diego (1830-1907) BHLA 293, 361; C 61; CG I, 289; CHL 14, 284; CL 132; CLH 241; HC 105; SASS 188 *Chil.*
Barros Borgoño, Luis C 61 *Chil.*
Barros Grez, Daniel (1834-1904) BHLA 403; C 2, 26, 44; CHL 271; CLH 231; HC 232; NC 17, 354; SASS 167 *Chil.*
Barros Lynch, Víctor C 26 *Chil.*
Barros Méndez, Luis C 26 *Chil.*
Barrutia, Salvador (1842-1889) CA 62; GPCA II, 303; PG 207 *Guat.*
Barry, Carlos A. A 8 *Arg.*
Barthalot, Irene A 8 *Arg.*
Bartolini, Ricardo V 35 *Venez.*
"Bartolito" (*pseud.*) *see* Mitre y Vedia, Bartolomé
Bartolomé, Higinia V 35 *Venez.*
Bartolomeis, Antonio de A 8 *Arg.*
Barzo, Carlos del CG I, 279; P 2 *Per.*
Bas, J. J. PR 16, 58 *P.R.*
Bas, Luis Ángel Cu 18 *Cu.*
Bas y Pí, R. PU 35 *Uru.*
Basa, Leopoldo A 8; CG I, 289 *Arg.*
Basadre, Jorge (1903-) BHLA 602; P 2; WLA 42 *Per.*
Basadre, Modesto P 2 *Per.*
Basail, Tomás Cu 18 *Cu.*
Basalenque, Diego de (1577-1651) HLM 208 *Mex.*
Basave del Castillo N., C. TM 527 *Mex.*
Basave y del Castillo Negrete, Agustín (1886-) CG I, 290; G 355; NM 1; WLA 42 *Mex.*
"Baset, George" (*pseud.*) *see* Miranda, Ignacio de

Basoa Marsella, Francisco Cu 18 *Cu.*
Basso Maglio, Vicente LU 64, 666; PIU III, 170; PoU 55; U 3 *Uru.*
Bassols, Narciso CG I, 291; TM 82, 425 *Mex.*
Bastar Sasso, José M. PM 22 *Mex.*
Bastidas, José B. E 10 *Ecua.*
Bastitta, José Pedro PU 252 *Uru.*
"Bastos, Rey de" (*pseud.*) *see* Tejera, Felipe
Basualdo, Benjamín A 8 *Arg.*
Basurto, Carmen G. TM 82 *Mex.*
Basurto, José Ignacio ACe 726; HLM 246 *Mex.*
Batalla, José Guillermo (1886-) AP 47; Pan 4 *Pan.*
Batallas, Leónidas E 10 *Ecua.*
Batrell, Ricardo ARC 43 *Cu.*
Batres, Juan CA 62 *Guat.*
Batres, Luis CA 62 *Guat.*
Batres, Manuel de CA 62 *Guat.*
Batres Jáuregui, Antonio (1847-) CA 62, 63 *Guat.*
Batres y Montúfar, José de (1809-1844) AEHA 885; BHLA 244; BLN 153; CA 63, 64; CG I, 294; CHL 506; CLH 446; FPA 291, 293; GPCA I, 221; HPHA I, 194; PG 88; PS 33 *Guat.*
Battle Ordóñez, José (1856-1930) BHLA 360 *Uru.*
Baturini, G. TM 527 *Mex.*
Baturoni, Gerónimo Ig 42; NM 10; TM 83 *Mex.*
Bauder, Ricardo Moisés V 35 *Venez.*
Baudón, Héctor Roberto A 8; CG I, 296 *Arg.*
Baudouin, Julio ("Julio de la Paz") (1888-) BHLA 551; P 2 *Per.*
Baudrit, Fabio CA 6, 7; IBCR IV, 34 *C.R.*
Bautista, Juan HLMex 51 *Mex.*
Bauzá, Francisco CG I, 297; CHL 224; CLH 170, 186; HSLU III, pt 4, 23; PIU I, 246; U 3; UL 123 *Uru.*
Bauzate Mesa, Jaime BHLA 149 *Arg.*
Bayón Herrera, Luis A 8, 80; CHL 199 *Arg.*
Bayona, L. TM 426 *Mex.*
Bayona Posada, Daniel (1886-1919) CG I, 301; CHL 355; Co 8, 29 *Col.*
Bayona Posada, Jorge (1888-) Co 8; PCo 54 *Col.*
Bayona Posada, Nicolás Co 8 *Col.*
Baz, Adolfo PM 22 *Mex.*
Baz, Gustavo HLM 466; PM 22; TM 83, 426, 427, 528 *Mex.*
Baz, J. TM 578 *Mex.*
Baz, Maximiliano TM 427 *Mex.*
"Baza, Xavier de" (*pseud.*) *see* Prado, Eladio
Bazán, Armando BAP 109 *Per.*
Bazán de Cámara, Rosa A 8; AT II, 859 *Arg.*
Bazán y Bustos, Abel (1887-) AT I, 21; CG I, 301 *Arg.*
Bazil, Osvaldo CG I, 301; GLO 242; PD 26; PR 6, 32; SD 5 *Dom.*
Bazorda, Nicolás Javier Co 9 *Col.*
Bazzano, Leonardo A. A 8 *Arg.*
Becchi, Constantino U 3; UL 123 *Uru.*
Becerra, Jerónimo HLM 187; TM 84 *Mex.*
Becerra, José PM 22 *Mex.*
Becerra, Marcos E. PM 22 *Mex.*

Becerra, Ricardo (1836-1905) CG I, 304; Co 9; LC 170; RHLC 200; V 35 *Col.*
Becerra, Vicente BC 71; Co 9; E 10 *Col.*
Becerra y Castro, Antonio PM 22; TM 84, 427 *Mex.*
Becerro de Bengoa, Miguel (1880-) CG I, 304; UT 69 *Uru.*
Béckert, Guillermo NC 426 *Chil.*
Becu, Carlos Albert CG I, 305; SAL 146 *Arg.*
Bechara, José U 3 *Uru.*
Bedoya, Manuel Augusto (1888-) BHLA 551; CG I, 305; CHL 307; CLH 261; LP 390; P 3 *Per.*
Bedregal, Juan Francisco (1883-) B 3; BT 51; G 320 *Bol.*
Behck, Jim von Cu 18 *Cu.*
Behety, Luis Ortiz A 66 *Arg.*
Béjar, José María BDC 5 *Cu.*
Bejarano, José Ramón (1879-) Co 9 *Col.*
Bejarano, Lázaro HPHA I, 322 *Dom.*
Belaúnde y Díez-Canseco, Víctor Andrés (1883-) BHLA 483; CG I, 307; P 3; PLHA 270; WLA 43 *Per.*
Belaval y Agostini, Amelia PR 11 *P.R.*
Belbey, José C. A 8 *Arg.*
Belelli, Antonio (hijo) A 8 *Arg.*
Belgrano, Manuel (1770-1820) A 8, 80; AA II, 33, 229; BHLA 183; GEA X; LA VIII, 830; SPLA 147 *Arg.*
Belgrano, Miguel de APA I, xlix, 245 *Arg.*
Belín Sarmiento, Augusto A 8; CG I, 309 *Arg.*
Belmonte, Pedro Luis Co 9 *Col.*
Belmonte Bermúdez, Luis de CHL 22; CLH 19; HPHA II, 173 *Sp.*
"Belsarina" (*pseud.*) *see* Sánchez Concha, María Isabel
Beltrán, Ángel TM 84 *Mex.*
Beltrán, Aurelio B 3 *Bol.*
Beltrán, José ACe 731; CG I, 310; TM 85 *Mex.*
Beltrán, Juan CG I, 311; Cu 19 *Cu.*
Beltrán, Oscar R. (1896-) A 8, 80 *Arg.*
Beltrán Ávila, Marcos B 3 *Bol.*
Beltrán de Alzate y Esquivel, Simón Estevan PM 22 *Mex.*
Beltrán Núñez, Rosario A 8 *Arg.*
Beltroy, Manuel (1890-) CG I, 313; P 3; SASS 421 *Per.*
Belzú de Dorado, Mercedes (1835?-1879) B 3; LB 590; PB 82 *Bol.*
Bellán, José Pedro CG I, 313; HSLU III, pt 3, 32; LU 64, 676, 690; PIU III, 288; U 3 *Uru.*
Belli, Ida Pan 4 *Pan.*
Bellido, Abilio Pan 4 *Pan.*
Bello, Andrés (1781-1865) AB 21; AEHA 145; BHLA 192, 210; C 61; CG I, 314; CHL 85, 237, 240; CL 135; CLH 72, 197; FPA 549, 552; G 391; HC 68, 132; HPHA I, 359; II, 357; LV 40, 122, 261; PLHA 68, 239; SAL 204, 231, 329; SASS 502; V 35; WSAL 16, 68 *Venez.*
Bello, Ángel (-1859) BDC 5; Cu 19 *Cu.*
Bello, Ernesto PM 22 *Mex.*
Bello, Federico PM 23 *Mex.*
Bello, Francisco CHL 239; CLH 199 *Chil.*
Bello, Francisco R. A 8 *Arg.*

"Bello, Inés" *see* Echeverría de Larraín, Inés
Bello, Leoncio N. CA 7 *C.R.*
Bello, Lope (1883-   ) PR 45; QPR (2) 31 *P.R.*
Bello y Boyland, Carlos (1815-1854) C 44; CHL 240; CLH 200; HC 133 *Chil.*
Bello y Dunn, Juan (1825-1860) CHL 240; CLH 200; HC 133 *Chil.*
Belloso, Abraham V 39 *Venez.*
Benares, Myriam C 3 *Chil.*
Benavente, Manuel CG I, 321; PU 40; U 3 *Uru.*
Benavente, Marcolino (1845-1910) LA VII, 311 *Arg.*
Benavente, Toribio de ("Motolinia") (-1568) BAMP 12; BHLA 57; CG I, 321; HLM 44; HLMex 25; TM 528 *Mex.*
Benavento, Gaspar L. A 8 *Arg.*
Benavides, M. Antonio C 45 *Chil.*
Benavides Ponce, Rafael V 39 *Venez.*
Bencomo, Diego PM 23 *Mex.*
Benchetrit, A. CG I, 321; V 39 *Venez.*
Benedetti, Albino (1848-   ) UT 75 *Uru.*
Benedetti, Antonio BC 72 *Bol.*
Benedetti, Carlos Co 9 *Col.*
Benet, Eduardo Cu 19 *Cu.*
Beney, Raúl A 8 *Arg.*
Benisia, Alejandro BP 522; PR 32 *P.R.*
Benítez, Alejandrina ("A. Carmen Hernández") (1819-1879) BHLA 244; CHL 499; CLH 439; PP 51; PR 33, 49 *P.R.*
Benítez, Cristóbal CG I, 323; V 39 *Venez.*
Benítez, José María (1898-   ) PM 23 *Mex.*
Benítez, Juan Aboy ARC 43; Cu 19 *Cu.*
Benítez, Justo Pastor CG I, 323; Par 7 *Para.*
Benítez, M. P. SD 5 *Dom.*
Benítez, María Bibiana (1783-1873) BDC 109; PR 11, 49 *P.R.*
Benítez, Mauricio Par 7 *Para.*
Benítez, Vicente HLNG II, 536 *Col.*
Benítez Artiles, Luis Cu 19 *Cu.*
Benítez del Cristo, Ignacio BDC 5; Cu 19 *Cu.*
Benítez Flores, Manuel PP 238 *P.R.*
Benítez López, Trinidad V 39 *Venez.*
Benítez y Guzmán, Dolores BDC 5 *Cu.*
"Benito Blanco" (*pseud.*) *see* Añez Luengo, J. de J.
Benitoa, Felipe de BDC 5; Cu 19 *Cu.*
Benot, Eduardo CG I, 327; PR 49 *P.R.*
Benuzzi, Santiago Ludovico Pan 4 *Pan.*
Benvenuto, Carlos HSLU III, pt 4, 46; PIU III, 310 *Uru.*
Benzoni, Girolamo (1519?-   ) SCL 96, 590 *Ital.*
Berdiales, Germán A 8; CG I, 329 *Arg.*
Berenguer y Sed, Antonio BDC 5; Cu 19 *Cu.*
Berganzo, Luis Alfonso PM 23; TM 85 *Mex.*
Bergaño y Villegas, Simón ACe 1005; CA 64; Cu 19 *Guat.*
Berges, Consuelo A 8 *Arg.*
Berges Bordas, Gustavo E. SD 5 *Dom.*
Bergrave, Donato P 3 *Per.*
Bergues Pruna, Manuel ARC 41 *Cu.*
Berisso, Emilio A 8, 80; CHL 199 *Arg.*
Berisso, Luis A 8; CG I, 331 *Arg.*

Beristáin de Souza, Vicente ACe 731 *Mex.*
Beristáin y Souza, José Mariano (1756-1817) ACe 99, 663; C 61; Cu 19; HLM 213; HLMex 119; HPHA I, 66; PM 23; SD 5; TM 528 *Mex.*
Berlanga, David G. TM 528 *Mex.*
Bermejo, Ildefonso Antonio (1820-1892) A 8; CG I, 332; Par 7 *Para.*
Bermejo, Manuel M. ("Luis Martín") PM 23, 56; TM 85, 621 *Mex.*
Bermúdez, Anacleto (1806-1852) HLC 126; RLC 92 *Cu.*
Bermúdez, Antonio NL 111; PN 175 *Nicar.*
Bermúdez, Federico PA 268; PD 30; SD 6 *Dom.*
Bermúdez, Francisca Ofelia CG I, 333; U 3 *Uru.*
Bermúdez, José Alejandro (1886-   ) Co 9 *Col.*
Bermúdez, Manuel María V 39 *Venez.*
"Bermúdez, Oscar C." (*pseud.*) A 9; CG I, 333 *Arg.*
Bermúdez, Pedro Pablo (1816-1860) CHL 208; CLH 172; U 3 *Uru.*
Bermúdez, Sergio Wáshington (1883-   ) UT 83 *Uru.*
Bermúdez, Wáshington P. (1847-   ) CHL 217; CLH 181; PIU I, 242; U 3 *Uru.*
Bermúdez Acevedo, P. U 3 *Uru.*
Bermúdez Ávila, Manuel María LV 136; V 39 *Venez.*
Bermúdez de Castro, Jacopo U 3 *Uru.*
Bermúdez de Castro, Rafael TM 427 *Mex.*
Bermúdez de Castro, Salvador HPHA II, 59 *Col.*
Bermúdez de la Torre y Solier, Pedro José (1665-   ) BHLA 97; P 3 *Per.*
Bernabó, Leonor V 39 *Venez.*
Bernal, Emilia (1885-   ) CG I, 334; CHL 489; Cu 19; IE 30; PA 12; PCu 38; TM 529 *Cu.*
Bernal, Evelio Cu 19 *Cu.*
Bernal, José Calixto (1804-1886) Cu 19, 20; RLC 175, 243 *Cu.*
Bernal, Juan José CHL 507; CLH 448; GPCA II, 323; PS 66 *Salv.*
Bernal Granados, Luis BC 73; Co 9 *Col.*
Bernal Orjuela, Raimundo BC 73; Co 9, 64 *Col.*
Bernard, J. M. PD 32; SD 6 *Dom.*
Bernárdez, Francisco Luis (1900-   ) A 9; APAM 442; APEH 1006; CG I, 336; LAC 149; NPA 249 *Arg.*
Bernárdez, Juan Carlos PU 253 *Uru.*
Bernárdez, Manuel (1868-   ) CG I, 336; CHL 227; CLH 190; LUr 472; PIU II, 30; U 3; UT 87 *Uru.*
Bernárdez de Ribera, José HPM 456 *Mex.*
Bernardini de la Huerta, Tomás (1871-   ) QPR (2) 33 *P.R.*
Bernat, Pedro Antonio U 3 *Uru.*
Berninsoni, Luis BAP 67 *Per.*
Berón, Sebastián C. A 9 *Arg.*
Berra Benítez, Héctor TM 86 *Mex.*
Berríos, José David (1849-   ) B 3 *Bol.*
Berríos Berdecia, Tomás (1888-   ) QPR (1) 33 *P.R.*
Berríos Herrero, Alfonso PR 32 *P.R.*

Berriz y Xiqués, José María   Cu 20; PCu 42; PJC 37   *Cu.*

Berrizbeitia, Carlos (1899-   )   QPR (2) 34 *P.R.*

Berro, Adolfo (1819-1841)   AEHA 163; BHLA 234; CHL 208; CLH 172; HCLU I, 236; HPHA II, 485; LUr 442; PIU I, 166; PLHA 73; U 3   *Uru.*

Berro, Aurelio   U 3   *Uru.*

Berro, Bernardo Prudencio (1803-1868) BHLA 213; CHL 211; CLH 174; HCLU I, 292; HPHA II, 483; PIU I, 92, 93   *Uru.*

Berroa Canelo, Quiterio   PD 33; SD 6 *Dom.*

Berruecos, Pedro   TM 86   *Mex.*

Berrutti, José J. (1871-   )   A 9, 80; WLA 49   *Arg.*

Bersetche, Pedro L.   U 3   *Uru.*

Berta Fernández, Virgilio   PU 254; U 3 *Uru.*

"Bertal, O." (*pseud.*)   A 9   *Arg.*

Bertani, Orsini   PIU II, 67   *Uru.*

Berthet, Elías   CG I, 339; E 10   *Ecua.*

Bertolé, Emilia   A 9; APAM 449; CG I, 339   *Arg.*

Bertoni, Moisés Santiago   CG I, 339; Par 8 *Para.*

Bertonio, Ludovico (-1628)   LA III, 389 *Arg.*

Bertrán, Alfonso   Cu 20   *Cu.*

Bertrán y Ferrari, José   BDC 6; Cu 20 *Cu.*

Best Maugard, Adolfo (1891-   )   WLA 50 *Mex.*

Betances, Ramón Emeterio ("Bin-tah") BDC 109; PR 8, 9, 11, 16, 45   *P.R.*

Betancourt   *see also* Bethencourt *and* Vetancourt

Betancourt, srita América (1878-   )   Cu 20 *Cu.*

Betancourt, Antonio M.   Cu 20   *Cu.*

Betancourt, Gerardo L.   BDC 6; Cu 20   *Cu.*

Betancourt, Isabel Esperanza   Cu 20   *Cu.*

Betancourt, Ismael   Cu 20   *Cu.*

Betancourt, José ("Dmitri Ivanovich") (1888-   )   CG III, 159; Co 9, 35   *Col.*

Betancourt, José Mercedes (-1866)   ARC 34; Cu 20   *Cu.*

Betancourt, José Ramón (1823-1890)   Cu 20; HLC 177; PR 49; RLC 139, 227   *Cu.*

Betancourt, José Victoriano (1813-1875) BDC 6; Cu 20; HLC 126; RLC 91, 143 *Cu.*

Betancourt, Luis G.   TM 428   *Mex.*

Betancourt, Luis Victoriano (1842-1885) CG I, 346; Cu 20; PCu 44; RLC 144, 227, 274   *Cu.*

Betancourt, Rómulo   V 39   *Venez.*

Betancourt Agramonte, Oscar   Cu 21   *Cu.*

Betancourt Cisneros, Gaspar (1803-1866) RLC 174   *Cu.*

Betancourt Figueredo, Francisco ("Pako") V 39, 110   *Venez.*

Betancourt Figueredo, María de   V 40 *Venez.*

Betancurt, Manuel   A 9   *Arg.*

Betanzo, Francisca ("Chanteclair")   CG I, 346; Ig 42; NM 10   *Mex.*

Betéa, José   Cu 21   *Cu.*

Beteta, José Antonio (1861-   )   CA 65; IE 31   *Guat.*

Bethencourt Apolinaris, Cayetano ("C. B. A.")   V 40, 54   *Venez.*

Betnaza, María Enriqueta (1909-   )   A 9 *Arg.*

Bettega, Claudio   A 9   *Arg.*

Bettelini, Luis   C 26   *Chil.*

Beye Cisneros y Quixano, Manuel Ignacio PM 23   *Mex.*

Beye de Cisneros, José   ACe 734   *Mex.*

Bezanilla Mier y Campa, José Mariano ACe 741; PM 23   *Mex.*

Biaggi y Díaz, Antonio   Cu 21   *Cu.*

Bianco, Francisco N.   A 9   *Arg.*

Bianchi, Alberto G.   CG I, 348; PM 23, 348; TM 86, 428   *Mex.*

Bianchi, Alfredo Antonio (1882-   )   A 9; AT II, 861; CHL 197; G 310; HLM 466; WLA 51   *Arg.*

Bianchi, Edmundo (1880-   )   A 9, 80; PIU III, 312; UT 99   *Uru.*

Bianchi, Enrique   PU 48; U 3   *Uru.*

Bianchi, Guillermo ("Shanty")   C 3, 45, 46; CG I, 348   *Chil.*

Bianchi, José Juan   A 9   *Arg.*

Bidó, Amado Franco   SD 6   *Dom.*

Bidone, Humberto   A 9   *Arg.*

Biedma, José Juan (1864-   )   AT II, 971; CG I, 358   *Arg.*

Biedma, María Isabel   A 9; CG I, 358   *Arg.*

Bielsa Vives, Manuel (1868-   )   Cu 21   *Cu.*

Bierstadt, Edward Hale   A 9, 80, 83   *Arg.*

Bigotte, Félix E. ("Akara")   CG I, 359; V 27, 40   *Venez.*

Bilbao, Francisco (1823-1865)   BHLA 288, 315; C 62; CG I, 359; CHL 249; CLH 209, 221; HC 92   *Chil.*

Bilbao, Manuel (1827-1895)   A 9; BHLA 341; C 3, 62; CG I, 359; CHL 264; CLH 224; LA VIII, 628; NC 31   *Chil.*

"Billiken" (*pseud.*)   *see* Callejas, Félix

Billini, Francisco Gregorio (1844-1898) CHL 495; CLH 435; LD 86; SD 6   *Dom.*

Billini, Hipólito   SD 6   *Dom.*

Billini, Miguel   SD 6   *Dom.*

Billini y Hernández, Francisco Xavier   SD 6   *Dom.*

"Billo" (*pseud.*)   *see* Zeledón, José María

Binayán, Narciso (1896-   )   A 73; CG I, 360; WLA 52   *Arg.*

"Bin-tah" (*pseud.*)   *see* Betances, Ramón Emeterio

Binvignat, Fernando   C 26   *Chil.*

Bisbé y Alberni, Manuel   Cu 21   *Cu.*

Bizeña, Irma   NM 11   *Mex.*

"Blanc, Charles" (*pseud.*)   *see* Blixen, Samuel

"Blanca" (*pseud.*)   *see* Pachano de Fombona, Ignacia

"Blanca C. de Hume" (*pseud.*)   *see* Colt de Hume, Blanca C. E.

"Blanca Milanés" (*pseud.*)   *see* Brenes Argüello de Rizo, Carlota

"Blanca y Margot" (*pseud.*)   *see* Pachano de Fombona, Ignacia *and* Pimentel, Margarita A. de

Blancas, Alberto (1859-   )   AT II, 974 *Arg.*

"Blanck, Willy de" (*pseud.*)   *see*

Blanck y Menocal, Guillermo de   CG I, 363; Cu 22   *Cu.*

Blanco, A.   CG I, 363; PR 16   *P.R.*

Blanco, Andrés Eloy BHLA 542, 581; V 40 *Venez.*
Blanco, Ángel Julio A 9 *Arg.*
Blanco, Antonio Nicolás BP 520; CG I, 363; PA 148; PP 263; PR 32, 49 *P.R.*
"Blanco, Benito" (*pseud.*) *see* Añez Luengo, J. de J.
1. Blanco, Benjamín (1832-1905) B 4 *Bol.*
2. Blanco, Benjamín (hijo) (1860-) B 4; CG I, 363; PB 87 *Bol.*
Blanco, Diego Alberto V 40 *Venez.*
Blanco, Eduardo (1838-) BHLA 411; CG I, 363; CHL 376; CLH 324; LV 7, 73, 370; V 40; VPF 39 *Venez.*
Blanco, Federico (1827-1896) B 4 *Bol.*
Blanco, Gerónimo Eusebio LV 114; V 40 *Venez.*
Blanco, José Félix V 41 *Venez.*
Blanco, José Trinidad V 41 *Venez.*
Blanco, Juan Carlos CG I, 363; PIU I, 232; UL 124 *Uru.*
Blanco, Leandro CG I, 363; TM 21, 87 *Mex.*
Blanco, Luis Alejandro V 41 *Venez.*
Blanco, Manuel Ig 43; NM 11 *Mex.*
Blanco, Marcial BC 74; Co 9 *Col.*
Blanco, Ramón Domingo V 41 *Venez.*
Blanco, Teodosio Adolfo V 41 *Venez.*
Blanco Cuartín, Manuel (1822-1890) B 4; C 26, 62; CG I, 365; CHL 255; CL 136; CLH 216; HC 171; PCh 57 *Chil.*
Blanco de Aguirre, Juan A 9 *Arg.*
Blanco Encalada, Ventura (1782-1856) B 4; HC 63; HPHA II, 279, 350; LA V, 491 *Chil.*
Blanco Fernández, Antonio PR 41 *P.R.*
Blanco Fombona, Horacio (1889-) CG I, 365; IE 34; V 41 *Venez.*
Blanco-Fombona, Rufino (1874-) AB 21; AEHA 754; APEH 444, 1186; BHLA 467, 472; C 62; CG I, 365; CHL 69, 91, 382, 541; CLH 327; FPA 550, 573; G 391; GLO 255; LAND 229, 285; LV 70, 241; PLHA 131, 260, 283; SAL 307 *et passim*; SASS 529; V 41; VPF 145; WLA 53; WSAL 59 *Venez.*
Blanco Viel, Ventura CL 137 *Chil.*
Blanco García, Francisco LV 98 *Venez.*
Blanco y Géiger, Enrique Tomás (1886-) QPR (1) 181; (2) 37 *P.R.*
Blanch S., Juan R. V 45 *Venez.*
Blanchard-Chessi, Enrique C 45 *Chil.*
Blanchet, Emilio (1829-1915) BDC 6, 109; CG I, 371; Cu 21; PA 149 *Cu.*
Blanchié y Palma, Francisco Javier (1822-1847) BDC 7; Cu 22; HLC 138; RLC 192 *Cu.*
Blanga Valenzuela, Miguel de la PM 23 *Mex.*
Blank, Carlos V 45 *Venez.*
Blanlot Holley, Anselmo A 9; C 3; CG I, 371; NC 34 *Chil.*
Blasco y Navarro, Tomás PM 23 *Mex.*
Blavatski, Helene Petrovno CG I, 376; V 45 *Venez.*
Blengio, Joaquín (1834-) PM 23; PMe I, 35 *Mex.*

Blest Gana, Alberto (1830-1923) BHLA 341; C 3, 4, 45, 62; CHL 264; CL 137; CLH 224; G 323; HC 186; NC 34, 491; SAL 339; SASS 165 *Chil.*
Blest Gana, Guillermo (1829-1905) BHLA 315; C 4, 26, 45, 62; CG I, 377; CHL 251; CLH 211; CMPC 7; HC 140; NC 102; PCh 47; SASS 143 *Chil.*
Blest Gana, Joaquín CL 138 *Chil.*
Blest Gana, Luis C 4; NC 355 *Chil.*
Bliss, Cornelio P. Par 8 *Para.*
Blixen, Samuel ("Charles Blanc") (1868-1911) CHL 231; CLH 192; HSLU I, pt 4, 9; III, pt 4, 28; LU 64, 689; LUr 471, 536; PIU II, 31; SAL 187, 228; U 3; UL 124 *Uru.*
Blómberg, Héctor Pedro (1890-) A 9; APAM 182; APEH 814; BHLA 507; CG I, 378; LAC 133; NPA 155; PPa 185 *Arg.*
Blondel, Enrique C 45 *Chil.*
Bobadilla, Emilio ("Fray Candil" *or* "Dagoberto Mármara") (1868-1921) AEHA 886; BHLA 474; CG I, 380, 504; CT 449; Cu 22, 30, 100; G 335; PA 14; PCu 46; RLC 352, 357, 364 *Cu.*
Bobadilla, Tomás SD 6 *Dom.*
Bobea, Joaquín M. SD 6 *Dom.*
Bobia Berdeyes de Carbó, América Cu 23 *Cu.*
Boca Ángel, Gabriel PM 24 *Mex.*
Bocanegra, Manuel M. PM 24 *Mex.*
Bocanegra, Matías de CHL 29; CLH 25; HLM 159; HLMex 70; HPM 221; PM 24; TM 88 *Mex.*
Bocanegra, Serafín Ig 44; NM 11 *Mex.*
Bocaranda, Francisco V 45 *Venez.*
Boissier, Carlos Alberto (1877-1897) RLC 273 *Cu.*
Boissier, Pedro Alejandro (1839-) BDC 7; Cu 23 *Cu.*
Boizard, Ricardo C 26 *Chil.*
Bojórquez, Juan de Dios ("Djed Bórquez") (1892-) G 355; IE 35; Ig 44; NM 11 *Mex.*
Bolaño, Manuel Cu 23 *Cu.*
Bolaños, Demetrio, Jr. TM 428 *Mex.*
Bolaños, Federico BAP 75; P 3 *Per.*
Bolaños, José BDC 7; Cu 23 *Cu.*
Bolaños, Luis de (1549-1629) LA III, 392 *Arg.*
Bolaños, María Christina Cu 23 *Cu.*
Bolaños Cacho, Miguel (1869-) CG I, 386; G 355; NM 11; PM 24; TM 88 *Mex.*
"Bolena, Lydia" (*pseud.*) *see* Pertuz, Julia de
Bolet Peraza, Nicanor (1838-1906) CHL 369; CLH 317; LV 386; V 45; VPF 51 *Venez.*
Bolio Ávila, Alberto PM 24 *Mex.*
Bolio Ávila, Antonio PM 24 *Mex.*
Bolio de Peón, Dolores (1880-) Cu 23; Ig 45; NM 11; PM 24 *Mex.*
Bolio Rendón, Eduardo PM 24 *Mex.*
Bolívar, Simón (1783-1830) ACe 1006; BHLA 178; CG I, 386; G 392; HLNG II, 445; LAND 285; RHLC 71; SAL 337 *et passim*; SASS 547; V 46 *Venez.*
Bolívar Álvarez, Rafael (1860-1900) CHL 379; CLH 327; V 46; VPF 69 *Venez.*

Bolívar Coronado, Rafael CG I, 387; V 51 *Venez.*

Boloña, Joaquín Cu 23 *Cu.*

Boluda y Roig, Emeterio (-1886) BDC 8; Cu 23 *Cu.*

Bollo, Sarah CG I, 388; HSLU II, pt 7, 11; PIU III, 242; U 3 *Uru.*

Bombalier, S. ARC 76 *Cu.*

Bonachea, José CG I, 388; Cu 23 *Cu.*

Bonafoux y Quintero, Luis CG I, 388, 389; PR 16, 41, 55 *P.R.*

Bonavita, María Adela HSLU II, pt 8, 23; PIU III, 234 *Uru.*

Bonazzola, Alcira (1904-) A 10; CG I, 390 *Arg.*

Bonesatti, Tobías A 10 *Arg.*

Bonet, Carmelo M. A 10; CG I, 390 *Arg.*

Bonifacino, Víctor U 4 *Uru.*

Bonilla, Carlos PS 142 *Salv.*

Bonilla, Juan (1869-) ARC 43 *Cu.*

Bonilla, Policarpo (1858-) CG I, 391; HL I, 665 *Hond.*

Bonilla Cornejo, Joaquín (1888-) WLA 56 *Hond.*

Bonilla Ruano, José María LAS 198 *Guat.*

Bonnat, Mario C 4 *Chil.*

Bonome, Rodrigo A 10 *Arg.*

Boquerizos, José N. A 10 *Arg.*

Borbolla y Gárate, Joaquín María de la PM 24 *Mex.*

Borbón, Luis de Cu 23 *Cu.*

Borda, Ignacio (1849-) BC 78; Co 9 *Col.*

Borda, José Joaquín (1835-1878) BC 75; CHL 338; CLH 290; Co 9, 10, 79; Cu 24; LC 158; RHLC 121, 125 *Col.*

Bordas, J. Rafael SD 6 *Dom.*

"Borge, Jorge" (*pseud.*) *see* López, José Heriberto

Borge C., Carlos CA 7; IBCR IV, 193 *C.R.*

Borges, Carlos V 51 *Venez.*

Borges, Jorge Luis (1900-) A 10; APAM 453; APEH 1149; BHLA 629; C 66; G 310; GLO 235; LAC 95, 150; LAS 198; MSAP 244, 338; NPA 263; PLHA 161; SASS 54; V 52; WLA 57 *Arg.*

Borges, Nicanor V 52 *Venez.*

Borgia, René V 52 *Venez.*

Borja, Arturo (-1912) E 11; G 343; PE 31; PLE 103 *Ecua.*

Borja, César (1852-1910) E 11; FPA 254, 272; PE 45; PLE 55 *Ecua.*

Borja, Filomeno Co 10 *Col.*

Borja, Luis Felipe (1845-1912) E 11; PLE 47 *Ecua.*

Borja Bolado, Francisco (1894-) IE 37; PM 24 *Mex.*

Borja Kuney, Francisco de E 11 *Ecua.*

Borja López, Juan E 11 *Ecua.*

Borja Martínez, Luz Elisa E 11 *Ecua.*

Borja Moncayo, Luis Alberto de CG I, 399; E 11 *Ecua.*

"Bórquez, Djed" (*pseud.*) *see* Bojórquez, Juan de Dios

Bórquez Solar, Antonio Nicanor (1874-) C 4, 26, 45; CG I, 399; CHL 262; CLH 222; FPA 192, 208; IE 38; PCh 169; WLA 57 *Chil.*

Bórquez Solar, Humberto C 4, 26, 45; PCh 385 *Chil.*

Borrero, Filomeno Co 10 *Col.*

Borrero, Juana (1878-1896) Cu 24; HLC 194; PA 15; RLC 285, 288 *Cu.*

Borrero de Luján, Dulce María (1883-) CHL 489; CLH 429; Cu 24; HLC 206; PA 17; PCu 51; SASS 287 *Cu.*

Borrero Echeverría, Esteban (1849-1906) CG I, 401; CHL 478; CLH 418; Cu 24; G 335; PCu 49; RLC 276 *et passim Cu.*

Borrero Echeverría, Manuel (-1894) Cu 24 *Cu.*

Borsani, Carlos Lorenzo A 10 *Arg.*

Borsella, Juan A 10 *Arg.*

Borunda, José Ignacio ACe 741 *Mex.*

Borzani, Carlos A 10 *Arg.*

Bosco Gaibisso, Amnerys A 10 *Arg.*

Bosch, Gonzalo (1885-) A 10, 80; AT II, 607; CG I, 402 *Arg.*

Bosch, José M. A 10, 81 *Arg.*

Bosch, Mariano G. (1865-) A 10, 81; AT II, 1041; CG I, 402 *Arg.*

Bosch, Pedro José P 3 *Per.*

Bosch, Rafael PR 32, 55 *P.R.*

Bosque, Carlos (1866-) CG I, 403; IE 40 *Per.*

Bossero, Luis G. TM 88, 428 *Mex.*

Bossi, B. A 10, 81 *Arg.*

Botella, Francisco A. TM 88 *Mex.*

Botello, Edmundo (1867-1911) AP 51; Pan 4 *Pan.*

Botero, Francisco Co 10 *Col.*

Botero, Juan José (1840-1926) Co 10 *Col.*

Botero Guerra, Camilo (1853-) Co 10 *Col.*

Botero Isaza, Horacio Co 10 *Col.*

Botero Saldarriaga, Roberto (1870-) CG I, 404; Co 10; RHLC 190; WLA 58 *Col.*

Boti y Barriero, Regino Eladio (1878-) APEH 963; ARC 44; BHLA 571; Cu 24; LH 124; PJC 39; RLC 364; WLA 58 *Cu.*

Botta, Vicente Raúl A 10 *Arg.*

Böttger, Adolf (1815-1870) Cu 23 *Cu.*

Boturini Benaduci, Lorenzo (1702?-1756?) HLM 200 *Mex.*

Bouilly, Enrique A 10 *Arg.*

Bouquet, Alejandro L. A 11, 81 *Arg.*

Bourgeois, Anicet V 37 *Venez.*

Bourguet, Lola S. B. de ("Angélica Farfalla") A 11, 78; CG I, 409 *Arg.*

Bove, Vicente A 11; CG I, 410 *Arg.*

Boveda, Xavier A 11; CG I, 410 *Arg.*

"Boy" (*pseud.*) *see* Prado, Eladio *and* Soto, Antonio

Boza, Ernesto G. P 3 *Per.*

Boza, Luis R. C 26 *Chil.*

Boza Masvidal, Aurelio A. (1900-) Cu 25; WLA 59 *Cu.*

Bozello y Guzmán, Carmen BDC 109; PR 11 *P.R.*

Bracale, Adolfo V 52 *Venez.*

Bracamonte, R. V 52 *Venez.*

"Bracy, Mauricio de" (*pseud.*) *see* Almendaro, José Pablo

Bracho, Saturnino ARC 36; BDC 8 *Cu.*

Bracho Vargas, A. E. V 52 *Venez.*

Brahms, Miguel A. A 11 *Arg.*

Braida, Telémaco (1855-) CG I, 417; UT 111 *Uru.*

Brambila, Alberto M. NM 11; PM 24 *Mex.*

Bramón, Francisco NM 11 *Mex.*

Brandán Caraffa, Alfredo (1898-) A 11; APAM 460; NPA 279; PLHA 165 *Arg.*
"Brander" (*pseud.*) A 11 *Arg.*
Brandi Vera, Pascual C 26 *Chil.*
Brannon, Carmen (189.-) FPA 502, 523 *Salv.*
Braña, José Marín A 11; CG I, 418 *Arg.*
Brañas, César A. CA 65; IBCR IV, 181 *C.R.*
Braschi, Juan PR 16 *P.R.*
Braschi, Mario PR 25 *P.R.*
Brasseur de Bourbourg, Carlos Esteban CG I, 418; TM 429, 529 *Mex.*
Brau, Salvador (1837-1912) BDC 109; BP 510, 521, 581; CG I, 418; PP 85; PR 11, 16, 17, 32, 49, 55 *P.R.*
Brau Zuzuarregui, Mario BP 521 *P.R.*
Braun Bonilla, Juan Diego (1859-1885) CA 7; EPCR 65 *C.R.*
"Bravito" (*pseud.*) *see* Bravo, Juan de
Bravo, Abel Pan 4 *Pan.*
Bravo, Alfredo Guillermo C 25, 26; CG I, 419; PCh 341 *Chil.*
Bravo, Bernabé ("Figarete") (1846-) Ig 45; NM 11; PoM 366 *Mex.*
Bravo, José E 11 *Ecua.*
Bravo, Juan de ("Bravito") ARC 44; Cu 25 *Cu.*
1. Bravo, Juan de Dios ("L. B. M.") C 45 *Chil.*
2. Bravo, Juan de Dios PCo 55 *Col.*
Bravo, Mario (1882-) A 11; APAM 188; AT I, 269; CG I, 419; G 310; NPA 45; WLA 60 *Arg.*
Bravo, Ramón Luis C 26; NC 412 *Chil.*
Bravo, Serapio Cu 25 *Cu.*
Bravo, Vicente M. ("Aerolito") E 11 *Ecua.*
Bravo Acosta, Antonio ARC 44 *Cu.*
Bravo Albornoz, Trinidad V 52 *Venez.*
Bravo de Lagunas y Castilla, José SCL 543, 591 *Per.*
Bravo Gallegos, Guillermo L. E 11 *Ecua.*
Bravo V., Aníbal M. C 45 *Chil.*
Brea, Manuel Cu 25 *Cu.*
Brea, Pedro V 52 *Venez.*
Breca, Juan José V 52 *Venez.*
Brenes, Edin CA 7 *C.R.*
Brenes, Rafael Andrés SD 6 *Dom.*
Brenes Argüello de Rizo, Carlota ("Blanca Milanés") (1905-) CA 7, 39; IBCR IV, 296; WLA 344 *C.R.*
Brenes Córdoba, Alberto CA 7; CG I, 421; EPCR 69 *C.R.*
Brenes Mesén, Roberto (1874-) APEH 749, 1190; CA 7, 8; CG I, 421; CHL 509; EPCR 264; FPA 122, 134; IBCR IV, 94, 226, 399; PC 161; SASS 128 *C.R.*
Bribiesca, Luis TM 89 *Mex.*
Briceño *see also* Briseño
Briceño, Antonio M. E 11 *Ecua.*
Briceño, Antonio S. V 52 *Venez.*
Briceño, Emilio (1857-1894) Pan 4 *Pan.*
Briceño, Manuel CG I, 422; Co 10, 64; PCo 56; V 52 *Venez.*
Briceño, Mariano de V 52 *Venez.*
Briceño, Sancho V 52 *Venez.*
Briceño Baltodano, Leónidas CA 8, 9 *C.R.*
Briceño Fernández, Manuel (1849-1885) Co 10; LC 174; RHLC 200 *Col.*

Briceño-Iragorry, Mario (1897-) V 52; WLA 61 *Venez.*
Briceño Méndez, Pedro V 53 *Venez.*
Briceño Ortega, Rafael V 53 *Venez.*
Briceño O'Ryan, Ramón Belisario C 4, 62; CL 138; NC 355, 412 *Chil.*
Briceño Picón, Adolfo V 53 *Venez.*
Briceño Valero, Américo CG I, 422; V 53 *Venez.*
Briceño y Briceño, Domingo V 53 *Venez.*
Brickles Velasco, René Isidoro C 4, 45; CHL 277; CLH 236; NC 102 *Chil.*
Brieba, Liborio E. ("Mefistófeles") (1841-1897) BHLA 403; C 4, 14; CHL 270; CLH 230; HC 241; NC 110, 492 *Chil.*
"Brigadier Alfa" (*pseud.*) *see* Velarde, César Augusto
Brigard Silva, Álvaro de Co 11 *Col.*
Brigé, Carmen V 53 *Venez.*
Brignardello, F. A 93 *Arg.*
Brignole, Carlos R. A 11 *Arg.*
Brindes Pérez, Clodoveo de V 53 *Venez.*
Bringas, César LAS 206 *Per.*
Bringas y Encinas, Diego Manuel ACe 127 *Mex.*
Brioso y Candiani, Manuel (1859-) IE 41; Ig 46; NM 11; WLA 62 *Mex.*
Briseño *see also* Briceño
Brisson, J. E. PR 41 *P.R.*
Brito, Álvaro TM 594 *Mex.*
Brito, Hilario C. ("C. L. Otardo") (1857-) Cu 25 *Cu.*
"Brito, Fray K." (*pseud.*) *see* López Loayza, Fernando
Brito de Donoso, Tilda ("María Monvel") (1897-) C 15, 36; CMPC 126; PCC xix, 203; PCU 85; WLA 261 *Chil.*
Brito N., Marcos C 5, 26 *Chil.*
Brizeño *see also* Briseño
"Brocha Gorda" (*pseud.*) *see* Jaimes, Julio Lucas
Broche, José Francisco BDC 8; Cu 25 *Cu.*
Broche, José P. Cu 25 *Cu.*
Brochero, Luis HLNG I, 140 *Col.*
Brondo Whitt, E. LAS 198 *Mex.*
Bros, C. TM 429, 430 *Mex.*
Brot, Alfonso Cu 25 *Cu.*
Brotchie *see* Páez Brotchie
Brown, Ed. A 11 *Arg.*
Browne, Miguel A 11 *Arg.*
Brughetti, Faustino A 11 *Arg.*
Brull y Caballero, Mariano (1891-) APEH 981; BHLA 568; CT 109; Cu 25; G 335; LH 130; PJC 45; PoC 36; WLA 62 *Cu.*
Brum, Blanca Luz PoU 65 *Uru.*
Brumana, Herminia C. A 11 *Arg.*
"Brummel" (*pseud.*) *see* Puga y Acal, Manuel
Brunet, Domingo A 11; CG I, 429 *Arg.*
Brunet, Marta C 5 *Chil.*
Bruno, Francisco Co 11 *Col.*
Bruno Dal Molin, Antonio A 11 *Arg.*
Brusa, Alejandro Cu 25 *Cu.*
Brusi y Font, Juan PR 45 *P.R.*
Bruzual, Narcisa V 53 *Venez.*
Bruzual López, Rafael CG I, 432; V 53 *Venez.*
Bruzual Serra, Claudio V 53 *Venez.*
Buccicardi, Ricardo A 11 *Arg.*

Buceta, Clotilde C. A 11 *Arg.*
Buceta, María Villar PJC 41 *Cu.*
Bucio, Víctor Manuel TM 89 *Mex.*
"Buenamar, Ricardo" (*pseud.*) *see* Cabrera, Raimundo
Buendía, José de (1644-1727) BHLA 117; LP 321; P 3; SCL 341, 591 *Per.*
Bueno, Cosme (1711-1798) BHC III, 54 *et passim Chil.*
Bueno, Luis Eduardo E 11; PLE 78 *Ecua.*
Bueno, Manuel Antonio (1808-1878) Co 11 *Col.*
Bueno, Marcelino V 53 *Venez.*
Bueno R., Joaquín Co 11 *Col.*
Buerga del Palacio, Manuel Cu 25 *Cu.*
Buero, Juan Antonio (1888-) UT 123 *Uru.*
Buesa, José Ángel (1910-) PoC 37 *Cu.*
Bufano, Alfredo R. (1895-) A 11; APAM 193; APEH 836; CG I, 437; LAC 146; NPA 199 *Arg.*
Bufarini, Juan E 12 *Ecua.*
Buhigas, Félix Cu 25 *Cu.*
Bujanda, Ezequiel V 53 *Venez.*
Bulnes, Francisco (1847-1924) CG I, 439; CHL 429; HLM 482; HLMex 232 *Mex.*
Bulnes, Gonzalo (1851-1936) BHLA 379 *Per.*
Bunge, Augusto (1877-) A 12; AT I, 113; CG I, 440; WLA 64 *Arg.*
Bunge, Carlos ("Thespis") (1875-1918) A 12, 78, 81; BHLA 500; CG I, 441; CLH 168; LA VII, 140 *Arg.*
Bunge de Gálvez, Delfina A 12, 78; AT I, 71; CG I, 441; LAC 153; WLA 158 *Arg.*
Buñols, J. Esteban SD 6 *Dom.*
Burbano, Rueda G. E 12 *Ecua.*
Burbano Vázquez, José Rafael E 12 *Ecua.*
Burdett O'Connor, Francisco (1791-1871) B 4; CG I, 442 *Bol.*
Burghi, Juan A 12; APAM 199; CHL 187 *Arg.*
Burgoa, Francisco (1605-1681) HLM 207 *Mex.*
Burgos, Antonio CG I, 443; Pan 4 *Pan.*
Burgos, Fausto A 12; CG I, 443; LAC 138 *Arg.*
Burgos, Nicolás Antonio *or* Nicolás Ambrosio de Co 11; HLNG II, 382 *Col.*
Burgos, Rafael Co 11; V 53 *Col.*
Burgos, Ricardo de Cu 25 *Cu.*
Burgos Acuña, Manuel ACe 745 *Mex.*
Burgos Jiménez, Filiberto (*also* Feliberto) APMM 6 *Mex.*
Burich, Antonio A 13, 81; CG I, 448; G 310 *Arg.*
Burton, A. Walter PCh 99 *Chil.*
"Burundulín" (*pseud.*) *see* Prado, Eladio
Burzio, Blas F. A. A 13 *Arg.*
Busqueto, Ernesto BP 498 *P.R.*
Bussett, Conrado de Cu 25 *Cu.*
Bustamante *see also* Bustamente
Bustamante, Guillermo E 12; PE 95 *Ecua.*
Bustamante, José Luis LA VI, 1074 *Arg.*
Bustamante, Juan P 4 *Per.*
Bustamante, Luis PB 56 *Bol.*
Bustamante, Montero PIU II, 66 *Uru.*
Bustamante, P. A 13 *Arg.*
Bustamante, Pedro PIU I, 208 *Uru.*
Bustamante, Ricardo (1880-) B 4 *Bol.*

Bustamante, Ricardo José (1821-1881) AEHA 182; B 4, 17; FPA 53, 57; G 320; HPHA II, 283; LB 587; PB 59, 221; SASS 97 *Bol.*
Bustamante Carlos, Calixto ("Concolorcorvo") (188.-) BHLA 105; CG I, 451; CHL 42; FPA 502, 515; LP 338; P 4; SCL 526, 591 *Per.*
Bustamante Rivero, José Luis BAP 37 *Per.*
Bustamante y Ballivián, Enrique (1883-1936) BAP 29; BHLA 539; CG I, 451; G 381; P 4; PPe 313; U 4; WLA 65 *Per.*
Bustamente *see also* Bustamante
Bustamente, Carlos María de (1774-1848) CHL 410; CLH 356; HLM 345; HLMex 132 *Mex.*
Bustamente, Francisco E. V 53 *Venez.*
Bustamente, P. A 13 *Arg.*
Bustillo, Carlos C. (1870-) HL II, 655 *Hond.*
Bustillo Oro, Juan CG I, 451; TM 529 *Mex.*
Bustillos, D. V 54 *Venez.*
Bustillos, José María (1866-1899) AMP 327; HLM 391; PM 25; PMe I, 37; PoM 371 *Mex.*
Busto, Francisco del ACe 746 *Mex.*
Busto, José G. del (1858-1904) CHL 219; CLH 182; PIU I, 244; U 4 *Uru.*
Bustos, Francisco de BHC II, 531 *Chil.*
Bustos, Julia A 13 *Arg.*
Bustos, Laura C 26 *Chil.*
Bustos, Zenón (1850-) AT II, 879; CG I, 452 *Arg.*
Buttari y Gaunaurd, J. ("Ornofay") Cu 26, 123 *Cu.*
Buxó, Eloi P. C 45 *Chil.*
Buxó, Eloy P. E 12 *Ecua.*
Buxó, Ramón P. TM 89 *Mex.*
Byrne, Bonifacio (1861-1937) BDC 8; BHLA 436; CG I, 453; CHL 487; CT 455; Cu 26; G 335; HLC 202; PA 19; PCu 54; RLC 272 *Cu.*

C

C., A. B. E 12 *Ecua.*
"C. B. A." *see* Bethencourt Apolinaris, Cayetano
C., G. Cu 26 *Cu.*
C., J. E 12 *Ecua.*
C., J. B. Cu 26 *Cu.*
C., M. P 19 *Per.*
"C. M." *see* Lamas, Andrés
Caamaño de Cárdenas, Francisco ARC 44 *Cu.*
Caamaño de Vivero, Ángela PE 39 *Ecua.*
Caballero, Eugenio B 4, 16 *Bol.*
Caballero, José CG I, 457; V 54 *Venez.*
Caballero, José Agustín (1762-1835) RLC 38, 44, 151, 168 *Cu.*
Caballero, José María CG I, 457; HLNG II, 405; RHLC 64 *Col.*
Caballero, Manuel (1851-) CG I, 457; HLM 398; PM 25; PMe I, 39; TM 89, 430 *Mex.*

Caballero, Manuel María B 4; LB 626 *Bol.*
Caballero, Pablo CG I, 457; E 12 *Ecua.*
Caballero, Pedro BP 502 *P.R.*
Caballero de la Paz, María Cu 26 *Cu.*
Caballero y Ontiveros, Félix Cu 26 *Cu.*
Caballero y Ramírez, Francisco C 45 *Chil.*
Caballero y Valero, Víctor (1838-1874) BDC 8; Cu 26 *Cu.*
Cabello, Salvador NM 11 *Mex.*
Cabello de Balboa, Miguel SCL 144, 592 *Per.*
Cabello de Carbonera, Mercedes AEHA 887; CHL 305; CLH 259; LP 369; P 4; PLHA 175 *Per.*
Cabello y Mesa, Francisco Antonio (-1812) BHLA 149; SCL 570 *Arg.*
Cabezas, Diego PN 123 *Nicar.*
Cabezas, Pedro ACe 753 *Mex.*
Cabildo, Raziel PM 25 *Mex.*
Caboteau, Clodomiro A 13 *Arg.*
"Cabotín" (*pseud.*) *see* Carrillo, Enrique A.
Cabral, Antonio PD 36; SD 6 *Dom.*
Cabral, Eulogio C. SD 7 *Dom.*
Cabral, Jorge (1886-) AT 170; CG I, 463 *Arg.*
Cabral de la Cerda, Manuel (1886-) CA 65; PG 435 *Guat.*
Cabrales, Gonzalo ARC 45 *Cu.*
Cabrales, Luis A. NL 202 *Nicar.*
Cabrales y Cabrales, S. V 54 *Venez.*
Cabrera, Arturo C 5; CG I, 463; NC 413 *Chil.*
Cabrera, Carlos Cu 26; PP 35 *P.R.*
Cabrera, Cristóbal HLM 82; HPM 83 *Mex.*
Cabrera, Daniel PM 25 *Mex.*
Cabrera, Francisco A. CG I, 464; Cu 26 *Cu.*
Cabrera, Gustavo PR 10 *P.R.*
Cabrera, Juan D. Cu 26 *Cu.*
Cabrera, Juan Nepomuceno (1745-) Co 11; HLNG II, 411 *Col.*
Cabrera, Luis ("Lucas Ribera") CG I, 464; PM 25, 73 *Mex.*
Cabrera, Miguel de PM 25 *Mex.*
Cabrera, Pablo (1857-) CG I, 464; WLA 66 *Arg.*
1. Cabrera, Rafael (-1859) Cu 26 *Cu.*
2. Cabrera, Rafael (1884-) APMM 7; G 355; HLM 522; PM 25; PNM 11; TM 430 *Mex.*
3. Cabrera, Rafael (-1885) GPCA III, 285; PS 43 *Salv.*
Cabrera, Raimundo ("Ricardo Buenamar") (1852-1923) BDC 9; CG I, 464; CT 193; Cu 27; PA 150; PCu 53; RLC 243, 245, 306; SASS 303 *Cu.*
Cabrera, Ramiro CG I, 464; Cu 28 *Cu.*
Cabrera, Raoul (Raúl) PD 34; SD 7 *Dom.*
Cabrera, Teodoro PJC 51 *Cu.*
Cabrera Guerra, Marcial (-1912) PCh 157 *Chil.*
Cabrera Malo, Rafael (1870-) CHL 378; CLH 326; LV 392; V 54; VPF 73 *Venez.*
Cabrera y Quintero, Cayetano HLM 187, 210; HPM 462; TM 90 *Mex.*
Cabrerizo, Francisco BDC 9; CG I, 466; Cu 28 *Cu.*
Cabrillo ACe 755 *Mex.*

Cabrisas, Hilarión (1883-) Cu 28; PCu 64; PJC 47 *Cu.*
Cáceres, Carlos A. A 13 *Arg.*
Cáceres, Esther de HSLU II, pt 8, 25; PIU III, 237; PoU 69; U 4 *Uru.*
Cáceres, Manuel G. Cu 28 *Cu.*
Cáceres, P. Nicolás CA 65 *Guat.*
Cáceres, Zoila Aurora ("Eva Angelina" *or* "Evangelina") (1877-) CG II, 467; G 381; P 4; WLA 67 *Per.*
Cacia, A. BDC 9; Cu 28 *Cu.*
"Cachidiablo" (*pseud.*) *see* Tejera, Felipe
Cacho, José María HL I, 155 *Hond.*
Cacho-Negrete, Eusebio BDC 9; Cu 28 *Cu.*
Cadavid Restrepo, Tomás Co 11 *Col.*
Cadena, Pedro de la HPHA II, 141 *Ecua.*
Cadena, Pedro Ignacio Co 11 *Col.*
Cadenazzi, Edgarda HSLU II, pt 8, 27 *Uru.*
Cadicamo, Enrique D. A 13; CG I, 470 *Arg.*
Cadilla Cadilla, Arturo (1895-) QPR (1) 43 *P.R.*
Cadilla de Martínez, María (1886-) BP 499; PR 41; QPR (1) 183; (2) 42 *P.R.*
Cadilla Matos, Arturo BP 521; PR 32 *P.R.*
Caicedo, Fernando Co 11 *Col.*
Caicedo, Juan Esteban BC 92; Co 11 *Col.*
Caicedo, María Clemencia (1707-) HLNG I, 406 *Col.*
Caicedo, Rodolfo (1868?-1905?) AP 61; Pan 4 *Pan.*
Caicedo D'Elhuyar, Alejandro BC 83; Co 11 *Col.*
Caicedo Ladrón de Guevara, Manuel de (1718-1781) Co 11; HLNG I, 384 *Col.*
Caicedo y Flores (Flórez), Fernando (1756-1832) Co 11; HLNG II, 150, 336 *Col.*
Caicedo y Rojas, José (1816-1898) AC I, 291; BC 83; CHL 336; CLH 289; Co 12; LC 142; RHLC 113, 185; SASS 250 *Col.*
Caillava, Domingo A. CG I, 471; U 4 *Uru.*
Caillet Bois, Horacio A 13 *Arg.*
Caisse, J. Oberto Cu 28 *Cu.*
Cajar, Mario Horacio Pan 5 *Pan.*
Cajaraville, José M. U 4 *Uru.*
Cajica, Juan SCL 452, 592 *Per.*
Cajigal, Juan Manuel V 54 *Venez.*
Calancha, Antonio de la (1584-1654) B 4; BHLA 117; LA III, 117; LB 571; SCL 304, 592 *Bol.*
Calancha, Francisco de la LA III, 117 *Arg.*
Calancha, Francisco María (1850-) Pan 5 *Pan.*
Calancha, José Leonardo Pan 5 *Pan.*
Calandrelli, Matías (1845-) A 13; CG I, 472 *Arg.*
Calandrelli, Susana (1904-) A 13; APAM 462; LAC 148 *Arg.*
Calápiz, Francisco TM 90 *Mex.*
1. Calcagno, Francisco (1827-1903) ARC 75; CG I, 473; Cu 28; RLC 312 *Cu.*
2. Calcagno, Francisco (1829-) BDC 9; Cu 29; RLC 248 *Cu.*
Calcáneo, Andrés Cu 29 *Cu.*
Calcáneo Díaz, Andrés PM 25 *Mex.*
Calcaño, Arístides LV 289; V 54 *Venez.*

Calcaño, Eduardo ("Epsilón Kappa") BHLA 325; CHL 367; CLH 316; LV 12, 290; V 54, 67 *Venez.*

Calcaño, José Antonio (1827-1897) AEHA 190; BHLA 325; CG I, 473; CHL 362; CLH 311; FPA 550, 567; LV 114, 282; Par 8; SASS 510; V 55 *Venez.*

Calcaño, Julio ("Régulo") (1840-1919) AEHA 193; BHLA 325, 410; CG I, 473; CHL 376; CLH 324; LV 43, 88, 367; V 55, 121; VPF 29 *Venez.*

Calcaño, Luis Camilo V 56 *Venez.*

Calcaño, Simón V 56 *Venez.*

Calcaño Herrera, Antonio José V 56 *Venez.*

Calcaño Sánchez, Juan Bautista V 57 *Venez.*

Calcaño y Paniza, Juan Bautista V 57 *Venez.*

Caldas y Tenorio, Francisco José de (1771-1816) BHLA 141; CG I, 474; CHL 40; CLH 34; Co 12; LC 101 *Col.*

Caldera, R. R. LAS 199 *Venez.*

Caldera y del Villar, Daniel (1852-1896) C 45; CHL 257; HC 213 *Chil.*

Calderón, Clímaco (1852-1913) RHLC 197 *Col.*

Calderón, Guadalupe PM 26 *Mex.*

Calderón, José Cu 29 *Cu.*

Calderón, José L. B 5 *Bol.*

Calderón, Luis (1848-1894) Ig 48; NM 11 *Mex.*

Calderón, Melchor BHC II, 5 *Chil.*

Calderón, Pedro B. B 5 *Bol.*

Calderón, Próspero CA 9; IBCR IV, 122 *C.R.*

Calderón, Salvador CA 9; IBCR IV, 25 *C.R.*

Calderón, Severo TM 92 *Mex.*

Calderón, Tomás Co 12 *Col.*

Calderón Aponte, José BP 499 *P.R.*

Calderón Ávila, Félix (1891-1924) CA 65; PG 441 *Guat.*

Calderón de Becerra, Pablo Ig 48; NM 11 *Mex.*

Calderón de la Barca, Carlos ACe 756 *Mex.*

Calderón de la Barca, Manuel ACe 756; HPM 477 *Mex.*

Calderón Escobar, Juan PR 32 *P.R.*

Calderón Figueroa, Juan de Dios C 27 *Chil.*

Calderón Pardo, Rodolfo (1885-) CA 65; PG 380 *Guat.*

Calderón R., Venancio (1844-1885) CA 9; EPCR 43 *C.R.*

Calderón Reyes, Carlos (1856-1916) Co 12 *Col.*

Calderón y Beltrán, Fernando (1809-1845) AMP 233; BHLA 240; CHL 390; CLH 337; G 355; HLM 304, 326; HLMex 149; HPHA I, 126; HPM 775; PM 25; PMe I, 45; SASS 349; TM 91 *Mex.*

Caldevilla, Samuel (1917-) PoC 44 *Cu.*

Calero, José Cu 29 *Cu.*

Calero Orozco, Adolfo NL 227 *Nicar.*

Calero Quintana, Vicente HPM 826; TM 529 *Mex.*

"Calibán" (*pseud.*) *see* Rodó, José Enrique *and* Santos, Enrique

Calisto, Antonio José E 12 *Ecua.*

Calisto, Belisario L. E 12 *Ecua.*

"Calisto el Ñato" (*pseud.*) *see* De María, Alcides

Calixto Pompa, Elías V 57 *Venez.*

Caló Berro, Ophelia A 13; HSLU II, pt 8, 19 *Uru.-Arg.*

Caloca, Lauro G. (1884-) Ig 48; NM 12 *Mex.*

Calou, Juan Pedro (-1923) A 13, 81; APAM 205; G 310 *Arg.*

Calsamiglia, Eduardo (-1918) CA 9; EPCR 271; IBCR IV, 402 *et passim C.R.*

"Calvini, Juan" (*pseud.*) *see* Fernández Morúa, Juan

Calvo, Daniel (1832-1880) B 5; CHL 310; CLH 262; PB 223; SASS 100 *Bol.*

Calvo, Joaquín Bernardo (1799-1865) EPCR 20 *C.R.*

Calvo, Luis María E 12 *Ecua.*

Calvo, Manuel BDC 9; Cu 30; TM 617 *Cu.*

Calvo, Ramón BC 93; Co 12; E 12 *Col.*

Calvo, René B 5 *Bol.*

Calvo de la Riva, Pedro Andrés Co 12; HLNG I, 339 *Col.*

Calvo Mora, Joaquín Bernardo (1852-1915) CA 9; EPCR 21 *C.R.*

Calzada, Bernardo María de TM 490 *Mex.*

Calzadilla, Santiago A 13; CG I, 482 *Arg.*

Calzadilla Váldez, Fernando V 57 *Venez.*

Calle, Ezequiel E 12 *Ecua.*

Calle, Jorge A 13; CG I, 483 *Arg.*

Calle, Manuel J. (1866?-1919) CG I, 483; E 12, 73; G 343; PLE 58; V 57 *Ecua.*

Calleja, Bernardo ARC 45 *Cu.*

Calleja, Francisco Cu 29 *Cu.*

Calleja, L. E. TM 93 *Mex.*

Callejas, Félix ("Billiken") (1878-) AP 65; CT 461; Cu 21, 29; HLC 204; PA 22; Pan 5; PCu 67 *Cu.*

Callejas y Bercera, José María (1782-1823) Cu 30; RLC 32 *Cu.*

Callejo, Fernando PR 7 *P.R.*

Callorda, Pedro Erasmo U 4 *Uru.*

Camacho, Francisco Cu 30 *Cu.*

Camacho, Joaquín HLNG II, 283 *Col.*

Camacho, José Leocadio (1833-1914) BC 95; Co 12 *Col.*

Camacho, José María B 5 *Bol.*

Camacho, Juan Vicente V 57 *Venez.*

Camacho, Simón ("Nazareno") LA VIII, 631; V 57, 106 *Venez.*

Camacho, Tomás Felipe Cu 30 *Cu.*

Camacho Carrizosa, Guillermo (1876-) CG I, 487; Co 13 *Col.*

Camacho de Figueredo, Pomiana (1841-1889) BC 96; Co 13; RHLC 184 *Col.*

Camacho G., Francisco Co 13 *Col.*

Camacho Pradilla, Pedro A. BC 95; Co 13 *Col.*

Camacho Ramírez, Arturo LAS 206 *Col.*

Camacho Roldán, Salvador (1827-1900) BC 94; Co 13; LC 172; RHLC 197 *Col.*

"Camagüey, Una Hija del" (*pseud.*) Cu 82 *Cu.*

"Camagüeyano, El" (*pseud.*) *see* Mitjans, Aurelio

Camaña, Raquel A 13; CG I, 488 *Arg.*

Cámara, F. S. NM 12 *Mex.*

Camarena, Francisco NM 12 *Mex.*

Camarena Perdomo, M. de J. SD 7 *Dom.*
Camargo, Agustín Co 13 *Col.*
Camargo, Rafael María ("Fermín Pimentel y Vargas") (1858-1926) Co 13, 56; RHLC 191 *Col.*
Camargo Ángulo, F. Co 13 *Col.*
Camargo Latorre, Miguel Co 13 *Col.*
Camarillo y Roa de Pereyra, María Enriqueta ("María Enriqueta") (1875-) AMP 110; APEH 895, 1192; APMM 116; CG I, 489; FPA 340, 354; G 356; GLO 248; HLM 430, 458; Ig 49; LAS 206; NM 12; PM 26, 40; PMe I, 141; PNM 170; TM 93; WLA 306 *Mex.*
Cambaceres, Eugenio (1843-1888) A 13; BHLA 397; CG I, 490; CHL 190; CLH 162; LA VIII, 633; SASS 58; SPLA 238 *Arg.*
Camberos, Manuela G. de Ig 52; NM 12 *Mex.*
Cambours Ocampo, Arturo A 13, 71 *Arg.*
Cambre, Manuel CG I, 491; NM 1 *Mex.*
Camejo, Rafael W. PR 32 *P.R.*
Camelino Vedoya, Manuel A 13 *Arg.*
Camera B., Gerardo V 57 *Venez.*
Camín, Alfonso CG I, 491; Cu 30 *Cu.*
Caminero Sánchez, Mario SD 7 *Dom.*
"Camino, Juan del" (*pseud.*) BHLA 576 *Hond.*
Camino, Miguel A. (1877-) A 13; APAM 214; APEH 561; BHLA 530; CHL 187; GLO 235; NPA 181; PLHA 156 *Arg.*
Cammarano, Salvador CG I, 492; Cu 30 *Cu.*
Campa, Gustavo E. CG I, 493; TM 604 *Mex.*
Campa, Joaquín A 14, 81; CG I, 493 *Arg.*
Campa, Miguel Ángel de la (1883-) Cu 30 *Cu.*
Campero, Eduardo B 5 *Bol.*
Campero, Isaac S. B 5 *Bol.*
Campero, Lindaura A. de ("El Novel") (1846-1898) B 5 *Bol.*
Campero, Manuel B 5 *Bol.*
Campero, Narciso (1815-1896) B 5 *Bol.*
Campero E., Octavio B 5 *Bol.*
"Campesino, El" (*pseud.*) Cu 30 *Cu.*
Campilongo, Carlos A. A 14 *Arg.*
Campo, Ángel de ("Micrós") (1868-1908) BAMP 35; G 356; HLM 448; HLMex 222; Ig 52; NM 12; PoM 367 *Mex.*
Campo, Astur de U 4 *Uru.*
Campo, Carlos al Cu 30 *Cu.*
"Campo, Carlos al" (*pseud.*) *see* Zum Felde, Carlos
Campo, Estanislao del ("Anastasio el Pollo") (1834-1880) A 19; BHLA 306; CG I, 495; CHL 161; CLH 141; G 310; HLA 396; HPHA II, 469; LA II, 665, 735; PLHA 81; SASS 26; SPLA 86; WSAL 39 *Arg.*
Campo, Isidro del PE 111 *Ecua.*
Campo, Juan del C 5 *Chil.*
Campo, Nicolás del HLA 36 *Arg.*
Campo de Barcellos, Lucía del C 5; CG I, 495 *Chil.*
Campo Larraondo y Valencia, Manuel Mariano del (1772-1860) BC 97; Co 13; HLNG II, 221; RHLC 83 *Col.*

Campo y Rivas, Manuel Antonio del (1750-) ACe 1006; CG I, 496; Co 13; HLNG II, 402 *Col.*
Campos, Daniel B 5 *Bol.*
Campos, Ernesto de los PU 50 *Uru.*
Campos, Francisco (1868-) CHL 320; CLH 272; E 13, 73 *Ecua.*
Campos, José Antonio ("Jack the Ripper") (1805-1884) E 13; G 344; PLE 78 *Ecua.*
Campos, Manuel Antonio E 14 *Ecua.*
Campos, Rubén M. (1876-1930) AMP 105; BHLA 524; CG I, 498; HLM 428, 458; IE 44; Ig 56; NM 12; PM 26; PMe I, 47; PNM 19; TM 93, 530; WLA 70 *Mex.*
Campos Díaz, Manuel TM 95 *Mex.*
Campos Marquetti, Generoso ARC 45 *Cu.*
Campos Martínez, Juan Gregorio PM 26 *Mex.*
Campos Ortega, Lino Ramón PM 26 *Mex.*
Campos Vicente, Ambrosio ARC 45 *Cu.*
Camprodón, Francisco Cu 30 *Cu.*
Camprodón y Lafont, Francisco CG I, 499; V 57 *Venez.*
Camprubi, José (1879-) QPR (1) 44; (2) 43 *P.R.*
Camps, Antonio Ignacio de HLNG I, 238 *Col.*
Campuzano, Juan de Dios E 14 *Ecua.*
Campuzano, Pío (1814-1873) BDC 9; Cu 30 *Cu.*
Campuzano, Ricardo (1826-) Co 13 *Col.*
Canabal, Clemente María (hijo) Co 13 *Col.*
Canales, Leonardo TM 604 *Mex.*
Canales, Nemesio R. PA 160; PP 208; PR 17, 26 *P.R.*
Canales Carazo, Juan Cu 30 *Cu.*
Canales Carrasco, Juan (1869-) ARC 45 *Cu.*
Canali, Diego HLNG II, 381 *Col.*
Canamaque, Antonio G 310 *Arg.*
"Cancán, Mr." (*pseud.*) *see* Gutiérrez Nájera, Manuel
Cancela, Arturo (1892-) A 14; AT II, 773; BHLA 507; CG I, 502; CrA 103; G 310; LAC 56, 134; OA 23; PLHA 217, 294; WLA 71 *Arg.*
Cancio, Miguel Galliano PJC 49 *Cu.*
Cancio Madrigal, César (-1922) Cu 30; PA 23; PCu 70 *Cu.*
Candelas, el Tío NM 12 *Mex.*
Candia, Romeo de PU 258 *Uru.*
"Candil, Fray" (*pseud.*) *see* Bobadilla, Emilio
Candil, Mario Co 14 *Col.*
"Candileja, Agapito" (*pseud.*) *see* Soiza Reilly, Juan José de
Candioti, Alberto María (1889-) CG I, 504; WLA 71 *Arg.*
Cané, Luis (1897-) A 14; APAM 466; LAC 147 *Arg.*
1. Cané, Miguel ("E") (1812-1863) A 14; BHLA 276; HSLU III, pt 4, 13; LA VI, 1107; SPLA 233 *Uru.*
2. Cané, Miguel (hijo) (1851-1905) A 14; BHLA 398; CG I, 504; CHL 186; GLO 235; LA VIII, 710; SPLA 244 *Arg.*
Canelas, Demetrio (1881-) B 5; C 5 *Bol.-Chil.*
"Canelón, Agapito" (*pseud.*) *see* Agostini, Rafael

Cánepa, Alejandro Rómulo (1865-) A 14, 81; CG I, 505 *Arg.*
Cannobbio G., Agustín C 29, 62; CG I, 506; CL 139 *Chil.*
Cano, Antonio José (1874-) Co 14 *Col.*
Cano, Fidel (1854-1919) BC 97; Co 14 *Col.*
Cano, Hilario U 4 *Uru.*
Cano, Julio Co 14 *Col.*
Cano, Miguel A. CG I, 506; Cu 30 *Cu.*
Cano, Rafael A 14; G 310 *Arg.*
Cano Gutiérrez, Diego P 4 *Per.*
Canseco, Enrique PM 26 *Mex.*
Canseco, Francisco R. PM 26 *Mex.*
Cantarell, C. PM 26 *Mex.*
Cantero, J. B. Cu 31 *Cu.*
Cantero y Altuna, Ricardo Cu 31 *Cu.*
Cantilo, José Luis (1871-) CG I, 511; WLA 71 *Arg.*
1. Cantilo, José María ("J. M. C.") (1816-1872) HLA 424; LA VI, 1104 *Arg.*
2. Cantilo, José María (hijo) (1840-1891) A 14; LA VIII, 758 *Arg.*
3. Cantilo, José María (hijo) (1877-) WLA 72 *Arg.*
Canto, José Dolores TM 95, 330 *Mex.*
Canto, Rufino del C 5; NC 113 *Chil.*
Cantú Corro, José (1884-) CG I, 513; G 356; Ig 57; NM 12 *Mex.*
Cañamaque, Antonio G 310 *Arg.*
Cañarte, Juan José Cu 31 *Cu.*
Cañas, Juan José (1826-1900) CHL 507; CLH 448; GPCA II, 49; PS 82 *Salv.*
Cañas, Tomás M. BDC 9; Cu 31 *Cu.*
Cañas Pinochet, Alejandro C 62; CG I, 513 *Chil.*
Cañellas, Francisco CG I, 513; Cu 31 *Cu.*
Cañizares, Daniel Alberto E 14 *Ecua.*
Cañizares, José de TM 490 *Mex.*
Cañizares, Nicolás A. PE 251 *Ecua.*
Caño y Pastor, Nicolás Cu 31 *Cu.*
Cao y Montiel, Manuel (-1884) Cu 31 *Cu.*
"Cap. José" (*pseud.*) *see* Rosas Londa
"Capacho" (*pseud.*) *see* Rodríguez Uscares, José
Capdevielle, Adolfo A 72 *Arg.*
Capdevila, Arturo (1889-) A 14, 81; APAM 224; APEH 754, 1190; AT I, 339; BHLA 528; CG I, 514; CHL 186; G 310; GLO 235; IE 45; LAC 76, 143; LAS 206, 207; NPA 101; PLHA 145; SASS 51; WLA 72 *Arg.*
Capece, José Andrés A 15, 81 *Arg.*
Capella Toledo, Luis (1838-) BC 97; Co 14 *Col.*
Capetillo, Luisa PR 17 *P.R.*
Capitaine Funes, Carlos A 15 *Arg.*
Capó, Claudio PR 17 *P.R.*
Capó Rodríguez, Pedro PR 49 *P.R.*
Capriles, Aníbal (1854-) B 5 *Bol.*
Capriles, Carlos L. V 57 *Venez.*
Capriles, Raúl V 58 *Venez.*
Caraballo, Gustavo (1885-) A 15, 81; APAM 243 *Arg.*
Caraballo y Sotolongo, Francisco (1891-) CG I, 519; Cu 31 *Cu.*
Carabaño, Miguel V 58 *Venez.*
Carabaño, R. M. PR 32 *P.R.*
Caravantes, Agustín de B. y PM 26 *Mex.*

Carbajal, Adeodato ARC 45 *Cu.*
Carballido, Pastor M. A 15 *Arg.*
Carballo, Manuel S. (-1898) Cu 31 *Cu.*
Carbia, Rómulo D. (1885-) AT I, 488; CG I, 520 *Arg.*
Carbo, Luis Felipe E 14 *Ecua.*
Carbo, Pedro (1813-1894) E 14 *Ecua.*
Carbo Viteri, Carlos E 14; PE 57 *Ecua.*
Carbonell, C. A 15 *Arg.*
Carbonell, Diego CG I, 521; V 58 *Venez.*
Carbonell, Miguel Ángel (1895-) ARC 76; Cu 33 *Cu.*
Carbonell y Rivero, José Manuel (1880-) CG I, 522; CHL 490; CT 279; Cu 31; HLC 205; PA 24; PCu 72; RLC 198, 270, 349, 362; WLA 73 *Cu.*
Carbonell y Rivero, Néstor (1883-) CG I, 522; CT 101; Cu 33; WLA 73 *Cu.*
Cárcano, Ramón J. (1860-) AT II, 543; CG I, 523; WLA 73 *Arg.*
Carcassés y Guerrero, José (-1883) Cu 33 *Cu.*
Cardenal, Armando CA 9 *C.R.*
Cardenal, José Francisco NL 255 *Nicar.*
Cardenal, Theodoro Cu 33 *Cu.*
Cárdenas, Alejandro E 14, 73 *Ecua.*
Cárdenas, Encarnación de (1790-1831) ACe 759 *Mex.*
Cárdenas Quintana, Julia (1919-) PoC 42 *Cu.*
Cárdenas y Chávez, Miguel de (1808-1890) BDC 10; Cu 33; PCu 77; RLC 88 *Cu.*
Cárdenas y Echarte, Raúl de (1884-) CT 211 *Cu.*
Cárdenas y León, Joaquín Velásquez de *see* Velásquez de Cárdenas y León, Joaquín
Cárdenas y Rodríguez, José María de (1812-1882) BDC 10; Cu 34; RLC 88, 142 *Cu.*
Cárdenas y Rodríguez, Nicolás (1814-1868) BDC 10; Cu 34 *Cu.*
Cardiel, José SCL 421, 592 *Arg.*
Cardona, Rafael (1893-) CA 10, 11; EPCR 537; FPA 122, 141; IBCR IV, 306; IE 47 *C.R.*
Cardona y Valverde, Jenaro (1863-) A 15; CA 10; EPCR 75; IBCR IV, 125 *et passim C.R.*
Cardoso, Francisco José HLNG I, 173 *Col.*
Cardoso, Saúl Par 8 *Para.*
Cardoza y Aragón, Luis CA 65; TM 430 *Guat.*
Cardozo, Ramón I. Par 8 *Para.*
Carduz Vierra, José U 4 *Uru.*
Carias, Alejandro V 58 *Venez.*
"Caribe, El" (*pseud.*) *see* Padilla, José Gualberto
"Caribe, La Hija del" (*pseud.*) *see* Padilla de Sanz, Trinidad
Cariola V., Carlos C 45 *Chil.*
Carlo, Celestino de E 15 *Ecua.*
Carlos, Pedro J. CL 139 *Chil.*
"Carlos al Campo" (*pseud.*) *see* Zum Felde, Carlos
"Carlos Díaz" (*pseud.*) *see* Rokha, Pablo de
Carmen, José de la V. del Co 14 *Col.*
"Carmen Hernández, A." (*pseud.*) *see* Benítez, Alejandrina

"Carmen Lira" (pseud.) see Carvajal, María Isabel

Carmona, Eduardo U 4 Uru.

Carmona, Hipólito Alfonso PM 27 Mex.

Carmona, Miguel ("Genaro Culmani") V 58, 75 Venez.

Carmona, Miguel Guillermo CL 139 Chil.

Carnelli, María Luisa A 15 Arg.

Carnero, Juan (1660-1723) PM 27 Mex.

Carnevali, Gonzalo PLHA 166; V 58 Venez.

Carnevali Monreal, Ángel V 58 Venez.

Carniado, Enrique NM 13; PM 27 Mex.

Carnicer, Francisco A 15 Arg.

Caro, Andrés L. A 15 Arg.

Caro, Antonio José (1783-1853) HLNG II, 106, 345 Sp.

Caro, Brigido TM 95 Mex.

Caro, Francisco Xavier (1750-1822) CG I, 530; Co 14; HLNG II, 104; HPHA II, 37; RHLC 65 Col.

Caro, José Eusebio (1817-1853) AC I, 21; II, 41; AEHA 227; ALC I, 105; BC 99; BHLA 214, 222; CHL 323; CLH 275; Co 14; CoL 268; FPA 81, 90; G 328; HPHA II, 46; LC 124; PCo 57; PLHA 75; RHLC 85; SASS 215; WSAL 43, 75 Col.

Caro, María HLNG II, 104 Col.

Caro, Miguel Antonio (1843-1909) AC I, 49; II, 59; AEHA 230; ALC I, 281; BC 101; BHLA 369; CG I, 530; CHL 79, 330, 339, 340; CLH 283, 291; Co 14, 21; FPA 42, 114; G 328; LC 162; PCo 65; RHLC 195; SASS 226; V 58 Col.

Caro, Tito Lucrecio HLNG II, 103 Col.

Caro, Víctor Eduardo (1885-) CG I, 530; Co 15; WLA 79 Col.

Caro de Torres, Francisco (1750-) BHC I, 167 et passim; HLNG II, 104; SCL 254, 593 Col.

Caro Grau, Francisco CG I, 531; Co 15 Col.

Carpena, Elías A 15 Arg.

Carpentier, Alejo LH 140, 167

"Carpio, Juan del" (pseud.) see Espinosa Saldaña, Adán

Carpio, Julio C. del CG I, 532; P 5 Per.

Carpio, Manuel (1791-1860) AEHA 888; AMP 228; CHL 392; CLH 339; G 356; HLM 292; HLMex 156; HPHA I, 148; HPM 702; NM 1, 13; PM 27; PMe I, 49; PoM 28 Mex.

Carpio, Miguel del (1795-) P 5 Per.

Carr, Oswaldo A. Cu 34 Cu.

Carrancá y Trujillo, Raúl (1897-) CG I, 536; WLA 79 Mex.

Carranza, Adolfo P. CG I, 536; Par 1 Para.

Carranza, Ángel Justiniano (1834-) CG I, 536; LA VI, 1085 Arg.

Carranza, José (-1813) ACe 760 Mex.

Carranza, Mario A. A 15 Arg.

Carranza, Rafael (1840-) CA 11; EPCR 41 C.R.

Carranza, Sienra PIU I, 246 Uru.

Carrasco, Alberto PCh 401 Chil.

Carrasco, Aliro C 5, 62; CL 139 Chil.

Carrasco, Ángel A 15 Arg.

Carrasco, Constantino (1841-1877) BHLA 320; HPHA II, 265; P 5 Per.

Carrasco, Gabriel A 15; CG I, 537 Arg.

Carrasco, Germán A 15; CG I, 537 Arg

Carrasco, José (1862-1921) B 5 Bol.

Carrasco, Josefa HL II, 269 Hond.

Carrasco, Julio Cu 34 Cu.

Carrasco, Rosendo C 5 Chil.

"Carrasco, Sansón" (pseud.) see Muñoz, Daniel

Carrasco M., Francisco Pan 5 Pan.

Carrasco Mojena, Esteban A. BDC 10; Cu 34 Cu.

Carrasco Núñez, Salustio PM 27 Mex.

Carrasco y Jelves, Rosendo C 27, 46 Chil.

Carrasquel, Federico V 58 Venez.

Carrasquel y Valverde, Raúl V 58 Venez.

Carrasquilla, Francisco de Paula (1855-) BC 109; Co 15; LC 181 Col.

Carrasquilla, Luis Co 15 Col.

Carrasquilla, Rafael María (1857-) BC 108; Co 15, 16; LAS 203; LC 178 Col.

Carrasquilla, Ricardo ("Rómulo") (1827-1886) AC I, 265; AEHA 888; BC 106; CHL 341; CLH 290, 292; Co 16, 41; HPHA II, 73; LC 149; PLHA 75; RHLC 121, 139 Col.

Carrasquilla, Tomás (1858-) BHLA 410; CG I, 538; CHL 353; CLH 303; Co 16; LAS 203; LC 191; RHLC 189; WLA 79 Col.

Carrasquilla Mallarino, Eduardo CA 11; CG I, 538; Pan 5; PC 21 C.R.

Carrencá, Ricardo A 15, 81 Arg.

Carreño, Alberto María (1875-) CG I, 539; WLA 79 Mex.

Carreño, Eduardo V 59 Venez.

Carreño, Franco Ig 59; NM 1, 13 Mex.

Carreño, Gabriel RHLC 193 Col.

Carreño, Miguel P 5 Per.

Carreño, Pedro BDC 10; Cu 34 Cu.

Carreño-Rodríguez, R. V 59 Venez.

Carrera, José Miguel CG I, 539, 642; HC 47 Chil.

Carrera Andrade, César PLE 124 Ecua.

Carrera Andrade, Jorge (1903-) APEH 1159, 1195; BHLA 598; CG I, 539; E 15; LAS 206; PE 146; PLE 115; WLA 80 Ecua.

Carreras, Carlos M. PR 11, 14 P.R.

Carreras, Carlos N. (1895-) PP 285; PR 41; QPR (1) 185; (2) 45 P.R.

Carreras, Ernesto BDC 110; PR 32 P.R.

Carreras, Roberto de las (1873-) CG I, 541; PIU II, 324; UT 149 Uru.

Carretero, Enrique CG I, 544; Cu 34 Cu.

Carreto, Rosa PM 27 Mex.

Carri Pérez, Julio (1894-) A 16, 81 Arg.

Carricarte y de Armas, Arturo R. de (1880-) CT 165; Cu 34; HLC 214 Cu.

Carriedo, Adalberto CG I, 546; Ig 60; NM 13; TM 96 Mex.

1. Carriego, Evaristo A 15; CG I, 546; LAC 78, 143 Arg.

2. Carriego, Evaristo (hijo) (1883-1912) A 16; APAM 245; APEH 820; BHLA 530; CHL 186; G 310; NPA 69; PLHA 146; SPLA 117 Arg.

Carrillo, Álvaro NM 13 Mex.

Carrillo, Braulio (1800-) CA 11 C.R.

"Carrillo, Charles" (*pseud.*) *see* Valladares y Rubio, Antonio

Carrillo, Enrique A. ("Cabotín") (1876-1936) BHLA 515; P 5; SAL 299, 301; WLA 80 *Per.*

Carrillo, Facundo ARC 40 *Cu.*

Carrillo, Horacio A 16; CG I, 546 *Arg.*

Carrillo, Julián TM 604 *Mex.*

Carrillo, Miguel NM 13 *Mex.*

Carrillo Guerra, Juan Bautista V 59 *Venez.*

Carrillo Márquez, Antonio José V 59 *Venez.*

Carrillo Ramírez, Salomón CA 65 *Guat.*

Carrillo Ruedas, Armando C 5, 27 *Chil.*

Carrillo y Ancona, Crescencio (1836-1897) Ig 60; NM 1, 13; PM 27; TM 531 *Mex.*

Carrillo y Navas, José Antonio V 59 *Venez.*

Carrillo y O'Farril, Isaac (1844-1901) BDC 11; Cu 34; RLC 278 *Cu.*

Carrillo y Pérez, Ignacio ACe 762 *Mex.*

Carrión, Agustín E 15 *Ecua.*

Carrión, Antonio (-1911) HLM 492; Ig 63; NM 13; PM 27 *Mex.*

Carrión, Benjamín BHLA 592; CG I, 547; G 344; PLE 123, 139 *Chil.*

Carrión Maduro, Tomás (1872-1920) ARC 41; BDC 110; PR 11, 17, 55 *P.R.*

Carrión y Cárdenas, Miguel de (1875-1929) CT 327; Cu 35; HLC 190; RLC 338, 355 *Cu.*

Carrión y Velasco, Nicolás Gerónimo E 73 *Ecua.*

Carrizo, César A 16; CG I, 547; LAS 203 *Arg.*

Carrizo, Juan Alfonso A 16, 71; CG I, 547 *Arg.*

Cartagena, Joaquín E 15 *Ecua.*

Cartey, Guido Anatolio A 16, 81 *Arg.*

Caruso, Juan A. (1890-) A 16, 81 *Arg.*

Carvacho, José A. C 5; NC 413 *Chil.*

Carvajal, Alberto (1882-) CG I, 535; Co 16; WLA 81 *Col.*

Carvajal, Alonso de HLNG I, 434 *Col.*

Carvajal, Aníbal C 46 *Chil.*

Carvajal, Fermín Francisco de BHC II, 566 *Chil.*

Carvajal, Juan (1914-) PoC 45 *Cu.*

Carvajal, Manuel A. PCo 78 *Col.*

Carvajal, María Isabel ("Carmen Lira") (1888-) BHLA 526; CA 11, 12; CHL 508; EPCR 449; IBCR IV, 139 *et passim*: SASS 133 *C.R.*

Carvajal, Rafael PE 277 *Ecua.*

Carvajal R., Walter B 5; CG I, 535 *Bol.*

Carvajal y Márquez, Ángela de (1880-) PCh 281 *Per.*

Carvajal y Robles, Rodrigo de HPHA II, 179 *Per.*

Carvallo, José A. C 27 *Chil.*

Carvallo Arvelo, María V 59 *Venez.*

Carvallo Arvelo, Salvador V 59 *Venez.*

Carvallo y Goyeneche, Vicente (1740-1816) HC 40; SCL 500, 503, 593 *Chil.*

Carve, Luis UL 124 *Uru.*

Casa Lug, Ramón P 5 *Per.*

Casabianca, Juan Par 8 *Para.*

Casaconcha, Marqués de P 5 *Per.*

Casacuberta, José (1799-1849) HLA 206 *Arg.*

Casacuberta, Juan Aurelio SPLA 145 *Arg.*

Casado, Francisco María Cu 35 *Cu.*

Casado, Luis Manuel CA 12 *C.R.*

Casado, Ricardo A. Cu 35 *Cu.*

Casal, Julián del (1863-1893) APEH 64, 1178; BHLA 453; CG I, 550; CHL 488, 514; CLH 453; Cu 35; FPA 162, 183; G 335; HLC 192; PA 28; PCu 80; PLHA 89; RLC 285 *et passim*; SAL 52 *et passim*; SASS 284 *Cu.*

Casal, Julio J. (1889-) APEH 981; BHLA 532; CG I, 550; HSLU II, pt 9, 35; LU 64, 667; PIU III, 197; PoU 75; PU 62; U 4 *Uru.*

Casal Carranza, Roque A 16 *Arg.*

Casal Castel, Alberto A 16 *Arg.*

Casal Cucalón, Bolívar E 15 *Ecua.*

Casals y Llorente, Jorge (1893-) Cu 35; PCu 84; PJC 65 *Cu.*

Casanova, Carlos BP 502, 585; PR 32, 42 *P.R.*

Casanova, José PM 27; TM 490 *Mex.*

Casanova, Luis R. P 5 *Per.*

Casanova, Mauricio de Cu 35 *Cu.*

Casanova, Pascual V 59 *Venez.*

Casanova Loor, Neptalí E 15, 73 *Ecua.*

Casanova Vicuña, Alfonso C 27; CG I, 552 *Chil.*

Casanova y Estrada, Ricardo (1844-1913) CA 66; PG 298 *Guat.*

Casanovas, Martí (1894-) IE 50 *Mex.*

Casañas J., Diego V 59 *Venez.*

Casaravilla Lemos, Enrique (1889-) CG I, 554; PIU III, 139; PoU 81; PU 55; SASS 469; U 4 *Uru.*

Casares, Manuel M. E 15 *Ecua.*

Casares, Manuel María Co 16 *Col.*

Casariego, Raúl A 16, 81 *Arg.*

Casas, Bartolomé de las (1474-1566) BHLA 56; CG I, 556; CHL 4; CLH 3; HLM 42; HLMex 21; SCL 29, 593 *Sp.-Mex.*

Casas, P. Las HPM 86 *Mex.*

Casas Araujo, Julio PIU III, 238; PU 257; U 4 *Uru.*

Casas Castañeda, José Joaquín (1866-) AC II, 357; ALC I, 327; BC 111; CG I, 556; CHL 348; Co 16; LC 182; RHLC 147; WLA 83 *Col.*

Casas López, Tomás de las Cu 35 *Cu.*

Casaseca, José Luis Cu 35 *Cu.*

Casasús, Joaquín Demetrio (1858-1916) AMP 136; CG I, 557; HLM 407; NM 1; PM 27; PMe I, 53; TM 532 *Mex.*

Casasús N., Carlos C 27 *Chil.*

Casavalle, Carlos A 73 *Arg.*

"Cascabel" (*pseud.*) *see* López Evia, Lorenzo

Cascabel, César C 5; CG I, 558 *Chil.*

Cascallares Gutiérrez, Isabel ("Quena") (1889-) A 16, 78 *Arg.*

Cascella, Armando (1900-) A 16 *Arg.*

Casco, R. PN 155 *Nicar.*

Casco Gadea, Pedro José A 16 *Arg.*

Casella, Edgardo A 16 *Arg.*

"Casimiro de la Barra" (*pseud.*) *see* Soto Borda, Clímaco

Caso, Antonio (1883-) BHLA 487; CG I, 561; G 356; HLM 510; LAND 121, 122; PM 28; WLA 84 *Mex.*

Caso y Sola, Luis Cu 35 *Cu.*

Casorla, J. R. CA 12 *C.R.*

Casós, Fernando (1828-1882) BHLA 338; P 5 *Per.*
Cassani, José (1673-) HLNG I, 350; RHLC 17; SCL 390, 595 *Col.*
Cassanova, José Cu 36 *Cu.*
Cassard, Andrés (1823-) Cu 36 *Cu.*
Casses de Xalo, Joaquín HLNG II, 383 *Col.*
Cassinelli, Amadeo A 16 *Arg.*
Castaing, Rodolfo CA 12; EPCR 556 *C.R.*
Castañeda, Ángel CG I, 563; TM 431 *Mex.*
Castañeda, Carlos E. TM 533 *Mex.*
Castañeda, Daniel PM 28 *Mex.*
1. Castañeda, Francisco (1776-1832) A 16; G 311; HLA 281 *Arg.*
2. Castañeda, Francisco (1856-) CG I, 563; GPCA III, 263; PS 54 *Salv.*
Castañeda Aragón, Gregorio (1887-) BHLA 518, 588; CG I, 564; CHL 354; IE 51; RHLC 193; WLA 84 *Col.*
Castañiza, José María (1744-1816) ACe 763 *Mex.*
Castañiza, Juan (1756-1825) ACe 764 *Mex.*
Castaño López, Ramón Cu 36 *Cu.*
Castaños, José María PM 28 *Mex.*
Castaños, Juan José TM 96 *Mex.*
Castelanos, Alberto ARC 46 *Cu.*
Castelar, Emilio Cu 36 *Cu.*
Castelblanco P., Agustín C 27 *Chil.*
Castelnuovo, Elías A 16, 82; CG I, 567; G 311; LAC 59, 135 *Arg.*
Castell, Manuel BDC 11; Cu 36 *Cu.*
Castell de López Rocha, Adela ("Zulema") UT 155 *Uru.*
Castellanos, Carlos A. R. ARC 46; Cu 36 *Cu.*
Castellanos, Carmen TM 96 *Mex.*
Castellanos, Francisco José (-1920) Cu 36 *Cu.*
Castellanos, Jesús (1879-1912) BHLA 525; CG I, 568; CHL 488; CLH 428; Cu 36; G 335; HLC 188; RLC 340, 351; SASS 291 *Cu.*
Castellanos, Joaquín ("Dharma") (1861-) A 16, 78; AT II, 1043; CG I, 568; G 311 *Arg.*
Castellanos, José SD 7 *Dom.*
Castellanos, José Guadalupe ARC 46 *Cu.*
Castellanos, José S. (1845-) Cu 36 *Cu.*
Castellanos, Juan de (1522-1606) AEHA 471; BHLA 61; CG I, 568; CHL 18; CLH 15; Co 17; CoL 263; HLNG I, 63; HPHA I, 354; II, 8, 12; LC 80; RHLC 6; SCL 214, 595; V 59 *Col.*
Castellanos, Julio A 16, 81; CG I, 568 *Arg.*
Castellanos, Lucio U 4 *Uru.*
Castellanos, Luis Alberto Co 17 *Col.*
Castellanos, María TM 96 Mex.
Castellanos, Mario ("Miro Cumbres") (1895-) CG I, 568; GLO 253; U 4 *Uru.*
Castellanos, Rafael C. SD 7 *Dom.*
Castellanos, Silvestre V 59 *Venez.*
Castellanos Abreu, Manuel Cu 37 *Cu.*
Castellanos García, Gerardo CG I, 568; Cu 37 *Cu.*
Castellanos Quinto, Erasmo PM 28 *Mex.*
Castello, Carlos Co 17 *Col.*
Castello, Manuel Co 17 *Col.*
Castellón, Pedro Ángel (1820-1860) G 335; PCu 85; RLC 186 *Cu.*

Castellot, José Felipe Ig 63; NM 13 *Mex.*
Casteñeda Aragón, Gregorio Co 16 *Col.*
Castera, Pedro (1838-1906) CA 66; HLM 457; HLMex 181; Ig 64; NM 13; PM 28 *Mex.*
Castex, Eusebio R. A 17; CG I, 570 *Arg.*
Castilla, Clodomiro PB 235 *Bol.*
Castilla, José María CA 66; CG I, 570 *Guat.*
Castilla, Ramón (1797-1867) CHL 289; CLH 244 *Per.*
Castilla Aguiar, A. A 17 *Arg.*
Castilla del Busto, Alberto Cu 37 *Cu.*
Castillero Reyes, Ernesto de Jesús WLA 85 *Pan.*
Castillo, Abel-Romeo E 74 *Ecua.*
Castillo, Cirilo R. del TM 431, 456 *Mex.*
Castillo, Diego Cu 37 *Cu.*
Castillo, Edmundo PM 28 *Mex.*
Castillo, Eduardo (1889-) ALC II, 241; Co 17; LC 195; PCo 79; RHLC 155; WLA 86 *Col.*
Castillo, Emilio del E 15 *Ecua.*
Castillo, Felipe Neri (1867-) G 356; PM 28, 60; TM 96 *Mex.*
Castillo, Félix R. AP 67; Pan 5 *Pan.*
Castillo, Florencio del (-1834) EPCR 14 *C.R.*
Castillo, Florencio M. del (1828-1863) BHLA 344; CHL 406; HLM 339; HLMex 174; Ig 68; NM 14; TM 533 *Mex.*
Castillo, Francisco del (1714-1770) LP 338 *Per.*
Castillo, Guillermo ("Jubilo") Ig 70; NM 14; TM 431, 480 *Mex.*
Castillo, I. D. del NM 14 *Mex.*
Castillo, Jesús V 59 *Venez.*
Castillo, José de la O. NM 14 *Mex.*
Castillo, José León CA 66 *Guat.*
Castillo, José R. del CG I, 572; Ig 71; NM 14; TM 433 *Mex.*
Castillo, José S. Co 17 *Col.*
Castillo, José Vicente ("Jotabé") Co 17 *Col.*
"Castillo, La Madre" (*pseud.*) see Castillo y Guevara, Francisca Josefa de la Concepción
Castillo, Luis C. del SD 7 *Dom.*
1. Castillo, Luis María PD 37; SD 7 *Dom.*
2. Castillo, Luis María V 59 *Venez.*
1. Castillo, Manuel (1814-1871) CG I, 572; III, 474; CHL 294; CLH 249; P 5 *Per.*
2. Castillo, Manuel HPM 464 *Mex.*
Castillo, María Piedad E 15 *Ecua.*
Castillo, Mario ARC 46 *Cu.*
Castillo, Moisés AP 69; Pan 5 *Pan.*
Castillo, Pedro (1859-) PCh 271 *Chil.*
Castillo, Pedro Pablo del V 59 *Venez.*
Castillo, Pío del PM 28 *Mex.*
Castillo, Rafael del (1847-1917) Ig 71; NM 14; PM 28 *Mex.*
Castillo, Regina Pía V 59 *Venez.*
Castillo, Ricardo José V 59 *Venez.*
Castillo de Clavijo, Elvira ARC 46; Cu 37 *Cu.*
Castillo de González, Aurelia (1842-1920) CHL 489; CT 263; Cu 37; GLO 242; HLC 165; PA 32; PCu 88; RLC 279, 281 *Cu.*
Castillo de Leví, Piedad PE 267 *Ecua.*

Castillo Ledón, Amalia González Caballero de (1902-) TM 533; WLA 86 *Mex.*

Castillo Ledón, Luis (1879-) APMM 11; CG I, 573; G 356; HLM 521; IE 52; NM 1; PM 28; PNM 25; TM 534; WLA 86 *Mex.*

Castillo Márquez, Francisco X. CG I, 573; SD 7 *Dom.*

Castillo Negrete, Emilio NM 1 *Mex.*

Castillo Peraza, Joaquín PM 28; TM 97 *Mex.*

Castillo Rada, José María del (1776-1833) HLNG II, 467 *Col.*

Castillo U., Eduardo C 27 *Chil.*

Castillo U., Pantaleón NC 413 *Chil.*

Castillo y Castillo, M. E. PE 215 *Ecua.*

Castillo y Guevara, Francisca Josefa de la Concepión ("La Madre Castillo") (1671-1742) AB 21; BHLA 95; CHL 33, 34; CLH 29; Co 17; CoL 264; G 328; HLNG I, 323; LC 95; RHLC 35; SCL 382, 595 *Col.*

Castillo y Justiz, Emiliano BDC 12; Cu 38 *Cu.*

Castillo y Lanzas, Joaquín María del (1781-1878) HLM 247; HPM 869; PM 28 *Mex.*

Castillo y Piña, José PM 28 *Mex.*

Castillo y Sucre, Rafael del (1741-1783) RLC 33 *Cu.*

Castiñeiras, Alejandro A 17; CG I, 574 *Arg.*

"Casto, Emiro" (*pseud.*) *see* Toro, Fermín

Castorena, Mercedes PM 28 *Mex.*

Castrejón, Eduardo A. Ig 72; NM 14 *Mex.*

Castro, Agustín de (1728-1790) ACe 662; HLM 185; HLMex 85; HPM 470 *Mex.*

Castro, Alfonso (1878-) Co 17, 18; RHLC 190 *Col.*

Castro, Aníbal de Co 18 *Col.*

Castro, Antonio ("Karez-i-Roshan") OA 133

Castro, Cipriano CG I, 575; V 59 *Venez.*

Castro, Constantino Cu 38 *Cu.*

Castro, Diego de (Titu Cussi Yupanqui) BHLA 65; P 7 *Per.*

Castro, Elías CA 12 *C.R.*

Castro, Enrique María V 60 *Venez.*

Castro, Ernesto L. A 17 *Arg.*

Castro, Francisco de HPM 456; PM 28 *Mex.*

Castro, Francisco de Asís (1860-) G 356; Ig 73; NM 14; PM 28 *Mex.*

Castro, Guillermo CA 12, 38 *C.R.*

Castro, J. C 5; NC 113 *Chil.*

Castro, J. Luis PM 29 *Mex.*

Castro, Jesús PM 28 *Mex.*

Castro, José Agustín de (-1814) ACe 49; HLM 238; HLMex 97; HPM 476; PM 29; TM 97 *Mex.*

Castro, José María (1818-1892) CA 12; EPCR 22 *C.R.*

Castro, José Mariano ACe 777 *Mex.*

Castro, Juan Bautista LV 54; V 60 *Venez.*

Castro, Juan S. (-1920) Ig 74; NM 15; PM 29; TM 98 *Mex.*

Castro, Julio (1836-) E 15 *Ecua.*

Castro, Julio Félix P 5 *Per.*

Castro, Luis Luvera V 60 *Venez.*

Castro, Manuel de CG I, 576; HSLU II, pt 6, 18; PIU III, 295; PU 67; U 4 *Uru.*

Castro, Martín B 6 *Bol.*

"Castro, O. Segura" (*pseud.*) *see* Araya, Juan Agustín

Castro, Rafael BP 521; CG I, 576; PR 32 *P.R.*

Castro, Ramón V 60 *Venez.*

Castro, Raúl de CG I, 576; U 4 *Uru.*

Castro, Ricardo (1833-1919) Co 18; TM 604 *Mex.*

Castro, Víctor M. SD 7 *Dom.*

Castro, Virgilio CA 12 *C.R.*

Castro A., Clodomiro C 27 *Chil.*

Castro Cambón, Vicenta (1885-1928) A 17; CG I, 577 *Arg.*

Castro Esquivel, Arturo ("Arcases") CA 5, 12; IBCR IV, 223 *et passim C.R.*

Castro Garín, Fabio C 46 *Chil.*

Castro Leal, Antonio (1895-) TM 434; WLA 88 *Mex.*

Castro Palomino, Rafael de Cu 38, 126 *Cu.*

Castro Saborío, Arturo (1883-1903) CA 12; IBCR IV, 110 *C.R.*

Castro Saborío, Claudio CA 12; EPCR 551 *C.R.*

Castro Saborío, Luis (1878-) CA 12; CG I, 580; EPCR 274 *C.R.*

Castro Saborío, Octavio CA 12 *C.R.*

Castro Salazar, Manuel TM 99 *Mex.*

Castro Santa-Anna, José Manuel TM 534 *Mex.*

Castro U., Elías CA 12 *C.R.*

Castro Ureña, Luis CA 12 *C.R.*

Castro y López, Luis PM 29; TM 98 *Mex.*

Castro y Oyanguren, Enrique (1875-) CG I, 580; P 5 *Per.*

Castro y Pulgar, Andrés TM 99 *Mex.*

Castro Zambrano, Francisco de ACe 778 *Mex.*

Castro Zamudio, Wenceslao C 5, 27; NC 356 *Chil.*

Castroverde, Mateo HPM 199 *Mex.*

Casuso, Teté (1912-) PoC 48 *Cu.*

Catá, Álvaro Cu 38 *Cu.*

Catalá, Valentín Cu 38 *Cu.*

Cataldo Marcial, Mario A 17 *Arg.*

Cataneo, Joaquín V. ARC 46; PJC 52 *Cu.*

Cateriano, Mariano A. P 6 *Per.*

Cato, Rubén EPCR 395 *C.R.*

"Cautivo, El" (*pseud.*) *see* Fajardo Ortiz, Desiderio

Cavada C., Darío C 5, 27 *Chil.*

Cavarri, Enrique TM 99 *Mex.*

Caviedes, Juan del Valle (1640-1695) BHLA 104 *Per.*

Caviglia, Buenaventura PU 58 *Uru.*

Cavo, Andrés (1739-1795?) ACe 662; HLM 206; HLMex 87 *Mex.*

Cayafa Soca, Domingo CG I, 595; U 4; UL 124 *Uru.*

Cayama Martínez, Rafael V 60 *Venez.*

Caycedo *see also* Caicedo

Caycedo y Velasco, Agustín de HLNG I, 296 *Col.*

Cayol, Roberto L. A 17, 82 *Arg.*

Cazade, Enrique A. Cu 38; PJC 50 *Cu.*

Ceballos, Celso TM 99, 380 *Mex.*

Ceballos, Ciro B. (1873-) CG I, 595; HLM 458; Ig 75; NM 15; WLA 89 *Mex.*
Ceballos Novelo, Roque Jacinto (1885-) IE 56; TM 99; WLA 89 *Mex.*
Cebollero, Pedro Ángel PA 162; PP 243 *P.R.*
Cebreco, Agustín ARC 47 *Cu.*
Cecchi, Emilio TM 535 *Mex.*
Cedillo, Víctor José V 60 *Venez.*
Ceijas, Julio R. (1884-) Cu 38 *Cu.*
Celada, Fernando G 357; PM 29; TM 100 *Mex.*
Celedón, Rafael (1831-1903) AC II, 209; BC 112; Co 18; LC 177; RHLC 204 *Col.*
Celedón C., Pedro Luis C 46 *Chil.*
"Celeste Lassabe de Cruz" (*pseud.*) see Lassabe, Celeste
"Celestino Hourcade" (*pseud.*) Ig 173; NM 28 *Mex.*
"Celinda P. Varmes" (*pseud.*) see Silva, Carmen P. de
Celis, Eduardo V 60 *Venez.*
Celis Aguilera, José de PR 17 *P.R.*
Celis Ríos, Trino V 60 *Venez.*
Celis Venegas, A. C 5 *Chil.*
Ceniceros y Villarreal, Rafael (1855-) CG I, 600; Ig 76; NM 15; TM 100 *Mex.*
Centeno, Francisco (1862-) CG I, 602; WLA 90 *Arg.*
Centeno, Lucas (1730-1812) ACe 779 *Mex.*
Centeno del Campillo, Lucrecia (1863-) A 17 *Arg.*
Centurión, Leopoldo (1893-) Par 9; PT 223 *Para.*
Centurión (y Martínez?), Juan Crisóstomo Par 8 *Para.*
Cepeda, Cecilia Co 18 *Col.*
Cepeda, Francisco de (1532-1602) HLM 21 *Mex.*
Cepeda, Josefina de (1907-) PoC 55 *Cu.*
Cepeda, Lorenzo de HPHA II, 80 *Ecua.*
Cepeda, Ruperto C 5; NC 356 *Chil.*
Cepeda Echemendía, Julio de ARC 47 *Cu.*
Cépero, Belén ("Hija del Yumurí") Cu 38, 83 *Cu.*
Cépero, Francisco Cu 38 *Cu.*
Ceppi, José ("Aníbal Latino") A 17, 78; CG I, 603 *Arg.*
Cerdá, Antonio Cu 38 *Cu.*
Cergoglio Boero, Violeta Blanca ("Alma") A 17 *Arg.*
Ceriola, Juan B. CG I, 605; E 15 *Ecua.*
Cerna, Ismael (-1901) CA 66; PG 221 *Guat.*
Cerna Sandoval, O. CP 688; PS 292 *Salv.*
Cernadas, Remigio (1779-1859) RLC 45, 152 *Cu.*
"Cero" (*pseud.*) see Riva Palacio, Vicente
Cerrados Lafuente, Enrique Cu 38 *Cu.*
Cerruto, Oscar BHLA 613; LAS 203 *Bol.*
Cerutti Crosa, Pedro CG I, 605; PIU III, 305 *Uru.*
Cervantes, Edmundo (1861-1917) Co 18; RHLC 150 *Col.*
Cervantes, Francisco ARC 47 *Cu.*
Cervantes, Pedro Pablo BC 113; Co 18; V 60 *Col.*
Cervantes, Rodrigo SD 7 *Dom.*
Cervantes de los Ríos, Pedro de CG I, 605; PM 29 *Mex.*

Cervantes de Salazar, Francisco (1513-1575) BHLA 116; CG I, 610; HLM 57, 78; HLMex 35; HPHA I, 26; HPM 89 *Mex.*
Cervera, Alejandro TM 594 *Mex.*
Cervera, Manuel CG I, 610; Co 39 *Col.*
Cervi, Segismundo TM 100 *Mex.*
"César, Julio" (*pseud.*) see Silva Endeiza, Hugo
"César de Guanabacoa" (*pseud.*) see Sos, Ciriaco
"César de Madrid" (*pseud.*) see Coronado y Álvaro, Francisco de Paula
"César Duayén" (*pseud.*) see Barra, Ema de la
"César Tiempo" (*pseud.*) see Zeitlin, Israel
Céspedes, Ángel María (1892-) ALC II, 303; Co 17, 18; PCo 81; PLHA 147; RHLC 172 *Col.*
Céspedes, Augusto BHLA 613 *Bol.*
Céspedes, Carlos Manuel de (1819-1874) ARC 76; CHL 468; CLH 408, 411; PCu 89 *Cu.*
Céspedes, José María Cu 38 *Cu.*
Céspedes B., Julián B 6 *Bol.*
Céspedes Casado, Emilio ARC 47 *Cu.*
Céspedes Casado, Miguel Ángel ARC 47 *Cu.*
Céspedes de Escanaverino, Ursula (1832-1874) Cu 39; PCu 90; RLC 221 *Cu.*
Céspedes Marín, Armando (1851-) CA 13 *C.R.*
Céspedes Rivero, Julián B 6 *Bol.*
Céspedes y Borges, Carlos M. Cu 39 *Cu.*
Céspedes y (de) Quesada, Carlos Manuel de (1871-) CG I, 612; WLA 92 *Cu.*
Cester, Ricardo (1855-) Cu 39 *Cu.*
Cestero, Ferdinand R. (1868-) BP 522; PA 161; PR 32; QPR (2) 180 *P.R.*
Cestero, Manuel Florentino CG I, 613; CHL 497; CLH 437; SD 7 *Dom.*
Cestero, Mariano Antonio LD 84; SD 7 *Dom.*
Cestero, Tulio Manuel (1877-) BDC 12; BHLA 526; CG I, 613; CHL 497; CLH 437; IE 57; LAND 153; LD 98; SASS 318; SD 8; WLA 92 *Dom.*
Cestero Burgos, T. A. SD 8 *Dom.*
Cesteros, Ferdinand R. see Cestero, Ferdinand R.
Cestino, Francisco A 17 *Arg.*
Cevallos, Pedro Fermín (1812-1893) CG I, 613; E 15; PLE 42 *Ecua.*
Cevallos Salvador, Pedro José E 16 *Ecua.*
Ciaño, Carlos BDC 12; Cu 39 *Cu.*
Cibils, José A 17 *Arg.*
Cichero, Félix Esteban ("Fray Linterna") A 17, 78; WLA 99 *Arg.*
Cid Baeza, Astenia C 27 *Chil.*
"Cid Fragueiro Fonseca" (*pseud.*) see Acuña de Figueroa, Francisco
Cieza de León, Pedro (1519-1560) BHLA 63; CG I, 615; LA III, 287; SCL 83, 596 *Arg.*
Cifuentes, Francisco de B. C 46 *Chil.*
Cifuentes, José María C 27 *Chil.*
Cifuentes, Pío de Jesús E 16 *Ecua.*
"Cifuentes, Rodrigo" (*pseud.*) see Prieto Yeme, Guillermo
Cifuentes Sepúlveda, Joaquín C 27 *Chil.*

"Cigarral, Lucas del" (*pseud.*) *see* Ruiz y Rodríguez, Manuel
Cintas Álvarez, Santiago Cu 39 *Cu.*
Cintora, Gregorio B 6 *Bol.*
Cintrón, Guillermo V. BP 522; PR 32, 33 *P.R.*
Cione, Otto Miguel ("Martín Flores") (1875-) A 17, 82; BHLA 548; CG I, 616; LU 64, 676; PIU III, 302; PLHA 295; U 4; UT 157 *Uru.*
Ciorolo, B. J. U 5 *Uru.*
"Cira" (*pseud.*) *see* Salazar de Robles, Caridad
Cirerol, M. TM 594, 595 *Mex.*
"Ciro Mendía" (*pseud.*) *see* Mejía Ángel, Carlos
Cisneros, Consuelo C. PJC 66 *Cu.*
Cisneros, Hipólito V 60 *Venez.*
Cisneros, Jeremías HL I, 611; II, 117 *Hond.*
Cisneros, José Antonio (1826-1880) HPM 873; TM 101 *Mex.*
Cisneros, José Eduardo A 17 *Arg.*
Cisneros, José Luis de (1710?-) CG I, 618; SCL 379, 597; V 60 *Venez.*
Cisneros, Luis Benjamín (1837-1904) AEHA 264; BHLA 319, 338; CHL 299; CLH 253; LP 361; P 6; PLHA 75; PPe 167 *Per.*
Cisneros, Luis Fernán (1883-) BAP 117; LP 389; P 6; PPe 251; WLA 99 *Per.*
Cisneros, María Guadalupe TM 535 *Mex.*
Cisneros, Rafael Antonio Cu 39 *Cu.*
Cisneros Cámara, Antonio TM 101, 595 *Mex.*
Cisneros de Colón, Consuelo CG I, 618; Cu 39 *Cu.*
Cisneros y Mendoza, Francisco José de Cu 39 *Cu.*
Citter Morosini, Emilia Helena A 17 *Arg.*
Ciudad, Pedro C 6; NC 356 *Chil.*
"Ciudadano que le acompaña en su desgracia, Un" TM 345 *Mex.*
"Clara, Diana" (*pseud.*) *see* Amador, María Ester
Clare, Enrique R. CA 13 *C.R.*
Clarencio, Don Cu 39 *Cu.*
Clarens, Ángel BDC 12; CG I, 620; Cu 39 *Cu.*
Claretie, Jules CG I, 621; NM 1 *Mex.*
Clarín, René de C 6 *Chil.*
"Claro, Julián del" (*pseud.*) *see* Hederra Concha, Francisco
"Claro-Oscuro, Don" (*pseud.*) *see* Asenjo, Federico
Claro Yépez, Edmundo C 6 *Chil.*
"Clary" (*pseud.*) *see* Polanco de Hoffman, Clarissa
"Claudio Coello" (*pseud.*) *see* Mitre y Vedia, Bartolomé
"Claudio de Alas" (*pseud.*) *see* Uribe, José Escobar
"Claudio Frollo" (*pseud.*) *see* Luchichí, Ignacio M.
"Claudio Mamerto Cuenca" (*pseud.*) *see* Cuenca, Claudio José del Corazón de Jesús
Clavell, Eusebio UT 159 *Uru.*
Claver, Pedro (1585-1654) RHLC 26; SCL 352 *Col.*

Clavería, Francisco TM 102 *Mex.*
Clavijero, Francisco Javier (1731-1787) HLM 194; HLMex 86; HPM 459 *Mex.*
Clavijo, J. Luis E 16 *Ecua.*
Clavijo Tisseur, Arturo (1886-) ARC 47; BDC 12; Cu 39; PJC 53 *Cu.*
"Cleta Masa" (*pseud.*) *see* Pereyra, Emilia A. de
Clifton, Jorge C 6; NC 114 *Chil.*
"Cloamón (*pseud.*) *see* Moncloa y Covarrubias, Manuel
Clulow, Alfredo S. CG I, 627; GLO 253; U 5 *Uru.*
Clúlow, Carlos Alberto CG I, 627; HSLU III, pt 6, 52; PIU III, 242 *Uru.*
Cobas, Francisco (-1911) Cu 40 *Cu.*
Cobas, José A. (1895-) Cu 40 *Cu.*
Cobo, Bernabé (1582-) SCL 307, 597 *Per.*
"Cobo, J. A." (*pseud.*) *see* Domínguez y Santi, Jacobo
Cobo, José BDC 13 *Cu.*
Cobo, Salustio C 46 *Chil.*
Cobos, Francisco A 17, 82 *Arg.*
Cobos Daract, Julio (1883-) A 17; CG I, 628 *Arg.*
Cobos Fuertes, Francisco V 60 *Venez.*
Coca, G. D. Par 9 *Para.*
Codazzi, Agustín (1772-1859) CG I, 629; Co 18 *Col.*
Coello, Adán (1891?-) FPA 318, 335 *Hond.*
Coello, Augusto C. (1891-) FPA 318, 336 *Hond.*
"Coello, Claudio" (*pseud.*) *see* Mitre y Vedia, Bartolomé
Coello Noritz, Manuel E 16 *Ecua.*
Coffin, José Ig 78; NM 15 *Mex.*
Cohen, Luis PD 38; SD 8 *Dom.*
Cohucelo y Collantes, Pedro José CG I, 639; Cu 40 *Cu.*
Coimbra, Ursula ARC 48 *Cu.*
Coirolo, Hipólito (1881-) UT 161 *Uru.*
"Colas, Fray" (*pseud.*) *see* Martínez, Luis A.
Cole, Domingo E 16 *Ecua.*
Colín, Eduardo (1880-) AMP 120; APMM 15; CG I, 646; G 357; HLM 520; PM 29; PNM 34; WLA 103 *Mex.*
Colina, Salvador de la A 17; CG I, 646 *Arg.*
Colindres, Jesús T. (1870-) HL II, 571 *Hond.*
Colman, Narciso Ramón ("Rosicran") (1878-) Par 9; WLA 103 *Para.*
Colmenare, Carmelo (Melo) V 60 *Venez.*
Colmo, Alfredo (1878-) AT II, 539; CG I, 647 *Arg.*
Colom, Pedro M. E 17 *Ecua.*
Colombi Publiari, José U 5 *Uru.*
Colombini y Camayori, Francisco María HPM 482 *Mex.*
Colón Baerga, Enrique (1877-) PR 33; QPR (2) 50 *P.R.*
Colón y Colón, Isidoro PR 9 *P.R.*
Colson, Jayme G 385; SD 8 *Dom.*
Colt de Hume, Blanca C. E. ("Blanca C. de Hume") (1879-) A 17, 78; CG III, 99 *Arg.*
Colta, Juan Manuel A 17 *Arg.*

Colunje, Gil (1831-1899) AP 71; Pan 5 *Pan.*
1. Colunje, Guillermo Pan 5 *Pan.*
2. Colunje, Guillermo (hijo) ("Lino Tipo") Pan 5, 12 *Pan.*
Coll Núñez, Pedro Emilio (1872-) CG I, 651; CHL 382; CLH 353; G 392; LV 424; SASS 527; V 60; VPF 196; WLA 103 *Venez.*
Coll Otero, Ignacio V 61 *Venez.*
Coll Vidal, José (1892-) QPR (1) 185; (2) 49 *P.R.*
Coll y Britapaja, José PR 11, 33 *P.R.*
Coll y Cuchí, Cayetano CG I, 652; PR 17 *P.R.*
Coll y Cuchí, José CG I, 652; PR 17 *P.R.*
Coll y Toste, Cayetano (1850-1930) CG I, 652; G 384; PA 151; PP 164; PR 24, 49, 50 *P.R.*
Coll (y) Vidal, Antonio (1898-) BP 510, 522; PR 11, 33; QPR (1) 185; (2) 49 *P.R.*
Collado, María PCu 92; PJC 56 *Cu.*
Collado Martell, A. PR 55 *P.R.*
Collante de Tapía, Lola Pan 5 *Pan.*
Collantes, José María (1877-) CT 223; Cu 40; PA 32; PCu 96 *Cu.*
Collantes y Buenrostro, Juan (1849-1916) Ig 78; NM 15 *Mex.*
Collar, Mateo Par 9 *Para.*
Collazo, Enrique (1849-1921) CG I, 652; RLC 344 *Cu.*
Collazo, Francisco E. A 17, 82 *Arg.*
Collazo, José Antonio Cu 40 *Cu.*
Comallonga y Mena, José ("Fray Tabarra") (1865-) CT 411; Cu 40, 158; PCu 97 *Cu.*
Comas, Juan Francisco (1837-1903) PR 33 *P.R.*
Comas Pagán, Ezequiel J. BP 522; PR 33 *P.R.*
Comas Ruiz, Mecha A 17 *Arg.*
Comes, Bernabé U 5 *Uru.*
Cominges, Juan de A 17 *Arg.*
Compte, Francisco María E 17 *Ecua.*
Compte y Rique, Enriqueta UT 163 *Uru.*
Comte, Damion Norberto A 17 *Arg.*
Conangla Fontanilles, J. CG I, 663; Cu 40 *Cu.*
Concepción, Francisca Josefa de la *see* Castillo y Guevara, Francisca Josefa de la Concepción
"Concepción Ríos" (*pseud.*) *see* Vázquez de Montiel, María del Carmen
Concetti, Nicolás E 17 *Ecua.*
"Concolorcorvo" (*pseud.*) *see* Bustamante Carlos, Calixto
Concha, Delfiu Cozar Espans de Cu 40 *Cu.*
Concha, Manuel C 6, 46; NC 357, 414 *Chil.*
Concha, Manuel Santiago C 46 *Chil.*
Concha Castillo, Francisco A. (1855-) C 62; CHL 260; CLH 220; PCh 125 *Chil.*
Concha y Marín, Hermógenes C 6; NC 114 *Chil.*
Condaminos, Salvador Cu 40 *Cu.*
Conde, Francisco Javier (1773-1799) RLC 32 *Cu.*
Conde, Joaquín ACe 780 *Mex.*
Conde, José Martínez SD 9 *Dom.*

Conde, Miguel CA 13; IBCR IV, 269 *C.R.*
"Conde Costra" (*pseud.*) Cu 43 *Cu.*
Conde de Casa Montalvo *see* Montalvo y Castillo, Juan
"Conde de la Cortina" (*pseud.*) *see* Gómez de la Cortina, José
Conde de la Granja *see* Oviedo y Herrera, Luis Antonio de
"Conde Kostia" (*pseud.*) *see* Valdivia, Aniceto
Conejares, Francisco HPM 499 *Mex.*
"Constantino Pla" (*pseud.*) *see* Arias Suárez, Eduardo
Constenla, José A 17 *Arg.*
Consuegra, Andrés López *see* López Consuegra, Andrés
Consuegra, Domingo Cu 41 *Cu.*
Consuegra, María Cristobalina ARC 35 *Cu.*
Contardo, Luis Felipe (1880-1921) APEH 645, 1188; C 27; CMPC 44; PCC xiii, 81; PCh 237 *Chil.*
Conte, F. A. CHL 483 *Cu.*
Conte, J. Antonio (1898?-) AP 75; Pan 5 *Pan.*
Conte, Juan Bautista (1887-1913) Pan 5 *Pan.*
Conte Bermúdez, Héctor (1879-) AP 77; Pan 5, 6 *Pan.*
Conto, César (1836-1892) AC I, 315; BC 116; CHL 345; CLH 296; Co 18; LC 151 *Col.*
Contreras, Álvaro (1839-1882) HL I, 315 *Hond.*
Contreras, Carlota TM 102 *Mex.*
Contreras, David PM 29 *Mex.*
Contreras, Felipe T. (1864-) AMP 321; PM 29; PMe I, 55 *Mex.*
Contreras, Francisco (1877-1932) C 6, 27, 63; CG I, 680; CHL 262; CLH 222; CMPC 15; G 323; N 61; PCC xii, 35; PCh 185; PLHA 148; SASS 149; SD 9 *Chil.*
Contreras, Juan Gabriel de E 17 *Ecua.*
Contreras Elizalde, Nicanor PM 30; TM 102 *Mex.*
Contreras Gómez, Domingo C 6, 28 *Chil.*
Cooper, Felipe S. (hijo) V 61 *Venez.*
Coorsi, Demetrio *see* Korsi, Demetrio
Cora, Luis M. A 17; CG I, 684 *Arg.*
Coral, Luciano E 17 *Ecua.*
Corao, Ángel V 61 *Venez.*
Corbalán, Juan Emilio C 6; NC 357 *Chil.*
Corbalán Melgarejo, Emiliano PCh 377 *Chil.*
Corces, José BDC 13; Cu 41 *Cu.*
Corchado y Juarbe, Manuel (1840-1884) BDC 13, 110; BP 522, 588; CG I, 685; CHL 501; CLH 442; PR 12, 17, 32, 33, 42, 50, 51, 55 *P.R.*
Corchero Carreño, Francisco (-1668) HPM 206; PM 30 *Mex.*
Cordero, Clodomiro A 17 *Arg.*
Cordero, Gregorio E 17 *Ecua.*
Cordero, J. Julio CA 66 *Guat.*
Cordero, José María PM 30 *Mex.*
Cordero, Juan N. (1851-) Ig 79; NM 15; PM 30 *Mex.*

Cordero, Luis (1833-1912) BHLA 321; CHL 317; CLH 269; E 17, 74; FPA 253, 267; PE 183; PLE 47 *Ecua.*
Cordero, Modesto BP 522; PR 33 *P.R.*
Cordero, Salvador (1876-) CG I, 686; G 357; HLM 457; IE 63; Ig 80; NM 15; PM 30; WLA 106 *Mex.*
Cordero Crespo, Luis E 18 *Ecua.*
Cordero Dávila, Gonzalo E 18; PE 89 *Ecua.*
Cordero Dávila, Miguel E 18 *Ecua.*
Cordero Leiva, Primitivo CG I, 686, 736; PJC 63 *Cu.*
Cordero Palacios, Alfonso E 18 *Ecua.*
Cordido Roo, J. A. V 61 *Venez.*
Cordiviola, Cleopatra A 17 *Arg.*
Córdoba *see also* Córdova
Córdoba, Diego V 61 *Venez.*
Córdoba, Juan de (1503-1595) HLM 21 *Mex.*
Córdoba, Matías de ACe 1006 *Mex.*
Córdoba, Tirso Rafael HPM 914; TM 103 *Mex.*
Córdoba Bocanegra, Fernando (1565-1589) HPM 94 *Mex.*
Córdoba de Aragón, María Josefa (1838-) CA 66; GPCA II, 295; PG 203 *Guat.*
Córdoba Salinas, Diego de (1591-) LA III, 113; P 6 *Per.*
Córdoba Vizcarrondo, Eugenio CG I, 686; PD 39; SD 9 *Dom.*
Córdoba y Figueroa, Pedro Pascual de (1692-1751?) HC 29; SCL 499, 599 *Chil.*
Córdoba y Urrutia, José María P 7 *Per.*
Cordone, Jacinta A 17 *Arg.*
Cordone, Matilde A 17 *Arg.*
Córdova *see also* Córdoba
Córdova, Alejandro (1889-) CA 66; IE 64; WLA 107 *Guat.*
Córdova, Federico CG I, 686; E 74 *Ecua.*
Córdova, Matías (1750-1828) CA 66; GPCA I, 3; PG 23 *Guat.*
Córdova, Ulpiano S. BP 523 *P.R.*
Córdova Dávila, Félix PA 159; PP 206; PR 33 *P.R.*
Córdova de Fernández, Sofia Cu 41 *Cu.*
Córdova Iturburu, C. (1899-) A 18; APAM 470; BHLA 640 *Arg.*
Córdova y Lebrija, Enrique BDC 13; Cu 41 *Cu.*
Córdova y Lebrija, Lorenzo BDC 13; Cu 41 *Cu.*
Cordovés, Simón (1831-) BC 117; C 28; Co 18 *Col.*
Cordovez, Mareval C 46 *Chil.*
Cordovez Moure, José María (1835-1918) BC 118; CG I, 686; Co 18 *Col.*
Cordovez Moure, Manuel Isodoro (1821-1848) BC 117; Co 18 *Col.*
Coria Gallegos, Elía A 18 *Arg.*
Cornejo, Aparicio E 18 *Ecua.*
Cornejo, David PS 255 *Salv.*
Cornejo, Manuel Alberto B 6 *Bol.*
Cornejo, Mariano H. (1867-) CG I, 687; P 7 *Per.*
Cornejo, Ricardo E 18 *Ecua.*
Cornejo, Vicente María (1863-1912) CG I, 687; Pan 6 *Pan.*
Cornejo Cevallos, Manuel E 18 *Ecua.*

Cornejo Franco, José TM 535 *Mex.*
Cornejo M., Pedro E 18 *Ecua.*
"Cornelio Hispano" (*pseud.*) *see* López, Ismael
Cornyn, Juan Humberto CG I, 688; NM 15 *Mex.*
Corona Raimundo, Manuel ARC 48; Cu 41 *Cu.*
Corona Salado, Juan Cu 41 *Cu.*
Corona y Ferrer, Mariano (1869-1912) BDC 13; Cu 41 *Cu.*
Coronado, Diego V 61 *Venez.*
Coronado, Enrique ("Henry") PR 12; V 61, 82 *Venez.*
Coronado, Martín (1840-1919) A 18, 71, 82; BHLA 441; CHL 171, 197; CLH 147; LA VIII, 865; SPLA 165 *Arg.*
Coronado, Nicolás A 18; CG I, 690; LAC 120, 155 *Arg.*
Coronado, Pedro José V 61 *Venez.*
Coronado, Trinidad CA 66 *Guat.*
Coronado, Vicente V 61 *Venez.*
Coronado J., Mariano CA 13 *C.R.*
Coronado y Álvaro, Francisco de Paula ("César de Madrid") (1870-) CT 481; Cu 41, 98; WLA 108 *Cu.*
Coronel, Juan BC 119; Co 19 *Col.*
Coronel, Julián CG I, 690; U 5 *Uru.*
Coronel, Manuel E 19 *Ecua.*
Coronel, Maximiliano E 19 *Ecua.*
Coronel G., Rafael C 28; CG I, 690; E 20; PLE 122 *Ecua.*
Corpancho, Manuel Nicolás (1830-1863) BHLA 318; CHL 294; CLH 249; HPHA II, 259; P 7 *Per.*
Corpancho, Teobaldo Elías P 7 *Per.*
Corral, F. del NM 15 *Mex.*
Corral, José María del C 46; CG I, 697 *Chil.*
Corral, Manuel TM 605 *Mex.*
Corral, Miguel Ángel (1833-1881) E 20; PE 237 *Ecua.*
Corral Calvo de la Torre, Juan del BHC II, 462 *Chil.*
"Corrales" (*pseud.*) *see* Palma, Clemente
Corrales, José María de los CG I, 698; NM 15 *Mex.*
Corrales, Juan Manuel V 61 *Venez.*
Corrales, Manuel Ezequiel Co 19 *Col.*
Corrales de Chavarría, Rosa CA 13 *C.R.*
Correa, Agustín PM 30 *Mex.*
Correa, Eduardo J. CG I, 698; NM 15; PM 30; TM 103 *Mex.*
Correa, G. A 18; CG I, 699 *Arg.*
Correa, Limbano TM 104 *Mex.*
Correa, Luis V 61, 62, 128 *Venez.*
Correa, Luis D. V 62 *Venez.*
Correa, Rafael CA 67 *Guat.*
Correa de Carter, Teutila Ig 81; NM 15 *Mex.*
Correa de Malvehy, Avelina Cu 41 *Cu.*
Correa de Rincón Soler, Evangelina Co 19; RHLC 184 *Col.*
Correa Luna, Carlos (1874-) AT I, 366; CG I, 699; WLA 108 *Arg.*
Correa Nieto, Juan TM 434 *Mex.*
Correa Sabatier, Felipe ARC 48 *Cu.*
Correa Zapata, Dolores (1853-) G 357; PM 30 *Mex.*
Correa Zapata, Juan PM 30 *Mex.*

Corredor, Víctor Julio Co 11, 19 *Col.*
Correoso Miranda, Ricardo Cu 41 *Cu.*
Corretjer, Juan Antonio PR 55 *P.R.*
Corro, Miguel Calixto del (1775-) HLA 277 *Arg.*
Cortada, Juan CG I, 690; NM 15 *Mex.*
Cortazar, A. C. de Cu 41 *Cu.*
Cortázar, Roberto (1884-) CG I, 691; Co 19, 20 *Col.*
Corte, José C. A 18 *Arg.*
Cortés, Alfonso NL 163 *Nicar.*
Cortés, Domingo C 28 *Chil.*
Cortés, Enrique (1838-1912) Co 19 *Col.*
Cortés, Francisco de Paula (1850-) BC 119; Co 19 *Col.*
Cortés, Hernán (1485-1547) BAMP 3; BHLA 56, 90; CG I, 692; HLM 33; HLMex 18; SAL 17, 318 *Sp.-Mex.*
Cortés, Íñigo A 18 *Arg.*
Cortés, Jenaro (1876-) QPR (1) 53 *P.R.*
Cortés, José CG I, 693; Cu 41 *Cu.*
Cortés, José Domingo (1839-1884) A 71; B 6; C 63; CL 141; E 20; NM 2; P 7; SD 9 *Chil.*
Cortés, León (1858-) CA 13 *C.R.*
Cortés, Lucila BC 118; Co 19 *Col.*
Cortés, Manuel José (1811-1865) AEHA 890; B 6; LB 580; PB 72, 225 *Bol.*
Cortés, María del Carmen PM 30 *Mex.*
Cortés, Martín H. Co 19 *Col.*
Cortés, Roberto CA 13 *C.R.*
Cortés, Rogelio Co 19 *Col.*
Cortés Ch., Rafael CA 13; IBCR IV, 215 *C.R.*
Cortés de Monroy, Juan BHC I, 198 *Chil.*
Cortés de Monroy, Pedro BHC II, 123 *et passim Chil.*
Cortés Lee, Carlos (1859-1928) Co 19 *Col.*
Cortés Vargas, Carlos (1883-) CG I, 694; Co 19 *Col.*
Corti, Alfonso A 18 *Arg.*
Cortina, José Gómez de la "Conde de la Cortina" *see* Gómez de la Cortina, José
Cortina, José Manuel CG I, 695; Cu 42; RLC 348 *Cu.*
Cortina Aravena, Augusto A 18 *Arg.*
"Cortina, Conde de la" (*pseud.*) *see* Gómez de la Cortina, José
Cortina y Sotolongo, José Antonio (1852-1884) CHL 477, 480; Cu 41; HLC 82; RLC 232, 244, 275 *Cu.*
Cortinas, Ismael (1884-) A 18, 82; CG I, 696; PU 256; UT 167 *Uru.*
Cortinas, Laura CG I, 696; HSLU II, pt 6, 25, 28 *Uru.*
Cortón, Antonio (1854-1913) CG I, 696; PR 8, 10, 17, 26, 33 *P.R.*
Corvacho, José P 7 *Per.*
Corvalán, Armando C 28 *Chil.*
Corvalán, José María A 18 *Arg.*
Corvalán Mendilharzu, Dardo CG I, 696; G 311 *Arg.*
Corzo, Ángel M. PM 30 *Mex.*
Corzo, Isidoro CG I, 696; Cu 42 Cu.
Corzo y Barrera, Antonio BDC 14; Cu 42 *Cu.*
Cos, José María (-1819) ACe 165; HLM
Cosío *see also* Cossío
Cosío, David A. PM 30 *Mex.* 251; HLMex 105 *Mex.*

Cosío, José Gabriel (1888-) P 7; WLA 109 *Per.*
Cosío, Pedro (1873-) CG I, 702; U 5; UT 169 *Uru.*
Cosío Villegas, Daniel Ig 82; NM 16 *Mex.*
Cosmé, Bernabé PU 59 *Uru.*
Cosmes, Francisco G. (1850-1907) AMP 306; PMe I, 57 *Mex.*
Cossío *see also* Cosío
Cossío, Carlos A 18; CG I, 702 *Arg.*
Cossío, David Alberto TM 104 *Mex.*
Cossío, Francisco de ("Pedro Lacor") CG I, 702; III, 263; Cu 87 *Cu.*
Costa, Adolfo C 46 *Chil.*
Costa, Cayetano Cu 42 *Cu.*
Costa, Fernando (-1893) BDC 14; Cu 42 *Cu.*
Costa, Julio A. A 18; CG I, 703 *Arg.*
Costa, Pablo della *see* Della Costa, Pablo
Costa Álvarez, Arturo C 63; CG I, 703 *Chil.*
Costa du Rels, Adolfo (1891-) WLA 110 *Bol.*
Costa Nogueras, Gabriel BDC 14; Cu 42 *Cu.*
Costales, Manuel (1815-1866) Cu 42 *Cu.*
Costales y Sotolongo, Bernardo BDC 14; Cu 42 *Cu.*
Costi, Luis G. Cu 43 *Cu.*
Costi y Erro, Candido Cu 43 *Cu.*
"Costra, Conde" (*pseud.*) Cu 43 *Cu.*
Coto Fernández, Rubén CA 13, 14; IBCR IV, 209 *C.R.*
Coto M., Fausto CA 14; EPCR 559 *C.R.*
Cotta, Juan Manuel A 18; CG I, 709 *Arg.*
Cousandier, Camilo A 18 *Arg.*
"Coustillac, Polifemo de" (*pseud.*) *see* Ruiz de Esparza, Juan
Coutaret, Emilio B. A 18 *Arg.*
Couto, José Bernardo (1803-1862) HLM 361; HLMex 163; HPM 838 Mex.
Couto Castillo, José Bernardo (1880-1901) HLM 458; Ig 82; NM 16 *Mex.*
Cova, J. A. V 62 *Venez.*
Cova, Rafael de la V 62 *Venez.*
Cova Maza, J. M. CG I, 713; V 62 *Venez.*
Covarrubias, Francisco (1774-1850) BDC 14; Cu 43; HLC 25; RLC 52 *Cu.*
Covarrubias, Luis C 63; CL 142; NC 415 *Chil.*
Covarrubias y Acevedo, Manuel Ig 83; NM 16 *Mex.*
Covo, Juan Cu 43 *Cu.*
Cox, Carlos Manuel (1902-) IE 66 *Mex.*
Cox Méndez, Ricardo C 46 *Chil.*
Cox-Stuven, Mariana ("Shade") C 6; NC 115 *Chil.*
Cox y Méndez, Guillermo C 63; NC 415 *Chil.*
Coyula, Pedro PM 30 *Mex.*
Cozar Espans de Concha, Delfín BDC 14 *Cu.*
Cransaz, Luis A. A 18 *Arg.*
Cravioto Mejorada, Alfonso (1883-) APMM 23; G 357; HLM 522; PM 30; WLA 111 *Mex.*
Crema, Eduardo V 62 *Venez.*
Crespo, Francisco BHC II, 268 *et passim Chil.*

Crespo, Ismael Co 19 *Col.*
Crespo, Joaquín V 62 *Venez.*
Crespo, José BDC 111; CG I, 716; PR 12, 33, 42 *P.R.*
Crespo, José D. Pan 6 *Pan.*
Crespo, Luis S. B 6, 7, 15; CG I, 716 *Bol.*
Crespo, Manuel A. V 62 *Venez.*
Crespo Báez, Nina V 62 *Venez.*
Crespo H., J. Miguel V 62 *Venez.*
Crespo Meléndez, Virgilio V 62 *Venez.*
Crespo Toral, Cornelio E 20 *Ecua.*
Crespo Toral, Remigio ("Stein") (1860-191.) CG I, 718; E 20; FPA 254, 277; G 344; PE 280; PLE 52 *Ecua.*
Crespo Vivas, R. V 62 *Venez.*
Crespo y Borbón, Bartolomé José ("Anfibio") (1811-1871) BDC 14; Cu 11, 23, 43 *Cu.*
Criado, Emilio Alonso (1883-) AT I, 231 *Arg.*
Criado, Matías Alonso Par 9 *Para.*
Criales, Isaac B 6 *Bol.*
"Crisantema" (*pseud.*) *see* Sansores, Rosario
Crispo Acosta, Osvaldo ("Lauxar" *or* "O.C.A,") (1884-) CG III, 303; CHL 224; HSLU III, pt 4, 44; LU 64, 685; PIU III, 313; U 5, 10; UL 125; WLA 111 *Uru.*
Cristi, Mauricio C 6; NC 415 *Chil.*
Cristiani, Esteban TM 605 *Mex.*
Cristo, Teresa de HPM 234 *Mex.*
"Cristóbal, Juan" (*pseud.*) *see* Parra del Riego, Juan
"Cronista de Antaño, El" (*pseud.*) *see* Urbina y Sánchez, Luis Gonzaga
Crosa, Enrique U 5 *Uru.*
Cruciani, Luis E 21 *Ecua.*
Cruchaga, Miguel C 46; CG I, 723 *Chil.*
Cruchaga Santa María, Ángel (1893-) APEH 778, 1191; C 6, 28; CMPC 120; PCC xvii, 153; PCh 343; PLHA 165; WLA 111 *Chil.*
Cruz, Alonzo de la HLNG I, 140 *Col.*
Cruz, Antonio de la ARC 33 *Cu.*
Cruz, Arquímedes PD 40; SD 9 *Dom.*
Cruz, Cornelio de la TM 105 *Mex.*
Cruz, Cupertino de la TM 108 *Mex.*
Cruz, Fernando (1845-1901) CA 67; GPCA II, 355; PG 211 *Guat.*
Cruz, Francisco (-1895) HL I, 211 *Hond.*
Cruz, Francisco de la SCL 451, 599 *Per.*
Cruz, Francisco Javier de la Cu 44 *Cu.*
Cruz, José C. PM 30 *Mex.*
"Cruz, Juana Inés de la" (*pseud.*) *see* Anabalón, Luisa V.
Cruz, Laudacio de la ARC 48 *Cu.*
Cruz, Luis BDC 15; Cu 44 *Cu.*
Cruz, Magdaleno TM 108 *Mex.*
Cruz, Manuel A 18, 82 *Arg.*
Cruz, Manuel de la ("Juan Sincero") (1861-1896) ARC 75; BHLA 414; CG I, 724; CHL 484; CLH 423; Cu 44, 155; G 336; GLO 242; RLC 301 *Cu.*
Cruz, María (1876-1915) CA 67; PG 360 *Guat.*
Cruz, Mario CA 14; IBCR IV, 134 *C.R.*
Cruz, Pablo PM 36 *Mex.*

Cruz, Pedro Nolasco C 6, 46, 63; CHL 275; CL 142; CLH 234; NC 115, 357, 416 *Chil.*
"Cruz, Sor Juana Inés de la" (*pseud.*) *see* Asbaje y Ramírez de Cantillana, Juana Inés de
Cruz Coke, Ricardo ("Juan Marsella") C 6; NC 116 *Chil.*
Cruz Ghio, Julio A 18 *Arg.*
Cruz Meza, Luis (1877-) CA 14; EPCR 280 *C.R.*
Cruz Ocampo, Luis D. ("Licenciado Vidriera") CL 142 *Chil.*
Cruz Paredes, José de la V 62 *Venez.*
Cruz Robles, Galileo PM 36 *Mex.*
Cruz Santos, Camilo (1888-) CA 14 *C.R.*
Cruz Varela, Juan (1794-1839) BHLA 208, 230; LA IV, 945 *Arg.*
Cruz y Bahamonde, Nicolás de la BHC III, 411 *et passim* *Chil.*
Cruzat, Federico C 63; P 7 *Per.-Chil.?*
Cuadra, José de la BHLA 594; E 21 *Ecua.*
Cuadra, Manolo NL 273 *Nicar.*
Cuadra, Pablo Antonio LAS 206; NL 276 *Nicar.*
"Cuasimodo" (*pseud.*) *see* Varela, José Pedro
"Cubano, El Trovador" (*pseud.*) *see* Poveda y Armenteros, Francisco José
"Cubano, Un Magistrado" (*pseud.*) *see* Franchi Alfaro y Lemaur, Antonio
Cubas, Ramón ARC 48 *Cu.*
Cubria, José Alejandro Cu 44 *Cu.*
"Cucalón" (*pseud.*) *see* Barahona Vega, Clemente
Cucalón, Inocencio (1848-) BC 122; Co 19 *Col.*
Cucalón, Rafael E 21 *Ecua.*
"Cuculambé, El" (*pseud.*) *see* Nápoles Fajardo, Juan Cristóbal
Cuéllar, Ángel A 18; CG I, 728 *Arg.*
Cuéllar, E. TM 435, 481 *Mex.*
Cuéllar, José Tomás de ("Facundo") (1830-1894) BAMP 38; BHLA 345, 413; CHL 406; G 357; HLM 438; HLMex 177; Ig 83; NM 16; PM 36, 42; TM 109 *Mex.*
Cuéllar, Juan María (1864-) GPCA III, 473; HL II, 503 *Hond.*
Cuéllar Chaves, Zoilo PCo 82 *Col.*
Cuéllar y Flores Verdad, José María PM 36 *Mex.*
Cuello, Julio A. SD 9 *Dom.*
Cuello, L. SD 9 *Dom.*
Cuenca, Agustín F. (1850-1884) AMP 308; CHL 402; CLH 350; HLM 390; HPM 881; PM 36; PMe I, 65; PoM 171; TM 109 *Mex.*
Cuenca, Claudio José del Corazón de Jesús ("Claudio Mamerto Cuenca") (1812-1852) A 18, 82; CHL 138; CLH 117; HLA 373; LA VI, 800; PB 192; SPLA 72, 152 *Arg.*
Cuenca, Héctor V 62 *Venez.*
Cuenca, Humberto V 62 *Venez.*
Cuenca, Salvador HPM 102 *Mex.*
Cuervo, Ángel (1838-1896) BC 125; Co 20; RHLC 168, 187 *Col.*
Cuervo, José Romualdo Co 20 *Col.*
Cuervo, Luis Augusto (1893-) CG I, 732; Co 20 *Col.*

Cuervo, Rufino (1801-1853) BC 122; Co 20; LAS 199; RHLC 108 *Col.*

Cuervo, Rufino José (1844-1911) AEHA 285; BC 127; BHLA 385; CG I, 732; CHL 354; CLH 303; Co 20, 21; G 328; GLO 240; LC 164; RHLC 203; SASS 253 *Col.*

Cuervo Márquez, Carlos (1858-) CG I, 732; CHL 354; Co 21 *Col.*

Cuervo-Márquez, Emilio (1874-) CG I, 732; Co 21; RHLC 211; WLA 112 *Col.*

Cuervo Márquez, R. Co 21 *Col.*

Cuervo Martínez, Francisco PM 36 *Mex.*

Cuesta, Juan María E 21 *Ecua.*

Cuesta, Justino de la U 5 *Uru.*

Cuesta, Ramiro ARC 48 *Cu.*

Cuesta, Vicente E 22 *Ecua.*

Cueto y Mena, Juan Co 21; HLNG I, 237 *Col.*

Cueva, Baltazar de la P 7 *Per.*

Cueva, Eusebio de la (1893-) CG I, 735; IE 66; Ig 88; NM 17; PM 36; TM 110 *Mex.*

Cueva Ponce de León, Alonso de la SCL 542, 599 *Per.*

Cueva V., Agustín E 22; PLE 93 *Ecua.*

Cuevas, Adán (1852-1895) HL II, 381 *Hond.*

Cuevas, Alejandro (1870-) G 357; Ig 88; NM 17; TM 110, 435, 605, 618 *Mex.*

Cuevas, Jesús HLM 467 *Mex.*

Cuevas, Jorge C 7; CG I, 735 *Chil.*

Cuevas, José de Jesús TM 113, 536 *Mex.*

Cuevas, Mariano CG I, 736; HLM 531; TM 536 *Mex.*

Cuevas, Raúl C 28 *Chil.*

Cuevas Puga, Santiago 2° C 7; NC 117 *Chil.*

Cuevas Zequeira, R. M. PA 159 *P.R.*

Cuevas Zequeira, Rafael PP 236 *P.R.*

Cuevas Zequeira, Sergio (1863-) CG I, 736; CT 185; Cu 44; PR 9, 17, 25, 45, 55 *Cu.*

Culebra, Anastasio U 5 *Uru.*

"Culmani, Genaro" (*pseud.*) *see* Carmona, Miguel

Cumbá, Candelario ARC 49 *Cu.*

"Cumbres, Miro" (*pseud.*) *see* Castellanos, Mario

Cumplido, Ignacio PM 37 *Mex.*

Cúneo, Celestino (1868-) UT 177 *Uru.*

Cúneo-Vidal, Rómulo ("Juan Pagador") (1869-) CG I, 737; IE 68; P 7 *Per.*

Cunha Dotti, Juan PoU 89 *Uru.*

Curbía, Francisco M. BDC 15; Cu 45 *Cu.*

Curbía y García, Juan Ignacio de Cu 45 *Cu.*

Curiel, Elías David V 62 *Venez.*

Curiel Coutiño, Ramón V 63 *Venez.*

Curotto, Ángel ("Ludovic") (1902-) A 18, 78, 82 *Arg.*

Cursach, Antonio A 18; CG I, 738 *Arg.*

Curtis, Carlos Daniel Ig 89; NM 17 *Mex.*

Cussi Yupangui Inca *see* Castro, Diego de

CH

Chabalier, Clotilde A 18 *Arg.*

Chabrillón, Andrés (1887-) A 18; APAM 251; LAC 147 *Arg.*

Chacón, Enrique CA 67 *Guat.*

Chacón, Federico 2° C 7; NC 114 *Chil.*

Chacón, Jacinto (1822-) CHL 247; CLH 207; PCh 21 *Chil.*

Chacón, Juan W. B 6; CG I, 744 *Bol.*

Chacón, Luis Antonio E 22 *Ecua.*

Chacón, Luis R. E 22 *Ecua.*

Chacón, Rodrigo V 63 *Venez.*

Chacón Chaverri, Tranquilino (1859-) CA 14, 15; EPCR 81 *C.R.*

Chacón González, Luis A. C 28 *Chil.*

Chacón Lorca, Luis Edo C 28 *Chil.*

Chacón Méndez, Euclides CA 15 *C.R.*

Chacón Trejos, Gonzalo ("Lorenzo Jiménez") CA 15, 34; IBCR IV, 294 *C.R.*

Chacón y Calvo, José María (1893-) CG I, 744; CHL 489; CT 339; Cu 45; G 335; GLO 242; HLC 217; LH 117; WLA 93 *Cu.*

"Chagrofilo" (*pseud.*) E 22 *Ecua.*

Chaigneau, Julio C 7, 46; NC 356 *Chil.*

Chamorro, Delfín (1863-) Par 9; PPa 47 *Para.*

Champion, Emilio LAS 206 *Per.*

"Chanteclair" (*pseud.*) *see* Betanzo, Francisca

1. "Chantecler" (*pseud.*) U 5 *Uru.*

2. "Chantecler" (*pseud.*) *see* Trullas y Aulet, Ignacio

Chaparro, Juan S. Par 9 *Para.*

Chaparro Albarracín, Hernando V 63 *Venez.*

Chapuseaux, Adalberto SD 8 *Dom.*

"Charles Blanc" (*pseud.*) *see* Blixen, Samuel

"Charles Carrillo" (*pseud.*) *see* Valladares y Rubio, Antonio

Charlier, Louis TM 491 *Mex.*

Charlín Correa, Carlos C 63 *Chil.*

Charras, Basilio B. de A 18 *Arg.*

Charras, Julián de A 18 *Arg.*

Chas de Chruz, Israel A 18 *Arg.*

Chassaing, Juan (1838-1864) HLA 458; LA VIII, 572 *Arg.*

Chaumer, Enrique V 63 *Venez.*

Chavarría, Lisímaco ("Rosa de Chavarría") (1877-1913) CA 15, 16; FPA 122, 139; EPCR 288; IBCR IV, 55; PC 123, 137 *C.R.*

"Chavarría, Rosa de" (*pseud.*) *see* Chavarría, Lisímaco

Chavero, Alfredo (1841-1906) BHLA 443; CG I, 751; CHL 410, 413; CLH 360; HLM 460, 490; Ig 90; NM 17; TM 113, 117, 434, 537 *Mex.*

Chaverri, Graciliano (1854-) CA 16; EPCR 89 *C.R.*

Chaverri, Virgilio CA 16 *C.R.*

Chaverri y Garibay, José TM 118 *Mex.*

Chaves *see also* Chávez

Chaves, Manuel W. (1878-) Par 1; PT 55 *Para.*

Chaves R., Max PCo 84 *Col.*

Chaves Torres, José María (1856-1915) BC 114; Co 21 *Col.*

Chávez *see also* Chaves

Chávez, Ángel Polibio (1855?-) E 22 *Ecua.*

Chávez, Ezequiel A. (1868-) CG I, 752; HLM 514; TM 537; WLA 95 *Mex.*

Chávez, Fernando BHLA 596; E 22; PLE 134 *Ecua.*

Chávez, Manuel A. PM 37 *Mex.*

Chávez, Mario BAP 79 *Per.*

Chávez Franco, Modesto (1872-) E 22, 74; PLE 78; WLA 96 *Ecua.*

Chávez Mata, José María E 22 *Ecua.*

Chávez Torres, José María E 22 *Ecua.*

Chávez y Martínez, Pedro BDC 15; Cu 45 *Cu.*

Cházari Fenochio, Andrés Ig 91; NM 17; PM 37 *Mex.*

Cházaro, Rafael M. PM 37 *Mex.*

Cházaro, Tirso W. PM 37 *Mex.*

Cherrutti, Pedro S. A 18 *Arg.*

Chesebrough Diez de Medina, Juan A. C 28 *Chil.*

Cheves, Adelaida (1846-) CA 67; GPCA III, 301; PG 279 *Guat.*

Cheves de Wyld Ospina, Amalia (1896-) CA 67; PG 459 *Guat.*

Chiappa, Víctor M. CL 274 *Chil.*

Chiappori, Atilio (1880-) A 19; AT II, 856; CG I, 755; LAC 45, 131 *Arg.*

Chiari, Eduardo Pan 6 *Pan.*

Chioino, José BAP 57; P 7 *Per.*

Chiossone, Tulio V 63 *Venez.*

Chirapozu, José A 19; CG I, 757 *Arg.*

Chiriboga, Gerardo PLE 127 *Ecua.*

Chiriboga, Joaquín E 22 *Ecua.*

Chiriboga, Julio E 23 *Ecua.*

Chiriboga Alvear, Manuel E 23 *Ecua.*

Chiriboga B., Francisco E 23; PE 88 *Ecua.*

Chirino, Jesús María V 63 *Venez.*

Chirveches Arróspide, Armando (1883-1926) B 7; BHLA 513; BT 81; CG I, 757; CHL 311; G 320; LB 617, 630; SASS 107 *Bol.*

Chocano, José Santos (1875-1934) AB 21; AEHA 290; APEH 427, 1186; BHLA 462; CG I, 758; CHL 536; CLH 469; CP 692; GLO 252; LP 383; MSAP 130, 306; PLHA 112; PPe 204; SAL 246 *et passim;* SASS 415; WLA 98; WSAL 55, 76 *Per.*

Chorroarín, Luis J. (1757-1823) LA V, 414 *Arg.*

Chouteau, Eugenio C 46 *Chil.*

Chumaceiro, David PC 165 *Chil.*

Chumillas, Ventura A 19; CG I, 758 *Arg.*

Churión, Juan José ("Bachiller Munguía") (1876-) V 33, 63; WLA 98 *Venez.*

Churión, Luis LV 343; V 63 *Venez.*

D

D., A.C. PM 17 *Mex.*

D.P.V. BDC 15 *Cu.*

D'Acosta, Diógenes U 5 *Uru.*

Dadey, José (1574-1660) HLNG I, 244; RHLC 27 *Col.*

Dagnino, Manuel V 63 *Venez.*

"Dagoberto Mármara" (*pseud.*) see Bobadilla, Emilio

Dahlquist, Juan R. (1884-) Par 9; PPa 147; PT 241 *Para.*

Daireaux, Godofredo A 19, 83; CG II, 2 *Arg.*

Daireaux, Max C 63 *Chil.*

D'Alençon, Emiliano C 7 *Chil.*

"Dalevuelta, Jacobo" (*pseud.*) see Ramírez de Aguilar, Fernando

"Daliza, Flor" (*pseud.*) see Moll, Mercedes

Dalmau Canet, Sebastián CG II, 2; PR 7, 9, 17, 33, 45 *P.R.*

Dallegri, Santiago CG II, 5; U 5 *Uru.*

"Dámaso Gil Aclea" (*pseud.*) see Márquez, Matías F.

Damirón, Rafael BDC 111; PA 274; PD 41; SD 9, 10, 20 *Dom.*

"Damón" (*pseud.*) see Ochoa y Acuña, Anastasio María de

Damos, L. E 23 *Ecua.*

Daneff, Stoyan A 19 *Arg.*

Danero, E.M.S. A 19; CG II, 5 *Arg.*

"Daniel" (*pseud.*) see Mansilla de García, Eduarda

Daniel, Francisco J. BDC 15; Cu 46 *Cu.*

"Daniel Morton" (*pseud.*) see Menéndez, Carlos R.

"Daniel Vásquez" (*pseud.*) see Gómez Rojas, Domingo

Danke, Jacobo (1905-) PCC xxi, 243 *Chil.*

Dantas Lacombe, Mercedes (1888-) A 19 *Arg.*

Dantés, Edmundo ("Manuel Guzmán Maturana") C 28 *Chil.*

Dantin, Clemente (-1904) ARC 49 *Cu.*

Danús, Juan C 7 *Chil.*

Darbois y León, René BDC 16; Cu 46 *Cu.*

1. Darío, Rubén (1867-1916) AB 21; AEHA 748; APEH 143, 1180; BHLA 459; CHL 510, 513, 516, 519, 540; CLH 221, 445, 450, 458; CP 689; FPA 357, 359; G 375; GLO 250; GPCA III, 205; LAND 33; MSAP 2, 38, 255; NC 227; NL 23; PLHA 95; PN 97; SA 37; SAL 101 *et passim;* SASS 119; SD 10; WSAL 47 *Nicar.*

2. Darío, Rubén (hijo) CA 16 *C.R.*

Darío Jaén, J. see Jaén, J. Darío

Darío Maldonado, Samuel CHL 375; CLH 323; LV 202 *Venez.*

D'Arlach, Adhemar PB 122 *Bol.*

Darquea, Secundino E 23 *Ecua.*

Darquea Cevallos, F. Alberto E 23 *Ecua.*

Darquer, S. P 7 *Per.*

Daubón, José Antonio BP 523, 591; PR 17, 33, 51 *P.R.*

"Daurico Marón" (*pseud.*) see Roca, Ramón

Dávalos, Balbino (1866-) AMP 326; APMM 30; CG II, 13; G 357; HLM 427; PM 37; PMe I, 81; PNM 47; PoM 354; SASS 368; TM 436 *Mex.*

Dávalos, Juan Carlos (1887-) A 19, 83; APAM 255; C 46; CG II, 13; G 311; LAC 137; LAS 207; NPA 207; PLHA 234; WLA 114 *Arg.*

Dávalos, Marcelino (1871-1923) CG II, 13; G 357; GLO 248; HLM 469; Ig 92; NM 17; PM 37; SASS 399; TM 118, 537 *Mex.*

Dávalos Mora, Rafael ("Dionisio Areopagita") (1888-) Ig 93; NM 17 *Mex.*

Dávalos y Figueroa, Diego BHLA 77 *Per.*

Dávalos y Lissón, Pedro (1863-) CG II, 13; P 7; WLA 115 *Per.*
Dávalos y Lissón, Ricardo P 8 *Per.*
Daverio de Bonavita, Layly CG II, 13; HSLU II, pt 8, 20; PU 261 *Uru.*
"David" (*pseud.*) *see* Guarín, José David
Dávila, Céleo (1890?-) FPA 318, 332 *Hond.*
Dávila, Eudoro C. E 23 *Ecua.*
Dávila, Guillermo CG II, 14; E 23 *Ecua.*
Dávila, Mariano TM 120 *Mex.*
Dávila, Pablo Aurelio E 23 *Ecua.*
Dávila, Vicente (1874-) CG II, 14; V 63; WLA 116 *Venez.*
Dávila, Virgilio (1869-) BP 523, 591; CP 693; PA 164; PP 231; PR 34; QPR (2) 57 *P.R.*
Dávila Boza, Ricardo C 28 *Chil.*
Dávila Caballero, Arturo PM 37 *Mex.*
Dávila Cordero, César PE 56 *Ecua.*
Dávila de Cordero, Jesús E 38 *Ecua.*
Dávila de Ponce de León, Waldina (-1900) BC 130; Co 21; RHLC 184 *Col.*
Dávila Garibi, J. Ignacio PM 37 *Mex.*
Dávila Larraín, Benjamín NC 416 *Chil.*
Dávila Martínez, José PR 45 *P.R.*
Dávila Padilla, Agustín (1562-1604) HLM 77 *Mex.*
Dávila Ricci, José (1904-) QPR (2) 57 *P.R.*
Dávila Silva, Ricardo ("Leo Par") C 64; CL 274 *Chil.*
Dávila y Arrillaga, Mariano NM 2 *Mex.*
Davin, Diego BHC II, 489 *Chil.*
Day, Emma A 19 *Arg.*
De Angelis, Pedro A 19, 71 *Arg.*
De Bellazi, Luis A 19 *Arg.*
De la Calle, Ceferino A 19 *Arg.*
De la Orga, Bernabé A 19 *Arg.*
De la Torre, Antonio A 19 *Arg.*
De la Vega, Alfonso M. A 19 *Arg.*
De las Carreras, Roberto U 5 *Uru.*
De María, Alcides ("Calisto el Ñato") (1858-1899) U 5 *Uru.*
De María, Alfonso C 7 *Chil.*
De Paola, Luis A 20 *Arg.*
De Pedro, Valentín A 20, 71, 83 *Arg.*
De Soto y Sagarra, Luis (1893-) CT 575 *Cu.*
De Vedia, Joaquín (1877-) AT I, 429 *Arg.*
De Vitis, Michael SD 10 *Dom.*
Debayle, León NL 238 *Nicar.*
Debayle, Luis H. NL 129 *Nicar.*
Decoud, Adolfo Par 9 *Para.*
Decoud, Diógenes (1863-) CG II, 16; Par 9 *Para.*
Decoud, Héctor Francisco (1855-) CG II, 16; PT 305 *Para.*
Decoud, José Secundo (1848-1909) Par 1, 10 *Para.*
Decoud, Juan José Par 10; PPa 41 *Para.*
Defilippis Novoa, Francisco (1890?-1930) A 19, 83 *Arg.*
Degetau y González, Federico (1862-1914) BP 503, 591; PR 6, 8, 17, 26, 42, 45, 55 *P.R.*
Deheza, José Abdías B 7 *Bol.*
Del Campo, Cosme (-1660) LA III, 63 *Arg.*

Del Campo, Cupertino (1873-) A 19; AT II, 785 *Arg.*
Del Campo, Estanislao *see* Campo, Estanislao del
Del Campo, Ricardo A 19 *Arg.*
Del Campo V., José Manuel C 64; NC 416 *Chil.*
Del Cioppo, Carlos María U 5 *Uru.*
Del Monte *see also* Delmonte *and* Monte del
Del Monte, Domingo *see* Monte, Domingo del
Del Monte, Félix María (1819-1899) BDC 16; BHLA 225; CHL 492; CLH 432; SD 10 *Dom.*
Del Plata, Rodolfo A 19 *Arg.*
Del Portal, Herminia Cu 46 *Cu.*
Del Valle, José Santos (1849-) HL II, 337 *Hond.*
Délano, Luis Enrique (1906-) BHLA 621; C 7; PCC xxiii, 281 *Chil.*
Delanoy, Oscar SD 10 *Dom.*
Delazerda, Fernando (1852-1885) Pan 6 *Pan.*
Delgadillo, Jorge B 7; PB 228 *Bol.*
Delgado, Asdrúbal E. (1880-) UT 185 *Uru.*
Delgado, Aurelio PB 109 *Bol.*
Delgado, Camilo S. ("Dr. Arcos") CG II, 27; Co 21 *Col.*
Delgado, Daniel CG II, 27; Co 21 *Col.*
Delgado, Eladio V 64 *Venez.*
Delgado, F. Javier P 8 *Per.*
Delgado, José María CG II, 27; LU 64, 668; PIU III, 192; PU 69; TM 120, 578; U 5 *Uru.*
Delgado, Juan B. (1868-1927) AMP 137; CG II, 27; G 357; HLM 408; IE 71; PM 37; PMe I, 89 *Mex.*
Delgado, Julio Esaú E 23 *Ecua.*
Delgado, Luis Humberto LAS 206 *Per.*
Delgado, Luis M. P 8 *Per.*
Delgado, Manuel de J. ARC 39 *Cu.*
Delgado, Manuel J. ARC 49 *Cu.*
Delgado, Nicolás V 64 *Venez.*
1. Delgado, Rafael (1853-1914) BAMP 48; BHLA 443; CG II, 27; CHL 423; CLH 367; G 357; HLM 445; HLMex 219, 225; Ig 94; NM 17; PMe I, 91; SASS 382; TM 121 *Mex.*
2. Delgado, Rafael (1890-) AMP 138 *Mex.*
Delgado, Samuel Co 21 *Col.*
Delgado Correa, Luis LV 114 *Venez.*
Delgado Fito, C. A 20 *Arg.*
Delgado y Buenrostro, Antonio PM 38 *Mex.*
Delheye, Pedro Mario (1894-1918) A 20; APAM 267 *Arg.*
Delhumeau, Viuda de Bolado, Julia TM 122, 436 *Mex.*
Deligne, Gastón Fernando (1861-1913) CG II, 30; CHL 497; CLH 437; FPA 228, 236; LD 92; PA 278; PD 44; SD 10 *Dom.*
Deligne, Rafael Alfredo (1863-1902) BDC 16; CG II, 30; CHL 497; CLH 437; FPA 228, 241; LD 97; PA 294; PD 68; SD 10 *Dom.*
Delino Cu 46 *Cu.*

"Delio" (*pseud.*) *see* Iturrondo, Francisco

"Delio Seravile" (*pseud.*) *see* Sarmiento, Ricardo

Deliz, Monserrate PR 34 *P.R.*

Delmar, Serafín (1901-) BHLA 605, 609; IE 72 *Per.*

Delmonte, Francisco Muñoz SD 10 *Dom.*

Delmonte y Mena, Jesús M. (1824-1877) BDC 16; Cu 46 *Cu.*

Delmonte y Portillo, Casimiro (1838-1887) BDC 16; Cu 46 *Cu.*

Delmonte y Portillo, Domingo (-1883) BDC 17; Cu 46 *Cu.*

Delmonte y Tejada, Antonio SD 10 *Dom.*

Delmotte, José Mariano PM 38 *Mex.*

Delofeu y Leonard, Manuel (1849-1911) Cu 46 *Cu.*

Delorme y Campos, Jorge PM 38; TM 122 *Mex.*

Delpino y Lamas, Francisco Antonio V 64 *Venez.*

Delpodio, Matilde A 20 *Arg.*

Della Costa, Pablo ("Severus") (1884-) A 20, 78; APAM 263; NPA 171 *Arg.*

Delle Ville, Carlos A 20 *Arg.*

Dellepiane, Antonio (1864-) AT I, 137; CG II, 31 *Arg.*

Demarchi, Andrés A 20, 83 *Arg.*

Demaría, Antonio M. LA VIII, 615 *Arg.*

Demaría, Bernabé A 20; CG II, 33 *Arg.*

Dengo, Omar (1888-1928) CA 16; EPCR 401; IBCR IV, 353 *C.R.*

Depons, François V 64 *Venez.*

"Derecho, Justo" (*pseud.*) *see* Monge, José María

Derkes, Eleuterio BDC 17, 111; BP 511, 591; PR 12, 17, 34 *P.R.*

D'Erzell, Catalina HLM 530; HLMex 248; Ig 109; NM 18; TM 122 *Mex.*

Deschamps, Enrique SD 10 *Dom.*

Deschamps, Eugenio SD 10 *Dom.*

"Desocupado, Un" (*pseud.*) *see* Díaz González, Olallo

Despradel, Lorenzo ARC 49; CG II, 41; SD 11 *Dom.*

Dessein Merlo, Justo S. A 20 *Arg.*

Dessús, Luis Felipe PP 188; PR 6, 34 *P.R.*

Destéffanis, Luigi HSLU III, pt 4, 21 *Uru.*

Destruge, Camilo CG II, 41; E 23; PLE 56 *Ecua.*

Destruge M., Guillermo CG II, 41; E 24 *Ecua.*

"Desval" (*pseud.*) *see* Valdés Machuca, Ignacio

Deulhumeau, Vda. de Bolado, Julia *see* Delhumeau

Deústua, Alejandro O. (1849-) IE 72 *Per.*

Dey, Josefina C 28 *Chil.*

Deza, Justo PU 263 *Uru.*

Deza y Ulloa, Francisco HPM 199; PM 38 *Mex.*

"Dharma" (*pseud.*) *see* Castellanos, Joaquín

"Diablofuerte" (*pseud.*) *see* Fermandois, José Luis

"Diana Clara" (*pseud.*) *see* Amador, María Ester

Díaz, Agustín TM 123 *Mex.*

Díaz, Alberto Alfonso A 20 *Arg.*

Díaz, Antolín LAS 204

Díaz, Antonio Américo U 5 *Uru.*

"Díaz, Carlos" (*pseud.*) *see* Rokha, Pablo de

Díaz, D. V 64 *Venez.*

Díaz, Eduardo U 5 *Uru.*

Díaz, Eligio J. *see* Díaz y Álvarez, Eligio J.

Díaz, Ezequiel A 20 *Arg.*

Díaz, Faustino V. A 20 *Arg.*

Díaz, Fernando Antonio V 64 *Venez.*

Díaz, Francisco (1812-1845) CG II, 46; GPCA I, 143 *Salv.*

Díaz, Joaquín (1843-1892) GPCA II, 385; HL II, 145 *Hond.*

Díaz, José Cornelio (1800-) Cu 46 *Cu.*

Díaz, José de Jesús (1809-1846) BHLA 227; CHL 395; CLH 342; HPM 818 *Mex.*

Díaz, José del Carmen ARC 36 *Cu.*

Díaz, José del Pilar Par 10 *Para.*

Díaz, José Domingo V 64 *Venez.*

Díaz, José María (-1888) Cu 46; TM 123 *Mex.*

Díaz, José V. U 5 *Uru.*

Díaz, Josefa Cu 46 *Cu.*

Díaz, Juan Par 10 *Para.*

Díaz, Juan E. Par 10 *Para.*

Díaz, Leopoldo (1862-) A 20; AEHA 493; APEH 119, 1179; BHLA 456; CHL 528; CLH 466; FPA 16, 42; GLO 235; SAL 325 *et passim;* SASS 43 *Arg.*

1. Díaz, Luis María A 21 *Arg.*

2. Díaz, Luis María V 64 *Venez.*

Díaz, Mantilla S. V 64 *Venez.*

Díaz, Pedro CG II, 46; TM 123 *Mex.*

Díaz, Pedro Pablo V 64 *Venez.*

Díaz, Porfirio SD 11 *Dom.*

Díaz, Ramón V 34, 64 *Venez.*

Díaz, Ramón M. HSLU III, pt 6, 36 *Uru.*

Díaz, Roberto de J. Co 21 *Col.*

Díaz, Rómulo PM 38 *Mex.*

Díaz, Salvadora PM 38 *Mex.*

Díaz, Sebastián (1741-1812) BHC III, 76; HC 44 *Chil.*

Díaz, Teófilo Eugenio ("Tax") CG II, 46; HSLU I, pt 4, 6; PIU I, 238; U 5 *Uru.*

Díaz, Víctor Miguel CA 67 *Guat.*

Díaz, Vigil SD 11 *Dom.*

Díaz Arrieta, Hernán ("Alone") (1891-) BHLA 617; C 1, 7, 28, 59; NC 417; WLA 123 *Chil.*

Díaz Barreiro, Francisco V 64 *Venez.*

Díaz Bolio, José PM 38 *Mex.*

Díaz C., Gerardo CA 67 *Guat.*

Díaz Calvillo, Juan Bautista ACe 781 *Mex.*

Díaz Caneja, Ignacio PR 10, 18, 45 *P.R.*

Díaz Caneja, Luis PR 12, 14 *P.R.*

Díaz Cardeña, Gonzalo TM 123 *Mex.*

Díaz Casanueva, Humberto (1905-) C 28; PCC xxiii,275 *Chil.*

Díaz Castro, Eugenio (1804-1865) BC 134; CHL 338; CLH 290, 291; Co 21; LC 145; RHLC 181; SAL 339 *Col.*

Díaz Covarrubias, Juan (1837-1859) AMP 260; BHLA 332; CHL 395, 407; CLH 343; G 357; GLO 248; HLM 318, 336; HLMex 173; HPM 831; Ig 99; NM 18; PM 38; PMe I, 63; PoM 158 *Mex.*

Díaz de Aguiar, Félix V 64 *Venez.*

"Díaz de Escobar, Zoraida" (*pseud.*) *see* Díaz de Ross *or* de Schtronn, Zoraida

Díaz de Gamboa, José María PM 39 *Mex.*

Díaz de Guzmán, Ruy (-1629) LA III, 327 *Arg.*

Díaz de la Quintana, Alberto A 21; CG II, 54; Cu 46

Díaz de la Rionda, Silverio (1898-) PoC 60 *Cu.*

Díaz de la Vega, Silvestre TM 538 *Mex.*

Díaz de León, Rafael NM 18; PM 39 *Mex.*

Díaz de Molina, Alfredo A 21 *Arg.*

Díaz de Poo, M. F. Cu 47 *Cu.*

Díaz de Rodríguez, Albertina ("Nenúfar") Cu 47 *Cu.*

Díaz de Ross *or* de Schtronn, Zoraida ("Zoraida Díaz de Escobar") (1881-) AP 83; Pan 6, 18 *Pan.*

Díaz del Castillo, Bernal (1492-1568) AEHA 295; BAMP 8; BHLA 58; CA 67; CG II, 48; HLM 35; HLMex 19; TM 538 *Sp.-Mex.*

Díaz del Castillo, Idelfonso (1856-1926) Co 21 *Col.*

Díaz del Gallego, Pascasio Cu 47 *Cu.*

1. Díaz Dufoo, Carlos (1861-) CG II, 49; G 358; HLM 458; Ig 102; NM 18; TM 123; WLA 123 *Mex.*

2. Díaz Dufoo, Carlos (hijo) TM 124 *Mex.*

Díaz Flores, Francisco V 64 *Venez.*

Díaz Flores, Rafael ("Modesto") V 64, 103 *Venez.*

Díaz Galano, Wilfrido Cu 47 *Cu.*

Díaz Gana, Pedro C 46 *Chil.*

Díaz Garcés, Joaquín ("Ángel Pino") C 7; CHL 282; G 323; NC 417 *Chil.*

Díaz González, Olallo ("Un Desocupado") BDC 17; Cu 46, 47 *Cu.*

Díaz Granados, Domingo (1835-1869) Co 22 *Col.*

Díaz Granados, Enrique Co 7 *Col.*

Díaz Guerra, Alirio (1862-) BC 136; Co 22; V 64 *Col.*

Díaz Jardón, S. Cu 47 *Cu.*

Díaz Lecuna, Eduardo V 64 *Venez.*

Díaz Leguizamón, Héctor (1892-) A 21; APAM 271; CG II, 52; LAC 147 *Arg.*

Díaz Lemus, Ángel María (1853-) Co 22 *Col.*

Díaz Meza, Aurelio C 7, 47; CG II, 52 *Chil.*

Díaz Mirón, Manuel (1821-1894) AMP 303; PM 39; PMe I, 99; TM 125 *Mex.*

Díaz Mirón, Salvador (1853-1928) AEHA 299; AMP 34; APEH 54, 1178; APMM 34; BHLA 451; CG II, 53; CHL 420, 513; CLH 365, 452; FPA 339, 343; G 358; GLO 248; HLM 413; HLMex 215; PLHA 87; PM 39; PMe I, 103; PMM 20; PNM 56; PoM 389; SAL 64 *et passim;* SASS 360 *Mex.*

Díaz Molina, Pedro ARC 49 *Cu.*

Díaz Olazábal, Rodolfo A 21 *Arg.*

Díaz Ordóñez, Virgilio ("Ligio Vizardi") SD 11, 31 *Dom.*

Díaz Páez, Enrique Cu 47 *Cu.*

Díaz-Pérez, Viriato CG II, 53; Par 10 *Para.*

Díaz Pombo, Gonzalo Co 22 *Col.*

Díaz Quijano, Máximo BDC 67; Cu 47 *Cu.*

Díaz Rodríguez, Manuel (1868-1927) AEHA 891; BHLA 471, 484; CG II, 54; CHL 381; CLH 332; G 392; GLO 255; LV 400; PLHA 195, 259; SAL 92, 316, 339; SASS 523; V 64; VPF 175 *Venez.*

Díaz Rojas, Teobaldo C 7 *Chil.*

Díaz Romero, Belisario B 7; CG II, 54 *Bol.*

Díaz Romero, Eugenio (-1926) A 21; AEHA 303; APAM 75; CHL 186; CLH 160 *Arg.*

Díaz Rugama, Alberto TM 436 *Mex.*

Díaz Sánchez, Ramón V 65 *Venez.*

Díaz Silveira, Francisco Cu 47; PA 34; PCu 98 *Cu.*

Díaz Usandivaras, Julio (1888-) A 21, 71; AT II, 653; CG II, 55 *Arg.*

Díaz Valdés, Laura ARC 49 *Cu.*

Díaz Volero, Francisco Cu 47 *Cu.*

Díaz y Álvarez, Eligio J. Cu 46, 47 *Cu.*

Díaz y Cruz, Manuel José (1855-1874) Cu 48 *Cu.*

Díaz Zapata, Francisco NL 13 *Nicar.*

Di Carlo, Adelia A 21 *Arg.*

Dickmann, Enrique (1874-) AT I, 461; CG II, 19, 69; WLA 124 *Arg.*

Dicoudray, J. Humberto PD 72; SD 11 *Dom.*

Didapp, Juan Pedro (1874-) Ig 103; NM 18 *Mex.*

Diego, José de (1866-1918) BP 524, 592; CG II, 70; FPA 461, 485; PA 167; PP 133; PR 18, 34, 45, 51, 55 *P.R.*

Diego, Pedro R. de ("Raúl de la Vega") BP 525; PR 34 *P.R.*

Diego, Rafael de A 21 *Arg.*

Diego Padró, J. I. de (1896-) BP 503, 524; CG II, 71; IE 75; PP 321; PR 34, 51, 55 *P.R.*

Diéguez, Luis Francisco A 21 *Arg.*

Diéguez Flores, Manuel (1856-1919) CA 67; CHL 508 *Guat.*

Diéguez y Olaverri, Juan (1813-1866) AEHA 891; BHLA 332; BLN 261; CA 67, 68; CHL 506; CLH 447; FPA 291, 294; GPCA I, 155; PG 121 *Guat.*

Diéguez y Olaverri, Manuel (1821-1861) AEHA 891; BLN 115; CA 68; GPCA I, 269; PG 139 *Guat.*

Dieste, Eduardo CG II, 72; HSLU III, pt 4, 45; PIU III, 272; U 6; UL 125 *Uru.*

Dieste, Enrique CG II, 72; HSLU III, pt 4, 45 *Uru.*

Diez, Domingo CG II, 73; TM 539 *Mex.*

Diez, Joseph PM 39 *Mex.*

Diez, Manuel Antonio V 65 *Venez.*

Díez Barroso, Francisco HLM 513 *Mex.*

Diez Barroso, Víctor Manuel (1890-) HLM 529; TM 125; WLA 124 *Mex.*

Diez-Canedo, Enrique CG II, 73; TM 437, 449 *Mex.*

Diez de Betanzos, Juan (-1576) P 8 *Per.*
Diez de Bonilla, Benjamín TM 127 *Mex.*
Diez de Medina, Ángel (1869-) B 7 *Bol.*
Diez de Medina, Eduardo (1882-) B 7; BT 97; CG II, 75; PB 115; WLA 124 *Bol.*
Diez de Medina, Fernando B 7; BHLA 613; G 320; LAS 199 *Bol.*
Diez de Medina, Francisco Tadeo BHC III, 133 *et passim Chil.*
Diez de Medina, Lucio B 7 *Bol.*
Diez de Medina, Raúl ("Gaston Nerval") (1909-) WLA 275 *Bol.*
Diez Gómez, Adolfo A 21; CG II, 74 *Arg.*
Dihigo, Ernesto Cu 48 *Cu.*
Dihigo y Mestre, Juan Miguel (1866-) CG II, 77; CT 493; Cu 48; WLA 125 *Cu.*
"Dilletante" (*pseud.*) E 24 *Ecua.*
Dillon, Luis Napoleón E 24 *Ecua.*
Dillon, María Luisa E 24 *Ecua.*
"Dinka" (*pseud.*) C 28 *Chil.*
"Diógenes, Nucleo" (*pseud.*) A 50 *Arg.*
Diogli, M. G. PM 39 *Mex.*
"Dionisio Areopagita" (*pseud.*) *see* Dávalos Mora, Rafael
Discépolo, Armando A 21, 61, 83, 90 *Arg.*
"Djed Bórquez" (*pseud.*) *see* Bojórquez, Juan de Dios
"Dmitri Ivanovich" (*pseud.*) *see* Betancourt, José
Dobal, Manuel de Jesús (1845-1914) RLC 240, 242 *Cu.*
Doblas, Gonzalo de (1741-1809) LA IV, 1013 *Arg.*
Dobles Segreda, Gonzalo CA 16; IBCR IV, 302 *C.R.*
Dobles Segreda, Luis CA 16; CHL 508; EPCR 408; IBCR IV, 170 *et passim;* IE 75 *C.R.*
Dobranich, Baldmar F. A 21; CG II, 83 *Arg.*
Dobranich, Horacio Heriberto (1897-) A 21; CG II, 83; WLA 125 *Arg.*
Dobrizhoffer, Martín (1717-1791) LA IV, 599; SCL 419, 599 *Arg.*
"Doctor Atl" (*pseud.*) *see* Murillo, Gerardo
"Doctor Valromey" (*pseud.*) *see* González, Francisco
Doldán, Andrés Par 10 *Para.*
Dolz, Marco Antonio (1889-) Cu 49 *Cu.*
Doll, Ramón A 21; BHLA 632; G 311 *Arg.*
Dollero, Adolfo CG II, 88; Co 22; Cu 49 *Cu.*
Domenech y Vinajeras, Francisco (1882-) BDC 17; CG II, 89; Cu 49 *Cu.*
"Domingo" (*pseud.*) BDC 18; Cu 50 *Cu.*
Domingo y Castellanos, Juan M. (1883-) Cu 50 *Cu.*
Domingues, Atahualpa V 66 *Venez.*
Domínguez, Agustín María Cu 50 *Cu.*
Domínguez, Ángel S. (1895-) WLA 126 *Venez.*
Domínguez, Catalina Q. de Par 10 *Para.*
Domínguez, Fermín Par 10 *Para.*
Domínguez, Francisco CG II, 94; Cu 50 *Cu.*
Domínguez, José Antonio (1869-) HL II, 516 *Hond.*
Domínguez, José de Jesús BP 528, 605; PR 9, 34 *P.R.*

Domínguez, José Manuel TM 127 *Mex.*
Domínguez, Juan de Dios Ig 104; NM 18; TM 127 *Mex.*
Domínguez, Juan Francisco (1725-1813) ACe 787 *Mex.*
Domínguez, Luis L. (1819-1898) A 21; BHLA 307; CHL 142; CLH 120; FPA 15, 24; G 311; HLA 374; LA VI, 1099 *Arg.*
1. Domínguez, Manuel (1830-1910) CHL 410; CLH 356; Ig 105; NM 18 *Mex.*
2. Domínguez, Manuel (1869-1935) CG II, 95; Par 10; PT 299 *Para.*
Domínguez, María Alicia (1908-) A 21; CG II, 94; G 311; GLO 235; LAC 148; LAS 199; WLA 127 *Arg.*
Domínguez, María de la Paz TM 128 *Mex.*
1. Domínguez, Rafael Ig 106; NM 18 *Mex.*
2. Domínguez, Rafael V 66 *Venez.*
3. Domínguez, Rafael V 66 *Venez.*
Domínguez, Ricardo PM 39 *Mex.*
Domínguez, Salvador A. Cu 50 *Cu.*
Domínguez, Silverio A 21; CG I, 94 *Arg.*
Domínguez, Teófilo ARC 42 *Cu.*
Domínguez Barrera, Juan Cu 50 *Cu.*
Domínguez Camargo, Hernando (-1656) CHL 26; CLH 22; Co 22; HLNG I, 181; HPHA II, 22; LC 81; RHLC 23; SCL 322, 600 *Col.*
Domínguez de Gironella, Máximo BDC 18; Cu 50 *Cu.*
Domínguez García, Antonio Cu 50 *Cu.*
Domínguez Illanes, Tomás TM 127 *Mex.*
Domínguez Monteleone, Augusto TM 128 *Mex.*
Domínguez-Paulín, José NM 19 *Mex.*
Domínguez-Pérez, Francisco Cu 50 *Cu.*
Domínguez Roche, José María (1788-1858) BC 137; Co 22; RHLC 158 *Col.*
Domínguez Roldán, Francisco (1864-) CG II, 96; CT 217 *Cu.*
Domínguez Roldán, Guillermo (1868-1923) CG II, 96; CT 617; Cu 50 *Cu.*
Domínguez Sierra, Jorge C 28 *Chil.*
Domínguez y Santi, Jacobo ("J. A. Cobo") (-1898) BDC 13, 18; Cu 51 *Cu.*
Domínici, Aníbal (1837-1897) LV 4, 60; V 66; VPF 62 *Venez.*
Domínici, Pedro César (1875-) AEHA 892; BHLA 520; CG II, 97; CHL 378; CLH 326; LV 200, 383; PLHA 203; SASS 516; V 66; VPF 189 *Venez.*
"Don Claro-Oscuro" (*pseud.*) *see* Asenjo, Federico
"Don Julio" (*pseud.*) *see* Arboleda, Julio
"Don Quijote de la Mancha" (*pseud.*) C 7 *Chil.*
"Don Simón" (*pseud.*) *see* Fernández, Manuel María
Dondo, Osvaldo A 21 *Arg.*
Donis, Manuel E 25 *Ecua.*
Donoso, Francisco C 28; CMPC 112; G 323 *Chil.*
Donoso, Hugo C 47 *Chil.*
Donoso, José Antonio HC 174 *Chil.*
Donoso, Ricardo (1896-) BHLA 493; C 64; CG II, 98; IE 78; V 67 *Chil.*
Donoso González, Francisco C 28, 64 *Chil.*

Donoso Novoa, Armando (1887-) BHLA 493; C 28, 64; CG II, 98; CHL 286, 526; CL 277; IE 77; SASS 195; SD 11; V 67; WLA 128 *Chil.*

Donoso Raventos, Vicente C 7; NC 417 *Chil.*

Doporto, Manuel Cu 51 *Cu.*

Dorantes, Baltasar HPM 103 *Mex.*

Dorantes, R. Maximiliano NM 19 *Mex.*

Doreste, Arturo Cu 51; PJC 67 *Cu.*

Dorraine, Julio A 21; CG II, 101 *Arg.*

"Dos-Pes" (*pseud.*) Cu 51 *Cu.*

Dotti, Da Cunha HSLU III, pt 6, 51 *Uru.*

Dotti, Víctor M. HSLU III, pt 2, 28; PIU III, 275; U 6 *Uru.*

Dou, Lino ARC 49 *Cu.*

Douverné Torres, Isolina Cu 51 *Cu.*

Downton García, Jorge A 83; C 47

Dozo, Ismael E. A 22 *Arg.*

Dozo Lebeaud, R. A 22 *Arg.*

"Dr. Arcos" (*pseud.*) *see* Delgado, Camilo S.

Drago-Bracco, Adolfo CA 68 *Guat.*

Drew, Arturo Samuel A 22 *Arg.*

Drinot, Pablo C 47 *Chil.*

Dromundo, Baltasar LAS 199 *Mex.*

Drouet, Virgilio E 25, 74 *Ecua.*

D'Sola, Juan V 67 *Venez.*

Dualde, Eduardo LU 64, 668; PIU III, 244; U 6 *Uru.*

Duany i Méndez, Pedro ARC 50 *Cu.*

Duarte, Félix Cu 51 *Cu.*

Duarte, Juan Pablo (1813-1875) CHL 491; SD 11 *Dom.*

Duarte Level, Lino CG II, 108; V 67 *Venez.*

"Duayén, César" (*pseud.*) *see* Barra, Ema de la

Dublán y Maza, Manuel PM 39 *Mex.*

Dublé Urrutia, Diego (1877-) C 28; CHL 263, 538; CLH 223; CMPC 16; FPA 192, 212; PCh 177; SASS 147 *Chil.*

Ducassi, Juan E. y Vidal ARC 50 *Cu.*

Ducoing, Heriberto C 47 *Chil.*

Ducondrai, S. Humberto PA 298 *Dom.*

Ducoudray, Félix Servio SD 11 *Dom.*

Ducoudray, J. Humberto SD 11 *Dom.*

Dueñas, Joaquín Andrés Cu 51 *Cu.*

Dueñes, Heliodoro TM 128 *Mex.*

Dufrechóu, Eduardo CG II, 112; U 6 *Uru.*

Duhalde, Eduardo *see* Dualde, Eduardo

Duhau, Alfredo A 22, 83 *Arg.*

Dulzaides del Cairo, Laura CG II, 113; Cu 51 *Cu.*

Dumont, Gabriel Par 11 *Para.*

Duncan, Jeptha B. Pan 6 *Pan.*

Duque, Manuel PB 101 *Bol.*

Duque, Matías (1869-) CG II, 120; Cu 51 *Cu.*

"Duque de Lerma" (*pseud.*) *see* Raldiris Guasp, Juan P.

"Duque Job, El" (*pseud.*) *see* Gutiérrez Nájera, Manuel

Duque Uribe, Rafael (-1862) Co 22 *Col.*

Duquesne, José Domingo (1747-1822) Co 22; HLNG II, 119, 149, 333 *Col.*

"Duralis Estars" (*pseud.*) *see* Barrios de los Ríos, José María

Durán, Alfonso A 22 *Arg.*

Durán, Carlos (hijo) CA 17 *C.R.*

Durán, Diego (1538?-1588) HLM 64; TM 540 *Mex.*

Durán, Juan C 7, 29 *Chil.*

Durán, Justo L. (1859-1924) Co 22 *Col.*

Durán, Leopoldo A 22, 71 *Arg.*

Durán, Nicolás (1570-1653) Par 11; SCL 406, 612 *Para.*

Durán, Pedro G. A 22 *Arg.*

Durán Canelas, J. M. B 7 *Bol.*

Durand, Luis C 7 *Chil.*

Durante de Cabarga, Guillermo PM 39 *Mex.*

Duranti, Reginaldo M. E 25 *Ecua.*

Durantón, Luciano P 8 *Per.*

Durbal Sarali, Pío U 6 *Uru.*

Duro, Rogelio A. A 22 *Arg.*

Durón, Rómulo E. (1865-) CG II, 124; HL II, 457; WH 189 *Hond.*

1. Durón, Valentín (1830-1874) HL I, 349 *Hond.*

2. Durón, Valentín (1870-) HL II, 607 *Hond.*

Durr, Federico P 8 *Per.*

Dutari (*or* Dutary), Alejandro ("Romeo") (1877-1911) AP 85; Pan 6 *Pan.*

"Duval, Armando" (*pseud.*) *see* Monteagudo Rodríguez, Joaquín

Duzán, Juan V 67 *Venez.*

E

"E" (*pseud.*) *see* Cané, Miguel

Eandi, Héctor I. A 22 *Arg.*

Echagüe, Juan Pablo ("Jean Paul") (1877-) A 22, 78; AT 1, 48; CG II, 131; G 311; GLO 235; LAC 112, 154; LAS 199; PLHA 290; WLA 129 *Arg.*

Echagüe, Pedro (1821-1889) A 22, 83; LA VI, 630, 1116; SPLA 153 *Arg.*

Echáiz, Jesús HLM 466; Ig 107; NM 19; PM 40; TM 128, 437 *Mex.*

Echaurren Herboso, Raquel C 47 *Chil.*

Echavarri, Luis A 22; CG II, 132 *Arg.*

Echavarría *see also* Echevarría *and* Echeverría

Echavarría, Colón SD 11 *Dom.*

Echegaray, Aristóbulo A 22 *Arg.*

Echemendía, Ambrosio (-1898) ARC 34; Cu 51 *Cu.*

Echevarría *see also* Echavarría *and* Echeverría

Echevarría, Jaime CA 17; PC 69 *C.R.*

Echevarría, Juan Manuel BP 525; PR 34, 36, 55 *P.R.*

Echeverri, Camilo Antonio (1827-1887) BC 138; Co 22; LC 171 *Col.*

Echeverría *see also* Echavarría *and* Echevarría

Echeverría, Aquileo J. (1866-1909) CA 17, 18; CG II, 135; CHL 508; CLH 449; EPCR 91; FPA 121, 130; G 332; PC 25 *C.R.*

Echeverría, Carlos E. V 67 *Venez.*

Echeverría, Eduardo (1873-) Co 23; PCo 87; RHLC 152 *Col.*

Echeverría, Esteban (1805-1851) A 22; AEHA 317; BHLA 230, 247; CG II, 136; CHL 125; CLH 107; FPA 15, 17; G 311; GEA XII, XIX; HLA 303; HPHA II, 442; LA V, 235, 293, 345; PIU I, 136; PLHA 71; SASS 11; SPLA 66, 225; WSAL 23, 70 *Arg.*

Echeverría, José Antonio (1815-1855) CHL 433; CLH 376; Cu 51; RLC 90, 127, 147, 217, 296; V 67 *Cu.*

Echeverría, Juan Abel (1853-) E 25; PE 160; PLE 48 *Ecua.*

Echeverría, Juan M. V 67 *Venez.*

Echeverría, Pedro T. PM 40 *Mex.*

Echeverría, Sinforiano, Jr. ("Vicente Echeverría del Prado") PM 40 *Mex.*

Echeverría de Larraín, Inés ("Inés Bello" *or* "Iris") C 3, 7, 11, 64, 66; CG III, 153; CL 278 *Chil.*

"Echeverría del Prado, Vicente" (*pseud.*) *see* Echeverría, Sinforiano, Jr.

Echeverría Morales, Moisés (1888-) QPR (2) 62 *P.R.*

Echeverría y Reyes, Aníbal C 29 *Chil.*

Echeverría y Veytia, Mariano *see* Fernández de Echeverría y Veytia, Mariano

"Edda" (*pseud.*) *see* Pombo, Rafael

Edelmann y Pinto, Federico (1869-) CT 235 *Cu.*

"Edén, Jacobo" (*pseud.*) *see* Egaña, Rafael

Ederra, Francisco NC 493 *Chil.*

"Edmundo del Vals" (*pseud.*) *see* Milla Chapelli, Julio

Edo, Enrique (-1913) BDC 18; Cu 51; PR 33 *Cu.*

Edreira, Oscar G. ARC 50 *Cu.*

Edreira Rodríguez, Angelina ARC 50 *Cu.*

Eduardo, Isaac G. (1861-) B 8; BT 103; CG II, 136 *Bol.*

Edwards, Alberto BHLA 619; C 64; CL 278 *Chil.*

Edwards, Ricardo C 47 *Chil.*

Edwards Bello, Joaquín (1888-) C 8, 64; CG II, 137; G 323; WLA 129 *Chil.*

Edwards y MacClure, Agustín BHLA 619; C 64; CG II, 137; NC 419 *Chil.*

"Efe Gómez" (*pseud.*) *see* Gómez, Francisco

1. Egaña, Juan (1769-1836) C 47, 50; HC 51 *Chil.*

2. Egaña, Juan (1896-1928) PCC xvii, 147 *Chil.*

Egaña, Mariano C 8; NC 358 *Chil.*

Egaña, Rafael ("Jacobo Edén") (1851-1923) C 47; CG II, 137; HC 137; NC 118 *Chil.*

Egas, José María E 25; PE 143 *Ecua.*

"Ego Polibio" (*pseud.*) P 8 *Per.*

Egosque, Carlos M. de A 23 *Arg.*

Egües y Villamar, José Alejandro E 74 *Ecua.*

Eguez, Vidal E 25 *Ecua.*

Egui, Jacinto A. A 67 *Arg.*

Egui, José Agustín V 67 *Venez.*

Eguía Muñoz, Beatriz (1899-1927) A 23 *Arg.*

Eguía Puentes, Ricardo PU 265 *Uru.*

Eguía y Lumbe, Jorge de BHC II, 305 *Chil.*

Eguiara y Eguren, Juan José de (1706-1763) ACe 663; HLM 211 *Mex.*

Eguiarreta, Juan Antonio V 67 *Venez.*

Eguiguren, José Miguel E 25 *Ecua.*

Eguiguren, Luis Antonio (1887-) CG II, 138; P 8 *Per.*

Eguiguren y Escudero, José Antonio E 25 *Ecua.*

Eguílaz, Luis de CG II, 138; TM 491 *Mex.*

Eguren, José María (1882-) AB 22; APEH 959; BAP 27; BHLA 538; FPA 436, 456; G 381; P 8; PLHA 154; SAL 296 *et passim;* SASS 419 *Per.*

Eichelbaum, Samuel A 23, 83 *Arg.*

Eizaguirre, José Manuel (1862-) AT I, 475; CG II, 142 *Arg.*

Eizaguirre y Portales, José Ignacio Víctor (1817-1875) HC 128 *Chil.*

"El viejo Pancho" (*pseud.*) *see* Alonso y Trelles, José

Eleboro, Justo BDC 19; Cu 52 *Cu.*

Elena, Walter J. A 23, 71 *Arg.*

Elera, Pedro (1820-) P 8 *Per.*

Elflein, Ada M. A 23; CG II, 145 *Arg.*

Elguera, Federico ("El Barón de Keef") (1860-) CG II, 146; P 8 *Per.*

Elguero, Francisco (1856-) CG II, 146; NM 19; PM 40; TM 129 *Mex.*

Elgueta de Ochsenius, Herminia C 64 *Chil.*

Elías, Adolfo A 14 *Arg.*

Elías, Daniel A 23 *Arg.*

Elías, María Eugenia de A 23 *Arg.*

Eliet, Simón Pan 6 *Pan.*

Elim, Miriam C 29 *Chil.*

Eliz, Leonardo ("Rodófilo") (1861-) C 29, 64; CG II, 148; CHL 261; CL 279; CLH 222; NC 419; PCh 297 *Chil.*

Elízaga, Lorenzo Ig 107; NM 19 *Mex.*

Elizalde, Martín BDC 19; Cu 52 *Cu.*

Elizalde y Escudero, Pedro PM 40 *Mex.*

Elizondo, José F. (1880-) G 358; HLM 468; PM 40; TM 129, 130, 216 *Mex.*

Elizondo, Víctor Manuel CA 18; EPCR 642 *C.R.*

Elmore, Edwin P 8 *Per.*

Elola, Federico Cu 52 *Cu.*

Elorduy, Aquiles CG II, 149; TM 131 *Mex.*

Elorduy, Ernesto TM 606 *Mex.*

"Eloy Falopio Mañod" (*pseud.*) *see* Olmedo, Adolfo

Elzaburu y Vizcarronda, Manuel HPHA I, 349 *P.R.*

"Emar, Jean" (*pseud.*) *see* Yáñez, Álvaro

"Emeth, Omer" (*pseud.*) *see* Vaïsse, Emilio

Emiliani, María ("Fanny Mery") (1882-) Co 23 *Col.*

"Emiro Casto" (*pseud.*) *see* Toro, Fermín

"Emiro Kastos" (*pseud.*) *see* Restrepo, Juan de Dios *or* Toro, Fermín

Enamorado, Calixto Cu 52 *Cu.*

Enamorado, Miguel Wenceslao de (-1884) BDC 19; Cu 52 *Cu.*

Encalada y Orozco, Diego de BHC II, 378 *Chil.*

Encina, Carlos (1838-1882) A 23; CHL 176; CLH 151; HPHA II, 465; LA VIII, 541 *Arg.*

Enciso, Cenobio I. (1849-1903) Ig 107; NM 19; PM 40 *Mex.*

Endara, Benjamín E 27 *Ecua.*

Endara, Carlos Honorato E 27 *Ecua.*

Endara, Javier E 27 *Ecua.*
Endara, José A. E 27 *Ecua.*
Endara, Julio CG II, 157; E 27, 74 *Ecua.*
Engaña, Juan C 47 *Chil.*
Engaña, Rafael C 47 *Chil.*
"Enrique Espinosa" (*pseud.*) *see* Glusberg, Samuel
"Enrique Rotres V." (*pseud.*) *see* Torres Valderrama, Enrique
"Enrique Somoyar" (*pseud.*) *see* Nariño, Antonio
"Enriqueta, María (*pseud.*) *see* Camarillo y Roa de Pereyra, María Enriqueta
Enríquez, Alonso HPHA II, 137 *Per.*
Enríquez, Juan M. Cu 52 *Cu.*
Enríquez de Guzmán, Alonso SCL 73, 600 *Per.*
Enríquez Montaño (hijo) PD 131; SD 23 *Dom.*
Enríquez Simoní, Guillermo PM 40 *Mex.*
Entrala, F. de P. Cu 52 *Cu.*
Entralgo y Mendoza, José de Cu 52 *Cu.*
Entralgo y Vallina, Elías José (1903-) Cu 52; WLA 132 *Cu.*
"Epsilón Kappa" (*pseud.*) *see* Calcaño, Eduardo
"Equis" (*pseud.*) *see* Prohías y Hernández, Juan
Eraso, Domingo de BHC II, 38 *Chil.*
Erazo, Salvador L. PS 238 *Salv.*
Erazo Armas, Héctor C 29 *Chil.*
Ercilla y Zúñiga, Alonso de (1533-1594) AEHA 327; BHC I, 16; III, 34; BHLA 71; C 29; CG II, 162; CHL 7; CLH 6; HC 7; HPHA II, 292; LA III, 194; SASS 141; SCL 159, 601; WSAL 8 *Chil.*
Ernalz, Plázido A 23 *Arg.*
Ernst, Adolfo LV 191; V 67 *Venez.*
Errazurez y Aldunate, Javier de BHC III, 438 *Chil.*
Errázuris de Subercaseaux, Amalia C 8 *Chil.*
Errázuriz, Crescente (1894-1931) BHLA 379; CL 279 *Chil.*
Errázuriz, Isidoro (1835-1898) BHLA 379; C 65; CG II, 163; CHL 250; CL 280; CLH 209; HC 177 *Chil.*
Errecart, Amadeo A 23 *Arg.*
"Errol Lionel" (*pseud.*) *see* Nin Frías, Alberto
Erseguer, Enrique CG II, 163; G 386; U 6 *Uru.*
Escala, Víctor Hugo (1887-) E 27, 74; PE 313; WLA 132 *Ecua.*
Escalante, Félix María HPM 826; PM 40; TM 131 *Mex.*
Escalante, Goyito CA 18 *C.R.*
Escalante, Manuel G. CA 18 *C.R.*
Escalante, Manuela EPCR 19 *C.R.*
Escalante, Tomás de NM 19 *Mex.*
Escalante Palma, Pedro TM 131, 216 *Mex.*
Escalona, Rafael de LV 100 *Venez.*
Escalona, Rafael E. BDC 111; PR 12 *P.R.*
Escamilla, Pedro CG II, 166; Cu 52 *Cu.*
Escanaverino de Linares, Ginés Cu 52 *Cu.*
Escardó, Florencio A 23; CG II, 167 *Arg.*
Escobar, Arcesio (1832-1867) AC I, 355; BC 140; Co 23; E 27, 30 *Col.*
Escobar, Avelino (1818-1881) Co 23 *Col.*

Escobar, Diego Antonio de PM 40 *Mex.*
Escobar, Eduardo A 23 *Arg.*
Escobar, Eloy (1824-1889) AEHA 332; LV 289; V 68 *Venez.*
Escobar, Emilio Antonio (1857-1885) Co 23; RHLC 171 *Col.*
Escobar, Federico (1861-1912) AP 89; Co 23; Cu 52; Pan 6, 7 *Pan.*
Escobar, Felipe Juan BHLA 577; CG II, 168; Pan 7 *Pan.*
Escobar, Felipe Santiago (-1921) Co 23 *Col.*
Escobar, Francisco CG II, 168; Co 23 *Col.*
Escobar, Germán Cu 52 *Cu.*
Escobar, Gerónimo de Co 23; HLNG I, 118 *Col.*
Escobar, José María TM 132 *Mex.*
Escobar, José N. C 29 *Chil.*
Escobar, Julio Filiberto (1892-) A 83; AT I, 493; CG II, 168 *Arg.*
Escobar, Manuel María NM 19 *Mex.*
Escobar, Napoleón (1866-) GPCA III, 433 *Nicar.*
Escobar, Simón A. V 68 *Venez.*
Escobar, Zoilo (1877-) C 29; PCC xii, 41 *Chil.*
Escobar Bravo, Pablo BC 141; Co 23 *Col.*
Escobar Macías, Emilio (1833-) Co 23 *Col.*
Escobar Mendoza, Antonio PM 41 *Mex.*
Escobar R., Eusebio Co 24 *Col.*
Escobar R., José Ignacio C 29 *Chil.*
Escobar Roa, Rafael PCo 91 *Col.*
Escobedo, Federico (1874-) CG II, 168; G 358; HLM 407; PM 41 *Mex.*
Escobedo, Nicolás M. (1795-1840) RLC 69, 146, 158 *Cu.*
Escobedo Urra, Antonio BDC 19; Cu 53 *Cu.*
Escofet, José CG II, 169; LAND 121, 132 *Mex.*
Escóiquiz, Juan de CG II, 169; CHL 20; CLH 17 *Mex.*
Escolano y Obregón, Francisco TM 132 *Mex.*
Escosura y Escosura, Francisco de la Cu 53 *Cu.*
Escoto Carrión, Saturnino (1874-) ARC 50; Cu 53 *Cu.*
Escoto y Castello, José Augusto (1864-) CG II, 170; CT 139; Cu 53; WLA 135 *Cu.*
Escovar, R. V 68 *Venez.*
Escovar, Simón A. V 68 *Venez.*
Escudero, Carlos HPM 868; TM 132 *Mex.*
Escudero, El Padre SCL 550, 601 *Chil.*
Escudero, Francisco HLNG II, 402 *Col.*
Escudero, Manuel Eduardo E 27 *Ecua.*
Escudero, Salvador PM 41 *Mex.*
Escudero Miranda, E. ARC 50 *Cu.*
Escudero Miranda, Juan PR 24, 35 *P.R.*
Escudero Moscoso, Gonzalo CG II, 174; E 27; PE 98; PLE 115 *Ecua.*
Escuti, Santiago 2° C 29 *Chil.*
Escuti M., Héctor C 29 *Chil.*
Escuti Orrego, Santiago C 29, 47 *Chil.*
Esguerra, Arsenio (1836-1875) BC 142; Co 24; PB 230 *Col.*
Esguerra, Joaquín Co 24. Col.

Eslava, Catalina de HPM 96 *Mex.*
Eslava, Rafael G. Cu 53 *Cu.*
Esmenard, José Alfonso TM 497 *Mex.*
Espaillat, Eliseo SD 11 *Dom.*
Espaillat, Ulises Francisco LD 85; SD 11 *Dom.*
España, Juan V 68 *Venez.*
España Núñez, J. M. V 68 *Venez.*
"Español Andante, El" (*pseud.*) E 27 *Ecua.*
Esparza, Miguel Ángel Ig 109; NM 19 *Mex.*
Esparza Martínez, Reinaldo PM 41 *Mex.*
Espasa, Ramón A 23 *Arg.*
Espejo, Francisco Javier Eugenio (1747-1795) AA II, 17, 83; BHLA 141; CG II, 179 *Ecua.*
Espejo, Jerónimo (1801-1889) LA VI, 1066 *Arg.*
Espejo, Juan Luis C 8; CG II, 179 *Chil.*
Espejo, María de los Ángeles PJC 70 *Cu.*
Espejo Ibáñez, Ángel Custodio C 8; CG II, 181; CLH 238; NC 359 *Chil.*
Espelozín, Eduardo V 68 *Venez.*
Esperón, Esteban E. PM 41 *Mex.*
Espinal, Valentín V 68 *Venez.*
Espíndola, Sofía (1904-) A 23; CG II, 184 *Arg.*
"Espinel, Juan de" (*pseud.*) *see* Marín Cañas, José
Espinel, Marcos B. E 27 *Ecua.*
Espino, Alfonso PS 262 *Salv.*
Espino, Lisandro (1861-) CG II, 184; Pan 7 *Pan.*
Espino, Rosa PMe I, 147 *Mex.*
1. Espínola, Francisco CG II, 184; HSLU III, pt 2, 10; LU 64, 676; PIU III, 275; U 6 *Uru.*
2. Espínola, Francisco (hijo) CG II, 184; HSLU III, pt 6, 48 *Uru.*
Espinosa *see also* Espinoza
Espinosa, Antonio R. Co 24 *Col.*
Espinosa, Aurelio R. E 27 *Ecua.*
"Espinosa, Enrique" (*pseud.*) *see* Glusberg, Samuel
Espinosa, García NL 212 *Nicar.*
Espinosa, Gervasio A 23 *Arg.*
Espinosa, Januario C 8; NC 119 *Chil.*
Espinosa, José María (1796?-1883) CG II, 185; Co 24 *Col.*
Espinosa, José Modesto (1833-1916) E 27; PLE 44 *Ecua.*
Espinosa, José Santiago C 47 *Chil.*
Espinosa, Juan CG II, 185; P 9 *Per.*
Espinosa, Julio (-1888) HLM 467; Ig 110; NM 19; TM 132 *Mex.*
Espinosa, Leoncio Ig 111; NM 19; PM 41 *Mex.*
Espinosa, Roberto (1842-) E 27; PE 312 *Ecua.*
Espinosa, Rodrigo TM 133 *Mex.*
Espinosa Altamirano, Horacio CA 68 *Guat.*
Espinosa Bustos, Anacleto C 8, 29; NC 120 *Chil.*
Espinosa de Cordero, Josefina E 39 *Ecua.*
Espinosa de los Monteros, Pedro P 9 *Per.*
Espinosa de los Monteros, Ramón ("Nomar") Cu 53, 120; TM 492, 500 *Cu.*

Espinosa de Rendón, Silveria (1815-1886) BC 144; CHL 349; CLH 299; Co 24 *Col.*
Espinosa Landaeta, Gabriel (1882-) CG II, 185; V 68; WLA 136 *Venez.*
Espinosa Manzón, Martín PM 41 *Mex.*
Espinosa Medrano, Juan de ("El Lunarejo") (1632-1688) BHLA 99, 110; CHL 27, 36; CLH 23; HPHA II, 189; LP 326; P 9 *Per.*
Espinosa Pólit, Aurelio PLE 126 *Ecua.*
Espinosa Saldaña, Adán ("Juan del Carpio") (1878-) BHLA 539; CHL 306; CLH 260; P 9; PPe 296; SASS 418 *Per.*
Espinosa Tamayo, Alfredo E 28, 74 *Ecua.*
Espinosa y Cutillas, Juan Pedro de Cu 53 *Cu.*
Espinosa y Socarrás, Fernando Cu 53 *Cu.*
Espinoza *see also* Espinosa
Espinoza, Enrique (1898-) WLA 137 *Arg.*
Espinoza, José Antonio V 69 *Venez.*
Espiñeira, Antonio (1855-1907) C 47, 48, 65; HC 253 *Chil.*
Esponda *see* Ezponda
Esquijarosa, Milagros P. PJC 71 *Cu.*
Esquirol, Ignacio Cu 53 *Cu.*
Esquiú, Mamerto (1826-1882) LA VII, 277 *Arg.*
Esquivel, José ARC 51 *Cu.*
Esquivel de la Guardia, Adolfo CA 18, 19; EPCR 417 *C.R.*
Esquivel Obregón, Toribio (1861-) CG II, 189; IE 82 *Mex.*
Esquivel Pren, José PM 41 *Mex.*
Estades, Avelino U 6 *Uru.*
"Estars, Duralis" (*pseud.*) *see* Barrios de los Ríos, José María
Este, Beatriz de Cu 53 *Cu.*
Esteban, Miguel Antonio Cu 53 *Cu.*
Estéevan, Alejandro C 8 *Chil.*
Esteller, Alfredo V 69 *Venez.*
Esteller, Antonia CG II, 199; V 69 *Venez.*
Esteller, Benito V 69 *Venez.*
Esténger, Rafael A. (1899-) Cu 53; PJC 73 *Cu.*
Estete, Miguel de CG II, 202; P 9 *Per.*
Esteva, Adalberto A. (1863-1914) AMP 317; CG II, 202; NM 19; PM 41; PMe I, 157 *Mex.*
Esteva, Guillermo A. APMM 46 *Mex.*
Esteva, José María (1818-1904) HLM 319; HLMex 152; Ig 111; NM 19; PM 41; PMe I, 177; TM 133 *Mex.*
Esteva, Roberto A. (1844-1899) HLM 466; Ig 112; NM 19; TM 133 *Mex.*
Esteva Ruiz, Roberto A. CG II, 202; TM 134 *Mex.*
Esteves, Felipe V 69 *Venez.*
Esteves, José de Jesús (187.-190.) BP 525; FPA 461, 490; PP 151; PR 35, 51 *P.R.*
Esteves, José Ignacio V 69 *Venez.*
Esteves, Juan D. V 69 *Venez.*
Estévez, Rafael Co 24 *Col.*
Estévez Travieso, José BDC 19; Cu 53 *Cu.*
Estévez y Valdés, Sofía Cu 53 *Cu.*
Estorch y Siqués, Miguel (1809-1868) BDC 19; Cu 53 *Cu.*
Estorino, Eusebio (1818-1902) Cu 53 *Cu.*

Estrada, Ángel de (hijo) (1872-1923) A 23; APAM 78; AT II, 939; CG II, 204; G 311; GLO 235; LAC 38, 130; PLHA 264; SPLA 254 *Arg.*

Estrada, Dardo CG II, 205; U 6; UL 126 *Uru.*

Estrada, Domingo (-1901) CA 68; Cu 53; FPA 291, 298; PG 230 *Guat.*

Estrada, Emilio E 28 *Ecua.*

Estrada, Francisco ACe 789; TM 588 *Mex.*

Estrada, Genaro (1887-1937) AMP 139; BAMP 91; BHLA 523, 558; CG II, 205; G 358; HLM 517, 527; IE 84; NM 19; PM 42; WLA 137 *Mex.*

Estrada, José Manuel (1843-1894) A 23; CG II, 205; HLA 435; LA VII, 360; Par 1 *Arg.*

Estrada, Juan Manuel Cu 54 *Cu.*

Estrada, Norberto CG II, 205; U 6; UL 126 *Uru.*

Estrada, Rafael APEH 1011; CA 19; EPCR 644 *C.R.*

Estrada, Santiago (1835-1892) A 24; CG II, 206; HLA 428; LA VIII, 629, 703, 915; SAL 110; SPLA 246 *Arg.*

Estrada, Temístocles J. E 28, 74 *Ecua.*

Estrada Paniagua, Felipe CA 69; CG II, 206 *Guat.*

Estrada y Ayala, Aurora E 28; PLE 121 *Ecua.*

Estrada y Cordero, Antonio TM 437 *Mex.*

Estrada y Cordero, Manuel TM 134, 438 *Mex.*

Estrada y Morales, Benjamín Cu 54 *Cu.*

Estrada y Zenea, Ildefonso (-1911) BDC 20; Cu 54; PM 42; TM 134 *Cu.*

Estrade, Eduardo C 54 *Chil.*

Estrella, Guillermo A 24; CG II, 207; LAC 134 *Arg.*

Estrella Gutiérrez, Fermín (1900-) A 24; APAM 480; BHLA 634; CG II, 207; LAC 145; LAS 206; WLA 138 *Arg.*

Etchart, Pablo A 24 *Arg.*

Etcheverts, Sara de A 24 *Arg.*

Etkin, Alberto M. A 24 *Arg.*

Eulate Sanjurjo, Carmela (1861-) CG II, 210; PR 26; QPR (2) 183 *P.R.*

Eusebio y de Diego, José HLNG II, 106

"Eva Angelina" *or* "Evangelina" (*pseud.*) *see* Cáceres, Zoila Aurora

Evia, Jacinto de (1620-) BHLA 97; CHL 26; CLH 22; E 28; HPHA II, 83; PE 268; PLE 13 *Ecua.*

Eyma, Javier (1816-1876) Cu 55 *Cu.*

Eyraud, José Hipólito C 48 *Chil.*

Eyzaguirre, José Ignacio Víctor CL 280 *Chil.*

Eyzaguirre S., J. Delfín B 8; GLO 239 *Bol.*

Ezcurra, E. de A 24; CG II, 214 *Arg.*

Ezcurra y Pardo, M. ("Muerdago") A 24, 78; CG II, 216 *Arg.*

Ezeta, Carlos NM 19 *Mex.*

Ezponda, Eduardo (1815-1887) Cu 53, 55 *Cu.*

F

F. F. P. Co 25 *Col.*

F. Ll. TM 141 *Mex.*

"F. M." (*pseud.*) *see* Medina, Filomeno

F. R. TM 141 *Mex.*

Fabela Alfaro, Isidro (1882-) CG II, 218; HLM 518; IE 85; NM 19; WLA 139 *Mex.*

Fabila, Alfonso G 358; Ig 113; NM 19 *Mex.*

Fabo y Campor, Pedro (1873-) CG II, 219; Co 24 *Col.*

Fabre, Joaquín BDC 20 *Cu.*

Fábrega, Demetrio (1881-) AP 93; Pan 7 *Pan.*

Fábrega, José Isaac CG II, 221; Pan 7 *Pan.*

Fábrega, Julio J. Pan 7 *Pan.*

Fábrega, Octavio AP 97; Pan 7 *Pan.*

Fábrega, Pedro (1872-) CG II, 221; Pan 7 *Pan.*

Fábrega de López, Sofía (1880-) Pan 7 *Pan.*

Facio, Justo A. (1859-1931) AP 101; BC 146; CA 19, 20; Co 24; EPCR 98; FPA 121, 124; Pan 7; PC 81 *Pan.-C.R.*

"Facundo" (*pseud.*) *see* Cuéllar, José Tomás de

Facha, José M. PM 42 *Mex.*

Fagetti, Juan A. (1898-) CG II, 224; IE 87 *Uru.*

Fait, Anny CA 20; IBCR IV, 285 *C.R.*

Fajardo, Carlos A. HCLU I, 361 *Uru.*

Fajardo, Elicier L. E 28 *Ecua.*

Fajardo, Heraclio C. (1833-1867) BHLA 312; CHL 212; CLH 175; HCLU I, 333; PIU I, 191; U 6; UL 126 *Uru.*

Fajardo, Luis V 69 *Venez.*

Fajardo Ortiz, Desiderio ("El Cautivo") (1862-1905) BDC 20; Cu 38, 55 *Cu.*

Falcao Espalter, Mario (1892-) CG II, 225; HSLU I, pt 2, 5; III, pt 4, 45; PIU III, 314; U 6; UL 126; UT 211 *Uru.*

Falco, Ángel (1885-) CG II, 225; HSLU II, pt 2, 24; IE 87; LU 64. 663; PIU II, 321; PU 72; U 6; UT 213; WLA 140 *Uru.*

Falco, Ricardo IBCR IV, 375 *C.R.*

Falcón, César CG II, 225; P 9 *Per.*

Falcón, Juan Crisóstomo V 69 *Venez.*

Falcón, Manuel Cu 55 *Cu.*

Falcón Roldán, Antonio NM 20; PM 42 *Mex.*

Falconí, Aurelio E 28; PE 23; PLE 86 *Ecua.*

Falconí Villagómez, Carlos E 28 *Ecua.*

Falconí Villagómez, J. A. PE 147 *Ecua.*

Falkner, Tomás (1707-1784) CG II, 227; LA IV, 604; SCL 419, 602 *Arg.*

Fálquez y Ampuero, Francisco J. (1880-) CG II, 227; E 28, 74; PE 79; PLE 91; WLA 141 *Ecua.*

"Falucho" (*pseud.*) *see* Bambill, Julio

Falla, Salvador CA 69 *Guat.*

Fallón, Diego (1834-1905) AC I, 103; AEHA 341; ALC I, 251; BC 146; BHLA 323; CHL 344; CLH 295; Co 24; FPA 82, 110; LC 161; PCo 93; RHLC 141; SASS 223 *Col.*

Fánger, Henrique V 69 *Venez.*
"Fanny Mery" (*pseud.*) *see* Emiliani, María
"Fardusi" (*pseud.*) C 8 *Chil.*
"Farfalla, Angélica" (*pseud.*) *see* Bourguet, Lola S. B. de
"Farfalla, V." (*pseud.*) *see* López-Portillo y Rojas, José
Farfán, Salvador PM 42 *Mex.*
Farfán Rosas, Joaquín PM 42 *Mex.*
Faría, Francisco María V 69 *Venez.*
Farías de Isassi, Teresa (1878-) CG II, 230; G 358; HLM 529; Ig 114; NM 20; TM 135 *Mex.*
Farina, Abel (-1921) Co 24 *Col.*
Fariña, Pío Alberto C 29 *Chil.*
Fariña Núñez, Eloy (1885-) FPA 402, 420; Par 11; PPa 197; PT 31 *Para.*
Farrera, Juan José V 69 *Venez.*
Farrés, Abelardo (-1906) Cu 56; PA 34; PCu 100 *Cu.*
Faura, Enrique CG II, 233; E 28 *Ecua.*
"Fausto" (*pseud.*) *see* Arocha, Pablo José
Febrés, Andrés BHC II, 573 *Chil.*
Febres Cordero, F. ("Hermano Miguel") (1854-) E 29 *Ecua.*
Febres Cordero, Joaquín L. E 29 *Ecua.*
Febres Cordero, Tulio (1860-) CG II, 236; LV 116, 416, 424; V 70; VPF 64; WLA 142 *Venez.*
Fehrmann, Juan Eduardo C 8, 29, 48; NC 120 *Chil.*
Feijóo, Samuel (1914-) PoC 64 *Cu.*
Feitoza, Isaac U 6 *Uru.*
"Felicia" (*pseud.*) *see* Auber, Virginia
Felipe, Gregorio A. SD 11 *Dom.*
Feliú, D. C 9; NC 499 *Chil.*
Feliú Cruz, Guillermo BHLA 618; C 65 *Chil.*
Fenochio, Arturo (1854-) Ig 115; NM 20; TM 136 *Mex.*
Fentanea, Benito PM 42 *Mex.*
Feo, Berta María CA 20; IBCR IV, 283, 357 *C.R.*
Feo, Ramón F. V 70 *Venez.*
Fermandois, José Luis ("Diablofuerte" or "Jotavé") C 9, 11; NC 117 *Chil.*
Fermandois Reyes, Mardoqueo C 9; NC 121 *Chil.*
Fermín Aycinena, Juan (1838-1898) PG 184 *Guat.*
"Fermín Pimentel y Vargas" (*pseud.*) *see* Camargo, Rafael María
Fernández, Cayetano CG II, 242; PM 42 *Mex.*
Fernández, Diego CG II, 242; HPHA II, 143; SCL 75, 602 *Per.*
Fernández, E. G. A 24 *Arg.*
1. Fernández, Emilio B 8 *Bol.*
2. Fernández, Emilio PM 42 *Mex.*
Fernández, Enrique ARC 51 *Cu.*
Fernández, Enrique W. (1858-) AC I, 345; II, 259; Co 24; PCo 108 *Col.*
Fernández, Eufrasio CG II, 256; Cu 56 *Cu.*
Fernández, Felipe A. A 24 *Arg.*
Fernández, Francisco BDC 20, 76; Cu 56 *Cu.*
Fernández, Francisco F. A 24, 83 *Arg.*
Fernández, H. V 70 *Venez.*
Fernández, Horacio A 24 *Arg.*

Fernández, J. C. A 24 *Arg.*
Fernández, José TM 136 *Mex.*
Fernández, Juan SCL 101, 602 *Per.*
Fernández, Juan de Dios BDC 20; Cu 56 *Cu.*
Fernández, Juan Patricio (1661-1733) Par 12; SCL 425, 602 *Para.*
Fernández, Juan Rómulo (1884-) A 24; CG II, 243; LAC 137; WLA 143 *Arg.*
Fernández, León CA 20; CG II, 256; EPCR 34 *C.R.*
Fernández, M. A 24 *Arg.*
Fernández, Manuel C 29 *Chil.*
1. Fernández, Manuel María ("Don Simón") V 67, 70 *Venez.*
2. Fernández, Manuel María (hijo) V 70 *Venez.*
Fernández, Mauro (1843-1905) CA 20; EPCR 35 *C.R.*
Fernández, Máximo (1859-) CA 20; CG II, 244; Cu 56 *C.R.*
Fernández, O. M. PR 51 *P.R.*
Fernández, Otelo J. CG II, 244; U 6 *Uru.*
Fernández, Pío C 48 *Chil.*
Fernández, Plácido José V 71 *Venez.*
Fernández, Rafael Antonio (1877-) CT 605 *Cu.*
Fernández, S. NM 20 *Mex.*
Fernández, Sabás V 71 *Venez.*
Fernández, Segundo A 24 *Arg.*
Fernández, Silvia (1857-) A 24 *Arg.*
Fernández, Trinidad (1830-1873) P 9 *Per.*
Fernández A., José M. Co 24 *Col.*
Fernández Alonso, Rodrigo A 25 *Arg.*
Fernández Arrondo, Ernesto (1897-) Cu 56; PoC 65 *Cu.*
Fernández Blanco, Antonio PR 45 *P.R.*
Fernández Bolandi, Tomás CA 20 *C.R.*
Fernández Bustamante, Adolfo TM 136 *Mex.*
Fernández Cabrera, Manuel CG II, 251; Cu 56 *Cu.*
Fernández Concha, Carlos C 29 *Chil.*
Fernández Córdova, Miguel Ángel CG II, 254; E 29 *Ecua.*
Fernández Coria, José A 25 *Arg.*
Fernández Cuesta, Nemesio CG II, 254; V 34, 71 *Venez.*
Fernández de Agüero y Echave, Juan Manuel APA I, xix, 5 *Arg.*
Fernández de Alfaro y Ramayo, María de Jesús PM 42 *Mex.*
Fernández de Campino, José SCL 512, 603 *Chil.*
Fernández de Castro, Jerónimo P 9 *Per.*
Fernández de Castro, José Cu 56 *Cu.*
Fernández de Castro, José Antonio (1897-) BDC 21; CG II, 253; Cu 56; IE 91; LH 115, 127 *Cu.*
Fernández de Castro, Rafael (1856-1920) Cu 56, 90; HLC 85; RLC 230, 236, 346 *Cu.*
Fernández de Córdova, Ignacio (1777-1816) ACe 791 *Mex.*
Fernández de Córdova Uriguen, Eliseo E 29 *Ecua.*
Fernández de Echeverría y Veytia, Mariano (1718-1779) ACe 663; HLM 88, 202 *Mex.*
Fernández de García Huidobro, M. Luisa C 9 *Chil.*

Fernández de (la) Lande, Pámela ("Rafaela") BDC 21; Cu 56, 136 *Cu.*

Fernández de la Puente, J. L. A 25 *Arg.*

Fernández de la Puente, Luis Fernán Par 12 *Para.*

Fernández de Lara, José (1840-1895) Ig 116; NM 20 *Mex.*

Fernández de Lizardi, José Joaquín ("El Pensador Mexicano") (1776-1827) AB 22; ACe 265; AMP 226; BAMP 23; BHLA 172, 174, 198; CG II, 268; CHL 103; CLH 87; G 358; GLO 248; HLM 262; HLMex 108; HPM 485; Ig 117; NM 20; PM 42, 65; PMe I, 187; SASS 393; TM 137; WSAL 13 *Mex.*

Fernández de los Reyes, A. A 25; CG II, 280 *Arg.*

Fernández de Madrid, José TM 492, 498 *Mex.*

Fernández de Mujía, Hercilla (*or* Heraclia) (1860-) B 8; BT 119 *Bol.*

Fernández de Oviedo y Valdés, Gonzalo (1478-1557) BHC I, 14; CG II, 275; HLM 34; HPHA I, 291; LA III, 99; SCL 37, 41, 603 *Sp.*

Fernández de Palazuelos, Antonio BHC III, 217 *Chil.*

Fernández de Piedrahita, Lucas (1624-1688) BHLA 65; Co 24; HLNG I, 202; LC 83; RHLC 14; SCL 212, 348, 604 *Col.*

Fernández de Quirós, Pedro (1565-) SCL 323, 604 *Port.-Per.*

Fernández de San Salvador, Agustín Pomposo (1756-1842) ACe 113; HLM 249; PM 42; TM 588 *Mex.*

Fernández de Soto, Mario (1899-) Co 24 *Col.*

Fernández de Soto, Pacífica CA 20 *C.R.*

Fernández de Sotomayor, Juan (1777-1849) Co 24; HLNG II, 543 *Col.*

Fernández de Tinoco, María ("Apaikán") CA 4, 20, 21; EPCR 341; IBCR IV, 83 *C.R.*

Fernández de Valenzuela, Pedro (-1660) Co 24; HLNG I, 163 *Col.*

Fernández de Velasco, Antonio Cu 56 *Cu.*

Fernández del Castillo, Francisco (1864-) CG II, 252; WLA 143 *Mex.*

Fernández del Rincón, Ramón (1736-1807) ACe 793 *Mex.*

Fernández Duque, L. A 25, 84 *Arg.*

Fernández Duro, Cesáreo CG II, 255; Cu 56 *Cu.*

Fernández Espadero, J. A 25 *Arg.*

Fernández Espiro, Diego (1872?-1912) A 25; APAM 90; CG II, 255; LA VIII, 557; SPLA 105 *Arg.*

Fernández Ferraz, Juan (1849-) CA 21; IBCR IV, 386 *C.R.*

Fernández Ferraz, Valeriano ("Hermógenes Novo") (1831-1929) CA ·21, 40; IBCR IV, 108 *C.R.*

Fernández Ferraz v. de Salazar, Juana CA 22, 25; IBCR IV, 99 *C.R.*

Fernández García, A. A 25 *Arg.*

Fernández García, Alejandro (1880-) SASS 533; V 71; VPF 201; WLA 144 *Venez.*

Fernández García, Eugenio PR 45 *P.R.*

Fernández González, Alfredo A 25 *Arg.*

Fernández Granados, Enrique ("Fernángrana") (1867-1920) AMP 43; CG II, 262; G 358; HLM 408; HLMex 219; PM 43; PMe I, 185; PNM 79; PoM 379 *Mex.*

Fernández Guardia, León CA 22; G 332 *C.R.*

Fernández Guardia, Ricardo (1867-) BHLA 526; CA 22, 23, 24; CG II, 262; CHL 508; EPCR 102; G 332; IBCR IV, 20, 257, 392 *et passim C.R.*

Fernández Güell, Rogelio (1883-1918) CA 24, 25; CG II, 262; EPCR 422; PC 119 *C.R.*

Fernández Juncos, Manuel (1846-) BP 499, 595; CG II, 265; CHL 503; CLH 443; PA 189; PP 157; PR 6, 9, 18, 24, 25, 42, 51, 52, 58 *P.R.*

Fernández Lechuga, Antonio PM 43 *Mex.*

Fernández Ledesma, Enrique (1888-) APMM 47; G 358; HLM 523; PM 43; PNM 324 *Mex.*

Fernández Ledesma, Gabriel CG II, 205; TM 543 *Mex.*

Fernández López, Manuel CG II, 268; Cu 56 *Cu.*

Fernández Mac-Gregor, Genaro (1883-) CG II, 269; G 359; HLM 518; Ig 127; NM 22; TM 543; WLA 144 *Mex.*

Fernández Madrid, José (1789-1830) AEHA 894; BC 147; BHLA 158; CHL 83; CLH 69; Co 24; HLNG II, 87, 214, 327; HPHA II, 39; LC 112; RHLC 53; SCL 545, 603 *Col.*

Fernández Madrid, Pedro (1817-1875) Co 25; CoL 268; LC 156; RHLC 110 *Col.*

Fernández Martínez, Luis TM 139, 196 *Mex.*

Fernández Mascaró, Guillermo (1872-) CG II, 270; CT 525 *Cu.*

Fernández Mato, Ramón CG II, 270; Co 29 *Col.*

Fernández Mendoza, Edmundo Ig 130; NM 22 *Mex.*

Fernández Montalva, Ricardo (1866-1899) C 9, 29, 48; HC 220; NC 121, 420; PCh 135 *Chil.*

Fernández Montalva, Samuel C 9, 29, 48; CG II, 271; NC 121; PCh 319 *Chil.*

Fernández Montes, José BP 526; PR 35 *P.R.*

Fernández Montúfar, Joaquín CA 25 *C.R.*

Fernández Mora, Carlos CA 25; IBCR IV, 344 *C.R.*

Fernández Moreno, A. CG II, 272; G 311 *Arg.*

Fernández Moreno, Baldomero (1886-) A 25; APAM 274; APEH 864, 1191; BHLA 530; CG II, 272; CHL 186; GLO 237; LAC 75, 142; NPA 127 *Arg.*

Fernández Morúa, Juan ("Juan Calvini") CA 9, 25; IBCR IV, 417 *C.R.*

Fernández N., Alfredo C 48 *Chil.*

Fernández Ortelano, Manuel HPHA II, 340; SCL 551, 604 *Chil.*

Fernández Ossorio, Alonso PM 43 *Mex.*

Fernández Ossorio, Pedro PM 43 *Mex.*

Fernández Otelo, J. PU 269 *Uru.*

Fernández Peralta, Ricardo CA 25; EPCR 562 *C.R.*

Fernández Pesquero, Javier C 9; CG II, 277 *Chil.*
Fernández Ríos, Ovidio CG II, 280; PU 89; U 6 *Uru.*
Fernández Rodella, Francisco C 48 *Chil.*
Fernández Rodríguez Cu 56 *Cu.*
Fernández Rodríguez, León CA 25 *C.R.*
Fernández Saavedra, Manuel (1796-1877) BC 151; Co 25 *Col.*
Fernández Salazar, Santiago ARC 51 *Cu.*
Fernández Sánchez, M. Par 12 *Para.*
Fernández Serrano, Tomás Ig 130; NM 22 *Mex.*
Fernández Silva, Berta E. C 29 *Chil.*
Fernández Soto, Francisco Cu 56 *Cu.*
Fernández Valdés, Manuel (1870-) Cu 56 *Cu.*
Fernández Vanga, E. PP 225 *P.R.*
Fernández Vázquez, Santiago C 29 *Chil.*
Fernández Villa, Ignacio TM 139 *Mex.*
Fernández y Díaz, Jesús María Cu 57 *Cu.*
Fernández y Fernández, José Cu 57 *Cu.*
Fernández y González, José CG II, 261; NM 22 *Mex.*
Fernández y González, Manuel CG II, 261; E 29 *Ecua.*
Fernández y Medina, Benjamín (1873-) CG II, 271; G 386; PIU II, 28; U 6; UL 127; UT 217; WLA 144 *Uru.*
Fernández y Menéndez, Rafael Antonio (1877-) WLA 146 *Cu.*
Fernández y Real, María Luisa Cu 57 *Cu.*
Fernández y Vega, Wilfredo (1881-) CT 323 *Cu.*
"Fernando de Ayala" (*pseud.*) *see* Ortega, Simón
"Fernando Jules Zea" (*pseud.*) *see* Alú Fernández, José
"Fernángrana" (*pseud.*) *see* Fernández Granados, Enrique
Fernás-Isern, A. P 35 *Per.*
Ferrada Labatut, Luis C 9 *Chil.*
Ferrand La Toison d'Or, Ángel Cu 57 *Cu.*
Ferrando, Federico PIU II, 39 *Uru.*
Ferrant, Natalia B. de Cu 57 *Cu.*
Ferrari, Antonio Rubén A 25; G 311 *Arg.*
Ferrari, Arístides de C 9; NC 122 *Chil.*
Ferrari, Trinidad (1836-) HL I, 791 *Hond.*
Ferrari Amores, Alfonso A 25 *Arg.*
Ferraría, Mayorino NPA 286 *Arg.*
Ferraz v. de Salazar, Juana *see* Fernández Ferraz v. de Salazar, Juana
Ferreira, Elvira A 25 *Arg.*
Ferreira, Francisco BHC I, 493 *Chil.*
Ferreira, Mariano (1834-) CG II, 296; UT 225 *Uru.*
Ferreira, Rosendo PU 267 *Uru.*
Ferreira y Artigas, Fermín (1837-1872) HCLU I, 364; PIU I, 194 *Uru.*
Ferreira y Correa, Eduardo (1869-) HSLU III, pt 4, 33; PIU II, 32; U 7; UL 127; UT 221; WLA 147 *Uru.*
Ferreiro, Alfredo Mario LU 64, 668; PIU III, 210; U 7 *Uru.*
Ferreiro, José M. PU 271 *Uru.*
Ferrel, José Ig 130; NM 22 *Mex.*
Ferrer, Elvira A 25 *Arg.*
Ferrer, Fidel SD 11 *Dom.*
Ferrer, Jesús Alfonso V 71 *Venez.*

Ferrer, Luis Cu 57 *Cu.*
Ferrer Buenaventura, Ventura Pascual (1772-1851) Cu 57; RLC 43, 146 *Cu.*
Ferrer Hernández (Fernández), Gabriel (1847-) BDC 21; PA 183; PP 209; PR 12, 18, 35, 52 *P.R.*
Ferrera, Francisco (1800-1852) HL I, 141 *Hond.*
Ferretis, Jorge LAS 204
Ferreyra, Alfredo D. A 25 *Arg.*
Ferreyra Díaz, Horacio A 25; CG II, 304 *Arg.*
Ferreyros, César E. LAS 206 *Per.*
Ferro Collazos, L. E. Co 25 *Col.*
Ferrufino, Juan Bautista Par 12 *Para.*
"Festivo, Oportuno" (*pseud.*) Cu 57 *Cu.*
Feuillet, Tomás Martín (1834-1862) AP 105; FPA 381, 383; Pan 7, 8 *Pan.*
Fiallo, Fabio F. (1865-) APEH 137; BHLA 457; CG II, 309; CHL 497; CLH 437; FPA 228, 247; G 385; LAND 143; LAS 204, 206; LD 93; PA 299; PD 73; SASS 317; SD 11 *Dom.*
Fiallo Cabral, Arístides CG II, 309; SD 12 *Dom.*
Fiallos, E. Constantino (1861-) HL I, 775 *Hond.*
Fiansón, José (189.-) FPA 436, 454 *Per.*
"Fidel" (*pseud.*) *see* Prieto, Guillermo
Fiel, León Federico A 25 *Arg.*
"Fierabas" (*pseud.*) *see* Sanz, J.
Fierro, Humberto E 29; PE 105; PLE 104 *Ecua.*
"Figarete" (*pseud.*) *see* Bravo, Bernabé
"Figarillo" (*pseud.*) *see* Alberdi, Juan Bautista
Figarola-Caneda, Domingo (1852-1926) CG II, 311; CHL 441; CLH 383; CT 91; Cu 57; GLO 242; RLC 352 *Cu.*
Figueira, Gastón (1905-) CG II, 312; G 386; IE 92; LAS 206; PU 272; U 7 *Uru.*
Figueira, José Henríques (1860-) CG II, 312; UT 235 *Uru.*
Figuer del Valle, José CA 26; CG II, 312; IBCR IV, 212 *C.R.*
Figuera Montes de Oca, M. V 71 *Venez.*
Figueredo, Carlos B. V 71 *Venez.*
Figueredo, Fernando (1846-1929) Cu 57; RLC 274, 344 *Cu.*
Figueredo Cisneros, Pedro (1816-1870) Cu 58 *Cu.*
Figueredo Lora, Viriato CA 26 *C.R.*
Figuerero, Jacinto A. A 25 *Arg.*
Figuerero, Manuel V. (1865-) AT I, 463; CG II, 313; WLA 148 *Arg.*
Figueroa (Licenciado) PR 45 *P.R.*
Figueroa, A. Cu 58 *Cu.*
Figueroa, Esperanza (1913-) PoC 67 *Cu.*
Figueroa, Francisco de (1612-1666) CG II, 314; Co 25; HLNG I, 237; RHLC 14 *Col.*
Figueroa, José Hernán A 25 *Arg.*
Figueroa, José Tomás TM 140 *Mex.*
Figueroa, Pedro Pablo C 9, 30, 65; CG II, 314; CL 281; Cu 58; NC 122, 362, 420 *Chil.*
Figueroa, Rodulfo PM 43 *Mex.*
Figueroa, Sotero (-1922) ARC 51; BDC 111; Cu 58; PR 9, 12 *Cu.-P.R.?*
Figueroa, Virgilio C 65; CG II, 314 *Chil.*

Figueroa y Miranda, Miguel (1851-1893) ARC 77; HLC 83; LAS 199; RLC 230, 231 *Cu.*

Figueros, Isabel A 25 *Arg.*

Filacciani, Domingo E 29 *Ecua.*

Filartigas, Juan M. CG II, 315; HSLU III, pt 6, 40; PIU III, 306; U 7 *Uru.*

Filatti, Rosa (1895-) CG II, 315; WLA 148 *Mex.*

Filio, Carlos TM 544 *Mex.*

Filomeno y Ponce de León, Francisco (-1835) BDC 21; Cu 58 *Cu.*

Finalés, Amado ARC 51 *Cu.*

Fingerit, Julio A 25; CG II, 316; LAC 60, 135 *Arg.*

Fingerit, Marcos A 26 *Arg.*

Finol, Guillermo V 71 *Venez.*

Finol, Sisoes V 71 *Venez.*

Finoqueto, Juan J. Par 12 *Para.*

Finot, Enrique (1891-) B 8; BT 121; CG II, 318; WLA 149 *Bol.*

Finot Franco, Emilio (1886-1905) B 8, 13; PB 124 *Bol.*

Fiorito, Francisco B. CG II, 319; U 7 *Uru.*

Flachebba, Alberto TM 606 *Mex.*

Flamenco, José (1865-1918) CA 69; PG 327 *Guat.*

"Flavio" (*pseud.*) *see* Noli Bautista, Antonio

Flax, Edmond A 26 *Arg.*

"Flor, Serafín de la" (*pseud.*) *see* Torres y Feria, Manuel

"Flor Daliza" (*pseud.*) *see* Moll, Mercedes

Florencia, Francisco de (1620-) HLM 208 *Mex.*

"Florencio" (*pseud.*) Cu 58 *Cu.*

Flores *see also* Flórez

Flores, Alejandro C 30 *Chil.*

Flores, Antonio (1833-) E 29, 74 *Ecua.*

Flores, Augusto G 311 *Arg.*

Flores, Benjamín TM 140 *Mex.*

Flores, Carlos Alberto CG II, 327; E 29 *Ecua.*

Flores, Diego de P 9 *Per.*

Flores, Domingo (1825-1864) CA 69; GPCA II, 41; PG 145 *Guat.*

Flores, Enrique E 29 *Ecua.*

Flores, Esteban APMM 50; PNM 326 *Mex.*

"Flores, Georgina de" (*pseud.*) *see* Rencurrell, Georgina

Flores, J. A. PN 243 *Nicar.*

Flores, Joaquín TM 438 *Mex.*

Flores, Jorge C 30 *Chil.*

Flores, José PM 43 *Mex.*

Flores, Juan José (1801-1864) CHL 82, 313; CLH 69; E 29; V 71 *Ecua.*

Flores, Juan Vicente ARC 39 *Cu.*

Flores, Lorenzo Cu 58 *Cu.*

Flores, Luis R. (1860-) CA 26; EPCR 110 *C.R.*

Flores, Manuel (1853-1924) HLM 497; HLMex 222, 239 *Mex.*

Flores, Manuel María (1840-1885) AEHA 355; AMP 272; BHLA 334; CG II, 327; CHL 401; CLH 348; G 359; HLM 394; HLMex 195; HPHA I, 163; HPM 882; PM 43; PMe I, 189; PoM 174; SASS 357; WSAL 45, 75 *Mex.*

"Flores, Martín" (*pseud.*) *see* Cione, Otto Miguel

Flores, Zoilo B 8 *Bol.*

Flores Aguirre, Jesús (1904-) PM 44 *Mex.*

Flores Alatorre, Francisco (1838-1897) Ig 131; NM 22 *Mex.*

Flores Alatorre, José Martín (1760-1805) ACe 796 *Mex.*

Flores Arenas, Guillermo PM 44 *Mex.*

Flores Chinarro, Francisco P 9 *Per.*

Flores de León, Diego BHC II, 246 *Chil.*

Flores Fernández, L. C 9; NC 123 *Chil.*

Flores Jijón, Antonio (1833-) E 29 *Ecua.*

Flores Maciel, Ignacio TM 140 *Mex.*

Flores Magón, Ricardo TM 140 *Mex.*

Flores Parra, José Ig 132; NM 22 *Mex.*

Flores Villar, Mariano Ig 132; NM 22 *Mex.*

Flores y Caamaño, Alfredo (1888-) CG II, 327; E 30; WLA 150 *Ecua.*

Flores y Galindo, Federico P 9 *Per.*

Flores y Oliva, Isabel (1586-1617) LP 312 *Per.*

Flores Z., J. Augusto NL 132 *Nicar.*

Flórez, Adolfo (-1895) Co 25 *Col.*

Flórez, Julio (1867-1923) AC I, 359; II, 277; ALC I, 389; BC 154; BHLA 431; CG II, 328; CHL 348; Co 25; G 329; LC 185; PCo 108; PLHA 77; RHLC 147; SASS 230; V 71 *Col.*

Flórez, Leónidas (1862-1892) Co 26 *Col.*

Flórez, Manuel de Jesús (1857-1896?) AC I, 367; BC 154; Co 26 *Col.*

Flórez Álvarez, Leónidas (1888-) CG II, 328; Co 26 *Col.*

Flórez de Ocaris (Ocáriz), Juan Co 26; HLNG I, 218; RHLC 15; SCL 353, 604 *Col.*

Florián, Dr. Par 12 *Para.*

Floridio, M. G. y Cu 58 *Cu.*

"Florimel" (*pseud.*) *see* Pichardo y Arredondo, Próspero

"Florisel" (*pseud.*) *see* Alcázar, Ricardo de

Florit de Roldán, Jorge Cu 58 *Cu.*

Florit y Sánchez de Fuentes, Eugenio (1903-) Cu 58; LH 126; PoC 72; WLA 150 *Cu.*

Floro Costa, Ángel CG II, 330; U 7; UL 127 *Uru.*

"Fogonero, Simón" (*pseud.*) C 9 *Chil.*

Fojas, Claudio A 26 *Arg.*

Fombona, Evaristo SAL 309; V 71 *Venez.*

Fombona Pachano, Jacinto BHLA 582; V 71 *Venez.*

Fombona Palacio, Manuel (1857-1903) AEHA 895; BHLA 433; CHL 375; CLH 322; LV 313; V 72 *Venez.*

Foncerrada y Ulibarri, Melchor ACe 797 *Mex.*

Foncueva, Esteban (1881-) Cu 58; PCu 102 *Cu.*

Fonseca, Amílcar V 72 *Venez.*

Fonseca, Doroteo (1869-) HL II, 663 *Hond.*

Fonseca, José Félix V 72 *Venez.*

Font, J. G. *see* González Font, José

Font, Ramón (1885-) CG II, 343; Cu 58 *Cu.*

Font y Barrena, Anselmo ARC 51 *Cu.*

Fontanarrosa, D. A 26 *Arg.*
Fontanella, Agustín A 26, 84 *Arg.*
Fontanilles y Quintanilla, Francisco Cu 58 *Cu.*
Fontanus, Andreas Didacus PM 44 *Mex.*
Fontecilla, Ignacio C 48 *Chil.*
Fontecilla Larraín, Arturo C 65 *Chil.*
Fontela, José A. UL 127 *Uru.*
Foppa, Tito Livio A 26, 84; CG II, 346 *Arg.*
Forero, Manuel José (1902-) Co 26; RHLC 201 *Col.*
Forero, Salomón (1838-) Co 26 *Col.*
Forero Román, Luis Co 26 *Col.*
Formas, Adolfo NC 424 *Chil.*
Fornaris, José (1827-1890) AEHA 895; BDC 21; BHLA 329; CHL 458; CLH 400; Cu 58; HLC 133; HPHA I, 288; PA 36; PCu 103; RLC 147, 191, 194, 207, 244, 245 *Cu.*
Foronda y Pinto, Ana María de HSLU II, pt 8, 20 *Uru.*
Fors, Luis Ricardo A 26; BDC 23; CG II, 350; Cu 59 *Cu.*
Fort, Gustavo PA 196; PP 251 *P.R.*
Fortín, Julio César (1866-1894) HL II, 587 *Hond.*
Fortín, Miguel A. (1863-) HL II, 439 *Hond.*
Fortique, Ana Guadelupe V 72 *Venez.*
Fortique, José F. V 72 *Venez.*
Fortique, L. César V 72 *Venez.*
Fortoul, Vicente V 72 *Venez.*
Fortoul Hurtado, Pedro V 72 *Venez.*
Fortuny Salvadó, José Cu 59 *Cu.*
Fortuño Sellés, Ramón (1889-) BP 526, 597; PR 35; QPR (2) 71 *P.R.*
Fossey, Mathieu de CG II, 353; TM 493 *Mex.*
Fournier, Ricardo CA 26; EPCR 566 *C.R.*
Foussats, Hebe A 26 *Arg.*
Foxá, Francisco Javier de (1816-) BDC 23; Cu 59 *Cu.*
Foxá y Lecanda, Narciso de (1822-1883) CHL 500; CLH 432, 440; Cu 59; HLC 142; HPHA I, 339; PR 35; RLC 193 *Cu.*
Fraccaroli, Arturo A 26, 84 *Arg.*
Fraga, Ventura C 9; CG II, 355; NC 123 *Chil.*
Fragachán, Félix R. V 72 *Venez.*
Fragueiro, Mariano (1795-1872) LA VI, 873 *Arg.*
Fragueiro, Rafael (1864-1914) A 26; CG II, 355; CHL 222; CLH 185 *Arg.*
Fragueiro-Olivera, Magdalena G 311 *Arg.*
Francasci, Amelia CG II, 356; SD 12 *Dom.*
Franceschi, Gustavo J. (1881-) AT II, 873 *Arg.*
Francia, Felipe CG II, 359; V 72 *Venez.*
Francisco, Julio de (1864-1903) Co 26; RHLC 151 *Col.*
Francisco, Ricardo de (1849-) BC 154; Co 26 *Col.*
Franck, Doctor BP 503; PR 26, 55, 56 *P.R.*
Franck, Francisco Javier (-1868) BDC 23; Cu 60 *Cu.*
Franco, Agustín José Ig 133; NM 22 *Mex.*
Franco, Alberto A 26 *Arg.*

Franco, Luis L. (1898-) A 26; APAM 484; APEH 988; G 311; IE 94; LAC 144; NPA 215 *Arg.*
Franco, Pedro B. A 71; CG II, 361 *Arg.*
Franco, Persio C. SD 12 *Dom.*
Franco, Ramón N. PM 44; TM 142 *Mex.*
Franco Bidó, Augusto SD 12 *Dom.*
Franco Quijano, J. F. CG II, 362; V 72 *Venez.*
Franco V., Constancio (1842-) BC 155; Co 26 *Col.*
Franchi, Alfredo C. ("Alfredo de Lery") CG II, 364; PU 96 *Uru.*
Franchi, Paolino TM 493 *Mex.*
Franchi Alfaro de H. Dávila, Luisa de (-1871) Cu 60 *Cu.*
Franchi Alfaro y Lemaur, Antonio ("Un Magistrado Cubano") Cu 60, 99 *Cu.*
Franky, Guillermo Co 27 *Col.*
Frau Marsal, Lorenzo (1885-) BDC 24; CT 523 *Cu.*
Fray Apenta C 65 *Chil.*
"Fray Candil" (*pseud.*) *see* Bobadilla, Emilio
"Fray Colas" (*pseud.*) *see* Martínez, Luis A.
"Fray Concierto" (*pseud.*) PR 18, 35 *P.R.*
"Fray K. Brito" (*pseud.*) *see* López Loayza, Fernando
"Fray Linterna" (*pseud.*) *see* Cichero, Félix Esteban
"Fray Mocho" (*pseud.*) *see* Álvarez, José Sixto
"Fray Tabarra" (*pseud.*) *see* Comallonga y Mena, José
"Fray Tomás" (*pseud.*) *see* Vidrio, Tomás L.
"Fray Verdades" (*pseud.*) *see* Arcos y Segovia, Luis de
Frean Amavet, José A 26 *Arg.*
Fregeiro, Clemente L. (1853-) AT II, 718; CG II, 367 *Arg.*
Fregones, Arnoldo A 26; CG II, 367 *Arg.*
Freire, Alberto J. CG II, 367; U 7 *Uru.*
Freire, Javier U 7 *Uru.*
Freire de Jaimes, Carolina LB 593; P 9
Freire Esteves, Gómez (1886-) Par 13; PPa 153 *Para.*
Freire Silvar, J. CG II, 367; U 7 *Uru.*
Freites Roque, Arturo LD 101; SD 12 *Dom.*
French, Alfredo A 26 *Arg.*
Fresneda, José Ricardo PCu 106 *Cu.*
Freyre *see also* Jaimes Freyre
Freyre Arango, Eugenio Cu 60 *Cu.*
Frías, A. C 9; NC 498 *Chil.*
Frías, Carlos Eduardo V 72 *Venez.*
Frías, Félix (1816-1881) A 26; CG II, 369; GEA XIII; LA VI, 623 *Arg.*
Frías, José D. (1891-) AMP 143; APMM 54; Cu 60; HLM 524; PNM 327 *Mex.*
Frías, Juan Antonio (1835-187.) ARC 34 *Cu.*
Frías, Valentín F. ("Alter") NM 23 *Mex.*
Frías Beltrán, Gonzalo PM 45 *Mex.*
Frías Collao, B. C 9; NC 425 *Chil.*
Frías Fernández, Luis TM 131, 142 *Mex.*
Frías y Soto, Heriberto (1870-1925) CG II, 369; CHL 428; HLM 457; HLMex 226; Ig 133; NM 22; TM 142 *Mex.*

Frías y Soto, Hilarión (-1895) CG II, 370; CLH 356; Ig 137; NM 23; TM 143 *Mex.*

Frías y Soto, Luciano TM 143 *Mex.*

Frimont Herrera, Celestino *see* Herrera Frimont, Celestino

"Frollo, Claudio" (*pseud.*) *see* Luchichí, Ignacio M.

Frontaura, Rafael BHLA 549; C 9, 45 *Chil.*

Frontaura Arana, José Manuel C 9; NC 425 *Chil.*

Frontaura Argandoña, Manuel (1906-) WLA 153 *Bol.*

Frugoni, Emilio (1881-) APEH 830, 1191; BHLA 498; CG II, 372; G 387; IE 95; HSLU II, pt 2, 32; LU 64, 667, 681; PIU III, 158; PLHA 157; U 7; UT 241 *Uru.*

Frydensberg, Adolfo V 72 *Venez.*

"Fuego" (*pseud.*) *see* Sánchez Arce, Abraham

Fuenmayor, Alejandro V 72 *Venez.*

Fuenmayor, Ángel V 72 *Venez.*

Fuenmayor, Juan C. V 72 *Venez.*

Fuensanta, Emiro CA 69 *Guat.*

Fuente, Antonio de la PM 45; TM 144 *Mex.*

Fuente, Nicanor de la BAP 113 *Per.*

Fuentes, Calistro U 7 *Uru.*

Fuentes, Filadelfo J. CA 69 *Guat.*

Fuentes, Hildebrando P 10 *Per.*

Fuentes, Juan Bautista P 10 *Per.*

Fuentes, Julio Ig 138; NM 23 *Mex.*

Fuentes, Manuel Atanasio ("El Murciélago") (1820-) AEHA 895; BHLA 320; P 10; PPe 32 *Per.*

Fuentes, Mariano CA 69; CG II, 375 *Guat.*

Fuentes, Miguel A. TM 144 *Mex.*

Fuentes, Rafael, Jr. TM 544 *Mex.*

Fuentes, Vicente V 72 *Venez.*

Fuentes C., Víctor CA 69 *Guat.*

Fuentes Carrillo, E. Cu 60 *Cu.*

Fuentes Castro, Paulino (1854-) P 10 *Per.*

Fuentes Vallejo, Victorino ACe 798 *Mex.*

Fuentes y Betancourt, Emilio de los Santos Cu 60; RLC 241 *Cu.*

Fuentes y Matous, Laureano (1822-1898) Cu 60 *Cu.*

Fuenzalida Grandón, Alejandro (1865-) C 66; CG II, 376; CL 284; WLA 154 *Chil.*

Fülöp-Miller, René CG II, 377; TM 547 *Mex.*

Funck de Fernández, María B. (1841-1904) Pan 8 *Pan.*

Funes, Celestina A 26 *Arg.*

Funes, Enrique López (1851-1904) Cu 61 *Cu.*

Funes, Gregorio (1749-1829) A 26; BHLA 166; CHL 56; CLH 47; HLA 166; LA IV, 779; V, 122; Par 1 *Arg.*

Furcy Pichardo, J. SD 12 *Dom.*

Furlong, P. A 73 *Arg.*

Furlong Cardiff, Guillermo (1889-) CG II, 378; Par 2; WLA 154 *Uru.*

Furt, Jorge M. A 26, 71; CG II, 378 *Arg.*

Fuselli, Angélica A 26 *Arg.*

G

G., J. A. E 30 *Ecua.*

G., J. V. E 31 *Ecua.*

G., L. A. Cu 61 *Cu.*

G. P. TM 547 *Mex.*

G. de Fortín, Celia C 30 *Chil.*

G. y Grave de Peralta, Fernando Cu 61 *Cu.*

Gabard, Bernardo U 7 *Uru.*

"Gabriel de Rimur" (*pseud.*) *see* Gómez, Santiago Carlos

Gabriel López, José (1896-) A 26; BHLA 631; WLA 155 *Arg.*

Gabriela, María PM 45 *Mex.*

"Gabriela Mistral" (*pseud.*) *see* Godoy Alcayaza, Lucila

Gabrielli, Ada (1912-) PoC 84 *Cu.*

Gabutti y Fausto, Miguel R. PR 33 *P.R.*

Gacitúa, Juan Nepomuceno C 48 *Chil.*

Gache, Alberto I. A 26; CG II, 386 *Arg.*

Gache, Roberto (1891-) A 26, 84; AT II, 679; CG II, 386; CHL 199; LAC 117, 154; PLHA 218 *Arg.*

Gagini, Carlos (1865-1929) CA 26, 27; CG II, 386; CHL 508; CLH 449; EPCR 115; IBCR IV, 12, 161, 395 *et passim C.R.*

Gaitán, José B. (1827-) BC 159 *Col.*

Gaitán, José María Ángel RHLC 121 *Col.*

Gaitán, Julio C. Co 27; PCo 118 *Col.*

Gaitán, Pantaleón Co 27 *Col.*

Gajardo, Oscar C 30 *Chil.*

Gajardo Cruzat, Pablo C 30 *Chil.*

Galán, Ángel María (1836-) BC 160; CG II, 387; Co 27 *Col.*

Galano, Francisco C 9 *Chil.*

Galarraga de Salazar, Concepción Cu 61 *Cu.*

Galarreta, Luis Adam Cu 61 *Cu.*

Galdames, Luis C 30; CG II, 389 *Chil.*

Gali, Arturo (1873-) Cu 61 *Cu.*

Galicchio, Domingo PU 273 *Uru.*

Galicia, Vicente A. TM 145, 440, 441 *Mex.*

Galíndez, Bartolomé (1896-) A 27; APAM 493; CG II, 391; G 311 *Arg.*

Galíndez, J. M. CG II, 391; V 73 *Venez.*

Galindo, Aníbal (1834-1901) Co 27; LC 170; RHLC 197 *Col.*

Galindo, Francisco E. (1850-1900) CHL 507; CLH 448; GPCA III, 67 *Salv.*

Galindo, Humberto Ig 138; NM 23; TM 130, 146 *Mex.*

Galindo, Marco Aurelio CG II, 392; Ig 138; NM 23; TM 146, 441 *Mex.*

Galindo, Miguel (1881-) G 359; IE 96; Ig 139; NM 2, 23; PM 45; TM 544, 619 *Mex.*

Galindo, Néstor (1830-1865) B 8; CHL 310; CLH 262; GLO 239; HPHA II, 285; PB 231; SASS 99 *Bol.*

Galindo Torres, Francisco CG II, 392; TM 146 *Mex.*

Galindo y Villa, Jesús (1867-) CG II, 392; WLA 156 *Mex.*

Galofre, Julio N. Co 27 *Col.*

Galván, Manuel de Jesús (1834-1911) BHLA 415; CG II, 393; CHL 495; CLH 435; G 385; GLO 253; LD 82; SD 13 *Dom.*

Galván, R. Octavio PD 82; SD 13 *Dom.*

Galván Moreno, C. A 27 *Arg.*
Galván y Socorro, Andrés Cu 61 *Cu.*
Galvarro, R. J. PB 234 *Bol.*
Galveg, Julio A. BC 164 *Col.*
Gálvez, Alfonso M. E 31 *Ecua.*
Gálvez, Aníbal CG II, 394; P 10 *Per.*
Gálvez, Javier J. CA 69 *Guat.*
Gálvez, José (1886-) AEHA 464; APEH 657; BAP 17; BHLA 537; CHL 306; CLH 260; FPA 436, 452; LP 389; P 10; PPe 274; SASS 417; WLA 159 *Per.*
Gálvez, Juan Ignacio ("Jig Gómez") (1874-) CG II, 394; Co 27; E 31 *Ecua.*
Gálvez, Lázaro ARC 41 *Cu.*
Gálvez, Manuel (1882-) A 27, 71, 84; AB 22; APAM 293; AT II, 596; BHLA 505; CG II, 394; CHL 186, 202; CLH 160; G 312; GLO 236; LAC 40, 130; LAS 199, 204; NPA 51; PLHA 196; SASS 70; WLA 159 *Arg.*
Gálvez, Ramón C 9 *Chil.*
Gálvez, Rosa TM 148 *Mex.*
"Gálvez, Víctor" (*pseud.*) *see* Quesada, Vicente G.
Gálvez Molina, Rodolfo CA 69 *Guat.*
Gálvez Otero, Julio PR 18 *P.R.*
Gálvez Portocarrero, Francisco CA 69 *Guat.*
Gálvez y Alfonso, Jesús Benigno (1838-) Cu 61 *Cu.*
Gálvez y Alfonso, José María (1835-) HLC 83 *Chil.*
Gálvez y del Monte, Wenceslao (1867-) CG II, 395; Cu 61 *Cu.*
Gallaga, Vicente TM 146 *Mex.*
Gallardo, Aurelio Luis (1831-1869) HLM 344; HPM 835; Ig 140; NM 23; PM 45; TM 148, 578 *Mex.*
Gallardo, Diego PM 45 *Mex.*
Gallardo, Guadalupe (1853-1894) HL II, 189 *Hond.*
Gallardo Sarmiento, Francisco A 27 *Arg.*
Gallego, Juan Manuel TM 148 *Mex.*
Gallego, Juan Nicasio (1777-1853) LA IV, 850 *Arg.*
Gallego y García, Tesifonte (1862-) Cu 61 *Cu.*
Gallegos, Gerardo E 31 *Ecua.*
Gallegos, Manuel Antonio (1860-) CA 27 *C.R.*
Gallegos, Manuel Modesto CG II, 402; V 73 *Venez.*
Gallegos Celis, Eduardo V 73 *Venez.*
Gallegos del Campo, Emilio CG II, 402; CHL 320; CLH 272; E 31; PE 68 *Ecua.*
Gallegos del Campo, Joaquín CG II, 402; E 31 *Ecua.*
Gallegos F., José Lorenzo (1857?-) Pan 8 *Pan.*
Gallegos Freire, Rómulo (1884-) BHLA 579; CG II, 402; G 392; LAS 204; LH 152; V 73; VPF 235; WLA 157 *Venez.*
Gallegos Lara, Joaquín BHLA 595; E 31 *Ecua.*
Gallegos Naranjo, Emilio CHL 320; CLH 272; E 31, 32 *Ecua.*
Gallegos Naranjo, Enrique (1836-1871) CG II, 402; E 31, 32, 74 *Ecua.*
Gallegos Naranjo, Manuel (1845-) CG II, 402; E 31, 32; PE 211 *Ecua.*

Galliano Cancio, Miguel (1890-) CG II, 402; Cu 61; PA 39; PCu 108 *Cu.*
Gallinal, Gustavo (1889-) CG II, 402; HSLU III, pt 4, 44; LU 64, 684; PIU III, 286; PU 275; U 8; UL 127 *Uru.*
"Gallo, Aniceto el" (*pseud.*) *see* Ascasubi, Hilario
Gallo, Vicente C. A 27; CG II, 403 *Arg.*
Gallo Almeida, Luis E 32 *Ecua.*
Gamarra, Abelardo ("El Tunante") (1857-1924) BHLA 406; P 11 *Per.*
Gamarra, Benito Díaz de (1745-1783) ACe 663 *Mex.*
Gamarra, P. Manuel (1887-) Par 13; PPa 187 *Para.*
Gamba, Carlos T. PU 99 *Uru.*
Gamba, Ramón (1792-) HLNG II, 537 *Col.*
Gamboa, Federico (1864-) BAMP 70; BHLA 524; CG II, 405; CHL 425; CLH 370; G 359; HLM 450; HLMex 227; IE 99; Ig 141; NM 2, 24; SAL 112; SASS 384; TM 148, 442; WLA 160 *Mex.*
Gamboa, José Joaquín (1878-1931) HLM 469; HLMex 249; TM 149, 442 *Mex.*
Gamboa, José María CG II, 405; TM 443 *Mex.*
Gamboa, Miguel TM 151 *Mex.*
Gamboa, Tobías Co 27 *Col.*
Gámez Monge, Manuel CA 27 *C.R.*
Gámez Monge, Matías CA 28; IBCR IV, 240 *C.R.*
Gamio, Manuel CG II, 406; NM 24 *Mex.*
Gamio, Rodrigo PM 45 *Mex.*
Gámiz, Abel PM 45 *Mex.*
Gana, Federico C 9; CHL 279; Cu 61 *Chil.*
Gana, Guillermo C 48 *Chil.*
Gancedo, Alejandro A 27, 84; CG II, 407 *Arg.*
Gandia, Enriqueta L. de A 27 *Arg.*
Gandía y Lebrero, Enrique de (1906-) A 27; CG II, 408; WLA 162 *Arg.*
Gando Bustamante, José Antonio V 73 *Venez.*
Gandolfo, Eduardo CG II, 408; U 8 *Uru.*
Gangotena y Jijón, Cristóbal de (1884-) BHLA 517; CG II, 408; E 32; PLE 94; WLA 162 *Ecua.*
Gante, Carlos de (1864-) CG II, 409; G 359; IE 102; Ig 146; NM 24 *Mex.*
Gante, Gregorio de PM 45 *Mex.*
Gaona, Roque PPa 267 *Para.*
Garacochea, Miguel W. (1816-1861) P 11 *Per.*
Garaicoa, Pedro P. E 32 *Ecua.*
Garasino, Ana María A 27; CG II, 410 *Arg.*
Garasino Brugo, C. A 28 *Arg.*
Gárate, Claudio Cu 61 *Cu.*
Garavito, José María (1860-1903) BC 164; Co 27; PB 232 *Col.*
Garay, Aurelio Ig 147; NM 25 *Mex.*
Garay, Blas Par 13 *Para.*
Garay, Narciso (1876-) IE 103; Pan 8 *Pan.*
Garay, Nicole *or* Nicolle (1873-1928) Pan 9 *Pan.*
Garay Díaz, María Nicolasa de las Mercedes *see* Garay, Nicole

Garbalosa, Graziella CG II, 411; Cu 61; PCu 110; PJC 83 *Cu.*

Garbán, Domingo V 73 *Venez.*

Garbi, Pedro Jorge A 28 *Arg.*

Garbiras, Arístides V 73 *Venez.*

Garbiras, Isaias V 73 *Venez.*

Garcerán, Buenaventura AP 109; Pan 9 *Pan.*

Garcés, G. E 33 *Ecua.*

Garcés, Miguel Gabriel E 32 *Ecua.*

Garcés, Modesto (1849-1906) Co 27 *Col.*

Garcés, Víctor M. E 32; PE 314 *Ecua.*

Garcés Álamo, Rafael V 73 *Venez.*

García, Adolfo (1872-1900) AP 115; FPA 381, 387; Pan 9 *Pan.*

García, Antonio (1912-) BHLA 590 *Col.*

García, Armando D. (1895-1918) Cu 62; PJC 79 *Cu.*

García, Benjamín Cu 62 *Cu.*

García, Carlos B 8 *Bol.*

García, Dionisio Cu 62 *Cu.*

García, Ernesto M. (1914-) PoC 86 *Cu.*

García, Ezequiel V 73 *Venez.*

García, Genaro (1867-1920) G 359; HLM 491; Ig 148; NM 25; TM 544 *Mex.*

García, Héctor Modesto V 74 *Venez.*

García, Hermes V 74 *Venez.*

García, Higinio C. TM 151 *Mex.*

García, Ismael TM 152 *Mex.*

García, Joaquín José (-1790?) Cu 62 *Cu.*

García, Jorge I. E 33 *Ecua.*

García, José Gabriel CG II, 416; LD 84; SD 13 *Dom.*

García, José Hermengildo V 74 *Venez.*

1. García, José Joaquín BDC 24 *Cu.*

2. García, José Joaquín (1849-1919) Co 27 *Col.*

García, Juan Agustín (hijo) (1862-1923) A 28, 84; AT I, 363; CG II, 416; SPLA 252 *Arg.*

García, Juan Crisóstomo Co 27 *Col.*

García, Luis CA 69 *Guat.*

García, Luis R. PM 45 *Mex.*

García, Manuel ARC 34; Cu 62 *Cu.*

García, Manuel Adolfo (1828-1883) CHL 298; CLH 252; P 11 *Per.*

García, Manuel O. PP 271 *P.R.*

García, Miguel Luis V 74 *Venez.*

García, Nicasio C 30 *Chil.*

García, Oscar Cu 62 *Cu.*

García, Porfirio SD 13 *Dom.*

García, Quintiliano CHL 455; CLH 397 *Cu.*

García, Rafael A. TM 152 *Mex.*

García, Rodolfo SD 13 *Dom.*

García, Sebastián Co 27 *Col.*

García, Silverio (1840-1920) Ig 149; NM 25 *Mex.*

García, Silvino M. PM 45 *Mex.*

García Acuña, Fernando Cu 62 *Cu.*

García Albuquerque, Manuel BDC 24 *Cu.*

García Arias, Isidoro Cu 13 *Cu.*

García Barcena, Rafael (1907-) PoC 92 *Cu.*

García Berenguer, José PR 12 *P.R.*

García Calderón, Francisco (1883-) BHLA 482; CG II, 428; CHL 307; CLH 261; G 381; IE 106; LAND 95, 265, 293; P 11; PLHA 251; SAL 92, 93, 335; SASS 433; SD 13, 30; WLA 164 *Per.*

García Calderón, Ventura (1887-) BAP 15; BHLA 515; CG II, 429; CHL 25, 41, 307; CLH 248; G 381; GLO 235, 252; P 11; PLHA 229; SAL 277, 295; SASS 435; WLA 164 *Per.*

García Capella, Estrella (1905-) QPR (1) 71 *P.R.*

García Copley, Federico Cu 62 *Cu.*

García Costa, Rosa (1892-) A 28; APAM 306; AT II, 968; CG II, 432 *Arg.*

García Cubas, Antonio (1832-1912) CG II, 432; HLM 459; NM 2, 25; TM 545 *Mex.*

García Cuevas, Francisco CG II, 433; TM 153 *Mex.*

García de Aguilar, Manuel Cu 62 *Cu.*

García de Arellano, Luis PM 45 *Mex.*

García de Carrasquedo, Isidro ("Mitilo") PM 45, 57 *Mex.*

García de Coronado, Domitila Cu 62 *Cu.*

García de Espinosa, Juan Co 28 *Col.*

García de la Huerta, Joaquín (1825-1875) Cu 62; PCu 111; TM 153 *Cu.*

García de la Linde, Juan M. (-1887) BDC 24; Cu 63 *Cu.*

García de León y Pizarro, José CG II, 447; E 33 *Ecua.*

García de Quevedo, José Heriberto (1819-1871) AEHA 379; CHL 359; CLH 308; HPHA I, 404; LV 73, 136, 274, 366; V 74 *Venez.*

García de Tarafa, Ignacia Cu 63 *Cu.*

García de Tejada, Juan Manuel (1774-1845) Co 28; RHLC 54 *Col.*

García del Río, Juan (1794-1856) BC 167; CHL 68, 199; CLH 74; Co 28; LC 116; LV 77; RHLC 76 *Col.*

García Domínguez, Antonio Cu 63 *Cu.*

García Enseñat, Ezequiel (1862-) CT 243 *Cu.*

García Escobar, Rafael PS 203 *Salv.*

García Espinel, Emilio Co 28 *Col.*

García Espinosa, Juan M. (1911-) PoC 98 *Cu.*

García-Figueroa, Agustín TM 153 *Mex.*

García Fominaya, Zoila (1912-) PoC 99 *Cu.*

García Fox, Leonardo (1892-) PoC 107 *Cu.*

García Games, Julia C 66 *Chil.*

García Garófalo y Mesa, Manuel CG II, 440; Cu 63 *Cu.*

García Garófalo y Morales, Francisco Cu 63 *Cu.*

García Gelaz, Juan Cu 63 *Cu.*

García Godoy, Federico (-1923) BHLA 415; CG II, 440; CHL 496; CLH 437; G 385; LD 104; SAL 100; SASS 324; SD 13, 14, 30 *Dom.*

García Gómez, Arístides LD 97; SD 14 *Dom.*

García González, Francisco Ig 151; NM 25 *Mex.*

García Gordo, Gregorio A 28 *Arg.*

García Goyena, Rafael (1766-1823) ACe 1007; BLN 1; CA 69; CHL 88; CLH 75; E 33; GPCA I, 17; PE 278; PG 36; PLE 20 *Ecua.*

García Granados, María Josefa (1796-1848) CA 70; GPCA I, 105; PG 78 *Guat.*

García Granados, Miguel (1825?-1898) CA 70 *Guat.*

García Gutiérrez, Antonio CG II, 442; TM 494 *Mex.*

García Herreros, Manuel (1894-) Co 28; RHLC 193 *Col.*

García Huidobro, Vicente *see* Huidobro, Vicente

García Icazbalceta, Joaquín (1825-1894) AEHA 378; CG II, 445; CHL 410; CLH 356; G 359; HLM 476; HLMex 168; HPHA I, 24; TM 545 *Mex.*

García Iglesia, Alfonso (1911-) PoC 109 *Cu.*

García Irigoyen, Carlos CG II, 445; P 12 *Per.*

García Irigoyen, Manuel P 12 *Per.*

García Kohly, Mario CG II, 447; Cu 63; IE 109 *Cu.*

García M., Octavio Adolfo V 75 *Venez.*

García Medina, Vicente A 28 *Arg.*

García Mella, Arístides SD 14 *Dom.*

García Mella, Moisés SD 14 *Dom.*

García Mendoza, Alberto BDC 24; Cu 63 *Cu.*

García Mérou, Martín (1862-1905) A 28; BHLA 421; CG II, 453; CHL 183, 185; CLH 159; LA VIII, 636, 655; SPLA 245 *Arg.*

García Monge (*or* Monje), Joaquín (1883-) BHLA 572; CA 28; CHL 509; EPCR 294; G 332; IBCR IV, 21 *et passim* *C.R.*

García Mongón, José PR 18 *P.R.*

García Montero, José (1836-) PM 45; TM 153 *Mex.*

García Moreno, Gabriel (1821-1875) BHLA 295; CHL 313; CLH 265; E 33; HPHA II, 133; PE 88; PLE 36 *Ecua.*

García Naranjo, Nemecio (*or* Nemesio) CG II, 457; NM 25; V 75 *Venez.*

"García Nieto, Alejandro" (*pseud.*) *see* Urbaneja, Alejandro

García Oldini, Fernando C 30, 66 *Chil.*

García Ortiz, Laureano Co 28 *Col.*

García Pérez, Luis (1832-1893) BDC 24; Cu 63 *Cu.*

García Pérez, Manuel BDC 25 *Cu.*

García Pompa, Agustín V 75 *Venez.*

García Prada, Carlos (1898-) Co 28; WLA 165 *Col.*

García Ramos, Francisco PM 45; TM 156 *Mex.*

García Reverón, Luis Felipe V 75 *Venez.*

García Robleto, D. NL 35 *Nicar.*

García Roel, José TM 157 *Mex.*

García Rojas, Heliodoro Cu 63 *Cu.*

García Rojas, Manuel TM 157 *Mex.*

García Sagastume, Baldomero CG II, 466; P 12 *Per.*

García Sáiz, Valentín CG II, 467; PIU III, 311; U 8 *Uru.*

García Salaberry, Adela A 28 *Arg.*

García Samudio, Nicolás (1892-) CG II, 467; Co 28; WLA 166 *Col.*

García Solano, Arturo CA 28; EPCR 568 *C.R.*

García Tejada, Juan Manuel (1774-1845) BC 167; Co 28; HLNG II, 115, 331; HPHA II, 37 *Col.*

García Tuduri de Coya, Mercedes (1904-) PoC 111 *Cu.*

García Vásquez, Demetrio Co 28 *Col.*

García-Vélez, Mario C. CG II, 473; Cu 63 *Cu.*

García Velloso, Enrique (1880-) A 29, 84; AT II, 593; CG II, 473; PLHA 293 *Arg.*

García Velloso, Juan José A 29; CG II, 474 *Arg.*

García y Cubas *see* García Cubas

García y García, Elvira (1872-) WLA 165 *Per.*

García y García, José Antonio Co 28 *Col.*

García y Mellid, Atilio (1901-) A 29; APAM 496 *Arg.*

García y Onrubia, Sarah Felisa (1909-) A 29 *Arg.*

García y Valdés, María Ig 151; NM 25 *Mex.*

García Zegers, M. E. PCh 295

Garcías, Rogelio Cu 63 *Cu.*

Garcilaso de la Vega ("el Inca") (1539-1616) AEHA 449; BHLA 59; CG II, 475; CHL 4; CLH 4; HPHA II, 145; LA III, 306; LP 307; P 12; SASS 430; SCL 113, 606 *Per.*

Garet Más, Julio PU 102; U 8 *Uru.*

Garibay, César PM 46 *Mex.*

Garibay K., Ángel María PM 46 *Mex.*

Garita, Juan (1859-1912) CA 28; EPCR 124 *C.R.*

Garland, Antonio G. LP 391; P 12 *Per.*

Garmendia, José Froilán V 75 *Venez.*

Garmendia, José Ignacio A 29; CG II, 477 *Arg.*

Garmendia, Julio PLHA 221; V 75 *Venez.*

Garmendia y Rodríguez, Miguel (1862-) CG II, 477; CT 233; Cu 63 *Cu.*

Garnier, José Fabio (1884-) CA 29, 30; CG II, 478; EPCR 431; IBCR IV, 90 *et passim* *C.R.*

Garrido, Bernardo TM 157 *Mex.*

Garrido, E. Víctor PA 311; PD 85; SD 14 *Dom.*

Garrido, Luis NM 25 *Mex.*

Garrido, Luis E. PD 83; SD 14 *Dom.*

Garrido, Miguel A. LD 96; SD 14, 18, 23, 29 *Dom.*

Garrido Alfaro, Vicente (1888-) G 359; PM 46 *Mex.*

Garrido Concha, Pedro N. C 30; NC 426 *Chil.*

Garrido Cuadri, Santos CG II, 481; U 8 *Uru.*

Garrido de la Peña, Carlota (1870-) AT I, 361; CG II, 482 *Arg.*

Garrido Merino, Edgardo BHLA 622; C 9; CG II, 482 *Chil.*

Garriga y Argandoña, Pablo (1853-1893) C 30, 48; CHL 260; CLH 220; HC 215; PCh 103 *Chil.*

Garrigó, Roque E. (1876-) Cu 64 *Cu.*

Garrigós Brun, Carlos A 29 *Arg.*

Garro, Juan Mamerto (1847-) A 29; AT I, 485 *Arg.*

Garrochótegui, Abelardo V 75 *Venez.*

Garza, Alma A 29 *Arg.*

Garza, Juan B. PM 46; TM 157 *Mex.*

Garza, María Luisa ("Lorely") PM 46, 55 *Mex.*

Garza, S. Antonio PM 46 *Mex.*
Garzón, Esteban S. A 29 *Arg.*
Garzón, Eugenio A 29; HSLU I, pt 4, 6; UT 251 *Uru.*
Garzón, Ricardo CG II, 479; U 8 *Uru.*
Garzón, Tobías A 29; CG II, 479 *Arg.*
Garzón de Tahuste, Alonso (1558-) Co 28; LC 90; RHLC 21 *Col.*
Gasca, José del Refugio PM 46 *Mex.*
Gassie, Julián (-1878) Cu 64 *Cu.*
Gastón, José María Cu 64 *Cu.*
"Gaston Nerval" (*pseud.*) see Diez de Medina, Raúl
Gatica Martínez, Tomás (1881-) C 9, 30, 66; CG II, 402; NC 123; PCh 323 *Chil.*
Gautier, Manuel María SD 14 *Dom.*
Gautier Benítez, José (1848-1880) CG II, 495; CHL 502; CLH 439; FPA 460, 462; G 384; GLO 253; HPHA I, 347; PA 205; PP 21; PR 35, 52; SASS 309 *P.R.*
Gavidia, Francisco A. (186.-) CG II, 496; FPA 501, 504; GPCA III, 441; PS 9; SAL 110, 127, 138 *Salv.*
Gavila, Fernando TM 158 *Mex.*
Gavira, Joaquín (-1870?) Cu 64 *Cu.*
Gavito, Francisco PM 46 *Mex.*
Gavito, Manuel Cu 64 *Cu.*
Gaxiola D., Antonio PM 46 *Mex.*
Gay, Luz Cu 64; PJC 78 *Cu.*
Gay, Ramón Cu 64 *Cu.*
Gay Calbó, Enrique (1889-) BDC 25; WLA 167 *Cu.*
Gaztelu, Angel (1915-) PoC 113 *Cu.*
Gazzano, Adolfo A 29 *Arg.*
Geada, Juan J. CG II, 503; Cu 64; PJC 84 *Cu.*
Geenzier, Enrique (1888-) AP 123; CG II, 503; FPA 382, 395; Pan 9; WLA 168 *Pan.*
Gelabert, Francisco de Paulo (1834-1894) Cu 64; RLC 144 *Cu.*
Gell, J. C. A 29 *Arg.*
Gemelli Carreri, Juan Francisco CG II, 504; TM 545 *Mex.*
"Genaro A. Groimemi" (*pseud.*) see Guerra, Gerónimo A.
"Genaro Culmani" (*pseud.*) see Carmona, Miguel
"Genaro E. Terrues" (*pseud.*) see Guerra, Ernesto E.
Gener, Lorenzo BDC 25; Cu 64 *Cu.*
Genovese, Blas S. A 29; CG II, 507 *Arg.*
Genta, Edgardo Ubaldo (1894-) CG II, 507; LU 64, 668; PU 104; U 8; UT 255 *Uru.*
Gentile, Alberto C. A 29 *Arg.*
"George Baset" (*pseud.*) see Miranda, Ignacio de
"Georgina de Flores" (*pseud.*) see Rencurrell, Georgina
Gerchunoff, Alberto (1883-) A 29; AT I, 252; BHLA 506; CG II, 509; LAC 107, 151 *Arg.*
Germán, Pedro M. SD 14 *Dom.*
Gez, Juan W. A 29; CG II, 512 *Arg.*
Ghinetti, Domingo (1808-1855) Cu 64 *Cu.*
Ghio, Haydée M. A 29 *Arg.*
Ghio, Julio Cruz A 29; CG II, 513 *Arg.*

Ghiraldo, Alberto (1874-) A 29, 84; APAM 93; BHLA 497, 506; CG II, 513; CHL 199; G 312; LAS 204, 207; PLHA 133; SAL 281; SASS 91; SD 14 *Arg.*
Giberga y Gali, Eliseo (1854-1916) Cu 64; HLC 84; RLC 230, 235 *Cu.*
Gibson, Percy (189.-) BAP 31; BHLA 539; FPA 436, 457 *Per.*
Gil, Adolfo V 75 *Venez.*
Gil, Enrique PM 46 *Mex.*
Gil, Juan A 30, 84 *Arg.*
Gil, Julián Cu 64 *Cu.*
Gil, Luis José BDC 25; Cu 65 *Cu.*
Gil, Manuel TM 595 *Mex.*
Gil, Martín A 30; CHL 197 *Arg.*
Gil, Pedro E. PCh 207 *Chil.*
Gil, Pío BHLA 521; CG II, 519; V 75 *Venez.*
"Gil, Salomé" (*pseud.*) see Milla y Vidaurre, José
Gil Borges, Esteban V 75 *Venez.*
Gil de Hermoso, Virginia CG II, 522; V 75 *Venez.*
Gil de Lamadrid, Jesús BP 527 *P.R.*
Gil Esquerdo, Francisco A 30; CG II, 520 *Arg.*
Gil Fortoul, José (1862-) BHLA 388; CG II, 521; CHL 377; CLH 325; LV 11, 72, 140, 379; PLHA 284; SASS 545; V 75; VPF 70 *Venez.*
Gil Gilbert, Enrique E 33 *Ecua.*
"Gil Got" (*pseud.*) see Subieta, Eduardo
"Gil Guero" (*pseud.*) see Barrios F., Ciriaco
Gil Rodríguez, Francisco Cu 65 *Cu.*
Gil Rodríguez, Manuel PM 46 *Mex.*
Giménez, Aníbal Marc Par 13 *Para.*
Giménez, Arturo A. U 8 *Uru.*
Giménez, Joaquín BDC 25; Cu 65 *Cu.*
Giménez Aquino, Miguel PR 35 *P.R.*
Giménez Martín, D. Par 13 *Para.*
Giménez Pastor, Arturo (1872-) A 30, 84; CHL 200; WLA 170 *Arg.*
Gimón Sterlings, Emilio V 76 *Venez.*
Giner, J. A. BDC 25; Cu 65 *Cu.*
Giral Ordóñez, Mario CG II, 530; Cu 65 *Cu.*
Giraldo, Federico U 8 *Uru.*
Giraldo, Francisco Co 28; PCo 119 *Col.*
Giralt, José A. Cu 65 *Cu.*
Giralt, Pedro Cu 65 *Cu.*
Giralt Moreno, Mario Cu 65 *Cu.*
Giraudy Betancourt, S. Cu 65 *Cu.*
Giró, Valentín PA 312; PP 86; SD 14 *Dom.*
Girón, Leopoldo V 76 *Venez.*
"Girón de Pinabete Alcornoque y Astragalo" (*pseud.*) see Tablada, José Juan
Girón y Cuevas, Manuel (1816-1892) Cu 65 *Cu.*
Girondo, Oliverio (1891-) A 30; APAM 503; APEH 993, 1193; BHLA 639; CG II, 534; G 312; LAC 148; NPA 259; PLHA 168 *Arg.*
Giusti, Roberto Fernando (1887-) A 30; AT I, 243; BHLA 631; CG II, 536; CHL 204; CrA 143; G 312; IE 114; LAC 109, 152; PLHA 272; WLA 170 *Arg.*
Givovich, Arturo C 10, 48; NC 126, 363 *Chil.*

Glusberg, Samuel ("Enrique Espinosa") A 30; BHLA 632; LAC 134 *Arg.*
Gneco Mozo, José Co 28 *Col.*
Gobeo de Victoria, Pedro (1560-1630) P 12; SCL 327, 607 *Per.*
Godoi, Juansilvano (Godoy, Juan Silvano) (1850-) CG II, 541; Par 13; PT 15 *Para.*
Godoy, Jorge de (1894-) CG II, 540; G 359; HLM 519; Ig 151; NM 25 *Mex.*
Godoy, José Francisco (1851-) CG II, 541; G 359; NM 2 *Mex.*
Godoy, Juan Gualberto (1793-1864) A 30; BHLA 168; CHL 71, 156; CLH 61; HLA 388; LA II, 573; SPLA 60 *Arg.*
Godoy, Manuel C. Ig 154; NM 25 *Mex.*
Godoy, Oscar C 10 *Chil.*
Godoy, Pedro A 30 *Arg.*
Godoy, Rodolfo G. A 30 *Arg.*
Godoy, Rosario P. de A 30 *Arg.*
Godoy Alcayaza, Lucila ("Gabriela Mistral") (1889-) AB 22; APEH 920, 1192; BHLA 536, 623; C 35; CG III, 806; CHL 287; CMPC 45; CP 695; CrA 37; FPA 193, 225; G 323; GLO 239; HSLU II, pt 8, 10; LH 25; MSAP 194, 320; OA 37; PCC xvi, 127; PCh 335; PCU 24; PLHA 169; SASS 157; WLA 255 *Chil.*
Godoy de Martínez, Concepción Cu 65 *Cu.*
Goenaga, Florentino (1859-) BC 169; CG II, 541; Co 28 *Col.*
Goenaga, José Manuel (1851-) CG II, 541; Co 29 *Col.*
Goicoclea Walton, Luis C 48 *Chil.*
Goicochea, César P 12 *Per.*
Goicoechea *see also* Goycoechea
Goicoechea, C. A 30, 85 *Arg.*
Goicouría, Domingo ARC 76 *Cu.*
Goldsack Guiñazú, Alfredo A 31; IE 116 *Arg.*
Golisciani, Enrique TM 158 *Mex.*
Gollaz, Francisco PM 46 *Mex.*
Gollury, Ramón F. ("Roger de Lauria") Cu 65 *Cu.*
Gomar, José María PS 175 *Salv.*
Gomensoro, Andrés T. CG II, 547; U 8 *Uru.*
Gómez, A. Co 29 *Col.*
Gómez, Adolfo E 34 *Ecua.*
Gómez, Adolfo León PCo 122 *Col.*
Gómez, Alberto M. PE 30 *Ecua.*
Gómez, Alfredo CA 70 *Guat.*
Gómez, Amiama PA 303; SD 14 *Dom.*
Gómez, Antonio Cu 65 *Cu.*
Gómez, Betsabe TM 159 *Mex.*
Gómez, César V 76 *Venez.*
"Gómez, Efe" (*pseud.*) *see* Gómez, Francisco
Gómez, Eusebio F. A 31; LA VIII, 628 *Arg.*
Gómez, Francisco ("Efe Gómez") (1875-) RHLC 190 *Col.*
Gómez, Gustavo TM 159 *Mex.*
Gómez, Hernán Félix (1888-) AT II, 583; CG II, 548 *Arg.*
Gómez, Ignacio PS 100 *Salv.*
"Gómez, Jig" (*pseud.*) *see* Gálvez, Juan Ignacio
Gómez, José TM 546 *Mex.*
Gómez, José Benito BDC 25; Cu 65 *Cu.*

Gómez, José Bernardo V 76 *Venez.*
Gómez, Juan Bautista A 31 *Arg.*
Gómez, Juan Carlos (1820-1884) BHLA 296; CHL 209; CLH 173; HCLU I, 248, 465; LA VI, 767; LUr 444; PIU I, 169; SAL 227, 231, 233; U 8; UL 128 *Uru.*
Gómez, Juan Eusebio ARC 51 *Cu.*
Gómez, Juan Gualberto (1854-) ARC 36, 37, 51; CT 509 *Cu.*
Gómez, Laureano Co 29 *Col.*
Gómez, Manuel María B 8 *Bol.*
Gómez, Manuel Ubaldo SD 14 *Dom.*
Gómez, Máximo ARC 75 *Cu.*
Gómez, Rafael PM 46 *Mex.*
Gómez, Ramón (1832-1890) Co 29 *Col.*
Gómez, Ruperto S. (1837-1910) AC II, 231; BC 175; Co 29; PCo 143 *Col.*
Gómez, Santiago Carlos ("Gabriel de Rimur") C 48 *Chil.*
Gómez Barrientos, Estanislao Co 29 *Col.*
Gómez Brioso, José PR 52 *P.R.*
Gómez Capirot, María Antoineta CG II, 552; Cu 65 *Cu.*
Gómez Carbonell, María Cu 66 *Cu.*
Gómez Cárdenas, Guadalupe TM 159 *Mex.*
Gómez Carrillo, Agustín (1842-) CA 70; CG II, 552 *Guat.*
Gómez Carrillo, Enrique (1873-1927) AEHA 400; BHLA 475; CA 70, 71, 72, 73, 74; CG II, 552; CHL 541; CLH 473; G 346; PLHA 276; SA 127; SASS 132 *Guat.*
Gómez Carvallo, Antonio PM 46 *Mex.*
Gómez Colón, José María BDC 29; Cu 66 *Cu.*
Gómez Corena, Luis Co 29 *Col.*
Gómez Corena, Pedro CG II, 554; Co 29 *Col.*
Gómez Costa, Arturo PA 205; PP 295; PR 35 *P.R.*
Gómez de Abadía, Herminia (1861-1926) BC 173; Co 29; RHLC 184 *Col.*
Gómez de Avellaneda y Arteaga, Gertrudis ("La Peregrina") (1814-1873) AB 21; BDC 25; BHLA 328; CG II, 550; CHL 463; CLH 405; Cu 15, 66; FPA 162, 171; G 336; GLO 242; HLC 95, 168; HPHA I, 265; PA 43; PCu 115; PUC 17; RLC 105, 207, 220; SAL 137; SASS 269 *Cu.*
Gómez de la Cortina, José ("Conde de la Cortina") (1779-1860) HLM 359; HLMex 160 *Mex.*
Gómez de la Parra, Joseph PM 46 *Mex.*
Gómez de Morante, Herminia Cu 69 *Cu.*
Gómez de Orozco, Federico CG II, 563; TM 546 *Mex.*
Gómez de Suárez, Guadalupe TM 162 *Mex.*
Gómez Estévez, Rafael ARC 52; Cu 69 *Cu.*
Gómez Flores, F. J. NM 25 *Mex.*
Gómez G., José B 8; CG II, 555 *Bol.*
Gómez García, E. Cu 69 *Cu.*
Gómez González, Luis E. PE 208 *Ecua.*
Gómez Haedo, Eduardo PU 277 *Uru.*
Gómez Haro, Eduardo (1871-) CG II, 556; G 359; IE 116; NM 25; PM 46; TM 159, 546; WLA 172 *Mex.*
Gómez Holguín, Heraclio C 10 *Chil.*
Gómez Ibáñez, Eduardo A 31 *Arg.*
Gómez Iparraguirre, Carlos A 31 *Arg.*

Gómez J., Alberto PLE 88 *Ecua.*
Gómez Jaime, Alfredo (1878-) AEHA 896; ALC II, 131; CG II, 557; CHL 349; Co 29; G 329; LC 193; PCo 123; RHLC 153; WLA 172 *Col.*
Gómez Luna, Ignacio ("Lucio Magez Nigona") Ig 154; NM 25 *Mex.*
Gómez Palacio, Martín (1893-) APMM 56; G 359; HLM 517; Ig 155; NM 25; PM 47; WLA 173 *Mex.*
Gómez Portugal, Manuel PM 47; TM 162 *Mex.*
Gómez Restrepo, Antonio María (1869-) AC I, 339; II, 239; ALC I, 411; BC 175; BHLA 431; CHL 34, 343, 347; CLH 298; Co 16, 30; G 329; PCo 141; RHLC 209; SAL 63, 64; SASS 232; WLA 173 *Col.*
Gómez Robelo, Ricardo CG II, 565; PM 47 *Mex.*
Gómez Rojas, Domingo ("Daniel Vásquez") (1896-) C 30; CMPC 125; PCC xix, 205 *Chil.*
Gómez Sánchez, Luis Cu 69 *Cu.*
Gómez Sicre, José (1915-) PoC 119 *Cu.*
Gómez Ugarte, José ("El Abate Benigno") (1874-) G 360; HLM 524; PM 17, 47 *Mex.*
Gómez Vergara, Joaquín (-1894) G 360; Ig 156; NM 25 *Mex.*
Gómez Victoria, Mercedes BC 174; Co 29; RHLC 184 *Col.*
Gómez y Arroyo, G. BDC 25; Cu 69 *Cu.*
Gómez y Gómez, Agapito Cu 69 *Cu.*
Gómez y Martínez, Luis CG II, 559; Cu 69 *Cu.*
Gomezanda, Antonio TM 606 *Mex.*
Gondra, Manuel (1872-) Par 14; PT 1 *Para.*
Gondrecourt, Arístides de (1815-1876) Cu 69 *Cu.*
Góngora, José Guadalupe TM 162 *Mex.*
Gonzaga Cuevao, Luis HLM 358; PM 47 *Mex.*
González, Abel C 30; PCh 391 *Chil.*
González, Adalberto Elías TM 163 *Mex.*
González, Agustín R. HLM 492; TM 163 *Mex.*
González, Alejandro C 10; NC 136 *Chil.*
González, Alfredo NM 26 *Mex.*
González, Anacarsis Polibio E 34 *Ecua.*
González, Ángel I. Par 14; PPa 191 *Para.*
González, Antonio BDC 29; Cu 69 *Cu.*
González, Antonio R. V 76 *Venez.*
González, Arévalo CHL 378; CLH 526; LV 414 *Venez.*
González, Ariosto Domingo (1901-) CG II, 575; U 8; WLA 174 *Uru.*
González, Arnaldo C 10, 30 *Chil.*
González, Arturo CG II, 575; Co 30 *Col.*
González, Aurelio C 10, 30; CG II, 575; NC 363, 426 *Chil.*
González, Benigno V 76 *Venez.*
González, Calixto V 76 *Venez.*
González, Carlos TM 163 *Mex.*
González, Celestino PM 47 *Mex.*
González, Eduardo Innes V 76 *Venez.*
González, Eloy Guillermo CG II, 576; LV 75; V 77 *Venez.*
1. González, Ernesto Co 30 *Col.*
2. González, Ernesto PM 47 *Mex.*

González, Esteban D. V 77 *Venez.*
González, Eugenio C 10; CG II, 576; LAS 204 *Chil.*
González, Ezequiel María LV 54; V 77 *Venez.*
González, F. B. P 13 *Per.*
González, Federico B 8; PCh 311 *Chil.*
González, Fernando BHLA 591; Co 30; G 329; PLHA 221 *Col.*
González, Filiberto C. TM 164 *Mex.*
González, Florentino (1805-1875) LC 121; RHLC 110 *Col.*
1. González, Francisco CG II, 576; Cu 69 *Cu.*
2. González, Francisco ("Doctor Valromey") CG II, 576; TM 164, 344 *Mex.*
"González, Gonzalo" (*pseud.*) see Quirós Blanco, Teodoro
González, J. Félix CA 30 *C.R.*
González, Joaquín Víctor (1863-1923) A 31; AT I, 149; BHLA 400; CG II, 577; CHL 196, 200; G 312; SPLA 251 *Arg.*
González, José Ignacio TM 168 *Mex.*
González, José María CG II, 578; SD 15 *Dom.*
González, José Silverio V 77 *Venez.*
González, Josefa Vivero de E 34 *Ecua.*
González, Juan B. A 31; CG II, 578; G 312 *Arg.*
González, Juan Luis Cu 69 *Cu.*
González, Juan Vicente (1808-1866) BHLA 298, 400; CHL 364; CLH 312; GLO 255; LV 6, 8, 28, 67, 131, 133; V 77 *Venez.*
González, Julián ARC 52; Cu 69 *Cu.*
González, Julián S. NM 26; PM 47 *Mex.*
González, Julio V. A 31; CG II, 578; LAC 138 *Arg.*
González, Lauro Ig 158; NM 26 *Mex.*
González, Luis Felipe (1882-) CA 30, 31; CG II, 578; EPCR 439; IBCR IV, 324 *C.R.*
González, M. Gelafio B 8 *Bol.*
González, Magdaleno BP 511 *P.R.*
González, Manuel TM 164 *Mex.*
González, Manuel Dionisio (1815-1863) BDC 29; Cu 69 *Cu.*
González, Manuel Pedro (1894-) WLA 175 *Cu.*
González, María Rosa C 10 *Chil.*
González, Mariano PM 47 *Mex.*
González, Miguel BDC 30 *Cu.*
González, Nicanor A. (1843-1898) BDC 30; Cu 69 *Cu.*
González, Nicolás Augusto (1858-1918) BHLA 517; CG II, 579; E 34; PE 252; PLE 58 *Ecua.*
González, Otilio (1895-) PM 47 *Mex.*
González, Pedro Antonio (1863-1903) APEH 117; BHLA 456; C 30; CHL 262; CLH 222; FPA 191, 194; PCh 145; SASS 145 *Chil.*
González, Refugio TM 164 *Mex.*
González, Ricardo CG II, 579; P 13 *Per.*
González, S. A. A 31 *Arg.*
González, Teodardo V 78 *Venez.*
González, Teresa BC 180; Co 30 *Col.*
González, Ulpiano (1815-1849) RHLC 116 *Col.*
González, Velasco V 78 *Venez.*
González, Vidal Cu 69; NM 26

González A., N. C 31 *Chil.*
González Alcorta, Leandro (1861-) CT 249 *Cu.*
González Arrili, Bernardo (1892-) A 31; AT II, 809; CG II, 582; IE 120; WLA 175 *Arg.*
González Bastías, Jorge (1879-) C 31; N 147; PCC xiii, 75; PCh 215 *Chil.*
González Bocanegra, Francisco HPM 827; TM 164 *Mex.*
González Calderón, Luciano A 31 *Arg.*
González Calixto, Pedro Rafael (1839-1904) E 35 *Ecua.*
González Camargo, Joaquín (1865-1886) AC I, 325; BC 177; CHL 347; CLH 298; Co 30; LC 183; RHLC 145 *Col.*
González Campo, Francisco (1832-1904) CA 74; GPCA II, 93; PG 161 *Guat.*
González Carbalho, José (1900-) A 31; APAM 512; APEH 680, 1189; NPA 231 *Arg.*
González Carrasco, Aurelio (1876-) CG II, 589; G 360; HLM 468; PM 47; TM 165 *Mex.*
González Castillo, José (1885-) A 32, 85; AT I, 497; CHL 199 *Arg.*
González Castro, Augusto A 32 *Arg.*
González Castro, Fermín TM 165 *Mex.*
González Cos, Jesús PM 47; TM 165, 443, 546 *Mex.*
González Costi, Luis Cu 70 *Cu.*
González Curquejo, Antonio CG II, 592; Cu 70 *Cu.*
González Chacón, Simón V 78 *Venez.*
González Chávez, Nicolás (1817-1878) Co 30 *Col.*
González Dávila, Gil HLM 209; PR 56 *Sp.*
González de Eslava, Fernán (1825-) BHLA 99, 108; CHL 38; CLH 32; HLM 120; HLMex 53; HPHA I, 47; HPM 130; PM 47; TM 166 *Mex.*
González de Fanning, Teresa ("María de la Luz") (1836-) P 13 *Per.*
González de Güemes, Bernardo Co 30 *Col.*
González de Güemes, Pedro Co 30 *Col.*
González de la Vega, Joseph Sixto PM 47 *Mex.*
González de Mendoza, J. M. NM 26 *Mex.*
González de Mesa, Narciso BDC 30; Cu 70 *Cu.*
González de Moscoso, Mercedes PLE 63 *Ecua.*
González de Sancha NM 26 *Mex.*
González de Soto, C. V 78 *Venez.*
González de Veranes, Pedro N. ARC 52 *Cu.*
González del Valle, Ángel Cu 70 *Cu.*
González del Valle, Francisco ARC 77; Cu 70 *Cu.*
González del Valle, José Zacarías (1820-1851) Cu 70; G 336; HLC 174; PCu 129; RLC 128, 146 *Cu.*
González del Valle, Manuel (1802-1884) Cu 70; G 336; RLC 70, 81, 173 *Cu.*
González del Valle, Martín, marqués de la Vega de Anzó (-1911) Cu 70 *Cu.*
González Díaz, Francisco CG II, 592; Cu 71 *Cu.*

González Dorticós, Arturo ARC 52 *Cu.*
González Eiris, Joaquín V 78 *Venez.*
González Elajalde, Teodomiro P 13 *Per.*
González Font, José CG II, 594; PR 6, 45 *P.R.*
González Franco, Francisco TM 168 *Mex.*
González G., Federico C 31 *Chil.*
González Gamargo, Juan V 78 *Venez.*
González Garay, Rafael TM 444 *Mex.*
González García, Manuel CG II, 596; PR 26, 35, 42, 52 *P.R.*
González García, Matías (1866-) BP 503, 527, 600; PR 27; QPR (1) 76; (2) 78 *P.R.*
González Gastellú, Pedro A 32 *Arg.*
González Ginorio, José BP 504, 600; PR 9, 27 *P.R.*
González Gomar, Manuel PM 47 *Mex.*
González González, Ricardo C 10; NC 136 *Chil.*
González Guerrero, Francisco AMP 145; APMM 59; G 360; HLM 524; PM 47; PNM 328 *Mex.*
González Guerrero, Luis C 10 *Chil.*
González Guinán, Francisco CG II, 597; LV 5; V 78 *Venez.*
González Guinán, Santiago CG II, 598; V 79 *Venez.*
González Gutiérrez, Juan (1660-) Co 30; HLNG I, 189; SCL 447, 608 *Col.*
González Hurtado, Rodolfo NM 26 *Mex.*
González Jiménez, Manuel ARC 52 *Cu.*
González Laguna, Francisco SCL 564, 608 *Per.*
González Lanuza, Eduardo (1900-) A 32; APAM 499; CG II, 600; PLHA 165 *Arg.*
González León, Francisco APMM 61; G 360; HLM 524; PM 47 *Mex.*
González Llorca, Enrique PM 48 *Mex.*
González Llorca, R. TM 168 *Mex.*
González M., G. C 31 *Chil.*
González Maldonado, Eugenio PM 48 *Mex.*
González Manrique, Mariano (1829-1870) Co 30 *Col.*
González Manrique, Venancio (1836-1889) LC 167; RHLC 204 *Col.*
González Martínez, Enrique (1871-1920) AB 23; AMP 45; APEH 488, 1187; APMM 63; BHLA 469, 543; CG II, 603; CHL 539; CLH 472; CP 691; FPA 340, 353; G 360; GLO 248; HLM 425; MSAP 146, 310; PM 48; PMe I, 205; PMM 67; PNM 89; SAL 82 *et passim*; SASS 375; WLA 177 *Mex.*
González Moncada, A. NL 216 *Nicar.*
González Moreno, Jesús LAS 199; TM 444 *Mex.*
González Murioles, Miguel Cu 71 *Cu.*
González N., Carlos SD 15 *Dom.*
González Narváez, J. I. Cu 71; V 79 *Cu.*
González Obregón, Luis (1865-) BAMP 61; CG II, 605; CHL 410; CLH 356; G 360; HLM 485; HLMex 239; NM 2, 26; SASS 387; TM 547; WLA 178 *Mex.*
González Ortiz, C. V 79 *Venez.*
González P., Alejandro C 31; NC 426 *Chil.*
González Pacheco, Rodolfo A 32, 85 *Arg.*
González Páez, M. A. E 35 *Ecua.*

González Peña, Carlos (1885-) CG II, 609; CHL 428; G 361; HLM 515; Ig 159; LAND 121, 130; NM 2, 26; TM 168, 444, 547; WLA 178 *Mex.*

González Peña, Simón V 79 *Venez.*

González Pérez, Salvador V 79 *Venez.*

González Prada, Alfredo (1891-) BHLA 540 *Per.*

González Prada, Manuel (1844-1918) AB 23; AEHA 691; APEH 3, 1175; BHLA 363, 428, 538; CHL 300; CLH 254; G 381; LAS 207; LP 377; P 13; PLHA 257; SA 177; SASS 432 *Per.*

González Pulido, J. Andrés A 32 *Arg.*

González Quiara, José E. BP 504, 601 *P.R.*

González Quiara, T. PR 27 *P.R.*

González Quintana, Octavio NL 248 *Nicar.*

González Rincones, Salustio ("Otal Susi") V 79, 108 *Venez.*

González Rodil, Jorge V 79 *Venez.*

González Rodríguez, J. Pan 9 *Pan.*

González Rojo, Enrique (1899-) AMP 98; APMM 71; CG II, 616; HLM 525; PM 49; PMM 163 *Mex.*

González Rucavado, Claudio (1878-1929) CA 31; CG II, 617; EPCR 302; IBCR IV, 20, 74 *et passim C.R.*

González Ruz de Montoro, Francisca (-1895) Cu 71; PCu 123 *Cu.*

González Sánchez, Flaviano CG II, 618; Cu 71 *Cu.*

González Sánchez, Marcelino TM 169 *Mex.*

González Santos, Francisco BDC 30; Cu 71 *Cu.*

González Saravia, Miguel CA 75 *Guat.*

González Soto, Miguel ("Gumiel") (1881-) CA 32; EPCR 447 *C.R.*

González Suárez, Federico (1844-1917) BHLA 384; CG II, 619; E 35; G 344; PLE 44 *Ecua.*

González Téllez y Ruiz, Luisa Cu 71 *Cu.*

González Toledo, Aureliano BC 176; Co 30 *Col.*

González Torres, Nicolás Co 30 *Col.*

González Tuñón, Enrique A 32 *Arg.*

González Tuñón, Raúl A 32; APAM 516; BHLA 640; LAC 149; PLHA 157 *Arg.*

González Varela, José Silverio V 79 *Venez.*

González Varela, Juan Manuel V 79 *Venez.*

González Vera, J. S. (1897-) C 10; GLO 239; IE 123 *Chil.*

González Verástegui, Esteban TM 169, 444 *Mex.*

González Vigil, Francisco de Paula P 13 *Per.*

González Víquez, Cleto (1858-) CA 32; CG II, 622; EPCR 127 *C.R.*

González y Menéndez, Piedad Cu 71 *Cu.*

González y Ugalde, Carlos C 31, 48; CG II, 478, 621 *Chil.*

González Zeledón, Manuel ("Magón") (1864-1936) CA 32, 37; CHL 508; EPCR 134; IBCR IV, 179; IE 124 *C.R.*

"Gonzalo González" (*pseud.*) *see* Quirós Blanco, Teodoro

Gonzalo Marín, Francisco (1863-1897) PP 118; PR 35 *P.R.*

Gonzalo-Salas, Tulio V 79 *Venez.*

Gooding, G. Co 51 *Col.*

"Goodman, H." (*pseud.*) CHL 473; CLH 414 *Cu.*

"Gorda, Brocha" (*pseud.*) *see* Jaimes, Julio Lucas

Gordils Vassallo, José PR 35 *P.R.*

Gordon, Eduardo G. U 8 *Uru.*

Gormaz Santander, Raúl E 36 *Ecua.*

Gornés MacPherson, Martín José (1884-) V 79; WLA 179 *Venez.*

Gorostiza, Celestino TM 169 *Mex.*

Gorostiza, Manuel Eduardo de ("el lic. Sánchez Vicuña") (1789-1851) AEHA 409; CHL 387; CLH 335; G 361; GLO 248; HLM 319; HLMex 126; HPHA I, 113; HPM 737; TM 169, 445, 480 *Mex.*

Gorostiza Alcalá, José (1901-) AMP 167; APEH 1145; APMM 76; BHLA 562; HLM 526; PM 49; PMM 189; TM 169, 445, 547; WLA 180 *Mex.*

Gorriño, Manuel E 36 *Ecua.*

Gorriti de Belzú, Juana Manuela (1819-1892) A 32; BHLA 350; CHL 188, 303; CLH 161, 257; LA VI, 1128; VIII, 787, 793; PLHA 176; SPLA 234 *Arg.*

Gorrochótegui, Abelardo V 79 *Venez.*

Gosdawa, Gustavo, Baron de Gostkowski TM 494 *Mex.*

Gostkowski, Alfredo G. TM 174, 448 *Mex.*

"Got, Gil" (*pseud.*) *see* Subieta, Eduardo

Goti, Leo A 32 *Arg.*

Gouchón Cané, Emilio A 32; CG II, 627 *Arg.*

Govantes, José Joaquín (-1881) BDC 30; Cu 71 *Cu.*

Govantes, Pedro Pablo Cu 71 *Cu.*

Govantes y Govantes, Vivino Cu 71 *Cu.*

Govea, Luis Guillermo V 80 *Venez.*

Goyc, Juan Ig 161; NM 26 *Mex.*

Goycoechea Menéndez, Martín de ("Lucio Stella") (1877-1906) A 31, 32, 78; APAM 102 *Arg.*

Goyena, Carlos P. A 32 *Arg.*

Goyena, Pedro (1843-1892) A 32; CG II, 631; HLA 437 *Arg.*

Goyena Peralta, Rafael (1852-1883) CA 75; GPCA II, 425; PG 251 *Guat.*

Graciani, Antonio A 32 *Arg.*

Grafe Calatrava, Eladio V 80 *Venez.*

Granada, Nicolás (-1915) A 32, 85; CG II, 638 *Arg.*

Granado, Félix A. del (1873?-) B 8 *Bol.*

Granados, Emilio CA 32 *C.R.*

Granados, Joaquín ARC 52 *Cu.*

Granados, Juan Antonio CA 32 *C.R.*

Granados, María Josefa G. (1796-1848) CA 75 *Guat.*

Granados Guarnizo, Carlos Francisco E 36; PE 58 *Ecua.*

Granados Guarnizo, M. A. E 37 *Ecua.*

Granados Maldonado, Francisco HPM 830; PM 49; TM 174 *Mex.*

Grande, Cayetano Alberto A 32 *Arg.*

Grande y Rossi, Federico Cu 71 *Cu.*

Grandmontagne, Francisco A 32; CG II, 639; LA VIII, 622 *Arg.*

Grané, Luis María A 33 *Arg.*

Granja, Conde de la *see* Oviedo y Herrera, Luis Antonio de

Granja Irigoyen, Agustín CG II, 642; NM 26; TM 174 *Mex.*

Gras, Mario César A 33; CG II, 642 *Arg.*
Graterol y Morles, J. V 80 *Venez.*
Grau, Jacinto (1877-) G 336; GLO 243 *Cu.*
Grau B., Daniel E 37 *Ecua.*
Gravier, Bernardo A 33 *Arg.*
Greca, Alcides A 33; CG II, 645 *Arg.*
Grecia, Pablo de CG II, 646; U 8; UL 128 *Uru.*
Gredilla y Gauna, Apolinar Federico (1859-) CG II, 646; Co 3 *Col.*
Greek, Alejandro C 10, 48; NC 136 *Chil.*
Gregor, J. TM 547 *Mex.*
Greiff, León de ("Leo de Gris") (1895-) ALC II, 317; BHLA 588; Co 31 *Col.*
Greve, Ernesto C 10 *Chil.*
Grez, Vicente (1847-1909) BHLA 404; C 10, 31, 66; CHL 273; CLH 232; HC 239; NC 137 *Chil.*
Grez P., Eduardo C 31 *Chil.*
Grez Torres, Carlos C 48 *Chil.*
Grillo, Augusto J. CA 32 *C.R.*
Grillo, Maximiliano (1868-) ALC II, 43; BC 180; CG II, 651; Co 31, 79; G 329; LC 188; PCo 147; RHLC 211; WLA 181 *Col.*
Griñán Peralta, Leonardo ARC 53 *Cu.*
"Gris, Leo de" (*pseud.*) *see* Greiff, León de
Grisanti, Ángel V 80 *Venez.*
Grodsinski, G. A 33 *Arg.*
"Groimemi, Genaro A." (*pseud.*) *see* Guerra, Gerónimo A.
Gronlier, Camilo E. Cu 71 *Cu.*
Groot, José Manuel ("Pacho") (1800-1878) BC 181; CHL 340; Co 31; LC 151; RHLC 121, 199 *Col.*
Groussac, Paul (1848-1929) A 33, 85; BHLA 358, 398; CG II, 654; CHL 192; CLH 164; G 312; GLO 235; LAC 100; SAL 110; SASS 87 *Arg.*
Grovares, Juan F. Cu 71 *Cu.*
Gruesso, José María (1779-1835) Co 31; HLNG II, 76, 297; RHLC 80; SCL 543, 608 *Col.*
Grullón, Eliseo SD 15 *Dom.*
Grünberg, Carlos M. A 33; APAM 519 *Arg.*
Grunberg, Raquel A 33 *Arg.*
Guachalla, José Manuel B 8 *Bol.*
Guadalajara, José Rafael (1863-1895) CG II, 655; G 361; HLM 457; Ig 161; NM 26 *Mex.*
Guadalajara, Julio E. V 80 *Venez.*
Guadalajara y Cosío, Joaquín M. PM 49 *Mex.*
Gual, Pedro CG II, 655; V 80 *Venez.*
Gualba Guerra, Miguel ARC 38 *Cu.*
Gualtieri, Luigi TM 448 *Mex.*
Guamorado, Miguel W. BDC 30 *Cu.*
"Guanabacoa, César de" (*pseud.*) *see* Sos, Ciriaco
Guanes, Alejandro Par 14; PPa 63 *Para.*
Guarderas, Francisco PE 81 *Ecua.*
Guardia, Harmodio Pan 9 *Pan.*
Guardia, Heraclio Martín de la (1829-1907) CHL 370; CLH 319; LV 285; V 80 *Venez.*
Guardia, Isidoro Rafael de la (-1912) Cu 71 *Cu.*

Guardia, José María (1883?-) Pan 9 *Pan.*
Guardia, Julio Pan 9 *Pan.*
Guardia G., Tomás Pan 9 *Pan.*
Guardia Quirós, Víctor CA 32; EPCR 307 *C.R.*
Guardia y Ayala, Víctor de la (1772-18?) CA 33; CG II, 657; EPCR 15; IBCR IV, 388 *C.R.*
Guardiola, Matilde A 55 *Arg.*
Guarín, José David ("David" *or* "El Tisgón") (1830-1890) AC II, 227; BC 187; CHL 338; Co 32, 46; LC 145; PCo 148; RHLC 124 *Col.*
Guasp, Ignacio PP 29 *P.R.*
"Guayabo" (*pseud.*) *see* Martínez, Domingo
Gucovsky, Victoria A 33; LAC 138 *Arg.*
Güell y Mercader, José ("Hortensio") CG II, 662; V 13, 84 *Venez.*
Güell y Renté, José (1819-1884) Cu 72 *Cu.*
Güell y Renté, Juan (1815-1875) Cu 72 *Cu.*
"Guero, Gil" (*pseud.*) *see* Barrios F., Ciriaco
Guerra, Adolfo F. A 33 *Arg.*
Guerra, Antonino de la BDC 31; Cu 73 *Cu.*
Guerra, Antonio E 37 *Ecua.*
Guerra, Armando ARC 53 *Cu.*
Guerra, Ernesto E. ("Genaro E. Terrues") NM 26, 54 *Mex.*
Guerra, Gerónimo A. ("Genaro A. Groimemi") ARC 41 *Cu.*
Guerra, Héctor Arnaldo C 31 *Chil.*
Guerra, Ignacio (hijo) PD 90; SD 15 *Dom.*
Guerra, J. Guillermo CL 285 *Chil.*
Guerra, José Eduardo (1894-) B 9; BT 131 *Bol.*
Guerra, José Joaquín (1873-) Co 32 *Col.*
Guerra, Juan Esteban C 48 *Chil.*
Guerra, Juan Rafael NL 126; PN 71 *Nicar.*
Guerra, Juvenal C 31 *Chil.*
Guerra, Mario E. SD 15 *Dom.*
Guerra, Martín (1840-) BC 189; Co 32 *Col.*
Guerra, Ramón Héctor ("Barón de Astrea") PR 18, 42, 46 *P.R.*
Guerra, Rosa (-1864) A 33, 85; LA VIII, 791 *Arg.*
Guerra Castro, Felipe PM 49 *Mex.*
Guerra G., Manuel A. C 31 *Chil.*
Guerra García, J. TM 175 *Mex.*
Guerra Marcano, Mateo V 80 *Venez.*
Guerra Massetti, Luciano A 33, 85 *Arg.*
Guerra Mondragón, Miguel CG II, 664; PR 25 *P.R.*
Guerra Núñez, Juan Cu 73; PA 41; PCu 133 *Cu.*
Guerra y García, José Cu 73; TM 175
Guerra y Sánchez, Ramiro (1881-) CG II, 665; CT 335; Cu 73 *Cu.*
Guerrero, Dolores (1833-1858) HPM 838; PM 49; PoM 298 *Mex.*
Guerrero, Doroteo José PS 110 *Salv.*
Guerrero, Eduardo A. PM 49 *Mex.*
Guerrero, Emilio Constantino LV 412; V 80 *Venez.*
Guerrero, Francisco C 31 *Chil.*
Guerrero, J. Agustín E 37 *Ecua.*
Guerrero, J. J. TM 175 *Mex.*
Guerrero, Juan José (-1867) BDC 31; Cu 73 *Cu.*
Guerrero, Julio (1862-) CG II, 665; PM 49 *Mex.*

Guerrero, Luis M. BDC 31; Cu 73. *Cu.*
Guerrero, Miguel A. PD 89; SD 15 *Dom.*
Guerrero, Pablo J. V 80 *Venez.*
Guerrero, Pacífico A 33 *Arg.*
Guerrero, Pascual Cu 73; PJC 89 *Cu.*
Guerrero, Teodoro (1820-1905) BDC 31; BP 504; CG II, 666; PR 27 *P.R.*
Guerrero Kramer, Concepción PM 49 *Mex.*
Guerrero y Pallares, Teodoro (1820-1905) Cu 73 *Cu.*
Guerro, Ortiz Par 14 *Para.*
Guevara, Bernardo de C 31 *Chil.*
Guevara, Bernardo José B 9 *Bol.*
Guevara, José (1719-1806) LA III, 524; Par 14; SCL 415, 608 *Para.*
Guevara, Juan de HLM 157; HPM 201; PM 49; TM 176 *Mex.*
Guevara, Maximiliano V 80 *Venez.*
Guevara, Tomás C 48, 66; CG II, 667; CL 285 *Chil.*
Guevara Carrera, J. M. V 80 *Venez.*
Guevara Labal, C. A 33 *Arg.*
Guevara Núñez, F. V 80 *Venez.*
Guevara Rojas, Felipe CG II, 667; V 81 *Venez.*
Guevara Santander, Francisco de Paula V 81 *Venez.*
Guevara Valdés, Antonio PS 60 *Salv.*
Guezúraga, Margot A 33 *Arg.*
Guezúraga Diez, V. C 31 *Chil.*
Guglielmi Urzúa, Juana C 31 *Chil.*
Guglielmini, Homero A 33; LAC 123, 155 *Arg.*
Guglieri, P. A 34 *Arg.*
Guibernao, Domingo BDC 32 *Cu.*
Guibourg, Edmundo A 34, 85 *Arg.*
Guido, Ángel (1896-) CG II, 685; WLA 184 *Arg.*
Guido, José Tomás A 34 *Arg.*
Guido, Juan B. PM 49 *Mex.*
Guido y Spano, Carlos (1827-1918) A 34; BHLA 311; CG II, 685; CHL 177; CLH 152; FPA 15, 30; LA VII, 424; PLHA 73; SASS 25; SPLA 101; WSAL 31, 72 *Arg.*
Guijo, Gregorio Martín de TM 548 *Mex.*
Guillén, Alberto (1900-) BAP 59; BHLA 606, 609; CG II, 687; CrA 101; E 37; G 381; IE 125; P 14; SASS 437 *Per.*
Guillén, Andrés ARC 53 *Cu.*
Guillén, Nicolás (1907-) APEH 1025; ARC 41, 53; BHLA 570; Cu 75; G 336; LH 81, 140; PJC 91; PoC 122 *Cu.*
Guillén Chaparro, Francisco Co 32; HLNG I, 119 *Col.*
Guillén y Mesa, Mariano (1846-) BDC 32; Cu 75 *Cu.*
Guillén y Sánchez, Antonio TM 176 *Mex.*
Guillén Zelaya, Alfonso (1889?-) CP 691; FPA 318, 330; G 347 *Hond.*
Guillot, Víctor Juan A 34; CG II, 690; GLO 236; LAC 134 *Arg.*
Guimerrá, Miguel P. Cu 76 *Cu.*
Guinán (or Guinand), Rafael V 81 *Venez.*
Guindilla, N. A 34 *Arg.*
Guindo, Máximo A 34 *Arg.*
Guiñazú, H. R. C 31 *Chil.*
Guiral Moreno, Mario (1882-) CG II, 692; Cu 76 *Cu.*

Güiraldes, Ricardo (1886-1927) A 34; APAM 523; APEH 964, 1192; BHLA 506, 635; CG II, 692; CHL 204; G 313; GLO 236; LAC 46, 132; LH 155; NPA 253; PLHA 209; SASS 75 *Arg.*
Guirao, Ramón (1908-) PoC 129 *Cu.*
Guiteras, Antonio Cu 76 *Cu.*
Guiteras, Eusebio (1823-1893) Cu 76 *Cu.*
Guiteras, Pedro José (1814-1890) CG II, 694; Cu 76; RLC 246 *Cu.*
Gullo, Antonio A 34 *Arg.*
"Gumiel" (*pseud.*) *see* González Soto, Miguel
Gumilla, José (1686-1750) CG II, 697; Co 32; HLNG I, 359; RHLC 17; SCL 390, 609 *Col.*
Gumilla, Joseph V 81 *Venez.*
Gurdiel Fernández, José TM 176 *Mex.*
Guridi y Alcocer, José Miguel (1763-1828) ACe 545; BAMP 20; BHLA 199; HLM 259; HLMex 117 *Mex.*
Guruceaga, Juan de V 81 *Venez.*
Gutiérrez, Alberto (1863-1928) B 9; BT 133; CG II, 698 *Bol.*
Gutiérrez, Alonso ("Alonso de la Veracruz") (1504-1584) HLM 24 *Mex.*
Gutiérrez, Carlos A. C 31; PCh 301 *Chil.*
Gutiérrez, César Mayo PU 280 *Uru.*
Gutiérrez, Eduardo (1853-1890) A 34; BHLA 411; CG II, 699; CHL 170; CLH 146; LA II, 875; SPLA 159, 235 *Arg.*
Gutiérrez, Eulogio C 10; NC 500 *Chil.*
Gutiérrez, Federico NM 26 *Mex.*
Gutiérrez, Federico A. A 35; APAM 104 *Arg.*
Gutiérrez, José C. TM 176 *Mex.*
Gutiérrez, José Margarito (1855-) ARC 39; Cu 76 *Cu.*
Gutiérrez, José Rosendo (1840-1883) B 9; LB 595 *Bol.*
Gutiérrez, Juan María (1809-1878) A 35, 71, 73; AEHA 417; BHLA 278; C 66; CG II, 700; CHL 129, 136, 145, 184, 188; CLH 123; G 313; GEA XXII; GLO 236; HLA 355, 362; HPHA II, 456; HSLU III, pt 4, 16; LA II, 933; VI, 1025; VII, 405; PLHA 72, 256; SAL 227; SPLA 74; TM 548; WSAL 26, 71 *Arg.*
Gutiérrez, Luis TM 176 *Mex.*
Gutiérrez, Manuel CG II, 700; TM 177, 448 *Mex.*
Gutiérrez, Marcelo Co 32 *Col.*
Gutiérrez, Miguel C. TM 178 *Mex.*
Gutiérrez, Pedro Elías V 81 *Venez.*
1. Gutiérrez, Ricardo (1836-1896) A 35; BHLA 310; CG II, 700; CHL 160; CLH 139; G 313; GLO 236; HLA 450; LA VII, 461; PLHA 82; SPLA 99 *Arg.*
2. Gutiérrez, Ricardo (1879-) APAM 310; CG II, 700; NPA 237 *Arg.*
Gutiérrez, Rigoberto PN 31 *Nicar.*
Gutiérrez, Rufino (1854-) Co 32 *Col.*
Gutiérrez, Severiano L. TM 179 *Mex.*
Gutiérrez, Tomás (-1881) A 35, 40; LA VIII, 628 *Arg.*
Gutiérrez, Valeriano G. Cu 76 *Cu.*
Gutiérrez Alea, Lino Cu 76; PA 51 *Cu.*
Gutiérrez Alfaro, Antonio A 35 *Arg.*
Gutiérrez Betancourt, Alfonso CG II, 701; V 81 *Venez.*

Gutiérrez Coll, Jacinto AEHA 420; CHL 374; CLH 322; LV 28, 42, 300; V 81 *Venez.*

Gutiérrez Cruz, Carlos (-1930) G 361; PM 49 *Mex.*

Gutiérrez Darío (1869-) B 9; BT 89 *Bol.*

Gutiérrez de Cos, Pedro (1750-1833) PR 18 *P.R.*

Gutiérrez de Gandarilla, Juan Cu 76 *Cu.*

Gutiérrez de Lara, L. NM 27 *Mex.*

Gutiérrez de Piñeres, Germán (1816-1872) BC 195; Co 32; LC 139; RHLC 99, 101 *Col.*

Gutiérrez de Piñeres, Vicente (1805-1877) RHLC 101 *Col.*

Gutiérrez Ferreira, J. A. Co 32 *Col.*

Gutiérrez González, Gregorio ("Antioco") (1826-1872) AC I, 1; II, 7; AEHA 423; ALC I, 171; BC 190; BHLA 322; CHL 332; CLH 284, 285; Co 32; FPA 82, 105; G 329; HPHA II, 60; LC 140; RHLC 93, 99; SASS 218 *Col.*

Gutiérrez Hermosillo, Alfonso PM 49 *Mex.*

Gutiérrez Nájera, Manuel ("El Duque Job," "Junius," "Mr. Cancán," "Puck," *or* "Recamier," *etc.*) (1859-1895) AB 23; AEHA 424; AMP 3; APEH 5, 1175; APMM 78; BHLA 452; CG II, 705; CHL 417, 512, 540; CLH 363, 364, 452; FPA 340, 349; G 361; GLO 249; HLM 409; HLMex 206, 221; NM 27; PLHA 88; PM 49; PMe I, 207; PNM 112; PoM 275; SAL 16 *et passim*; SASS 364; TM 179 *Mex.*

Gutiérrez Ortiz, Víctor PR 46 *P.R.*

Gutiérrez Podestá LAS 207 *Arg.*

Gutiérrez Ponce, Ignacio (1850-) Co 33 *Col.*

Gutiérrez Quintanilla, Emilio (1858-1935) BHLA 406; P 14 *Per.*

Gutiérrez Quirós, Manuel Cu 76 *Cu.*

Gutiérrez Vergara, Ignacio (1806-1877) RHLC 109 *Col.*

Gutiérrez Zamora, José Manuel PM 50 *Mex.*

Guzmán, Alcibíades (1862-1919) B 9; BT 145; CG II, 707 *Bol.*

Guzmán, Antonio Leocadio LV 16; V 81 *Venez.*

Guzmán, César C. (1840-) Co 33 *Col.*

Guzmán, Diego Rafael de (1848-1920) BC 198; CG II, 708; Co 33; LAS 199; LC 173 *Col.*

Guzmán, Ernesto A. (1877-) APEH 702, 1189; C 31; CG II, 708; N 229; PCC xii, 43; PCh 219 *Chil.*

Guzmán, F. Benjamín SD 15 *Dom.*

Guzmán, Francisco de Paula (1844-1884) HLM 303; HPM 882; PM 50 *Mex.*

Guzmán, Guadelupe V 82 *Venez.*

Guzmán, José Benito B 9 *Bol.*

Guzmán, Juvenal C 10; NC 165 *Chil.*

Guzmán, L. B. V 82 *Venez.*

Guzmán, Leonardo B 10 *Bol.*

Guzmán, Luis Mariano B 10 *Bol.*

Guzmán, Luis Ramón LV 110, 392; V 82 *Venez.*

Guzmán, Ricardo BHLA 613 *Bol.*

Guzmán, Salvador R. de TM 179 *Mex.*

Guzmán, Víctor Manuel (1884-) WLA 186 *Ecua.*

Guzmán Aguilera, Antonio CG II, 708; PM 50; TM 180 *Mex.*

Guzmán Blanco, Antonio (1830-1899) CHL 369; CLH 318; LV 159; V 82 *Venez.*

Guzmán C., Benjamín (1873-) B 10; LB 614 *Bol.*

Guzmán Cruchaga, Juan (1896-) APEH 672; BHLA 535; C 32, 49; CMPC 122; MSAP 182, 319; PCC xviii, 191; PCh 383 *Chil.*

"Guzmán Maturana, Manuel" (*pseud.*) *see* Dantés, Edmundo

Guzmán Téllez, Roberto (1894-) WLA 187 *Bol.*

Guzmán y Benítez, José PR 18 *P.R.*

Guzmán y Franco, Martín Luis (1887-) BHLA 558; CG II, 709; G 363; HLM 518; NM 27; TM 449; WLA 186 *Mex.*

H

"Habanero, Un Vate" (*pseud.*) Cu 173 *Cu.*

"Halmar, Augusto d'" (*pseud.*) *see* Thomson, Augusto

Hall, Eduardo (1832-1885) CA 75; GPCA II, 205; PG 152 *Guat.*

Hall, Guillermo F. CA 75; GPCA III, 461 *Guat.*

Hammeken y Mejía, Jorge TM 449 *Mex.*

"Harmodio" (*pseud.*) *see* Tijerina, Juan B.

Haro y T., Agustín NM 27 *Mex.*

Hárriett, Ramón 2° C 10; NC 165, 499 *Chil.*

"Hatuey" (*pseud.*) Cu 76 *Cu.*

Haucke, J. von TM 595 *Mex.*

Havestadt, Bernardo (-1781) BHC III, 55 *Chil.*

Haya de la Torre, Víctor Raúl (1895-) BHLA 601 *Per.*

Hederra Concha, Francisco ("Julián del Claro") C 6, 11, 49 *Chil.*

"Heim, Víctor" (*pseud.*) *see* Márquez, Antonio José

Helguera, Álvaro de la TM 449, 495 *Mex.*

Helú, Antonio Ig 165; NM 27; TM 180 *Mex.*

Hemmingsen, Víctor A 11 *Arg.*

Henao, Januario (1850-) Co 33 *Col.*

Henao y Melguizo, Jesús María (1868-) Co 33 *Col.*

Henares y Briega, Francisco (1872-) CT 303 *Cu.*

Henis, Tadeo Xavier (1711-) Par 14 *Para.*

Henríquez, Camilo ("Quirino Lemachez") (1769-1825) A 35, 85; BHLA 162, 176; C 49; CHL 59, 67; CLH 50, 58; HC 48; HPHA II, 342; LA IV, 924 *Arg.*

Henríquez, Enrique (*or* Enríquez) LD 97; PA 314; PD 91; SD 15 *Dom.*

Henríquez, Gustavo J. PD 110; SD 15 *Dom.*

Henríquez, José Ramón V 82 *Venez.*

Henríquez, Juan Antonio (1860-) Pan 9 *Pan.*

Henríquez de Guzmán, Alonso BHLA 81 *Per.*

Henríquez Pérez, Honorio (1879-) C 11, 32; NC 363; PCh 257 *Chil.*

Henríquez Ureña, Max (1885-) BDC 32; BHLA 491; C 66; CG III, 21; CHL 497; CLH 428, 438; CT 97; Cu 76; FPA 228, 250; HLC 215; IE 128; LD 100; NM 2; PA 326; PD 100; SAL 201 *et passim*; SASS 323; SD 15 *Dom.*

Henríquez Ureña, Pedro (1884-) BDC 33; BHLA 491; CG III, 21; CHL 38, 417, 497; CLH 32, 362, 438; G 385; LAND 121, 127, 177; LD 99; OA 67; PA 328; PD 106; SAL 160, 244; SASS 321; SD 16; TM 548; WLA 187 *Dom.*

Henríquez y Carvajal, Federico (1848-) BHLA 390; CHL 495; CLH 436; Co 33; Cu 77; IE 131; LD 85; PA 322; PD 97; SD 17 *Dom.*

Henríquez y Carvajal, Francisco (1859-) CHL 494; LD 85; SD 18 *Dom.*

"Henry" (*pseud.*) *see* Coronado, Enrique

"Heráclito" (*pseud.*) *see* Muñoz Rivera, Luis

Heredia, Antonio de (fl.1700) PM 50; TM 180 *Mex.*

Heredia, Carmen LAS 199 *Mex.*

Heredia, José Félix E 37 *Ecua.*

Heredia, José María de (1803-1839) BDC 33; BHLA 172; CG III, 26; CHL 107; CLH 90; Cu 77; FPA 161, 163; G 337; GLO 243; HLC 38; HPHA I, 228; HPM 813; PA 54; PCu 136; RLC 57, 70, 90, 146, 177, 192; SAL 13, 113, 295; SASS 262; TM 449, 495; WSAL 18, 69 *Cu.*

Heredia, Manuel de J. PD 111; SD 18 *Dom.*

Heredia, Severiano (1839-1895) ARC 35 *Cu.*

Heredia y Mota, Nicolás (1859-1901) CG III, 26; Cu 79; G 337; HLC 187; LD 87; RLC 230, 308 *Cu.*

Herize y Salinas, Martín de (1626-) BHC I, 523 *Chil.*

"Hermano Miguel" (*pseud.*) *see* Febres Cordero, F.

Hermes García, G. V 82 *Venez.*

"Hermes Nahuel" (*pseud.*) *see* Arriaza, Armando

"Herminia" (*pseud.*) *see* Ureña de Henríquez, Salomé

"Hermógenes Novo" (*pseud.*) *see* Fernández Ferraz, Valeriano

Hermosa, J. Cu 80 *Cu.*

Hermosa, Jesús Ig 166 *Mex.*

Hermoso, R. R. V 82 *Venez.*

Hermoso de Álvarez, Josefina V 82 *Venez.*

"Hernández, A. Carmen" (*pseud.*) *see* Benítez, Alejandrina

Hernández, Basilio ARC 53 *Cu.*

Hernández, Belisario A 35 *Arg.*

Hernández, Blas Co 33 *Col.*

Hernández, Carlos PM 50 *Mex.*

Hernández, Carmen BDC 37, 112; PR 12 *P.R.*

Hernández, Domingo Ramón (1829-1893) BHLA 326; CHL 366; CLH 314; LV 136, 286; SASS 511; V 82 *Venez.*

Hernández, Efrén G 363; NM 27 *Mex.*

Hernández, Emiliano CG III, 30; V 83 *Venez.*

Hernández, Enrique Soriano PR 25 *P.R.*

Hernández, Fortunato (1862-) CG III, 30; Ig 166; NM 27 *Mex.*

Hernández, Francisco J. PR 18, 46 *P.R.*

Hernández, Gaspar Octavio (1893-1918) AP 131; CG III, 30; Cu 80; FPA 382, 396; Pan 10 *Pan.*

Hernández, Gaston B. (1866-) Cu 80 *Cu.*

Hernández, Genaro Cu 80 *Cu.*

Hernández, Hilarión V 83 *Venez.*

Hernández, J. R. Ig 168; NM 27 *Mex.*

Hernández, Jacinto Cu 80 *Cu.*

Hernández, Jesús Co 33 *Col.*

Hernández, José (1834-1886) A 35; AB 23; AEHA 437; BDC 37; BHLA 419; CHL 165; CLH 143; Cu 80; G 313; GLO 236; HLA 405; HPHA II, 473; LA I, 66; II, 757; PLHA 80; SASS 28; SPLA 88; WSAL 39 *Arg.*

Hernández, José Elías Cu 80 *Cu.*

Hernández, José Gregorio V 83 *Venez.*

Hernández, José P. H. BP 527; PP 341; PR 35 *P.R.*

Hernández, Manuel H. ("Hernando d'Aquino") Cu 12, 80 *Cu.*

Hernández, Manuel María Cu 80 *Cu.*

Hernández, Marcial CG III, 31; V 83 *Venez.*

Hernández, Octavio V 83, 113 *Venez.*

Hernández, Pablo BDC 37; Cu 80; PCu 142 *Cu.*

Hernández, Pedro José CHL 368; CLH 317; V 83 *Venez.*

Hernández, Pero LA III, 145 *Arg.*

Hernández, Reynel NM 27 *Mex.*

Hernández, Roberto C 66 *Chil.*

Hernández, Soledad V 83 *Venez.*

Hernández Alemán, Antonio E. BDC 38; Cu 80 *Cu.*

Hernández Alonso, Gregorio TM 180, 220 *Mex.*

Hernández Ayala, Vicente BDC 38; Cu 81 *Cu.*

Hernández Blanco, Héctor Horacio (1885-) CG III, 32; Co 33; WLA 188 *Col.*

Hernández Capote, Antonio CG III, 33; Cu 81 *Cu.*

Hernández-Catá, Alfonso (1885-) BDC 38; BHLA 525; CG III, 34; CHL 488; Cu 81; G 337; GLO 244; PLHA 234; RLC 343; WLA 188 *Cu.*

Hernández Crespo, Manuel (-1886) BDC 39 *Cu.*

Hernández de Alba, Alfonso Co 33 *Col.*

Hernández de Alba, Guillermo Co 33 *Col.*

Hernández de Alba, Rafael BDC 37, 112; Cu 82 *Cu.*

Hernández de León, Federico (1883-) CA 75; CG III, 37; WLA 189 *Guat.*

Hernández de Rosario A 36 *Arg.*

Hernández Fombona, Juan F. ARC 53 *Cu.*

Hernández Franco, Tomás Rafael SD 18 *Dom.*

Hernández Giro, Juan E. CG III, 36; Cu 82 *Cu.*

Hernández Gutiérrez, Rafael V 83 *Venez.*

Hernández Gwynne, B. A 36 *Arg.*

Hernández Lapido, Pablo Cu 82 *Cu.*

Hernández Millares, E. PCu 143 *Cu.*

Hernández Miyares, Enrique (1859-1914) CG III, 38; CHL 490; CLH 429; Cu 82; FPA 162, 190; G 338; PA 51, 58; RLC 245, 270; SASS 283 *Cu.*

Hernández Otero, Saturno Cu 82 *Cu.*

Hernández Pavolini, Pedro Cu 82 *Cu.*

Hernández Portela, Ramiro PA 53; PCu 140 *Cu.*

Hernández Torres, Eusebio BC 199; Co 33 *Col.*

Hernández Usera, Rafael CG III, 45; PR 18, 46 *P.R.*

Hernández y García, Julio Severiano (-1909) ARC 40 *Cu.*

Hernández y Rodríguez, Juan Cu 82 *Cu.*

"Hernando d'Aquino" (*pseud.*) *see* Hernández, Manuel H.

Herrán y Bolado, José TM 181 *Mex.*

Herrasti, Francisco de P. (1879-) HLM 514; IE 133; PM 50; WLA 189 *Mex.*

Herrera, Adela Ig 168; NM 27 *Mex.*

Herrera, Alberto CG III, 50; PM 50 *Mex.*

Herrera, Alejandro TM 181 *Mex.*

Herrera, Alejandro N. P 14 *Per.*

Herrera, Alfredo A 36 *Arg.*

1. Herrera, Armando A 36; CG III, 50 *Arg.*

2. Herrera, Armando P 14 *Per.*

Herrera, Ataliva (1888-) A 36; APAM 315; CG III, 50 *Arg.*

Herrera, Bartolomé (1808-1864) BHLA 294 *Per.*

Herrera, Carlos CA 75 *Guat.*

Herrera, Darío (1877-1914) AP 145; FPA 381, 389; Pan 10 *Pan.*

Herrera, Dionisio de (-1850) HL I, 73 *Hond.*

Herrera, Ernesto (-1917) A 36, 85; CG III, 50; HSLU III, pt 3, 17; LU 64, 689; PIU III, 249; PU 107; U 8 *Uru.*

Herrera, Federico (1874-1905) CA 75; PG 354 *Guat.*

Herrera, Flavio (1892-) BHLA 573; CA 75; CG III, 50; FPA 292, 311; LAS 204; PG 449; WLA 190 *Guat.*

Herrera, Francisco TM 181 *Mex.*

Herrera, Héctor TM 595 *Mex.*

Herrera, Ignacio Cu 82 *Cu.*

Herrera, Jenero P 14 *Per.*

Herrera, José de la Cruz (1876-) AP 161; Pan 10; WLA 190 *Pan.*

Herrera, José Manuel de ACe 827 *Mex.*

Herrera, Luis Alberto de (1873-) CG III, 51; UL 128; UT 263; WLA 190 *Uru.*

Herrera, Luis Pío V 84 *Venez.*

Herrera, Manuel Antonio CA 75 *Guat.*

Herrera, Manuel J. A 36; CG III, 51 *Arg.*

Herrera, Pablo (1820-1896) CG III, 52; E 37; PLE 44 *Ecua.*

Herrera, Porfirio PA 331; PD 113; SD 18 *Dom.*

Herrera, Primitivo PA 332; PD 117; SD 18 *Dom.*

Herrera, Tomás (1804-1854) Co 33 *Col.*

1. Herrera, Vicente ACe 828 *Mex.*

2. Herrera, Vicente EPCR 27 *C.R.*

Herrera Alarcón, J. M. NM 27 *Mex.*

Herrera de León, Ignacio TM 181, 451 *Mex.*

Herrera del C., José Antonio Co 33 *Col.*

Herrera Frimont, Celestino NM 23, 27 *Mex.*

Herrera Irigoyen, Jesús María LV 117; V 84 *Venez.*

Herrera Oliver, Raúl A 36 *Arg.*

Herrera S., Demetrio AP 159; Pan 10 *Pan.*

Herrera Tejeda, Luis PM 50 *Mex.*

Herrera Toro, Antonio V 84 *Venez.*

Herrera y Espinosa, Manuel UL 129 *Uru.*

Herrera y Ogazón, Alba (1891-) CG III, 53; IE 137 *Mex.*

Herrera y Puente, Eduardo TM 549 *Mex.*

Herrera y Reissig, Julio (1875-1910) AB 23; APEH 469, 1187; BHLA 464; CG III, 53; CHL 532; CLH 468; CP 696; CrA 69; FPA 528, 539; G 387; GLO 254; HSLU I, pt 8, 5; LU 64, 656; LUr 511; MSAP 126, 301; PIU II, 117; PLHA 108; PoU 97; SA 79; SAL 92, 187, 355; SASS 459; U 8; UL 128 *Uru.*

Herrera y Tordesillas, Antonio de (1549-1625) BHLA 51; CG III, 54; HLM 32; LA III, 103 *Mex.*

Herrera y Vergara, Ignacio (1769-1840) HLNG II, 498 *Col.*

Herrero, Antonio A 36; CG III, 54 *Arg.*

Herrero, Vicente BDC 39; Cu 82 *Cu.*

Herrero Ducloux, Enrique CG III, 55; G 313 *Arg.*

Herrero y Espinosa, Manuel HSLU III, pt 4, 27 *Uru.*

Herreros, Pedro (1890-) A 36; APAM 317 *Arg.*

Heureaux, Belisario ARC 53 *Cu.*

1. Heureaux, Ulises BDC 40, 112; SD 18 *Dom.*

2. Heureaux, Ulises (hijo) SD 18 *Dom.*

Hicken, Ricardo A 36, 85 *Arg.*

Hidalgo, Alberto (1893-) BAP 43; BHLA 606; C 66; GLO 236; P 14; PLHA 162 *Per.*

Hidalgo, Aurelio TM 182 *Mex.*

Hidalgo, Bartolomé (1788-1823) BHLA 169; CHL 71; G 313; HCLU I, 38; HLA 390; HPHA II, 468; HSLU I, pt 2, 31; LA I, 67; II, 495; LUr 421; PIU I, 73; PLHA 67; SASS 453; SPLA 48 *Uru.*

Hidalgo, Enrique A. (1876-1915) CA 75, 76; PG 357 *Guat.*

1. Hidalgo, Félix A 36 *Arg.*

2. Hidalgo, Félix Cu 82 *Cu.*

Hidalgo, José PM 50 *Mex.*

Hidalgo, José Manuel (-1896) HLM 458; Ig 168; NM 27 *Mex.*

Hidalgo de Morán, Delfina C 32, 36 *Chil.*

Hidalgo N., J. CA 76 *Guat.*

Hidalgo y Costilla, Miguel HLMex 103; TM 451 *Mex.*

Hierro, Castor Cu 82 *Cu.*

Higuera, Ernesto PM 50 *Mex.*

"Hija del Camagüey, Una" (*pseud.*) Cu 82 *Cu.*

"Hija del Caribe, La" (*pseud.*) *see* Padilla de Sanz, Trinidad

"Hija del Yumurí" (*pseud.*) *see* Cépero, Belén

Híjar y Haro, Juan B. PM 50 *Mex.*

Himiob, Nelson V 84 *Venez.*

Hine, David (1858-) CA 33 *C.R.*
Hine, Luis CA 33 *C.R.*
Hine Saborío, Enrique PC 115 *Chil.*
Hinestrosa, León (1816-1880) BC 201; Co 33 *Col.*
Hinojosa, Antonio de HLM 23 *Mex.*
Hiroux Funes, Teófilo A 36 *Arg.*
Hirsfield, Dorothy TM 549 *Mex.*
"Hispano, Américo" (*pseud.*) *see* Pozo, José Miguel
"Hispano, Cornelio" (*pseud.*) *see* López, Ismael
Hita, Antonio A 36 *Arg.*
Hofmann, Antonio (hijo) TM 183 *Mex.*
Hogg, Ricardo A 36 *Arg.*
Hojeda, Diego de *see* Ojeda, Diego de
Holguín, Carlos (1832-1894) Co 34; LC 169 *Col.*
Holguín, Jorge Co 34 *Col.*
Holguín Burboa, Joaquín G. TM 183 *Mex.*
Holmberg, Eduardo Ladislao (1852-) A 36; AT II, 107; CG III, 73; LA VIII, 630; WLA 192 *Arg.*
Holmberg de Bracht, Laura A 36 *Arg.*
"Holmes, Sherlock" (*pseud.*) C 20 *Chil.*
Hooper, Ofelia AP 163; Pan 10 *Pan.*
Horta, Eulogio (-1912) Cu 83 *Cu.*
Horta, Manuel (1897-) G 363; HLM 519; IE 139; Ig 171; NM 28 *Mex.*
Horta y Hernández, Juana de BDC 40; Cu 83 *Cu.*
"Hortensio" (*pseud.*) *see* Güell y Mercader, José
Hostos, Adolfo J. de (1887-) QPR (2) 87 *P.R.*
Hostos y Bonilla, Eugenio María de (1839-1903) AB 23; BHLA 375; BP 504, 603; CG III, 83; CHL 494, 502; CLH 442; G 384; LD 87; PR 9, 18, 19, 27, 52, 56; SAL 330; SASS 314; SD 18 *Sp.-P.R.*
"Hourcade, Celestino" (*pseud.*) Ig 173; NM 28 *Mex.*
House, Guillermo A 36 *Arg.*
Hoyos, Enrique PS 106 *Salv.*
Huaman Poma de Ayala, Felipe (1583-1613) BHLA 66 *Per.*
Huarpe, Segundo A 36 *Arg.*
Hubbe, Enrique TM 595 *Mex.*
Hübner, Carlos Luis C 66; NC 427, 493 *Chil.*
Hübner, Manuel Eduardo BHLA 619 *Chil.*
Hübner Bezanilla, Jorge (1892-) APEH 776, 1191; C 7, 28; CMPC 107; G 325; NC 417; PCC xvi, 137; PCh 345 *Chil.*
Huergo, Palemón (1820-) A 36; LA VIII, 590 *Arg.*
Huerta, Gualberto Cardús (1878-) PT 281 *Para.*
Huerta, J. G. de la TM 184 *Mex.*
Huertas, Ignacio CG III, 92; TM 183 *Mex.*
"Hugo Aníbal" (*pseud.*) *see* Acevedo, Pedro Tadeo
"Hugo Sol" (*pseud.*) *see* Manzanilla, Anastasio
"Hugo Wast" (*pseud.*) *see* Martínez Zuviria, Gustavo Adolfo

Huidobro, Vicente (1893-) APEH 1127, 1194; BHLA 624; C 11, 32, 66; CG III, 97; CMPC 115; G 325; MSAP 236, 334; PCC xviii, 167; PCh 359; PLHA 159; SASS 162 *Chil.*
"Hulda" (*pseud.*) *see* Andrade Berti, Josefa
Humanes y Mora, Luis BDC 40; Cu 83 *Cu.*
Hume, B. B. de G 313 *Arg.*
"Hume, Blanca C. de" (*pseud.*) *see* Colt de Hume, Blanca C. E.
Huneeus Gana, Jorge C 11, 66; CG III, 99; CHL 286; CL 286; CLH 242; NC 366 *Chil.*
Huneeus Gana, Roberto C 32, 49; CG III, 99; NC 427 *Chil.*
Hungría, José Antonio SD 19 *Dom.*
Hungría Lovelace, L. A. SD 19 *Dom.*
Hurtado, Antonio Co 34 *Col.*
Hurtado, Leopoldo A 36 *Arg.*
Hurtado, Manuel A. C 32 *Chil.*
Hurtado, Maximiliano V 84 *Venez.*
Hurtado, Ramón CG III, 101; V 84 *Venez.*
Hurtado Baquedano, Jorge C 32; CG III, 101 *Chil.*
Hurtado Borne, René C 11, 49; CG III, 101 *Chil.*
Hurtado de Álvarez, Mercedes (1840-1890) BC 203; Co 34; RHLC 184 *Col.*
Hurtado del Valle, Antonio (1842-1877) Cu 83; PCu 145; RLC 269 *Cu.*
Hurtado L., Luis A. C 32; PCh 331 *Chil.*
Hurtado Machado, J. M. V 84 *Venez.*
Hurtado Sánchez, Ramón V 84 *Venez.*
Hurtado y Arias, Enrique G. C 49 *Chil.*
Huyke, Emilio E. (1912-) QPR (2) 186 *P.R.*
Huyke, Juan Bernardo (1880-) BDC 113; BP 499, 504, 511, 528; PR 7, 9, 12, 13, 19, 27, 36, 42, 46, 52; QPR (1) 87 *P.R.*

I

Ibáñez, Emmy (1887-) G 363; PM 51 *Mex.*
Ibáñez, Fermín Co 34 *Col.*
Ibáñez, Francisco P 14 *Per.*
Ibáñez, Pedro María (1854-1919) CG III, 105; Co 34, 58; RHLC 200 *Col.*
Ibáñez, Roberto CG III, 105; HSLU III, pt 8, 5; PIU III, 215; U 9 *Uru.*
Ibáñez, Víctor M. B 10 *Bol.*
Ibáñez de Echavarri, Bernardo Par 15 *Para.*
Ibarbourou, Juana de (1895-) AB 23; APEH 941, 1192; BHLA 533; CG III, 107; CHL 234; CP 697; CrA 127; FPA 528, 541; G 387; GLO 254; HSLU II, pt 5, 5; III, pt 4, 46; LU 64, 666; PCU 195; PIU III, 77; PLHA 180; PoU 113; PU 113; SASS 462; U 9; WLA 193 *Uru.*
Ibarguren, Carlos (1877-) A 36; AT I, 46; BHLA 633; CG III, 107; LAC 121, 156 *Arg.*
Ibarra, Alejandro V 84 *Venez.*
Ibarra, Felipe GPCA III, 493 *Nicar.*
Ibarra, Luis A. V 84 *Venez.*
Ibarra de Anda, F. LAS 200 *Mex.*

Ibarra R., Juan C 49 *Chil.*
Ibarzábal, Federico de (1893-   ) APEH 817; CG III, 108; Cu 83; GLO 243; PCu 148; PJC 97 *Cu.*
Iberri, Alfonso PM 51 *Mex.*
Icaza *see also* Ycaza
Icaza, Alonso de NM 28 *Mex.*
Icaza, Amelia Denis de (1836-1911) AP 167; FPA 381, 385; Pan 10 *Pan.*
Icaza, Francisco A. de (1863-1925) AMP 88; APEH 111, 1179; APMM 97; BHLA 439; G 363; HLM 429, 494, 496; HLMex 218, 235; PM 51; PMe I, 237; PMM 35; PNM 141; PoM 370; TM 550; V 84 *Mex.*
Icaza (Ycaza), Hortensio de (1883-   ) AP 173; CG III, 113; FPA 382, 393; Pan 11, 20 *Pan.*
Icaza, Jorge BHLA 595; LAS 204 *Ecua.*
Icaza y Lopez Negrete, Xavier, Jr. ("Xavier Icaza") (1892-   ) CG III, 113; G 363; Ig 173; NM 28; TM 185; WLA 194 *Mex.*
Ichaso Díaz, León (1869-   ) BDC 40; CG III, 114; Cu 83 *Cu.*
Ichazo, Francisco BHLA 568; LAS 200 *Cu.*
Igaravídez Arnau, José M. PR 52 *P.R.*
Iglesia y Santos, Álvaro de la ("A. L. Baró") (1859-   ) CG III, 116; CT 59; Cu 18, 84 *Cu.*
Iglesias, Eugenio Julio A 36; CG III, 116 *Arg.*
Iglesias, Francisco María CA 33; EPCR 28 *C.R.*
Iglesias, Luis Samalea PR 46 *P.R.*
Iglesias Calderón, Fernando (1856-   ) WLA 195 *Mex.*
Iglesias Hogan, Rubén CA 33, 34; EPCR 646 *C.R.*
Iglesias Infante, José ARC 53; Cu 84 *Cu.*
Iglesias Mascareño, Augusto ("Julio Talanto") (1895-   ) BHLA 618; C 11, 32; CMPC 130; WLA 195 *Chil.*
Iglesias Paz, César A 36, 85; CHL 199; CG II, 119; PLHA 294 *Arg.*
"Ignotus" (*pseud.*) *see* Peña, Ignacio A. de la
Iguíniz, Juan B. CG III, 121; G 363; HLM 531; NM 2 *Mex.*
Ilabaca León, Alfredo C 32 *Chil.*
Ildefonso, T. TM 246 *Mex.*
Illanes, Bernardo B. C 32 *Chil.*
Illanes, Bernardo Victorino C 11; NC 166 *Chil.*
Illingworth, Juan (1859?-   ) CG III, 123; E 38; PE 162 *Ecua.*
Imbernó, José Cu 84 *Cu.*
Imendia, Carlos A. PS 165 *Salv.*
Imhof, Francisco A 36, 86; CG III, 123; LU 64, 690; PIU III, 299 *Uru.*
Imperiale, Aníbal J. A 36; CG III, 123 *Arg.*
"Inca, El" (*pseud.*) *see* Garcilaso de la Vega
Inclán, Luis Gonzaga (1816-1875) BHLA 345; CHL 404; HLM 342; HLMex 174; Ig 174; NM 28; PM 51 *Mex.*
Inchaustegui, Joaquín SD 19 *Dom.*
Indarte, Rivera (1814-1844) HLA 336 *Arg.*
"Inés Bello" (*pseud.*) *see* Echeverría de Larraín, Inés

"Inés de la Cruz, Juana" (*pseud.*) *see* Anabalón, Luisa V.
"Inés de la Cruz, Sor Juana" *see* Asbaje y Ramírez de Cantillana, Juana Inés de
Infante, José Miguel (1778-1844) HC 54 *Chil.*
Infante, Ramón Antonio V 84 *Venez.*
Infante de Palacios, Santiago Cu 84 *Cu.*
Ingenieros, José (1877-1926) BHLA 496; CG III, 132; CHL 201; G 313; GLO 236; PLHA 267; SASS 84 *Arg.*
"Ingenio de esta corte, Un" (*pseud.*) TM 345 *Mex.*
"Ingenio de esta villa, Un" (*pseud.*) TM 345 *Mex.*
"Inístoga" (*pseud.*) *see* Agostini, Rafael
Inostroza, José María C 49 *Chil.*
Insúa, Alberto (1885-   ) BDC 41; CG III, 143; GLO 244 *Cu.*
Insúa, Waldo A. (1858-   ) CG III, 143; Cu 85 *Cu.*
Intriago, Carlos E. E 38 *Ecua.*
Inza Ochoa, Anastasio (-1901) ARC 39; BDC 43; Cu 85 *Cu.*
"Íñigo" (*pseud.*) *see* Acosta, Ignacio María de
Iñiguez, Dalia (1911-   ) PoC 136 *Cu.*
Iñíguiz Vicuña, Antonio C 32; NC 428 *Chil.*
"Ipandro Acaico" (*pseud*) *see* Montes de Oca y Obregón, Ignacio
Ipuche, Pedro Leandro BHLA 642; CG III, 149; LAS 204; LU 64, 667; PIU III, 182; PoU 119; U 9 *Uru.*
Irabién Rosado, Manuel CG III, 149; Ig 177; NM 29 *Mex.*
Irabién Rosado, Perfecto NM 29 *Mex.*
Iracheta y Mascort, Francisco de CG III, 149; Cu 85 *Cu.*
Iraizoz y del Villar, Antonio (1890-   ) CG III, 150; CT 295; Cu 85; RLC 353; WLA 195 *Cu.*
Irarrázabal Zañartu, Alfredo (1864-   ) C 32; PCh 133 *Chil.*
Iregui, Antonio José Co 34 *Col.*
"Irene, Antici" (*pseud.*) A 36 *Arg.*
Iriarte Heredia, Gregorio (1878-   ) PCh 287 *Chil.*
Irigoyen, Gustavo A. TM 185 *Mex.*
Irigoyen, Salvador A 37 *Arg.*
Irio y Bausá, Octavio BDC 43; CG III, 153; Cu 85 *Cu.*
"Iris" (*pseud.*) *see* Echeverría de Larraín, Inés
Irisarri, Antonio José de (1786-1868) ACe 1007; AEHA 898; BHLA 226; C 11; CA 76, 77; CG III, 153; CHL 88, 504; CLH 74, 207, 445; GPCA I, 75; HPHA I, 202; PG 65; V 84 *Guat.*
Irisarri, Martín T. U 9 *Uru.*
Irisarri y Trucios, Hermógenes de (1819-1886) CHL 247; CLH 207; HC 134; PCh 43 *Chil.*
Irizarri (*or* Irizarry), Francisco BDC 43; PR 13 *P.R.*
Irribaren, Eduardo V 85 *Venez.*
Irulegui, Agustín (1917-   ) PoC 138 *Cu.*
Irusta, Héctor M. (1899-   ) A 37; APAM 526; CG III, 154 *Arg.*
Irwin, Carlos T. V 85 *Venez.*

Isaac, María de la Victoria   Par 15   *Para.*
Isaacs, Jorge (1837-1895)   AC I, 321; AEHA 898; ALC I, 265; BC 207; BHLA 408; CG III, 155; CHL 352; CLH 300, 302; Co 34; CoL 270; G 329; LC 135; PCo 159; PLHA 189; RHLC 182; SASS 242; WSAL 28   *Col.*
Isaza, Emiliano (1850-1930)   CG III, 155; Co 35; RHLC 205   *Col.*
Isaza, José Joaquín   BC 212; Co 35   *Col.*
Isern, Jacinto   CG III, 156; Cu 85   *Cu.*
Isernia, Francisco   A 37; APAM 530   *Arg.*
Isnardi, Francisco   V 85   *Venez.*
Isova, Faustino   PR 19   *P.R.*
Ispizúa, Segundo   E 38   *Ecua.*
Israel de Portela, Luisa   A 37   *Arg.*
Itolararres, José T.   P 14   *Per.*
Ituarte, Alberto   TM 451   *Mex.*
Ituarte, Julio   TM 606   *Mex.*
Ituarte, Luis Gonzaga   PM 51   *Mex.*
Iturbe, Alberto   TM 185   *Mex.*
Iturbe, Maximiliano   LV 338; V 85   *Venez.*
Iturburu, Córdoba (1899-   )   APEH 682
Iturralde, Abelardo G.   E 38   *Ecua.*
Iturralde, José María   ACe 829; PM 51   *Mex.*
Iturri, Francisco (1738-1822)   LA IV, 573   *Arg.*
Iturri, Francisco Javier (1767-   )   HLA 222   *Arg.*
Iturriaga, Manuel   HPM 461   *Mex.*
Iturriaga, Miguel Mariano (1728-1814)   ACe 662, 830   *Mex.*
Iturriaga y Alzaga, Manuel (-1810)   ACe 829   **Mex.**
Iturriaga y López, Ramón de   A 37   *Arg.*
Iturricha, Agustín (1863-   )   B 10   *Bol.*
Iturrino, Antonio   P 14   *Per.*
Iturrino, José Eugenio   P 15   *Per.*
Iturrondo, Francisco ("Delio") (1800-1868)   Cu 46, 85; RLC 72, 74   *Cu.*
"Ivanovich, Dmitri" (*pseud.*)   *see* Betancourt, José
Ixtlilxóchitl, Fernando de Alva (1568-1648)   BHLA 65; CHL 5; CLH 4; HLM 75; HLMex 23   *Mex.*
Iza, Luis G.   Ig 182; NM 29; TM 185   *Mex.*
Izaguirre, César   CA 77   *Guat.*
Izaguirre, José M. (1830-1905)   Cu 86   *Cu.*
Izaguirre Rojo, Baltasar   PM 51   *Mex.*
Izaguirre Valero, Ildefonso M.   V 85   *Venez.*
Izcúa Barbat de Muñoz Ximénez, María Carmen   CG III, 160; HSLU II, pt 8, 11; PIU III, 200; PU 119; U 9   *Uru.*
Izcue, José Augusto de (1872-   )   P 15   *Per.*
Izchudi (*or* Izchudy), Fernando   BDC 43; Cu 86   *Cu.*
Izgaga, José Aniceto (1794-1860)   Cu 86   *Cu.*
Izquierdo, Domingo A.   A 33, 49   *Arg.*
Izquierdo, Francisco   CG III, 160; Cu 86   *Cu.*
Izquierdo, Joaquina   LA VIII, 774   *Arg.*
Izquierdo, José Ignacio   Cu 86   *Cu.*
Izquierdo Brown, Juan   A 37   *Arg.*
Izquieta, Amadeo (1858-   )   E 38   *Ecua.*

J

"J. M. C." (*pseud.*)   *see* Cantilo, José María
J. M. G.   C 33   *Chil.*
J. M. S. E.   TM 189   *Mex.*
J. W. R.   C 11   *Chil.*
"Jabino" (*pseud.*)   *see* Mármol, Miguel
"Jacán" (*pseud.*)   *see* López, José Florencio
"Jacinto Amores" (*pseud.*)   *see* Ascasubi, Hilario
"Jack the Ripper" (*pseud.*)   *see* Campos, José Antonio
"Jacob, Porfirio Barba" (*pseud.*)   *see* Osorio, Miguel Ángel
"Jacobo Dalevuelta" (*pseud.*)   *see* Ramírez de Aguilar, Fernando
"Jacobo Edén" (*pseud.*)   *see* Egaña, Rafael
Jácome, D.A.   Co 35   *Col.*
Jacome, José Amadeo   E 38   *Ecua.*
Jaén, J. Darío   AP 175; Pan 6, 11   *Pan.*
Jaén, Manuel   V 85   *Venez.*
Jahn, Alfredo   CG III, 169; V 85   *Venez.*
Jaimes, Julio Lucas ("Brocha Gorda") (1840-1910)   B 10; CHL 310; LB 597; PB 126; SASS 114   *Bol.*
Jaimes Freyre, Julio   B 10   *Bol.*
Jaimes Freyre, Raúl (1886-   )   BT 151   *Bol.*
Jaimes Freyre, Ricardo (1868-1933)   APEH 365, 1185; B 10; BHLA 466; BT 153; CG III, 170; CHL 310, 529; CLH 263, 466; FPA 54, 70; G 320; GLO 238; LB 621 MSAP 88, 286; PLHA 137; SAL 92, 146, 271, 281; SASS 102   *Bol.*
James   *see* Jaimes
Janer y Soler, Felipe   BDC 43; PR 7, 13; SD 19   *P.R.*
Jaques y Aguado, Federico (1846-   )   CG III, 173; Cu 86   *Cu.*
Jara, Max (1886-   )   APEH 651, 1188; C 33; CMPC 88; PCC xiv, 111; PCh 241   *Chil.*
Jaramillo, Esteban   RHLC 197   *Col.*
Jaramillo, Hernán   C 33   *Chil.*
Jaramillo, L. Benjamín   E 38   *Ecua.*
Jaramillo, Marco A.   Co 35   *Col.*
Jaramillo Alvarado, Pío   CG III, 174; E 38, 74; PLE 94   *Ecua.*
Jaramillo Isaza, Manuel   Co 35   *Col.*
Jaramillo Meza, J. B.   CG III, 174; Co 35; LAS 207   *Col.*
Jarrige, Juan Francisco   A 37; CG III, 176   *Arg.*
Jarrín H., Misael   E 38   *Ecua.*
Jáuregui, Fernando   A 37; CG III, 177   *Arg.*
Jáuregui, J. M.   V 85   *Venez.*
Jáuregui, José A. de   B 11   *Bol.*
Jáuregui Rosquellas, Alfredo (1880-   )   B 11; BT 155; CG III, 177   *Bol.*
Jáuregui Urigen, Ricardo   E 38   *Ecua.*
Javier, Eugenio Francisco (1747-1795)   PLE 20   *Ecua.*
Javier Alegre, Francisco (1729-1788)   ACe 662   *Mex.*
Javier Clavijero, Francisco (1731-1787)   ACe 662   *Mex.*
"Jean Emar" (*pseud.*)   *see* Yáñez, Álvaro
"Jean Paul" (*pseud.*)   *see* Echagüe, Juan Pablo

Jemio, Luis Francisco B 11 *Bol.*

Jens, Federico Carlos Ig 183; NM 29; PM 51 *Mex.*

Jens, Juan Federico TM 452, 453 *Mex.*

Jerez, Bernardo C 33 *Chil.*

Jerez (*or* Xerés), Francisco de (1504-   ) LA III, 291; SCL 61, 611 *Arg.*

Jerez, Gerardo B. CA 77 *Guat.*

Jerez Villareal, Juan (1890-   ) ARC 54; Cu 86 *Cu.*

Jesús, Felipe Co 35 *Col.*

Jesús, Mariano de ACe 832; PM 51 *Mex.*

Jesús Lizol, José de PR 46 *P.R.*

"Jig Gómez" (*pseud.*) *see* Gálvez, Juan Ignacio

Jijena Sánchez, Rafael A 37 *Arg.*

Jijón Pallarés, Carlos E 39 *Ecua.*

Jijón y Caamaño, Jacinto CG III, 181; E 38 *Ecua.*

Jijón y León, Tomás de (1712-   ) E 38 *Ecua.*

"Jil, Salomé" (*pseud.*) *see* Milla y Vidaurre, José

"Jim, Lord" (*pseud.*) *see* Subercaseaux, Benjamín

Jiménez, Auristela C. de CA 34 *C.R.*

Jiménez, Blanca Rosa Cu 86 *Cu.*

Jiménez, Camilo V 85 *Venez.*

Jiménez, Ghiraldo (1892-   ) ARC 54; Cu 86 *Cu.*

Jiménez, Guillermo (1891-   ) CG III, 183; G 364; Ig 183; NM 29; WLA 200 *Mex.*

Jiménez, Jesús (1832-1897) CA 34; CG III, 183; EPCR 26 *C.R.*

Jiménez, José Cu 86 *Cu.*

Jiménez, José María PA 334; PD 125; SD 19 *Dom.*

Jiménez, Julio C 11 *Chil.*

"Jiménez, Lorenzo" (*pseud.*) *see* Chacón Trejos, Gonzalo

Jiménez, Manuel de Jesús (1854-   ) CA 34; EPCR 147 *C.R.*

Jiménez, Max CA 34; IBCR IV, 263 *et passim* *C.R.*

Jiménez, Miguel A. SD 19 *Dom.*

Jiménez, Nicolás E 39 *Ecua.*

Jiménez, Octavio CA 34; EPCR 569 *C.R.*

Jiménez, Rafael S. (1895-   ) Cu 86 *Cu.*

Jiménez, Ramón Emilio PD 119; SD 19 *Dom.*

Jiménez, Ricardo (1859-   ) CA 34 , 35; EPCR 162; PM 51 *C.R.*

Jiménez, Samuel E 39 *Ecua.*

Jiménez Acebedo, Nepomuceno Co 35 *Col.*

Jiménez Arraiz, Francisco CG III, 185; V 85 *Venez.*

Jiménez Arrechea Co 35 *Col.*

Jiménez D., Enrique TM 453 *Mex.*

Jiménez de Enciso, Salvador (-1841) HLNG II, 512 *Col.*

Jiménez de la Romera, Waldo PR 7 *P.R.*

Jiménez de Quesada, Gonzalo (1506-1579) BHLA 60; Co 35; HLNG I, 34; HPHA II, 7; LC 79; RHLC 5; SCL 211, 612 *Col.*

Jiménez Espinosa, Daniel PPa 161 *Para.*

Jiménez Grullón, Juan I. G 385; SD 19 *Dom.*

Jiménez Lamar, Gabriel (1878-   ) Cu 86; PCu 153; PJC 102 *Cu.*

Jiménez López, Miguel Co 35 *Col.*

Jiménez Núñez, Enrique CA 35 *C.R.*

Jiménez-Placer, Carlos TM 496 *Mex.*

Jiménez Rojas, Elías (1869-   ) CA 35; EPCR 174 *C.R.*

Jiménez Rueda, Julio (1896-   ) CG III, 196; G 364; GLO 249; HLM 516, 528; Ig 146; NM 2, 29; SASS 401; TM 187, 454, 553; WLA 200 *Mex.*

Jiménez y de León, Ramón (-1850) Cu 86 *Cu.*

Jiménez y Mendizábal, Juan N. TM 186 *Mex.*

Jinesta, Carlos CA 35; CG III, 202; EPCR 572; IBCR IV, 325 *C.R.*

Jinesta, Ricardo (1891-   ) CA 35; CG III, 202; EPCR 574 *C.R.*

Jirón, Luis C 33 *Chil.*

"Joaner" (*pseud.*) *see* Arvelo, José Antonio

Joanicó, Cándido HCLU I, 419 *et passim* *Uru.*

"Job, Duque" (*pseud.*) *see* Gutiérrez Nájera, Manuel

"Job Pim" (*pseud.*) *see* Pimentel, Francisco

Jodar y San Martín, Luis Co 36 *Col.*

Jofré, Hermójenes B 11 *Bol.*

Jofré C., Emilia H. C 33 *Chil.*

Joglar Cacho, M. PR 36 *P.R.*

"John S. War" (*pseud.*) *see* Ravignani, Emilio

Jolís, José (1728-   ) SCL 421, 613 *Para.*

Jordán, Camilio (1839-   ) LA VII, 303 *Arg.*

Jordán, Francisco Cu 86 *Cu.*

Jordán, Luis María (1883-   ) A 37; APAM 321; CG III, 206; NPA 147 *Arg.*

Jordán, Manuel María B 11 *Bol.*

Jordán y G., Federico BDC 44; Cu 86 *Cu.*

Jordana y Alonso, Eudaldo Cu 86 *Cu.*

"Jorge Borge" (*pseud.*) *see* López, José Heriberto

"Jorge Nelke" (*pseud.*) A 37 *Arg.*

"Jorge Useta" (*pseud.*) *see* Ugarte, José

"Jorje Alberto" (*pseud.*) A 37 *Arg.*

Jorquera, Laura C 11; CG III, 209 *Chil.*

Jorquera Villarroel, J. A. C 11; CG III, 209 *Chil.*

Jorrín, José Silverio (1816-1897) Cu 86; RLC 70, 146, 243 *Cu.*

Jorrín y Díaz, Rafael S. BDC 44; Cu 86 *Cu.*

"José, Cap." (*pseud.*) *see* Rosas Londa

"José Arce" (*pseud.*) *see* Martínez, Manuel

"José Nigreros" (*pseud.*) *see* Ortiz, José Joaquín

"Jotabé" (*pseud.*) *see* Castillo, José Vicente

"Jotabeche" (*pseud.*) *see* Vallejo, José Joaquín

"Jotavé" (*pseud.*) *see* Fermandois, José Luis

Joublanc Rivas, Luciano (1896-   ) AMP 147; APMM 101; CG III, 211; Ig 187; NM 29; PM 51; TM 190 *Mex.*

Jouvin de Llona, Zoila Aurora E 39 *Ecua.*

Jouy, José Esteban de TM 497 *Mex.*

Jova, María Dámasa ARC 54; Cu 87 *Cu.*

Jové Masqué, Ramón Cu 87 *Cu.*

Jovel, Pedro (1851-1877) CA 35; EPCR 43 *C.R.*

Jover, Gonzalo E 39 *Ecua.*

Jover, Rafael C 49 *Chil.*

Juan, Alejandro de Cu 87 *Cu.*
Juan, Jorge BHLA 131; P 34 *Per.*
"Juan Calvini" (*pseud.*) *see* Fernández Morúa, Juan
"Juan Cristóbal" (*pseud.*) *see* Parra del Riego, Juan
"Juan de Arona" (*pseud.*) *see* Paz Soldán y Unánue, Pedro
"Juan de Espinel" (*pseud.*) *see* Marín Cañas, José
"Juan del Camino" (*pseud.*) BHLA 576
"Juan del Carpio" (*pseud.*) *see* Espinosa Saldaña, Adán
"Juan del Páramo" (*pseud.*) *see* Vargas Márquez, Juan
"Juan Marsella" (*pseud.*) *see* Cruz Coke, Ricardo
"Juan Negro" (*pseud.*) *see* Aguirre, Juan
"Juan Pagador" (*pseud.*) *see* Cúneo-Vidal, Rómulo
"Juan Perales" (*pseud.*) *see* Pereda, Setembrino Ezequiel
"Juan Sincero" (*pseud.*) *see* Cruz, Manuel de la
Juan y Santacilla, Jorge SCL 361, 613 *Sp.*
"Juana Inés de la Cruz" (*pseud.*) *see* Anabalón, Luisa V. *and* Asbaje y Ramírez de Cantillana, Juana Inés de
"Juancé" (*pseud.*) *see* Martínez, Juan Cristóbal
Juanes G., Joaquín PM 52 *Mex.*
Juárez (*or* Xuárez), Gaspar (1731-1804) LA IV, 562; SCL 422, 613 *Arg.*
Juárez Muñoz, J. Fernando CA 77; CG III, 217 *Guat.*
Juárez Muñoz, J. J. CA 36 *C.R.*
Juárez Núñez, Rodolfo A 37; GLO 236 *Arg.*
Juarros, Domingo (1752-1820) CA 77 *Guat.*
"Jubilo" (*pseud.*) *see* Castillo, Guillermo
Juglaris, Enrique Juan A 37 *Arg.*
Jugo Ramírez, Diego V 85 *Venez.*
"Jules Wallas" (*pseud.*) *see* Valdés, Julio César
Juliá, Tomás A. BDC 44 *Cu.*
Julián, Antonio Co 36; HLNG I, 387; RHLC 19; SCL 392, 613 *Col.*
"Julián del Claro" (*pseud.*) *see* Hederra Concha, Francisco
"Julián Martel" (*pseud.*) *see* Miró, José
"Julio, Don" (*pseud.*) *see* Arboleda, Julio
Julio, Juan José E 39 *Ecua.*
"Julio César" (*pseud.*) *see* Silva Endeiza, Hugo
"Julio de la Paz" (*pseud.*) *see* Baudouin, Julio
"Julio Talanto" (*pseud.*) *see* Iglesias Mascareño, Augusto
"Julio Vives Guerra" (*pseud.*) *see* Velásquez García, José
Julio y Elizalde, Juan José (1866-) P 15; PCh 273 *Chil.*
Junco, Alfonso (1896-) APMM 104; CG III, 223; HLM 524; IE 141; PM 52; WLA 201 *Mex.*
Junco de la Vega, Celedonio CG III, 223; PM 52 *Mex.*
Juneman, Guillermo E 39 *Ecua.*
Jünemann, Guillermo C 33 *Chil.*

"Junius" (*pseud.*) *see* Gutiérrez Nájera, Manuel
Junoy, Ramón CA 36; CG III, 224; IBCR IV, 252 *et passim* *C.R.*
Jurado Avilés, J. J. E 39 *Ecua.*
Jurado Quintero, Isaías (1881-) Pan 11 *Pan.*
Jurado y Tort, Ignacio César BDC 44; Cu 87 *Cu.*
"Just, Saint" (*pseud.*) *see* Lafosse, Alfredo P.
Jústiz y del Valle, Tomás Juan de (1871-) BDC 44; CG III, 227; CT 153; Cu 87 *Cu.*
"Justo" (*pseud.*) *see* Sales Pérez, Francisco de
"Justo Adalid" (*pseud.*) *see* Monterde García Icazbalceta, Francisco
"Justo de Lara" (*pseud.*) *see* Armas y Cárdenas, José de
"Justo Derecho" (*pseud.*) *see* Monge, José María
Juvenal Rosa, Pedro PR 56 *P.R.*
"Jymb" (*pseud.*) Cu 87 *Cu.*

K

"Kadosh, A." (*pseud.*) *see* Quiñones, Francisco Mariano
Kantor, Moisés A 37, 86; CG III, 230 *Arg.*
"Kappa, Epsilón" (*pseud.*) *see* Calcaño, Eduardo
"Karez-i-Roshan" (*pseud.*) *see* Castro, Antonio
Karker, Simón S. Co 36 *Col.*
"Kaskabel" (*pseud.*) *see* Padilla, Benjamín
"Kastos, Emiro" (*pseud.*) *see* Restrepo, Juan de Dios *or* Toro, Fermín
"Keef, El Barón de" (*pseud.*) *see* Elguera, Federico
Kégel, Federico Carlos (-1907) CG III, 232; Ig 187; NM 29; TM 190 *Mex.*
Keller R., Carlos (1898-) WLA 201 *Chil.*
Kennedy, Elena ARC 54 *Cu.*
Keratry, Ernesto ("Nadie") Ig 231; NM 36 *Mex.*
Key Ayala, Santiago CG III, 235; V 86 *Venez.*
Keymer B., Carlos E. C 33; CG III, 235 *Chil.*
Killen, Carlos V 86 *Venez.*
Kirs, Manuel A 37; CG III, 237
Klickmann, Jorge C 49 *Chil.*
Kloques Campos, Julio C 11, 33; CG III, 239; NC 493 *Chil.*
Kloz, Ernesto E 39 *Ecua.*
Köhnenkampf Cisternas, Guillermo C 33 *Chil.*
König, Abraham C 11; CG III, 243; CL 287; NC 366 *Chil.*
Korn, Alejandro (1860-1936) BHLA 499 *Arg.*
Korn Villafañe, Adolfo A 37; CG III, 243 *Arg.*
Korsi (*or* Coorsi), Demetrio (1899-) AP 181; BHLA 542; CG III, 244; FPA 382, 398; Pan 6, 11 *Pan.*

"Kostia, Conde" (pseud.) see Valdivia, Aniceto
Kramer, Pedro B 11 Bol.
Kruger, Rosa (-1881) Cu 87 Cu.
Krupkin, Ilka A 37, 86; CG III, 250; G 314 Arg.
Kubly, Enrique U 9 Uru.
Kurth, Gisberta S. de A 37; CG III, 252 Arg.
"Kyn Taniya" (pseud.) see Quintanilla, Luis

L

"L. B. M." (pseud.) see Bravo, Juan de Dios
L., E. J. de Cu 87 Cu.
L. R., J. E 39 Ecua.
La Cruz see Cruz, la
La Fuente, J. M. A 38 Arg.
La Fuente Benavides, Rafael de ("Martín Adán") BAP 119; BHLA 606 Per.
La Gandara, José de SD 19 Dom.
La Madrid, F. A. A 38 Arg.
La Rea, Alonso de (1624-) HLM 208 Mex.
La Torre, José María de (1777-1840) HC 52 Chil.
La Villa, Sergio PCu 313 Cu.
Labarca Hubertson, Amanda Pinto de (1886-) C 11; CG III, 256; NC 429; WLA 202 Chil.
Labarca Hubertson, Guillermo (1880-) C 12; CG III, 256; CLH 238; NC 367; PLHA 235; SASS 169; WLA 202 Chil.
Labarca Labarca, Eugenio (1898-) C 11; WLA 203 Chil.
Labardén, Manuel José de (1754-1809) BHLA 143; CHL 44; CLH 37; HPHA II, 398; LA IV, 701; VIII, 851; SPLA 28, 138; SASS 4 Arg.
Labarthe, Pedro Juan (1906-) QPR (1) 90, 186 P.R.
Laborde, Hernán (1894-) PM 52 Mex.
Labougle, Eduardo CG III, 258; Cu 87 Cu.
Labra y Cadrana, Rafael M. de (1843-) ARC 75; CG III, 258; PR 9, 19, 46 P.R.
Labroue, P. Esteban C 49 Chil.
Lacalle, Servando C 12 Chil.
Lacasa, Pedro A 38; CG III, 261 Arg.
"Lacor, Pedro" (pseud.) see Cossío, Francisco de
Lacroix Esain, Miguel B. PU 282 Uru.
Lacunza, Juan María ACe 834; HLM 246 Mex.
Lacunza, Manuel (1731-1801) BHLA 118; CG III, 263; HC 38; SCL 456, 613 Chil.
Lachner Sandoval, Vicente (1868-) CA 36; EPCR 184 C.R.
Ladrón de Guevara, Pablo CG III, 263; Co 36 Col.
Lafargue, Paul ARC 36, 37 Cu.
Laferrère, Alfonso de A 38; CG III, 264 Arg.
Laferrère y Roca, Gregorio de (1867-1913) A 38, 86; BHLA 548; CG III, 264; CHL 199; LA VIII, 899; PLHA 293; SPLA 172 Arg.
Laffón, Rafael Cu 87 Cu.

Lafinur, Juan Crisóstomo (1797-1824) BHLA 167, 186; CHL 53; CLH 59; HLA 213; HPHA II, 407; LA IV, 913 Arg.
Lafinur, Melián PIU I, 235 Uru.
Lafita Navarro, María Cu 87 Cu.
Lafita y Blanco, Francisco de Asís Cu 87 Cu.
Lafone Quevedo, Samuel (1835-) LA VII, 226 Arg.
Lafosse, Alfredo P. ("Saint Just") CG III, 266; P 15 Per.
Lafragua, José María (1813-1875) HPM 866; NM 29, 43; TM 454, 469, 553 Mex.
Lafuente Machain, Ricardo de (1882-) WLA 203 Arg.
Lagarder, Humberto Co 36 Col.
Lagardere, Rodolfo ARC 38 Cu.
Lagarrigue, Juan Enrique C 33; CG III, 268; NC 429 Chil.
Laggar, Mary A 38 Arg.
Lago, Jesús María PA 213; PP 227; PR 52 P.R.
Lago, Tomás (1903-) C 12; PCC xxii, 253 Chil.
Lagomaggiore, Francisco A 38, 71 Arg.
Lagomarsino, Carlos E 39 Ecua.
Lagorio, Arturo A 38 Arg.
Lagos, Luis A. (1885-) PCh 329 Chil.
Lagos, Roberto C 33, 37; CG III, 269 Chil.
Lagos A., Leónidas C 33 Chil.
Lagos Lisboa, Jerónimo (1883-) C 33; CG III, 270; PCC xiv, 99; PCh 231 Chil.
Lagrolet, Chicho ARC 40 Cu.
Lagunas, Juan Bautista de HLM 21 Mex.
Láinez, Manuel (1852-) AT II, 689 Arg.
Lainfiesta, Francisco (1837-1912) CA 77; GPCA II, 269; PG 181 Guat.
Lallana, Joseph de PM 52 Mex.
Lama, Tomás CG III, 273; P 15 Per.
Lamadrid, Gregorio Aráoz de see Aráoz de Lamadrid, Gregorio
Lamadrid Moya, Lukas (1919-) PoC 139 Cu.
Lamar Schweyer, Alberto (1902-) BHLA 566; CG III, 274; Cu 87; IE 142; PCu 156; PJC 106; RLC 355 Cu.
Lamarca Bello, Arturo C 12, 33, 49; CG III, 274 Chil.
Lamarca y Bello, Carlos C 12 Chil.
Lamarche, Juan Bautista PA 336; PD 127; SD 20 Dom.
Lamarque, Adolfo (1852-1888) A 38; LA VIII, 601 Arg.
Lamarque, Nydia (1906-) A 38; CG III, 274; LAC 148 Arg.
Lamas, Alejandro (1871-) CG III, 275; UT 289 Uru.
Lamas, Andrés ("C. M.") (1817-1891) CG III, 275; CHL 210; HCLU I, 213; HSLU III, pt 4, 8; LA VI, 666; LUr 450; PIU I, 163 et passim; U 9; UL 129 Uru.
Lamas, Benito PIU I, 56 Uru.
Lamas, José Ángel V 86 Venez.
Lamas, Pedro S. A 38; CG III, 276 Arg.
Lamas Carísimo de Rodríguez Alcalá, Teresa (1889-) G 380; Par 15 Para.
Lamas García, Eduardo CL 288 Chil.
Lamberti, Antonino (-1926) A 38 Arg.
Lameda, Juan Bautista CG III, 276; V 86 Venez.

Lameda, León V 86, 87 *Venez.*
Lamedo, Lisandro V 86 *Venez.*
Lamuchi, Vicente BHLA 76 *Mex.*
Lamus G., Ramón CG III, 278; Co 36; E 40 *Ecua.*
Lana, Braulio de BHC I, 171 *Chil.*
Lanas, Oscar C 12 *Chil.*
Lancaster Jones, Alfonso TM 191, 578 *Mex.*
Land, R. O. C 12 *Chil.*
Landa, Jaime (1886?-1911) PPe 288 *Per.*
Landaeta, José D. V 86 *Venez.*
Landaeta, Juan J. V 86 *Venez.*
Landaeta, Leopoldo V 86 *Venez.*
Landaeta, Rafael de Jesús V 86 *Venez.*
Landaeta Rosales, Manuel CG III, 279; V 86 *Venez.*
Landaluce, Patricio TM 455 *Mex.*
Landaluce, Patricio de V 87, 102 *Venez.*
Landaluce, Víctor TM 490, 497 *Mex.*
Landázuri, Isabel A. de *see* Prieto de Landázuri, Isabel A.
Landázuri, Pedro TM 191 *Mex.*
Landázuri, Salvador TM 191, 340 *Mex.*
Landívar y Caballero, Rafael (1731-1793) ACe 662; AEHA 899; BHLA 106; CA 77, 78; CG III, 281; CHL 33, 504; CLH 28, 445; E 40; G 346; HLM 183; HLMex 83; HPHA I, 184; HPM 475; PG 12; PM 52; WSAL 12, 66 *Guat.*
Landó, L. Juan U 9 *Uru.*
Lange, Norah A 38; LAC 149; NPA 283 *Arg.*
Languasco, Bernardo Cu 88 *Cu.*
Lannot, León A 38 *Arg.*
Lanuza, Agustín (1870-) CG III, 283; PM 52 *Mex.*
Lanuza, Cayetano Cu 88 *Cu.*
Laña Santillana, Pilar WLA 204 *Per.*
Laparra, Jesús (1820-1887) CA 78; GPCA I, 323; PG 135 *Guat.*
Laparra de la Cerda, Vicenta (1834-1905) CA 78; GPCA III, 1; PG 257 *Guat.*
Lapuente, Laurindo R. A 38; CHL 217; CLH 179; LA VIII, 582, 628 *Arg.*
Lara, Eladio V 87 *Venez.*
Lara, Francisco J. PM 52 *Mex.*
Lara, Francisco V. PM 52 *Mex.*
Lara, Jesús B 11 *Bol.*
Lara, Juan A. B 11 *Bol.*
"Lara, Justo de" (*pseud.*) *see* Armas y Cárdenas, José de
Lara, María Julia ARC 54 *Cu.*
Lara, Othón TM 621 *Mex.*
Lara, Raúl C 33 *Chil.*
Lara A., Manuel María ("Pujavante") B 11 *Bol.*
Lardé de Venturino, Alice (189.-) C 12; CG III, 287; FPA 502, 524 *Chil.*
Lardizábal y Uribe, Manuel de (1739-1820) ACe 489; CG III, 287; HLMex 118 *Mex.*
Lardizábal y Uribe, Miguel HLMex 118 *Mex.*
Laredo, Bernardo TM 191, 284 *Mex.*
Lares, José Ignacio CG III, 287; LV 119; V 87 *Venez.*
Laria y Caso, Antonio Cu 88 *Cu.*
Larios, Manuel (1824-1895) Pan 11 *Pan.*
Laris, José Trinidad G. CG III, 287; TM 191 *Mex.*

Larmig, Eduardo Par 15 *Para.*
Larrabure, José Vicente P 15 *Per.*
Larrabure y Unánue, Eugenio (1844-) CG III, 291; P 15 *Per.*
Larrahondo y Valencia, Mariano Co 36 *Col.*
Larraín, Jacob A 38 *Arg.*
Larraín, Tomás (1703-) PLE 19 *Ecua.*
Larraín Barra, Bruno C 12; CG III, 292; NC 166, 371 *Chil.*
Larraín C., Raimundo C 12; NC 429 *Chil.*
Larraín Zañartu, Luis C 12; NC 170, 499 *Chil.*
Larráinzar, Enriqueta NM 30 *Mex.*
Larráinzar, Ernestina NM 30 *Mex.*
Larran de Vere, Alberto A 38 *Arg.*
Larrañaga, Bruno Joseph de (-1816) ACe 851; HPM 471; PM 52 *Mex.*
Larrañaga, Dámaso Antonio (1771-1846) BHLA 169; CG III, 292; HCLU I, 48; PIU I, 52; U 9 *Uru.*
Larrañaga, Gonzalo CG III, 292; TM 192 *Mex.*
Larrañaga, José Rafael ACe 851; HLM 185; HPM 471; PM 53 *Mex.*
Larrañaga Portugal, Manuel (1868-) AMP 104; PMe I, 263; PoM 381 *Mex.*
Larrazábal, Felipe (1816-1873) BHLA 348; CG III, 293; LV 6, 131, 134; V 87 *Venez.*
Larrea, J. B. E 40 *Ecua.*
Larrea, Julio C. E 74 *Ecua.*
Larrea Alvarado, Venancio S. CG III, 293; E 40 *Ecua.*
Larrea Ch., Alberto E 40; PE 14; PLE 88 *Ecua.*
Larrea León, Teodoro E 40 *Ecua.*
Larrea Lizarzaburu, Joaquín E 40 *Ecua.*
Larreta, Eduardo R. U 9; UL 129 *Uru.*
Larreta, Enrique ("Rodríguez") (1875-) A 38; AT II, 843; BHLA 505; CG III, 293; CHL 204; CLH 168; G 314; GLO 237; LAC 39, 124, 130; PLHA 200; SASS 67; WLA 206 *Arg.*
Larriera Varela, Diego PU 287 *Uru.*
Larriva, Juan Francisco (1830-) P 16 *Per.*
Larriva de Llona, Lastenia (1848-) CG III, 293; E 43, 74; P 16 *Ecua.*
Larriva y Ruiz, José Joaquín (1780-1832) BHLA 160, 198; CHL 65; CLH 56; HPHA II, 240; P 16 *Per.*
Larrondo y Maza, E. Cu 88 *Cu.*
Larrosa de Ansaldo, Lola A 38 *Arg.*
Larrosa Pizarro, José Domingo A 38 *Arg.*
Lasauca Ibieta, Antonio Cu 88 *Cu.*
Lascano *see also* Lazcano
Lascano, Antenor TM 192 *Mex.*
Lascano Tegui, Emilio ("Vizconde de Lascano Tegui") A 38, 78; APAM 327 *Arg.*
Laso de los Vélez, Pedro Cu 88; PR 36 *Cu.*
Lasplaces, Alberto CG III, 297; G 388; PIU III, 292; PU 122; U 9; UL 130 *Uru.*
Lassabe, Celeste ("Celeste Lassabe de Cruz") C 12; NC 171 *Chil.*
Lassaletta, Bernardo BHC III, 530 *Chil.*
Lasso, Elías E 40 *Ecua.*
Lasso de la Vega, Gabriel CHL 20; CLH 17; SCL 210, 616 *Mex.*

Lasso de la Vega, Leoncio CG III, 298; U 10 *Uru.*

Lasso de la Vega, Melchor AP 193; Pan 11 *Pan.*

Lasso de la Vega, Rafael CG III, 298; HLNG II, 148, 336 *Col.*

Lastarria, José Victorino (1817-1888) BHLA 286, 340; C 12, 50, 66; CG III, 299; CHL 238, 240, 252; CL 288; CLH 200, 212; HC 85; NC 171, 371, 430, 499; SASS 183 *Chil.*

Lastarria, Miguel LA IV, 1010 *Arg.*

Lastarria Cavero, Berta C 12 *Chil.*

Lastra, Carlos M. A 39 *Arg.*

Lastra, Juan Julián A 39; CG III, 299; G 314 *Arg.*

Latapier, Juan Tranquilino ARC 54 *Cu.*

Latapie, Olga C 12 *Chil.*

Latcham, Ricardo A. BHLA 618; C 12, 67; CG III, 301; CMPC 163 *Chil.*

Lathrop, Carlos 2° (1853-) C 12, 33, 34, 50; CLH 216; NC 173, 431 *Chil.*

"Latino, Aníbal" (*pseud.*) *see* Ceppi, José

"Latino, Simón" (*pseud.*) *see* Pareja, Carlos Henrique

Lato-monte, Ludovico HPM 805 *Mex.*

Latorre *see also* La Torre

Latorre, Demetrio Co 36 *Col.*

Latorre, Gabriel (1868-) Co 36; RHLC 190 *Col.*

Latorre, Germán CG III, 301; PR 8 *P.R.*

Latorre, Mariano (1886-) AB 24; BHLA 512, 619; C 13; CG III, 301; CHL 280; LAS 200, 204 *Chil.*

Laurent, Armando C 13 *Chil.*

"Lauria, Roger de" (*pseud.*) *see* Gollury, Ramón F.

"Lauset, Violette" (*pseud.*) *see* Vilarés, Tauler

"Lauxar" (*pseud.*) *see* Crispo Acosta, Osvaldo

Lavagnini, Juan Pablo PU 289; U 10 *Uru.*

Laval Alvear, Ramón A. (1862-) C 13, 67; CG III, 304; IE 144; NC 432 *Chil.*

Lavalle, Enrique Richard (1884-) AT II, 589; CG III, 304 *Arg.*

Lavalle, José Antonio (1833-1893) CG III, 304; P 16 *Per.*

Lavalle, Juan Bautista de (1887-) CG III, 304; P 16 *Per.*

Lavarden, Juan Manuel de SCL 553, 614 *Arg.*

Lavat, Juan (-1911) Ig 187; NM 30 *Mex.*

Laverde Amaya, Isidoro (1852-1903) CHL 341; Co 36; LC 175; RHLC 207 *Col.*

Laverde Liévano, Manuel Co 36 *Col.*

Lavie, Luis Adrián PM 53 *Mex.*

Lavigne, Arturo D. Par 15 *Para.*

Lay, Joaquín BDC 44 *Cu.*

Laya, Carlos M. V 88 *Venez.*

Lázaro, Ángel CG III, 308; Cu 88 *Cu.*

Lázaro, Obdulia C. de PR 19, 46 *P.R.*

Lazcano *see also* Lascano

Lazcano, Eliezer PM 53 *Mex.*

Lazcano Colodrero, Godofredo A 39; CG III, 308 *Arg.*

Lazo, José Esteban (1845-1894) HL I, 631 *Hond.*

Lazo, Raimundo Cu 88 *Cu.*

Lazo Baeza, Olegario C 13; CG III, 308 *Chil.*

Lazo Martí, Francisco CG III, 308; CHL 376; CLH 323; V 88 *Venez.*

Le Compte, Eugenio PR 19 *P.R.*

Le Gouhir y Rodas, José CG III, 330; E 39 *Ecua.*

Le Quesne, María Antonieta C 34; CMPC 113 *Chil.*

Leal, Emilio R. TM 192 *Mex.*

Leal, José R. Cu 88 *Cu.*

Leal, Teófilo V 88 *Venez.*

Leante, Eugenio CG III, 310; Cu 88 *Cu.*

Lebredo de Blanco, Dolores G. Cu 88 *Cu.*

Lebrón Rodríguez, Ramón (1868-) QPR (1) 91; (2) 93 *P.R.*

Lecaro de Muñoz V., Zoila C. E 41 *Ecua.*

Lecuanda, José Ignacio SCL 564, 614 *Per.*

Lecuna, Vicente CG III, 317; V 88, 117 *Venez.*

Lecuna Bejarano, Antonio CG III, 317; V 88 *Venez.*

Lechón, Rafael S. CG III, 318; TM 192 *Mex.*

Ledesma, Luis G. G 364; PM 53 *Mex.*

Ledesma, Roberto (1901-) A 39; APAM 532 *Arg.*

Ledrú, Andrés Pierre PR 46 *P.R.*

Leduc, Alberto (1867-1908) CG III, 320; HLM 458; HLMex 228; Ig 188; NM 30; TM 193 *Mex.*

Leduc, Renato PM 53 *Mex.*

Lee de Muñoz Marín, Muna (1895-) QPR (1) 92; (2) 94 *P.R.*

Lefebre, Enrique PR 7, 19, 25 *P.R.*

Lefèvre, Ernesto T. (-1922) AP 197; Pan 11 *Pan.*

Lefevre, Julio Alejandro TM 497 *Mex.*

Legorreta, Luis Cu 88 *Cu.*

Leguía, Jorge Guillermo (1898-1934) BHLA 603; CG III, 331; G 381; IE 145; P 16 *Per.*

Leguía y Martínez, Germán (1861-1928) BHLA 382; P 17 *Per.*

Leguizamón, Martiniano P. (1858-) A 39, 86; AT II, 115; BHLA 502; CG III, 332; CHL 196; CLH 168; G 314; WLA 209 *Arg.*

Leguizamón Díaz, Fidel A 39 *Arg.*

Lehardy, Karl A 39 *Arg.*

Lehmann-Nitsche, Robert A 39; G 314 *Arg.*

Leiseca, Juan M. Cu 88 *Cu.*

Leiva, Julián LA IV, 780 *Arg.*

Lejarza, Juan José PM 53 *Mex.*

Lejos Taseyar, Tomás Cu 88 *Cu.*

Lelio, Carlos Par 15 *Para.*

"Lemachez, Quirino" (*pseud.*) *see* Henríquez, Camilo

Lemoine, Joaquín de (-1923) B 11 *Bol.*

Lemos Ramírez, Gustavo (1878-) WLA 210 *Ecua.*

Lendían, Evelio Rodríguez (1860-) CT 43 *Cu.*

Lenis, Andrés J. Co 36 *Col.*

Lenz, Benjamín (1836-1878) B 12; CHL 309; CLH 262; LB 593 *Bol.*

Lenz, Rodolfo (1863-) C 67; CG III, 337; WLA 210 *Chil.*

Lenzi, Carlos César CG III, 388; PU 124 *Uru.*

Lenzoni, Marcos A 39 *Arg.*

"Leo" (*pseud.*) *see* Martínez, Leoncio

"Leo de Gris" (*pseud.*) *see* Greiff, León de

"Leo Par" (*pseud.*) *see* Dávila Silva, Ricardo

León, Álvaro de CG III, 339; TM 193 *Mex.*

León, Antonio de CG III, 339; HLNG II, 147 *Col.*

León, Aquilino (1839-) BC 216; Co 37 *Col.*

León, Carlos Arturo (1886-) E 41; WLA 211 *Ecua.*

León, Carlos Emilio C 13; NC 432 *Chil.*

León, Carlos Manuel E 41 *Ecua.*

León, César A. C 58; CG III, 339; V 88 *Venez.*

León, César Luis de PJC 126 *Cu.*

León, Daniel E 41 *Ecua.*

León, Gonzalo E. de PM 53 *Mex.*

León, Gregorio SCL 276, 614 *Chil.*

León, J. B. V 89 *Venez.*

León, José E. C 50; CG III, 339 *Chil.*

León, José Socorro de (1831-1869) Cu 88 *Cu.*

León, Juan de la Luz Cu 88; G 338 *Cu.*

León, Luis Emilio P 17 *Per.*

León, Miguel Ángel E 41 *Ecua.*

León, Nicolás CG III, 341; HLM 492; IE 146; NM 2; TM 554 *Mex.*

León, Pedro de CG III, 341; Ig 191; NM 30 *Mex.*

León Gómez, Adolfo (1857-1927) BC 216; CG III, 342; Co 37; RHLC 170 *Col.*

León Gómez, Ernesto (-1892) BC 217; Co 37 *Col.*

León Pinelo, Antonio de (-1660) BHLA 122; CG III, 343; P 17 *Per.*

León Pinelo, Diego BHLA 122; LA III, 62; P 17 *Per.*

León S., Víctor A. de AP 205; Pan 11 *Pan.*

León y Bezerra, Antonio de (-1708) SCL 354, 615 *Pan.*

León y Garabito, Andrés de SCL 410, 615 *Arg.*

Leonard, Chita de A 39 *Arg.*

"Leonardo Penna" (*pseud.*) *see* Pérez Kallens, Ignacio

"Leoncito" (*pseud.*) *see* López Evia, Lorenzo

Lepino, K. NM 30 *Mex.*

Lera, Carlos Américo Cu 89 *Cu.*

Lerdo, Francisco A. HLM 467; TM 194 *Mex.*

Lerdo, Francisco de A. PM 53 *Mex.*

Lerdo de Tejada, Francisco TM 194 *Mex.*

Lerdo de Tejada, Miguel TM 554 *Mex.*

Lerena Acevedo, Andrés Héctor HSLU III, pt 6, 21; PU 126; U 10 *Uru.*

Lerena Flores, Juan P 17 *Per.*

Lérida, Juan de C 50 *Chil.*

"Lerma, Duque de" (*pseud.*) *see* Raldiris Guasp, Juan P.

"Lery, Alfredo de" (*pseud.*) *see* Franchi, Alfredo C.

Letelier, Sandalio C 34 *Chil.*

Letelier, Valentín (1852-1919) BHLA 392; CG III, 351; G 325 *Chil.*

Letelier-Maturana C 34 *Chil.*

Letts, María Montemayor de V 89 *Venez.*

Leturia, Pedro CG III, 352; V 89 *Venez.*

Leumann, Carlos Alberto (1887-) A 39, 86; APAM 330; CG III, 352; LAC 132 *Arg.*

Leumur, Gil TM 193 *Mex.*

Level, Andrés A. V 89 *Venez.*

Level, Lino Duarte V 89 *Venez.*

Level de Goda, Luis LV 4; V 89 *Venez.*

Levene, Ricardo (1885-) AT I, 187; CG III, 352; CHL 201; WLA 212 *Arg.*

Levillier, Roberto (1883-) AT II, 625; CG III, 353; PLHA 286; WLA 214 *Arg.*

Levis Bernard, José Elías (1871-) BP 504; PR 27, 56, 59; QPR (1) 93; (2) 95 *P.R.*

Lewis, Samuel (1871-) AP 199; CG III, 355; Pan 12 *Pan.*

Leyva, Armando (1888-) Cu 89 *Cu.*

Leyva, Francisco *see* López Leiva, Francisco

Leza, Walterio F. PJC 116 *Cu.*

Lezama Lima, José (1912-) PoC 142 *Cu.*

Lezcámez, Antón de Co 37 *Col.*

Lezcano de Podetti, Amelia A 39 *Arg.*

Liacho, Lázaro A 39; BHLA 632 *Arg.*

Libonati, Vicente J. A 39; CG III, 374 *Arg.*

"Lic. Sánchez Vicuña" (*pseud.*) *see* Gorostiza, Manuel Eduardo de

Liccioni, Antonio V 89 *Venez.*

"Licenciado Vidriera" (*pseud.*) *see* Cruz Ocampo, Luis D.

"Lidia, Palmiro de" (*pseud.*) *see* Valle, Adrián del

Liendo y Goicoechea, José Antonio de (1735-1814) CA 36, 78; EPCR 13 *C.R.*

Liern, Rafael María Cu 89 *Cu.*

Lietti, José C 50 *Chil.*

Liévana, Pedro de G 346 *Guat.*

"Ligio Vizardi" (*pseud.*) *see* Díaz Ordóñez, Virgilio

Lillo, Ángel C. C 34 *Chil.*

Lillo, Baldomero (1867-1923) C 13; CG III, 380; CHL 279; CLH 238; N 25; NC 372; SASS 177; WSAL 57 *Chil.*

Lillo, Eusebio (1827-1910) BHLA 315; C 34, 50; CHL 250; CLH 210; HC 136; PCh 37; PCU 21 *Chil.*

Lillo, Victoriano C 13 *Chil.*

Lillo Catalán, Victoriano (1892-) A 39; CG III, 381; WLA 215 *Arg.*

Lillo Figueroa, Samuel A. (1870-) C 34, 67; CG III, 381; CHL 263; CLH 223; FPA 191, 197; PCh 159; PCU 22; WLA 215 *Chil.*

Lima de Castillo, Polita V 89 *Venez.*

Limardo, Ricardo Ovidio V 89 *Venez.*

Limón de Arce, José Ramón (1877-) BDC 113; PR 13, 36 *P.R.*

Limosín, Febo de Pan 12 *Pan.*

Linares, José Antonio CG III, 382; V 89 *Venez.*

Linares, Julio NL 233 *Nicar.*

Linares, Victorio A 39 *Arg.*

Linares Rivas, Manuel (-1909) CG III, 385; Cu 90 *Cu.*

Lindo y Zelaya, Juan Nepomuceno Fernández (-1856) HL I, 127 *Hond.*

Lindsay, Santiago C 67 *Chil.*

Linnig, Samuel A 39, 86 *Arg.*

"Lino Sutil" (*pseud.*) *see* Silva, Rafael M.

"Lino Tipo" (*pseud.*) *see* Colunje, Guillermo (hijo)

"Linterna, Fray" (*pseud.*) *see* Cichero, Félix Esteban

"Lionel, Errol" (*pseud.*) *see* Nin Frías, Alberto

"Lira, Carmen" (*pseud.*) *see* Carvajal, María Isabel

Lira, Luciano (-1840) HSLU I, pt 1, 10; PIU I, 85 *Uru.*

Lira, Martín José (1833-1867) C 34; CHL 253; CLH 213; HC 161 *Chil.*

Lira, Máximo R. (1845-1916) C 13; HC 183; NC 377 *Chil.*

Lira, Miguel Nicolás (1905-) G 364; PM 53; WLA 217 *Mex.*

Lira Girón, Luis Felipe (1903-) WLA 217 *Bol.*

Lira Smith, Luis C 50 *Chil.*

Lirio, D. Cu 90 *Cu.*

Lisoni, Tito V. C 34; CG III, 390; NC 433 *Chil.*

List Arzubide, Germán PM 53 *Mex.*

"Listo, K." (*pseud.*) *see* Pompa, Elías Calixto

Liubaro, Aisick A 39 *Arg.*

Lizana D., Desiderio C 34; CG III, 393 *Chil.*

"Lizárraga, Reginaldo de" (*pseud.*) *see* Obando, Baltasar de

Lizarralde, Fernando A 39; CG III, 394 *Arg.*

Lizarzaburu, Pedro I. E 42 *Ecua.*

Lizaso, Félix (1891-) BHLA 568; CG III, 394; Cu 90; G 338; IE 148; LH 115, 127 *Cu.*

Lizol, José Jesús PR 36 *P.R.*

Lizondo Borda, Manuel (1889-) AT I, 107; CG III, 395 *Arg.*

Loaiza, Guillermo C. (1870-1924) B 12; BT 167; CG III, 395 *Bol.*

Loayza, Francisco A. P 17 *Per.*

Loayza, Luis Aurelio P 17 *Per.*

Lobé, Gerónimo Cu 90 *Cu.*

Lobera y Castro, Rafael V 89 *Venez.*

Lobo, Octavio E. A 39 *Arg.*

Lobos O., Redumiro C 34; CG III, 396 *Chil.*

Lobosco, Angelina A 39 *Arg.*

Loera y Chávez, Agustín (1895-) CG III, 397; NM 3; WLA 219 *Mex.*

Logroño, Arturo SD 10, 20 *Dom.*

Lohengrín, Camilo de Cu 90 *Cu.*

Loiseau, Ernesto O. A 39 *Arg.*

Loma Ossorio, José María de Cu 90 *Cu.*

Lomba, José María BP 529; PR 19 *P.R.*

Lombard, Aquilino ARC 54 *Cu.*

Lombardo, Alberto Ig 191; NM 30; TM 194 *Mex.*

Lombardo, María L. de TM 455 *Mex.*

Lombardo, Oscar Cu 90 *Cu.*

Lombardo Toledano, Vicente (1894-) CG III, 399; WLA 220 *Mex.*

Lomboy, Reinaldo C 13 *Chil.*

Lomely y Jáuregui, María R. PM 53 *Mex.*

Londoño, Víctor M. (1876-1936) ALC II, 111; Co 38, 79; CoL 274; RHLC 153; SASS 239 *Col.*

Longhi, Leopoldo A 39, 86; CG III, 401 *Arg.*

Lonzarich, Enrique U 10 *Uru.*

López, Ambrosio Co 38 *Col.*

López, Ambrosio V. (1854-) Cu 90 *Cu.*

López, Carlos Enrique E 42 *Ecua.*

López, Carlos L. (1879-) Pan 12 *Pan.*

López, Casto Fulgencio V 89 *Venez.*

López, Casto R. V 89 *Venez.*

López, Clara (1860-) A 40 *Arg.*

López, El Padre SCL .550, 616 *Chil.*

López, Eliseo V 89 *Venez.*

López, Enrique A 40; Par 16 *Para.*

López, Enrique E. PM 53 *Mex.*

López, Ernestina A. A 40 *Arg.*

López, Eufrasio A 40 *Arg.*

López, Eugenio Gerardo A 40, 86 *Arg.*

López, Felicísimo CG III, 404; E 42 *Ecua.*

López, Heriberto C 51 *Chil.*

López, Ismael ("Cornelio Hispano") (1880-) APEH 715, 1189; BHLA 541; CG III, 66; Co 33, 38, 79; CrA 63; G 329; IE 138; LC 194; PCo 153; PLHA 144, 283; RHLC 211; SASS 239; WLA 192 *Col.*

López, J. Alejandro (1863-1917) E 42 *Ecua.*

López, Jacinto LV 70, 420; V 90 *Venez.*

López, Jesús F. TM 194 *Mex.*

López, Jesús J. (1889-) Cu 90 *Cu.*

López, José Antonio (1850-) Cu 91; HL I, 731 *Hond.*

López, José Florencio ("Jacán") (1821-1892) BDC 45; Cu 86, 91 *Cu.*

López, José Francisco A 40 *Arg.*

López, José Heriberto ("Jorge Borge") CG III, 405; V 51, 90 *Venez.*

López, José Hilario (1798-1869) CHL 326; CLH 279; Co 38 *Col.*

López, José Ramón LD 99; SD 20 *Dom.*

López, Libardo Co 38 *Col.*

López, Lina ("Zulima") V 90, 145 *Venez.*

López, Luciano NM 30 *Mex.*

López, Lucio BHLA 503 *Arg.*

López, Lucio Vicente (1848-1894) A 40; BHLA 397; CHL 191; CLH 164; GEA VIII; LA VIII, 642; SPLA 240 *Arg.*

López, Luis Carlos (1885-) ALC II, 181; APEH 851, 1191; BHLA 541, 587; CG III, 406; CHL 354; Co 38; CP 693; G 329; GLO 240; IE 151; LAND 169; PCo 162; RHLC 154; SASS 241; WLA 221 *Col.*

López, Manuel Antonio (1803-1891) CG III, 406; Co 39; E 42; V 90

López, María Dolores ACe 864 *Mex.*

López, Miguel ARC 55 *Cu.*

López, Modesto E 42 *Ecua.*

López, Patricio Antonio PM 53 *Mex.*

López, Pedro Alejandro (1881-) ARC 55; Cu 91 *Cu.*

López, R. TM 195 *Mex.*

López, Rafael (1875-) AMP 74; APMM 106; G 364; HLM 519; PM 54; PMe I, 265; PMM 52; PNM 149; TM 455 *Mex.*

López, Rafael M. SD 20 *Dom.*

López, René (1884-1909) PA 60; PCu 158; RLC 361 *Cu.*

López, Román I. A 40 *Arg.*

López, Sabatino A 40, 86; CG III, 407 *Arg.*

López, Sotero TM 596 *Mex.*
López, Venancio Víctor (1862-   ) Par 16; PPa 45; PT 21 *Para.*
López, Vicente (1691-   ) HPM 460 *Mex.*
López, Vicente Fidel (1815-1903) A 40; BHLA 275, 285; CG III, 438; CHL 143, 188; CLH 121, 161; GEA XXIII; HLA 425; LA V, 335, 477; VI, 989; VII, 154; VIII, 613, 631; PLHA 278; SPLA 233 *Arg.*
López Albújar, Enrique (1872-   ) BHLA 516; WLA 222 *Per.*
López Álvarez, Leopoldo Co 39 *Col.*
López Aretillar, Eduardo BDC 45; Cu 91 *Cu.*
López Ávilez, José HLM 157; HPM 203 *Mex.*
López Bago, Eduardo CG III, 411; U 10; UL 130 *Uru.*
López Ballesteros, Luis (1869-   ) BP 505; CG III, 411; PR 27 *P.R.*
López Ballesteros, Sixto (186?-1906) B 12; FPA 54, 65; LB 616; PB 133 *Bol.*
López Baralt, Rafael V 90 *Venez.*
López Benedito, F. A 40 *Arg.*
López Blanco, Marino CG III, 413; Cu 91; PJC 122 *Cu.*
López Blomberg, C. A. A 40, 86 *Arg.*
López Borreguero, Ramón V 90 *Venez.*
López Carvajal, Francisco TM 455, 471 *Mex.*
López Castañón, Rafael (1875-   ) WLA 222 *Mex.*
López Castro, Manuel PR 36 *P.R.*
López Consuegra, Andrés BDC 45; Cu 41, 91 *Cu.*
López Contreras, Eleazar CG III, 415; V 90 *Venez.*
López de Avilés, Joseph PM 54 *Mex.*
López de Ayala, Ramón Cu 91 *Cu.*
López de Barandier, Venancia A 40; CG III, 412 *Arg.*
1. López de Briñas, Felipe (1822-1877) CHL 454; CLH 396; Cu 25, 91; HLC 140; RLC 191, 192, 205 *Cu.*
2. López de Briñas, Felipe (hijo) (-1899) BDC 45; Cu 91 *Cu.*
López de Cogolludo, Diego HLM 209 *Mex.*
López de Gómara, Francisco (1510-   ) LA III, 297 *Arg.*
López de Gómara, Justo S. (1859-1923) A 40, 86; CG III, 418 *Arg.*
López de Haro, Damián PR 46 *P.R.*
López de Heredia, Miguel CG III, 422; Ig 192; NM 30 *Mex.*
López de la Serna, Rafael CG III, 445; Ig 197; NM 31 *Mex.*
López de Lisboa, Diego P 17 *Per.*
López de Maturana, José A 40 *Arg.*
López de Mendoza, Rafael PM 54; TM 195 *Mex.*
López de Mesa, Luis (1888-   ) BHLA 47, 473; CG III, 428; Co 36, 39; G 330; PLHA 270; WLA 222 *Col.*
López de Molina A 40 *Arg.*
López de Nelson, Ernestina (1879-   ) AT II, 651 *Arg.*
López Decoud, Arsenio (1868-   ) CG II, 416; Par 2, 16; PT 211 *Para.*

López Dorticós, Pedro Cu 91; GLO 244 *Cu.*
López Estremera, Juan BDC 45; Cu 91; TM 195
López Evia, Lorenzo ("Cascabel" *or* "Leoncito") PM 27, 53, 54 *Mex.*
López Fortún, P. TM 455 *Mex.*
López García de Peralta, María A 40 *Arg.*
López Gómez, Adel (1901-   ) Co 39; RHLC 190 *Col.*
López Ituarte, Alfonso CG III, 422; Ig 192; NM 30 *Mex.*
López Landrón, Rafael PR 19 *P.R.*
López Leiva, Francisco Cu 89, 91 *Cu.*
López Lira, José CG III, 423; TM 196 *Mex.*
López Loayza, Fernando ("Fray K. Brito") C 51; CG III, 423; P 17 *Chil.*
López Martínez, Celestino B 12; CG III, 427 *Bol.*
López Matoso, Antonio ACe 864 *Mex.*
López Méndez, Luis CHL 382; CLH 333; LV 133, 140; V 90 *Venez.*
López Méndez, R. Vargas SD 20 *Dom.*
López Merino, Francisco (1904-1928) A 40; APAM 535; APEH 683, 1189; CG III, 428 *Arg.*
López Negrete, Ladislao CG III, 432; G 364; TM 196 *Mex.*
López Ozeguera, Aurelio BDC 45; Cu 92 *Cu.*
López Palmero, M. A 40 *Arg.*
López-Penha, A. Z. Co 39; LAND 201 *Col.*
López-Portillo y Rojas, José ("V. Farfalla") (1850-1923) BAMP 44; BHLA 523; CG III, 440; CHL 403, 421; CLH 366; G 364; HLM 443; HLMex 225; Ig 192; NM 3, 30; PM 42, 54; PoM 343; TM 196, 197, 555 *Mex.*
López Prieto, Antonio (1847-1893) Cu 92 *Cu.*
López Rivas, Eduardo LV 117; V 90 *Venez.*
López Rocha, Carlos A 40; CG III, 443 *Arg.*
López Ruiz, Mariano (1871-   ) CG III, 443; G 364; NM 32 *Mex.*
López Sánchez, Carlos Par 16 *Para.*
López Sánchez, Francisco (1883-   ) QPR (1) 96; (2) 99 *P.R.*
López Seña, Juan (-1912) Cu 92 *Cu.*
López Silvero, Jesús ARC 55; Cu 92 *Cu.*
López Torres, Francisco A 40; LA VIII, 628 *Arg.*
López Traspaderne, Domingo C 34 *Chil.*
López Trujillo, Clemente PM 54 *Mex.*
López Vega, Carlos A 40 *Arg.*
López Velarde, Ramón (1888-1921) AMP 66; APEH 967, 1193; APMM 110; BHLA 559; G 364; HLM 524; HLMex 244; LAS 207; NM 31; PM 54; PMM 94; PNM 159 *Mex.*
López y Fuentes, Gregorio (1895-   ) APMM 109; BHLA 560; CG III, 417; G 365; IE 151; Ig 191; LAS 204; NM 31; PM 54 *Mex.*
López y Lugo, Andrés Cu 92 *Cu.*
López y Muñiz, Lorenzo Cu 92 *Cu.*

López y Planes, Vicente (1785-1856) A 40; BHLA 167, 397; CHL 49, 53; CLH 42, 45; HLA 154; HPHA II, 405; LA IV, 815; SPLA 32 *Arg.*

López Zamora de Torres, Dora A 41; CG III, 451 *Arg.*

Lora, Juan José BAP 105; BHLA 610 *Per.*

Lora, Miguel B 12 *Bol.*

Lora y Lora, José (-1907) AEHA 521; P 18; PPe 266; PR 56 *Per.*

"Lord Jim" (*pseud.*) *see* Subercaseaux, Benjamín

"Lorely" (*pseud.*) *see* Garza, María Luisa

Lorente, Sebastián (-1884) BHLA 383 *Per.*

Lorento, Severiano A 41 *Arg.*

Lorenzana, Carlos PCo 166 *Col.*

Lorenzana, Máximo Co 39 *Col.*

"Lorenzo Jiménez" (*pseud.*) *see* Chacón Trejos, Gonzalo

Lorenzo Rodríguez, Tirso (1877-) WLA 223 *Arg.*

Loreto, Agustín NM 31 *Mex.*

Loría Iglesias, Ramón CA 36, 37; IBCR IV, 8 *C.R.*

Lorié, Antonio María BDC 45; Cu 92 *Cu.*

Lorié Bertot, Francisco Cu 92 *Cu.*

Lorient, Myrtil ARC 55; Cu 92 *Cu.*

Lorusso, Arturo A 41, 86; CG III, 456 *Arg.*

Losada *see also* Lossada *and* Lozada

Losada, Alcides CG III, 456; V 90 *Venez.*

Losada, Francisco Cu 92 *Cu.*

Losada, Hedilio V 90 *Venez.*

Losada, Juan Miguel de BDC 46; Cu 92; TM 498 *Cu.*

Loscar BDC 46; Cu 93 *Cu.*

Lossada, Eduardo Matthyas V 90 *Venez.*

Lossada, Jesús Enrique CG III, 457; V 90 *Venez.*

Lossada Piñeres, Juan Antonio V 90 *Venez.*

Lotero Quintana, Ramón Antonio ("C. B. Ralg") Co 39, 59 *Col.*

Loubayssin de la Marca, Francisco BHC I, 113 *et passim Chil.*

Loudaiz y Arriete, Nicolás TM 197 *Mex.*

"Louis, Saint" (*pseud.*) *see* Pérez Fuentes, Francisco

Loveira y Chirino, Carlos (1882-1928) BHLA 526, 565; CG III, 458; CHL 488; Cu 93; G 338; GLO 244; HLC 189; LH 109; RLC 342; SASS 293 *Cu.*

Lovera, Armando V 90, 111 *Venez.*

Loynaz, Carlos (1906-) PoC 150 *Cu.*

Loynaz, Enrique (1903-) PoC 161 *Cu.*

Loynaz y Muñoz, Dulce María (1902-) PCu 159; PJC 108; PoC 151 *Cu.*

Loyola, Bernabé Ig 197; NM 31 *Mex.*

Loyola, Toribio C 51 *Chil.*

Loza, Belisario B 12 *Bol.*

Loza, José Manuel (1799-1862) B 12; LB 580 *Bol.*

Loza, León M. B 12 *Bol.*

Lozada *see also* Losada *and* Lossada

Lozada, Enrique NM 31 *Mex.*

Lozada, Pedro L. P 18 *Per.*

Lozano, Abigaíl (1821-1866) AEHA 523; BHLA 324; CG III, 459; CHL 360; CLH 308, 310; FPA 550, 564; HPHA I, 408; LV 221; SASS 508; V 90 *Venez.*

Lozano, José G. (-1888) BDC 47 *Cu.*

Lozano, M. J. V 91 *Venez.*

Lozano, Pedro (1697-1752) CG III, 460; LA III, 515; Par 16; SCL 411, 426, 617 *Para.*

Lozano, Pedro A. Co 39 *Col.*

Lozano, Rafael (1899-) AMP 166; APMM 115; CG III, 460; G 365; PM 55 *Mex.*

Lozano Casado, M. PB 136 *Bol.*

Lozano Casado, Manuel CG III, 461; Cu 93 *Cu.*

Lozano Casado, Miguel Cu 93 *Cu.*

Lozano de Valderas, Juan de Dios TM 198 *Mex.*

Lozano de Vilches, Enriqueta CG III, 464; TM 197 *Mex.*

Lozano García, Carlos (1902-) CG III, 461; HLM 528; TM 198 *Mex.*

Lozano García, Ernesto CG III, 461; TM 197 *Mex.*

Lozano García, Lázaro (1899-) HLM 528; TM 198 *Mex.*

Lozano y Lozano, Fabio Co 39 *Col.*

Lozano y Lozano, Juan (1902-) ALC II, 437; Co 39; P 18; WLA 223 *Col.*

Luaces, Joaquín Lorenzo (1826-1867) AEHA 526; BDC 47; BHLA 330; CHL 461; CLH 403; Cu 93; FPA 162, 175; G 338; HLC 147, 172; HPHA I, 272; PA 63; RLC 147, 196, 203, 206, 245; SASS 273 *Cu.*

"Luca" (*pseud.*) B 12 *Bol.*

Luca y Patrón, Esteban de (1786-1824) BHLA 168, 186; CHL 66; CLH 57; HLA 157, 216; HPHA II, 407; LA IV, 895; SPLA 52 *Arg.*

"Lucas del Cigarral" (*pseud.*) *see* Ruiz y Rodríguez, Manuel

"Lucas Ribera" (*pseud.*) *see* Cabrera, Luis

Lucentó, Vicente E 43 *Ecua.*

Lucero, Juan Carlos A 41 *Arg.*

"Lucero, Paulino" (*pseud.*) *see* Ascasubi, Hilario

"Luciano Pulgar" (*pseud.*) *see* Suárez, Marco Fidel

Lucio, Manuel Jesús Co 39 *Col.*

"Lucio Magez Nigona" (*pseud.*) *see* Gómez Luna, Ignacio

"Lucio Stella" (*pseud.*) *see* Goycoechea Menéndez, Martín de

Luco Cruchaga, Germán C 13 *Chil.*

Luchichí, Ignacio M. ("Claudio Frollo") (1850-) AMP 299; PMe I, 267; PoM 347 *Mex.*

"Ludovic" (*pseud.*) *see* Curotto, Ángel

Luengas, Carlos TM 456 *Mex.*

Luera Fernández, Andrés CG III, 471; Cu 94 *Cu.*

Lufríu y Alonso, René (1890-) CG III, 471; G 338; GLO 244; WLA 224 *Cu.*

Lugo, Américo (1871-) BDC 47; CG III, 471; CHL 497; CLH 437; LD 97; SD 20 *Dom.*

Lugo, Bernardo de HLNG I, 243; LC 91; RHLC 27 *Col.*

Lugo, Cristián SD 21 *Dom.*

Lugo, Eleuterio BP 529; PR 36 *P.R.*

Lugo, Eusebio A. (1890-) Par 17; PT 155 *Para.*

Lugo, Francisco Aniceto CG III, 471; V 91 *Venez.*
Lugo, Raziel de PM 55 *Mex.*
Lugo Viña, Ruy de BDC 48; CG III, 471; Cu 94; PCu 166; PJC 123 *Cu.*
Lugones, Arturo A 41 *Arg.*
Lugones, Manuel A 41 *Arg.*
Lugones Argüello, Leopoldo (1874-) A 41; AB 24; AEHA 528; APAM 11; APEH 369, 1185; AT II, 903; BHLA 464; CG III, 471; CHL 165, 186, 530; CLH 467; CrA 7; FPA 16, 43; G 314; GLO 237; LAC 141; MSAP 96, 290; NPA 9; PLHA 123; SAL 92 *et passim;* SASS 44; WLA 224 *Arg.*
"Luis del Valle" (*pseud.*) *see* Varona y Pera, Enrique José
"Luis Martín" (*pseud.*) *see* Bermejo, Manuel M.
"Luis Ruiz" (*pseud.*) *see* Olavarría, Domingo Antonio
"Luis Tablanca" (*pseud.*) *see* Pardo Farelo, Enrique
Luisi, Luisa (189.-) BHLA 533; CG III, 473; FPA 528, 546; G 388; HSLU II, pt 7, 22; III, pt 4, 46; LAS 207; PIU III, 190; PU 129; SASS 463; TM 556; U 10; UT 307; WLA 225 *Uru.*
Luisi de Podestá, Clotilde HSLU II, pt 8, 31; UT 305 *Uru.*
Lujambio de Mecías, María J. PU 291 *Uru.*
Luján, Agustín CA 37; EPCR 317; PC 181 *C.R.*
Luján, E. C 51 *Chil.*
"Lunarejo, El" (*pseud.*) *see* Espinosa Medrano, Juan de
Luperón, Gregorio SD 21 *Dom.*
Luque, Mario (1880-) BDC 48; CG III, 476; Cu 94 *Cu.*
Luquín, Eduardo CG III, 478; Ig 198; NM 31 *Mex.*
Lussich, Antonio D. U 10 *Uru.*
Lussich, Juan (-1885) A 41, 71 *Arg.*
Lutz, Otto Pan 12 *Pan.*
"Luz, María de la" (*pseud.*) *see* González de Fanning, Teresa
Luz de la Madrid, Francisco de la Cu 94 *Cu.*
Luz y Caballero, José Cipriano de la (1800-1862) BHLA 225, 252; CG III, 478; CHL 466; CLH 407; Cu 94; G 338; GLO 244; HLC 55; RLC 38, 44, 71, 151, 168 *Cu.*
Luz y Duarte, Francisco de la CG III, 478; Cu 94 *Cu.*
Luzuriaga Agote, G. A 41 *Arg.*
Luzuriaga y Bribiesca, Guillermo de ("Solón de Mel") (1895-) IE 152; NM 31; PM 55, 79 *Mex.*
"Lydia Bolena" (*pseud.*) *see* Pertuz, Julia de
Lynch, Benito (1885-) A 41; CG III, 480; CHL 202; GLO 237; LAC 48, 132; PLHA 196; WLA 226 *Arg.*
Lyra *see* Lira

LL

Llaguno, J. Orión CG III, 484; E 43 *Ecua.*
Llamosas y de Cépeda, Antonio (-1892) Cu 94 *Cu.*

Llamozas, Salvador N. V 91 *Venez.*
Llanas, Pedro L. Ig 198; NM 31 *Mex.*
Llanes, Ricardo M. A 42 *Arg.*
"Llano, Américo" (*pseud.*) *see* Vasseur, Álvaro Armando
Llano, Juan C. Co 39 *Col.*
Llano, Teodomiro BC 222; Co 39 *Col.*
Llano y Martínez, Sergio Cu 94 *Cu.*
Llano y Zapata, José Eusebio CG III, 486; P 18; SCL 491, 616 *Per.*
Llanos, Adolfo TM 199 *Mex.*
Llanos, Bernardino (-1639) HPM 195 *Mex.*
Llanos, Julio A 42; CG III, 486; LA VIII, 629 *Arg.*
Llanos y Alcaraz, Adolfo CG III, 486; TM 199 *Mex.*
Llanos y Valdés, F. de E 43 *Ecua.*
Llata, Manuel de la PM 55 *Mex.*
Llavaneras, Jesús Antonio V 91 *Venez.*
Llave, Fernando de la PM 55 *Mex.*
Llaverías, Federico (1888-) CG III, 489; IE 155; SD 21 *Dom.*
Llaverías y Martínez, Joaquín (1875-) CG III, 489; Cu 94; WLA 218 *Cu.*
Lleó y Abad, Lorenzo Cu 94 *Cu.*
Llera, F. José P 18 *Per.*
Lleras, José Manuel (1843-1879) BC 225; CA 37; Co 39; IBCR IV, 385; RHLC 168 *C.R.*
Lleras, Lorenzo María (1811-1868) AC I, 299; BC 223; Co 39; RHLC 99, 162 *Col.*
Lleras Acosta, Carlos Alberto CG III, 490; Co 40 *Col.*
Lleras Codazzi, Ricardo (1869-) CG III, 490; Co 40 *Col.*
Llerena, Agustín R. de CG III, 490; Cu 94 *Cu.*
Lles y Berdayes, Fernando (1883-) BDC 48; CG III, 490; CT 137; Cu 94; IE 157; PCu 171; PJC 130; RLC 354; WLA 219 *Cu.*
Lles y Berdayes, Francisco (1888-1921) CG III, 490; Cu 95; PCu 169; PJC 128 *Cu.*
Llona, Gonzalo CG III, 493; E 43 *Ecua.*
Llona, Lastenia Larriva de *see* Larriva de Llona, Lastenia
Llona Runosa, Numa Pompilio (1832-1907) AEHA 537; BHLA 321, 430; CHL 316; CLH 268; E 43, 74; FPA 253, 259; PE 255; PLE 47; SASS 332 *Ecua.*
Llop, Francisco TM 200 *Mex.*
Lloréns Torres, Luis (1878-) APEH 752, 1190; BP 529, 608; CG III, 496; FPA 461, 491; G 384; LAS 207; PA 215; PP 193; PR 13, 19, 36, 56; QPR (2) 100; SASS 310 *P.R.*
Llorent, José AP 209; Pan 12 *Pan.*
Llosa, José Mariano P 18 *Per.*

M

M., J. B. S. E 43 *Ecua.*
"M. de Saavedra Z." (*pseud.*) *see* Saavedra Zelaya, Mercedes
M. J. P. Co 44 *Col.*
"M. O." (*pseud.*) *see* Ortega, Miguel

"M. Sasor" (*pseud.*) *see* Rivera, Mercedes de Rosas

Macau, Miguel Ángel (1886-) BDC 48; CG III, 502; Cu 95; PJC 135 *Cu.*

Macchi, José E 43 *Ecua.*

MacDouall, Roberto (1842-1921) AC I, 349; II, 299; BC 226; Co 40; PCo 176; RHLC 149 *Col.*

MacDowald, P. Salcedo E 43 *Ecua.*

Macedo, Miguel NM 31 *Mex.*

Macedo y Arbeu, Eduardo PM 55; TM 200, 456 *Mex.*

Maceo, Antonio ARC 35, 55 *Cu.*

Maceo Verdecia, J. Cu 95 *Cu.*

Macía, Federico Cu 95 *Cu.*

Macías, Francisco Ig 199; NM 31 *Mex.*

Maciel, Ernesto PM 55 *Mex.*

Maciel, Santiago (1863-) BHLA 423; CG III, 506; CHL 223; CLH 186; PLHA 235; U 10 *Uru.*

Mackay, Jermán C 51 *Chil.*

Mackenna Subercaseaux, Alberto C 51; NC 433 *Chil.*

Mackenna y Eyzaguirre, Juan C 13; CG I, 642; III, 507; IBCR IV, 261; NC 174, 433 *Chil.*

Macpherson, Telasco A. ("Pío Tenazas") V 91, 117 *Venez.*

Machado, Francisco de P. CG III, 509; Cu 95 *Cu.*

Machado, Francisco Javier SD 21 *Dom.*

Machado, José E. (1868-) CG III, 509; IE 159; V 92 *Venez.*

Machado, Manuel Arturo SD 21 *Dom.*

Machado, Mario SD 22 *Dom.*

Machado, Ofelia HSLU II, pt 7, 4 *Uru.*

Machado, Reinaldo R. (1889-) CG III, 509; Cu 96 *Cu.*

Machado de Arredondo, Isabel (1838-) CG III, 509; Cu 96 *Cu.*

Machado de Chávez, Juan (-1653) SCL 454, 467, 618 *Ecua.*

Machado Hernández, Alfredo V 92 *Venez.*

Machado Jáuregui, Rafael (1834-) CLH 449; GPCA II, 235; PG 169 *Guat.*

Machado y Gómez, Eduardo (1836-1877) CG III, 510; Cu 96 *Cu.*

Machaly, Ramón (Ramón Machali Cazón) A 42 *Arg.*

Machiavelo, José Ángel PR 36 *P.R.*

Machoni, Antonio (1671-1753) BHC II, 387; LA III, 372; Par 17 *Arg.*

Madán y García, Augusto E. (1853-1915) BDC 49; CG III, 512; Cu 96 *Cu.*

Madariaga, José María ACe 865 *Mex.*

Madera, Elías Liborio CG III, 514; E 44 *Ecua.*

Madera, Luis F. E 44 *Ecua.*

Madiedo, Manuel María (1815-1888) BC 227; CHL 342; CLH 293; Co 40; HPHA II, 74; LC 131; RHLC 99, 160, 177; V 92 *Col.*

Madrazo, Mariano Ignacio ("Noriama Giciona Mazorda") ACe 866 *Mex.*

"Madre Castillo" (*pseud.*) *see* Castillo y Guevara, Francisco Josefa de la Concepción

Madrid, Carlos (-1895) HL I, 603 *Hond.*

"Madrid, César de" (*pseud.*) *see* Coronado y Álvaro, Francisco de Paula

Madrid, F. de la BDC 44; Cu 99 *Cu.*

Madrid, J. F. de *see* Fernández de Madrid, José

Madrid, Samuel E. de A 42 *Arg.*

Madrigal, Policarpo ARC 55 *Cu.*

Madrigal, Vitalia CA 37; CG III, 517 *C.R.*

Madrueño y Palacios, Germán TM 201 *Mex.*

Maduro, Alejandro V 92 *Venez.*

Maduro, Eduardo AP 213; Pan 12 *Pan.*

Maduro, Jesús M. V 92 *Venez.*

Maduro, Rómulo V 92 *Venez.*

Maeso Tognochi, Carlos M. ("Máximo Torres") CG III, 518; HSLU I, pt 4, 5; LU 64, 669; PIU III, 217; PoU 127; U 10 *Uru.*

Magallanes, Manuel C 51 *Chil.*

Magallanes Moure, Manuel (1878-1924) APEH 637, 1188; BHLA 535; CG III, 521; CHL 263, 286; CLH 223; CMPC 24; FPA 192, 215; G 325; PCC xii, 49; PCh 189; SASS 150 *Chil.*

Magalli, José María E 44 *Ecua.*

Magallón, E. PJC 133 *Cu.*

Magariños Borja, Mateo A. LU 672; PIU III, 319; U 10 *Uru.*

Magariños Cervantes, Alejandro (1825-1893) BHLA 313, 339; CHL 213; CLH 176; HPHA II, 486; HSLU III, pt 4, 16; LA VIII, 621; LU 64, 670; LUr 456; PIU I, 181; SASS 472; U 10; UL 130 *Uru.*

Magariños Solsona, Mateo CG III, 521; CHL 227; CLH 190; LU 64, 672; PIU III, 318; U 10 *Uru.*

Magdaleno, Mauricio BHLA 563; LAS 204; NM 31; TM 556 *Mex.*

"Magez Nigona, Lucio" (*pseud.*) *see* Gómez Luna, Ignacio

"Magistrado Cubano, Un" (*pseud.*) *see* Franchi Alfaro y Lemaur, Antonio

Magnani, Virgilio A 42 *Arg.*

Magnasco, Osvaldo A 42; CG III, 522 *Arg.*

Mago González, F. CG III, 523; V 92 *Venez.*

"Magón" (*pseud.*) *see* González Zeledón, Manuel

Magrassi, Alejandro A 42; CG III, 523 *Arg.*

Magri, Valeriano CG III, 523; PU 292; U 10 *Uru.*

Maillefert, Alfredo (1889-) IE 162 *Mex.*

Maitín, Federico V 93 *Venez.*

Maitín, José Antonio (1804-1874) AEHA 541; BHLA 239, 324; CHL 360; CLH 308; FPA 549, 555; HPHA I, 410; LV 221; V 93 *Venez.*

"Maître Renard" (*pseud.*) *see* Solano, Armando

Maiz, Fidel (1828-) Par 17 *Para.*

Malabear, José TM 621 *Mex.*

Malaret, Augusto CG III, 526; PR 52 *P.R.*

Malbrán A., Pedro J. C 35, 51; CG III, 527 *Chil.*

Malda, José Gabriel Ig 199; NM 31 *Mex.*

Malde Vizoso, Enrique Cu 99 *Cu.*

Maldonado, Alfonso M. (1849-) CG III, 527; CHL 409; CLH 356; Ig 200; NM 31 *Mex.*

Maldonado, Angela C. de PE 40 *Ecua.*

Maldonado, Bruno (1890-) BC 230 *Col.*
Maldonado, Dolores TM 201 *Mex.*
Maldonado, Francisco Severo (-1832) ACe 149; HLM 250 *Mex.*
Maldonado, Gerónimo (hijo) V 93 *Venez.*
Maldonado, Horacio O. (1884-) CG III, 528, 529; G 388; HSLU III, pt 4, 44; IE 163; LU 64, 677, 685; Par 17; PIU III, 315; U 11; UT 313 *Uru.*
Maldonado, Julio S. A 42 *Arg.*
Maldonado, Manuel NL 63; PN 49 *Nicar.*
Maldonado, Samuel Darío CG III, 528; LV 325; SASS 515; V 93; VPF 115 *Venez.*
Maldonado, Vicente (1710-1748) BHLA 134; PLE 16 *Ecua.*
Maldonado, Víctor V. CG III, 528; V 94 *Venez.*
Maldonado Melíndez, Bruno (-1890) Co 40 *Col.*
Maldonado Plata, J. CG III, 529; PCo 168 *Col.*
Malpica La Barca, Domingo (1836-1894) Cu 99 *Cu.*
Maltos, Juan NM 32 *Mex.*
Maltrana C 35 *Chil.*
Maluenda Labarca, Rafael (1885-) BHLA 511; C 13, 51; CG III, 531; N 161; NC 378 *Chil.*
Mallarino, Manuel María (1808-1872) LC 157 *Col.*
Mallea, Eduardo A 42; BHLA 634; LAC 135 *Arg.*
Mallevigne, A. Cu 99 *Cu.*
Mallo, Nicanor B 13; CG III, 534; V 94 *Bol.*
"Mamerto Cuenca, Claudio" (*pseud.*) *see* Cuenca, Claudio José del Corazón de Jesús
Manacorda, Telmo (1893-) IE 163; PU 293; WLA 231 *Uru.*
Mancera, Gabriel CG III, 535; PM 55 *Mex.*
Mancera, Octavio Ig 201; NM 32 *Mex.*
Mancero V., Luis E 44 *Ecua.*
Mancisidor, José CG III, 536; LAS 200; NM 32 *Mex.*
"Manco Paz" (*pseud.*) *see* Paz, José María
Mandiola, Ambrosio Segundo C 51 *Chil.*
Mandiola, Rómulo ("M. Richard," *or* "R. Roco," *or* "Roque Roca") (1848-1881) C 67; CL 290; HC 252 *Chil.*
Mandolini, Hernani A 42; CG III, 536 *Arg.*
Maneiro, Juan Luis (1759-1802) ACe 867; HLM 185 *Mex.*
Manera, Enrique A 42 *Arg.*
"Manfredo" (*pseud.*) *see* Micolao y Sierra, Vicente
Mangel Mesnil, Emilio de C 14; NC 498 *Chil.*
Maniau y Torquemada, Francisco ACe 869 *Mex.*
Manquilef G., Manuel C 67; CG III, 540 *Chil.*
Manrique C 14; NC 499 *Chil.*
Manrique, Adina V 94 *Venez.*
Manrique, Aurelio, Jr. PM 55 *Mex.*
Manrique, José Ángel (1777-) BC 233; HLNG II, 253 *Col.*

Manrique, José María (1846-1907) BHLA 411; CHL 376; CLH 324; LV 74; V 94; VPF 31 *Venez.*
Manrique, Juan Manuel V 94 *Venez.*
Manrique, Maldonado G. Co 41 *Col.*
Manrique, Mariano G. (1829-1870) BC 235; Co 40 *Col.*
Manrique, Venancio G. (1836-1889) BC 234; CG III, 540; Co 40; LC 167 *Col.*
Manrique Arvelo, Pedro CG III, 540; E 44; V 94 *Venez.*
Manrique Jérez, Juan V 94 *Venez.*
Manrique Jérez, Manuel Co 41; V 94
Manrique Terán, Guillermo (1890-) CG III, 541; Co 41; PCo 174; WLA 231 *Col.*
Mansilla, Lucio Víctor (1831-1914) A 42, 86; CG III, 541; CHL 186; GEA III, IX; GLO 237; LA VIII, 691 *Arg.*
Mansilla de García, Eduarda ("Daniel") (1838-1892) A 42, 78, 86; BHLA 398; CHL 189; CLH 161; LA VIII, 788 *Arg.*
"Manso, Severo" (*pseud.*) *see* Martínez, Demetrio Benjamín
Manso de Noronha, Juana Paula (1820-1875) A 42; CG III, 541; LA VIII, 792 *Arg.*
Mansoulet, Juan C 14; CG III, 542 *Chil.*
Mantecón y González, Enrique Cu 99 *Cu.*
Manterola, Ramón HLM 467; TM 201 *Mex.*
Mantilla, Daniel (1836-1868) BC 235; Co 41 *Col.*
Mantilla, Manuel Florencio A 42; CG III, 542 *Arg.*
Mantilla, Víctor P 18 *Per.*
"Manuel Guzmán Maturana" (*pseud.*) *see* Dantés, Edmundo
Manzanet, Santiago Cu 99 *Cu.*
Manzanilla, Anastasio ("Hugo Sol") (1892-) CG III, 557; Ig 201; NM 28, 32 *Mex.*
Manzanilla, José Matías (1870-) CG III, 557; P 18 *Per.*
Manzano, José Francisco CHL 434; CLH 377 *Cu.*
Manzano, Juan Francisco (1797-1854) ARC 33; BDC 54; Cu 99; HPHA I, 257; RLC 70, 72, 73, 146 *Cu.*
Manzano, Lucas V 94 *Venez.*
Manzano Hernández, Tomás PR 56 *P.R.*
Manzanos, Arturo TM 202 *Mex.*
Manzanos Gutiérrez, Ezequiel TM 203 *Mex.*
Manzeles, Gonzalo Cu 99 *Cu.*
Mañach y Robato, Jorge (1898-) BHLA 567; CG III, 558; Cu 99; GLO 244; IE 164; WLA 232 *Cu.*
"Mañod, Eloy Falopio" (*pseud.*) *see* Olmedo, Adolfo
Mañón, Manuel TM 556 *Mex.*
Maples Arce, Manuel (1898-) AMP 159; CG III, 559; HLM 527; PM 55; PMM 130 *Mex.*
Maqueo Castellanos, Esteban CG III, 559; Cu 99; HLM 517; Ig 202; NM 32; PM 55 *Mex.*
Maquet, Augusto CG III, 559; Cu 99; V 95
Mar, María del IE 165; NM 32 *Mex.*
Mar, Serafín del BAP 81 *Per.*

Mar, Sofía   TM 203   *Mex.*
Mar y Rotti, Luis de la   NC 119   *Chil.*
Marasso, Bautista   A 43; CG III, 562   *Arg.*
Marasso Rocca, Arturo   (1890-   )   A 42; APAM 334; APEH 718; CG III, 562; LAC 144   *Arg.*
"Maravelo"   (*pseud.*)   *see* Valero Méndez, Agustín
Marcano, Gaspar   CG III, 563; V 95   *Venez.*
Marcano, Vicente ("Tito Salcedo")   V 95, 127, 136   *Venez.*
Marcano Villanueva, Jesús   CG III, 563; V 95   *Venez.*
Marcellino, Antonio F.   A 43   *Arg.*
Marcial Quiñones, José   PR 9, 19   *P.R.*
Marcio, Anco   PB 23   *Bol.*
Marcó, Alejandro   A 86   *Arg.*
Marcos, Agustín   CG III, 566; Ig 203; NM 32   *Mex.*
Marcos, Fernando L.   CG III, 566; Cu 99   *Cu.*
Marcos, José Antonio   E 44   *Ecua.*
Marcos, Mateo   V 95   *Venez.*
Marcos Suárez, Miguel de   CG III, 566; Cu 99   *Cu.*
Marcucci, Ángel R.   PR 36   *P.R.*
Marchán García, Francisco   E 44   *Ecua.*
Marchant Pereira, Ruperto   C 14, 51; CG III, 567; NC 176   *Chil.*
Marchena, Héctor de   SD 22   *Dom.*
Marchena, Julián   (1897-   )   CA 37; EPCR 577   *C.R.*
Marchito, N.   PC 183   *Chil.*
Marecos, Séver   Par 17; PPa 263   *Para.*
Marechal, Leopoldo   (1900-   )   A 43; APAM 539; APEH 1166; LAC 149; NPA 271; PLHA 165   *Arg.*
Marfany, A. Carlos   A 43   *Arg.*
Margalli, Felipe A.   TM 204   *Mex.*
Margallo y Duquesne, Francisco   (1765-1837)   HLNG II, 484   *Col.*
Margarita, Blanca   BAP 121   *Per.*
"Margot"   (*pseud.*)   *see* Pimentel, Margarita A. de
María, Alicia   Cu 100   *Cu.*
María, Ana   Cu 100   *Cu.*
"María de la Luz"   (*pseud.*)   *see* González de Fanning, Teresa
"María Enriqueta"   (*pseud.*)   *see* Camarillo y Roa de Pereyra, María Enriqueta
María Josefa de los Ángeles   (1770-   )   V 95   *Venez.*
"María Monvel"   (*pseud.*)   *see* Brito de Donoso, Tilda
María y Campos, Antonio de   TM 606   *Mex.*
María y Campos, Armando de   CG III, 571; NM 32; PM 55; TM 456   *Mex.*
"Marianela"   (*pseud.*)   *see* Palma, Angélica
Mariani, Roberto   A 43; APAM 342   *Arg.*
Mariátegui, Francisco Javier   P 18   *Per.*
Mariátegui, José Carlos   (1886-1930)   BHLA 599; G 382; LH 47; P 18.   *Per.*
Maribona, Armando R.   (1894-   )   CG III, 572; Cu 100   *Cu.*
Marín, Abel   PCo 182   *Col.*
Marín, Carlos Luis   V 95   *Venez.*
Marín, Domingo   SCL 391, 618   *Chil.*
Marín, Francisco   V 95   *Venez.*

Marín, Francisco Gonzalo   (1869-1897)   ARC 40; BP 530, 609; PA 223; PR 36; SD 22   *P.R.*
Marín, J. A.   V 95   *Venez.*
Marín, Juan   (1897-   )   BHLA 621; C 35; CG III, 575; PCC xx, 215   *Chil.*
Marín, Manuel Antonio (hijo)   V 95, 96   *Venez.*
Marín, Ramón   (1832-1902)   BDC 54; PR 13, 19, 33, 46   *P.R.*
Marín, Rufino   A 43   *Arg.*
Marín Calderón, Isidro   CA 37   *C.R.*
Marín Cañas, José ("Juan de Espinel")   CA 18, 37; CG III, 577; IBCR IV, 341, 424 *et passim*   *C.R.*
Marín de Poveda, Bartolomé   BHC II, 335   *Chil.*
Marín del Solar, Mercedes   (1804-1866)   C 35; CHL 247; CLH 207; HC 65; HPHA II, 368; PCh 19; PCU 15   *Chil.*
Marín i Recabarren, Buenaventura   (1806-1877)   HC 56   *Chil.*
Marín Loya, Luis   CG III, 577; IE 166; Ig 203; NM 32; PM 56   *Mex.*
Marinello Vidaurreta, Juan   (1899-   )   APEH 1016, 1193; BHLA 567; Cu 100; WLA 234   *Cu.*
Mariño, Cosme   (1847-   )   AT 160   *Arg.*
Mariño, Juan Agustín   (-1873)   Cu 100   *Cu.*
Mariño de Lovera, Pedro   SCL 152, 618   *Chil.*
Mariño de Riverón, Adelina ("Yolanda")   PJC 146   *Cu.*
Mariño Estrada, Adolfo   CG III, 582; Cu 100   *Cu.*
"Mario, Salvador"   (*pseud.*)   *see* Ocampo, Luis
"Mariquita, Misia"   (*pseud.*)   *see* Sánchez, Mariano
Mariscal, Agustín   Cu 100   *Cu.*
Mariscal, Federico E.   CG III, 583; HLM 513   *Mex.*
Mariscal, Ignacio   (1829-1910)   AMP 241; G 365; PMe I, 275; TM 204   *Mex.*
Markes, José Krus   TM 204   *Mex.*
"Mármara, Dagoberto"   (*pseud.*)   *see* Bobadilla, Emilio
Mármol, Francisco   V 96   *Venez.*
Mármol, Francisco J.   V 96   *Venez.*
Mármol, Francisco Manuel   V 96   *Venez.*
Mármol, José   (1818-1871)   A 43, 86; AEHA 557; BHLA 276, 308; CG III, 585; CHL 134, 295; CLH 114; G 315; HLA 346; HPHA II, 458; LA VI, 693; PLHA 71, 187; SAL 248, 339; SASS 16; SPLA 69, 155, 226; VPF 15; WSAL 27, 72   *Arg.*
Mármol, Luis Enrique   V 96   *Venez.*
Mármol, Luis M.   V 96   *Venez.*
Mármol, Miguel ("Jabino")   LV 424; V 85, 96   *Venez.*
Mármol, Tomás   LV 344; V 96   *Venez.*
Mármol y Muñoz, José   V 96   *Venez.*
Marmolejo, Luis   (-1893)   BC 237; Co 41   *Col.*
"Maroff, Tristán"   (*pseud.*)   *see* Navarro, Gustavo Adolfo
"Marón, Daurico"   (*pseud.*)   *see* Roca, Ramón
Maroni, Enrique P.   A 43   *Arg.*
Maroto de Quirós, Eduardo   Cu 100   *Cu.*

Marqués de Dos Hermanas *see* Velasco y Rojas, Matías de

Marqués de la Vega de Anzó *see* González del Valle, Martín

Marqués de San Francisco *see* Romero de Terreros y Vinent, Manuel

Márquez, Antonio José ("Víctor Heim") BC 237 *Chil.*

Márquez, Coriolano, Coronel A 43; LA VIII, 628 *Arg.*

Márquez, José Arnaldo (1830-1904) BHLA 319; CHL 296; CLH 250; FPA 435, 440; P 19; PPe 99 *Per.*

Márquez, José de Jesús (1837-1902) CG III, 587; Cu 100 *Cu.*

Márquez, Matías F. ("Dámaso Gil Aclea") Cu 8, 100 *Cu.*

Márquez, Pedro M. TM 204 *Mex.*

Márquez Bustillos, V. CG III, 587; V 96 *Venez.*

Márquez Cañizales, Augusto V 96 *Venez.*

Márquez de la Romana, P. E 44 *Ecua.*

Márquez Eyzaguirre, Luis E. C 67 *Chil.*

Márquez Sterling y Loret de Mola, Manuel (1872-1934) CG III, 589; CT 579; Cu 100; WLA 236 *Cu.*

Márquez Valdez, Doroteo UL 130 *Uru.*

Marquina, Pedro (-1886) Cu 101 *Cu.*

Marrero, Jacinto BP 530 *P.R.*

Marrero Marengo, Ricardo Par 17; PPa 149 *Para.*

Marrero y Caro, Rosa Cu 101 *Cu.*

Marroquí, José María (1824-1898) CG III, 658; HLM 490; Ig 208; NM 33 *Mex.*

Marroquín, Andrés María (1796-1833) HLNG II, 472; LC 115 *Col.*

Marroquín, José Manuel (1827-1908) AC I, 275; BC 238; BHLA 343, 368; CHL 339; CLH 291; Co 41; LAS 200; LC 148; RHLC 139, 187 *Col.*

Marroquín, Lorenzo (1856-1918) BC 242; BHLA 410; CG III, 658; CHL 353; CLH 303; Co 35, 41; G 330; LC 192; RHLC 171, 188; SASS 243 *Col.*

Marroquín y Osorio, José Manuel (1874-) Co 42 *Col.*

"Marsella, Juan" (*pseud.*) *see* Cruz Coke, Ricardo

"Marset, Adán" (*pseud.*) *see* Mata, Andrés A.

Martel, José María V 96 *Venez.*

"Martel, Julián" (*pseud.*) *see* Miró, José

Martel Larruscaín, P. V 96 *Venez.*

Martes de Oca, Ignacio (1840-1924) AMP 271 *Mex.*

Martí, Carlos (1855-) CG III, 594; Cu 101 *Cu.*

Martí, José Julián (1853-1895) APEH 34, 1176; BDC 54; BHLA 371, 450; CG III, 595; CHL 485, 540; CLH 320, 424, 473; CrA 13; Cu 101; FPA 162, 185; G 338; GLO 245; HLC 196; LH 13; LV 153; PA 66; PCu 174; PLHA 88; RLC 251 *et passim*; SAL 46 *et passim*; SASS 278; TM 498, 557, 619 *Cu.*

Martín, Diego BDC 57; CG III, 601; PR 13 *P.R.*

Martín, Ernesto (1880-) CA 37, 38; CG III, 601; EPCR 319; IBCR IV, 10, 107 *et passim C.R.*

Martín, Gabriel Vergara SD 22 *Dom.*

Martín, Gregorio (hijo) CA 38 *C.R.*

Martín, Guillermo E. Co 42 *Col.*

Martín, Hermenegildo CG III, 601; V 96 *Venez.*

Martín, José Reyes Cu 104 *Cu.*

Martín, Lorenzo HPHA II, 9 *Col.*

"Martín, Luis" (*pseud.*) *see* Bermejo, Manuel M.

Martín, Mariano Cu 104 *Cu.*

Martín, Pedro Pablo CG III, 602; Cu 104 *Cu.*

Martín, Ramón Cu 104 *Cu.*

Martín, Tulio B. PR 9 *P.R.*

"Martín Adán" (*pseud.*) *see* La Fuente Benavides, Rafael de

"Martín Alva" (*pseud.*) *see* Martínez Álvarez, Rafael

Martín de la Guardia, Heraclio (1836-) AEHA 562; V 96, 97 *Venez.*

"Martín Flores" (*pseud.*) *see* Cione, Otto Miguel

Martín-Maillefer, P. D. V 97 *Venez.*

Martín y de Castro, Luis Cu 104; IBCR IV, 5 *C.R.*

Martín y Manero, Vicente C 14; CG III, 609; NC 178, 499 *Chil.*

Martín y Villalta, Meliotón CG III, 614; Cu 105 *Cu.*

Martínez, Albert F. PR 19 *P.R.*

Martínez, Alberto B. (1868-) AT II, 671; CG III, 615 *Arg.*

Martínez, Alfredo PLE 114 *Ecua.*

Martínez, Alfredo E. PLE 124; PU 134; U 11 *Uru.*

Martínez, Anselmo Inés Cu 105 *Cu.*

Martínez, Benigno T. CG III, 615; U 11; UL 130 *Uru.*

Martínez, Carlos H. (1885-) PG 389 *Guat.*

Martínez, Celestino V 97 *Venez.*

Martínez, César A. BC 243; Co 42 *Col.*

Martínez, Cirilo J. CG III, 615, 734; Pan 12 *Pan.*

Martínez, Cristóbal ("Simón Rivas") (1867-1914) AP 215; Pan 12, 14 *Pan.*

Martínez, Demetrio Benjamín ("Severo Manso") (1864-) AT I, 324 *Arg.*

Martínez, Diego PM 56 *Mex.*

Martínez, Domingo ("Guayabo") (1863-1896) Cu 72, 105; V 97, 98 *Venez.*

Martínez, Domingo Narciso V 98 *Venez.*

Martínez, Félix (1832-) BDC 58; Cu 105 *Cu.*

Martínez, Félix M. PM 56 *Mex.*

Martínez, Florentino Cu 105 *Cu.*

1. Martínez, Francisco LUr 533 *Uru.*

2. Martínez, Francisco (1736-1794) Co 42; HLNG II, 399 *Col.*

Martínez, Gonzalo Ig 205; NM 32 *Mex.*

Martínez, Graciano Cu 105 *Cu.*

Martínez, Guillermo CG III, 616; Ig 205; NM 32 *Mex.*

Martínez, José Luciano CG III, 616; UT 317 *Uru.*

Martínez, José María ARC 37; BDC 58; CG III, 616; Cu 105 *Cu.*

Martínez, Josefa PR 19, 42 *P.R.*

Martínez, Juan Cristóbal ("Juancé") Co 42 *Col.*

Martínez, Juan Francisco CHL 49; CLH 42; HCLU I, 27; HSLU I, pt 1, 23; U 11 *Uru.*
Martínez, Juan José PIU I, 57 *Uru.*
Martínez, Juan P. CG III, 617; Cu 105 *Cu.*
Martínez, Leoncio ("Leo") V 98 *Venez.*
Martínez, Luis A. ("Fray Colas") (1868-1909) CG III, 617; E 44; PLE 62 *Ecua.*
Martínez, Luisa V 98 *Venez.*
Martínez, M. Pérez Par 18 *Para.*
Martínez, Manuel ("José Arce") BDC 58, 114; Cu 105; PR 13
Martínez, Manuel Vicente CG III, 617; V 98 *Venez.*
Martínez, Mariano C 14; NC 179 *Chil.*
Martínez, Mariano R. Co 42 *Col.*
Martínez, Miguel Gerónimo (1817-1870) AMP 236; HLM 303; HLMex 157; HPM 844 *Mex.*
Martínez, Miguel Víctor U 11; UL 130 *Uru.*
Martínez, Modesto CA 38; CG III, 617; G 332; IBCR IV, 338 *C.R.*
Martínez, Nicolás G. E 44 *Ecua.*
Martínez, Onofre Ángel (1867-) Ig 204; NM 32 *Mex.*
Martínez, Pepe C 51 *Chil.*
Martínez, Quiles U 11 *Uru.*
Martínez, Raquel C 35 *Chil.*
Martínez, Rodrigo PM 56 *Mex.*
Martínez, Rufino M. CG III, 617; SD 22 *Dom.*
Martínez, Saturnino (1840-1905) CHL 465; CLH 406; Cu 105 *Cu.*
Martínez, Ventura (1823-1872) LA VII, 306 *Arg.*
Martínez Acosta, Carmelo (1879-) PR 19, 46; QPR (1) 100 *P.R.*
Martínez Albín, Homero HSLU III, pt 6, 38; PIU III, 241; U 11 *Uru.*
Martínez Alfaro, L. CG III, 618; PM 56 *Mex.*
Martínez Alomía, Salvador PM 56 *Mex.*
Martínez Alonso, Evaristo CG III, 618; Cu 105 *Cu.*
Martínez Álvarez, Antonio PR 20, 46 *P.R.*
Martínez Álvarez, Rafael ("Martín Alva") (1882-) BP 505, 512, 610; PA 225; PP 301; PR 13, 16, 27, 56; QPR (2) 102 *P.R.*
Martínez Amores, Manuel E. CG III, 620; Cu 105 *Cu.*
Martínez Arauna, Susana de TM 205 *Mex.*
Martínez Astudillo, Francisco E 44 *Ecua.*
Martínez Barreiro, Manuel E 44 *Ecua.*
Martínez Bello, A. M. (1911-) PoC 164 *Cu.*
Martínez Bosch, M. SD 22 *Dom.*
Martínez Casado, Luis BDC 58; Cu 105 *Cu.*
Martínez Casado, Manuel BDC 58 *Cu.*
Martínez Cordero, Eliseo A. Cu 105 *Cu.*
Martínez Córdova, Luis Eduardo E 45 *Ecua.*
Martínez Cuadra, José ("B. de Sandemar") C 14; NC 178 *Chil.*
Martínez Cuitiño, Vicente (1887?-) A 86; BHLA 548; CG III, 625; CHL 199 *Arg.*
Martínez Chable, W. Cu 106 *Cu.*

Martínez de Aldunate, Vicente (1769-) BHC III, 251 *Chil.*
Martínez de Arredondo y Castro, José PM 56 *Mex.*
Martínez de Avileira, Lorenzo (1722-) HLC 15; RLC 25 *Cu.*
Martínez de Bernabé, Pedro Usauro (1732-) SCL 509, 619 *Chil.*
Martínez de Castro, Manuel Ig 205; NM 32 *Mex.*
Martínez de Cervera, Leonor Cu 106 *Cu.*
Martínez de la Rosa, Francisco (1789-1852) CHL 433; CLH 376; Cu 106 *Cu.*
Martínez de la Torre, Ricardo CG III, 649; P 19 *Per.*
Martínez de la Vega, Miguel E 45 *Ecua.*
Martínez de Lacosta, Rosa CG III, 630; Cu 106 *Cu.*
Martínez de los Ríos, Ramón Esteban ACe 880; TM 588 *Mex.*
Martínez de Rozas, Juan (1776-1813) AA II, 41, 309
Martínez de San Vicente, Felipe E 45 *Ecua.*
Martínez Dolz, Félix PM 56 *Mex.*
Martínez Domínguez, Manuel CG III, 625; Cu 106; PCu 179 *Cu.*
Martínez Estrada, Ezequiel (1895-) A 43; APAM 344; APEH 885, 1191; CG III, 626; LAC 85, 146; WLA 238 *Arg.*
Martínez Fortún, Carlos A. Cu 106 *Cu.*
Martínez Gracida, Manuel CG III, 629; NM 32 *Mex.*
Martínez Izquierdo, Simón P 19 *Per.*
Martínez Lazzeri, Eugenio CG III, 630; Ig 206; NM 32 *Mex.*
Martínez López, Eduardo (1867-) CG III, 631; HL I, 823 *Hond.*
Martínez Lorenzo, José Cu 106 *Cu.*
Martínez M., Luis G. V 98 *Venez.*
Martínez Marcos, L. A 44 *Arg.*
Martínez Márquez, G. R. BDC 58 *Cu.*
Martínez Méndez, José Antonio CG III, 632; V 98 *Venez.*
Martínez Méndez, Nemecio NC 434 *Chil.*
Martínez-Moles, Manuel CG III, 633; Cu 106 *Cu.*
Martínez Montesino, Francisco Cu 106, 116 *Cu.*
Martínez Mutis, Aurelio (1884-) ALC II, 219; Co 42; G 330; PCo 183; RHLC 155; SASS 237; WLA 239 *Col.*
Martínez Nadal, Rafael ("Armando Ruido") (1879-) BP 500; PR 20, 42; QPR (1) 103 *P.R.*
Martínez Nolasco, Gustavo CG III, 633; Ig 207; NM 33 *Mex.*
Martínez Orozco, A. Co 42 *Col.*
Martínez Otero, Manuel BDC 58; Cu 106 *Cu.*
Martínez Payva, Claudio (1890-) A 44, 87 *Arg.*
Martínez Quevedo, Mateo C 14, 51, 52; CG III, 638; NC 382 *Chil.*
Martínez Rendón, Miguel D. (1891-) APMM 122; PM 56 *Mex.*
Martínez Reyna (Reina), Virgilio PD 128; SD 22 *Dom.*
Martínez Riestra, Ceferino CG III, 639; Ig 207; NM 33 *Mex.*

Martínez Rivas, Federico CG III, 639; Co 42; PCo 184 *Col.*

Martínez Rivas, Víctor Co 42 *Col.*

Martínez Roselló, M. G 384; PR 20 *P.R.*

Martínez Rubio, Luis (1880-) PCh 289 *Chil.*

Martínez Salas, Luis CG III, 642; V 98 *Venez.*

Martínez Siliceo, Ernesto TM 205 *Mex.*

Martínez Silva, Carlos (1847-1903) CG III, 647; CHL 34; Co 42 *Col.*

Martínez Sotomayor, José NM 33 *Mex.*

Martínez Tamáriz, Joaquín E 45 *Ecua.*

Martínez Urrutia, Luis A 44; CG III, 650 *Arg.*

Martínez Valadez, Manuel (1893-) PM 56 *Mex.*

Martínez Velasco, Juan ARC 56 *Cu.*

Martínez Vélez, Felicia PJC 145 *Cu.*

Martínez Vigil, Carlos CG III, 651; Par 18 *Para.*

Martínez Vigil, Daniel (1867-) CG III, 651; HSLU III, pt 4, 34; PIU II, 21; SAL 189; U 11; UL 131; UT 329 *Uru.*

Martínez Villena, Rubén GLO 245; PCu 176; PJC 142; RLC 367 *Cu.*

Martínez Villergas, Juan (1817-1894) CHL 151; CLH 129; Cu 106, 178 *Cu.*

Martínez y Cordero, Miguel Cu 106 *Cu.*

Martínez y Cortés, Eliseo CG III, 624; Ig 206; NM 32 *Mex.*

Martínez y Vela, Bartolomé B 13; CHL 309; LB 565; SASS 113 *Bol.*

Martínez Zaldúa, Ramón Co 42 *Col.*

Martínez Zuviría, Gustavo Adolfo ("Hugo Wast") (1883-) A 44, 78, 87; AB 24; AT I, 189; BHLA 504; CG III, 652; CHL 203; G 315; GLO 237; LAC 51, 132; LAS 205; PLHA 210; SASS 73; WLA 240 *Arg.*

Martinto, Domingo D. (1859-1898) A 44; CHL 185; LA VIII, 598 *Arg.*

Mártir de Angleia, Pedro PR 46 *P.R.*

Martorello, Noé S. G 316 *Arg.*

Martos, Adrián PM 56 *Mex.*

Martos, Miguel A 45 *Arg.*

Marure, Alejandro (1809-1851) BLN 343 *Guat.*

Márvez, Pacífico V 98 *Venez.*

Mas, Juan B 13 *Bol.*

Mas de Ayala, Isidro PIU III, 309 *Uru.*

Mas Miranda, Arturo PR 13 *P.R.*

Mas y Pérez, José ("G. Naro") BP 530 *P.R.*

Mas y Pi, Juan (-1916) A 45; CG III, 662; CLH 160; U 11 *Uru.*

"Masa, Cleta" (*pseud.*) *see* Pereyra, Emilia A. de

Mascaró y Reissig, Pedro CG III, 663; U 11 *Uru.*

Masdeu, Jesús Cu 106 *Cu.*

Masferrer, Alberto CG III, 665; IBCR IV, 15, 200 *C.R.*

Masferrer Berríos, Joaquín BDC 114; PR 13 *P.R.*

Masi, Alceste A 45; CG III, 666 *Arg.*

Masó, Bartolomé (1834-1907) CG III, 667; Cu 107 *Cu.*

Mason C., Orlando C 35; CG III, 667 *Chil.*

Maspons Franco, Juan Cu 107 *Cu.*

Massardo, Francisco C 52 *Chil.*

Massini Correas, Carlos A 45 *Arg.*

Mastronardi, Carlos (1900-) A 45; CG III, 673; NPA 294 *Arg.*

Masústegui, Pedro Co 43; HLNG II, 381; RHLC 22 *Col.*

Mata, Andrés A. ("Adán Marset") CHL 375; CLH 323; G 392; LV 315; PLHA 132; V 98 *Venez.*

Mata, Efrén N. PM 56 *Mex.*

Mata, G. Humberto E 74 *Ecua.*

Mata, Gonzalo de la TM 205 *Mex.*

Mata, Juan de Cu 107 *Cu.*

Mata, Rafael M. E 45 *Ecua.*

Mata Gamboa, Jesús CA 38 *C.R.*

Mata Guevara, Alejandro CA 38; CG III, 675 *C.R.*

Mata Silva, M. A. V 98 *Venez.*

Mata Valle, Félix (1857-1915?) CA 38, 39; EPCR 188 *C.R.*

Matamoros, Gerardo CA 39 *C.R.*

Matamoros, Lino CG III, 676; Ig 209; NM 33 *Mex.*

Matamoros, Mercedes (1858-1906) BDC 59; CG III, 676; Cu 107; HLC 162; PCu 181; RLC 281 *Cu.*

Matamoros Olvera, J. E 45 *Ecua.*

Mataro, Pelegrín de CA 39; CG III, 676 *C.R.*

Mateizan, Manuel de SD 22 *Dom.*

Mateos, Esteban TM 208 *Mex.*

Mateos, Juan Antonio (1831-1913) BHLA 413; CG III, 677; CHL 407; CLH 354; HLM 456, 465; HLMex 225; Ig 209; NM 33; PM 56; TM 208, 300, 456 *Mex.*

Mateos, Manuel (1869-) CG III, 677; Cu 107 *Cu.*

Mateus, Alejandro E 45 *Ecua.*

Matéus, Jorge (1889-) Co 43; CP 693; PCo 185; WLA 242 *Col.*

Matías Quintana, José (1767-1841) ACe 921 *Mex.*

Matienzo, Juan de LA III, 265 *Arg.*

"Matilde Elena Wili" (*pseud.*) A 45 *Arg.*

Matos, M. A. CG III, 682; V 98 *Venez.*

Matos Arvelo, Martín CG III, 682; V 98, 99 *Venez.*

Matos Bernier, Félix (1869-) BP 500, 530, 611; PR 9, 10, 20, 27, 36, 42, 46, 60; QPR (2) 106 *P.R.*

Matos Bernier, Rafael PR 13 *P.R.*

Matos-Díaz SD 22 *Dom.*

Matos-Hurtado, B. Co 43 *Col.*

Matovelle, Julio (1852-) E 45; PE 173 *Ecua.*

Matra, Mathilde de TM 457 *Mex.*

Matta, Manuel Antonio C 35; CL 293 *Chil.*

Matta Vial, Enrique C 67 *Chil.*

Matta y Goyenechea, Guillermo (1829-1899) BHLA 316; C 35; CHL 253; CLH 213; HC 144; PCh 29 *Chil.*

Matthyas Lossada, E. V 99 *Venez.*

Matto de Turner, Clorinda (1854-1909) AEHA 901; BHLA 405; CG III, 682; CHL 304; CLH 258; P 19 *Per.*

Maturana, José de (1884-1917) A 45, 87; BHLA 548; CG III, 683; CHL 197; LA VIII, 878 *Arg.*

"Maturana, Manuel Guzmán" (*pseud.*) *see* Dantés, Edmundo

Maturana, Víctor C 67; CG III, 683; CL 294 *Chil.*

Matus, J. de Dios CA 39 *C.R.*

Matute, Santiago Co 43 *Col.*

Maubé, José Carlos A 45, 72 *Arg.*

Maurente, Luis T. TM 499 *Mex.*

Mauret Caamaño, Alberto (1880-) C 35; CG III, 687; PCh 193 *Chil.*

Mauri, Isabel P. de V 99 *Venez.*

"Mauricio de Bracy" (*pseud.*) *see* Almendaro, José Pablo

Maury, José W. BDC 59; Cu 107 *Cu.*

"Máximo Torres" (*pseud.*) *see* Maeso Tognochi, Carlos M.

Maya, Aurelio TM 210 *Mex.*

Maya, Juan C. TM 211 *Mex.*

Maya, Rafael (1898-) ALC II, 345; APEH 1013, 1193; BHLA 585; Co 43; G 330; RHLC 155; WLA 243 *Col.*

Mayea, Eduardo Cu 107 *Cu.*

Mayo, Hugo PLE 121 *Ecua.*

Mayol, Luis A 45 *Arg.*

Mayol Martínez, Jaime (1849-) BDC 59; CG III, 690; Cu 107 *Cu.*

Mayorga, Arístides NL 94 *Nicar.*

Mayorga, José Manuel Cu 108 *Cu.*

Mayorga, Ventura Cu 108 *Cu.*

Mayorga Rivas, Román (1862-) GPCA III, 367; NL 17; PN 45; PS 152 *Nicar.*

Maytín, José Antonio V 99 *Venez.*

"Maz, R. E." (*pseud.*) *see* Meza y Suárez Inclán, Ramón

Maza, Gregorio de la PM 56 *Mex.*

Mazas Garbayo, Gonzalo Cu 108 *Cu.*

Maziel, Juan Baltasar (1727-1788) APA I, xxvii, 31; BHLA 139; CHL 44; CLH 36; HLA 29; LA II, 556; SPLA 26 *Arg.*

Mazo, Carlos Co 43 *Col.*

Mazo, Marcelo del A 45 *Arg.*

"Mazorda, Noriama Giciona" (*pseud.*) *see* Madrazo, Mariano Ignacio

Mazzoni, R. Francisco A 45, 87; CG III, 693 *Arg.*

McGrigor, Julieta P. de IBCR IV, 72 *C.R.*

McKay, Guillermo Pan 12 *Pan.*

McKay, Santiago D. (1898-) AP 219; CG III, 507; Pan 12 *Pan.*

Meany y Meany, Carlos (1871-1921) CG III, 694; PG 339 *Guat.*

Meaño, Francisco V 99 *Venez.*

Meaño Velázquez, J. A. V 99 *Venez.*

Mederos de Pellón, Leonor Cu 108 *Cu.*

Medín Arango, Enrique ARC 41 *Cu.*

Medina, A. V. CG III, 696; Cu 108 *Cu.*

Medina, Antonio (1824-1886) ARC 34; BDC 59, 114; Cu 108 *Cu.*

Medina, Baltasar de (1600-1670) HLM 208 *Mex.*

Medina, Bernardo de P 19 *Per.*

Medina, Filomeno ("F. M.") TM 141, 212 *Mex.*

Medina, Francisco PM 56 *Mex.*

Medina, José HPM 233 *Mex.*

Medina, José Toribio (1852-1931) A 73; C 67; CG III, 699; CHL 13, 15, 285; CL 294; CLH 12, 242; G 325; GLO 240; OA 181; PR 8, 60; SASS 190; SD 22 *Chil.*

Medina, Juan de TM 212 *Mex.*

Medina, Lucila Gamero Moncada de (1873-) WLA 244 *Hond.*

Medina, Rafael HLM 468; TM 214, 216 *Mex.*

Medina, Sergio V 99 *Venez.*

Medina, Tristán de Jesús (1833-1886) Cu 108; RLC 239, 312 *Cu.*

Medina, Vicente A 45; CG III, 699 *Arg.*

Medina Betancort, Manuel (1882-) A 45; CG III, 697; U 11; UT 337 *Uru.*

Medina Chirinos, Carlos CG III, 697; V 99 *Venez.*

Medina de la Torre, F. PM 56 *Mex*

Medina J., Gilberto Pan 12 *Pan.*

Medina Onrubia, Salvadora (1895-) A 45, 87; CG III, 698 *Arg.*

Medina Ruiz, Pedro V 99 *Venez.*

Medina Solís, Antonio TM 217 *Mex.*

Medina Valdés, Antonio ARC 56 *Cu.*

Medina y González, Adolfo BP 531; PR 37 *P.R.*

Medina y González, Zenón PR 20, 37 *P.R.*

Médiz Bolio, Antonio (1884-) AMP 132; CA 39; CG III, 703; Cu 108; G 365; HLM 527; NM 34; PM 56; PMe I, 277; TM 217, 596; WLA 244 *Mex.*

Medrano, Antonio NL 71; PN 141 *Nicar.*

Medrano, Francisco de SCL 378, 619 *Col.*

Medrano, Gerardo C. Cu 108 *Cu.*

Medrano, José Domingo V 99 *Venez.*

Medrano, Manuel APA I, xliii, 177 *Arg.*

"Mefistófeles" (*pseud.*) *see* Brieba, Liborio E.

Megía, Diego HPM 111 *Mex.*

Meireles, Eduardo (1865-) BDC 59; Cu 108; PR 13

Mejía, Abigail CG III, 704; SD 22 *Dom.*

Mejía, Demetrio (-1913) CG III, 704; Ig 215; NM 34 *Mex.*

Mejía, Epifanio (1838-1913) AC I, 231; II, 217; Co 43; LC 141; RHLC 141 *Col.*

Mejía, Estanislao TM 607 *Mex.*

Mejía, Félix E. PD 129; SD 22 *Dom.*

Mejía, Francisco V 99 *Venez.*

Mejía, Gustavo Adolfo CG III, 704; SD 22 *Dom.*

Mejía, Isauro TM 218 *Mex.*

Mejía, Juan Tomás PD 130; SD 22 *Dom.*

Mejía, Vidal WLA 245 *Hond.*

Mejía Álvarez, Luis María (1846-) Co 43 *Col.*

Mejía Ángel, Carlos ("Ciro Mendía") (1894-) Co 43; WLA 245 *Col.*

Mejía de Ovando, Pedro P 20 *Per.*

Mejía González, Raúl (1891-1919) PG 437 *Guat.*

Mejía Nieto, Arturo (1900-) CG III, 705; WLA 245 *Hond.*

Mejía Robledo, Alfonso (1897-) CG III, 705; Co 43; G 330; WLA 245 *Col.*

Mejía y Lequerica, José (1775-1813) CG III, 704; E 45; PLE 27 *Ecua.*

"Mel, Solón de" (*pseud.*) *see* Luzuriaga y Bribiesca, Guillermo de

Meléndez, Concha (1904-) BHLA 573; CG III, 706; G 384; PA 226; PP 203; PR 20, 56; QPR (2) 107; TM 557 *P.R.*

Meléndez, Juan P 20 *Per.*

Meléndez, Manuel Antonio CG III, 706; V 99 *Venez.*

Meléndez, Simón V 99 *Venez.*

Meléndez Muñoz, Miguel (1884-) BP 500, 505, 612; PR 7, 20, 27, 56, 60; QPR (1) 104; (2) 107 *P.R.*
Meléndez y Muñoz, Mariano Ig 217; NM 36 *Mex.*
Melero, José Lino BDC 60; Cu 108 *Cu.*
Melfi, Domingo BHLA 617; C 68 *Chil.*
Melgar, Mariano (1791-1814) BHLA 161; CHL 64; CLH 55; HPHA II, 237; LP 353; P 20; PLHA 67; SASS 409 *Per.*
Melgarejo, Bartolomé HPM 87 *Mex.*
Melián Lafinur, Álvaro (1891-) A 45; APAM 355; AT I, 457; CG III, 709; CLH 160; LAC 119, 155; WLA 246 *Arg.*
Melián Lafinur, Luis (1850-) CG III, 709; CHL 219; CLH 182; U 11; UL 131; UT 339 *Uru.*
Melo, Carlos F. (1873-1931) A 45; AT I, 179; CG III, 712 *Arg.*
Melo, Juan de (1825-) Cu 109 *Cu.*
Melo, Rosendo P 20 *Per.*
Melo Cruz, Flaminio C 52 *Chil.*
Mellado, Guillermo CG III, 713; Ig 218; NM 34 *Mex.*
Mellado, Manuel (-1892) BDC 60; Cu 109 *Cu.*
Membreño, Alberto (1859-) CG III, 713; CHL 504; G 347; HL I, 799; WH 187 *Hond.*
Mena, Filiberto de LA IV, 1006 *Arg.*
Mena, Juan de Dios A 45 *Arg.*
Menasché, Marcelo A 45 *Arg.*
Mencos, Alberto (1863-1922) CG III, 727; PG 315 *Guat.*
Mencos F., Agustín (-1902) CG III, 727; PG 323 *Guat.*
Menchaca, Ángel A 45, 87; CG III, 727; Par 18 *Arg.*
Méndez, Alejandro P 20 *Per.*
Méndez, Amado CG III, 728; Cu 109 *Cu.*
Méndez, Andrés SCL 277, 620 *Chil.*
Méndez, Delfor B. A 45 *Arg.*
Méndez, Evar (1888-) A 45; APAM 360; APEH 665; BHLA 530; NPA 123 *Arg.*
Méndez, Gervasio (1848-1898) A 46; BHLA 421; CHL 184; CLH 158; HLA 459; LA VIII, 549 *Arg.*
Méndez, Joaquín GPCA III, 319; PS 117 *Salv.*
Méndez, José Ignacio Co 43 *Col.*
Méndez, Juan de Dios (hijo) V 99 *Venez.*
Méndez, Juan J. Pan 12 *Pan.*
Méndez, Luis LA VI, 1120; U 11 *Arg.*
Méndez, Luis Augusto ARC 56; Cu 109; PJC 163 *Cu.*
Méndez, Manuel Pan 12 *Pan.*
Méndez, Manuel Isidro (1884-) CG III, 730; Cu 109 *Cu.*
Méndez, Mariano B 13 *Bol.*
Méndez A., Santiago TM 218 *Mex.*
Méndez Bravo, Alberto C 35; CG III, 732; PCh 373 *Chil.*
Méndez Caldeira, Alfredo A 46, 87 *Arg.*
Méndez Calzada, Enrique (1898-) A 46; APAM 545; APEH 890; CG III, 733; G 316; LAC 57, 135; NPA 241; WLA 247 *Arg.*
Méndez Capote de Solís, René Cu 109 *Cu.*
Méndez Cuesta, Concha A 46 *Arg.*

Méndez de Cuenca, Laura (1853-1928) AMP 316; CG III, 732; G 365; HLM 398; Ig 218; NM 34; PMe I, 281; PoM 172, 318 *Mex.*
Méndez del Yermo, José E 45 *Ecua.*
Méndez González, Andrés BP 531; PR 56 *P.R.*
Méndez Loinaz (*or* Loynaz), Augusto CG III, 733; V 99 *Venez.*
Méndez Nieto, Juan HPHA I, 314 *Col.*
Méndez P., Alejandro CG III, 733; Pan 12 *Pan.*
Méndez Pereira, Octavio (1887-) AP 221; CG III, 733; Pan 12, 13; WLA 248 *Pan.*
Méndez Plancarte, Gabriel PM 57 *Mex.*
Méndez Quiñones, Ramón BDC 61; BP 513; PR 13 *P.R.*
Méndez Reissig, Ernestina U 11 *Uru.*
Méndez Rivas, Federico Ig 219; NM 34 *Mex.*
Méndez Rivas, Joaquín (1888-) HLM 522; PM 57; TM 219 *Mex.*
Méndez y Mendoza, Eugenio LV 56, 210, 338, 424; V 99 *Venez.*
Méndez y Mendoza, Juan de Dios CG III, 733; V 100 *Venez.*
"Mendía, Ciro" (*pseud.*) *see* Mejía Ángel, Carlos
Mendible, Juan Vicente V 100 *Venez.*
Mendible, Lorenzo José V 100 *Venez.*
Mendiburu, Manuel de (1805-1885) BHLA 381; CG III, 735; P 20 *Per.*
Mendieta, Jerónimo de (1525-1604) HLM 61 *Mex.*
Mendilaharsú, Julio Raúl (1887-1924) CG III, 735; HSLU II, pt 1, 16; LU 64, 660; PIU III, 199; PLHA 152; PU 139; U 11; UT 343 *Uru.*
Mendiondo, Raúl ARC 56 *Cu.*
Mendioroz, Alberto (-1924) A 46; APAM 364; CG III, 735 *Arg.*
Mendive, Felipe de Cu 109 *Cu.*
Mendive y Daumy, Rafael María de (1821-1886) AEHA 579; BDC 61; BHLA 300, 328; CHL 455; CLH 395, 396; Cu 109; G 340; HLC 155; HPHA I, 281; PA 76; PCu 183; RLC 147, 192, 203 *et passim;* SASS 272 *Cu.*
Mendizábal, Emilio Rodolfo A 46 *Arg.*
Mendizábal, Horacio (1837-) A 46; LA VIII, 586 *Arg.*
Mendizábal, Luis de ACe 253; HLM 246; HPM 481 *Mex.*
Mendizábal, Miguel O. de (1890-) CG III, 736; IE 173 *Mex.*
Mendoza, Carlos (1822-1880) V 100 *Venez.*
Mendoza, Carlos A. (1856-1916) Pan 13 *Pan.*
Mendoza, Cristóbal L. V 100 *Venez.*
Mendoza, Daniel (1823-1867) BHLA 252; CHL 368; CLH 316; LV 386; V 100, 101; VPF 47 *Venez.*
Mendoza, Jaime (1873-) B 13; BT 175; CG III, 738; LB 631 *Bol.*
Mendoza, Javier de V 101 *Venez.*
Mendoza, Juan José V 101 *Venez.*
Mendoza, Manuel CG III, 738; V 101 *Venez.*
Mendoza, María Josefa ACe 882; HPM 491 *Mex.*

Mendoza, Tomás (-1869) BDC 61; Cu 109 *Cu.*

Mendoza Buroz, Cristóbal LV 113, 140; V 100, 143 *Venez.*

Mendoza Guerra, Pedro (1862-) CG III, 739; Cu 110 *Cu.*

Mendoza López, Ramiro TM 219 *Mex.*

Mendoza Ortiz, L. A 46, 87 *Arg.*

Mendoza Pérez, Diego (1857-) Co 43; IE 176; WLA 250 *Col.*

Mendoza y Monteagudo, Juan de C 35; CHL 15; CLH 12; HPHA II, 325; SCL 197, 620 *Chil.*

Menéndez, Carlos R. ("Daniel Morton") (1872-) IE 177; PM 57, 59; WLA 250 *Mex.*

Menéndez, José Luis A 46, 55 *Arg.*

Menéndez, Juan (-1684) LA III, 115 *Arg.*

Menéndez, Leonor E. de P 20 *Per.*

Menéndez, Mario CG III, 739; PU 145; U 11 *Uru.*

Menéndez, Miguel Ángel PM 57 *Mex.*

Menéndez, Ramón María (-1913) CG III, 739; Cu 110 *Cu.*

Menéndez Barriola, Emilio A 46; CG III, 740 *Arg.*

Menéndez Roque, Vicente Cu 110; PJC 160 *Cu.*

Menéndez y Serpa, G. CG III, 747; Cu 110 *Cu.*

Meneses, Francisco de BHC I, 549 *Chil.*

Meneses, Guillermo BHLA 581 *Venez.*

Meneses, Miguel TM 607 *Mex.*

Meneses, Olegario V 101 *Venez.*

Menotti Sposito, Emilio CG III, 748; V 101 *Venez.*

Mera, Eduardo (1876-1926) E 45 *Ecua.*

Mera, J. Trajano (1862-1919) CG III, 749; E 45; PE 156 *Ecua.*

Mera, Juan León (1832-1894) AEHA 583; BHLA 321, 342, 384; CG III, 343; CHL 318; CLH 270; E 46, 74; FPA 253, 258; G 344; HPHA II, 102, 132; PE 162; PLE 40; SASS 334 *Ecua.*

Mera y Cobo, Aurelio Elías E 47 *Ecua.*

Mercadillo, Manuel (-1825) ACe 882 *Mex.*

Mercado, C. Pedro de (1618-1701) Co 44 *Col.*

Mercado, Guillermo BAP 111 *Per.*

Mercado, Jorge Co 44 *Col.*

Mercado, José ("Momo") (1863-1911) FPA 461, 486; PP 128; PR 37, 56 *P.R.*

Mercado, Julio ("Momo") Co 44; IE 181; PR 37 *Col.*

Mercado, Pedro de HLNG I, 238 *Col.*

Mercado, Ramón Co 44 *Col.*

Mercado Moreira, Miguel B 13; CG III, 750 *Bol.*

Mercante, Víctor (1870-) AT I, 332; CG III, 750; U 12; WLA 251 *Arg.*

Merchán, Antonio PE 39 *Ecua.*

Merchán, Rafael María (1844-1905) BC 247; CG III, 751; CHL 470, 473; CLH 410, 413; Co 44; Cu 110; G 340; RHLC 208; RLC 214, 243, 300 *Col.*

Merino, Carlos PM 57 *Mex.*

Merino, Isidoro Virgilio PJC 158 *Cu.*

Merino, Manuel CG III, 753; Ig 220; NM 34 *Mex.*

Merino Correa, Fausto PM 57 *Mex.*

Merino de Heredia, Pedro BHC II, 589; C 35; CG III, 755 *Chil.*

Meriño, Fernando Arturo de LD 83; SD 22 *Dom.*

Merizalde, José Félix (1787-1868) BC 249 *Col.*

Merizalde y Santisteban, Joaquín Co 44 *Col.*

Merlin, Mercedes Jaruco (1788-1852) Cu 110 *Cu.*

Merlino, Salvador A 46; CG III, 756 *Arg.*

Merlos, Salvador R. CG III, 756; IBCR IV, 123 *C.R.*

Mertens, Federico (1886-) A 46, 87 *Arg.*

"Mery, Fanny" (*pseud.*) see Emiliani, María

Mery, Saturnino C 14; NC 180 *Chil.*

Mesa, Domingo ARC 56 *Cu.*

Mesa, Enrique de CG III, 759; Cu 111 *Cu.*

Mesa, Ignacio C 14; NC 382 *Chil.*

Mesa, Joaquín Cu 111 *Cu.*

Mesa Nichols, Alejandro (1896-1920) Co 44; RHLC 173 *Col.*

Mesa Nichols, Salvador Co 44 *Col.*

Mesa Ortiz, Rafael M. CG III, 759; Co 44 *Col.*

Mesía Venegas, Alonso (1557-1649) SCL 313, 620 *Per.*

Mestre, Arístides CG III, 761; Cu 111 *Cu.*

Mestre, José Manuel Cu 111; G 340 *Cu.*

Mestre, Laura CG III, 761; Cu 111 *Cu.*

Mestre de Silva, Concepción PU 295 *Uru.*

Mestre Fuenmayor, Aníbal V 101 *Venez.*

Mestre i Tolón, Anjel (1841-1873) Cu 111 *Cu.*

Metalli, Antonio E 47 *Ecua.*

Mexía, Diego CHL 25; CLH 22; HPHA II, 163, 166 *Per.*

Mexía de Hammeken, Adela TM 457 *Mex.*

"Mexicana, Una Señorita" (*pseud.*) TM 480 *Mex.*

"Mexicano, El Pensador" (*pseud.*) see Fernández de Lizardi, José Joaquín

"Mexicano, Un" (*pseud.*) see Ochoa y Acuña, Anastasio María de

Meyer Arana, Alberto A 46; CG III, 768 *Arg.*

Meza, Diego V 101 *Venez.*

Meza, Ladislao F. BHLA 551 *Per.*

Meza, S. PN 163 *Nicar.*

Meza Fuentes, Roberto (1899-) C 35; CG III, 769; CMPC 94; LAS 200; PCC xix, 209; PCh 439; WLA 253 *Chil.*

Meza y Suárez Inclán, Ramón ("R. E. Maz") (1861-1911) BDC 62; CG III, 769; CHL 484; CLH 423; Cu 108, 111; G 340; RLC 309 *Cu.*

Mialhe, Federico Cu 112 *Cu.*

Micolao y Sierra, Vicente ("Manfredo") V 87, 94, 101, 102 *Venez.*

"Micrós" (*pseud.*) see Campo, Ángel de

Michel, Alberto (1867-) G 365; HLM 468; Ig 221; NM 35; TM 219, 457 *Mex.*

Michel, Concha TM 220, 329, 558 *Mex.*

Michelena, Arturo V 102 *Venez.*

Michelena, Francisco V 102 *Venez.*

Michelena, Guillermo V 102 *Venez.*
Michelena, Santiago V 102 *Venez.*
Michelena, Santos V 102 *Venez.*
Michelena, Tomás (1835-) BHLA 411;
CG III, 773; CHL 377; CLH 325; LV 200,
377; V 102; VPF 67 *Venez.*
Michelena Fortoul, Rafael V 102 *Venez.*
Micheo, Juan José (1847-1869) GPCA II,
403; PG 236 *Guat.*
"Michoacano, Un" (*pseud.*) CG III, 774; Ig
376; NM 55 *Mex.*
Mier, Elpidio de CG III, 774; PR 46 *P.R.*
Mier, Servando Teresa de (1765-1827) AA
II, 20, 109; ACe 417; CG III, 775; HLM
254; HLMex 113 *Mex.*
"Miguel, Hermano" (*pseud.*) *see* Febres Cor-
dero, F.
Migueles, María Lorenzo BDC 62 *Cu.*
Míguez, Doelia C. A 46; CG III, 777 *Arg.*
Mijares, Augusto V 102 *Venez.*
Milá de la Roca, Bartolomé V 102 *Venez.*
Milá de la Roca Díaz, J. M. V 103 *Venez.*
"Milanés, Blanca" (*pseud.*) *see* Brenes Ar-
güello de Rizo, Carlota
Milanés, Federico (1815-1890) BDC 62; Cu
112 *Cu.*
Milanés, Manuel G. Cu 113 *Cu.*
Milanés y Fuentes, José Jacinto (1814-1863)
AEHA 584; BDC 62; BHLA 223; CG
III, 779; CHL 437; CLH 379; Cu 112;
FPA 161, 169; G 340; GLO 245; HLC 115,
170; HPHA I, 253; PA 79; PCu 186; RLC
70, 93, 146, 182; SASS 267 *Cu.*
Milanesio, Pedro José E 47 *Ecua.*
Miláns, Alcides PU 297 *Uru.*
Milesi, María Esther (1906-) A 46; CG
III, 779 *Arg.*
Milhe, José Leopoldo (1857-) BC 251
Col.
Milián, Joaquín PJC 164 *Cu.*
Milla Chapellí, Julio ("Edmundo del Vals")
(1896-) ARC 56; CG III, 780; Cu 113,
169 *Cu.*
Milla y Vidaurre, José ("Salomé Gil *or* Jil")
(1822-1882) BHLA 344; CA 70, 77, 81;
CG III, 780; CHL 506; CLH 447; GPCA
II, 3 *Guat.*
"Millaleubu, Pancho" HPHA II, 339; SCL
548, 621 *Chil.*
Millán, Augusto C 14 *Chil.*
Millán, Blas V 103 *Venez.*
Millán, José Agustín BDC 64; Cu 113 *Cu.*
Millán, Ricardo BC 252; Co 44 *Col.*
Millán y M., Ignacio NM 35 *Mex.*
Millet, Gabriel (1823-1899) Cu 114 *Cu.*
Mimenza Castillo, Ricardo (1888-) CG
III, 788; IE 182; PM 57; TM 220; WLA
254 *Mex.*
Minelli González, Pablo CG III, 788; PIU
II, 44; U 12 *Uru.*
Minvielle, Rafael (1800-1887) C 52; CHL
240; CLH 200 *Chil.*
Mira, Policarpo ARC 56; CG III, 795; Cu
114 *Cu.*
Mirabal, Antonio BP 532; PR 37, 56; SD 23
P.R.
Mirabel, Lugarda Cu 114 *Cu.*
Mirabet, Juan J. CG III, 796; Cu 114 *Cu.*

Miralla, José Antonio (1789-1825) G 316;
GLO 237; HLA 223; HLNG II, 421;
HPHA II, 408; LA VI, 1090 *Arg.*
Miralles, Francisco C 14; NC 180 *Chil.*
Miramontes, Arnulfo TM 607 *Mex.*
Miramontes y Zuázola, Juan de BHLA 80;
CG III, 798; P 20 *Per.*
Miranda, A. Cu 115 *Cu.*
Miranda, Arecio CG III, 798; V 103 *Venez.*
Miranda, Armando A. PR 37 *P.R.*
Miranda, Belén de BDC 65; Cu 115 *Cu.*
Miranda, Blas Par 18 *Para.*
Miranda, César (1884-) CG III, 798; PIU
II, 48; U 12; UT 353 *Uru.*
Miranda, Francisco de (1750-1816) AA II,
5, 49; BHLA 155; SASS 542; V 103
Venez.
Miranda, Francisco Mariano de E 47 *Ecua.*
Miranda, Ignacio BDC 66; Cu 115 *Cu.*
Miranda, Ignacio de ("George Baset") TM
458, 480 *Mex.*
Miranda, José de HLNG I, 170 *Col.*
Miranda, Leandro Co 80 *Col.*
Miranda, Luis Antonio BP 532; PP 326;
PR 20, 37 *P.R.*
Miranda, Luis de LA III, 131 *Arg.*
Miranda, Manuel María CG III, 799; Cu
115 *Cu.*
Miranda, Raúl (1875-) CG III, 799; Cu
115 *Cu.*
Miranda, Roque de Co 44 *Col.*
Miranda A., Alamiro G. C 35 *Chil.*
Miranda Archilla, Graciany PR 37 *P.R.*
Miranda Klix, José Guillermo (1907-1931)
A 46, 72 *Arg.*
Miranda Larco, Carlos Alfredo C 14; CG
III, 800; PCh 409 *Chil.*
Miranda M., Roberto C 35 *Chil.*
Miranda Velásquez, Pilar NC 434 *Chil.*
Miranda y Marrón, Manuel M. CG III, 800;
NM 35; PM 57 *Mex.*
Mirau, José M. A 46 *Arg.*
Miravalles, Heriberto CG III, 801; PM 57
Mex.
Miró, José ("Julián Martel") A 46, 78;
CHL 193; LA VIII, 668; SCL 434, 618;
SPLA 242 *Arg.*
Miró, Ricardo (1883-) AP 227; CG III,
802; FPA 382, 391; Pan 13 *Pan.*
"Miro Cumbres" (*pseud.*) *see* Castellanos,
Mario
Miró Quesada, Oscar P 20 *Per.*
Miró Quezada, César Alfredo BAP 97
Per.
Miró y Argenter, José Ignacio (1857-1925)
ARC 75; BDC 66; CG III, 803; CT 545;
Cu 115; RLC 344 *Cu.*
Miserol, Pedro José V 103 *Venez.*
"Misia Mariquita" (*pseud.*) *see* Sánchez,
Mariano
"Mistral, Gabriela" (*pseud.*) *see* Godoy Al-
cayaza, Lucila
"Mitilo" (*pseud.*) *see* García de Carrasquedo,
Isidro
Mitjans, Aurelio ("El Camagüeyano")
(1863-1889) BHLA 390; CG III, 807;
CHL 478; CLH 418, 419; Cu 115; RLC
206, 207, 212, 303; SASS 305 *Cu.*
Mitre, Adolfo (1859-1884) A 46; CHL 185;
CLH 159; HLA 455; LA VIII, 577 *Arg.*

Mitre, Bartolomé (1821-1906) A 47, 72, 73, 88; BHLA 273; CG III, 807; CHL 139, 157; CLH viii, 117; G 316; GEA XI; GLO 237; HLA 460; LA II, 918; VI, 953; VIII, 616; PLHA 279; SAL 97 *et passim;* SASS 18 *Arg.*

Mitre, Jorge M. (1852-1870) A 47; HLA 454; LA VIII, 575 *Arg.*

Mitre, Julio E. CLH 159 *Arg.*

Mitre y Vedia, Bartolomé (Bartolito) ("Claudio Coello") (1851-1900) A 47, 78; LA VII, 154; VIII, 749; SPLA 246 *Arg.*

Mityans, Aurelio *see* Mitjans, Aurelio

Miura Pérez, Elisa NM 35 *Mex.*

Mixco, José C. PS 252 *Salv.*

Mobellán, Sebastián de TM 500 *Mex.*

"Mocho, Fray" (*pseud.*) *see* Álvarez, José Sixto

"Modesto" (*pseud.*) *see* Díaz Flores, Rafael

Mogollón Araque, Luis Francisco Co 44 *Col.*

Mogollón Carrizosa, R. PCo 187 *Col.*

Mohr, Luis A. A 47; CG III, 809 *Arg.*

Mola, Abelardo ARC 56 *Cu.*

Molas Terán, Alberto A 47; CG III, 810 *Arg.*

Moleiro, Rodolfo V 103 *Venez.*

Molestina, Juan Eusebio E 47 *Ecua.*

Molestina, Vicente Emilio (1846-1871) E 48 *Ecua.*

Molina, A. C 14 *Chil.*

Molina, Alonso de (-1585) HLM 20 *Mex.*

Molina, Eugenia V 103 *Venez.*

Molina, Eulogio de los L. B 13 *Bol.*

Molina, Felipe CA 39 *C.R.*

Molina, Felipe Antonio RHLC 193 *Col.*

Molina, Gaspar ("Severino Amaro") P 20 *Per.*

Molina, José Agustín A 47 *Arg.*

Molina, Juan Agustín (1773-1837) LA IV, 925 *Arg.*

Molina, Juan Ignacio (1740-1829) BHLA 134; HC 33; SCL 185, 512, 621 *Chil.*

Molina, Juan José (1838-) BC 252; Co 44 *Col.*

Molina, Juan Ramón (1877-1908) CG III, 813; FPA 317, 320; HL II, 679 *Hond.*

Molina, Luis T. B 13 *Bol.*

Molina, Luisa (1826-1887) Cu 115 *Cu.*

Molina, Osvaldo B 13 *Bol.*

Molina, Roberto C 14 *Chil.*

Molina de Cuzco, Cristóbal de P 20; SCL 140, 621 *Per.*

Molina de R. Lezama, Calixta Cu 115 *Cu.*

Molina de Santiago, Cristóbal (1594-) P 20; SCL 71, 139, 621 *Per.*

Molina Garmendía, Enrique (1871-) CG III, 814; IE 184; WLA 256 *Chil.*

Molina Herrera, Evaristo PCh 355 *Chil.*

Molina M., Plácido B 13 *Bol.*

Molina Núñez, Julio C 35, 68; CG III, 816; PCh 399 *Chil.*

Molina Vijil, Manuel (1853-1883) HL II, 213 *Hond.*

Molina y López Cepero, Marina L. (1898-) QPR (2) 112 *P.R.*

Molina y Vedia de Bastianini, Delfina (1879-) A 47; AT I, 253; WLA 42 *Arg.*

Molina y Villafañe, José Agustín (1773-1838) HLA 279 *Arg.*

Molinari, Diego Luis (1889-) AT II, 981 *Arg.*

Molinari, Ricardo E. A 47; G 316; LAC 149 *Arg.*

Molinari, Víctor Luis A 47 *Arg.*

Molinas Rolón, Guillermo Par 18; PPa 250 *Para.*

Molins, Wenceslao Jaime A 47; CG III, 818 *Arg.*

Moll, Mercedes ("Flor Daliza") PP 275 *P.R.*

Moll Boscana, Arístides (1885-) QPR (1) 108 *P.R.*

Mom, Arturo S. (1894-) A 47; LAC 134 *Arg.*

"Momo" (*pseud.*) *see* Mercado, José *and* Mercado, Julio

Monagas, Rafael H. PR 52 *P.R.*

Monasterio, Esther A 48; CG III, 820 *Arg.*

Monasterio, Luis María V 103 *Venez.*

Moncada, Belisario CG III, 821; V 103 *Venez.*

Moncada, Liberato (1855-1886) HL I, 641 *Hond.*

Moncada, Vicente Elías V 104 *Venez.*

Moncada G., Arturo CA 39; CG III, 821 *C.R.*

Moncada Gamboa, Arturo Cu 115 *Cu.*

Moncayo, Abelardo ("Athos") (1848-1917) BHLA 367; CG I, 214; E 48; PLE 48 *Ecua.*

Moncayo, Carlos E. E 48 *Ecua.*

Moncayo, Gabriel L. E 48 *Ecua.*

Moncayo, Hugo PLE 123 *Ecua.*

Moncayo, José G. E 48 *Ecua.*

Moncayo, Pedro (1804-1888) CG III, 821; E 48, 74; PLE 34 *Ecua.*

Moncla y Santander, Antonia LA III, 61 *Arg.*

Moncloa y Covarrubias, Manuel ("Cloamón") (1859-1911) BHLA 442; P 20 *Per.*

Mondaca C., Carlos R. (1881-1928) APEH 653, 1188; C 35; CMPC 71; FPA 192, 204; N 213; PCC xiii, 83; PCh 249; SASS 153 *Chil.*

Monegal, Casiano (Osiano) PU 147; U 12 *Uru.*

Mones, Ángel A 48 *Arg.*

Monge, D. CA 39 *C.R.*

Monge, José María ("Justo Derecho") (1840-1891) BDC 66; BP 532, 613; Cu 115; PP 81; PR 13, 37, 40, 52 *P.R.*

Monge Navarrete, Celiano (1855-) BHLA 367; CG III, 824; E 48; PE 55; PLE 55; WLA 257 *Ecua.*

Monge Wilhelms, Ernesto C 14; NC 382 *Chil.*

Monje, Manuel Elías E 49 *Ecua.*

Monje, P. Benjamín B 13 *Bol.*

Monna Lissa C 14 *Chil.*

Monreal, Carnevali LV 140, 410, 412 *Venez.*

Monroy, A. Cu 115 *Cu.*

Monroy, Joel L. E 49 *Ecua.*

Monroy, José PM 57; TM 221 *Mex.*

Monroy, Perico A. V 104 *Venez.*

Monroy Garaicoa, Gustavo (1891-) WLA 258 *Ecua.*

Monsalve, Carlos A 48 *Arg.*

Monsalve, José Dolores (1862-1935) BC 253; CG III, 829; Co 45; RHLC 200 *Col.*

Monserrat, Darío V 104 *Venez.*

"Monsieur Perrichon" (*pseud.*) *see* Thévenin, Leopoldo

Mont y Prado, Pedro BHC III, 113 *et passim Chil.*

Montagne, Edmundo (1880-) A 48; APAM 367; CG III, 831 *Arg.*

Montagú y Vivero, Guillermo de (1882-) CG III, 831; CT 287; Cu 115; PA 81; PCu 189; PJC 175 *Cu.*

Montalbán, Leonardo ("Tom Tío") (1887-) CG III, 831; IBCR IV, 207, 219; WLA 259 *C.R.*

Montalvo, Ángel T. CG III, 832; Ig 222; NM 35 *Mex.*

Montalvo, Antonio PLE 124 *Ecua.*

Montalvo, Domingo de Cu 116 *Cu.*

Montalvo, Francisco CG III, 832; Co 45 *Col.*

Montalvo, Francisco J. CG III, 832; E 49 *Ecua.*

Montalvo, José Miguel (1782-1816) BC 254; Co 45; HLNG II, 86 *Col.*

Montalvo, Juan (1833-1889) AB 24; BHLA 366; CG III, 832; CHL 314; CLH 266; E 49, 74; G 344; GLO 246; LAS 207; PLE 36; PLHA 240; SAL 204 *et passim*; SASS 337 *Ecua.*

Montalvo, Miguel Ángel CG III, 832; E 50; PLE 97 *Ecua.*

Montalvo M., Jorge Isaacs E 50 *Ecua.*

Montalvo y Castillo, Juan (Conde de Casa Montalvo) Cu 116 *Cu.*

Montalvo y Morales, Domingo BDC 66 *Cu.*

Montaña, Luis (1755-1820) ACe 887; HPM 481 *Mex.*

Montañez, Francisco E. PR 20 *P.R.*

Montaño, Enríquez (hijo) *see* Enríquez Montaño (hijo)

Montaos y Robillard, Francisco Cu 116 *Cu.*

Monte, Félix María del LD 79; PA 337; PD 133; SD 23 *Dom.*

Monte, Laureano del (-1908) BDC 16; Cu 116 *Cu.*

Monte, Ricardo del (1828-1908) Cu 116; PA 82; PCu 191; RLC 299 *Cu.*

Monte Domecq, Ramón CG III, 834; Par 2 *Para.*

Monte y Aponte, Domingo del ("Bachiller Toribio Sánchez de Almodóvar") (1804-1853) CG III, 834; CHL 435, 439, 449, 499; CLH 376, 377, 381; Cu 46, 116; G 336; GLO 255; HPHA I, 250; PCu 192; RLC 59, 69, 81 *et passim*; V 104 *Cu.*

Monte y Tejada, Antonio del LD 76; SD 23 *Dom.*

Monteagudo, Bernardo de (1785-1825) AA II, 22, 141; BHLA 184; CG III, 834; CHL 57; CLH 49; HLA 172; LA V, 50 *Arg.*

Monteagudo Rodríguez, Joaquín ("Armando Duval") BP 532 *P.R.*

Montebruno, López (1871-) WLA 259 *Chil.*

Montejo, Manuel A. Cu 116 *Cu.*

Monteleone, Augusto D. TM 221 *Mex.*

Montenegro, Carlos BHLA 565; Cu 116 *Cu.*

Montenegro, Ernesto BHLA 621; G 325; PCh 245 *Chil.*

Montenegro, Lola GPCA III, 93

Monténegro, Lorenzo CA 39 *C.R.*

Montenegro, M. V. V 104 *Venez.*

Montenegro Colón, Feliciano LV 16, 106; V 104 *Venez.*

Montenegro de Méndez, Dolores (1857-) PG 261 *Guat.*

Monterde García Icazbalceta, Francisco ("Justo Adalid") (1894-) AMP 130; APMM 124; CG III, 838; G 365; HLM 516, 528; IE 185; Ig 222; NM 3, 35; Par 2; PM 58; TM 221, 458, 480, 558; WLA 260 *Mex.*

Monteressi, Octavio J. BDC 66 *Cu.*

Montero, Belisario J. (-1919) A 48; CG III, 839 *Arg.*

Montero, José Ángel V 104 *Venez.*

Montero, Marco Arturo Cu 116 *Cu.*

Montero Barrantes, Francisco (1864-) CA 39, 40; CG III, 839; EPCR 191 *C.R.*

Montero Brown, Ramón CG III, 839; U 12 *Uru.*

Montero Bustamante, Raúl (1881-) CG III, 839; HSLU III, pt 4, 42; LU 64, 684; U 12; UL 131; UT 355 *Uru.*

Montes, Lorenzo C 36 *Chil.*

Montes, Ramón Isidro LV 366; V 104; VPF 24 *Venez.*

Montes, Victoriano E. (1830-) A 48; CHL 217; CLH 180; FPA 527, 531 *Arg.*

Montes de Oca, Álvaro (1768-1848) RLC 46 *Cu.*

Montes de Oca, Figuera V 104 *Venez.*

Montes de Oca, José G. CG III, 843; IE 187; Ig 226; NM 35 *Mex.*

Montes de Oca, José Navarro PJC 177 *Cu.*

Montes de Oca de Cárdenas, Sara (1892-) A 48; CG III, 843 *Arg.*

Montes de Oca y Obregón, Ignacio ("Ipandro Acaico") (1840-1921) AEHA 903; CG III, 843; G 365; HLM 398; HLMex 198; PM 51, 58; PoM 131 *Mex.*

Montes del Valle, Agripina (1844-1915) AC I, 241; BC 254; CHL 350; CLH 299; Co 45; PCo 189 *Col.*

Montes Flores, Francisca TM 223 *Mex.*

Montesino, Francisco M. BDC 66 *Cu.*

Montesinos, J. de J. V 104 *Venez.*

Montesinos, Pedro V 104 *Venez.*

Montesinos, Roberto (1890-) V 104; WLA 261 *Venez.*

Montesinos C., Egidio A. V 104 *Venez.*

Monteverde, Juan (1855-) UT 359 *Uru.*

Monti, Antonio A 48; CG III, 846 *Arg.*

Montiel, Carlos R. V 104 *Venez.*

Montiel, Julián PM 58; TM 224 *Mex.*

Montiel, Manuel V 104 *Venez.*

Montiel, Rafael PN 5 *Nicar.*

Montiel, Susana A 48 *Arg.*

Montiel Ballesteros, Adolfo G 388; GLO 253; LAS 205; LU 64, 674; PIU III, 264; PLHA 236; PU 151; U 12 *Uru.*

Montiel Maciel, Luciano Par 18 *Para.*

Montilla, Mariano V 104 *Venez.*

Montilla de Arroyo, Julia A. PR 37 *P.R.*

Montilla Troanes, Ramón V 105 *Venez.*
Montolío, Andrés Julio SD 23 *Dom.*
Montori de Céspedes, Arturo (1878-) CG III, 849; CHL 489; CT 367; Cu 116; GLO 245 *Cu.*
Montoro, Rafael (1852-) CG III, 849; CT 7; Cu 117; G 341; HLC 66; RLC 234 *Cu.*
Montoya, Arturo P 21 *Per.*
Montoya, José Co 45 *Col.*
Montoya, Matilde PoM 297 *Mex.*
Montt, Enrique C 14; CHL 275; CLH 234; NC 181 *Chil.*
Montt, Luis (1848-1909) C 36, 68; CG III, 852; CHL 285; CL 516; CLH 242 *Chil.*
Montt, Pedro Nolasco NC 435 *Chil.*
Montt de Marambio, N. C 36 *Chil.*
Montt i Luco, Ambrosio (1830-1899) HC 169 *Chil.*
Montt y Montt, Ambrosio (1860-) C 36; CG III, 852; CHL 259; CLH 219; PCh 305 *Chil.*
Montúfar, Manuel (1859-) GPCA III, 533; PG 292 *Guat.*
"Monvel, María" (*pseud.*) see Brito de Donoso, Tilda
Moock Bousquet, Armando (1894-) BHLA 550; C 15, 52; CG III, 853; WLA 262 *Chil.*
Mora, Alfonso María E 50 *Ecua.*
Mora, Augustín de PM 58 *Mex.*
Mora, Emiliano A. E 50 *Ecua.*
Mora, Ernesto TM 224 *Mex.*
Mora, Federico CA 40; CG III, 854 *C.R.*
Mora, José Joaquín de (1783-1864) BHLA 227; CG III, 854; CHL 236; CLH 196; Cu 117; HPHA II, 280, 351; LA VI, 821 *Arg.*
Mora, Juan Antonio PM 58 *Mex.*
Mora, Juan José Luis de (1794-1850) BHLA 253; HLMex 140, 183 *Mex.*
Mora, Juan Rafael (1814-1860) CA 40 *C.R.*
Mora, Luis María (1869-1936) ALC I, 433; Co 45, 59; LC 194; RHLC 152 *Col.*
Mora, Samuel E 50 *Ecua.*
Mora López, José E 50 *Ecua.*
Mora P., Gustavo C 36; PCh 407 *Chil.*
Mora Tovar, Luis PM 58 *Mex.*
Morador, Federico CG III, 857; PU 300; U 12 *Uru.*
Moral, Salvador L. CG III, 858; Ig 226; NM 35 *Mex.*
Morales, Agustín TM 224 *Mex.*
Morales, Alejo Co 45 *Col.*
Morales, Alfredo Martín (-1921) Cu 117 *Cu.*
Morales, Celso TM 224 *Mex.*
Morales, Delio A 48; CG III, 859 *Arg.*
Morales, Emilio B. (1865-) A 48; AT I, 127; CG III, 859 *Arg.*
Morales, Ernesto (1890-) A 48, 72; APAM 373; BHLA 634; CG III, 859; G 316; IE 188; LAC 139; WLA 264 *Arg.*
Morales, Ernesto A. Pan 14 *Pan.*
Morales, Eusebio Antonio Pan 14 *Pan.*
Morales, Fernando V 105 *Venez.*
Morales, G. Alfredo SD 23 *Dom.*
Morales, José Agustín B 13; CG III, 860 *Bol.*
Morales, José D. PN 183 *Nicar.*

Morales, José Pablo (1828-) PR 20, 56 *P.R.*
Morales, Juan Alberto Pan 14 *Pan.*
Morales, Juan de Dios V 105 *Venez.*
Morales, Juan M. CG III, 860; Cu 117 *Cu.*
Morales, Julio M. TM 607 *Mex.*
Morales, Justo BDC 67; Cu 117 *Cu.*
Morales, Melesio TM 608 *Mex.*
Morales, Pedro HPM 90 *Mex.*
Morales, Raimundo C 36, 37; CG III, 860 *Chil.*
Morales, Ramón I. Cu 117 *Cu.*
Morales, Ramón S. BDC 67 *Cu.*
Morales, Sebastián Alfredo de Cu 117 *Cu.*
Morales, Sixto P 21 *Per.*
Morales, Vicente CG III, 860; HLM 467; Ig 226; NM 35; TM 225, 459 *Mex.*
Morales Berti, F. Co 45 *Col.*
Morales Cabrera, Pablo (1866-1933) BP 500; CG III, 861; PR 10; QPR (1) 15 *P.R.*
Morales de la Torre, Raimundo (1885-) LP 391; P 21 *Per.*
Morales de Rivera, Renato BAP 33; P 21; Par 18 *Per.*
Morales Díaz, Modesto (1871-) CT 171 *Cu.*
Morales Ferrer, Abelardo (1864-1894) BDC 67; PR 13, 27, 37 *P.R.*
Morales Gómez, Julio (1912-) PoC 170 *Cu.*
Morales Lara, Julio V 105 *Venez.*
Morales Lemus, José (1808-1871) CHL 475; CLH 415; G 341 *Cu.*
Morales Marcano, Fernando V 105 *Venez.*
Morales Marcano, Jesús María LV 12; V 105 *Venez.*
Morales Marcano, Pío V 105 *Venez.*
Morales O., L. Joaquín C 52 *Chil.*
Morales Pastrana, Antonio HPM 208 *Mex.*
Morales Puente, Armando NM 35; TM 226 *Mex.*
Morales V., Néstor B 13 *Bol.*
Morales y Álvarez, Ramón (1852-1910) BDC 67; CG III, 860; Cu 117 *Cu.*
Morales y Miranda, José Pablo PR 25 *P.R.*
Morales y Morales, Vidal (1848-1904) CG III, 863; Cu 117; RLC 167, 247 *Cu.*
Morán, Alberto C 36 *Chil.*
Morán, José I. TM 459 *Mex.*
Morán de Butrón, Jacinto Basilio (1688-1749) E 50, 75; PLE 14 *Ecua.*
Morán y Seidel, Antonio Cu 117 *Cu.*
Morandeyra, Mary Cu 117 *Cu.*
Morante, Ambrosio A 49, 88 *Arg.*
Morante, Luis Ambrosio C 52 *Chil.*
Morante, Pedro G. A 49, 88 *Arg.*
Morantes, Pedro María V 105 *Venez.*
Moratel, Enrique P. Par 18 *Para.*
Moratorio, Orosmán (1852-1898) CG III, 869; CHL 217; CLH 180; PIU I, 240; PU 158; U 12 *Uru.*
Morazán, Francisco (1792-1842) HL I, 89 *Hond.*
More, Ernesto BAP 55 *Per.*
More, Federico (1889-) B 13; CG III, 870 *Bol.*
Moré, José R. CG III, 870; Cu 117 *Cu.*
Moré, Manuel ("M. Remo") Cu 117, 137 *Cu.*

Moreda, Clara Cu 117 *Cu.*
Morel, Emilio A. CG III, 870; PA 339; PD 137; SD 23 *Dom.*
Morel, Regino (*or* Rejino) ARC 57; Cu 118 *Cu.*
Morel Campos, J. PR 12 *P.R.*
Morelos, José María CHL 96 *Mex.*
Morelos González PM 58 *Mex.*
Morell de Santa Cruz, Pedro Agustín (1694-1768) CG III, 871; Cu 118; RLC 20, 30 *Cu.*
Moreno, Alberto C 36; PCh 353 *Chil.*
Moreno, Antonio CG III, 871; E 50 *Ecua.*
Moreno, Antonio de Paula (1848-1920) CG III, 872; Ig 228; NM 35; PM 58; TM 226 *Mex.*
Moreno, Babil E 50 *Ecua.*
Moreno, Ceslao M. E 50 *Ecua.*
Moreno, Delfino C. PM 58 *Mex.*
Moreno, F. BDC 67; Cu 118 *Cu.*
Moreno, Francisco ARC 57 *Cu.*
Moreno, Francisco P. (1852-1919) LA VII, 96 *Arg.*
Moreno, Fulgencio R. (1872-) CG III, 873; Par 18; PPa 57; PT 163 *Para.*
Moreno, Ismael A 49; CG III, 873 *Arg.*
Moreno, José Ignacio (1767-1841) E 50; SCL 568, 622 *Ecua.*
Moreno, José María ACe 893; PM 58; TM 608 *Mex.*
Moreno, Juan Eduardo C 36 *Chil.*
Moreno, Julio E. Par 18; PE 166; PLE 85 *Ecua.*
Moreno, Manuel (1790-1857) HLA 297; LA V, 199 *Arg.*
Moreno, María (1882-) G 365; PM 58 *Mex.*
Moreno, Mariano (1778-1811) A 49; BHLA 164, 177, 196; CG III, 873; CHL 51; CLH 43; HLA 115; LA V, 30 *Arg.*
Moreno, Miguel (1851-1910) CG III, 873; E 50; G 345; PE 244; PLE 50 *Ecua.*
Moreno, Pablo (1773-1833) ACe 901 *Mex.*
Moreno, René (-1898) BHLA 380 *Bol.*
Moreno, Segundo A 49, 88; CG III, 873 *Arg.*
Moreno Alba, M. V 105 *Venez.*
Moreno Calderón, Antonio CG III, 874; PR 20 *P.R.*
Moreno Cantón, Delio (-1916) CG III, 874; Ig 230; NM 36; PM 58; TM 229; V 105 *Mex.*
Moreno Cora, Silvestre CG III, 875; CHL 423; CLH 368 *Mex.*
Moreno de Fuentes, José (1835-1892) CG III, 876; Cu 118 *Cu.*
Moreno del Cristo, Gabriel B. LD 96; SD 23 *Dom.*
Moreno Garzón, Pedro CG III, 876; Co 45 *Col.*
Moreno Jiménez, Domingo SD 23 *Dom.*
Moreno S., Miguel Ángel E 50, 51 *Ecua.*
Moreno Solano, Fernando C. (1849-1878) BDC 67; Cu 118 *Cu.*
Moreno y Buenvecino, José María HPM 810; TM 228 *Mex.*
Moreno y Contreras, Arturo PM 59 *Mex.*
Moreno y Escandón, Francisco Antonio (1736-1792) HLNG I, 415 *Col.*

Moreno y Oviedo, Antonio CG III, 878; G 365; PM 59 *Mex.*
Moret, Eduardo Cu 118 *Cu.*
Moret, Pantaleón TM 226 *Mex.*
Moret Pérez, Francisco (1863-) BDC 67; CG III, 882; Cu 118 *Cu.*
Morey, Héctor Adolfo V 105 *Venez.*
Morey Otero, Sebastián (1894-) CG III, 883; WLA 266 *Uru.*
Morgado, Benjamín C 36 *Chil.*
Morillas, Pedro J. Cu 118 *Cu.*
Morillo, Gabriel A. PD 136; SD 24 *Dom.*
Morillo, Providencia PR 37 *P.R.*
Morla Vicuña, Carlos (1849-1908) C 36; HC 248 *Chil.*
Morno, El Abate PR 52 *P.R.*
Moro, Pedro E 51 *Ecua.*
Moroni, Arturo R. A 49 *Arg.*
Morosoli, Juan José CG III, 887; PIU III, 228 *Uru.*
Mortgat, Guillermo Cu 118 *Cu.*
"Morton, Daniel" (*pseud.*) *see* Menéndez, Carlos R.
Morúa, José Enrique ARC 57 *Cu.*
Morúa, Martín de P 21 *Per.*
Morúa Contreras, Ildefonso ARC 57 *Cu.*
Morúa Delgado, Martín (-1910) ARC 36, 40, 57; CG III, 888; Cu 118 *Cu.*
Moscarda, E. B. Par 18 *Para.*
Moscoso, Alfonso E 51; PE 15; PLE 86 *Ecua.*
Moscoso, Juan Elías (hijo) PD 139; SD 24 *Dom.*
Moscoso, Mercedes González de (1860-1911) CG II, 605; E 51; PE 228 *Ecua.*
Moscoso, Octavio B 13 *Bol.*
Moscoso, Rafael M. SD 24 *Dom.*
Moscoso y Chávez, Felisa P 21 *Per.*
Moscote, José Dolores CG III, 889; Pan 14 *Pan.*
Mosqueira, Silvano (1875-) CG III, 890; Par 18; PT 311 *Para.*
Mosquera, Alberto Co 45 *Col.*
Mosquera, Alfonso J. CG III, 890; E 51 *Ecua.*
Mosquera, José Rafael (-1843) HLNG II, 519 *Col.*
Mosquera, Manuel José de (1800-) LC 119 *Col.*
Mosquera, Rubén J. (1860-1913) BC 256; CG III, 890; Co 45; PCo 193 *Col.*
Mosquera, Tomás Cipriano de (1798-1878) Co 45 *Col.*
Mossi, Miguel Ángel (1819-1895) LA VII, 235 *Arg.*
Mostajo, Francisco P 21 *Per.*
Mota, Félix (1822-1861) BHLA 331; CHL 492; CLH 433; HPHA I, 309; SD 24 *Dom.*
Mota, Fernando TM 499 *Mex.*
Mota Padilla, Matías de la (1688-1776) HLM 209 *Mex.*
"Motolinia" (*pseud.*) *see* Benavente, Toribio de
Motta Salas, Julián (1892-) RHLC 212 *Col.*
Mouliá, Enrique de A 49; CG III, 892 *Arg.*
Moxó y de Francoli, José Antonio BHC III, 273 *Chil.*
Moya, Casimiro N. de SD 24 *Dom.*

Moya, Ismael A 49 *Arg.*
Moya, Marcelino de Cu 119 *Cu.*
Moya, Nicolás Felipe Co 46 *Col.*
Moziño, José HPM 478 *Mex.*
Mozzi, Alfred A 49 *Arg.*
Mozzi, Clemente A 49 *Arg.*
"Muerdago" (*pseud.*) *see* Ezcurra y Pardo, M.
Mugaburu, Francisco de (1647-) P 21 *Per.*
Mugaburu, José de (1601?-1686) P 21 *Per.*
Mujía, María Josefa (1813-1888) B 13; FPA 53, 55; LB 583; PB 142; PLHA 175 *Bol.*
Mujía, Ricardo (1861-) B 13; BT 191; CG III, 898; FPA 53, 61; PB 143; WLA 268 *Bol.*
Mujica y García, Elías Cu 119 *Cu.*
"Mulato, El" (*pseud.*) *see* Urriola, José Dolores
"Munguía, Bachiller" (*pseud.*) *see* Churión, Juan José
Munguía, Clemente de Jesús (1810-1868) HLM 362; HLMex 191 *Mex.*
Munguía, Enrique TM 460 *Mex.*
Munguía, Felipe S. Ig 231; NM 36 *Mex.*
Muniagurria, Camilo A 49, 88; CG III, 901 *Arg.*
Munita, Roberto C 15; NC 435 *Chil.*
Munita M., Francisco C 36 *Chil.*
Munizaga Aguirre, Roberto C 36 *Chil.*
Munizaga Ossandón, Julio C 36; CG III, 902; PCh 379 *Chil.*
Munizaga Varela, Policarpo C 36; CG III, 902 *Chil.*
Munló, Ramiro C 15; CG III, 902 *Chil.*
Muntadas, Miguel TM 608 *Mex.*
Muñiz, Carlos María CG III, 903; P 21 *Per.*
Muñiz, Francisco Xavier (1795-1871) LA VII, 64 *Arg.*
Muñiz de Quevedo, José CG III, 904; Cu 119 *Cu.*
Muñoz, Alfonso PM 59 *Mex.*
Muñoz, Antonio Co 46 *Col.*
Muñoz, Bonifacio E 51 *Ecua.*
Muñoz, Daniel ("Sansón Carrasco") (1869-1930) CG III, 904; HSLU I, pt 4, 4; PIU I, 237; U 12; UL 132; UT 369 *Uru.*
Muñoz, Francisco de Paula (1840-) Co 46 *Col.*
Muñoz, Gabriel E. AEHA 595; CHL 375; CLH 322; LV 10, 318; V 105, 106 *Venez.*
Muñoz, José Antonio (1899-) APMM 126; CG III, 904; G 365; PM 59 *Mex.*
Muñoz, Juan Pablo PLE 124 *Ecua.*
Muñoz, Juan Ramón U 13 *Uru.*
Muñoz, María Elena CG III, 905; HSLU III, pt 7, 3; LU 64, 667; PIU III, 196; U 13 *Uru.*
Muñoz, Rafael F. BHLA 560; CG III, 905; NM 36 *Mex.*
Muñoz, Tomás M. P 21 *Per.*
Muñoz, Víctor (1873-) CG III, 905; CT 237; Cu 119 *Cu.*
Muñoz Bustamente, Mario (1881-1921) CG III, 906; CT 157; Cu 119; PA 75; PCu 194 *Cu.*

Muñoz Cabrera, Juan Ramón (1816-1869) LA VI, 1119 *Arg.*
Muñoz-Camargo, Diego (1526?-) HLM 77 *Mex.*
Muñoz Cornejo, Humberto (1887-) B 14; BT 199; CG III, 907 *Bol.*
Muñoz de Castro, Pedro HLM 158; HPM 205 *Mex.*
Muñoz de Molina, Juan HPM 197; PM 59 *Mex.*
Muñoz del Monte, Francisco (1800-1868) CHL 492; CLH 432; Cu 119; HPHA I, 305; RLC 72, 74; SD 24 *Cu.*
Muñoz del Valle, María Luisa (1909-) PoC 172 *Cu.*
Muñoz Donoso, Esteban (1844-1907) C 36; HC 249 *Chil.*
Muñoz Ginarte, Benjamín ARC 57 *Cu.*
Muñoz Igartúa, Ángel PR 37 *P.R.*
Muñoz Ledo, Luis F. TM 230 *Mex.*
Muñoz Llosa, César J. C 36 *Chil.*
Muñoz Maines, O. A 49 *Arg.*
Muñoz Maldonado, José (1807-1875) CG III, 910; Cu 119 *Cu.*
Muñoz Marín, Luis (1898-) BP 500; CG III, 910; PR 10, 20; QPR (1) 111; (2) 116; WLA 268 *P.R.*
Muñoz Morales, Luis PR 52 *P.R.*
Muñoz Rivera, Luis ("Heráclito") (1859-1916) BDC 68; BP 533, 615; CG III, 912; FPA 460, 473; G 384; PR 14, 37, 53 *P.R.*
Muñoz Rubalcaba, Francisco Cu 119 *Cu.*
Muñoz Tébar, Jesús CG III, 919; LV 130; V 106 *Venez.*
Muñoz V., Alberto E 51 *Ecua.*
Muñoz y Castro, Juan Cu 119 *Cu.*
Muñoz y Castro, Manuel V 106 *Venez.*
Muñoz y García, José BDC 67; Cu 119 *Cu.*
Muñoz y Marrero, Armando Cu 119 *Cu.*
Murcia, Luis María Co 46 *Col.*
Murcia Riaño, Jorge Co 46 *Col.*
"Murciélago, El" (*pseud.*) *see* Fuentes, Manuel Atanasio
Murga, Bernadino CG III, 921; P 21 *Per.*
Murga, Romeo (1904-) PCC xxii, 259 *Chil.*
Muriel, Domingo (1718-1795) LA IV, 581; SCL 422, 623 *Arg.*
Muriel Reveco, Fernando C 52; CG III, 922 *Chil.*
Murillo, Gerardo ("Doctor Atl") (1875-) CG III, 922; HLM 513; NM 9, 36; PM 21, 59; WLA 269 *Mex.*
Murillo, José BHLA 98; E 51; PLE 18 *Ecua.*
Murillo, Juan E 51 *Ecua.*
Murillo, Juan María CA 40 *C.R.*
Murillo, Ruperto C 15, 36; G 325 *Chil.*
Murillo, Valentín C 15, 52; CHL 275; CLH 234; NC 183, 435 *Chil.*
Murillo Toro, Manuel (1816-1880) LC 157; RHLC 112 *Col.*
Muro, Manuel CG III, 923; HLM 492 *Mex.*
Mustelier, Gustavo E. (1880-) CG III, 926; Cu 119 *Cu.*
Mutis Durán, Facundo CG III, 927; Co 46 *Col.*

Muzilli, José   A 49   *Arg.*
Muzio Sáenz-Peña, Carlos   A 49   *Arg.*
Múzquiz, F.   NM 39   *Mex.*
Múzquiz Blanco, Manuel   CG III, 927; Ig 231; NM 36; PM 59; TM 231   *Mex.*

N

N. y Esteban, Juan   BDC 70; Cu 119   *Cu.*
Naboulet, León   A 49   *Arg.*
Nacarato, Vicente   A 49   *Arg.*
Nadal, Hilarión   V 106   *Venez.*
"Nadie" (*pseud.*) *see* Keratry, Ernesto
Nagerilla, Valentín de   BDC 70; Cu 119 *Cu.*
"Nahuel, Hermes" (*pseud.*) *see* Arriaza, Armando
"Nahuinca" (*pseud.*)   A 49   *Arg.*
Najarro, Antonio   GPCA III, 481   *Salv.*
Nalé Roxlo, Conrado (1898-   )   A 49; APAM 553; APEH 1007; NPA 290   *Arg.*
Nandino, Elías   PM 59   *Mex.*
Naón, Pedro J. (-1913)   A 49   *Arg.*
Naón, Rómulo S.   A 49   *Arg.*
Napal, Dionisio R.   A 49, 72   *Arg.*
Nápoles Fajardo, Juan Cristóbal ("El Cuculambé") (1829-1862)   BDC 71; BHLA 329; CHL 459; CLH 402; Cu 119; PCu 195; RLC 198   *Cu.*
Nápoles Fajardo, Manuel (1836-1871)   Cu 120   *Cu.*
Nápoles y Fajardo, Antonio J.   Cu 120   *Cu.*
Naranjo, F. D.   BDC 71; Cu 120   *Cu.*
Naranjo, Héctor (1889-   )   CA 40; EPCR 457   *C.R.*
Naranjo, J.   Ig 232; NM 36   *Mex.*
"Narciso Valor y Fé" (*pseud.*) *see* Valerio, Juan Francisco
Nariño, Antonio ("Enrique Somoyar") (1765-1823)   AA II, 38, 267; BHLA 156; Co 46; HLNG II, 52 *et passim*; LC 108; RHLC 58; SCL 539, 623   *Col.*
"Naro, G." (*pseud.*) *see* Mas y Pérez, José
Narváez, Enrique de   Co 46   *Col.*
Narváez, Juan Salvador de (1826-1868)   BC 261   *Col.*
"Natal del Pomar" (*pseud.*) *see* Almazán, Pascual
Natalicio González, Juan   Par 2, 18   *Para.*
Natiello, Miguel V.   A 49   *Arg.*
Nattes, Enrique   Cu 120   *Cu.*
Nava, Ciro   V 106   *Venez.*
Nava de Rui Sánchez, Julia   Ig 232; NM 36; TM 231   *Mex.*
Navarrete, Luis A.   C 68; NC 436   *Chil.*
Navarrete, Manuel de (1768-1809)   ACe 1; AMP 225; BHLA 134, 138; CHL 39; CLH 43; HLM 175; HLMex 94; HPHA I, 102; HPM 389; PM 59; PMe I, 283; WSAL 12   *Mex.*
Navarrete, María C.   V 106   *Venez.*
Navarrete, Miguel V.   Cu 120   *Cu.*
Navarrete, Ramón María de   TM 232   *Mex.*
Navarrete, Raúl   ARC 57   *Cu.*
Navarrete C., M.   C 36   *Chil.*
Navarrete Tejeda, Manuel   CA 40   *C.R.*
Navarrete y Landa, Ramón   TM 232   *Mex.*

Navarrete y Romay, Carlos Valdés (1837-1893)   Cu 120; PCu 198; RLC 222   *Cu.*
Navarrette, Augustín   PR 53   *P.R.*
Navarro, Francisco   TM 232   *Mex.*
Navarro, Gabriel   NM 36   *Mex.*
Navarro, Gustavo Adolfo ("Tristán Maroff")   B 14; BHLA 611; SD 24   *Bol.*
Navarro, José Gabriel   E 51, 75; PLE 93   *Ecua.*
Navarro, Juan Nepomuceno (1834-1890)   BC 262; Co 46   *Col.*
Navarro, Mariano   NM 36   *Mex.*
Navarro, Nicolás E.   V 106   *Venez.*
Navarro, Rosa   PM 59   *Mex.*
Navarro, Rubén Aguilar (1886-1918)   PJC 180   *Cu.*
Navarro, Rubén C.   PM 59   *Mex.*
Navarro Almanza, Félix   PR 14, 16, 20   *P.R.*
Navarro Fuentes, Guillermo (1897-   )   QPR (2) 117   *P.R.*
Navarro Luna, Manuel (1895-   )   Cu 120; LH 134; PJC 115; PoC 176; WLA 273   *Cu.*
Navarro Martín de Villodres, Diego Antonio (1758-1820?)   BHC III, 448 *et passim*   *Chil.*
Navarro Montes de Oca, José   Cu 120   *Cu.*
Navarro Monzó, Julio   WLA 273   *Arg.*
Navarro Neyra, Luis   P 21; PPe 306   *Per.*
Navarro Velarde, Fernando (1868-   )   Ig 233; NM 36   *Mex.*
Navarro Viola, Alberto (1858-1885)   A 49, 73; CHL 185; CLH 159; LA VIII, 579   *Arg.*
Navarro Viola, Miguel   CHL 188; CLH 160   *Arg.*
Navarro y Muñoz, Pascual   E 51   *Ecua.*
Navas, Federico   Par 19   *Para.*
Navas E., Juan de Dios   E 51   *Ecua.*
Navas Spínola, Domingo   LV 28; V 106   *Venez.*
Navas V., José Buenaventura   E 51, 75   *Ecua.*
Navea, Ángel   A 49   *Arg.*
Nazaré, Jacobo   C 15   *Chil.*
"Nazareno" (*pseud.*) *see* Camacho, Simón
Nazario Rivera, Ramón   PR 37   *P.R.*
Nebel, Fernando   HSLU II, pt 1, 24; PIU III, 194; U 13   *Uru.*
Nébel Álvarez, Miguel   A 88; PU 161; U 13   *Uru.*
Necochea, Marco   C 15   *Chil.*
Negret, R.   Co 46   *Col.*
Negrete, José (1855-1883)   Ig 235; NM 36; TM 460   *Mex.*
Negrín, Ignacio (1825-   )   Cu 120   *Cu.*
"Negro, Juan" (*pseud.*) *see* Aguirre, Juan
Negrófilo Concienzudo   PR 46   *P.R.*
Negrón, Andrés   P 21   *Per.*
Negrón Collazo, M.   PR 46   *P.R.*
Negrón Flores, Ramón (1867-   )   BP 533; QPR (2) 118   *P.R.*
Negrón Sanjurjo, José A.   BP 533; PA 227; PP 216; PR 37   *P.R.*
Negrón Sanjurjo, Quintín   PA 227   *P.R.*
Negrón Ugarte, María   P 21   *Per.*
Negroni Mattei, F.   PP 240   *P.R.*
Neira, Miguel E.   E 51; PE 240   *Ecua.*
Neira Acevedo, José Ignacio   BC 264; Co 46   *Col.*

Neira Acevedo, Pedro (1829-1858) BC 265; Co 46 *Col.*

Neira de Calvo, Esther Pan 14 *Pan.*

"Nelke, Jorge" (*pseud.*) A 37 *Arg.*

Nelson, Ernesto (1873-) AT II, 703; WLA 275 *Arg.*

Nemidoru Cu 120 *Cu.*

Nemo, Celso C 15 *Chil.*

"Nenúfar" (*pseud.*) *see* Díaz de Rodríguez, Albertina

Nepomuceno Lacunza, Juan (1822-1843) HPM 818 *Mex.*

Nercasseaux y Morán, Enrique C 15, 68; CL 517; NC 437 *Chil.*

Nereo, Marco A 49 *Arg.*

Neruda, Pablo (1904-) APEH 1154, 1195; C 15, 36; CMPC 138; G 326; LH 75; MSAP 226, 330; PCC xxii, 261; PLHA 166; SASS 163; WLA 275 *Chil.*

"Nerval, Gaston" (*pseud.*) *see* Diez de Medina, Raúl

Nervo, Amado (1870-1919) AB 24; AEHA 602; AMP 57; APEH 396, 1185; APMM 127; BHLA 430, 468; CHL 532; CLH 469; FPA 340, 352; G 365; GLO 249; HLM 419; HLMex 213; Ig 237; MSAP 76, 276; NM 36; PM 60; PMe I, 285; PMM 45; PNM 180; SAL 75 *et passim;* SASS 371 *Mex.*

Nervo, Rodolfo PM 61 *Mex.*

Nestares, Francisco H. P 22 *Per.*

Netzahualcóyotl (-1470?) CHL 393, 402; SASS 346 *Mex.*

Neumann Gandía, Eduardo PR 10, 53 *P.R.*

Neve, Francisco C. TM 233 *Mex.*

Neves, Ana C 52 *Chil.*

Neyra, Domingo de LA VII, 266 *Arg.*

Neyra y Lanza, Ramiro ARC 58 *Cu.*

Nicodemi, Darío V 106 *Venez.*

Nieto, José E 51 *Ecua.*

Nieto, Juan José (1804-1866) BC 266; Co 46; RHLC 176 *Col.*

Nieto, Máximo Co 47 *Col.*

Nieto, Pablo E. Co 47 *Col.*

Nieto, Rafael TM 460 *Mex.*

Nieto, Ricardo (1879-) ALC II, 157; Co 47; LC 194; PCo 195; RHLC 154; WLA 276 *Col.*

Nieto Caballero, Agustín Co 47 *Col.*

Nieto Caballero, Luis Eduardo (Lenc) (1888-) Co 47; G 330; IE 194; RHLC 212; WLA 276 *Col.*

Nieto de Herrera, Carmela (1879-) CT 363; Cu 120 *Cu.*

Nieto del Río, Félix C 68 *Chil.*

Nieto O., Vicente E 51 *Ecua.*

Nieto Polo, Andrés E 52 *Ecua.*

Nieves, Rafael G. TM 233 *Mex.*

Nieves y Bustamante, María P 22 *Per.*

"Nigreros, José" (*pseud.*) *see* Ortiz, José Joaquín

"Nigromante, El" (*pseud.*) *see* Prieto, Guillermo *and* Ramírez, Ignacio

Nimer, Aquiles SD 24 *Dom.*

Nin Frías, Alberto ("Sordello Andrea" *or* "Errol Lionel") (1882-) CHL 233; HSLU II, pt 6, 24; III, pt 4, 40; IE 195; U 13; UL 132, 186; UT 377; WLA 277 *Uru.*

Nin y Tudó, Joaquín Cu 120 *Cu.*

"Nísidas" (*pseud.*) *see* Ureña, Nicolás

Noboa, Rafael E 52 *Ecua.*

Noboa, Teodoro PD 142; SD 24 *Dom.*

Noboa, Tomás H. E 52 *Ecua.*

Noboa Caamaño, Alfredo BHLA 540 *Ecua.*

Noboa Caamaño, Ernesto (1891-) E 52; FPA 254, 290; PE 69; PLE 104 *Ecua.*

Nochea, B. Cu 120 *Cu.*

Nodarse, Belisario Cu 120 *Cu.*

Nodarse y Nodarse, Joaquín Cu 120 *Cu.*

Noé, Eugenio C. A 49 *Arg.*

Noé, Julio (1893-) A 49, 72; AT I, 206; BHLA 631; IE 197; LAC 120, 155; WLA 278 *Arg.*

Noel, Carlos M. (1886-) AT I, 271; G 326; WLA 278 *Arg.*

Nogales, Rafael de (1879-) G 392; WLA 279 *Venez.*

Noguera, Bernardino A 49 *Arg.*

Noguera, María de CA 40; IBCR IV, 225 *C.R.*

Noguera, Miguel L. A 49 *Arg.*

Noguera, Rodrigo Co 48 *Col.*

Nolasco, Salvador O. PD 145; SD 24 *Dom.*

Nolasco Préndez, Pedro (-1907) PCh 91 *Chil.*

Noli Bautista, Antonio ("Flavio") AP 237; Pan 8, 14 *Pan.*

"Nomar" (*pseud.*) *see* Espinosa de los Monteros, Ramón

Noreña, Carlos (1859-) BDC 71; Cu 121 *Cu.*

"Noriama Giciona Mazorda" (*pseud.*) *see* Madrazo, Mariano Ignacio

Noriega, Eduardo HLM 467; PM 61; TM 233 *Mex.*

Noriega, Félix F. CA 40 *C.R.*

Noriega, José Antonio HLNG II, 147 *Col.*

Noriega, Luis A. Co 48 *Col.*

Noriega, M. TM 596 *Mex.*

Noriega, Rómulo (1868-) Cu 121 *Cu.*

Noriega Hope, Carlos (1896-) G 367; HLM 529; Ig 240; NM 37; TM 234 *Mex.*

Noriega y Ruiz, Eloy TM 234 *Mex.*

Nosari, Elvira TM 234 *Mex.*

Nouel, Bienvenido S. PA 343; PD 140; SD 24 *Dom.*

Nouel, Carlos SD 24 *Dom.*

Novajas y Solano, Casimiro P 22 *Per.*

Novás Calvo, Lino (1903-) WLA 279 *Cu.*

"Novel, El" (*pseud.*) *see* Campero, Lindaura A. de

Novelo, Adonay PM 61 *Mex.*

Novelo, Holda PM 61 *Mex.*

Novelo, José Inés PM 61 *Mex.*

Novelo, José J. (1867-) AMP 331; PMe I, 303 *Mex.*

Novillo Quiroga, Diego A 49, 72 *Arg.*

Novión, Alberto A 50, 88; CHL 199 *Arg.*

"Novo, Hermógenes" (*pseud.*) *see* Fernández Ferraz, Valeriano

Novo, Salvador (1904-) AMP 187; BAMP 88; G 367; HLM 526; IE 198; NM 38; PM 61; PMM 176; TM 235, 461, 560; WLA 279 *Mex.*

Novo y Gálvez, Lorenzo Cu 121 *Cu.*

Novo y García, José Cu 121 *Cu.*

Nucete, Manuel Vicente V 106 *Venez.*

Nucete-Sardi, José (1897-) V 106; WLA 280 *Venez.*
"Nucleo Diógenes" (*pseud.*) A 50 *Arg.*
Núñez, Agustín Alfredo PM 62; TM 462 *Mex.*
Núñez, Álvar Par 19 *Para.*
Núñez, Enrique Bernardo BHLA 581; V 106; VPF 126 *Venez.*
Núñez, Félix Armando C 37; V 106 *Venez.*
Núñez, Francisco María CA 40; EPCR 579 *C.R.*
Núñez, Ignacio (1792-1846) LA V, 205 *Arg.*
Núñez, J. Cu 121 *Cu.*
Núñez, José María A 50 *Arg.*
Núñez, Rafael (1825-1894) AC I, 181; ALC I, 147; BC 269; BHLA 297, 368; CHL 342, 523; CLH 294; Co 48; CoL 270; FPA 82, 101; LC 132; PCo 196; RHLC 161, 202; SASS 220 *Col.*
Núñez, Ruperto C 53 *Chil.*
Núñez, Serafina (1913-) PoC 180 *Cu.*
Núñez, Sergio E 52; PLE 102 *Ecua.*
Núñez, Solón (1883-) CA 41; EPCR 465 *C.R.*
Núñez Cabeza de Vaca, Álvar SCL 395, 624 *Sp.*
Núñez D., J. E. C 53 *Chil.*
Núñez de Aguiar, Federico V 107 *Venez.*
Núñez de Aguilera, Pedro Co 48 *Col.*
Núñez de Cáceres, José María CLH 317; HPHA I, 304; LV 12, 239; SD 24; V 107 *Venez.*
Núñez de Pineda y Bascuñán, Francisco (1607-1682) BHLA 63; CHL 16; CLH 14; HC 16, 23; HPHA II, 333; PCh 13; SCL 249, 331, 548, 624 *Chil.*
Núñez del Prado, Jorge B 14 *Bol.*
Núñez Olano, Andrés ARC 58; PJC 181 *Cu.*
Núñez Ponte, J. M. V 107 *Venez.*
Núñez Regueiro, Manuel (1883-) A 50; LU 64, 685; UL 187; UT 381; WLA 281 *Uru.*
Núñez y Domínguez, José de Jesús (1887-) APMM 134; G 367; HLM 523; IE 200; Ig 241; NM 3, 38; PM 62; PNM 199; TM 560; WLA 280 *Mex.*

Ñ

"Ñato, Calisto el" (*pseud.*) *see* De María, Alcides

O

O., A. A. E 52 *Ecua.*
"O. C. A." (*pseud.*) *see* Crispo Acosta, Osvaldo
Obaldía, José Domingo (1891-) Pan 15 *Pan.*
Obaldía, María Olimpia de (1891-) AP 241; BHLA 542; Pan 15 *Pan.*

Obando, Baltasar de ("Reginaldo de Lizárraga") (1545-1615) LA III, 239; SCL 428, 615 *Arg.*
Obando, José María (1795-1861) Co 48 *Col.*
Obelar, Raimundo D. (1878-) Par 19 *Para.*
Obeso, Candelario (1849-1884) BC 273; Co 48; PCo 204; RHLC 146 *Col.*
Obligado, Carlos (1890-) A 50; APAM 376; CHL 187; WLA 281 *Arg.*
Obligado, Jorge (1903-) A 50; APAM 557 *Arg.*
Obligado, Pastor S. (1841-) A 50; AT I, 105 *Arg.*
Obligado, Pedro Miguel A 50; APAM 381; APEH 677; LAC 147; NPA 175; PLHA 146 *Arg.*
Obligado, Rafael (1851-1920) A 50; AEHA 613; CHL 168, 173; CLH 145, 148; FPA 16, 39; G 316; GLO 237; LA VII, 478; SASS 38; SPLA 94 *Arg.*
Oblitas, Arturo (1873-) B 14; BT 201 *Bol.*
Obregón, Adolfo M. TM 235 *Mex.*
Obregón, Agustín A 50 *Arg.*
Obregón, Gregorio (1825-1888) Co 49 *Col.*
Obregón Lizano, Miguel A. (1861-) CA 41; EPCR 197 *C.R.*
Obregón Silva, Pedro V 107 *Venez.*
O'Brien, Eduardo V 107 *Venez.*
"Observador, Un" (*pseud.*) *see* Villanueva, Laureano
Ocadiz Arnaud, Emilio TM 462 *Mex.*
Ocampo, Antonio M. Co 49 *Col.*
Ocampo, Carlos A 50 *Arg.*
Ocampo, Eduardo María A 50 *Arg.*
Ocampo, José Gabriel APA I, xxvi, 13 *Arg.*
Ocampo, Luis ("Salvador Mario") A 50, 78; CHL 185; CLH 159; LA VIII, 600 *Arg.*
Ocampo, María Luisa HLM 530; TM 235, 561 *Mex.*
Ocampo, Victoria BHLA 634; LAC 111, 153 *Arg.*
Ocampo y Morán, Juana HPM 839 *Mex.*
Ocantos, Carlos María (1860-) A 50; AEHA 615; BHLA 399; CHL 193; CLH 165; LAS 205; SASS 62 *Arg.*
Ocio, José de Jesús (-1862) BDC 71; Cu 121 *Cu.*
O'Connor D'Arlach, Ademar (-1902) B 14 *Bol.*
O'Connor D'Arlach, Alberto (-1902) B 14 *Bol.*
O'Connor D'Arlach, Amable (1885-) B 14; BT 91 *Bol.*
O'Connor D'Arlach, Tomás (1855-) B 14; BHLA 404; BT 93 *Bol.*
Ochagavia, Rufina Margarita A 52 *Arg.*
Ochart, Bolívar PR 46 *P.R.*
Ochoa, Álvaro Leonor PM 62 *Mex.*
Ochoa, Antonio de NM 38 *Mex.*
Ochoa, Clementina de C 15; NC 174 *Chil.*
Ochoa, Eugenio de TM 463 *Mex.*
Ochoa, Francisco V 107 *Venez.*
Ochoa, Guillermo T. V 107 *Venez.*
Ochoa, José Manuel V 107 *Venez.*
Ochoa, José Vicente (1858-1898) B 14; PB 160 *Bol.*

Ochoa y Acuña, Anastasio María de ("Un Mexicano" or "Damón") (1783-1833) ACe 67; CHL 102; CLH 85; HLM 235; HLMex 98; HPHA I, 112; HPM 501; PM 37, 57, 63; TM 236, 463 *Mex.*

Odriozola, Manuel de P 22 *Per.*

O'Farril, Alberto (1899-) BDC 71 *Cu.*

O'Gabán, Juan B. (1782-1838) RLC 157 *Cu.*

Oiz, Matilde de *see* Troncoso de Oiz, Matilde

Ojea, Hernando de HLM 77 *Mex.*

Ojeda, Daniel de Jesús E 52 *Ecua.*

Ojeda (*or* Hojeda), Diego de (1571-1615) AEHA 442; BHLA 79; CG III, 72; CHL 21; CLH 18; HPHA II, 170; P 14, 22 *Per.*

Ojeda Gallinato, Diego de P 22 *Per.*

Ojeda Orozco, Indalecio TM 237 *Mex.*

Ojeda V., Alejandro E 52 *Ecua.*

Olaguíbel, Francisco Manuel de (1874-1924) AMP 107; G 367; HLM 428; Ig 242; NM 38; PM 63; PMe II, 5 *Mex.*

Olaguibel, Manuel AMP 108; PMe II, 9 *Mex.*

Olano, Antonio Co 49; E 53 *Col.*

Olano, Ricardo Co 49 *Col.*

Olavarría, Domingo Antonio ("Luis Ruiz") LV 15; V 107, 127 *Venez.*

Olavarría, Miguel de SCL 276, 625 *Chil.*

Olavarría y Ferrari, Enrique de (1844-1918) HLM 456 *et passim;* NM 3, 38; PM 63; PoM 368; TM 237, 347, 463, 561 *Mex.*

Olavarrieta, Antonio SCL 569, 625 *Per.*

Olaverría, Tomás de SCL 277, 625 *Chil.*

Olavide y Jáuregui, Pablo Antonio José de (1725-1803) BHLA 135; HPHA II, 221; LP 348; P 22 *Per.*

Olaya Merejón, Francisco Antonio de HLNG I, 349 *Col.*

O'Leary, Daniel Florencio (1800?-1854) BHLA 348; Co 49; V 107, 108 *Col.*

O'Leary, Simón B. V 108 *Venez.*

O'Leary de Urdapilleta, Juan Emiliano (1882-) FPA 401, 415; IE 208; Par 19; PPa 117; PT 113; WLA 285 *Para.*

Oliete, Vicente BDC 72; Cu 121 *Cu.*

Oliva, Anello de la SCL 345, 625 *Per.*

Oliva, Miguel E. PA 84; PCu 201 *Cu.*

Olivares, Francisco V 108 *Venez.*

Olivares, José (188.-) FPA 358, 372 *Nicar.*

Olivares, José C. Cu 121 *Cu.*

Olivares, José T. NL 115; PN 37 *Nicar.*

Olivares, Juvenal C 15; NC 383 *Chil.*

Olivares, Miguel de (1672-1786) HC 31; SCL 193, 494, 626 *Chil.*

Olivares B., José Antonio C 15, 53 *Chil.*

Olivares T., J. Gregorio C 53 *Chil.*

Olivari, Nicolás A 52; BHLA 639 *Arg.*

Oliveira, Cézar Filiberto de A 52; U 13

Oliveira, Pedro A 52 *Arg.*

Olivella, Francisco (-1893) BDC 72; Cu 121 *Cu.*

Oliver, José María (hijo) PU 167; U 13 *Uru.*

Oliver, Manuel María A 52 *Arg.*

Oliver, Prego de PIU I, 62 *Uru.*

Oliver, Ramón (1860-1897) A 52; LA VIII, 604 *Arg.*

Oliver y Casares, José María TM 561 *Mex.*

Olivera, Carlos A 52 *Arg.*

Olivera, Enrique C. PM 63 *Mex.*

Olivera Lavié, Héctor A 52; LAC 134 *Arg.*

Oliviari, Ulises PR 37 *P.R.*

Olivo, Leonte V 108 *Venez.*

Olivo Pino, Antonio BC 277; Co 49 *Col.*

Olivos y Carrasco, Horacio C 37; PCh 223 *Chil.*

Olmedo, Adolfo ("Eloy Falopio Mañod") (1865-1922) G 367; Ig 244; NM 32, 39 *Mex.*

Olmedo, Antonio José PJC 184 *Cu.*

Olmedo y Maruri, José Joaquín de (1780-1847) AEHA 616; BHLA 185, 215; CHL 76; CLH 64; E 53, 75; FPA 253, 255; G 345; GLO 252; HPHA II, 101; LV 38; PE 112; PLE 30; PLHA 66; SASS 329; WSAL 14, 67 *Ecua.*

Olmos, Andrés de HPM 89; TM 237 *Mex.*

Olmos, Mateo Segundo A 52 *Arg.*

Olmos y Zapián, Juan Francisco de Co 49; HLNG I, 297 *Col.*

Olona, Luis TM 238, 464 *Mex.*

Olvera, Francisco TM 99, 238 *Mex.*

Oller, Francisco de P. BDC 72; Cu 121 *Cu.*

Oller, José (1882-) AP 247; Pan 15 *Pan.*

Oller, Juana Raquel Pan 15 *Pan.*

Olleros, Mariano L. Par 20 *Para.*

Omaña, Manuel ACe 904 *Mex.*

"Omer Emeth" (*pseud.*) *see* Vaisse, Emilio

Omiste, Modesto B 15 *Bol.*

"Onateyac" (*pseud.*) *see* Rodríguez Beltrán, Cayetano

O'Neill, Arturo PP 278 *P.R.*

O'Neill, Gonzalo PR 37 *P.R.*

O'Neill de Milán, Luis (1893-) PP 267; QPR (1) 202; (2) 121 *P.R.*

Onel, Absalón C 53 *Chil.*

Onetti, Carlos María A 52; PU 302 *Uru.*

Onetti Lima, Luis PU 164; U 13 *Uru.*

Onrubia, Emilio A 52, 88 *Arg.*

Onrubia, Felisa de A 52 *Arg.*

Ontaneda, J. Virgilio E 53 *Ecua.*

Ontaneda, Mariano (1740-) E 53 *Ecua.*

Oña, Pedro de (1570-1643) AEHA 618; BHC I, 42; BHLA 73; C 37; CHL 12; CLH 10; HC 9; HPHA II, 309; PCh 11; SCL 189, 626 *Chil.*

Oñate, Agustín TM 238 *Mex.*

Oñate Gómez, Enrique de Cu 121 *Cu.*

Opazo F., Pepe C 15, 53 *Chil.*

"Oportuno Festivo" (*pseud.*) Cu 57 *Cu.*

Oquendo, Calendario V 108 *Venez.*

Oquendo de Amat, Carlos BAP 95; BHLA 610; P 23 *Per.*

Oramas, Luis R. V 108 *Venez.*

Orantes V., Alfonso (1898-) PG 463 *Guat.*

Orbe, Diógenes del SD 24 *Dom.*

Orbea, Fernando de Co 49; HLNG I, 120 *Col.*

Orcolaga, Diego Ambrosio HPM 453 *Mex.*

Ordóñez Chávez, César P 23 *Per.*

Ordóñez de Hara, Santiago (1868-) ARC 58 *Cu.*

Ordóñez López, Manuel B 15 *Bol.*

Ordóñez Mata, Alfonso E 53 *Ecua.*

Ordóñez Zamora, Aurelio V. E 53 *Ecua.*

Oré, Luis Jerónimo de (1554-1627) BHC I, 83, 101 *et passim;* SCL 435, 626 *Chil.*
Oreamuno, Nicolás CA 41 *C.R.*
Orellana, Agustín M. TM 238, 246 *Mex.*
Orellana, Delfín E 53 *Ecua.*
Orellana, Ildefonso T. TM 242, 464 *Mex.*
Orellana, J. Gonzalo E 54, 75 *Ecua.*
Orgallez, Manuel Cu 121 *Cu.*
Orgaz, Alfredo A 52 *Arg.*
Orgaz, Arturo A 52 *Arg.*
Orgaz, Francisco de Paula (1815-1873) BDC 72; BHLA 241; CHL 450; Cu 122; HLC 124; HPHA I, 285; PCu 203; RLC 92 *Cu.*
Orgaz, R. A. A 52 *Arg.*
Oria y Senties, Enrique de Ig 245; NM 39 *Mex.*
Oribe, Emilio (1883-) APEH 982, 1193; BHLA 532; G 388; LU 64, 665; PIU III, 121; PU 172; SASS 465; U 13 *Uru.*
Orihuela, Andrés A. Cu 122 *Cu.*
Orihuela, Miguel A. (1802-1834) BDC 72 *Cu.*
Orihuela Grez, Borja C 15, 37; CHL 276; CLH 235; NC 187, 383 *Chil.*
Orjuela, Luis Co 49 *Col.*
Ormaechea, Fernando de (-1892) Cu 122; PR 14, 46
Orman Tu-caes BDC 73 *Cu.*
Ornelas Hernández, Adolfo LAS 207 *Mex.*
"Ornofay" (*pseud.*) *see* Buttari y Gaunaurd, J.
Oropeza, Elías V 108 *Venez.*
Orosz, Ladislao (1697-1773) LA IV, 597; SCL 421, 626 *Arg.*
Oroz Scheibe, Rodolfo (1895-) WLA 286 *Chil.*
Orozco, Crescencio TM 246 *Mex.*
Orozco, José (1733-1786) HPHA II, 90; PLE 25; SCL 552, 627 *Ecua.*
Orozco, Juan A 52 *Arg.*
Orozco Castro, Carlos CA 41 *C.R.*
Orozco Muñoz, Francisco APMM 138; HLM 519 *Mex.*
Orozco R., Efrén TM 246 *Mex.*
Orozco y Berra, Fernando (1822-1851) BHLA 344; CHL 406; CLH 353; G 367; HLM 334; HPM 822; Ig 245; NM 39; TM 247 *Mex.*
Orozco y Berra, Manuel (1816-1881) HLM 472; HLMex 165; TM 247 *Mex.*
Orqueda, Liberato A 52 *Arg.*
Orrantia, Rafael E 54, 75 *Ecua.*
Orrego, Rafael C 37 *Chil.*
Orrego Barros, Antonio (1880-) C 16, 37, 53, 68; PCh 327 *Chil.*
Orrego de Uribe, Rosario (1834-1879) C 16; CHL 254; CLH 215; NC 196, 499; PCh 25 *Chil.*
Orrego Espinoza, Antenor (1892-) BHLA 602; IE 215; WLA 287 *Per.*
Orrego G., Rafael C 16; NC 196 *Chil.*
Orrego Luco, Augusto C 68; CL 518 *Chil.*
Orrego Luco, Luis (1866-) BHLA 509; C 16; CHL 278; CLH 237; G 326; NC 197, 383, 437; WLA 287 *Chil.*
Orrego Vicuña, Eugenio (1900-) C 53, 68; G 326; LAS 201; WLA 288 *Chil.*
Orrico i Caparroso, Miguel PM 64. 84 *Mex.*

Orta y Fernández, Juana de Cu 123 *Cu.*
Ortea, Juan Isidro PA 345; PD 147; SD 24 *Dom.*
Ortea, Virginia Elena PD 148; SD 25 *Dom.*
Ortega, Abelardo E 54 *Ecua.*
Ortega, Alfredo Tomás BC 277; Co 49 *Col.*
Ortega, Andrés PM 63 *Mex.*
Ortega, Aniceto TM 609 *Mex.*
Ortega, Aparicio (1852-1910) E 55 *Ecua.*
Ortega, Carlos M. TM 247 *Mex.*
Ortega, Eduardo Co 49; LC 195; PCo 209; V 108 *Col.*
Ortega, Eugenio Co 49 *Col.*
Ortega, Febronio NM 3 *Mex.*
Ortega, Francisco (1793-1849) ACe 619; BHLA 171; CHL 102; CLH 86; HLM 243; HLMex 121; HPHA I, 109; HPM 537; PM 63; TM 248, 464 *Mex.*
Ortega, G. TM 464 *Mex.*
Ortega, José Juan PM 63 *Mex.*
Ortega, Juan PJC 188 *Cu.*
Ortega, Juan Gualberto de Cu 123 *Cu.*
Ortega, M. J. C 16 *Chil.*
Ortega, Manuel Valerio TM 248 *Mex.*
Ortega, Miguel ("M. O.") A 52, 78, 88; LA VIII, 584, 848 *Arg.*
Ortega, Ramón (1890?-) FPA 318, 333; PM 63 *Mex.*
Ortega, Simón ("Fernando de Ayala") V 71, 108 *Venez.*
Ortega, Torcuato A. (1865-1893) BC 278; Co 49 *Col.*
Ortega B., Ismael Pan 15 *Pan.*
Ortega Belgrano, Raúl A 52 *Arg.*
Ortega Figueredo, R. V 108 *Venez.*
Ortega Folch, Joaquín C 16 *Chil.*
Ortega Martínez, José María V 108 *Venez.*
Ortega Ricaurte, José Vicente Co 49 *Col.*
Ortega Sanz, Atilano A 52 *Arg.*
Ortega y de la Flor, Luis (1814-1894) BDC 73; Cu 123 *Cu.*
Ortega y Gironés, Juan (-1900) Cu 123 *Cu.*
Ortegaray, Jacobo NL 260 *Nicar.*
Ortelli, Roberto A. A 52 *Arg.*
Ortiz, Alberto NL 181; PN 11 *Nicar.*
Ortiz, Carlos (1870-1910) A 52; APAM 107; NPA 29; SPLA 116 *Arg.*
Ortiz, Fernando (1881-) ARC 76; BHLA 500; Cu 123; IE 210; RLC 351, 353, 355 *Cu.*
Ortiz, Francisco Cu 123; TM 250 *Mex.*
Ortiz, Gabino (1819-1885) HPM 905; PM 63; TM 250 *Mex.*
Ortiz, José Joaquín ("José Nigreros") (1814-1892) AC I, 161; AEHA 630; ALC I, 77; BC 282; CHL 334; CLH 275, 286; Co 49; FPA 81, 83; HPHA II, 64; LC 127; PCo 214; RHLC 91, 96, 121, 158, 175; SASS 213 *Col.*
Ortiz, Juan Buenaventura (1840-1894) BC 278; Co 50; LC 180 *Col.*
Ortiz, Juan Francisco (1808-1875) BC 286; Co 50; RHLC 115 *Col.*
Ortiz, Luis Gonzaga (1835-1894) HLM 398; Ig 247; NM 39; PM 63; PMe II, 15; PoM 137; TM 464 *Mex.*
Ortiz, Manuel J. C 16; NC 384 *Chil.*
Ortiz, Melitón BC 289; Co 51 *Col.*

Ortiz, Nicolás (1834-) Co 51 *Col.*
Ortiz, Pedro PN 89 *Nicar.*
Ortiz, Rafael (1844-) BC 289; Co 51 *Col.*
Ortiz, Ricardo E 55 *Ecua.*
Ortiz, Venancio (1818-1891) Co 51 *Col.*
Ortiz Alibrán, J. J. PR 27, 47 *P.R.*
Ortiz Ávila, Raúl PM 63 *Mex.*
Ortiz Barrera, Francisco ("Patroclo") RHLC 122 *Col.*
Ortiz de Cervantes, Juan (-1629) HLNG I, 235 *Col.*
Ortiz de Montellano, Bernardo (1899-) AMP 164; APMM 140; G 367; HLM 525; LAS 201; NM 3, 39; PM 64; PMM 154; TM 251; WLA 289 *Mex.*
Ortiz de Morales, Joseph Co 51; HLNG I, 296 *Col.*
Ortiz de Torres, Juan HLM 187; HPM 217; PM 64 *Mex.*
Ortiz de Zárate, Juan HPHA II, 374 *Arg.*
Ortiz Grognet, Emilio (-1932) A 52, 88 *Arg.*
Ortiz Guerrero, Manuel (188.-) FPA 403, 432; Par 20; PPa 219 *Para.*
Ortiz Marín, Juan BDC 73; Cu 123 *Cu.*
Ortiz Olavarrieta, Luis C 16; NC 389 *Chil.*
Ortiz Pacheco, Daniel B 15 *Bol.*
Ortiz Sáenz, Ricardo BC 291; Co 51 *Col.*
Ortiz Saralegui, Juvenal HSLU III, pt 6, 49; PIU III, 243; U 13 *Uru.*
Ortiz Stella, Cruz BP 534; PR 37, 38 *P.R.*
Ortiz Vidales, Alfredo G 368; PM 64 *Mex.*
Ortiz Vidales, José PM 64 *Mex.*
Orts-Ramos, Tomás Cu 123 *Cu.*
"Ortsac" (*pseud.*) PM 64 *Mex.*
Ortuño, Esperanza TM 251 *Mex.*
Ortúzar G., Agustín C 37 *Chil.*
Orue y Vivanco, Salustiano de Cu 124 *Cu.*
Ory, Eduardo de Co 51 *Col.*
"Oscar C. Bermúdez" (*pseud.*) A 9; CG I, 333 *Arg.*
"Oscar Tiberio" (*pseud.*) A 53, 66 *Arg.*
Osejo, Rafael Francisco EPCR 16 *C.R.*
Osío, Manuel I. V 108 *Venez.*
Osio y Ocampo, Magdaleno (1746-) ACe 905 *Mex.*
Osorio *see also* Ossorio
Osorio, José Salomón PM 64 *Mex.*
Osorio, Luis Enrique (1896-) Co 51; RHLC 173; WLA 290 *Col.*
Osorio, Miguel Ángel ("Ricardo Arenales" *or* "Porfirio Barba Jacob") (1883-) ALC II, 199; AMP 70; APEH 739, 1190; BHLA 586; Co 6, 8, 51; PLHA 151; PMM 87; RHLC 154 *Col.*
Osorio Casas, Adolfo BC 291; Co 51 *Col.*
Osorio Lizarazo, J. A. (1900-) Co 51; LAS 205; RHLC 193 *Col.*
Osorio y Bernard, D. M. TM 465 *Mex.*
Osorno, Mariano TM 252 *Mex.*
Ospina, Eduardo Co 51 *Col.*
Ospina, Hernando de Co 51; HLNG I, 139 *Col.*
Ospina, Joaquín Co 51 *Col.*
Ospina de Navarro, Sofía Co 51 *Col.*
Ospina Rodríguez, Mariano (1805-1885) Co 51; LC 121; RHLC 111 *Col.*
Ossa, Jerónimo (1847-1907) AP 251; Pan 15 *Pan.*

Ossa, José Gregorio C 53 *Chil.*
Ossandón de la Peña, Arturo C 53 *Chil.*
Ossandón González, R. C 68 *Chil.*
Ossorio *see also* Osorio
Ossorio de las Peñas, Antonio Co 51; HLNG I, 174 *Col.*
Ossorio Nieto de Paz, José Co 52 *Col.*
Osuna, Heraclio D. V 108 *Venez.*
Osuna, Manuel BDC 73; Cu 124 *Cu.*
Osuna, Tomás Par 20 *Para.*
Osuna de Mutis, Elena C 37 *Chil.*
"Otal Susi" (*pseud.*) *see* González Rincones, Salustio
Otamendi, Roque C. A 53 *Arg.*
"Otardo, C. L." (*pseud.*) *see* Brito, Hilario C.
Otazo, Rafael V 108 *Venez.*
"Oteiza, Agustín" (*pseud.*) *see* Oteiza y Dongo, Manuel José de
Oteiza, José Simeón de B 15 *Bol.*
Oteiza Quirno, R. A 53 *Arg.*
Oteiza y Dongo, Manuel José de ("Agustín Oteiza") (1742-1798) HC 17 *Chil.*
Otel y R., Remigio TM 465 *Mex.*
Oteriño, Felipe A. A 53 *Arg.*
Otero, Daniel PJC 191 *Cu.*
Otero, Gustavo Alonso (1896-) B 15 *Bol.*
Otero, José Pacífico (1874-) A 53; WLA 291 *Arg.*
Otero, Luis Alfredo Co 52 *Col.*
Otero D'Acosta, Enrique (1883-) Co 52; RHLC 201; WLA 291 *Col.*
Otero de Morales, Justo Cu 124 *Cu.*
Otero Durán, J. J. Co 52 *Col.*
Otero Muñoz, Gustavo (1894-) Co 52; LAS 201; WLA 292 *Col.*
Otero Novo, Antonio (-1913) Cu 124 *Cu.*
Otero Vértiz, Gustavo Adolfo (1896-) B 7; BHLA 612; BT 207 *Bol.*
Otero y Castroverde, Rafael (1859-1892) Cu 124 *Cu.*
Otero y Gómez, José (-1910) Cu 124 *Cu.*
Otero y María, Rafael (1827-1876) BDC 73; Cu 124 *Cu.*
Otero y Pimentel, Luis Cu 125 *Cu.*
Oteza Bustamante, José A 53 *Arg.*
Othón, Manuel José (1858-1906) AMP 39; APEH 29, 1176; APMM 142; BHLA 438; CHL 415; CLH 362; FPA 339, 345; G 368; HLM 405, 466; HLMex 210; NM 39; PM 64; PMe II, 19; PMM 11; PNM 210; PoM 331; SASS 362; TM 253 *Mex.*
Outes, Carlos F. A 73 *Arg.*
Ovalle, Alonso de (1601-1651) BHC I, 458; HC 21; SCL 260, 627 *Chil.*
Ovalle, Esteban BC 296 *Col.*
Ovalle, Manuel J. C 48 *Chil.*
Ovalle, Samuel C 48 *Chil.*
Ovalle Castillo, Francisco Javier C 16, 68; CL 519 *Chil.*
Ovalle I., Martín C 53 *Chil.*
Ovalles, V. M. V 108 *Venez.*
Ovando, Leonor de SD 25 *Dom.*
Oviedo, Basilio Vicente de (1699-) Co 52; HLNG I, 308; LC 92; SCL 377, 628 *Col.*
Oviedo, Juan Antonio de (1670-1757) Co 52 *Col.*
Oviedo, Pedro Fernando P 23 *Per.*
Oviedo, Rodrigo de E 55 *Ecua.*

Oviedo de Baños y Sotomayor, José Antonio de (1674-1757) Co 53; HLNG I, 304, 306; HPHA I, 355; LC 86; SCL 376, 628; V 108 *Col.-Venez.*

Oviedo Martínez, Benjamín C 37; PCh 415 *Chil.*

Oviedo Reyes, I. Aug. NL 244 *Nicar.*

Oviedo y Herrera, Luis Antonio de, Conde de la Granja (1636-1717) BHLA 81, 101; CHL 22; CLH 19; HPHA II, 203; SCL 333, 628 *Per.*

Oviedo y Romero, A. de NM 3 *Mex.*

Oviedo y Valdés, Gonzalo Fernández de *see* Fernández de Oviedo y Valdés, Gonzalo

Ovilo, Felipe Cu 125 *Cu.*

Owen, Gilberto (1904-) AMP 210; BHLA 562; IE 216; NM 39; PM 64; PMM 212 *Mex.*

Oxiacan, Miguel PM 64 *Mex.*

Oyhanarte, Raúl A 53 *Arg.*

Oyuela, Calixto (1857-1935) A 50, 53, 72; AT I, 96; BHLA 420; C 68; CHL 176; CLH 150, 151; SASS 42; SD 25 *Arg.*

P

P. C. V 108 *Venez.*

P., D. Cu 125 *Cu.*

P., H. A. E 55 *Ecua.*

P., T. J. M. de E 55 *Ecua.*

Paadin y Tolosa, Juan Cu 125 *Cu.*

Pabello Acosta, Amalia PM 64 *Mex.*

Pablo, Ramón de TM 255 *Mex.*

Paci, Domingo C 51 *Chil.*

Pacífico Gallegos E 55 *Ecua.*

Pachano, Jacinto Regino LV 7; V 108, 109 *Venez.*

Pachano de Fombona, Ignacia ("Blanca") V 40, 71, 109, 116 *Venez.*

Pacheco, Abelardo ARC 58 *Cu.*

Pacheco, Antonio José V 109 *Venez.*

Pacheco, Armando Oscar SD 25 *Dom.*

Pacheco, Carlos M. A 53, 88 *Arg.*

Pacheco, J. Marcelino CA 41 *C.R.*

Pacheco, J. R. NM 39 *Mex.*

Pacheco, José R. V 109 *Venez.*

Pacheco, Leónidas CA 41 *C.R.*

Pacheco, Ramón (1845-1888) BHLA 403; C 16; CHL 271; CLH 231; NC 206, 494, 499 *Chil.*

Pacheco C., Carlos CA 41 *C.R.*

Pacheco Cooper, Emilio (1865-) CA 41; CLH 449; EPCR 209 *C.R.*

Pacheco Cruz, Santiago TM 255 *Mex.*

Pacheco Miranda, Andrés (1885-) V 109; WLA 293 *Venez.*

Pacheco S., Napoleón CA 41, 42; EPCR 648 *C.R.*

Pacheco y Obes, Melchor (1809-1851) CHL 216; CLH 179; HCLU I, 303; LUr 432 *Uru.*

"Pacho" (*pseud.*) *see* Groot, José Manuel

Pachuca, Francisco de PM 64 *Mex.*

Padilla, Benjamín ("Kaskabel") NM 39; TM 256 *Mex.*

Padilla, Diego (1754-) Co 53; HLNG II, 146, 335 *Col.*

Padilla, Emiliano CA 42 *C.R.*

Padilla, José Gualberto ("El Caribe") (1829-1896) BP 534, 620; FPA 460, 469; PP 63; PR 10, 20, 38, 47, 53 *P.R.*

Padilla, José P. PM 64 *Mex.*

Padilla, Luis Cu 125 *Cu.*

Padilla, Oscar CA 42 *C.R.*

Padilla Atoche, Hilarión B 15 *Bol.*

Padilla Bernabeu, Luis ARC 58 *Cu.*

Padilla Castro, Guillermo CA 42 *C.R.*

Padilla Castro, Noé CA 42; IBCR IV, 267 *C.R.*

Padilla Dávila, Manuel PA 230; PP 109; PR 38, 53 *P.R.*

Padilla de Sanz, Trinidad ("Trini Sanz" or "Hija del Caribe") (1868-) BP 528; PA 214; PP 178; PR 38; QPR (2) 124 *P.R.*

Padín, José PR 9, 53 *P.R.*

Padró, Humberto PR 56 *P.R.*

Padrón, Candelario V 109 *Venez.*

Padua Bosch, Antonio de BDC 8; Cu 125 *Cu.*

Paes Brohi, Luis TM 257 *Mex.*

Páez, Adriano (1844-1890) Co 53; LC 173 *Col.*

Páez, Alfonso E. (1892-) Cu 125 *Cu.*

Páez, José Antonio LV 12, 14; V 109 *Venez.*

Páez, Julián M. Co 53 *Col.*

Páez, Justiano de J. Co 53 *Col.*

Páez, Manuel Modesto PN 219 *Nicar.*

Páez, Marco Tulio V 109 *Venez.*

Páez, Ramón V 109; VPF 49 *Venez.*

Páez Brotchie, Luis NM 11, 39 *Mex.*

"Pagador, Juan" (*pseud.*) *see* Cúneo-Vidal, Rómulo

Pagador, Mariano P 24 *Per.*

Pagán, Bolívar BP 500; PR 20, 42, 53 *P.R.*

Pagán, Vicente PR 25 *P.R.*

Pagano, Adolfo U 13 *Uru.*

Pagano, José León (1878-) A 53, 89; AT II, 917; LAC 114, 152 *Arg.*

Pagaza, Joaquín Arcadio (1839-1918) AMP 269; CHL 415, 504; CLH 362; FPA 339, 342; G 368; HLM 401; HLMex 198; PM 64; PMe II, 41; PoM 128 *Mex.*

Pagés, Federico Cu 125 *Cu.*

Paguaga Núñez, Cristino NL 268 *Nicar.*

Pais, Pedro PM 65; TM 257 *Mex.*

País León, C. Rubén E 55 *Ecua.*

Pajés, Emilio Cu 125 *Cu.*

"Pako" (*pseud.*) *see* Betancourt Figueredo, Francisco

Palacio, Alberto ARC 58 *Cu.*

Palacio, Julio H. Co 53 *Col.*

Palacio, Manuel A. de Ig 249; NM 39 *Mex.*

Palacio, Manuel del PR 38 *P.R.*

Palacio, Pablo BHLA 597; E 55, 75; G 345; PLE 135 *Ecua.*

Palacio, Ramón M. V 110 *Venez.*

Palacios, Alfredo BHLA 497 *Arg.*

Palacios, B. (hijo) V 110 *Venez.*

Palacios, Eustaquio (1830-1898) Co 53; RHLC 185 *Col.*

Palacios, Florencio D. Ig 250; NM 39 *Mex.*

Palacios, Francisco ACe 908 *Mex.*

Palacios, García Reyes C 17 *Chil.*
Palacios, Jacinto de Jesús E 55 *Ecua.*
Palacios, Miguel de C 53 *Chil.*
Palacios, Natalia (-1918) B 15 *Bol.*
Palacios, Pedro Bonifacio ("Almafuerte") (1854-1917) A 53, 78; APEH 126; BHLA 456; CG I, 68; CHL 187; FPA 15, 22; G 317; GEA XIV, XXI; GLO 238; LA VII, 499; NPA 27; PLHA 138; SA 143; SASS 40; SPLA 106 *Arg.*
Palacios, Senén C 17 *Chil.*
Palacios Bravo, Manuel María E 55 *Ecua.*
Palau, Lisímaco Co 53 *Col.*
Palavicini, Félix F. NM 39 *Mex.*
Palavicini, Laura PM 65 *Mex.*
Palazzi, José B 15 *Bol.*
Palazzolo, Octavio A 53 *Arg.*
Palcos, Alberto A 53 *Arg.*
Palencia, Tranquilino ARC 58 *Cu.*
Palermo, Miguel A. Par 20 *Para.*
Palés, J. A. Vicente PR 38 *P.R.*
Palés Matos, Luis APEH 1020; BHLA 574; G 384; PP 219; PR 56 *P.R.*
Palés Matos, Vicente (1903-   ) PP 223; QPR (1) 117; (2) 125; WLA 296 *P.R.*
Paliza, Juan L. PM 65 *Mex.*
Palma, Angélica ("Marianela") (1883-1935) BHLA 514; CHL 306; G 382; P 24; WLA 297 *Per.*
Palma, Benigno (1882-   ) Pan 15 *Pan.*
Palma, Clemente ("Corrales") (1872-   ) AEHA 904; BHLA 474, 514; CHL 306; CLH 260; P 24; WLA 297 *Per.*
Palma, Francisco Luis ARC 58 *Cu.*
Palma, José Joaquín (1844-1911) Cu 125; G 341; PA 86; PG 9; RLC 267; SAL 136 *Cu.*
Palma, Luis N. (1863-1894) LA VIII, 603 *Arg.*
Palma, Martín (1821-1884) BHLA 342, 402; C 17, 69; CHL 269; CLH 228; HC 240; NC 212 *Chil.*
Palma, Ricardo (1833-1919) AB 24; AEHA 649; BHLA 320, 336; CHL 300; CLH 254; G 382; GLO 252; LB 597; LC 203; LP 370; P 24; PLHA 224, 283; PPe 34, 89; SA 93; SAL 355; SASS 423; SCL 226, 355, 628; VPF 17 *Per.*
Palma y Campos, Miguel NM 39; TM 257 *Mex.*
Palma y Palma, Eulogio (1851-   ) Ig 250; NM 39 *Mex.*
Palma y Riesco, Agustín I. C 69 *Chil.*
Palma y Romay, Ramón de (1812-1860) BDC 74; BHLA 224; CHL 449; CLH 391; Cu 125; HLC 123, 175; HPHA I, 286; RLC 70, 89, 135, 146 *Cu.*
Palma y V., José (1870-   ) B 15; BT 209 *Bol.*
"Palmiro de Lidia" (*pseud.*) *see* Valle, Adrián del
Palomares, Justino N. NM 39; PM 65 *Mex.*
Palomeque, Alberto (1852-   ) CHL 227; CLH 189; UL 187; UT 391 *Uru.*
Palomeque, Ignacio E 55 *Ecua.*
Palomeque, José Gabriel HCLU I, 406 *Uru.*
Palomino, Rafael de Castro *see* Castro Palomino, Rafael de

Palomino, Rafael Leopoldo BDC 75; Cu 126 *Cu.*
Palomo, Francisco de P. Ig 251; NM 40; TM 258 *Mex.*
Palou y Vivanco, Cayetano BDC 75; Cu 126 *Cu.*
Pallais, Azarías H. (188.-   ) FPA 358, 367; NL 146 *Nicar.*
Pallarés, Alfonso PE 40 *Ecua.*
Pallarés Arteta, Leónidas (1859-1932) E 55; PE 182; PLE 56 *Ecua.*
Pallarés Peñafiel, Vicente (1864-1894) E 56 *Ecua.*
Pampín, Manuel Lorenzo Cu 126 *Cu.*
Pancheco Zegarra, Gavino P 24 *Per.*
"Pancho, El viejo" (*pseud.*) *see* Alonso y Trelles, José
"Pancho Millaleubu" (*pseud.*) HPHA II, 339; SCL 548, 621 *Chil.*
Pando, J. M. B 17 *Bol.*
Pando, José María de (1787-1840) BHLA 190, 213; HPHA II, 245; P 25 *Per.*
Pando y Valle, Jesús (1849-1911) Cu 126 *Cu.*
Pane, Ignacio Alberto (-1919) FPA 401, 409; Par 20; PPa 101 *Para.*
Pane, Justo A. Par 21 *Para.*
Panes, Manuel M. (-1903) Ig 252; NM 40 *Mex.*
Paniagua, Cenobio TM 609 *Mex.*
Paniagua, Flavio Antonio (1844-1911) Ig 253; NM 40 *Mex.*
Paniagua, Héctor Eduardo PM 65 *Mex.*
Paniagua, Manuel M. TM 610 *Mex.*
Paniagua Prado, Ismael (Israel?) NL 235 *Nicar.*
Panizo y Orbegozo, Federico P 25 *Per.*
Panizza, Delio A 53 *Arg.*
Pantaleón Castillo, José SD 25 *Dom.*
Pantoja, Mardoqueo C 37 *Chil.*
"Paolo" (*pseud.*) *see* Romero, Paulo Emilio
Papini y Zas, Guzmán LUr 524; PIU III, 202; U 13 *Uru.*
Papo, Eduardo A 54, 89 *Arg.*
"Par, Leo" (*pseud.*) *see* Dávila Silva, Ricardo
Parada León, Ricardo HLM 529; TM 258 *Mex.*
"Páramo, Juan del" (*pseud.*) *see* Vargas Márquez, Juan
Paravey HLNG I, 249 *Col.*
Pardo, Francisco Guaycaypuro (1829-1882) BHLA 326; CHL 370; CLH 319; FPA 550, 569; LV 298; V 110 *Venez.*
Pardo, Leonardo R. Ig 254; NM 40; TM 258 *Mex.*
Pardo, María Esperanza Ig 254; NM 40 *Mex.*
Pardo, Miguel Eduardo (1868-1905) CHL 381; CLH 332; LV 396, 422; PLHA 194; SASS 521; V 110, 111; VPF 122 *Venez.*
Pardo, Nicolás (1834-1881) Co 53 *Col.*
Pardo, Ramón TM 258 *Mex.*
Pardo Farelo, Enrique ("Luis Tablanca") (1883-   ) Co 53; RHLC 193 *Col.*
Pardo García, Germán (1902-   ) ALC II, 453; BHLA 586; Co 53 *Col.*
Pardo Pimentel, Nicolás BDC 75; Cu 126 *Cu.*
Pardo Suárez, Vicente (1870-   ) CT 15 *Cu.*

Pardo y Aliaga, Felipe (1806-1868) AEHA 652; BHLA 212, 219; CHL 289; CLH 244; FPA 435, 437; HPHA II, 249; LP 363; P 25; PPe 7; SASS 443; V 111; WSAL 62, 79 *Per.*

Pardo y Fernández, Carlos BDC 75; Cu 126 *Cu.*

Pardo y Mangino, Antonio TM 259 *Mex.*

Paredes, Antonio V 111 *Venez.*

Paredes, Félix Gonzalo E 56 *Ecua.*

Paredes, Juan Pastor AP 255; Pan 16 *Pan.*

Paredes, Manuel Rigoberto (1871-) B 16 *Bol.*

Paredes Larrea, Enrique E 56 *Ecua.*

Paredes Ramírez, J. M. E 56 *Ecua.*

Pareja, Aníbal E 56 *Ecua.*

Pareja, Carlos Henrique ("Simón Latino") (1900-) Co 54; IE 143 *Col.*

Pareja, Wenceslao E 56; PE 325 *Ecua.*

Pareja y Artacho, Francisco BDC 75; Cu 126 *Cu.*

Pareja y Diez-Canseco, Alfredo E 56 *Ecua.*

Parejo, Antonio ("Rosina Pérez") V 111, 113 *Venez.*

París, José Joaquín Co 54 *Col.*

París, R. Manuel Co 54 *Col.*

Parisi, Antonio BHC II, 210 *Chil.*

Parodi, Enrique D. (186.-) A 54; FPA 401, 404; Par 21; PPa 37 *Para.*

Parodi, Gustavo V 90, 111 *Venez.*

Parodi, Humberto C 17; NC 390 *Chil.*

Parodi Uriarte, Esther R. HSLU II, pt 8, 16; PU 303; U 14 *Uru.*

Parra, Aquileo (1825-1900) Co 54 *Col.*

Parra, C. V 111 *Venez.*

Parra, Hernando de la RLC 19, 42 *Cu.*

Parra, Manuel de la (1878-1930) AMP 95; APMM 155; HLM 521; Ig 254; NM 40; PM 65; PMM 82; PNM 243 *Mex.*

Parra, Pedro María V 111 *Venez.*

Parra, Porfirio (1856-1912) CHL 424; CLH 369; HLM 457; Ig 255; NM 40; PM 65; PMe II, 47; PoM 258; TM 259 *Mex.*

"Parra, Teresa de la" (*pseud.*) *see* Parra Sanojo, Ana Teresa

Parra del Riego, Juan ("Juan Cristóbal") (1894-1925) BAP 39; HSLU II, pt 9, 5; LU 64, 659; PoU 133 *Uru.*

Parra Mege, Alejandro C 17; NC 390 *Chil.*

Parra Pérez, Caracciolo V 111 *Venez.*

Parra Pineda, José V 111 *Venez.*

Parra Sanojo, Ana Teresa ("Teresa de la Parra") (1895-1936) BHLA 580; G 392; PLHA 213; SASS 537; V 111, 112; VPF 214; WLA 118 *Venez.*

Parra y Freire, Héctor PU 178 *Uru.*

Parraga, Ernesto V 112 *Venez.*

Parráguez, Ismael C 17, 37; NC 390; PCh 397 *Chil.*

Parravicini, Florencio (1876-) A 54, 89; AT II, 799 *Arg.*

Parreño, José J. ARC 76 *Cu.*

Parrilla, M. de Jesús Cu 126 *Cu.*

Pasalagua, Carlos F. PM 65 *Mex.*

Pasán, José BDC 76; Cu 126 *Cu.*

Pasarell, Emilio J. (1891-) QPR (2) 127 *P.R.*

Pascali, Justo A 54 *Arg.*

Pascarella, Luis A 54, 89 *Arg.*

Paseyro, Ricardo PU 305 *Uru.*

Paso y Troncoso, Francisco del (1842-1916) HLM 491; HLMex 237; TM 465 *Mex.*

Pasos, Joaquín NL 284 *Nicar.*

Pasquel Monge, M. Enrique E 56 *Ecua.*

Passi García, Ricardo CL 520 *Chil.*

Pástor, César Alfonso PLE 94 *Ecua.*

Pastor, J. Miguel Ig 256; NM 40 *Mex.*

Pastor, Juan (1580-1658) LA III, 503 *Arg.*

Pastor, Juana ARC 33 *Cu.*

Pastor, Modesto X. U 14 *Uru.*

Pastrana, Prudencio Ig 257; NM 40 *Mex.*

"Pater" (*pseud.*) *see* Paterson, Roberto G.

Paterson, Roberto G. ("Pater") A 54, 78 *Arg.*

Patín Maceo, Manuel A. SD 25 *Dom.*

Patiño, Arístides SD 25 *Dom.*

Patiño, Heliodoro AP 257; Pan 16 *Pan.*

Patiño, Joaquín TM 468 *Mex.*

Patiño, Pedro Pablo ACe 911 *Mex.*

Patiño Jaramillo, Carlos Co 54 *Col.*

"Patroclo" (*pseud.*) *see* Ortiz Barrera, Francisco

Patrón, Pablo (1855-1910) P 25 *Per.*

Patrón Peniche, Prudencio TM 260, 562 *Mex.*

Patterson, Angélica Ch. de Pan 16 *Pan.*

Patterson, Guillermo Jr. (1844-) AP 273; Pan 16 *Pan.*

Pauke, Florián (1719-) LA IV, 596; SCL 419, 628 *Arg.*

"Paul, Jean" (*pseud.*) *see* Echagüe, Juan Pablo

Paula Pardo, Federico de V 112 *Venez.*

"Paulino Lucero" (*pseud.*) *see* Ascasubi, Hilario

Pauta R., Luis E 56 *Ecua.*

Pautret, Andrés BDC 76; Cu 126 *Cu.*

Pávez, Antonio C 37 *Chil.*

Pavía, Lázaro NM 40 *Mex.*

Pavletich, Esteban (1906-) BAP 93; IE 218 *Per.*

Pavón, M. A. SD 25 *Dom.*

Payno, Manuel (1810-1894) BHLA 345; CHL 404; CLH 352; G 368; HLM 431; HLMex 176; Ig 257; NM 3, 40; TM 262, 469 *Mex.*

Payno y M., M. PM 65 *Mex.*

Payró, Roberto Jorge (1867-1928) A 54, 89; AT II, 1052; BHLA 504; CHL 196, 201; CLH 168; G 317; LAC 35, 129; PLHA 292; SASS 64 *Arg.*

Paz, Arturo (1867-1915) G 368; Ig 261; NM 41 *Mex.*

Paz, Ireneo (1836-1924) G 368; Ig 263; NM 3, 41; PM 65; TM 262 *Mex.*

Paz, Jorge A 54, 89 *Arg.*

Paz, José María ("Manco Paz") (1791-1854) LA VI, 1060 *Arg.*

"Paz, Julio de la" (*pseud.*) *see* Baudouin, Julio

Paz, Luis (1854-) B 16; BHLA 381; BT 215 *Bol.*

"Paz, Manco" (*pseud.*) *see* Paz, José María

Paz, Martín (1890?-) FPA 318, 334; PM 65 *Mex.*

Paz, Ricardo A. A 54, 89 *Arg.*

Paz Castillo, Fernando V 112 *Venez.*

Paz Díaz, Ezequiel P. (1871-) WLA 302 *Arg.*

Paz García, Carlos V 112; VPF 208 *Venez.*

Paz Soldán, Juan Pedro (1869-) P 26 *Per.*

Paz Soldán, Mariano Felipe (1821-1886) BHLA 382; P 26 *Per.*

Paz Soldán y Unánue, Pedro ("Juan de Arona") (1839-1895) AEHA 659; BHLA 320, 383; CHL 296; CLH 251; LP 365; P 2, 26; PPe 28; SASS 412 *Per.*

Paz y Figueroa, María Antonia de la (1730-) LA IV, 613 *Arg.*

Paz y Miño, Luis Telmo (1884-) E 56 *Ecua.*

Pazós Kanki, Vicente (1780-1851?) B 16; BHLA 164; CHL 309; LB 575 *Bol.*

Pedreira, Antonio Salvador (1899-) PR 20, 53; QPR (1) 119; WLA 303 *P.R.*

Pedro, Valentín de V 112 *Venez.*

"Pedro Lacor" (*pseud.*) *see* Cossío, Francisco de

"Pedro Sienna" (*pseud.*) *see* Pérez Cordero, Pedro

Pedroni, José (1899-) A 54; APAM 561; LAC 83, 144 *Arg.*

Pedroso, Regino (1897-) LH 135; PJC 194; PoC 186 *Cu.*

Pedroso de Arriaza, A. Cu 126 *Cu.*

Peinado Arguíndegui, Pedro V 112 *Venez.*

Peire, José E. A 54 *Arg.*

Peláez, José G. Cu 126 *Cu.*

Peláez, María Cristina C 17 *Chil.*

Peláez C., Aurelio Co 54 *Col.*

Peláez y Tapia, J. C 37 *Chil.*

Pelayo, Félix M. A 54 *Arg.*

Pelissot, Felisberto (*or* Filiberto) A 54; LA VIII, 628 *Arg.*

Pellegrini, Carlos (1845-1906) A 55; LA VII, 340 *Arg.*

Pellerano, Arturo B. SD 25 *Dom.*

Pellerano, Fernando A. SD 25 *Dom.*

Pellerano, Isabel A. de PA 349; SD 25 *Dom.*

Pellerano, José Francisco SD 25 *Dom.*

Pellerano, Juan José (1888-) A 55, 89 *Arg.*

Pellerano Alfau, Arturo J. SD 25 *Dom.*

Pellerano Castro, Arturo B. (1865-1916) CHL 497; CLH 437; FPA 228, 243; LD 93; PA 346; PD 149; SD 25 *Dom.*

Pellés, Erasmo Cu 126; PCu 207 *Cu.*

Pellicciotti, Raimundo T. M. E 56 *Ecua.*

Pellicer, Eustaquio A 55 *Arg.*

Pellicer Cámara, Carlos (1897-) AMP 149; APEH 1137; APMM 160; BHLA 559; HLM 526; PM 65; PMM 141; SASS 378 *Mex.*

Pelliza, Mariano A. (1837-1902) A 55 *Arg.*

Pelliza de Sagasta, Josefina (1848-1888) A 55; LA VIII, 784 *Arg.*

"Pena, Leonardo" (*pseud.*) *see* Pérez Kallens, Ignacio

Penagos, Ranulfo Ig 269; NM 42 *Mex.*

Penella, Manuel TM 500 *Mex.*

Peniche, P. Ig 270; NM 42; TM 264, 469 *Mex.*

Penichet, A. Cu 127 *Cu.*

"Penna, Leonardo" (*pseud.*) *see* Pérez Kallens, Ignacio

"Pensador Mexicano, El" (*pseud.*) *see* Fernández de Lizardi, José Joaquín

Pensón, César Nicolás (1855-1902) CHL 495; CLH 435; FPA 227, 234; LD 96; PA 350; PD 158; SD 25 *Dom.*

Penzini Hernández, J. V 112 *Venez.*

Peña, Belisario (1834-1906) AC I, 219; II, 157; ALC I, 237; Co 54; E 56, 75; RHLC 142 *Col.*

Peña, Benedicto V 112 *Venez.*

Peña, Carlos María de PIU I, 220 *Uru.*

Peña, David (1863-1930) A 55, 89; AT I, 386; CHL 199; G 317; GLO 238 *Arg.*

Peña, Enrique (1849-) AT I, 305 *Arg.*

Peña, Ignacio A. de la ("Ignotus") (1860-1916) Ig 270; NM 28, 42 *Mex.*

Peña, Israel V 112 *Venez.*

Peña, J. Santiago Co 54 *Col.*

Peña, José Zeferino de la TM 264 *Mex.*

Peña, Lorenzo R. (1849-1898) E 57 *Ecua.*

Peña, Miguel V 112 *Venez.*

Peña, Pedro A. Co 54 *Col.*

Peña, Rafael Ángel de la (1837-1906) HLM 497; NM 3 *Mex.*

Peña Barrenechea, Enrique BAP 85; BHLA 610 *Per.*

Peña Barrenechea, Ricardo BAP 61 *Per.*

Peña de Calderón, Jacinta E 57 *Ecua.*

Peña Munizaga, Nicolás C 53, 69; CL 520 *Chil.*

Peña Peralta, Alonso de la PM 43, 66 *Mex.*

Peña Rodríguez, Manuel A 55 *Arg.*

Peña Viuda de González, Mercedes V. Cu 127 *Cu.*

Peña y Reinoso, Manuel de Jesús PA 370; PD 187; SD 26 *Dom.*

Peña y Reyes, Antonio de la (1869-1928) HLM 497; IE 219; NM 3; TM 562 *Mex.*

Peña y Troncoso, Gonzalo Ig 271; NM 42 *Mex.*

Peñafiel, Antonio PM 65 *Mex.*

Peñalosa Mondragón, Benito SCL 70, 629 *Per.*

"Peñalva, Simón" (*pseud.*) *see* Ascasubi, Hilario

Peñalver, F. V. V 112 *Venez.*

Peñaranda, Carlos PR 25 *P.R.*

Peñaranda, Claudio (1883-) B 16; BT 219; FPA 54, 75 *Bol.*

Peñaranda, F. Co 54 *Col.*

Peñas, Germán G. de las Cu 127 *Cu.*

Peñuela, Cayo Leónidas Co 54 *Col.*

Peñuela, Ramón I. V 112 *Venez.*

Peoli, Alejandro LV 114; V 112 *Venez.*

Peoli, Gonzalo (1835-1871) Cu 127 *Cu.*

Peón Cisneros, Arturo PM 66; TM 264 *Mex.*

Peón del Valle, José (1866-1924) AMP 281; Cu 127; G 368; NM 42; PM 66; PMe II, 61; PoM 376 *Mex.*

Peón y Contreras, José (1843-1907) AEHA 661; AMP 280; BHLA 443; CHL 411; CLH 357; Cu 127; HLM 461; HLMex 199; Ig 272; NM 42; PM 66; PMe II, 51; PoM 121; TM 117, 264, 562 *Mex.*

Peón y Varona, Alicia Cu 127; Ig 273; NM 42 *Mex.*

Pepper, Eduardo V 112 *Venez.*

"Pequén, El" (*pseud.*) C 37 *Chil.*

Pequeño, Pedro Néstor BDC 76; Cu 127 *Cu.*

Pequet, J. F. U 14 *Uru.*

104 A REFERENCE INDEX

"Perales, Juan" (*pseud.*) *see* Pereda, Setembrino Ezequiel

Peralta, Alejandro BAP 71; P 27 *Per.*

Peralta, Eduardo M. CA 42 *C.R.*

Peralta, Eleodoro (1881-) A 55, 89 *Arg.*

Peralta, Hernán G. CA 42; EPCR 586 *C.R.*

Peralta, José Francisco (1788-1844) EPCR 19 *C.R.*

Peralta, Manuel María de (1847-1930) CA 42, 43; EPCR 38; GPCA II, 373 *C.R.*

Peralta, María Isabel PCU 64 *Uru.*

Peralta, Maximiliano (-1922) CA 43 *C.R.*

Peralta, Pablo A 55 *Arg.*

Peralta Barnuevo Rocha y Benavides, Pedro José de (1663-1743) BHLA 97, 125; CHL 21, 28; CLH 24; G 382; GLO 252; HPHA II, 207; LP 340; P 27; SCL 383, 629 *Per.*

Peralta Flores, Jerónimo C 53 *Chil.*

Peramás, José Manuel (1732-1793) LA IV, 590; SCL 421, 629 *Arg.*

Peramás, Manuel HPHA II, 387 *Arg.*

Peraza, Celestino V 113 *Venez.*

Peraza de Zell, Rosa L. Cu 127 *Cu.*

Perazzo, Nicolás V 113 *Venez.*

Perdomo, Apolinar PA 352; PD 177; SD 26 *Dom.*

Perdomo, José R. SD 26 *Dom.*

Perdomo, Josefa A. SD 26 *Dom.*

Perdomo, Rosendo V 113 *Venez.*

Pereda, Clemente PR 38 *P.R.*

Pereda, Enrique Ig 273; NM 42 *Mex.*

Pereda, Fernando HSLU III, pt 6, 34; PIU III, 235; PoU 143 *Uru.*

Pereda, Laura de NM 42 *Mex.*

Pereda, Setembrino Ezequiel ("Juan Perales") (1859-) U 14; UL 187; UT 399; WLA 305 *Uru.*

Pereda Valdés, Ildefonso (1899-) BHLA 642; HSLU II, pt 9, 30; PIU III, 204; PLHA 164; PU 306; U 14 *Uru.*

Peredo, Manuel HLM 466; PMe II, 69; TM 273, 427, 469, 562 *Mex.*

Peredo y Gallegos, José (1733-1813) ACe 914 *Mex.*

"Peregrina, La" (*pseud.*) *see* Gómez de Avellaneda y Arteaga, Gertrudis

"Peregrino, Un" (*pseud.*) B 16 *Bol.*

Pereira *see also* Pereyra

Pereira, A. Cu 127 *Cu.*

Pereira, Antonio N. U 14 *Uru.*

Pereira, Juan de (-1682) Co 54; HLNG I, 189 *Col.*

Pereira Álvarez, Ismael V 113 *Venez.*

Pereira Gamba, Benjamín (1834-) Co 54 *Col.*

Pereira Gamba, Fortunato Co 54; E 57

Pereira Gamba, Próspero (1825-) Co 54; RHLC 98 *Col.*

Pereira Machado, Manuel V 113 *Venez.*

Pereira Medina, Leopoldo Cu 127 *Cu.*

Pereira Ocejo, Florentino PM 66; TM 273 *Mex.*

Pereira Rodríguez, José PU 308 *Uru.*

Pereira y Medina, Manuel Cu 127 *Cu.*

Perera, José Félix V 113 *Venez.*

Pereyra *see also* Pereira

Pereyra, Carlos (1871-) HLM 487; HLMex 239; SASS 391; WLA 306 *Mex.*

Pereyra, Emilia A. de ("Cleta Masa") (1891-) A 55, 78 *Arg.*

Pereyra, Francisco (hijo) SD 26 *Dom.*

Pereyra, Isabel A. A 55 *Arg.*

Pereyra, Miguel TM 273 *Mex.*

Pereyra, Rodrigo LA III, 182 *Arg.*

Pereyra y Pacheco, Miguel P 27 *Per.*

Pérez, Alfonso Macario PM 66 *Mex.*

Pérez, Álvaro TM 596 *Mex.*

Pérez, Arbonio V 113 *Venez.*

Pérez, Bartolomé Olegario (1868?-191.) FPA 228, 245; PA 369; PD 201; SD 26 *Dom.*

Pérez, Emeterio A 55 *Arg.*

Pérez, Emma (1901-) PoC 197 *Cu.*

Pérez, Enrique Co 54 *Col.*

Pérez, Eusebio L. Cu 127 *Cu.*

Pérez, Federico Cu 127 *Cu.*

Pérez, Federico Benigno SD 26 *Dom.*

Pérez, Felipe (1834-1891) BHLA 322; CHL 336; CLH 288; Co 54; HPHA II, 74; LC 138; PCo 219; RHLC 179 *Col.*

Pérez, Florencio R. A 55 *Arg.*

Pérez, Francisco de Sales CHL 368; CLH 317; V 113 *Venez.*

Pérez, Gregorio Ig 274; NM 42 *Mex.*

Pérez, Isidoro Mariano (1832-) P 27 *Per.*

Pérez, J. A. V 113 *Venez.*

Pérez, J. Alejandro Co 55 *Col.*

Pérez, Joaquín María Co 55; E 57 *Col.*

Pérez, José Antonio C 17; NC 390, 437 *Chil.*

Pérez, José E. BDC 76; Cu 128 *Cu.*

Pérez, José Joaquín (1845-1900) BHLA 436; CHL 494; CLH 434; FPA 227, 229; HPHA I, 310; LD 90; PA 353; PD 160; SD 26 *Dom.*

Pérez, José T. PM 66; TM 274 *Mex.*

1. Pérez, Juan E 57 *Ecua.*

2. Pérez, Juan NM 43; TM 596 *Mex.*

Pérez, Juan Francisco (1873-) Par 21; PPa 51 *Para.*

Pérez, Justo (1830-) HL II, 75 *Hond.*

Pérez, Lázaro María (1824-1892) Co 55; LC 139; PCo 225; PLHA 76; RHLC 98, 165 *Col.*

Pérez, Lucila Estrada de (1856-) HL II, 393 *Hond.*

Pérez, Luis G. Cu 128 *Cu.*

Pérez, Luis Ignacio C 17 *Chil.*

Pérez, Luis Marino (1882-) CT 227; Cu 128 *Cu.*

Pérez, Manuel Antonio V 113 *Venez.*

Pérez, Manuel José (1830-1888) Co 55; Pan 16 *Pan.*

Pérez, Marcelino C. U 14 *Uru.*

Pérez, Miquelángel V 113 *Venez.*

Pérez, P. C 17; NC 499 *Chil.*

Pérez, Pedro Par 21 *Para.*

Pérez, Pedro Ildefonso (1826-1869) HPM 835 *Mex.*

Pérez, Ponciano PM 66 *Mex.*

Pérez, Rafael Félix PJC 192 *Cu.*

Pérez, Renato V 113 *Venez.*

Pérez, Ricardo NM 43 *Mex.*

"Pérez, Rosina" (*pseud.*) *see* Parejo, Antonio

Pérez, S. U 14 *Uru.*

Pérez, Santiago (1830-1900) BHLA 322; CHL 336; CLH 288; Co 55; LC 137; PCo 229; RHLC 164 *Col.*

Pérez, Trinidad Manuel P 27 *Per.*
Pérez, Ubdón A. V 113 *Venez.*
Pérez, Udón BHLA 542; LV 337; V 83, 113 *Venez.*
Pérez Alfonseca, Eurípides SD 26 *Dom.*
Pérez Alfonseca, Ricardo PA 362; PD 189; SD 26 *Dom.*
Pérez Ambulagen, Juan PM 66 *Mex.*
Pérez Beato, Manuel (1857-) Cu 128 *Cu.*
Pérez Bello, Rolando C 37 *Chil.*
Pérez Bermúdez, Juan F. V 113 *Venez.*
Pérez Bibbins, Manuel HLM 467; PM 66; TM 274, 471 *Mex.*
Pérez Bonalde, Juan Antonio (1846-1892) AEHA 668; BHLA 432; CHL 371, 511; CLH 319; FPA 550, 570; G 393; LV 67, 69, 304; PLHA 77; SAL 13, 48, 113; SASS 512; V 113 *Venez.*
Pérez Cabello, Rafael ("Zerep") Cu 128, 183; PA 90 *Cu.*
Pérez Calama, José E 57, 75 *Ecua.*
Pérez Calvo, J. A. V 114 *Venez.*
Pérez Canto, Julio (1867-) WLA 307 *Chil.*
Pérez Castellanos, ? (-1915) PIU I, 51 *Uru.*
Pérez Cobati, José Antonio A 55 *Arg.*
Pérez Colman, Enrique A 55 *Arg.*
Pérez Cordero, Marcial (-1915) PCh 427 *Chil.*
Pérez Cordero, Pedro ("Pedro Sienna") (1893-) APEH 881; C 20, 40; PCC xviii, 163; PCh 423 *Chil.*
Pérez Coronado, José Antonio LV 28 *Venez.*
Pérez de Alejo, Miguel A. (1842-1898) Cu 128 *Cu.*
Pérez de Carvajal, Emma (1890-) B 16; BT 221 *Bol.*
Pérez de Gálvez, Miguel TM 275 *Mex.*
Pérez de la Vega, Serapio PM 66 *Mex.*
Pérez de León, Herminia Ig 274; NM 43 *Mex.*
Pérez de León, J. A. NM 43 *Mex.*
Pérez de Luarca, Manuel Cu 128 *Cu.*
Pérez de Menacho, Juan SCL 453, 630 *Per.*
Pérez de Morales, Emilio Cu 128 *Cu.*
Pérez de Oliva, Manuel Cu 128 *Cu.*
Pérez de Vargas, José P 28 *Per.*
Pérez de Zambrana, Luisa (1837-1922) BHLA 328; CHL 454; CLH 395; Cu 128, 129; HLC 163; PCu 208; PJC 279 *Cu.*
Pérez Díaz, Lucila Luciani de V 114 *Venez.*
Pérez Enamorado, Eduardo Cu 129 *Cu.*
Pérez Flores, Manuel V. E 57 *Ecua.*
Pérez Freites, Mercedes de V 114 *Venez.*
Pérez Freytes, Francisco J. PR 38 *P.R.*
Pérez Fuente, José Antonio HPM 452 *Mex.*
Pérez Fuentes, Francisco ("Saint Louis") Cu 129 *Cu.*
Pérez Gallardo, Ricardo M. PM 66 *Mex.*
Pérez Garcés, Luis E. SD 27 *Dom.*
Pérez García, José (1721-) SCL 500, 630 *Chil.*
Pérez Gomar, Gregorio HSLU III, pt 4, 20 *Uru.*

Pérez González, Eusebio BDC 76; Cu 129 *Cu.*
Pérez Guevara, Ada V 114 *Venez.*
Pérez Hernández, H. V 114 *Venez.*
Pérez Kallens, Ignacio ("Leonardo Penna or Pena") C 17; NC 494; PLHA 267 *Chil.*
Pérez Lazo, Mauricio V 114 *Venez.*
Pérez Lopes, A. Cu 129 *Cu.*
Pérez Losada, José (1879-) BDC 114; BP 505, 514, 623; PR 14, 20, 27; QPR (1) 203 *P.R.*
Pérez Martínez, Marcelino (187.-) FPA 402, 417; Par 21; PPa 165 *Para.*
Pérez Matos, Mary de V 115 *Venez.*
Pérez Milicua, Ernesto TM 276 *Mex.*
Pérez Montes de Oca, Julia (-1875) Cu 129 *Cu.*
Pérez Morales, Emilio Cu 129 *Cu.*
Pérez Moris, José (1840-1881) PR 27 *P.R.*
Pérez Nieto, Estanislao CHL 218; CLH 181 *Uru.*
Pérez Pazmiño, Ismael (1876-) E 57; WLA 307 *Ecua.*
Pérez Peña, Aurelio TM 276 *Mex.*
Pérez Perozo, Víctor Manuel E 57; V 115 *Ecua.*
Pérez Petit, Víctor (1871-) A 55, 89; BHLA 444, 508, 549; CHL 231; CLH 192, 193; HSLU III, pt 4, 34, 39; IE 220; LU 64, 676, 683, 691; LUr 496, 539; PIU II, 313; PLHA 271; PU 186; SAL 187, 189; SASS 489; U 14; UL 187; UT 405; WLA 308 *Uru.*
Pérez-Pierret, Antonio PA 232; PP 246; PR 38 *P.R.*
Pérez Piña, Pedro I. AMP 285; NM 43 *Mex.*
Pérez Quiñónez, Ulpiano (-1918) E 57 *Ecua.*
Pérez Ramírez, Juan (1544?-) HLM 116, 121; HPM 89; TM 277 *Mex.*
Pérez Reinoso, Ramiro BAP 47; P 28 *Per.*
Pérez Rioja, Bonifacio TM 471 *Mex.*
Pérez Ríos, E. PP 343 *P.R.*
Pérez Rosales, Vicente (1807-1886) BHLA 217, 380; C 17; CHL 285; CLH 242; HC 202; NC 391, 438 *Chil.*
Pérez Salazar y Osorio, Ignacio ("Alidauro Zacintio") PM 66, 85 *Mex.*
Pérez Salazar y Venegas, Manuel HPM 846; PM 67; TM 471 *Mex.*
Pérez Santana y Reyes Messa, A. C 37 *Chil.*
Pérez Soto, V. V 115 *Venez.*
Pérez Taylor, Rafael LAS 208; TM 277 *Mex.*
Pérez Triana, Santiago (1858-1916) Co 56; LC 190; PCo 235 *Col.*
Pérez Valencia, Enrique G 368 *Mex.*
Pérez Velasco, Antonio ACe 917 *Mex.*
Pérez Verdía, Antonio TM 278 *Mex.*
Pérez Verdía, Benito Javier PM 67 *Mex.*
Pérez Verdía, José María TM 472 *Mex.*
Pérez Verdía, Luis HLM 490, 492; TM 563 *Mex.*
Pérez y Curis, Manuel (-1920) PIU II, 65; PU 181; U 14 *Uru.*
Pérez y Hernández, José María Cu 129 *Cu.*

Pérez y Montes de Oca, Luisa *see* Pérez de Zambrana, Luisa

Pérez y Ontiveros, Esther PM 67 *Mex.*

Pérez y Ramírez, Manuel María (1781-1853) Cu 128; HLC 25; RLC 47, 52 *Cu.*

Pérez y Santa Cruz, Laureano ARC 33; Cu 129 *Cu.*

Pérez y Soto, Atenójenes (1886-) G 368; Ig 275; NM 43 *Mex.*

Pérez y Soto, Juan Bautista (1834?-) Co 56; E 57, 75; V 115

Pérez Zambrano, Arturo Cu 129 *Cu.*

Pérez Zamora, Aurelio Cu 129 *Cu.*

Pérez Zeledón, Pedro (1854-) EPCR 213 *C.R.*

Pérez Zúñiga, Santiago ARC 41 *Cu.*

Perfecto de Salas, José BHC II, 452 *Chil.*

Perigault, Manuela Pan 16 *Pan.*

"Perogrullo" (*pseud.*) E 58 *Ecua.*

Peroni, José C 53 *Chil.*

Perotti, Italo Eduardo U 14 *Uru.*

Perozo, César N. SD 27 *Dom.*

Perozo, L. PD 200; SD 27 *Dom.*

"Perrichon, Monsieur" (*pseud.*) *see* Thévenin, Leopoldo

Perrier, José Luis PR 8 *P.R.*

Perrin, Tomás G. TM 501 *Mex.*

Perrius, Guillermo C 53 *Chil.*

Perroblillos NM 43 *Mex.*

Perry, David Enrique (1899-) C 38; PCC xvii, 151; PCh 357 *Chil.*

Pertuz, Julia de ("Lydia Bolena") CA 7, 43; IBCR IV, 335 *C.R.*

Perygny, Maurice de IBCR IV, 241 *C.R.*

Pesado, Isabel HLM 398 *Mex.*

Pesado, José Joaquín (1801-1861) AEHA 683; BHLA 227; CHL 392; CLH 339; HLM 288; HLMex 152; HPHA I, 134; HPM 664; NM 43; PM 67; PMe II, 73; TM 563 *Mex.*

Pesquera Vallenilla, Vicente V 115 *Venez.*

Petit de Murat, Ulises A 55 *Arg.*

Petit Marfan, Magdalena BHLA 550; WLA 309 *Chil.*

Petit Senn, J. IBCR IV, 267 *C.R.*

Petray, Antonio A 55, 90 *Arg.*

Petrovik, Juan BAP 115 *Per.*

Petrovitch, Bartolomé Javier PR 38 *P.R.*

Peynado, Francisco J. SD 27 *Dom.*

Peyret, Bernardo L. A 72 *Arg.*

Peza, Juan de Dios (1852-1910) AEHA 686; AMP 311; BHLA 438; CHL 415; CLH 361; G 368; HLM 387; HLMex 196; NM 3, 43; Par 21; PM 67, 73; PMe II, 83; PoM 231; TM 279 *Mex.*

Pezoa Véliz (*or* Velis), Carlos (1879-1908) APEH 515; BHLA 467; C 38; CMPC 86; FPA 192, 217; G 326; HC 229; MSAP 168, 316; N 181; PCC xiii, 57; PCh 203; SASS 152 *Chil.*

Pezuela y Lobo, Jacobo de la (1811-1882) PR 20; RLC 38, 177 *Sp.*

Pi, Wifredo Francisco (1893-) U 15 *Uru.*

Piaggio, Juan A. A 55 *Arg.*

Piaggio de Tucker, Juana María A 55 *Arg.*

Piar, Manuel V 115 *Venez.*

1. Picado, Teodoro CA 43; EPCR 651; IBCR IV, 148 *C.R.*

2. Picado, Teodoro (hijo) CA 43 *C.R.*

Picado Twight, Clodomiro (1887-) EPCR 476 *C.R.*

Piccirilli, Ricardo A 55 *Arg.*

Pico, Manuel A 55 *Arg.*

Pico, Pedro E. A 55, 90 *Arg.*

Picón, Antonio I. V 115 *Venez.*

Picón, Juan de Dios V 115 *Venez.*

Picón-Febres, Gabriel (hijo) LV 119; V 116 *Venez.*

Picón-Febres, Gonzalo (1860-1919) AEHA 905; CHL 379; CLH 329; SASS 519; V 115; VPF 81 *Venez.*

Picón Lares, Eduardo V 116 *Venez.*

Picón Lares, Roberto V 116 *Venez.*

Picón Salas, Mariano (1901-) BHLA 581, 583; G 393; LAS 201; V 116; WLA 310 *Venez.*

Picone, José C. A 55, 90 *Arg.*

Pichardo, Bernardo SD 27 *Dom.*

Pichardo, Emilio (1816-1870) Cu 129 *Cu.*

Pichardo, Esteban (1799-1879) Cu 129; RLC 139 *Cu.*

Pichardo, Francisco J. (1873-) Cu 130; PA 95 *Cu.*

Pichardo, J. Furcy PD 182 *Dom.*

Pichardo, José Francisco SD 27 *Dom.*

Pichardo, José M. SD 27 *Dom.*

Pichardo, Manuel Serafín (1869-) CHL 489; CLH 429; Cu 130; PA 91; PCu 210; SASS 286 *Cu.*

Pichardo B., Eliodoro BDC 77; Cu 130 *Cu.*

Pichardo Moya, Felipe (1892-) APEH 841; BDC 77; Cu 130; PCu 213; PJC 168; PoC 207; RLC 365 *Cu.*

Pichardo y Arredondo, Próspero ("Florimel") Cu 58, 130 *Cu.*

Pié y Faura, Fernando (1831-1868) Cu 130 *Cu.*

Piedra, Francisco S. Cu 130 *Cu.*

Piedra, José Antonio E 58 *Ecua.*

Piedra Blanco, Ramón Cu 130 *Cu.*

Piedra-Bueno, Andrés de (1903-) Cu 130; HLC 207 *Cu.*

Piedrahita, José Gregorio RHLC 99 *Col.*

Piedrahita, Vicente (1833-1878) E 58 *Ecua.*

Pieter, Dionisio SD 27 *Dom.*

Pietri, Juan V 116 *Venez.*

Pildaín, Pablo (1848-) BDC 77; Cu 130 *Cu.*

Pillado, José A. A 73 *Arg.*

"Pim, Job" (*pseud.*) *see* Pimentel, Francisco (2.)

Pimentel, Eduardo A 55 *Arg.*

1. Pimentel, Francisco (1832-1893) CHL 410; CLH 357; HLM 496; HPM 3; NM 3; TM 564 *Mex.*

2. Pimentel, Francisco ("Job Pim") (1889-) LV 132, 338; V 116; WLA 310 *Venez.*

Pimentel, José A. Cu 130 *Cu.*

Pimentel, Margarita A. de ("Margot") V 40, 109, 116 *Venez.*

Pimentel Coronel, Manuel (1863-1907) AEHA 905; CHL 375; CLH 323; LV 321; V 116 *Venez.*

Pimentel de Marvez, Isabel Teresa V 117 *Venez.*

Pimentel Ixtlilxochil, Fernando Alva (1580-1649) HPM 119 *Mex.*

"Pimentel y Vargas, Fermín" (*pseud.*) *see* Camargo, Rafael María

Pina Domínguez, Mariano (1840-1895) Cu 130 *Cu.*

"Pinabete Alcornoque y Astragalo, Girón de" (*pseud.*) *see* Tablada, José Juan

Pinares, Lucio Ig 276; NM 43 *Mex.*

Pineau, Nacha A 55 *Arg.*

"Pineda, A." (*pseud.*) *see* Aquenza, Jacinto

Pineda, Antonio B. (1837-1869) Co 56 *Col.*

Pineda, Celso TM 282 *Mex.*

Pineda, José M. SD 27 *Dom.*

Pinelo Río, Fausto TM 610 *Mex.*

Pini, César A. (1874-) A 56, 90 *Arg.*

Pinilla, Claudio (1859-) B 16; BT 223; Par 21 *Bol.*

Pinilla, Sabino (1857-1909) B 16 *Bol.*

Pinilla Urrutia, José María (1881-) AP 261; Pan 16 *Pan.*

Pinincho U 15 *Uru.*

"Pino, Ángel" (*pseud.*) *see* Díaz Garcés, Joaquín

Pino, Reinaldo E 58 *Ecua.*

Pino de la Cruz y Penichet, María del Cu 130 *Cu.*

Pino Roca, J. Gabriel E 58 *Ecua.*

Pino Suárez, José María PM 68 *Mex.*

Pinochet Lebrún, Tancredo C 18 *Chil.*

Pinto, Benigno C 18; NC 213 *Chil.*

Pinto, José Joaquín E 58 *Ecua.*

Pinto, Manuel María (hijo) (1871-) B 16; PB 163 *Bol.*

Pinto, Mercedes HSLU II, pt 6, 25; LAS 201 *Uru.*

Pinto, Octavio (1890-) A 56; APAM 390 *Arg.*

Pinto, P. N. C 18; NC 439 *Chil.*

Pinto y Valdemoro BDC 77 *Cu.*

Pinuer, Ignacio SCL 511, 630 *Chil.*

Pinzón, José Rafael (1843-) Co 56 *Col.*

Pinzón, Ricardo V. Co 56 *Col.*

Pinzón Rico, José María (1834-1886) AC I, 305; CHL 345; CLH 296; Co 56; HPHA II, 74; LC 159 *Col.*

Pinzón Uzcátegui, M. V 117 *Venez.*

Piña, Ramón (1819-1861) BDC 77; Cu 130; RLC 139 *Cu.*

Piña y Varona, Andrés de Cu 131 *Cu.*

Piñango Ordóñez, Juan V 117 *Venez.*

Piñeiro *see also* Piñeyro

Piñeiro Chazas, Manuel HSLU III, pt 4, 34 *Uru.*

Piñera Llera, Virgilio (1914-) PoC 211 *Cu.*

Piñeres, Raúl CA 43 *C.R.*

Piñérez, J. G. Co 56 *Col.*

Piñero, Francisco M. NPA 268 *Arg.*

Piñero, Norberto A 55 *Arg.*

Piñero, Sergio (hijo) A 56; LAC 124 *Arg.*

Piñeyro *see also* Piñeiro

Piñeyro, Julio A. PD 185; SD 27 *Dom.*

Piñeyro del Campo, Luis CHL 222; CLH 185; U 15 *Uru.*

Piñeyro y Barri, Enrique (1839-1911) AEHA 689; BHLA 389; CHL 467, 471, 474; CLH 411, 415; Cu 131; G 341; GLO 245; HLC 70; RLC 295 *et passim Cu.*

"Pío Tenazas" (*pseud.*) *see* Macpherson, Telasco A.

Piquet, Juan Francisco HSLU III, pt 4, 47; UL 188 *Uru.*

Pirón, Alexis TM 501 *Mex.*

Pirovano, Emilio A 56 *Arg.*

Pisón y Vargas, Juan TM 282 *Mex.*

Pita, Santiago HLC 24 *Cu.*

Pita Rodríguez, Félix (1901-) LH 132; PoC 213 *Cu.*

Pitaluga y Delgado, Rafael (-1857) BDC 77; Cu 131 *Cu.*

Pittier de Fábrega, Henri François (1857-) CA 43 *C.R.*

Piwonka Gilaberto, Ricardo C 18; NC 391 *Chil.*

Pizano Restrepo, Roberto Co 56 *Col.*

Pizarro, Domingo L. PU 310; U 15 *Uru.*

Pizarro, Manuel Alonso PR 14 *P.R.*

Pizarro, Martín Cu 131 *Cu.*

Pizarro, Nicolás Ig 276; NM 43; PM 68 *Mex.*

Pizarro, Pedro SCL 70, 630 *Per.*

Pizarro, Ramona BDC 78; Cu 132 *Cu.*

Pizarro Espoz, Luis C 46 *Chil.*

Pizarro y Morejón, Juan Cu 132 *Cu.*

Pizzi de Porras, Enrique Cu 132 *Cu.*

Pizzurno, Pablo A. (1865-) AT II, 711 *Arg.*

"Pla, Constantino" (*pseud.*) *see* Arias Suárez, Eduardo

Pla, José Armando ARC 58, 75 *Cu.*

Placencia, Alfredo R. (1873-) G 368; PM 68 *Mex.*

"Plácido" (*pseud.*) *see* Valdés, Gabriel de la Concepción

Planas, Juan Manuel (1877-) Cu 132; G 341 *Cu.*

Planas, Miguel TM 610 *Mex.*

Planas, Simón V 117 *Venez.*

Planas y Hernández, Emilio ARC 59 *Cu.*

Plancarte, José HPM 475 *Mex.*

Planchart, Enrique PLHA 149; V 117 *Venez.*

Planchart, Julio V 88, 117; VPF 113 *Venez.*

"Platón" (*pseud.*) E 58 *Ecua.*

Plaza, Antonio (1833-1882) CLH 351; HPM 874; PM 69; PMe II, 115; PoM 159 *Mex.*

Plaza, José Antonio de (1809-1854) Co 56; RHLC 178, 198 *Col.*

Plaza, Ramón de la V 117 *Venez.*

Plaza y Jaén, Cristóbal Bernardo TM 564 *Mex.*

Plumbensis, Nicolaus PM 69 *Mex.*

Pobeda *see* Poveda

Pobess Chavarría, Ángel C 53 *Chil.*

Poblet Cruzat, M. PCh 283 *Chil.*

Poblete, Aníbal PCh 325 *Chil.*

Poblete, Egidio ("Ronquillo") C 20; G 326; NC 440 *Chil.*

Poblete Garín, Alberto C 18; NC 391 *Chil.*

Poblete Garín, Manuel C 38; PCh 165 *Chil.*

Pocaterra, José Rafael (1890-) BHLA 520; PLHA 273; V 117; VPF 129; WLA 313 *Venez.*

Podestá, Arturo (1883-) A 56, 90 *Arg.*

Podestá, Carlos María A 56 *Arg.*

Podestá, José J. A 56, 90 *Arg.*

Podestá, Manuel T. (1853-1918) A 56; CHL 193; LA VIII, 681 *Arg.*

Podetti, José Ramiro A 56 *Arg.*

Poëy, Andrés (1826-) Cu 132 *Cu.*

Poëy, Felipe (1799-1891) Cu 132; PA 99; PCu 220; RLC 70, 89, 147, 159 *et passim Cu.*

Poëy, Rodolfo D. (1847-1911) Cu 132 *Cu.*
Poirier, Eduardo NC 227 *Chil.*
Pol, José B 17 *Bol.*
Pola, Rafael BDC 78 *Cu.*
Polanco, J. Onésimo PD 188; SD 27 *Dom.*
Polanco, Manuel E 58 *Ecua.*
Polanco Casanova, Rodolfo (1868-) C 69; NC 440; PCh 263 *Chil.*
Polanco de Hoffman, Clarissa ("Clary") C 6 *Chil.*
Polar, Jorge P 28 *Per.*
Polar, Juan Manuel G 382 *Per.*
Poleo, Manuel María V 118 *Venez.*
Poleo Gonell, Luis V 118 *Venez.*
"Polibio, Ego" (*pseud.*) P 8 *Per.*
Policarpo, Juan TM 282 *Mex.*
"Polidoro" (*pseud.*) *see* Valdés, José Policarpo
"Polifemo de Coustillac" (*pseud.*) *see* Ruiz de Esparza, Juan
Pólit, Manuel María E 58 *Ecua.*
Polo, Ángel M. Par 21 *Para.*
Polo, José Toribio P 28 *Per.*
"Polo, Sancho" (*pseud.*) *see* Rabasa, Emilio
Polo de Ondegardo, Juan SCL 135, 631 *Per.*
Polo Taforó, María Dolores PR 27 *P.R.*
"Pollo, Anastasio el" (*pseud.*) *see* Campo, Estanislao del
Pollo Darraque, Ricardo PU 311; U 15 *Uru.*
"Pomar, Natal del" (*pseud.*) *see* Almazán, Pascual
Pombo, Beatriz Albertina U 15 *Uru.*
Pombo, Jorge (1857-1912) Co 56; RHLC 144 *Col.*
Pombo, Lino de (1797-1862) Co 57; RHLC 111 *Col.*
Pombo, Manuel (1827-1898) Co 57; LC 144; RHLC 126 *Col.*
Pombo, Manuel de (1769-) HLNG II, 341 *Col.*
Pombo, Miguel de HLNG II, 267, 341 *Col.*
Pombo, Rafael ("Edda") (1833-1912) AC I, 75; II, 87; AEHA 689; ALC I, 191; BHLA 323; CHL 345; CLH 296; Co 57; CoL 269; FPA 82, 108; G 328, 330; GLO 240; LC 133; PCo 237; PLHA 76; RHLC 130; SASS 222 *Col.*
Pompa, Elías Calixto ("K. Listo") V 89, 118 *Venez.*
Pompa, Gerónimo V 118 *Venez.*
Ponce, Aníbal A 56; LAC 120, 155 *Arg.*
Ponce, Carlos A 56 *Arg.*
Ponce, Caupolicán C 18, 38 *Chil.*
Ponce, Enrique C 38 *Chil.*
Ponce, J. M. V 118 *Venez.*
Ponce, José E. Cu 132 *Cu.*
Ponce, Luis (1839-1875) HPM 865; PM 69 *Mex.*
Ponce, Manuel M. TM 610 *Mex.*
Ponce, Mateo TM 282 *Mex.*
Ponce, Nicolás Clemente (1866-) E 59; PE 251 *Ecua.*
Ponce Aguilera, Salomón (1868-) AP 263; Pan 16 *Pan.*
Ponce de León, Francisco BHC I, 420; SCL 275, 631 *Chil.*
Ponce de León, José María (1845-1882) Co 57; RHLC 169 *Col.*

Ponce de León, Juan Bautista (-1875?) Cu 132 *Cu.*
Ponce de León, Leonardo A. BDC 78; PR 14, 38 *P.R.*
Ponce de León, Leonardo H. PR 28 *P.R.*
Ponce de León, Néstor Cu 132 *Cu.*
Ponce de León, Pedro PM 69 *Mex.*
Ponce de León, Rafael PM 69 *Mex.*
Ponce de León, Santiago V 118 *Venez.*
Ponce y Font, Bernardo NM 43; PM 69; TM 565 *Mex.*
Poncet y de Cárdenas, Carolina CT 559; Cu 132; G 341 *Cu.*
Pondal, José Agustín Cu 133 *Cu.*
Ponferrada, Juan Oscar A 56 *Arg.*
Pons, J. B. Cu 133 *Cu.*
Pons Lezica, Cipriano A 56 *Arg.*
Pons Lezica, Héctor A 56, 90 *Arg.*
Ponte, Andrés F. V 118 *Venez.*
Ponte, Esteban V 118 *Venez.*
Ponte, José Antonio V 119 *Venez.*
Ponte, Manuel María V 119 *Venez.*
Pontón, Nicolás Co 57 *Col.*
Ponvert, Hermenegildo ARC 59 *Cu.*
Poo, José de (1831-1898) BDC 78; Cu 133 *Cu.*
Popolizio, Enrique A 56 *Arg.*
Porcel, Agustín de B 17 *Bol.*
"Porfirio Barba Jacob" (*pseud.*) *see* Osorio, Miguel Ángel
Porras, Belisario (1856-) AP 277; Pan 16 *Pan.*
Porras, Emilio V 119 *Venez.*
Porras, José Ángel (1859-) Co 57 *Col.*
Porras, José Lizardo Co 57 *Col.*
Porras, Manuel María V 119 *Venez.*
Porras Barrenechea, Raúl (1895-) BHLA 603; P 28 *Per.*
Porras Troconis, Gabriel (1880-) Co 57; WLA 314 *Col.*
Porrata, Luis PR 20 *P.R.*
Porro Freire, Alicia HSLU II, pt 8, 19; LU 64, 669; U 15 *Uru.*
Porta Mencos, Humberto (1905-) PG 467 *Guat.*
Porta y Arellanos, Alfredo (1863-1925) PG 301 *Guat.*
Portal, Herminia del (1910-) PoC 216 *Cu.*
Portal, Magda (1901-) BAP 69; BHLA 608; IE 224 *Per.*
Portal Espinosa, Ismael (1863-) P 28; WLA 315 *Per.*
Portales, Diego CHL 248, 272 *Chil.*
Portilla, Anselmo de la (1816-1879) HLM 362 *Mex.*
Portilla, Juan R. de la TM 128, 283 *Mex.*
Portillo, Andrés Ig 278; NM 43; TM 283 *Mex.*
Portillo, Esteban L. TM 565 *Mex.*
Portillo, Jesús María V 119 *Venez.*
Portillo, Julio M. de P 29 *Per.*
Portillo, Miguel (1856-) Ig 278; NM 43; TM 283 *Mex.*
Portnoy, Antonio (1907-) WLA 316 *Arg.*
Porto de Fernández, Guadalupe Ig 280; NM 44 *Mex.*
Porto y Zárate, Miguel Francisco de ("Querubín de la Ronda") (1825-1858) BDC 78; Cu 133, 145 *Cu.*

Portugal de Salinas, Beatriz **Carlota** PM 69 *Mex.*

Portuondo, América ARC 59 *Cu.*

Posada, Adolfo GLO 238 *Arg.*

Posada, Carlos (1845-1887) Co 57; RHLC 171 *Col.*

Posada, Eduardo (1862-) Co 58; IE 225; PCo 256; RHLC 200; WLA 316 *Col.*

Posada, Guillermo Co 58 *Col.*

Posada, Joaquín Pablo (1825-1880) AC I, 247; CHL 344; CLH 295; Co 58; HPHA II, 72; LC 151; RHLC 102 *Col.*

Posada Arango, Andrés Co 58 *Col.*

Posada Gutiérrez, Joaquín Pablo (1797-1881) BHLA 349; Co 58; LC 154; RHLC 199 *Col.*

Posadas, Gervasio Antonio de (-1846) HLA 293 *Arg.*

Posnansky, Arturo B 17; BT 229 *Bol.*

Posse Martínez, Alejo (1839-1898) Co 58 *Col.*

Posso, Abelardo (1854-) E 59 *Ecua.*

Postigo, E. Par 21 *Para.*

Potentini, Tomás Ignacio LV 338; V 119 *Venez.*

Potrie, Enrique E. U 15 *Uru.*

Potts, René (1908-) PoC 219 *Cu.*

Pous, Arquimedes BDC 78 *Cu.*

Poveda, Arístides ARC 59 *Cu.*

Poveda, José Manuel (1888-1926) APEH 979; ARC 59; BHLA 571; Cu 133; LH 124; PA 96; PCu 227 *Cu.*

Poveda, Luis Aguiar PJC 199 *Cu.*

Poveda Ferrer, Antonio ARC 59; Cu 133 *Cu.*

Poveda Ferrer, Simeón ARC 41, 60; Cu 133 *Cu.*

Poveda y Armenteros, Francisco José ("El trovador cubano") (1796-1881) BDC 79; BHLA 223; CHL 436; CLH 379; Cu 14, 133, 162; RLC 73 *Cu.*

Povedano, Diego CA 43; IBCR IV, 347 *C.R.*

Povedano, Tomás CA 43 *C.R.*

Power, Daniel de Cu 133 *Cu.*

Pozo, Gonzalo PLE 115 *Ecua.*

Pozo, José Martín de Cu 133 *Cu.*

Pozo, José Miguel ("Américo Hispano") E 69 *Ecua.*

Pozo Monzalvo, Teófilo E 59 *Ecua.*

Pozos, Maximino PM 69 *Mex.*

Pozos Dulces, Conde de los (1809-1877) CLH 423; RLC 147, 176 *Cu.*

Prado, Amado TM 284 *Mex.*

Prado, Eladio ("Boy", "Xavier de Baza", or "Burundulín") (1880-) CA 43, 44; EPCR 323; IE 226 *C.R.*

Prado, Julio del BAP 123 *Per.*

Prado Calvo, Pedro (1886-) APEH 649, 1188; BHLA 510, 535; C 18, 38, 53, 69; CHL 287; CMPC 101; CrA 29; FPA 193, 220; G 326; MSAP 154, 313; PCC xiv, 101; PCh 253; SASS 155; WLA 318 *Chil.*

Prado Orrego, Juan José E 59 *Ecua.*

Prado Orrego, Miguel E 59 *Ecua.*

Prado Salinas, Bernardo NL 74 *Nicar.*

Prado y Ugarteche, Javier (1871-1921) P 29 *Per.*

Prando, Alberto A 56 *Arg.*

Prats, **Carlos** (1891-1917) Cu 133; PJC 201 *Cu.*

Prats Ramírez, Francisco SD 27 *Dom.*

Prego de Oliver, José APA I, xxix, 57; HPHA II, 401; HSLU I, pt 1, 14 *Arg.*

Prellezo, José M. ("R. P. Zöell") Cu 133, 183 *Cu.*

Préndez, Pedro Nolasco (1853-1906) BHLA 424; C 38; CHL 260; CLH 220; HC 217; PCh 91 *Chil.*

Préndez Saldías, Carlos (1892-) APEH 670, 1189; BHLA 536; C 38; CMPC 114; IE 227; PCC xvi, 139; PCh 431; WLA 319 *Chil.*

Price, Jorge W. Co 58, 59 *Col.*

Prida, Pablo TM 247, 284 *Mex.*

Prida y Díaz, Antonio PR 14 *P.R.*

Prieta Aravena, Carlos C 38 *Chil.*

Prieto, Aguada Cu 133 *Cu.*

Prieto, Alejandro HLM 492 *Mex.*

Prieto, Guillermo ("El Nigromante" or "Fidel") (1818-1897) AMP 237; BHLA, 333; CHL 398; CLH 346; G 369; HLM 309; HLMex 196; NM 3, 44; PM 69; PMe II, 127; PoM 33; TM 284, 430, 472, 565 *Mex.*

Prieto, Jenaro BHLA 622; C 18; PLHA 219 *Chil.*

Prieto, Víctor Manuel C 18; NC 228 *Chil.*

Prieto de Landázuri, Isabel A. (1833-1876) G 369; HLM 316, 333; HLMex 152; HPM 867; PM 70; PoM 305; TM 191, 285, 472 *Mex.*

Prieto de Valdés, Casimiro A 56 *Arg.*

Prieto del Egido, Ignacio A 56 *Arg.*

Prieto del Río, Luis Francisco (1857-1918) HC 252 *Chil.*

Prieto Yeme, Guillermo ("Rodrigo Cifuentes") APMM 162; HLM 524; PM 70; TM 287, 343 *Mex.*

Primo de Rivera, Miguel TM 565 *Mex.*

Prince, Carlos P 29 *Per.*

Príncipe, Miguel Agustín E 59 *Ecua.*

Princivalle, Carlos María LU 64, 691; PIU III, 270; U 15 *Uru.*

Prinz, Hernán A 56 *Arg.*

Priori, Genoveva B. de NC 358 *Chil.*

Proaño, Daniel Enrique (1853-) E 59 *Ecua.*

Proaño, Federico (1848-1894) E 59; PLE 54 *Ecua.*

Proaño, Filemón E 59 *Ecua.*

Proaño, Juan Félix E 60 *Ecua.*

Proaño, Manuel José E 60 *Ecua.*

Proaño, Rafael E 60 *Ecua.*

Proaño y Vega, Eloy E 60 *Ecua.*

Procel, Aurea TM 287 *Mex.*

Prohías y Hernández, Juan ("Equis") Cu 134 *Cu.*

Provedano, Diego NM 44 *Mex.*

Provins, Miguel Ig 281; NM 44 *Mex.*

Prudencio, Almanzor B 17 *Bol.*

Prud'homme, Emilio CHL 496; CLH 436; PD 198; SD 27 *Dom.*

Pruneda, Alfonso G 369 *Mex.*

Prunell Alzáibar, Elbio HSLU III, pt 8, 18; PIU III, 220; U 15 *Uru.*

"Puck" (*pseud.*) *see* Gutiérrez Nájera, Manuel

Puelma Laval, Ricardo C 38 *Chil.*

Puelma Tupper, Guillermo C 38 *Chil.*

Puelles, Pedro E 61 *Ecua.*
Puente, Agustín de la P 29 *Per.*
Puente, Antonio María Eligio de la (1887-) Cu 134 *Cu.*
Puente, Francisco de la PR 20 *P.R.*
Puente, José Félix de la BHLA 514; P 29 *Per.*
Puente, Julieta IBCR IV, 355 *C.R.*
Puente y Acosta, Lorenzo Cu 134; PR 10, 38
Puente y Apezechea, Fermín de la (1821-1875) AEHA 906; HLMex 158 *Mex.*
Puerta, Bernardo Co 59 *Col.*
Puerta de Vera y C., Francisco C 53 *Chil.*
Puga de Losada, Amalia BHLA 429; P 29 *Per.*
Puga y Acal, Manuel ("Brummel") (1860-1930) APMM 164; G 369; HLM 429, 493; HLMex 239; PM 70; PMe II, 143; PoM 350; TM 288 *Mex.*
Puig, Juan de la Cruz A 56, 72 *Arg.*
Puig Casauranc, José Manuel (1888-) G 369; HLM 517; IE 229; Ig 281; NM 44; PM 70 *Mex.*
Puig y Cárdenas, Félix (1835-1896) Cu 134 *Cu.*
Puig y de la Puente, Francisco Cu 134 *Cu.*
Pujals Santana, Joaquín (1877-) PR 47; QPR (1) 124; (2) 132 *P.R.*
"Pujavante" (*pseud.*) *see* Lara A., Manuel María
Pujato Crespo de Camelino Vedoya, Mercedes A 56, 90 *Arg.*
Pujol, Gaspar M. PM 70 *Mex.*
Pujol y de Camps, Marcelo Cu 134 *Cu.*
"Pulgar, Luciano" (*pseud.*) *see* Suárez, Marco Fidel
Pulgarón, Eduardo BDC 79 *Cu.*
Pulido, José Ignacio V 119 *Venez.*
Pulido, Lucio V 119 *Venez.*
Pulido, Luis V 119 *Venez.*
Pulido de León, Nicolás V 119 *Venez.*
Puncet de Jiménez, M. BDC 79; Cu 134 *Cu.*
Puñal, Luis de Juan Cu 134 *Cu.*
Pusalgas, Ignacio Cu 134 *Cu.*

Q

"Quena" (*pseud.*) *see* Cascallares Gutiérrez, Isabel
Queremel, Ángel Miguel V 119 *Venez.*
Queremel, Luisa V 119 *Venez.*
Queremel, Pedro M. V 119 *Venez.*
"Querubín de la Ronda" (*pseud.*) *see* Porto y Zárate, Miguel Francisco de
Quesada, Antonio Cu 134 *Cu.*
Quesada, Cristóbal de LV 100 *Venez.*
Quesada, Ernesto (1858-) A 56; AT I, 89; CHL 193; CLH 165; GLO 238; LA VIII, 615 *Arg.*
Quesada, Héctor A 56, 90 *Arg.*
Quesada, José León ARC 60 *Cu.*
Quesada, Josué (1885-) A 56, 90 *Arg.*
Quesada, Julio A. A 56 *Arg.*
Quesada, R. E 61 *Ecua.*

Quesada, Ramón Matías (-1916) CA 44; EPCR 228 *C.R.*
Quesada, Vicente G. ("Víctor Gálvez") (1830-1913) A 57, 78; CHL 142; CLH 120; LA VII, 192; PLHA 225 *Arg.*
Quesada Castillo, Ignacio de BDC 79; Cu 134 *Cu.*
Quesada S., Napoleón (1874-) CA 44; EPCR 328 *C.R.*
Quesada Torres, Salvador Cu 134 *Cu.*
1. Quesada y Miranda, Gonzalo (1868-1915) CHL 487; CLH 426; Cu 134; G 341; HLC 92 *Cu.*
2. Quesada y Miranda, Gonzalo (1900-) WLA 322 *Cu.*
Quevedo Cu 134 *Cu.*
Quevedo, Antonio José (1869-1902) E 61 *Ecua.*
Quevedo, Belisario PLE 89 *Ecua.*
Quevedo, Julio A 57; B 17
Quevedo, Quintín (1823-) B 17; LB 589 *Bol.*
Quevedo y Zubieta, Salvador (1859-) G 369; HLM 458; Ig 283; NM 44; TM 288 *Mex.*
Quevedo Z., Guillermo Co 59 *Col.*
Quijano, Alejandro (1883-) G 369; HLM 513; WLA 323 *Mex.*
Quijano, Arturo Co 59 *Col.*
Quijano, Franco V 119 *Venez.*
Quijano, Manuel de Jesús Pan 17 *Pan.*
Quijano, Víctor M. E 61 *Ecua.*
Quijano Hernández, Manuel (1871-) IE 230; WLA 323 *Salv.*
Quijano Mantilla, Joaquín (1875-) Co 59; WLA 323 *Col.*
Quijano Otero, José María (1836-1883) Co 59; LC 173; RHLC 200 *Col.*
Quijano Otero, R. Co 59 *Col.*
Quijano Torres, A. PCo 257 *Col.*
Quijano Torres, Gustavo Co 59 *Col.*
Quijano Wallis, José María (1847-) Co 59 *Col.*
Quimper Requena, José M. P 29 *Per.*
Quintana, Antonio M. Cu 135 *Cu.*
Quintana, Cuca (1912-) PoC 229 *Cu.*
Quintana, Emilio NL 225 *Nicar.*
Quintana, José María de BDC 79; Cu 135 *Cu.*
Quintana, Pedro Alejandro (1916-) PoC 232 *Cu.*
Quintana del Acebo, Ramón ACe 922; HLM 246; PM 70 *Mex.*
Quintana Menéndez, Juan A 57 *Arg.*
Quintana Róo, Andrés (1787-1851) ACe 185; BHLA 171, 188; CHL 98; CLH 84; HLM 239; HLMex 106, 125; HPHA I, 106; HPM 809; PM 70 *Mex.*
Quintanilla, Luis ("Kyn Taniya") (1900-) PM 71, 80; TM 566 *Mex.*
Quintero, Ángel V 119 *Venez.*
Quintero, Domingo V 119 *Venez.*
Quintero, J. Humberto V 120 *Venez.*
Quintero, Joaquín V 120 *Venez.*
Quintero, José Agustín (1829-1885) CHL 461; RLC 189 *Cu.*
Quintero, Manuel A 57; G 317 *Arg.*
Quintero, Mercedes (189.-) FPA 503, 525 *Salv.*
Quintero Rojas, Antonio V 120 *Venez.*

Quintero y Almeyda, José Mauricio   Cu 135 *Cu.*
Quiñones, Antonio de   HC 14   *Chil.*
Quiñones, F.   PM 71   *Mex.*
Quiñones, Francisco   Par 21   *Para.*
Quiñones, Francisco Mariano ("A. Kadosh")   BP 506, 625; PR 20, 25, 28   *P.R.*
Quiñones Sunsín, Francisco   GPCA I, 67; NL 11   *Nicar.*
"Quirino Lemachez" (*pseud.*) *see* Henríquez, Camilo
Quiroga, Adán (1863-1904)   A 57; LA VII, 251   *Arg.*
Quiroga, Alfonso   NM 44   *Mex.*
Quiroga, Carlos B.   A 57; G 388; GLO 238, 254; LAC 136   *Arg.*
Quiroga, Horacio (1879-1937)   A 57, 90; AB 24; BHLA 507; G 388; GLO 254; HSLU III, pt 9, 5; LAC 45, 131; LAS 205; PIU II, 40; PLHA 233; SASS 480; U 15; UT 421   *Uru.*
Quiroga, Jerónimo de   BHC III, 121; SCL 343, 632   *Chil.*
Quiroga, José   SCL 421, 633   *Arg.*
Quiroga, Malvina Rosa (1900-   )   A 57   *Arg.*
Quiroga, Ricardo   B 17   *Bol.*
Quirós, Adolfo   C 18   *Chil.*
Quirós, Ángel Fernando (1799-1862)   P 29   *Per.*
Quirós, Gonzalo   BDC 80; Cu 135   *Cu.*
Quirós, José M.   Cu 136   *Cu.*
Quirós, Justo R.   AP 287; Pan 17   *Pan.*
Quirós Blanco, Teodoro ("Gonzalo González" *or* "Yoyo") (1876-1902)   CA 30, 44, 57; CG II, 576; EPCR 336; IBCR IV, 45   *C.R.*
Quirós y Camposagrado, Manuel de   PM 71; TM 288   *Mex.*
Quiroz, Bernardino de Jesús   Ig 284; NM 45   *Mex.*

R

Rabasa, Emilio ("Sancho Polo") (1856-1930)   BAMP 66; CHL 422; CLH 367; HLM 440; HLMex 226; IE 232; Ig 285; NM 45   *Mex.*
Rabasa, Manuel   NM 45   *Mex.*
Rabell, Francisco J. (1853-1899)   Cu 136   *Cu.*
Rabí, Jesús   ARC 60   *Cu.*
Rabín, Noé   A 57   *Arg.*
Rabufetti, L. E.   A 57, 90   *Arg.*
Racamonde, Víctor   AEHA 856; CHL 375; CLH 323; LV 337; V 120   *Venez.*
Rada y Gamió, Pedro José (1873-   )   P 29   *Per.*
Rada y Paz Soldán, Pedro   P 30   *Per.*
Rafael, Carlos   Cu 136   *Cu.*
"Rafaela" (*pseud.*) *see* Fernández de (la) Lande, Pámela
Rahausen, Roberto   C 18; NC 228   *Chil.*
Rahavánez, Rodrigo de   Co 59   *Col.*
Raldiris Guasp, Juan P. ("Duque de Lerma")   PR 38   *P.R.*

"Ralg, C. B." (*pseud.*) *see* Lotero Quintana, Ramón Antonio
Ramallo, Jacobo (1850?-1906)   B 17   *Bol.*
Ramallo, Mariano (1817-1876)   B 17; HPHA II, 282; LB 583   *Bol.*
Ramallo, Miguel   B 17   *Bol.*
Ramasso, Ambrosio Luis (1873-   )   UT 423   *Uru.*
Ramella, Pablo A.   A 57   *Arg.*
Ramírez, Abraham   V 120   *Venez.*
Ramírez, Alfonso Francisco (1896-   )   NM 3; PM 71; WLA 325   *Mex.*
Ramírez, Carlos Aníbal   P 30   *Per.*
Ramírez, Carlos María (1848-1898)   BHLA 400; CHL 224; CLH 187; LUr 465; PIU I, 231; U 15   *Uru.*
Ramírez, Dimas   V 120   *Venez.*
Ramírez, Francisco Javier   SCL 392, 633   *Chil.*
Ramírez, Ignacio ("El Nigromante") (1818-1879)   AMP 239; BHLA 300, 332; CHL 398; CLH 345; G 369; HLM 297; HLMex 185; HPM 870; PM 71; PMe II, 147; PoM 64; SASS 353; TM 469, 472   *Mex.*
Ramírez, José   V 120   *Venez.*
Ramírez, José Fernando (1804-1871)   HLM 359 *et passim*; HLMex 168; TM 566   *Mex.*
Ramírez, José María (1834-1892)   HLM 345; Ig 287; NM 45; PM 71   *Mex.*
Ramírez, José Oberto   Cu 136   *Cu.*
Ramírez, Juan C. (1860-1914)   RHLC 150   *Col.*
Ramírez, Juan Vicente (1877-   )   Par 22; PT 123   *Para.*
Ramírez, Julio   C 18   *Chil.*
Ramírez, Manuel   PM 71   *Mex.*
Ramírez, Miguel Toro   V 120   *Venez.*
Ramírez, Noel   Co 59   *Col.*
Ramírez, Octavio   HSLU III, pt 4, 46   *Uru.*
Ramírez, Pedro Antonio   C 53   *Chil.*
Ramírez, Rafael W.   PR 25   *P.R.*
Ramírez, Ramón   V 120   *Venez.*
Ramírez, Santiago   NM 4   *Mex.*
Ramírez, Serafín   Cu 136   *Cu.*
Ramírez, Zenón   Par 22   *Para.*
Ramírez Aparicio, Manuel (1831-1867)   HLM 358; Ig 294; NM 45; PM 71   *Mex.*
Ramírez Araujo, M. A.   V 120   *Venez.*
Ramírez Arriaga, Manuel   PM 52, 71   *Mex.*
Ramírez B., Roberto   Co 59   *Col.*
Ramírez Brau, E.   BP 536; PR 38   *P.R.*
Ramírez Cabañas, Joaquín (1886-   )   G 369; HLM 524; Ig 295; NM 45; PM 71   *Mex.*
Ramírez Cortés, Mariano   C 69   *Chil.*
Ramírez de Aguilar, Fernando ("Jacobo Dalevuelta") (1887-   )   CG II, 2; Ig 292; NM 45; TM 287, 290, 343; WLA 326   *Mex.*
Ramírez de Arellano, Clemente (188.-   )   FPA 461, 496; PR 39   *P.R.*
Ramírez de Arellano, Domingo   PR 39   *P.R.*
Ramírez de Arellano, José   TM 472   *Mex.*
Ramírez de Arellano, Rafael   PR 42   *P.R.*
Ramírez de Rodríguez, Agustina   PoM 297   *Mex.*
Ramírez de Vargas, Alfonso ("Alonso")   HLM 187; HPM 219; PM 71; TM 290   *Mex.*
Ramírez L., Arturo   Cu 136   *Cu.*

Ramírez Noblia, Solano PU 314 *Uru.*
Ramírez R., Juan (1885-) AP 289; Pan 17 *Pan.*
Ramírez Romano, Francisco PM 71 *Mex.*
Ramírez Ros, Primitivo ARC 60 *Cu.*
Ramírez Santibáñez, José PR 11, 14, 47, 60 *P.R.*
Ramírez Santibáñez, Juan Antonio PM 72 *Mex.*
Ramírez y Vargas *see* Ramírez de Vargas
Ramírez Zúñiga, Teresa C 18 *Chil.*
Ramiro y Corrales, Mariano (1834-1886) Cu 136 *Cu.*
"Ramón Román" (*pseud.*) *see* Barreto, José María
"Ramoncito" (*pseud.*) *see* Urrutia y Guzmán, José María
Ramos, Domingo Santos V 120 *Venez.*
1. Ramos, Eduardo C 38 *Chil.*
2. Ramos, Eduardo NM 46 *Mex.*
Ramos, Emiliano A. BDC 81; PR 14 *P.R.*
Ramos, José Antonio (1885-) BDC 81; BHLA 571; Cu 136; GLO 245; HLC 219; LAS 201; WLA 327 *Cu.*
Ramos, José Luis CHL 357; CLH 306; LV 41, 104, 126; V 120, 121 *Venez.*
Ramos, José Manuel PM 72; TM 473 *Mex.*
Ramos, Juan Bautista A 57 *Arg.*
Ramos, Juan P. G 317; LAC 124 *Arg.*
Ramos, Julio César V 121 *Venez.*
Ramos, Leopoldo PM 72 *Mex.*
Ramos, Luis R. Cu 137 *Cu.*
Ramos, Mariano E. TM 291 *Mex.*
Ramos, Melchor José (1805-1832) HC 55 *Chil.*
Ramos, Ramón Alejandro V 121 *Venez.*
Ramos, Roberto NM 4; TM 567 *Mex.*
Ramos Carrión, Teresa (-1898) A 57 *Arg.*
Ramos Duarte, Félix Cu 137 *Cu.*
Ramos Ernandes, Enrike Rafael PM 72 *Mex.*
Ramos Giménez, Leopoldo (1896-) FPA 402, 426; Par 22; PPa 205; WLA 328 *Para.*
Ramos Martín, José TM 297 *Mex.*
Ramos Mejía, Francisco (1847-1893) LA VII, 203 *Arg.*
Ramos Mejía, José María (1849-1914) LA VII, 106, 203 *Arg.*
Ramos Pedrueza, Rafael TM 297 *Mex.*
Ramos Sucre, José Antonio V 121 *Venez.*
Ramos V., Lilia CA 45 *C.R.*
Ramos y Braus, José PR 14 *P.R.*
Ramos y García, Dioclesiano V 121 *Venez.*
Rander, Francisco Cu 137 *Cu.*
Rangel, Nicolás (1864-) HLM 530; IE 233; TM 567; WLA 329 *Mex.*
Rangel Báez, Carlos V 121 *Venez.*
Rangel Lamus, Amenodoro V 121 *Venez.*
Ranjel, Luis HLNG I, 176 *Col.*
Rapoport, Nicolás A 57 *Arg.*
"Raquel" (*pseud.*) *see* Troncoso de Oiz, Matilde
Rasch Isla, Miguel (1889-) ALC II, 261; BHLA 541; CHL 355; Co 59, 60; PCo 257; WLA 329 *Col.*
Rastignac, Enrique de E 61 *Ecua.*
"Raúl de la Vega" (*pseud.*) *see* Diego, Pedro R. de

"Raúl Waleis" (*pseud.*) *see* Varela, Luis Vicente
Raveau, Rafael C 54, 57 *Chil.*
Ravenet de Hechavarría, Joaquín Cu 137 *Cu.*
Ravignani, Emilio ("John S. War") (1886-) AT I, 121; IE 234 *Arg.*
Rawson, Guillermo A 57; GEA XV, XX *Arg.*
Raynaud, Georges TM 567 *Mex.*
Razetti, Luis V 121 *Venez.*
Read, Horacio SD 27 *Dom.*
Real, Cristóbal BP 536; PR 10, 39, 47 *P.R.*
Real, Matías BP 536; PR 39 *P.R.*
Real, Romualdo PR 53 *P.R.*
Real de Azúa, Gabriel Alejandro (1803-) LA V, 492 *Arg.*
Rebaque Thuillier, E. A 57 *Arg.*
Rebella, Juan U 15 *Uru.*
Réboli, Ida L. A 58 *Arg.*
Rebollar, Jesús María Ig 296; NM 46 *Mex.*
Rebolledo, Efrén (1877-1929) AMP 92; APMM 168; G 369; HLM 428; HLMex 219; Ig 297; NM 46; PM 72; PMM 57; PNM 251; TM 297, 473 *Mex.*
Reboredo, Eduardo M. A 58 *Arg.*
Recalde, Facundo (189.-) FPA 403, 434; Par 22; PPa 247 *Para.*
Recalde, Francisco Aurelio E 61 *Ecua.*
"Recamier" (*pseud.*) *see* Gutiérrez Nájera, Manuel
Rechani, L. (Luis Rechani Agrait?) PR 14, 39 *P.R.*
Rega Molina, Horacio (1899-) A 58; APAM 566; BHLA 640; G 317; NPA 245 *Arg.*
Rega Molina, María Esther A 58 *Arg.*
"Reginaldo de Lizárraga" (*pseud.*) *see* Obando, Baltasar de
Regüeiferos y Boudet, Erasmo (1863-) BDC 82; Cu 137 *Cu.*
Regules, Elías (1860-1929) BHLA 423; CHL 223; FPA 527, 533; HSLU I, pt 2, 41; LUr 468; PIU I, 239; SASS 457; U 15; UT 431 *Uru.*
Regúlez y Sanz del Río, Alberto PR 7, 47 *P.R.*
"Régulo" (*pseud.*) *see* Calcaño, Julio
Rei *see also* Rey
Rei, Max E 61 *Ecua.*
Reina, Jerónimo J. (1876-) HL II, 725 *Hond.*
Reina, José María V 121 *Venez.*
Reina, Leopoldo E 61 *Ecua.*
Reina, Librado Cu 137 *Cu.*
Reinales, Buenaventura (1836-) B 17 *Bol.*
Reinaudi Grossi, Teresa A 58 *Arg.*
Reinoso, I. C 18; NC 500 *Chil.*
Reinoso, Juan José (1852-) P 30 *Per.*
Reissig, Luis A 58 *Arg.*
Rejón García, Manuel Ig 298; NM 46 *Mex.*
Rejón Tejero, E. TM 596 *Mex.*
Reko, Víctor A. (1880-) IE 238 *Mex.*
Relaño, Alfonso Cu 137 *Cu.*
Remesal, Antonio HLM 208 *Mex.*
Remírez, Teodoro J. TM 502 *Mex.*
"Remo, M." (*pseud.*) *see* Moré, Manuel
Remos y Rubio, Juan José (1896-) BDC 82; CT 431; Cu 137; LAS 201 *Cu.*
Rémusat, Albert Cu 137 *Cu.*

"Renard, Maître" (*pseud.*) *see* Solano, Armando

Rencurrell, Georgina ("Georgina de Flores") Cu 58, 138 *Cu.*

Rendic I., Antonio C 38 *Chil.*

1. Rendón C 54 *Chil.*

2. Rendón PM 72 *Mex.*

Rendón, Francisco de Paula (1855-1917) Co 60; RHLC 190 *Col.*

Rendón, Vicente A. V 121 *Venez.*

Rendón, Víctor Manuel (1859-) E 61, 75; G 345; PE 317; PLE 63 *Ecua.*

Rendón, Zoila C. E 62 *Ecua.*

Rendón Pérez, Carlos E 62 *Ecua.*

Rendón Sarmiento, Raimundo V 121 *Venez.*

René, Rubén C 18 *Chil.*

René-Moreno, Gabriel (-1898) B 17; LB 600 *Bol.*

Rengel, Manuel E. E 62 *Ecua.*

Rengifo, Francisco M. Co 60 *Col.*

Renjifo, Ramón C 54 *Chil.*

Renté y Villa, José Cu 138 *Cu.*

Requena, Rafael V 121 *Venez.*

Requena Legarreta, Pedro (1893-1918) APMM 171; G 369; PM 72 *Mex.*

Restán, Juan Nepomuceno TM 298 *Mex.*

Restivo, Paulo (1658-1741) Par 22 *Para.*

Restrepo, Antonio José (1856-) Co 60, 73; G 330; PCo 260 *Col.*

Restrepo, Enrique Co 60 *Col.*

Restrepo, Felipe Co 60 *Col.*

Restrepo, José Luis Co 60 *Col.*

Restrepo, José Manuel (1782-1863) BHLA 255, 349; CHL 341; CLH 303; Co 60; HLNG II, 209, 340; LC 119; RHLC 75 *Col.*

Restrepo, Juan de Dios ("Emiro Kastos") (1823-1894) Co 36, 60; LC 143; RHLC 118 *Col.*

Restrepo, Juan Pablo Co 60 *Col.*

Restrepo, Lisandro Co 60 *Col.*

Restrepo, Manuel Canuto Co 60, 61 *Col.*

Restrepo, Santiago Co 61 *Col.*

Restrepo, Vicente (1837-1899) Co 61; RHLC 200 *Col.*

Restrepo E., Emilano Co 61 *Col.*

Restrepo Euse, Álvaro Co 61 *Col.*

Restrepo Gómez, Francisco PCo 276 *Col.*

Restrepo Jaramillo, José Co 61; RHLC 191 *Col.*

Restrepo Mejía, Félix (1887-) RHLC 205; WLA 334 *Col.*

Restrepo Mejía, Luis Co 61 *Col.*

Restrepo Rivera, J. PCo 278 *Col.*

Restrepo Sáenz, José María Co 61 *Col.*

Restrepo Tamayo, Joaquín PCo 281 *Col.*

Restrepo Tirado, Ernesto (1862-) Co 61; RHLC 201; WLA 334 *Col.*

Revello de Torre, José P 30 *Per.*

Revilla, Manuel G. HLM 497; NM 4 *Mex.*

Revolledo, Álvaro Co 61 *Col.*

Revollo del Castillo, Ernesto Co 61 *Col.*

Revuelta, Pedro BDC 82 *Cu.*

Rey, Alfredo V 121 *Venez.*

Rey, Emilio Ig 298; NM 46; PM 72; TM 299 *Mex.*

Rey, Fermín del Cu 138 *Cu.*

Rey, Miguel A 58, 90 *Arg.*

"Rey de Bastos" (*pseud.*) *see* Tejera, Felipe

Rey de Castro, José María E 62 *Ecua.*

Rey de Garriga, Mercedes (1913-1936) PoC 237 *Cu.*

Rey Soto, Antonio (1879-) IE 240 *Guat.*

Rey y Leanes, Julián del ARC 61 *Cu.*

Reybaud, Ch. Cu 138 *Cu.*

Reyes, Alfonso (1889-) AMP 122; APEH 724, 1189; APMM 176; BAMP 74; BHLA 490, 558; FPA 340, 355; G 369; GLO 249; HLM 512; Ig 298; LAND 121, 126, 247; LAS 207; NM 46; PM 72; PMe II, 153; PMM 110; PNM 263; SASS 396; TM 299, 569; WLA 335 *Mex.*

Reyes, Antonio V 122 *Venez.*

Reyes, Antonio de los (-1603) HLM 21 *Mex.*

Reyes, Arturo C 18 *Chil.*

Reyes, Bernardo TM 300 *Mex.*

Reyes, César (1885-) AT II, 681 *Arg.*

Reyes, F. de P. PR 47 *P.R.*

Reyes, Fernando (-1886) Cu 138 *Cu.*

Reyes, Germán Co 61 *Col.*

Reyes, J. Ascención Ig 299; NM 46 *Mex.*

Reyes, Jorge BHLA 597; E 62, 75; PLE 141 *Ecua.*

Reyes, José V 122 *Venez.*

Reyes, José Antonio ACe 930 *Mex.*

Reyes, José Luis B 18 *Bol.*

Reyes, José Trinidad (1797-1855) HL II, 5; HPHA I, 206 *Hond.*

Reyes, Juan de Jesús PD 202; SD 28 *Dom.*

Reyes, Juan Justo Cu 138 *Cu.*

Reyes, Juan Ramón (1848-1881) HL II, 171 *Hond.*

Reyes, Leopoldo (1863-1899) Cu 138 *Cu.*

Reyes, Menardo CA 45 *C.R.*

Reyes, Oscar Efrén E 62, 75; LAS 201; PLE 124, 139 *Ecua.*

Reyes, Rafael (1851-1921) Co 61 *Col.*

Reyes, Ramón (1861-1886) HL I, 809; II, 419 *Hond.*

Reyes, Rodolfo NM 46 *Mex.*

Reyes, Salvador (1899-) C 18, 39; LAS 205; PCC xx, 223 *Chil.*

Reyes, Víctor Cu 138 *Cu.*

Reyes Lovio, Horacio ARC 61 *Cu.*

Reyes Ortiz, Félix (1828-) B 18; LB 591 *Bol.*

Reyles, Carlos (1868-) BHLA 472, 508; CHL 228; CLH 190; G 388; GLO 254; HSLU I, pt 6, 5; LU 64, 672; LUr 499; PIU II, 261; PLHA 192; SA 163; SAL 187; SASS 476; U 16; UT 437; WLA 336; WSAL 59 *Uru.*

Reyna Almandos, Luis A 58 *Arg.*

Reyna Zeballos, Miguel de CHL 22; CLH 19; HLM 171; HPM 457 *Mex.*

Reynal O'Connor, Arturo A 58 *Arg.*

Reynolds, Gregorio (1882-) B 18; BT 243; FPA 54, 79; G 320; LB 623 *Bol.*

Reza, Felícitas TM 300 *Mex.*

Rezabal y Ugarte, José de BHC III, 406 *et passim Chil.*

Riaño Cualla, Eduardo Co 61 *Col.*

Riba y Rada, José María (1760-) ACe 933 *Mex.*

Ribadeneyra y Barrientos, Antonio Joaquín de (1710-) HPM 459; PM 73 *Mex.*

Ribas, José Félix V 122 *Venez.*

Ribas y Ribas, Fidel V 122 *Venez.*

Ribera   *see also* Rivera
Ribera, Diego de   PM 73   *Mex.*
Ribera, José   HPM 480   *Mex.*
Ribera, José Joaquín   PP 339; PR 39   *P.R.*
"Ribera, Lucas" (*pseud.*) *see* Cabrera, Luis
Ribera, Luis de   HPHA II, 273   *Bol.*
Ribera Flórez, Dionisio de   HPM 110   *Mex.*
Ribó, José Joaquín   Cu 138   *Cu.*
Ribot, Héctor   Ig 300; NM 46   *Mex.*
Ricalde, Domingo M.   TM 610   *Mex.*
Ricard, Robert   TM 569   *Mex.*
"Ricardo Arenales" (*pseud.*) *see* Osorio, Miguel Ángel
"Ricardo Buenamar" (*pseud.*) *see* Cabrera, Raimundo
Ricaurte y Terueros, Juan de   Co 61   *Col.*
Riccio, Gustavo   A 58   *Arg.*
Rico, José Adrián María   PM 73   *Mex.*
"Richard, M." (*pseud.*) *see* Mandiola, Rómulo
Richard Lavalle, Enrique   A 58   *Arg.*
Ried, Alberto   C 18, 39; G 326; PCh 347   *Chil.*
Riépele Pretto, Pío M. (1872-   )   PG 345; WLA 338   *Guat.*
Riera, Alberto (1901-   )   PoC 238   *Cu.*
Riera Aguinagalde, Ildefonso   V 122   *Venez.*
Riera Palmer, Mariano   BP 537, 628; PR 39, 47   *P.R.*
Riesco de Gaymer, Sara   C 54   *Chil.*
Riesco y Riesco, Alfredo   C 39   *Chil.*
Riesgo, Pascual   BDC 83; Cu 138   *Cu.*
Rijo, Baldemaro   PD 203; SD 28   *Dom.*
"Rimur, Gabriel de" (*pseud.*) *see* Gómez, Santiago Carlos
Rincón, Antonio del (-1601)   HLM 22   *Mex.*
Rincón, Baldomera   V 122   *Venez.*
Rincón, Luis   Co 62   *Col.*
Rincón, Manuel E. (1841-1902)   PM 73; PMe II, 157; TM 300   *Mex.*
Rincón Soler, Evangelina C. de   BC 119; Co 62   *Col.*
Rinsky, Benjamín   A 58   *Arg.*
Río, Andrés del   PM 73   *Mex.*
Río, Guillermo del   P 30   *Per.*
Río, Rosa   A 58   *Arg.*
Río Valenzuela, Raimundo del   NC 442   *Chil.*
Riobamba, Agustín de   PE 83   *Ecua.*
Riofrío, Francisco J.   E 63   *Ecua.*
Rioja, Luis de   Cu 139   *Cu.*
Ríonegro, Froilán de   V 122   *Venez.*
Ríos, Andrés   Cu 139   *Cu.*
"Ríos, Concepción" (*pseud.*) *see* Vázquez de Montiel, María del Carmen
Ríos, Epitacio J. de los (1833-1860)   HPM 832; PM 73   *Mex.*
Ríos, Fabio   Pan 17   *Pan.*
Ríos, José Manuel de los   V 122   *Venez.*
Ríos, Juan Pablo de los   Ig 300; NM 46; PM 73   *Mex.*
Ríos, Julia   U 16   *Uru.*
Ríos, Rafael de los   V 122   *Venez.*
Ríos, Ricardo de los   V 122   *Venez.*
Ríos Cárdenas, María   NM 46   *Mex.*
Ríos D., Aníbal   Pan 17   *Pan.*
Ríos González, Tomás   C 18; NC 392, 442   *Chil.*

Ríos Guzmán, Rodolfo   C 18; NC 443   *Chil.*
Ríos Ríos, Max   PR 28   *P.R.*
Ríos Ugarte, Lorenzo de los   HPM 118   *Mex.*
Ripa Alberdi, Héctor (1897-1923)   A 58; APAM 393; BHLA 630; G 317   *Arg.*
"Ripper, Jack the" (*pseud.*) *see* Campos, José Antonio
Riquelme, Ernesto   C 39   *Chil.*
Riquelme y Venegas, Daniel (1857-1912)   BHLA 380; C 18; CHL 281; CLH 239; HC 209; NC 444   *Chil.*
Risopatrón, Bolívar   C 19   *Chil.*
Risopatrón, Francisco   C 19; NC 443   *Chil.*
Risopatrón Sánchez, Alberto   NC 443   *Chil.*
Risquet, Juan Felipe (1874-   )   ARC 61; Cu 139   *Cu.*
Rísquez, Francisco R.   V 122   *Venez.*
Riú, Francisco Aníbal   A 58   *Arg.*
Riva, Francisco Manuel   A 58   *Arg.*
Riva, Maro   C 39   *Chil.*
Riva Agüero y Osma, José de la (1885-   )   BHLA 190; CHL 307; CLH 261; LAND 107; LAS 201; LC 203; P 30   *Per.*
Riva Agüero y Sánchez Boquete, J. de la   BHLA 52   *Per.*
Riva Palacio, Vicente ("Cero") (1832-1896)   AMP 243; BHLA 413; CHL 408; CLH 354; HLM 361, 434, 490; HLMex 179; Ig 300; NM 4, 46; PM 73; PMe II, 159; PoM 98; TM 300, 535, 569; WLA 339   *Mex.*
Rivadavia, Bernardino (1780-1845)   AA II, 9, 67; BHLA 206; CHL 122   *Arg.*
Rivadeneyra   *see* Ribadeneyra
Rivarola, Enrique E. ("Santos Vega") (1862-   )   A 58, 78; AT I, 181; CHL 186; CLH 160   *Arg.*
Rivarola, Pantaleón (1754-1821)   APA I, xxxvii, 83; BHLA 166; CHL 49; CLH 42; LA II, 535, 539; SASS 9; SPLA 34   *Arg.*
Rivarola, Rodolfo   A 58   *Arg.*
Rivas, Ángel César   V 122   *Venez.*
Rivas, Benjamín   B 18   *Bol.*
Rivas, Eduardo F.   A 58   *Arg.*
Rivas, Ernesto A.   P 30   *Per.*
Rivas, Francisco Manuel   A 59   *Arg.*
Rivas, Gabry   NL 144   *Nicar.*
Rivas, José María   V 122   *Venez.*
Rivas, José P.   Cu 139   *Cu.*
Rivas, José Pablo (1865-1919)   AMP 324; PMe II, 163   *Mex.*
Rivas, Juan Bautista   Cu 139   *Cu.*
Rivas, Martín   C 19   *Chil.*
Rivas, Medardo (1825-1901)   Co 62; LC 171; PCo 284; RHLC 119   *Col.*
Rivas, Miguel   B 18   *Bol.*
Rivas, Nicolás   PR 39, 47   *P.R.*
Rivas, Pedro (1825-1888)   A 59; LA VIII, 588   *Arg.*
Rivas, R. Jorge   SD 28   *Dom.*
Rivas, Raimundo (1889-   )   Co 62; V 122; WLA 341   *Col.*
Rivas, Ricardo   Co 62   *Col.*
"Rivas, Simón" (*pseud.*) *see* Martínez, Cristóbal
Rivas Bonilla, Alberto   PS 295   *Salv.*
Rivas Cherif, Cipriano   TM 570   *Mex.*
Rivas Dávila, Andrés   NL 214   *Nicar.*
Rivas Frade, Federico (1858-1922)   Co 18, 62; RHLC 149   *Col.*

Rivas Groot, José María (1864-1923) AC II, 285; Co 55, 62; LC 182; PCo 287; RHLC 211 *Col.*
Rivas Mundarain, Jesús María V 122 *Venez.*
Rivas Ortiz, Octavio NL 118; PN 25 *Nicar.*
Rivas Vázquez, Alejandro V 123 *Venez.*
Rivas Vicuña, Francisco V 123 *Venez.*
Rivas Vicuña, Pedro C 19, 54; NC 392 *Chil.*
Rivera *see also* Ribera
Rivera, Daniel PR 39 *P.R.*
Rivera, David Maximiliano E 63 *Ecua.*
Rivera, Diego HPM 214 *Mex.*
Rivera, Felipe TM 473 *Mex.*
Rivera, José Cu 139 *Cu.*
Rivera, José Eustasio (1889-1928) ALC II, 289; APEH 837, 1191; BHLA 591; CHL 355; Co 62; G 330; GLO 241; LH 147; PLHA 211; RHLC 191; SASS 247 *Col.*
Rivera, José María PM 73; TM 302 *Mex.*
Rivera, José P. TM 473 *Mex.*
Rivera, Juan C. BDC 83 *Cu.*
Rivera, Luis M. TM 570 *Mex.*
Rivera, Marcos Antonio de HLNG II, 384 *Col.*
Rivera, Mercedes de Rosas ("M. Sasor") A 63, 78 *Arg.*
Rivera Astengo, Agustín P. A 59 *Arg.*
Rivera Cambas, Manuel HLM 490, 492 *Mex.*
Rivera (*or* Ribera) Chevremont, Evaristo BP 537, 628; PA 236; PP 254; PR 53 *P.R.*
Rivera Chevremont, José Joaquín BP 537; PR 39 *P.R.*
Rivera G., José Antonio PM 74 *Mex.*
Rivera Garrido, Luciano (1846-) Co 62, 63 *Col.*
Rivera Indarte, José (1814-1844) A 59; BHLA 234; CHL 137; CLH 116; HPHA II, 458; LA VI, 777; SPLA 72 *Arg.*
Rivera Maestre, Francisco GPCA I, 121; PG 82 *Guat.*
Rivera Otero, Rafael PR 39 *P.R.*
Rivera R., Juan AP 291; Pan 17 *Pan.*
Rivera Santiago, Rafael (1900-) QPR (2) 139
Rivera y Río, José HLM 345; Ig 307; NM 47; PM 74 *Mex.*
Rivera y Sanromán, Agustín (1824-1916) HLM 490; PM 73; TM 570 *Mex.*
Rivero, Alejandro TM 302 *Mex.*
Rivero, Atanasio Cu 139 *Cu.*
Rivero, F. PA 234; PP 312 *P.R.*
Rivero, Gelasio V 123 *Venez.*
Rivero, Juan (1681-1736) Co 63; HLNG I, 338; RHLC 16; SCL 388, 634 *Col.*
Rivero, Néstor Eduardo Par 22; PPa 264 *Para.*
Rivero, Nicanor V 123 *Venez.*
Rivero, Nicolás (1849-) CT 75; Cu 139 *Cu.*
Rivero, Pedro V 123 *Venez.*
Rivero, Victorino B 19 *Bol.*
Riverol y Campos, Aurora ("Aurora") Cu 15, 139 *Cu.*
Riviera Maestre, Francisco *see* Rivera Maestre, Francisco

Rivodó, Baldomero V 123 *Venez.*
Rivodó, Ermelindo V 123 *Venez.*
Roa, Raimundo Par 22 *Para.*
Roa, Ramón (1844-1912) BHLA 414; CHL 483; CLH 423; RLC 243, 269 *Cu.*
Roa Bárcena, José María (1827-1908) AMP 240; CHL 394; CLH 341; HLM 300; HLMex 190; Ig 311; NM 4, 48; PM 74; PMe II, 171; PoM 134; SASS 354; TM 474, 570 *Mex.*
"Rob Roy" (*pseud.*) *see* Silva Endeiza, Hugo
Robainas, Francisco Cu 139; PJC 210 *Cu.*
Robalina Dávila, Luis PLE 93 *Ecua.*
Robatto, Domingo A. (-1917) A 59 *Arg.*
Robelo, Cecilio Agustín PM 74; TM 475 *Mex.*
Robert y Sagarra, Magín (-1902) Cu 139 *Cu.*
Roberts, Sergio C 19 *Chil.*
Robillot, Luis Cu 139 *Cu.*
Robleda y Troncoso, Cayetano Ig 314; NM 48 *Mex.*
Robledo, Alfonso Co 63 *Col.*
Robledo, Emilio (1875-) Co 63; LAS 201 *Col.*
Robledo, Francisco TM 303 *Mex.*
Robledo, Miguel HPM 469 *Mex.*
Roblejo, Manuel ARC 35; Cu 139 *Cu.*
Robles, Alejandro Mariano (-1807) ACe 934 *Mex.*
Robles, Antonio de TM 571 *Mex.*
Robles, Joselyn (-1916) PCh 435 *Chil.*
Robles, Pablo HLM 456; Ig 314; NM 48 *Mex.*
Robles, Ricardo NM 48 *Mex.*
Robles, Sebastián Alfredo LV 338 *Venez.*
Robles Gil, Emeterio TM 303 *Mex.*
Robleto, Hernán BHLA 576; IE 246; NM 49; TM 502 *Mex.*
Robreño, Gustavo Cu 139 *Cu.*
Robreño, José BDC 83 *Cu.*
Roca, Ignacio PE 107 *Ecua.*
Roca, Luis J. A 59 *Arg.*
Roca, Ramón ("Daurico Marón") PM 74; TM 304, 344 *Mex.*
"Roca, Roque" (*pseud.*) *see* Mandiola, Rómulo
Roca Boloña, José Antonio E 63 *Ecua.*
Rocafuerte, Vicente (1783-1847) BHLA 256; E 63, 75 *Ecua.*
Rocamonde, Víctor V 123 *Venez.*
"Roco, R." (*pseud.*) *see* Mandiola, Rómulo
Rocuant Figueroa, Miguel Luis C 69; LAS 205 *Chil.*
Rocuant Hidalgo, J. Félix C 39; NC 445 *Chil.*
Rocuant Mendoza, Emilio C 69 *Chil.*
Rocuant Sir, Miguel Luis (1880-) C 19, 39; CHL 263; CLH 223; NC 392; PCh 197; WLA 345 *Chil.*
Rocha, Diego Andrés HLNG I, 238 *Col.*
Rocha, Hermenegildo A 59, 90 *Arg.*
Rocha, José V. A 59 *Arg.*
Rocha, Miguel V 123 *Venez.*
Rocha, Octavio NL 282 *Nicar.*
Rocha de Lizardi, Natalia TM 304 *Mex.*
Rocha y Chabre, Manuel TM 304 *Mex.*
Roche, Andrés Co 63 *Col.*
Roche, José Domingo Co 63 *Col.*
Rodas, Olivastro ARC 61 *Cu.*

Rodaso, Federico Cu 139 *Cu.*
Rode, Guillermo TM 304 *Mex.*
Rodó, José Enrique ("Calibán") (1872-1917)
AB 25; BHLA 469; CHL 134, 314, 542;
CLH 474; G 388; GLO 254; HSLU I, pt
7, 5; III, pt 4, 35; LAS 201; LU 64, 678;
LUr 485; PIU II, 71; PLHA 249; PU
191; SA 9; SAL 184 *et passim;* SASS 484;
U 16; UL 189; WSAL 53 *Uru.*
"Rodófilo" (*pseud.*) *see* Eliz, Leonardo
Rodrigo, Luis de BAP 87 *Per.*
Rodrigo, Saturnino (1894-) B 19; WLA
346 *Bol.*
"Rodrigo Cifuentes" (*pseud.*) *see* Prieto
Yeme, Guillermo
"Rodríguez" (*pseud.*) *see* Larreta, Enrique
Rodríguez, Agustín PM 74 *Mex.*
Rodríguez, Agustín Baldomero (1826-1862)
ARC 34; Cu 140 *Cu.*
Rodríguez, Alberto A. NM 49; TM 305
Mex.
Rodríguez, Alberto M. E 63 *Ecua.*
Rodríguez, Alfonso TM 305 *Mex.*
Rodríguez, Amada Rosa PJC 216 *Cu.*
Rodríguez, Antonio E. Co 63 *Col.*
Rodríguez, Augustín A 59 *Arg.*
Rodríguez, Aureliana V 123 *Venez.*
Rodríguez, Bernardino TM 307 *Mex.*
Rodríguez, Carlos TM 441, 476 *Mex.*
Rodríguez, Carlos Alberto C 54 *Chil.*
Rodríguez, Catalina (1853-1894) Cu 140
Cu.
Rodríguez, Cayetano (1761-1823) BHLA
167; CHL 65; CLH 56; HLA 182; LA IV,
909 *Arg.*
Rodríguez, César A. (189.-) A 59; BAP
35; FPA 436, 458 *Per.*
Rodríguez, Cesáreo A 59, 71 *Arg.*
Rodríguez, Clodomiro V 123 *Venez.*
Rodríguez, Clotilde de Carmen (-1880)
Cu 140; PA 104 *Cu.*
Rodríguez, Cristóbal Pan 17 *Pan.*
Rodríguez, Diego TM 307 *Mex.*
Rodríguez, Elías V 123 *Venez.*
Rodríguez, Emilio Gaspar (1889-) Cu 140;
G 341; GLO 245; HLC 216 *Cu.*
Rodríguez, Eulogio V 123 *Venez.*
Rodríguez, Evangelina SD 28 *Dom.*
Rodríguez, Federico Cu 140 *Cu.*
Rodríguez, Francisco Antonio (1750-1817)
Co 63; HLNG II, 71; SCL 543, 634 *Col.*
Rodríguez, Francisco de P. ARC 36, 40
Cu.
Rodríguez, Ignacio TM 309 *Mex.*
Rodríguez, J. M. A. E 63 *Ecua.*
Rodríguez, José Cu 140 *Cu.*
Rodríguez, José Ignacio (1831-1907) CHL
483; CLH 423; Cu 140; RLC 244, 248 *Cu.*
Rodríguez, José Manuel Cu 140 *Cu.*
Rodríguez, José Santiago V 123 *Venez.*
Rodríguez, Juan Francisco (1848-1887)
GPCA II, 417; PG 246 *Guat.*
Rodríguez, Juan José V 123 *Venez.*
Rodríguez, Juan M. C 39, 54; PCh 365
Chil.
Rodríguez, Juan Zacarías BP 506; PR 39,
47 *P.R.*
Rodríguez, Julio Ariel A 59 *Arg.*
Rodríguez, Luis Ángel PM 74 *Mex.*

Rodríguez, Manuel (1633-1701) Co 63; LC
85; RHLC 13; SCL 357, 634 *Col.*
Rodríguez, Manuel del Socorro (1758-1818)
BHLA 144; Co 63; HLNG I, 375; HPHA
II, 33; RHLC 46; RLC 26; SCL 543, 635
Col.
Rodríguez, Manuel Filomeno (-1884) Ig
315; NM 49 *Mex.*
Rodríguez, Manuel L. V 123 *Venez.*
Rodríguez, María Luisa (1891-1913) PJC
213 *Cu.*
Rodríguez, Martín GEA X *Arg.*
Rodríguez, Máximo A. E 63 *Ecua.*
Rodríguez, Miguel Antonio (1777-) PLE
28 *Ecua.*
Rodríguez, Pablo E. PR 10 *P.R.*
Rodríguez, Paulino PR 47 *P.R.*
Rodríguez, Pedro Manuel P 30 *Per.*
Rodríguez, Simón (1771-1854) AA II, 46,
343; V 123 *Venez.*
Rodríguez, Teófilo V 123 *Venez.*
Rodríguez, Tomás Co 63 *Col.*
Rodríguez, Yamandú HSLU I, pt 2, 49;
Par 21; PU 196; U 16 *Uru.*
Rodríguez, Zorobabel (1839-1901) C 19;
CL 522; HC 180; NC 228, 445 *Chil.*
Rodríguez Acasuso, Luis A 59 *Arg.*
Rodríguez Acosta y García, Ofelia Cu 140
Cu.
Rodríguez Alcalá, José (1884-) Par 22
Para.
Rodríguez Alcalá, Teresa Lamas Carisimo
de (1889-) PT 71 *Para.*
Rodríguez B., Manuel de Jesús SD 28
Dom.
Rodríguez Barril, Alejandro PR 39 *P.R.*
Rodríguez Beltrán, Cayetano ("Onateyac")
(1866-) CHL 425; HLM 457; Ig 315;
NM 39, 49; PM 74 *Mex.*
Rodríguez Braida, Manuel F. PM 74 *Mex.*
Rodríguez Bravo, Joaquín CL 522 *Chil.*
Rodríguez C., Armando PD 204; SD 28
Dom.
Rodríguez Cabrero, Luis (186.-190.) FPA
460, 472; PR 14, 39 *P.R.*
Rodríguez Cáceres, Ricardo Cu 140; PA
107; PCu 230 *Cu.*
Rodríguez Calderón, Juan PR 39 *P.R.*
Rodríguez Carrasco, Manuel C 39 *Chil.*
Rodríguez Carreño, Generoso PJC 212 *Cu.*
Rodríguez Castells, Pura Cu 140 *Cu.*
Rodríguez Castro, José PR 47 *P.R.*
Rodríguez Cerna, Carlos (1894-) PG 456
Guat.
Rodríguez Cerna, José TM 476 *Mex.*
Rodríguez Correa, Ramón (1837-1894) Cu
140; NM 49
Rodríguez de Arizpe, Pedro José PM 74;
TM 307 *Mex.*
Rodríguez de Armas, Rodolfo (1874-)
BDC 84; CT 159; Cu 141 *Cu.*
Rodríguez de Cornick, Corina CA 45;
EPCR 656; IBCR IV, 303 *C.R.*
Rodríguez de Guzmán, Diego P 30 *Per.*
Rodríguez de la R., Carolina C 39 *Chil.*
Rodríguez de Ledesma y Cornejo, Felipe
TM 310 *Mex.*
Rodríguez de León, Alonso P 30 *Per.*
Rodríguez de León, Anastasio José ACe
941; PM 75 *Mex.*

Rodríguez de León, Juan P 31 *Per.*

Rodríguez de Morales, Catalina BDC 84; Cu 141 *Cu.*

Rodríguez de Tió, Lola (1862-1924) BP 538, 630; CHL 502; CLH 443; Cu 141; PA 242; PCu 231; PR 40, 54 *Cu.*

Rodríguez del Castillo, José Mariano ACe 935; HLM 245 *Mex.*

Rodríguez del Valle, Manuel Cu 141 *Cu.*

Rodríguez Díaz, José PJC 211 *Cu.*

Rodríguez Domínguez, Juan Antonio V 123 *Venez.*

Rodríguez-Embil y Urioste, Luis (1879-) Cu 141; PCu 232; WLA 348 *Cu.*

Rodríguez Fábregat, Enrique PU 201; U 16 *Uru.*

Rodríguez Faildes, José Cu 141 *Cu.*

Rodríguez Ferrer, Miguel Cu 141 *Cu.*

Rodríguez Fresle, Juan (1566-) BHLA 61; CHL 34; Co 64; HLNG I, 150; LC 88; RHLC 10; SCL 320, 635 *Col.*

Rodríguez Gabutti, Miguel PM 75 *Mex.*

Rodríguez Galván, Ignacio (1816-1842) AEHA 907; BHLA 240; CHL 387, 394; CLH 335; HLM 306, 331; HLMex 150; HPHA I, 129; HPM 630; NM 43, 49; PM 75; PMe II, 181; SASS 350; TM 308, 476; WSAL 44 *Mex.*

Rodríguez Gamboa, Luis C 19; NC 393 *Chil.*

Rodríguez García, José Antonio (1864-) BDC 84; CT 407; Cu 141; HLC 213; PR 17; RLC 244, 351, 355; WLA 348 *Cu.*

Rodríguez Godoy, Francisco Cu 143 *Cu.*

Rodríguez González, José TM 571 *Mex.*

Rodríguez Guichou, Rodolfo A 59 *Arg.*

Rodríguez Gutiérrez, Juan (-1863) E 63 *Ecua.*

Rodríguez Hernández, Luis V 124 *Venez.*

Rodríguez Iglesia, Emilio Ig 320; NM 49 *Mex.*

Rodríguez J., Carlos E. E 63 *Ecua.*

Rodríguez Juárez, Nicolás TM 311 *Mex.*

Rodríguez Larreta, Augusto A 59 *Arg.*

Rodríguez Larreta, Carlos A 59, 90 *Arg.*

Rodríguez Legrand, Luis U 16 *Uru.*

Rodríguez Lendián, Evelio Cu 143; RLC 344 *Cu.*

Rodríguez León, Amado Cu 143 *Cu.*

Rodríguez López, Francisco (1881-) QPR (1) 137 *P.R.*

Rodríguez López, Rafael V 124 *Venez.*

Rodríguez López, Rosa (1907-) IE 248 *Guat.*

Rodríguez Lucena, Mina de V 124 *Venez.*

Rodríguez Lucena, R. V 124 *Venez.*

Rodríguez Llamosas, Manuel V. V 124 *Venez.*

Rodríguez Manzo, José Antonio TM 312 *Mex.*

Rodríguez Méndez, José (1914-) PoC 246 *Cu.*

Rodríguez Mendoza, Emilio (1876-) BHLA 474, 509; C 19, 69; CHL 277; CLH 236; G 326; NC 232, 393, 446, 495 *Chil.*

Rodríguez Moguel, Heberto PM 75 *Mex.*

Rodríguez Objío, Manuel LD 80; SD 28 *Dom.*

Rodríguez Osterling, Enrique P 31 *Per.*

Rodríguez Pastor, J. PR 28 *P.R.*

Rodríguez Peña, Manuel A 59 *Arg.*

Rodríguez Peña, Román PM 75 *Mex.*

Rodríguez Pérez, Tomás Cu 143 *Cu.*

Rodríguez Pintos, Carlos HSLU II, pt 9, 39; PU 316 *Uru.*

Rodríguez Portillo, Armando (1880-1915) FPA 501, 513; PS 230 *Salv.*

Rodríguez Pujol, Héctor A 59 *Arg.*

Rodríguez Ramos, Manuel Cu 143 *Cu.*

Rodríguez Rendueles, M. PA 106 *Cu.*

Rodríguez Rivera, Ramón Ig 320; NM 49; TM 312 *Mex.*

Rodríguez Rivera, Vicente (1884-) BP 538, 629; PP 315; PR 40; QPR (2) 145 *P.R.*

Rodríguez Rivero, Crescencio BDC 84 *Cu.*

Rodríguez Rodríguez, Luis Felipe (1889-) Cu 140; LH 67, 95, 110; WLA 351 *Cu.*

Rodríguez S., Antonio E 63 *Ecua.*

Rodríguez Santos, Justo (1915-) PoC 250 *Cu.*

Rodríguez Santos, Luis Cu 143 *Cu.*

Rodríguez Socas, R. U 16 *Uru.*

Rodríguez Tejada, Manuel J. NM 4; TM 571 *Mex.*

Rodríguez Tomeu, Julia (1913-) PoC 256 *Cu.*

Rodríguez Torises, Manuel (1788-) HLNG II, 99 *Col.*

Rodríguez Tovar, Manuel E 63 *Ecua.*

Rodríguez Ucares (Uscarrel), José ("Capacho") BDC 83; Cu 143; HLC 18; RLC 25 *Cu.*

Rodríguez V., Amadeo Co 64 *Col.*

Rodríguez Velasco, Luis (1838-1919) C 39, 54; CHL 257; CLH 216; HC 150; PCh 53 *Chil.*

Rodríguez Xuárez, Nicolás PM 75 *Mex.*

Rodríguez y Barroso, Manuel Cu 143 *Cu.*

Rodríguez y Cos, José María PM 75; TM 310, 474 *Mex.*

Rodríguez y Jiménez, Emilio Gaspar (1889-) Cu 140; RLC 354, 363; WLA 349 *Cu.*

Roenicunt y Zenitrám, J. C. *see* Centurión, Juan Crisóstomo

"Roger de Lauria" (*pseud.*) *see* Gollury, Ramón F.

Roger y Roca, Miguel Cu 143 *Cu.*

Rohán, Ena de Cu 143 *Cu.*

Rohán, L. de Cu 143 *Cu.*

Rohde, Jorge Max (1893-) A 59; APAM 398; G 317; LAC 116, 153; WLA 353 *Arg.*

Röhl, Eduardo V 124 *Venez.*

Roig, Pablo BP 539; PR 40 *P.R.*

Roig de Leuchsenring, Emilio (1889-) BHLA 566; CT 567; Cu 144 *Cu.*

Roig y Grau, Jaime Cu 144 *Cu.*

Roiz, Domingo TM 312, 313 *Mex.*

Rojas, Alberto M. Cu 144 *Cu.*

Rojas, Arístides (1826-1894) BHLA 387; LV 12, 84; V 124; VPF 18 *Venez.*

Rojas, Casto (1880-) B 19; BT 251 *Bol.*

Rojas, Ezequiel (1801-) Co 64; LC 123 *Col.*

Rojas, Federico SD 28 *Dom.*

Rojas, Francisco M. Ig 320; NM 49 *Mex.*

Rojas, Jacobo Mariano TM 313 *Mex.*

Rojas, José María LV 29, 86; V 125 *Venez.*

Rojas, Juan Ramón (-1824) CHL 67, 197, 200; CLH 58; HLA 190, 192 *Arg.*
Rojas, Liberato Par 23; PPa 49 *Para.*
Rojas, Marco Aurelio V 125 *Venez.*
Rojas, Marqués de V 125 *Venez.*
Rojas, Pedro TM 477 *Mex.*
Rojas, Pedro Emilio V 125 *Venez.*
1. Rojas, Pedro José V 125 *Venez.*
2. Rojas, Pedro José (hijo) V 125 *Venez.*
Rojas, Pepe G 393 *Venez.*
Rojas, Ricardo (1882-) A 59, 90; APAM 114; APEH 743, 1190; AT II, 555; BHLA 489; CHL 43, 50, 70, 197, 200; G 317; LAC 103, 151; LAS 201; NPA 35; PLHA 266; SASS 46; WLA 354 *Arg.*
Rojas, Teófilo LV 113 *Venez.*
Rojas, Víctor Manuel CA 45 *C.R.*
Rojas Carrasco, Guillermo C 69 *Chil.*
Rojas Corrales, Ramón CA 45 *C.R.*
Rojas Cortés, Matías C 19 *Chil.*
Rojas de Herdocia, María Cristina CA 45 *C.R.*
Rojas de Oquendo, Mateo LA III, 64 *Arg.*
Rojas Garrido, José María (1824-1883) Co 64; LC 170; PCo 289 *Col.*
Rojas Giménez, Alberto C 19 *Chil.*
Rojas Gómez, Roberto Co 64 *Col.*
Rojas González, Francisco G 370; NM 49 *Mex.*
Rojas Guardia, Pablo V 125 *Venez.*
Rojas Jiménez, Alberto (1900-) PCC xxi, 235 *Chil.*
Rojas Meza, Héctor V 125 *Venez.*
Rojas Molina, A. C 39 *Chil.*
Rojas Paúl, Juan Pablo V 126 *Venez.*
Rojas Paz, Pablo A 60; BHLA 634, 636; LAC 122, 156 *Arg.*
Rojas Segovia, Juan C 39 *Chil.*
Rojas Sepúlveda, Manuel (1896-) AB 25; C 19, 39; PCC xx, 213; SASS 179; WLA 355 *Chil.*
Rojas Villalobos, Néstor C 39 *Chil.*
Rojas Vincenzi, Ricardo CA 45; IBCR IV, 332 *C.R.*
Rojas y Cañas, Ramón P 31 *Per.*
Rojas y Fuentes, José Basilio de SCL 499, 635 *Chil.*
Rojas y R., V. C 19; NC 500 *Chil.*
Rojas y Rocha, Francisco ACe 945; HPM 474 *Mex.*
Rojas y Rocha, Josefa Elvira ACe 946 *Mex.*
Rojas y Roélas, Elvira HPM 479 *Mex.*
Rojo, José R. Ig 321; NM 49 *Mex.*
Rojo García, Emilio Ig 321; NM 49 *Mex.*
Rokha, Pablo de ("Carlos Díaz") (1894-) C 39; CMPC 136; PCC xviii, 179 *Chil.*
Rokha, Winett de (1896-) C 39; CMPC 154; PCC xix, 197 *Chil.*
Rolando, Carlos A. E 63, 76 *Ecua.*
Roldán, Belisario J. (1873-1922) A 60, 90; AT I, 347 *Arg.*
Roldán, Eutimio Ig 321; NM 49 *Mex.*
Roldán, José Gonzalo (1822-1856) BDC 84; CHL 454; CLH 395, 396; Cu 144; RLC 191, 205 *Cu.*
Roldán Oliarte, E. V 126 *Venez.*
Roldán Sánchez, E. A 61 *Arg.*
Román, Alberto Cu 144 *Cu.*
Román, Aurelio PE 29 *Ecua.*

Román, Hugo E 63 *Ecua.*
Román, José Antonio (1873-) P 31 *Per.*
Román, Luis C 19, 39, 54; NC 240 *Chil.*
Román, Luis Antonio C 39 *Chil.*
Román, Manuel Antonio C 54, 69 *Chil.*
"Román, Ramón" (*pseud.*) *see* Barreto, José María
Román de Nieves, Josefa BP 506 *P.R.*
Román de Palma, Cristina P 25 *Per.*
Román Valdés, Justo P 31 *Per.*
Román y Rodríguez, Miguel SD 28 *Dom.*
Romana y Herrera, Felipe HLNG I, 297 *Col.*
Romanacce, Sergio (1898-) QPR (2) 147 *P.R.*
Romanace, Alejandro LV 338; V 126 *Venez.*
Romano, Manuel A 61 *Arg.*
Romay, Tomás (1764-1849) Cu 144; RLC 38, 39 *Cu.*
"Romeo" (*pseud.*) *see* Dutari (*or* Dutary), Alejandro
Romero, Antonio M. TM 314 *Mex.*
Romero, Calixto PR 54 *P.R.*
Romero, Carlos A. A 61 *Arg.*
Romero, Carlos Alberto (1863-) P 31, 35 *Per.*
Romero, Carlos V. B 19 *Bol.*
Romero, Cristóbal TM 314 *Mex.*
Romero, Enrique T. A 61 *Arg.*
1. Romero, Francisco Cu 144 *Cu.*
2. Romero, Francisco Co 64 *Col.*
Romero, Jesús C. TM 620 *Mex.*
Romero, José María BDC 84; Cu 144 *Cu.*
Romero, José Rubén PM 75 *Mex.*
Romero, Juan (1559-1630) LA III, 502 *Arg.*
Romero, Luis TM 597 *Mex.*
Romero, Manuel María HLM 466; TM 315, 477 *Mex.*
Romero, Manuel Salvador V 126 *Venez.*
Romero, Miguel J. V 126 *Venez.*
Romero, Paco Cu 144 *Cu.*
Romero, Paulo Emilio ("Paolo") LV 338; V 110, 126 *Venez.*
Romero, R. A. TM 315 *Mex.*
Romero, Rafael A. TM 315 *Mex.*
Romero, Romualdo B 19 *Bol.*
Romero, Rómulo A. A 61 *Arg.*
Romero Arnay, I. PM 75 *Mex.*
Romero Bermúdez, Rafael Co 64 *Col.*
Romero Cordero, Alberto (1896-) BHLA 620; C 19; WLA 357 *Chil.*
Romero Cordero, R. E 63 *Ecua.*
Romero de Terreros y Vinent, Manuel, Marqués de San Francisco (1880-) BAMP 79; HLM 530; IE 249; Ig 322; NM 50; TM 317, 477, 572; WLA 357 *Mex.*
Romero Fajardo, Fernando BHLA 605; Cu 144 *Cu.*
Romero Flores, Jesús (1885-) IE 251; PM 75 *Mex.*
Romero Gallardo, Luis M. A 61 *Arg.*
Romero García, Alejandro V 126 *Venez.*
Romero García, Manuel Vicente BHLA 412; CHL 378; CLH 326; LV 390; SASS 525; V 126; VPF 78 *Venez.*

Romero León, Remigio E 63; PE 310 *Ecua.*
Romero Menéndez, Emilio (1895?-) BHLA 603; E 63 *Ecua.*
Romero Menéndez, Héctor E 63 *Ecua.*
Romero Pérez, B. Cu 144 *Cu.*
Romero y Campa, Alfredo TM 316 *Mex.*
Romeu, Rafael PR 24 *P.R.*
Romeu y Aguayo, Domingo PR 21 *P.R.*
"Rómulo" (*pseud.*) *see* Carrasquilla, Ricardo
Ron Pedrique, M. L. V 126 *Venez.*
Ron Sierra, Eliseo E 63 *Ecua.*
"Ronda, Querubín de la" (*pseud.*) *see* Porto y Zárate, Miguel Francisco de
Rondón Sotillo, M. V 126 *Venez.*
"Ronquillo" (*pseud.*) *see* Poblete, Egidio
Roosen Rabalía, Carlos U 16 *Uru.*
Roosen Regalia, Germán HSLU II, pt 6, 21 *Uru.*
Roqué Geigel de Duprey, Ana (1853-) BP 506, 630; PR 28; QPR (1) 140 *P.R.*
"Roque Roco" (*pseud.*) *see* Mandiola, Rómulo
Roquendo, Miguel A 61, 90 *Arg.*
Roquero y Domínguez, Juan ("El Vate Arrugado") (1825-1885) BDC 85; Cu 145, 173 *Cu.*
Ros de Olano, Antonio (1802-1887) CHL 360; HPHA I, 400; V 126 *Venez.*
Rosa, Andrés Eloy de la V 126 *Venez.*
Rosa, Baltasar Juan Co 64 *Col.*
Rosa, Felipe de la PM 75 *Mex.*
Rosa, José Nicolás de la HLNG I, 348; RHLC 18; SCL 392, 636 *Col.*
Rosa, Rafael de A 61, 90 *Arg.*
Rosa, Ramón (1848-1893) HL I, 481; II, 179 *Hond.*
"Rosa de Chavarría" (*pseud.*) *see* Chavarría, Lisímaco
Rosa Nieves, Cesáreo PR 40 *P.R.*
"Rosa Té" (*pseud.*) *see* Trujillo y Arredondo, Rosa
Rosado Vega, Luis (1876-) AMP 118; APMM 182; G 370; HLM 429; Ig 325; NM 50; PM 75; PNM 274 *Mex.*
Rosado y Brincau, Federico (-1894) Cu 145; PR 33
Rosales, Antonio (1844-1902) ARC 35, 61; Cu 145 *Cu.*
Rosales, Aurora PM 76 *Mex.*
Rosales, Diego de (1603-1677) BHLA 63; SCL 281, 636 *Chil.*
Rosales, Hernán (1893-) IE 254 *Mex.*
Rosales, José Miguel Co 64 *Col.*
Rosales, Julio Horacio (1889-) V 127; VPF 112 *Venez.*
Rosales, Justo Abel C 20; NC 447 *Chil.*
Rosales, Ramón Co 64 *Col.*
Rosales de la Rosa, B. Co 64 *Col.*
Rosales y Morera, Francisco ARC 61; BDC 85; Cu 145 *Cu.*
Rosas, Avelino E 63 *Ecua.*
Rosas, Julio (1839-) Cu 145 *Cu.*
Rosas, Justo U 16 *Uru.*
Rosas Londa ("Cap. José") NM 50 *Mex.*
Rosas Moreno, José Ignacio (1838-1883) AEHA 908; AMP 264; CHL 401; CLH 348; HLM 397, 459; HLMex 195; HPHA I, 157; HPM 879; Ig 326; NM 50; PM 76; PMe II, 191; PoM 169; TM 318 *Mex.*

Roscio, Juan Germán V 127 *Venez.*
Rosell, Agustín Cu 146 *Cu.*
Rosell, Federico Ángel A 61 *Arg.*
Rosell y Carbonell, A. PR 21 *P.R.*
Roselló, Arturo Alfonso PJC 202 *Cu.*
Roselló, Héctor PIU III, 307 *Uru.*
Rosello de Salarido, Nieves A 61, 91 *Arg.*
"Rosicran" (*pseud.*) *see* Colman, Narciso Ramón
Rosillo y Meruelo, Andrés (1758-1835) HLNG II, 478 *Col.*
"Rosina Pérez" (*pseud.*) *see* Parejo, Antonio
Rosquellas, Luis Pablo (1823-) B 19; LB 589 *Bol.*
Rosquellas, Ramón B 19 *Bol.*
Ross, María Luisa G 370; Ig 328; NM 50; TM 477 *Mex.*
Ross Mujica, Luis NC 447 *Chil.*
Rossani, A. B. A 61 *Arg.*
Rossel, Ricardo (1841-1909) CHL 298; CLH 252; FPA 435, 445; LP 368; P 31; PPe 145; SASS 414 *Per.*
Rossi, Agustín (hijo) A 61; Par 23
Rossi, César A. U 17 *Uru.*
Rossi, José A 61 *Arg.*
Rossi, Lauro TM 610 *Mex.*
Rossi, Rómulo PIU III, 316 *Uru.*
Rossi, Vicente A 61 *Arg.*
Rossi Denevi, Alfredo C. A 61 *Arg.*
Rostand, Aura NL 199 *Nicar.*
Rothschuh, Guillermo NL 205 *Nicar.*
"Rotres V., Enrique" (*pseud.*) *see* Torres Valderrama, Enrique
Rotundo, José A 61 *Arg.*
Rouge, Delie C 20 *Chil.*
Roura Owen, Ramón PR 40 *P.R.*
Rousset de San Martín, Ángela A 61 *Arg.*
Roussilhe, J. Félix E 64 *Ecua.*
Rovira Vilella, R. A 61 *Arg.*
"Roxane" (*pseud.*) *see* Santa Cruz y Ossa, Elvira
Roxlo, Armando Víctor (-1912) PU 203 *Uru.*
Roxlo, Carlos (1860-1926) BHLA 423; CHL 223; CLH 186; FPA 527, 535; HSLU II, pt 1, 6; III, pt 4, 27; LU 64, 659; LUr 470; PIU II, 317; SASS 483; U 17; UL 190; UT 465 *Uru.*
Roy, Manuel Pan 17 *Pan.*
"Roy, Rob" (*pseud.*) *see* Silva Endeiza, Hugo
Royo, José Manuel Co 64; RHLC 159 *Col.*
Rozo, Jesús S. (1835-) Co 64; RHLC 186 *Col.*
Ruano, Jesús María Co 64 *Col.*
Ruanova, Francisco de P. Ig 329; NM 50 *Mex.*
Rubalcaba, Gilberto PM 76 *Mex.*
Rubalcava (Ruvalcaba), Manuel Justo (1769-1805) AEHA 908; CHL 106; CLH 89; Cu 146; HLC 35; HPHA I, 224; PR 56; RLC 46, 51 *Cu.*
Rubén, Abel ARC 35 *Cu.*
"Rubén Rubí" (*pseud.*) *see* Barra, Eduardo de la
Rubianes, Raúl A 61 *Arg.*
Rubiera, Ramón (1894-) Cu 146; PJC 220 *Cu.*
Rubiera y Casas, Leopoldo PM 76 *Mex.*

Rubín, Luis G. (1837-) G 370; Ig 329; NM 50; TM 321 *Mex.*
Rubín, Lupe NM 50 *Mex.*
Rubín de Celis, Antonio ACe 948 *Mex.*
Rubio, Alberto (1882-) PG 420 *Guat.*
Rubio, Darío HLM 514; TM 321 *Mex.*
Rubio, David P 31 *Per.*
Rubio, Ignacio R. PM 76 *Mex.*
Rubio, Luz Cu 146 *Cu.*
Rubio, Ozías H. Co 10, 64 *Col.*
Rubio Giménez, María Susana A 61 *Arg.*
Rubio J., Rafael TM 130, 321 *Mex.*
Rubio Marroquín, Jorge Co 64 *Col.*
Rubio v. de Robles, Laura (1886-) PG 432 *Guat.*
Rucabado, José Simón AP 293; Pan 17 *Pan.*
Rück, Ernesto O. B 19 *Bol.*
Rudas, Juan Manuel (1849-) Co 64 *Col.*
Ruderick, Alberto Cu 146 *Cu.*
Rueda, Evaristo Co 64 *Col.*
Rueda, F. TM 321 *Mex.*
Rueda R., Ramón Co 9, 64 *Col.*
Rueda Vargas, Tomás (1879-) Co 64, 65; RHLC 211 *Col.*
Rueda y Berañejos, Casandro de ACe 948 *Mex.*
Ruedas, Lisandro V 127 *Venez.*
Ruí, Francisco Aníbal AT II, 750 *Arg.*
"Ruido, Armando" (*pseud.*) *see* Martínez Nadal, Rafael
Ruilópez, Ramón Cu 146 *Cu.*
Ruiseco, Tomás TM 503 *Mex.*
Ruiz, Ángela L. PR 47 *P.R.*
Ruiz, Aureliano TM 322 *Mex.*
Ruiz, Eduardo (1839-1902) HLM 492; Ig 331; NM 50; PoM 366; TM 326 *Mex.*
Ruiz, Francisco (1817-1858) RLC 176 *Cu.*
Ruiz, Gustavo A. (189.-) FPA 502, 522; PS 241 *Salv.*
Ruiz, Joaquín Cu 146 *Cu.*
Ruiz, José María Co 65; HLNG II, 416 *Col.*
Ruiz, Julio TM 326 *Mex.*
"Ruiz, Luis" (*pseud.*) *see* Olavarría, Domingo Antonio
Ruiz, Telésforo PM 77 *Mex.*
Ruiz, Tomás Antonio PM 77 *Mex.*
Ruiz Aguilera, Ventura PR 40, 56, 61 *P.R.*
Ruiz Aldea, Pedro C 20; NC 393 *Chil.*
Ruiz Araujo, Isaac (1850-1881) CHL 507; CLH 448 *Salv.*
Ruiz Bravo, José Co 65; HLNG II, 390 *Col.*
Ruiz Cabañas, Samuel (1885-) APMM 191; G 370; HLM 524; PM 77; PNM 328 *Mex.*
Ruiz de Alarcón y Mendoza, Juan (1581?-1639) AEHA 30; AMP 217; BHLA 107; CHL 417; CLH 32; HLM 123; HLMex 57; HPHA I, 62; HPM 118; PoM 17; SAL 17; TM 322; WSAL 9 *Mex.*
Ruiz de Esparza, Juan Manuel ("Polifemo de Coustillac") AMP 200; NM 50; PM 77 *Mex.*
Ruiz de Gilbert, Carlota Cu 146 *Cu.*
Ruiz de León, Francisco CHL 21, 33; CLH 18, 28; Co 65; HLM 171; HLMex 78; HLNG II, 397; HPM 328 *Mex.*

Ruiz de Montoya, Antonio (1583-1652) HPHA II, 386; LA III, 382; Par 23; SCL 407, 636 *Para.*
Ruiz de Quevedo, Adolfo Co 146 *Col.*
Ruiz Díaz, Manuel HSLU III, pt 6, 31 *Uru.*
Ruiz é Irure, Luis Cu 146 *Cu.*
Ruiz Gandía, Manuel PR 54 *P.R.*
Ruiz García, Zoilo BP 507 *P.R.*
Ruiz Guerra y Rivera, Rafael PM 77 *Mex.*
Ruiz López, Rafael A 61; Par 23
Ruiz Morales, Salvador NL 123; PN 137 *Nicar.*
Ruiz Quiñones, Antonio PR 37, 40 *P.R.*
Ruiz Suárez, Bernardo ARC 62; Cu 146 *Cu.*
Ruiz Vernacci, Enrique Pan 17 *Pan.*
Ruiz y Galdós, César C 54 *Chil.*
Ruiz y Rodríguez, Manuel ("Lucas del Cigarral") (1874-) CT 361; Cu 39, 146 *Cu.*
Rumazo González, Alfonso (1903-) E 76; PLE 126; WLA 361 *Ecua.*
Rumazo González, José PLE 126 *Ecua.*
Rumbea, Tobías E. E 64 *Ecua.*
Runken, J. E. ("Joaquín de Zurriaga") editor of *Espectador Habanero Cu.*
Ruvalcaba *see* Rubalcava
Ruviñagras, Elías TM 326 *Mex.*
Ruz de Cea, G. TM 572 *Mex.*
Ruzo, Daniel (1900-) BAP 53; P 31 *Per.*

S

S., F. J. E 64 *Ecua.*
S., J. G. Cu 146 *Cu.*
"Saavedra, Antón Martín" (*pseud.*) *see* Salaverri, Vicente A.
Saavedra, Cornelio (1760-1819) GEA X; LA V, 209 *Arg.*
Saavedra, Gregorio G. A 61 *Arg.*
Saavedra, Rafael M. TM 326 *Mex.*
Saavedra Basavilbaso, María Helena (1908-) A 61 *Arg.*
Saavedra Galindo, José M. Co 65 *Col.*
Saavedra Guzmán, Antonio de BHLA 89; CHL 19; CLH 17; HLM 102; HLMex 48; HPHA I, 42; HPM 171; PM 77 *Mex.*
Saavedra y Bessey, Rafael GLO 249 *Mex.*
Saavedra y Guzmán, Martín de HLNG I, 236 *Col.*
Saavedra Zelaya, Mercedes ("M. de Saavedra Z.") (1893-) A 61, 78 *Arg.*
Sabas Aloma, Mariblanca (1901-) PoC 258 *Cu.*
Sábat Ercasty, Carlos (1887-) APEH 783; BHLA 532; G 390; LAS 208; LU 64, 664; PIU III, 164; PU 208; SASS 467; U 17 *Uru.*
Sábat Pebet, Juan Carlos HSLU III, pt 4, 46; LU 64, 685; U 17 *Uru.*
Sabater, José PR 25 *P.R.*
Sabella Gálvez, Andrés C 39 *Chil.*
Sablón, Jesús ARC 62 *Cu.*
Saborío, Adán CA 45 *C.R.*
Saborío, Francisco José CA 45 *C.R.*
Saborío, Joaquín CA 45 *C.R.*

Saborío Montenegro, Alfredo CA 46; EPCR 658 *C.R.*
Sabvini, Jermán B 19 *Bol.*
Sacasa S., Joaquín NL 197 *Nicar.*
Sacasa S., Salvador NL 193 *Nicar.*
Saco, José Antonio (1797-1879) ARC 75; BHLA 251; CHL 440, 451; CLH 381, 392; Cu 146; G 341; HLC 47; RLC 70, 86, 146, 160 *et passim*; SASS 299 *Cu.*
Sacrameña, Juan José TM 329 *Mex.*
Sacuy Morales, Ramón PN 145 *Nicar.*
Sáenz, Antonio (1780-1825) HLA 275 *Arg.*
Sáenz, Eduardo (1858-1900) A 61; LA VIII, 605 *Arg.*
Sáenz, Justo P. (hijo) A 61; LAC 137 *Arg.*
Sáenz, Mario (1879-) AT I, 249 *Arg.*
Sáenz, Máximo U 17 *Uru.*
Sáenz, Raquel HSLU II, pt 8, 11; LU 64, 668; U 17; WLA 363 *Uru.*
Sáenz, Tranquilino CA 46 *C.R.*
Sáenz, Vicente (1896-) CA 46; EPCR 668; IBCR IV, 175; IE 259 *C.R.*
Sáenz Azcorra, Franz AMP 204; PM 77 *Mex.*
Sáenz Cordero, Efraín CA 46 *C.R.*
Sáenz Cordero, Jorge CA 46 *C.R.*
Sáenz Cordero, Manuel (1882-) CA 46; EPCR 491 *C.R.*
Sáenz E., Carlos Luis CA 46; EPCR 666 *C.R.*
Sáenz Echeverría, Carlos (1853-1893) Co 65; RHLC 170 *Col.*
Sáenz Hayes, Ricardo A 61; LAC 108, 152 *Arg.*
Sáenz Morales, Ramón (1891-) FPA 358, 374; IE 260; NL 95 *Nicar.*
Sáenz Ovecurry, Diego CHL 22; CLH 19 *Guat.*
Sáenz Peña, Roque A 61 *Arg.*
Sáez, Amable Cu 147 *Cu.*
Sáez, Benjamín B. A 61 *Arg.*
Sáez Sanjuan, Carlos V 127 *Venez.*
Sagárnaga, Elías B 19 *Bol.*
Sagarra, Juan Bautista Cu 147 *Cu.*
Sagarra Magín, Roberto BDC 85 *Cu.*
"Sagitario" (*pseud.*) *see* Scott, Daniel R.
Sagra, Ramón de la (1798-1871) RLC 177 *Cu.*
Saguí, Juan Francisco A 61 *Arg.*
Sahagún, Bernardino de (1499?-1590) BHLA 59, 65; HLM 50; HLMex 14 *Mex.*
Sains de la Peña, Francisco C 39 *Chil.*
"Saint Just" (*pseud.*) *see* Lafosse, Alfredo P.
"Saint Louis" (*pseud.*) *see* Pérez Fuentes, Francisco
Sainte-Marie, Victoria C 39 *Chil.*
Sainz, José Antonio de (1894-) B 19; BT 261 *Bol.*
Sainz de la Peña, Dulce Ma., Vda. de Mena Cu 147 *Cu.*
Sainz Peña, Enrique SD 28 *Dom.*
Saiz de la Mora, Jesús Cu 147 *Cu.*
Salado Álvarez, Victoriano (1867-1931) BAMP 55; HLM 453; HLMex 227; Ig 332; NM 51; TM 478 *Mex.*
Salafranca, José Par 23 *Para.*
Salamanca T., Demetrio Co 65 *Col.*
1. Salas, Ángel B 19 *Bol.*
2. Salas, Ángel TM 329 *Mex.*

Salas, Carlos J. (1864-) AT II, 579 *Arg.*
Salas, Enrique B 19 *Bol.*
Salas, José (1862-) Cu 147 *Cu.*
Salas, Juan N. PM 77 *Mex.*
Salas, Julio C. V 127 *Venez.*
Salas, Manuel de (1745-1841) AA II, 25, 159; C 69 *Chil.*
Salas, Mariano B 19 *Bol.*
Salas Aloma, Mariblanca PCu 242; PJC 226 *Cu.*
Salas Errázuriz, Juan R. C 54 *Chil.*
Salas González, Eliodoro C 69; NC 454 *Chil.*
Salas Lavaqui, Manuel C 69 *Chil.*
Salas Pérez, José Joaquín CA 46 *C.R.*
Salas Subirat, J. A 62 *Arg.*
Salas y Quiroga, Jacinto de NM 51 *Mex.*
Salas y Quiroga, José Jacinto de (1813-1849?) Cu 148 *Cu.*
Salas y Valdés, Agustín P 31 *Per.*
Salaverri, Vicente A. ("Antón Martín Saavedra") (1889-) G 390; GLO 255; IE 260; LU 64, 675; PIU III, 281; PLHA 204; U 17; UL 190 *Uru.*
Salaverry, Carlos Augusto (1831-1890) AEHA 767; BHLA 318; CHL 295; CLH 250; FPA 435, 443; G 382; HPHA II, 263; LP 361; P 31; PLHA 75; PPe 57; SASS 410 *Per.*
Salazar, Abel C. (1878-1925) G 371; Ig 337; NM 51; PM 77 *Mex.*
Salazar, Agustín E 64 *Ecua.*
Salazar, Antonio de PM 77 *Mex.*
Salazar, Arturo CA 46 *C.R.*
Salazar, Buenaventura E 64 *Ecua.*
Salazar, Constantino R. P 31 *Per.*
Salazar, Elías (1866-1922) CA 46, 47 *C.R.*
Salazar, Eugenio de (1530?-) HLM 91; HPHA I, 295; HPM 104 *Mex.*
Salazar, Federico G. CA 47 *C.R.*
Salazar, Francisco Javier (1824-1891) E 64 *Ecua.*
Salazar, José María de (1785-1828) BHLA 159; CHL 84; CLH 71; Co 65; CoL 268; HLNG II, 85, 325; HPHA II, 35; LC 111; RHLC 53; V 127 *Col.*
Salazar, Luis A. E 64 *Ecua.*
Salazar, María Esther PM 77 *Mex.*
Salazar, Matías V 127 *Venez.*
Salazar, Rosendo PM 77 *Mex.*
Salazar, Virginia CA 47 *C.R.*
Salazar Álvarez, Raúl CA 47; EPCR 592 *C.R.*
Salazar de Alarcón, Eugenio BHLA 77; HPHA I, 28 *Mex.*
Salazar de Robles, Caridad ("Cira") CA 13, 47; IBCR IV, 185, 275 *C.R.*
Salazar Domínguez, José V 127 *Venez.*
Salazar G., F. I. E 65 *Ecua.*
Salazar Gagini, Carlos CA 47; EPCR 672 *C.R.*
Salazar Mallén, Rubén TM 329 *Mex.*
Salazar Muñoz, Alejandro Co 65 *Col.*
Salazar y Roig, Salvador (1892-) BDC 85; CLH 429; CT 397; Cu 148; LAS 202; WLA 367 *Cu.*
Salazar y Torres, Agustín (1642-) HLM 187; HPM 217; TM 329 *Mex.*
Salcedo, Luis TM 330 *Mex.*

"Salcedo, Tito" (*pseud.*) *see* Marcano, Vicente
Salcedo de Villar, Pedro Co 65 *Col.*
Salcedo Mantilla de los Ríos, Juan BDC 86 *Cu.*
Saldanha, E. de Co 65 *Col.*
Saldías, Adolfo (1850-1914) A 62; LA VII, 211; SASS 80 *Arg.*
Saldías, José Antonio (1891-) A 62, 91 *Arg.*
Saldías Vásquez, José C 20 *Chil.*
Sales, José Joaquín EPCR 590 *C.R.*
Sales Cepeda, Manuel Ig 338; NM 51 *Mex.*
Sales Pérez, Francisco de ("Justo") LV 387; V 85, 127, 128; VPF 53 *Venez.*
Sales Soto, F. de E 65 *Ecua.*
Salgado, Antonio ACe 949 *Mex.*
Salgado, José LAS 201; U 18 *Uru.*
Salgado, Luis A. E 65 *Ecua.*
Salgado, Teresina SD 28 *Dom.*
Salgueiro, Aristeo A 62; G 318 *Arg.*
Salgueiro, Juan José B 19 *Bol.*
Salias, Vicente LV 28; V 128 *Venez.*
Salicrup, A. PR 7, 40 *P.R.*
Salinas, Cesáreo NL 21 *Nicar.*
Salinas, Marcelo RLC 369 *Cu.*
Salinas, Miguel IE 262; NM 51; PM 77 *Mex.*
Salinas Aguilar, Norberto NL 218 *Nicar.*
Salinas Boquin, José NL 60 *Nicar.*
Salinas y Cabrera, Diego de BHC III, 302 *Chil.*
Salmón, Demetrio B 19 *Bol.*
Salom, Diwaldo (1879-) Cu 148; PA 107; PCu 244 *Cu.*
"Salomé Gil *or* Jil" (*pseud.*) *see* Milla y Vidaurre, José
Salteraín, Joaquín de (1856-) CHL 217; CLH 180; PIU I, 246; UT 469 *Uru.*
Salteraín y Herrera, Eduardo de (1892-) HSLU II, pt 6, 24; III, pt 4, 46; U 18; UL 191; WLA 368 *Uru.*
Saluzzo, Marco Antonio LV 296; V 128 *Venez.*
Salvador, C. E. E 65 *Ecua.*
Salvador, Humberto BHLA 595 *Ecua.*
"Salvador Mario" (*pseud.*) *see* Ocampo, Luis
Salvador Ulloa, M. A 62 *Arg.*
Salvagno (*or* Salvaño) Campos, Carlos LU 692; PIU III, 308 *Uru.*
Salvat, Angélica de (1866-) Pan 18 *Pan.*
Salvat, M. A. A 62 *Arg.*
Salvatierra, Fernando C 20 *Chil.*
Salvatierra y Garnica, Bernardino de PM 77 *Mex.*
Salvent, E. M. Cu 149 *Cu.*
Sallo, Pedro ARC 62 *Cu.*
Sama, Manuel María (1850-1913) BDC 86; PP 114; PR 8, 14, 37, 40, 61 *P.R.*
Samadhy, Allan C 39; PCh 315 *Chil.*
Samaniego, Carlos TM 611 *Mex.*
Samaniego, Francisco HPM 198; PM 77 *Mex.*
Samaniego, Pedro P. Par 23 *Para.*
Sámano, Carlos HPM 118 *Mex.*
Sámano, Juan Co 45 *Col.*
Samatan, Marta E. A 62 *Arg.*
Samonati, Alfredo (1887-) UT 475 *Uru.*
Samper, Carlos M. PM 77 *Mex.*
Samper, Darío (1909-) BHLA 589 *Col.*

Samper, José María (1828-1888) CHL 336; CLH 289; Co 65, 66, 67; HPHA II, 75; LC 129; RHLC 166, 184, 199 *Col.*
Samper, Miguel (1825-1899) Co 67; LC 171; RHLC 197 *Col.*
Samper Ortega, Daniel (1895-) CHL 355; Co 67; RHLC 192; WLA 369 *Col.*
Samper Ortega, Eduardo BHLA 519 *Col.*
Samperiz Janín, José Cu 149 *Cu.*
San Cayetano, Joseph de PM 77 *Mex.*
San Cremente, Jorge A 62, 91 *Arg.*
San Cristóval, Evaristo (1894-) WLA 373 *Per.*
San Emilio, Marqués de Cu 149 *Cu.*
San Francisco, José de Cu 149 *Cu.*
San Francisco, Marqués de *see* Romero de Terreros y Vinent, Manuel
San Germán, Arnulfo Ig 339; NM 51 *Mex.*
San Javier, Vizconde de U 18 *Uru.*
San Juan, Manuel A. P 31 *Per.*
San Juan, Manuel H. (1864-1917) HLM 457; Ig 339; NM 51 *Mex.*
San Lorenzo, Felipe Par 24 *Para.*
San Martín, Ataulfo de A 62 *Arg.*
San Martín, José de (1780-1850) A 62; BHLA 183 *Arg.*
San Martín, Manuel de Par 24 *Para.*
San Martín, Tomás de SCL 67, 638 *Dom.*
San Nicolás, Andrés de (-1666) Co 67; HLNG I, 168, 190; LC 87; SCL 447, 638 *Col.*
San Pedro M. Cu 149 *Cu.*
Sanabia, Rafael Emilio SD 28 *Dom.*
Sanabria, Martín José V 128 *Venez.*
Sanamé, José Policarpo (1760-1806) RLC 33 *Cu.*
Sanavria Hernández, José Tomás V 128 *Venez.*
Sanctis, Alfredo de TM 478 *Mex.*
Sánchez, Alonso B. V 128 *Venez.*
Sánchez, C. B. E 65 *Ecua.*
Sánchez, Eusebio TM 427, 478 *Mex.*
Sánchez, Florencio (1875-1910) A 62, 91; BHLA 547; CLH 198; G 390; GLO 255; HSLU II, pt 4, 5; LU 64, 686; LUr 528; PIU II, 153; PLHA 293; SASS 491; SPLA 175; U 18 *Uru.*
Sánchez, Flores José Par 24 *Para.*
Sánchez, Francisco del R. SD 29 *Dom.*
Sánchez, J. Juan S. TM 332 *Mex.*
Sánchez, Joaquín A. (-1890?) BDC 87; Cu 149 *Cu.*
Sánchez, José (-1917) ARC 62 *Cu.*
Sánchez, José C. (Jr.) TM 330 *Mex.*
Sánchez, José Manuel A 62, 92 *Arg.*
Sánchez, Juan Bautista (1714-1774) BHLA 106; SCL 393, 637 *Per.*
Sánchez, Juan de M. PM 77; TM 331 *Mex.*
Sánchez, Juan F. (1874-) Cu 149 *Cu.*
Sánchez, Juan José SD 29 *Dom.*
Sánchez, Julián ARC 62 *Cu.*
Sánchez, Julio C. PLE 114 *Ecua.*
Sánchez, Luis Alberto LAS 202; P 31 *Per.*
Sánchez, Luis Aníbal E 65 *Ecua.*
Sánchez, Luis P. A 62 *Arg.*
Sánchez, Manuel A. PM 77 *Mex.*
Sánchez, Manuel María (1890?-) FPA 254, 288; PE 211; PLE 86 *Ecua.*
Sánchez, Manuel Segundo V 128 *Venez.*

Sánchez, María ("Misia Mariquita") LA VIII, 776 *Arg.*

Sánchez, Mariano TM 332 *Mex.*

Sánchez, Quintiliano (1848-) E 65; PE 275; PLE 48 *Ecua.*

Sánchez, R. Augusto PD 205; SD 29 *Dom.*

Sánchez, Ricardo U 18 *Uru.*

Sánchez, Serafín Cu 149 *Cu.*

Sánchez Agramonte, Elpidio (1892-) Cu 149 *Cu.*

Sánchez Arce, Abraham ("Fuego") Ig 341; NM 51 *Mex.*

Sánchez Azcona, Héctor Ig 342; NM 51 *Mex.*

Sánchez Azcona, Juan (1876-) IE 263 *Mex.*

Sánchez Barra, José María (1806-1855) P 32 *Per.*

Sánchez Bolaños, Roberto C 40 *Chil.*

Sánchez Bonilla, Gonzalo (1884-) CA 47; EPCR 483; IBCR IV, 92 *et passim C.R.*

Sánchez Bustamante, Daniel (1871-) B 19 *Bol.*

Sánchez Capiro, Andrés Cu 149 *Cu.*

Sánchez Carrión, José Faustino BHLA 176 *Per.*

Sánchez Concha, María Isabel ("Belsarina") P 32 *Per.*

"Sánchez de Almodóvar, Bachiller Toribio" (*pseud.*) *see* Monte y Aponte, Domingo del

Sánchez de Bustamente, Antonio (1865-) CT 127; HLC 209; RLC 346 *Cu.*

Sánchez de Fuentes, Eduardo Cu 149 *Cu.*

1. Sánchez de Fuentes, Eugenio (1826-1894) BP 515, 539; Cu 149; PR 14, 15, 40 *P.R.*

2. Sánchez de Fuentes, Eugenio (1865-) BDC 87 *Cu.*

Sánchez de Fuentes, Fernando (1871-) CT 505; PCu 247 *Cu.*

Sánchez de Fuentes, María (1879-) PoC 263 *Cu.*

Sánchez de Tagle, Francisco Manuel (1782-1847) ACe 577; BHLA 187; CHL 101; CLH 85; GLO 249; HLM 241; HLMex 124; HPHA I, 108; HPM 596; PM 77 *Mex.*

Sánchez de Velasco, Manuel B 20 *Bol.*

Sánchez Escobar, Rafael PM 78 *Mex.*

Sánchez Figueras, Silverio ARC 62 *Cu.*

Sánchez Fuentes, Andrés PM 78 *Mex.*

Sánchez Galarraga, Gustavo (1892-) BDC 87; CT 311; Cu 150; HLC 207; PCu 248; PJC 75; RLC 366, 368; WLA 372 *Cu.*

Sánchez Gardel, Julio (-1936) A 62, 92; BHLA 546; CHL 199; PLHA 293 *Arg.*

Sánchez Gómez, Gregorio Co 67 *Col.*

Sánchez Gratereaux, Rafael SD 29 *Dom.*

Sánchez Guerrero, J. C 40 *Chil.*

Sánchez Labrador, José (1719-1798) LA IV, 586; SCL 423, 637 *Arg.*

Sánchez Lustrino, Gilberto SD 29 *Dom.*

Sánchez Lustrino, Ricardo V. LD 101; SD 29 *Dom.*

Sánchez Mármol, Manuel (1839-1912) BHLA 414; CHL 373, 408; CLH 355; HLM 457; NM 4, 51; TM 572 *Mex.*

Sánchez Montenegro, Víctor Co 67 *Col.*

Sánchez Ortiz, Ernesto (1899-) QPR (1) 145 *P.R.*

Sánchez Pérez, D. A. TM 332 *Mex.*

Sánchez Pérez, Nicolás (-1864) Cu 151 *Cu.*

Sánchez Pesquera, Miguel (1851-) AEHA 772; BHLA 432; CHL 373; CLH 321; LV 230, 308; PR 40; V 128, 129 *Venez.*

Sánchez Rubio, Elías V 129 *Venez.*

Sánchez Santos, Mariano TM 332 *Mex.*

Sánchez Santos, Trinidad PM 78 *Mex.*

Sánchez Sotomayor, José PR 40 *P.R.*

Sánchez Valverde, Antonio SD 29 *Dom.*

Sánchez Varona, Ramón HLC 219 *Cu.*

"Sánchez Vicuña, el lic." (*pseud.*) *see* Gorostiza, Manuel Eduardo de

Sánchez y Sánchez, Carlos SD 29 *Dom.*

Sancho, Francisco BDC 90; Cu 151 *Cu.*

Sancho, Mario CA 47, 48; EPCR 596; IBCR IV, 155 *C.R.*

Sancho, Pedro (-1547) P 32; SCL 64, 637 *Per.*

"Sancho Polo" (*pseud.*) *see* Rabasa, Emilio

"Sandemar, B. de" (*pseud.*) *see* Martínez Cuadra, José

Sandino Hernández, Antenor NL 229 *Nicar.*

Sandó y Vederia, Bernardo ARC 62 *Cu.*

Sandoval Palma, A. R. V 129 *Venez.*

Sandoval y Zapata, Luis de HLM 156; HPM 200 *Mex.*

Sanfuentes y Torres, Salvador (1817-1860) BHLA 314; C 40, 54; CHL 240, 242, 246; CLH 202; HC 73; HPHA II, 364; PCh 15 *Chil.*

Sanguily y Arizti, Manuel Cu 151 *Cu.*

Sanguily y Garrett (*also* Garrite *and* Garritte), Manuel (1848-1925) CHL 448, 484; CLH 391, 424; CT 313; Cu 151; G 341; HLC 89; RLC 315 *et passim Cu.*

Sanguinetti, Carlos C. A 62, 92 *Arg.*

Sanguino Sánchez, Ernesto C 20 *Chil.*

Sanhueza, Jorge C 20 *Chil.*

Saniere, S. de C 20 *Chil.*

Sanín Cano, Baldomero (1861-) BHLA 473; Co 67, 68; G 330; IE 266; LC 188; RHLC 210 *Col.*

Sanjenis, Avelino Cu 151 *Cu.*

Sanjinés, Fernando de M. B 20 *Bol.*

Sanjinés, Jenaro (1844-) B 20 *Bol.*

Sanjinés, José Ignacio B 20 *Bol.*

Sanjinés Uriarte, Modesta E. (1832-1873) B 20 *Bol.*

Sanmiguel, José Ignacio HLNG II, 460 *Col.*

Sanmiguel, Peregrino (1812-) Co 68 *Col.*

Sanojo, Luis V 129 *Venez.*

Sanromán, Mario PM 78 *Mex.*

"Sansón Carrasco" (*pseud.*) *see* Muñoz, Daniel

Sansone, Fusco PIU III, 226; U 18 *Uru.*

Sansores, Rosario ("Crisantema") Cu 152; E 65; PCu 255; PJC 228; PM 78 *Cu.*

Santa Anna, Antonio TM 336 *Mex.*

Santa Cruz, Elena Sabina Cu 152 *Cu.*

Santa Cruz, María de Cu 152 *Cu.*

Santa Cruz, Ricardo Cu 152 *Cu.*

Santa Cruz Pachacuti, Juan P 32 *Per.*

Santa Cruz y Espejo, Francisco Javier Eugenio (1747-1797) CHL 40; CLH 35; E 66; PLE 20 *Ecua.*

Santa Cruz y Ossa, Elvira ("Roxane") C 20, 54 *Chil.*
Santa Eulalia, Francisco F. Cu 152 *Cu.*
Santa Fe, Alberto PM 78 *Mex.*
Santa María, Fernando C 20; NC 454 *Chil.*
Santa María, Javier HLM 398, 467; PM 78; TM 478 *Mex.*
Santacilia, Pedro NM 4, 51 *Mex.*
Santacilia y Palacios, Pedro Antonio (1826-1910) BHLA 301, 329; CHL 460; Cu 152; G 341; HLC 129; RLC 187, 269 *Cu.*
Santacruz, J. Felicísimo E 65 *Ecua.*
Santaella, José Blas (1832-1880) PM 78 *Mex.*
Santaella, Juan V 129, 139 *Venez.*
Santamaría, Francisco Javier Antonio de (1710-) E 66; TM 573
Santamaría, Gonzalo de Co 68 *Col.*
Santamaría, J. TM 393 *Mex.*
Santamaría de Manrique, Manuela HLNG II, 81 *Col.*
Santana, Arturo V 129 *Venez.*
Santana, Pedro SD 29 *Dom.*
Santander, Alejandro Co 68 *Col.*
Santander, Francisco de Paula (1792-1840) BHLA 247; Co 68; HLNG II, 502; LC 118 *Col.*
Santander, José Antonio P 32 *Per.*
Santander, R. G. E 66 *Ecua.*
Santander, Rafael Eliseo (1809-1883) RHLC 120 *Col.*
Santander H., Modesto Co 68 *Col.*
Santelices E., Lisandro C 40 *Chil.*
Santelices Valenzuela, Augusto (1907-) C 40; PCC xxiv, 287; WLA 374 *Chil.*
Santiago, Ramón de (1833-) HCLU I, 361; PIU I, 193 *Uru.*
Santibáñez *see also* Santiváñez
Santibáñez, Enrique TM 573 *Mex.*
Santibáñez, Fernando *see* Santiván, Fernando
Santibáñez, J. Ramírez PR 11 *P.R.*
Santibáñez Rojas, Antonio C 69; NC 454 *Chil.*
Santiesteban, J. B. de TM 337 *Mex.*
Santillán, Fernando (-1575 or 1576) P 32 *Per.*
Santillán, José M. de Cu 152 *Cu.*
Santín Rossi, Carlos PIU III, 304 *Uru.*
Santisteban, Luis Enrique Cu 152 *Cu.*
Santisteban y Osorio, Diego de BHC I, 82, 90; CHL 12; CLH 10; HPHA II, 323; SCL 208, 638 *Chil.*
Santistevan, José María de E 66 *Ecua.*
Santiván, Fernando (Santibáñez, Fernando) C 20; CHL 280; CLH 238; N 195; NC 394; WLA 374 *Chil.*
Santiváñez, José María (1815-) B 20 *Bol.*
Santo Domingo, R. Co 35, 68 *Col.*
Santos, Aníbal CA 48 *C.R.*
Santos, Carlos R. Par 24 *Para.*
Santos, Enrique ("Calibán") (1887-) WLA 374 *Col.*
Santos, Luis R. Cu 152 *Cu.*
Santos, Rafael C 20, 40 *Chil.*
Santos, Tomás de los Par 24 *Para.*
Santos Coy, J. M. TM 337 *Mex.*

Santos Chocano, José (1876-) FPA 436, 450; G 383; P 32; PPe 204; SA 109 *Per.*
Santos González, Claudio Cu 152 *Cu.*
Santos Machicado, José (1844-) B 20; BT 171 *Bol.*
Santos Marmolejo C., Manuel Co 68 *Col.*
Santos Ramos, Domingo LV 52, 114; V 129 *Venez.*
Santos Salazar, Manuel HPM 452 *Mex.*
Santos Ugarte, Francisco Cu 152 *Cu.*
"Santos Vega" (*pseud.*) *see* Rivarola, Enrique E.
Santos y Salazar, Manuel de los TM 337 *Mex.*
Santovenia y Echaide, Emeterio Santiago (1889-) CT 103; Cu 152; WLA 375 *Cu.*
Santoyo, Felipe de PM 78 *Mex.*
Santrustegui, Cecilia PB 181 *Bol.*
Sanz, Gerónimo (1836-1882) Cu 153 *Cu.*
Sanz, J. ("Fierabas") Ig 343; NM 52 *Mex.*
Sanz, Julián (1886-1924) BDC 40, 90 *Cu.*
Sanz, Mariano José (1810-1868) P 33 *Per.*
Sanz, Miguel José CHL 357; CLH 306; LV 92; V 129 *Venez.*
"Sanz, Trini" (*pseud.*) *see* Padilla de Sanz, Trinidad
Sanz y García, Julián (1886-) Cu 153; HLC 220 *Cu.*
Sañudo, José Rafael Co 68 *Col.*
Sarachaga, Ignacio (-1900) BDC 91; Cu 153 *Cu.*
Sarasti, Manuel E 66 *Ecua.*
Saraví, Guillermo A 62 *Arg.*
Saravia, Buenaventura GPCA III, 383; PG 288 *Guat.*
Sardá y Salvany, Félix E 66, 76 *Ecua.*
Sardi, Julio V 129 *Venez.*
Sardiña y Villa, Juan (-1916) ARC 62 *Cu.*
Sargenti, Salvador B 20 *Bol.*
Sariñana, Severo María PM 78; TM 338 *Mex.*
Sariol, Juan F. PJC 235 *Cu.*
Sarlat, Simón TM 338 *Mex.*
Sarmiento, Domingo Faustino (1811-1888) A 62; BHLA 264, 283; CHL 147; CL 524; CLH 125, 198; G 318; GEA I, VI, XVIII; GLO 238; HLA 221, 375; HPHA II, 359; LA V, 497; PLHA 244; SAL 204, 231, 330; SASS 56; SPLA 228 *Arg.*
Sarmiento, José Miguel (1875-) G 371 *Mex.*
Sarmiento, Marciano TM 339 *Mex.*
Sarmiento, Nicanor A 63 *Arg.*
Sarmiento, Ricardo ("Delio Seravile") (1885-) Co 68 *Col.*
Sarmiento de Gamboa, Pedro (1532?-) SCL 125, 638 *Per.*
Sarracent, Carmelina ARC 62 *Cu.*
Sarret, Cecilio V. ARC 63; PJC 234 *Cu.*
Sartorio, José Manuel Mariano Aniceto (1746-1829) ACe 19; HLM 173; HLMex 95; HPM 362; PM 78 *Mex.*
Sartorio, Juan Manuel TM 339 *Mex.*
"Sasor, M." (*pseud.*) *see* Rivera, Mercedes de Rosas
Sasso, Ana B. de V 129 *Venez.*
Sasso, Domingo A 63 *Arg.*

Sassone, Felipe (1884-) AEHA 909; BAP 21; BHLA 515; CHL 306; CLH 261; G 383; LP 390; P 33; PPe 294 *Per.*

Sastre, Marcos (1809-1887) A 63; BHLA 235; CHL 211; LA VI, 1125; LUr 452 *Arg.*

Sastre Robles, Pablo BP 540; PR 40 *P.R.*

Sauza González, Jesús TM 340 *Mex.*

Saviñón, Altagracia PA 370; PD 206; SD 29 *Dom.*

Sbariggi, C. A 63 *Arg.*

Scaffo, Carlos HSLU III, pt 8, 25 *Uru.*

Scalabrini Ortiz, Raúl (1898-) A 63; BHLA 633 *Arg.*

Scalese, Luis E. A 63 *Arg.*

Scandroglio, R. U 18 *Uru.*

Scanlan, Eduardo V 129 *Venez.*

Scarone, Arturo (1885-) Par 24; U 18; UL 191; UT 483 *Uru.*

Scarpeta, Adriano (-1881) Co 68 *Col.*

Scarpetta, José Co 68 *Col.*

Scarpetta, M. Leónidas Co 68 *Col.*

Scarzolo Travieso, Luis U 18 *Uru.*

Scefano, G. di PM 78 *Mex.*

Scola y Robles, Adalio (-1873) BDC 91; Cu 153 *Cu.*

Scornick, Isabelino A 63 *Arg.*

Scott, Daniel R. ("Sagitario") V 127, 129 *Venez.*

Scotto, José Antonio U 18 *Uru.*

Schaefer Gallo, Carlos A 63, 92; CHL 199 *Arg.*

Schecker, Luis SD 29 *Dom.*

Schiaffino, Eduardo (1858-) A 63 *Arg.*

Schiavo, Horacio A. A 63 *Arg.*

Schiffino, José SD 29 *Dom.*

Schinca, Francisco Alberto HSLU III, pt 4, 46; PU 212; U 18; UL 191 *Uru.*

Schmidel de Straubing, Ulrich LA III, 165; SCL 398, 640 *Arg.*

Schmidke, Jorge V 129 *Venez.*

Schoenrich, Otto SD 29 *Dom.*

Schtronn, Zoraida de *see* Díaz de Ross *or* de Schtronn, Zoraida

Schulz, Enrique E. (1875-) IE 267 *Mex.*

Schumacher, Pedro E 66 *Ecua.*

Secas, Justo A. P 33 *Per.*

Secco Illa, Joaquín (1879-) UT 491 *Uru.*

Seco, José A. A 63 *Arg.*

Seda, J. TM 340 *Mex.*

Sedano, Francisco (1742-1812) ACe 951; HLM 209 *Mex.*

Segale, Atenógenes (1865-1903) Ig 343; NM 52; PM 78; TM 340 *Mex.*

Segarra, Julio G. TM 342 *Mex.*

Segovia, Teófilo C. E 66 *Ecua.*

Segovia Rocaberti, Enrique Cu 153; TM 504 *Cu.*

Seguel, Gerardo C 40 *Chil.*

Seguier, Conde de TM 479 *Mex.*

Segundo, José Pedro (1887-) PU 317; UT 493 *Uru.*

Segura, Emilio Co 68 *Col.*

Segura, Faustino (1853-1920) RHLC 205 *Col.*

Segura, José Sebastián (1822-1889) HLM 303; HLMex 158; HPHA I, 172; HPM 911; PM 78; PMe II, 203; TM 342 *Mex.*

Segura, Manuel CA 48; EPCR 673 *C.R.*

Segura, Manuel Ascencio (1805-1871) BHLA 221; CHL 292; CLH 247; HPHA II, 253; LP 364; P 33; PPe 22; SASS 440 *Per.*

Segura, Salvador G. CA 36 *C.R.*

Segura Argüelles, Vicente TM 342 *Mex.*

"Segura Castro, O." (*pseud.*) *see* Araya, Juan Agustín

Segura y Cabrera, Francisco ARC 41 *Cu.*

Segurola, Saturnino (1776-1854) LA IV, 785 *Arg.*

Segurola, Sebastián (1740-) B 20; SCL 517, 640 *Bol.*

Seguy, León U 18 *Uru.*

Seijas, Magdalena V 129 *Venez.*

Seijas, Rafael V 130 *Venez.*

Seijas, Rafael Fernando V 130 *Venez.*

Seijas Cook, Rafael ("El Arquitecto-poeta") V 31, 130 *Venez.*

Seijas García, J. M. V 130 *Venez.*

Sein PR 56 *P.R.*

Seixas y Lobera, Francisco de BHC I, 614 *Chil.*

"Selim-Adbel" (*pseud.*) *see* Urbaneja, Alejandro

Selva, Salomón de la NL 188; PLHA 166 *Nicar.*

Sellén, Antonio (1839-1889) CHL 477; CLH 417; Cu 153; PCu 259; RLC 222 *Cu.*

Sellén, Francisco (1838-1907) BDC 91; BHLA 434; CHL 477; CLH 417; Cu 154; G 341; PCu 263; RLC 222 *Cu.*

Sempértegui y R., Jorge B 20 *Bol.*

Semprum, Jesús V 130 *Venez.*

Sendras y Burin, Antonio PR 47 *P.R.*

Senet, Rodolfo (1872-) AT II, 695 *Arg.*

"Señorita de Avellaneda, La" TM 344 *Mex.*

"Señorita Mexicana, Una" TM 480 *Mex.*

Seoane, Buenaventura G. P 34 *Per.*

Seoane, Juan BHLA 605 *Per.*

Seoane Corrales, Manuel Alejandro (1900-) WLA 380 *Per.*

Seoane García, Guillermo F. P 34 *Per.*

Sepp (von Reinegg), Antón (1655-1733) Par 24 *Para.*

Sepúlveda, Antonio M. Co 68 *Col.*

Sepúlveda, Luis G. Co 68 *Col.*

Sepúlveda, Oscar (-1910) C 54; PCh 181 *Chil.*

Sepúlveda Leytón, Carlos BHLA 623; LAS 205 *Chil.*

Sepúlveda S., Juan C 40 *Chil.*

Sequeira, Anselmo NL 131; PN 127 *Nicar.*

Serafín C 20 *Chil.*

"Serafín de la Flor" (*pseud.*) *see* Torres y Feria, Manuel

Serán, Carlos Hipólito HPM 824; TM 343, 479 *Mex.*

Serantes, Marta A 63 *Arg.*

"Seravile Delio" (*pseud.*) *see* Sarmiento, Ricardo

Serna, Rafael de la HLNG II, 492 *Col.*

Serpa, Enrique (1899-) Cu 154; PJC 236 *Cu.*

Serra, José M. SD 29 *Dom.*

Serra, Rafael (1858-1909) ARC 37, 63; Cu 154 *Cu.*

"Serra, Tito" (*pseud.*) *see* Serrato Palma, Orestes
Serra y Heredia, Consuelo ARC 63 *Cu.*
Serradell, Luz María PM 78 *Mex.*
Serrano, Adolfo Benjamín E 66; PE 10 *Ecua.*
Serrano, Alejandro O. E 66 *Ecua.*
Serrano, Francisco CA 48; PC 121 *C.R.*
Serrano, Francisco P. Cu 154 *Cu.*
Serrano, José Mariano (1788-1851) B 20 *Bol.*
Serrano, Joseph Par 24 *Para.*
Serrano, Juan V 130 *Venez.*
Serrano de Vernengo, Marisa A 63 *Arg.*
Serrano P., Agustín C 54 *Chil.*
Serrano y Díez, Apolinar (1833-1876) Cu 154 *Cu.*
Serrano y Domínguez, Antonia, duquesa de la Torre Cu 155 *Cu.*
Serrato Palma, Orestes ("Tito Serra") C 20, 40 *Chil.*
Servet, Juan Co 68 *Col.*
Servín, María de Jesús TM 479 *Mex.*
Sesto, Julio NM 52 *Mex.*
Setaro, Ricardo M. (1903-) A 63 *Arg.*
"Severino Amaro" (*pseud.*) *see* Molina, Gaspar
"Severo Manso" (*pseud.*) *see* Martínez, Demetrio Benjamín
"Severus" (*pseud.*) *see* Della Costa, Pablo
Sevilla C., Alcibíades E 66 *Ecua.*
Sevilla Serdán, Natalia TM 347 *Mex.*
Seyxo, José Ignacio (-1838) BDC 92 *Cu.*
Sforza, Ángel E. A 63 *Arg.*
"Shade" (*pseud.*) *see* Cox-Stuven, Mariana
"Shanty" (*pseud.*) *see* Bianchi, Guillermo
"Sherlock Holmes" (*pseud.*) C 20 *Chil.*
Sherwell, Guillermo A. PM 78 *Mex.*
Sibaja, José Joaquín CA 48 *C.R.*
Sicard, Luciano M. A 63 *Arg.*
Sicard Briceño, Pedro Co 68 *Col.*
Sicard Pérez, Adolfo Co 68 *Col.*
Sicardi, Francisco A. (1856-1927) A 63; AT II, 895 *Arg.*
Sichar y Salas, Mariano PR 47 *P.R.*
"Sienna, Pedro" (*pseud.*) *see* Pérez Cordero, Pedro
Sienra, Roberto PIU III, 278; U 18 *Uru.*
Sienra Carranza, José (1843-) U 19; UT 499 *Uru.*
Sierra, Antonio BDC 92; Cu 155 *Cu.*
Sierra, José M. PM 78 *Mex.*
Sierra, Julián V. (1853-) ARC 63 *Cu.*
1. Sierra, Justo (padre) (1814-1861) CHL 405; CLH 352; HLM 344; Ig 346; NM 52; TM 347 *Mex.*
2. Sierra, Justo (hijo) (1848-1912) AEHA 789; AMP 287; BAMP 32; BHLA 371; CHL 405; CLH 353; G 371; HLM 383, 466; HLMex 229; Ig 348; NM 52; PM 78; PMe II, 209; PNM 281; PoM 146; SAL 93 *et passim*; SASS 380 *Mex.*
Sierra, Luis G. de la Ig 349; NM 52 *Mex.*
Sierra, Manuela (1892-1911) Pan 18 *Pan.*
Sierra, Ramón de la NM 19 *Mex.*
Sierra, Santiago J. (1850-1880) PMe II, 225; TM 347 *Mex.*
Sigüenza, Carlos de PR 10 *P.R.*

Sigüenza, Julio Cu 155 *Cu.*
Sigüenza y Góngora, Carlos de (1645-1700) BAMP 16; BHLA 124; CHL 29; CLH 25; G 371; GLO 249; HLM 158, 191; HLMex 68; HPM 209; NM 52; PM 79 *Mex.*
Silió y Gutiérrez, Evaristo (1842-1874) Cu 155 *Cu.*
Silva, Agapito (1850-1896) Ig 350; NM 52; PM 79; TM 348 *Mex.*
Silva, Andrés Antonio V 130, 131 *Venez.*
Silva, Arturo S. PU 216; U 19 *Uru.*
Silva, Carlos Alberto A 63 *Arg.*
Silva, Carmen P. de ("Celinda P. Varmes") GPCA III, 179; PG 273 *Guat.*
Silva, Domingo G. A 63 *Arg.*
Silva, Fidel PM 79 *Mex.*
Silva, Francisco Antonio V 131 *Venez.*
Silva, Gerardo TM 348 *Mex.*
Silva, Gustavo C 20; NC 256 *Chil.*
Silva, Januario Co 68; HLNG II, 430 *Col.*
Silva, José (1703-) SCL 451, 640 *Per.*
Silva, José Asunción (1865-1896) AEHA 793; ALC II, 5; APEH 79, 1178; BHLA 454; CHL 371, 516; CLH 304, 455; Co 69; CoL 274; FPA 82, 116; G 330; GLO 240; LC 184; MSAP 6, 25, 32; PCo 300; PLHA 91; RHLC 133; SA 29; SAL 57 *et passim*; SASS 228 *Col.*
Silva, Juan Vicente V 131 *Venez.*
Silva, Julio HSLU III, pt 6, 50 *Uru.*
Silva, López GLO 237 *Arg.*
Silva, Manuel María V 131 *Venez.*
Silva, Medardo Ángel (1899-1921) APEH 793; BHLA 540; E 66, 76; PE 222; PLE 108; PLHA 151 *Ecua.*
Silva, Rafael M. ("Lino Sutil") V 89, 131, 133; VPF 206 *Venez.*
Silva, Ricardo (1836-1887) Co 69; LC 144; RHLC 125 *Col.*
Silva A., L. Ignacio C 69 *Chil.*
Silva Bolívar, Columbo V 131 *Venez.*
Silva Castro, Raúl (1903-) BHLA 617; C 69; IE 269; LAS 202 *Chil.*
Silva Cotapos, Carlos CL 525 *Chil.*
Silva de la Fuente, Alejandro C 21; CHL 275; CLH 234; LAS 202; NC 256 *Chil.*
Silva de la Fuente, Samuel C 55 *Chil.*
Silva de Quiñones, Rosita PR 7 *P.R.*
Silva D'Herbil, Mario R. A 63 *Arg.*
Silva Endeiza, Hugo ("Julio César" *or* "Rob Roy") (1892-) WLA 384 *Chil.*
Silva Endeiza, Jorge Gustavo (1881-) WLA 383 *Chil.*
Silva Endeiza, Víctor Domingo (1882-) APEH 747, 1190; BHLA 510; C 20, 40, 54; CHL 263, 280; CLH 223; CMPC 147; FPA 192, 218; MSAP 172, 316; N 103; PCC xiv, 95; PCh 213; SASS 202; WLA 384 *Chil.*
Silva Gandolphi, Marco Antonio V 131 *Venez.*
Silva Humeres, Andrés C 40, 55; CMPC 149 *Chil.*
Silva Palma, Alberto NC 454 *Chil.*
Silva Renard, Ricardo NC 455 *Chil.*
Silva Román, Ernesto C 21 *Chil.*
Silva Serrano, Julián U 19 *Uru.*
Silva Uranga, Héctor U 19 *Uru.*

Silva Valdés, Fernán (1887-) APEH 974, 1193; BHLA 532, 642; G 390; GLO 238; HSLU III, pt 1, 5; LU 64, 665; PIU III, 98, 105; PLHA 164; PU 222; SASS 470; U 19; WLA 384 *Uru.*

Silva Vidal, Ismael P 34 *Per.*

Silva Vildósola, Carlos (1870-) C 21, 70; NC 289; SASS 194; WLA 385 *Chil.*

Silva y Aceves, Mariano (1887-) BAMP 86; G 371; HLM 518; Ig 351; NM 53; TM 349, 481 *Mex.*

Silván Fernández, Joaquín U 19 *Uru.*

Silveira, Inocencia ARC 63 *Cu.*

Silveira, Vicente (1841-1924) ARC 35, 63; Cu 155 *Cu.*

Silvestre, Francisco (1734-) Co 69; HLNG II, 387; RHLC 20 *Col.*

Silvestre, Luis Segundo de (1838-1887) Co 69; LC 181; RHLC 186 *Col.*

Silvestre de Feliú, Aurora Cu 155 *Cu.*

Silvestre de Luna, Miguel HLNG I, 169 *Col.*

Simois y Melitón, I. PU 219; U 19 *Uru.*

"Simón, Don" (*pseud.*) *see* Fernández, Manuel María

Simón, Francisco Cu 155; PJC 245 *Cu.*

Simón, Pedro (1574-) Co 69; HLNG I, 142; RHLC 10; SCL 314, 640; V 131 *Col.*

"Simón Ayanque" (*pseud.*) *see* Terralla y Landa, Esteban de

"Simón Fogonero" (*pseud.*) C 9 *Chil.*

"Simón Latino" (*pseud.*) *see* Pareja, Carlos Henrique

"Simón Peñalva" (*pseud.*) *see* Ascasubi, Hilario

"Simón Rivas" (*pseud.*) *see* Martínez, Cristóbal

Simoniello, Paulina A 63 *Arg.*

Sinán, Rogelio Pan 18 *Pan.*

'Sincero, Juan" (*pseud.*) *see* Cruz, Manuel de la

Sinués, María del Pilar Cu 155 *Cu.*

Sioen, A. A 63 *Arg.*

Siré Valenciano, Manuel (1896-) ARC 63; Cu 155 *Cu.*

Sirgado y Zequeira, Pedro (1799-1869) Cu 155 *Cu.*

Sirolli, Amadeo Rodolfo A 63 *Arg.*

Sisniega, Gerardo NM 53 *Mex.*

Sistiaga, Jesús María (1823-1889) V 131; VPF 50 *Venez.*

Sixto, Andrés A 63 *Arg.*

Smirna, Federico A 63 *Arg.*

Smith, Alberto V 131 *Venez.*

Smith, Roberto A 64 *Arg.*

Smith Monzón, Esteban V 131 *Venez.*

Sobrado y Martínez, J. Cu 155 *Cu.*

Sobreyra, Manuel PM 79 *Mex.*

Sobreyra Ortiz, J. PM 79 *Mex.*

Sobrino, Gaspar BHC II, 140 *Chil.*

Sobrino, Juan HPHA II, 274 *Bol.*

Socorro de León, José BDC 92 *Cu.*

Sodi, Federico Ig 352; NM 53 *Mex.*

Soffía y Argomedo, José Antonio (1848-1886) BHLA 425; C 40; CHL 258; CLH 218; Co 62; HC 154; LC 178; PCh 77 *Chil.*

Soiza Reilly, Juan José de ("Agapito Candileja") (1883-) WLA 387 *Arg.*

"Sol, Hugo" (*pseud.*) *see* Manzanilla, Anastasio

Sol, J. Álvaro A 64 *Arg.*

Sol, Manuel del (1824-1854) Cu 155 *Cu.*

Sola, José Sixto de Cu 155; GLO 255 *Cu.*

Sola, Juan de Cu 155 *Cu.*

Sola, Juan María Cu 156 *Cu.*

Solá de Castellanos, Sara A 64 *Arg.*

Solá de Solá, Emma A 64 *Arg.*

Solano, Abraham Co 69 *Col.*

Solano, Aquilles Cu 156 *Cu.*

Solano, Armando ("Maître Renard") (1887-) Co 69; WLA 387 *Col.*

Solano, Franco TM 589 *Mex.*

Solano, Pedro María ACe 953 *Mex.*

Solano, Vicente (1793-1865) E 66; PLE 34 *Ecua.*

Solano, Zenón (1822-1881) Co 69 *Col.*

Solano de Entralgo, Francisco Cu 156 *Cu.*

Solar, Alberto del (1860-) A 64, 92; C 21; CHL 282; CLH 239; NC 299, 465; PCh 117 *Chil.*

Solar, Fidelis P. del C 70 *Chil.*

Solar Armstrong, Juan Enrique del (1844-1922) C 21, 40, 55; CHL 282; CLH 239; NC 290, 308, 464, 465 *Chil.*

Solar Aspillaga, Hernán del C 40 *Chil.*

Solar Avaria, Bernardo C 40 *Chil.*

Solar Correa, A. E 67 *Ecua.*

Solar Correa, Eduardo (1891-) E 70; WLA 387 *Ecua.*

Solar de Claro, Amelia C 40, 55 *Chil.*

Solar y Marín, Enrique del (1844-1893) C 21; HC 246; NC 455 *Chil.*

Solares, Dionisio G. Cu 156 *Cu.*

Solari, Benjamín T. A 64 *Arg.*

Solari, Fidel A 64 *Arg.*

Solé Rodríguez, Oriol U 19 *Uru.*

"Soledad" (*pseud.*) *see* Zamudio, Adela

Soler, Ambrosio PR 40 *P.R.*

Soler, Darás A 64 *Arg.*

Soler, Francisco (-1920) CA 48; EPCR 600 *C.R.*

Soler, Francisco Javier Cu 156 *Cu.*

Soler, Juan J. Par 24 *Para.*

Soler y Gabarda, Gerónimo BDC 92; Cu 156 *Cu.*

Soler y Martorell, Manuel PR 7, 40 *P.R.*

Soler y Meriño, Mariano SD 29 *Dom.*

Solera, Rafael Ángel CA 48 *C.R.*

Solera, Tito Livio CA 48 *C.R.*

Solés, Pedro José BDC 92 *Cu.*

Solís, Antonio de (1610-1686) HLM 32 *Mex.*

Solís, Eudoro NL 253 *Nicar.*

Solís, Fidel Ig 353; NM 53 *Mex.*

Solís, José María APMM 193; G 371; PM 79 *Mex.*

Solís, Manuel PR 40 *P.R.*

Solís, Pedro TM 597 *Mex.*

Solís Cámara, Fernando (1884-) Ig 353; NM 53 *Mex.*

Solís y Valenzuela, Bruno de Co 69 *Col.*

Solís y Valenzuela, Pedro de Co 69; HLNG I, 165 *Col.*

"Solón de Mel" (*pseud.*) *see* Luzuriaga y Bribiesca, Guillermo de

Soloni, Félix Cu 156; SASS 296 *Cu.*

Solórzano, Juan Antonio PS 190 *Salv.*

Solórzano, Juan de Co 69 *Col.*

Solórzano, Mariano CA 48 *C.R.*
Solórzano y Correoso, Antonio BDC 92; Cu 156 *Cu.*
Somines, Luis M. Cu 156 *Cu.*
"Somoyar, Enrique" (*pseud.*) *see* Nariño, Antonio
Sonderéguer, Pedro Co 69 *Col.*
Sopo Barreto, Rogelio Cu 156; PJC 242 *Cu.*
"Sor Juana Inés de la Cruz" (*pseud.*) *see* Asbaje y Ramírez de Cantillana, Juana Inés de
"Sordello Andrea" (*pseud.*) *see* Nin Frías, Alberto
Soria, Ezequiel A 64, 92 *Arg.*
Soria, Francisco de HLM 187; HPM 465; TM 349 *Mex.*
Soria, Francisco de Paula E 67 *Ecua.*
Soria, José E. B 20 *Bol.*
Soria Galvarro, Rodolfo B 20 *Bol.*
Soriano, Juan Antonio Cu 157 *Cu.*
Soriano, M. Germán SD 29 *Dom.*
Soriano Letelier, Héctor C 22 *Chil.*
Sorondo y Tolón, Mario F. BDC 93; Cu 157 *Cu.*
Sort de Sanz, Enrique PM 79 *Mex.*
Soruco C., J. B 20 *Bol.*
Sorzano-Jorrín, Leonardo CT 73 *Cu.*
Sos, Ciriaco ("César de Guanabacoa") Cu 71, 157 *Cu.*
Sosa, Cornelio NL 89 *Nicar.*
Sosa, Enrique Juan Pan 18 *Pan.*
Sosa, Francisco (1848-1925) CHL 305, 410; CLH 357; Cu 157; G 371; HLM 496; HLMex 236; Ig 354; NM 4, 53; PM 79; PMe II, 229; PoM 142; TM 574 *Mex.*
Sosa, Gabriel Pan 18 *Pan.*
Sosa, Jesualdo LAS 202; LU 64, 668 *Uru.*
Sosa, Jonás A 64 *Arg.*
Sosa, Juan Bautista Pan 18 *Pan.*
Sosa, Julio María (1879-) UT 505 *Uru.*
Sosa, Pedro de BHC II, 132 *et passim Chil.*
Sosa Muñoz, Juan PM 80 *Mex.*
Sosa y Ávila, Francisco Ig 356; NM 53 *Mex.*
Sossa, Antonio de Cu 157 *Cu.*
Sota, José Severino de la Ig 357; NM 53 *Mex.*
Sotela, Rogelio (1894-) CA 48, 49; EPCR 607; FPA 123, 155; IBCR IV, 165 *et passim;* IE 270 *C.R.*
Soteldo, Eliseo V 131 *Venez.*
Sotillo, Pedro V 131, 132 *Venez.*
Soto, Antonio ("Boy") HSLU I, pt 4, 14; PIU III, 283; U 19 *Uru.*
Soto, Cipriano CA 50 *C.R.*
Soto, Fausto C 40 *Chil.*
Soto, Felipe S. de SD 30 *Dom.*
Soto, Foción Co 69 *Col.*
Soto, Francisco (1789-1846) HLNG II, 531 *Col.*
Soto, Humberto Co 69 *Col.*
Soto, Jesús S. PM 80 *Mex.*
Soto, José C. A 64, 92 *Arg.*
Soto, Juan B. PR 21, 47, 61 *P.R.*
Soto, León A. (1874-1902) AP 297; FPA 381, 388; Pan 18 *Pan.*
Soto, Ludovico ARC 63 *Cu.*
Soto, M. Belisario P 34 *Per.*

Soto, Marco Aurelio (1846-) HL I, 437 *Hond.*
Soto, Máximo (-1870) HL I, 189 *Hond.*
Soto, Salvador NC 466 *Chil.*
Soto Aguilar, Matías C 55 *Chil.*
Soto Alfaro, Bernardo (1854-1931) CA 49, 50 *C.R.*
Soto Ayala, Luis Carlos C 40, 70; NC 466; PCh 287 *Chil.*
Soto Borda, Clímaco ("Casimiro de la Barra") (1870-1919) Co 8, 56, 69, 70; LC 193; PCo 306; RHLC 152 *Col.*
Soto Hall, Máximo (1871-) BHLA 526; IBCR IV, 25 *et passim;* LAS 205; PG 341; WLA 389 *Guat.*
Soto Quesada, Luis CA 50 *C.R.*
Soto y Calvo, Edelina (1844-1932) A 64 *Arg.*
Soto y Calvo, Francisco (1860-1936) A 64; BHLA 419; CHL 169; CLH 145 *Arg.*
Soto y Villanueva, Julio Cu 157 *Cu.*
Sotomayor, Dámaso PM 80 *Mex.*
Sotomayor, Dolores PM 80 *Mex.*
Sotomayor, Fernando P 34 *Per.*
Sotomayor, José Francisco (1831-1898) Ig 356; NM 53 *Mex.*
Sotomayor de Concha, Graciela C 55 *Chil.*
Sotomayor Valdés, Ramón (1830-1903) HC 122 *Chil.*
Sotta, Nicanor de la C 55 *Chil.*
Soublette, Carlos V 132 *Venez.*
Soublette, Enrique (1888-1912) V 132; VPF 114 *Venez.*
Soublette, Félix LV 114, 280; V 132 *Venez.*
Spelucín, Alcides (1896-) BAP 49; BHLA 607 *Per.*
Spikermann y Mullins, Celina U 19 *Uru.*
Spinetti Dini, Antonio V 132 *Venez.*
Spinetti Dini, Humberto V 132 *Venez.*
Spínola, Agustín Cu 157 *Cu.*
Spontini, Gaspare Luigi Pacífico TM 504 *Mex.*
Stahl, Agustín PR 47, 56 *P.R.*
Stanchina, Lorenzo A 64 *Arg.*
"Stein" (*pseud.*) *see* Crespo Toral, Remigio
"Stella, Lucio" (*pseud.*) *see* Goycoechea Menéndez, Martín de
Stella, María L. BP 507 *P.R.*
Stenfanich, Juan (1889-) Par 24; PT 81 *Para.*
Stevens Romero, José Cu 157 *Cu.*
Stock, Guillermo A 64 *Arg.*
Storini Raimondi, P. A 65 *Arg.*
Stork, Juan Caspar CA 50 *C.R.*
Storni, Alfonsina (1892-) A 65; APAM 405; APEH 932, 1192; AT II, 603; BHLA 529; CHL 187; CP 697; FPA 16, 49; G 318; HSLU II, pt 8, 10; LAC 147; MSAP 220, 328; NPA 161; PLHA 179; SASS 53; WLA 391 *Arg.*
"Stravos" (*pseud.*) Ig 358; NM 53 *Mex.*
Stresov, Samuel D. A 65 *Arg.*
Striddels, Enrique SD 30 *Dom.*
Struque, Francisco P 34 *Per.*
Su, Kwang Cu 157 *Cu.*
Suáiter Martínez, Francisco A 65; LAC 138 *Arg.*
Suáiter Martínez, R. A 65 *Arg.*
Suara, Antonio TM 349 *Mex.*
Suárez, Arturo Co 70; WLA 392 *Col.*

Suárez, Constancio S. TM 349, 481 *Mex.*
Suárez, Constantino Cu 157 *Cu.*
Suárez, Jesús María V 132 *Venez.*
Suárez, José Manuel U 19 *Uru.*
Suárez, Manuel Octavio P 34 *Per.*
Suárez, Marco Fidel ("Luciano Pulgar") (1855-1927) BHLA 410; Co 70; G 331; LAS 205; LC 168; RHLC 203 *Col.*
Suárez, María (1899-) PM 80 *Mex.*
Suárez, Miguel (hijo) PM 80 *Mex.*
Suárez, Octavio M. PJC 243 *Cu.*
Suárez, Pelayo ACe 955 *Mex.*
Suárez, Sofía (1893-) AT II, 587 *Arg.*
Suárez Calimano, Emilio A 65; LAC 155; WLA 392 *Arg.*
Suárez Corvo, Yaya A 65 *Arg.*
Suárez de Mendoza, A. PR 47 *P.R.*
Suárez de Mendoza, Juan Co 70 *Col.*
Suárez de Peralta, Juan (1535?-) HLM 39 *Mex.*
Suárez Fernández, Francisco Cu 157 *Cu.*
Suárez Gómez, Antonio PJC 247 *Cu.*
Suárez Inclán, Estanislao PR 47 *P.R.*
Suárez Inclán, Nicolás Cu 157 *Cu.*
Suárez López, Miguel Cu 157 *Cu.*
Suárez Orozco A 65 *Arg.*
Suárez Osorio de Cepeda, Juan BHC I, 373 *Chil.*
Suárez Solís, Rafael Cu 157 *Cu.*
Suárez y Romero, Anselmo (1818-1878) BHLA 224; CHL 441; CLH 383; Cu 157; HLC 183; RLC 70, 137, 142 *Cu.*
Subercaseaux, Benjamín ("Lord Jim") BHLA 622 *Chil.*
Subercaseaux, Francisco A. C 22, 40, 55; NC 468 *Chil.*
Subercaseaux, Ramón C 70; NC 468 *Chil.*
Subieta, Eduardo ("Gil Got") B 20 *Bol.*
Subieta Sagárnaga, Luis B 20 *Bol.*
Subirats, Pedro G. Cu 158 *Cu.*
Sucre, Antonio José de (1790-1830) AA II, 27, 191; V 133 *Venez.*
Sucre, Dolores CHL 320; CLH 272; E 67; PLE 62 *Ecua.*
Sucre, Luis Alberto V 133 *Venez.*
Sudy, Carlos C 22; NC 398, 498 *Chil.*
Suero, Pablo (1899-) A 65; APAM 574 *Arg.*
Sulbarán, Eduardo V 133 *Venez.*
Suncar, Manuel E. SD 30 *Dom.*
Supervielle, Jules (1884-) HSLU III, pt 5, 3; PIU III, 178; PoU 19; PU 206; U 19 *Uru.*
Supparo, Atilio A 65; PU 318; U 19 *Uru.*
Surí, Rafael Justino ARC 64 *Cu.*
Surí y Aguila, José Cu 158; RLC 25 *Cu.*
Surí y González, José (1696-) HLC 15 *Cu.*
Surinach Senties, R. Cu 158 *Cu.*
"Sus, G." (*pseud.*) Cu 158 *Cu.*
"Susi, Otal" (*pseud.*) *see* González Rincones, Salustio
Sustaita, Alberto (1863-1909) Ig 359; NM 53 *Mex.*
Susto Lara, Juan Antonio (1896-) Pan 18; WLA 393 *Pan.*
"Sutil, Lino" (*pseud.*) *see* Silva, Rafael M.
Sux, Alejandro (1888-) IE 273; SD 30; U 19 *Uru.*
Sylva, César E 67 *Ecua.*
Sylva, Rafael *see* Silva, Rafael M.

T

"Tabarra, Fray" (*pseud.*) *see* Comallonga y Mena, José
Tablada, José ARC 64 *Cu.*
Tablada, José Juan ("Girón de Pinabete Alcornoque y Astragalo") (1871-) AMP 77; APEH 461, 1187; APMM 195; BHLA 543; CHL 420; CLH 365; G 372; HLM 424; Ig 361; NM 54; PM 80; PMe II, 235; PMM 62; PNM 289; PoM 384; SAL 69; SASS 376; TM 344, 352, 482; WLA 393 *Mex.*
"Tablanca, Luis" (*pseud.*) *see* Pardo Farelo, Enrique
Taborda, Saúl Alejandro (1885-) A 65; AT II, 574 *Arg.*
Taborga, Benjamín (1889-1918) APAM 416; APEH 877 *Arg.*
"Taceo" (*pseud.*) TM 344 *Mex.*
"Tag" (*pseud.*) C 40 *Chil.*
Tagliaferro, José A. V 133 *Venez.*
Tain de Traba, Martha A 65 *Arg.*
Tajes, Roque U 19 *Uru.*
Talachini, Félix E 67 *Ecua.*
Talamantes, Melchor de (1765-1809) ACe 1009 *Mex.*
"Talanto, Julio" (*pseud.*) *see* Iglesias Mascareño, Augusto
Talavera, Manuel Antonio BHC III, 117 *Chil.*
Talavera, Natalicio (1837-) Par 24; PPa 33 *Para.*
Talavera, R. TM 482 *Mex.*
Talavera León, José TM 597 *Mex.*
Talavera Luco, Vicente C 22; NC 309 *Chil.*
Talavera y Garcés, Mariano de LV 130; V 134 *Venez.*
Talavera y Patrón, Cipriano U 19 *Uru.*
Talero, Eduardo A 65 *Arg.*
Talero Núñez, Eduardo Co 70; G 331; PCo 307 *Col.*
Talquino, Virgilio C 55 *Chil.*
Tallet, José Zacarías (1893-) APEH 882; BHLA 568; LH 140; PoC 266 *Cu.*
Tallón, José Sebastián (1904-) A 65; APAM 576; NPA 276 *Arg.*
Tamáriz Crespo, Remigio (1890?-) E 67; FPA 254, 281 *Ecua.*
Tamayo, Alfredo TM 600 *Mex.*
Tamayo, Franz (1879-) B 21; BHLA 483; BT 289; FPA 54, 72; IE 277; LB 619; PB 165; SASS 103 *Bol.*
Tamayo, Isaac B 21 *Bol.*
Tamayo, Rafael (1851-1926) AC I, 331; Co 70 *Col.*
Tamayo, Víctor Hugo Cu 158 *Cu.*
Tamayo y Mendoza, García de BHC I, 441 *Chil.*
Tambolleo, D. A 65 *Arg.*
Tanco, Félix M. (1797-1871) RLC 72, 74 *Cu.*
Tanco, Jenaro Santiago Co 70 *Col.*
Tanco Armero, Nicolás Co 70 *Col.*
"Taniya, Kyn" (*pseud.*) *see* Quintanilla, Luis
Tapia, Francisco Par 24 *Para.*
Tapia, José L. TM 352 *Mex.*
Tapia de Castellanos, Esther (1842-) HLM 398; PM 80; PoM 308 *Mex.*

Tapia y Rivera, Alejandro (1827-1882) BDC 93; BHLA 332; BP 501, 507, 515, 635; CHL 500; CLH 440; G 385; HPHA I, 340; PR 10, 15, 25, 28, 40, 42, 47, 54 *P.R.*

Taracena, Alfonso (1899-) NM 54; WLA 394 *Mex.*

Tarnica, K. CA 50; IBCR IV, 9 *C.R.*

Tarrago, Torcuato U 19 *Uru.*

Tarruella, Alfredo C. A 65 *Arg.*

Tarzia, Miguel A 65 *Arg.*

Tascón, Julio Enrique (1888-) Co 70; WLA 394 *Col.*

Tatay, José María BDC 94; Cu 158 *Cu.*

Tatén, Doctor A 65 *Arg.*

Tavera Acosta, Bartolomé V 134 *Venez.*

Tavira, Pedro de BDC 94; Cu 158 *Cu.*

Tavolara, José Antonio U 19 *Uru.*

"Tax" (*pseud.*) *see* Díaz, Teófilo Eugenio

Taybo, Antonio C. Cu 158 *Cu.*

Taylhardat, Concepción de V 134 *Venez.*

"Té, Rosa" (*pseud.*) *see* Trujillo y Arredondo, Rosa

Teceyga, G. E 67 *Ecua.*

Techo, Nicolás del (1611-1685) LA III, 507; Par 24; SCL 396, 408 *et passim Para.*

Teijeiro Martínez, Benigno Par 25 *Para.*

Teixidor, Felipe NM 4 *Mex.*

Teja Zabre, Alfonso (1888-) G 372; HLM 515; Ig 363; NM 54; PM 81; TM 353, 434, 482 *Mex.*

Tejada, Luis Co 70 *Col.*

Tejada, Valentín (1914-) PoC 272 *Chil.*

Tejada U., Efraín Pan 19 *Pan.*

Tejeda, Félix A. (1866-1896) GPCA III, 541; HL II, 629 *Hond.*

Tejeda y Guzmán, Luis José de (1604-1680) A 65; BHLA 92; G 318; LA III, 125, 434; SPLA 24 *Arg.*

Tejedor, Carlos (1817-1903) LA VI, 1144 *Arg.*

Tejera, Apolinar SD 30 *Dom.*

Tejera, Diego Vicente (1848-1903) BDC 94; BHLA 435; CHL 478, 487; CLH 419; Cu 158; FPA 162, 178; G 341, 342; HLC 160; PA 130; PCu 267; RLC 223, 274; SASS 277; WSAL 63, 79 *Cu.*

Tejera, Emiliano LD 85; SD 30 *Dom.*

Tejera, Felipe ("Cachidiablo" or "Rey de Bastos") CHL 371; CLH 319; LV 28, 56 *et passim;* V 54, 122, 134, 135 *Venez.*

Tejera, Francisco Miguel V 135 *Venez.*

Tejera, Humberto (1890-) IE 279; V 135 *Venez.*

Tejera, José Domingo V 135 *Venez.*

Tejera, Miguel LV 8, 12; V 135 *Venez.*

Tejera de la Mota, Vicente V 135 *Venez.*

Tejerizo, Manuel Cu 158 *Cu.*

Tellería, Trinidad V 135 *Venez.*

Téllez, Joaquín (1823-) AMP 135; G 372; HPM 907; PM 81; PMe II, 245 *Mex.*

Téllez Girón, Rafael PM 81; TM 354 *Mex.*

Téllez Rendón, María Nestora (1828-1890) Ig 365; NM 54 *Mex.*

Tello, Antonio HLM 208 *Mex.*

Tello, Dolores TM 353 *Mex.*

Tello, Julio C. P 25 *Per.*

Tello, Rafael J. TM 611 *Mex.*

Tello Mendoza, Ramón V 135 *Venez.*

Temístocles, Salera IBCR IV, 385 *C.R.*

Tena, Alberto A 66 *Arg.*

"Tenazas, Pío" (*pseud.*) *see* Macpherson, Telasco A.

Tenorio Suárez, Ignacio TM 354 *Mex.*

Terán, Emilio María E 67 *Ecua.*

Terán, Juan Benjamín Manuel (1880-) A 66; AT I, 483; IE 281; WLA 397 *Arg.*

Terán, Rafael V 135 *Venez.*

Terán Guerrero, José M. E 67 *Ecua.*

Tercero, Juan Luis PM 81 *Mex.*

"Teresa de la Parra" (*pseud.*) *see* Parra Sanojo, Ana Teresa

Terradas Lafuente, Enrique Cu 158 *Cu.*

Terralla y Landa, Esteban de ("Simón Ayanque") BHLA 105; CHL 41; CLH 35; LP 335 *Per.*

Terraza y Rejón, Dionisio (Antonio José de Irizarri) E 76 *Ecua.*

Terrazas, Francisco de AMP 215; CHL 20; CLH 17; HLM 97; HLMex 46; HPHA I, 37; HPM 97; PM 81 *Mex.*

Terrazas, José Joaquín (-1931) PM 81 *Mex.*

Terre, Leonardo G. PJC 258 *Cu.*

Terreforte y Arroyo, Juan P. BDC 95; PR 15, 41, 42 *P.R.*

Terrero, Blas José V 136 *Venez.*

Terrero, Leopoldo V 136 *Venez.*

Terrero-Atienza, Alfredo V 136 *Venez.*

"Terrues, Genaro E." (*pseud.*) *see* Guerra, Ernesto E.

Teruel, José G. Ig 369; NM 54 *Mex.*

Terwilliger, L. Roy Cu 158 *Cu.*

"Tesh" (*pseud.*) TM 344 *Mex.*

Tesillo, Santiago de BHC I, 466; SCL 285, 497, 643 *Chil.*

Tessi, Francisco S. A 66 *Arg.*

Testena, Folco A 66, 72, 92 *Arg.*

Teúma, Emilio BDC 94 *Cu.*

Teúrbe de Tolón, Miguel de (1820-1858) AEHA 909; BDC 94; CHL 460; CLH 402; Cu 158; HLC 144; HPHA I, 284; PCu 272; RLC 147, 183 *Cu.*

Texeira y Mena, José de Co 70; HLNG II, 383 *Col.*

Teysera, Faustino M. PU 319; U 19 *Uru.*

Tezozomoc, Hernando de Alvarado HLM 73; TM 536 *Mex.*

Thayer Ojeda, Luis (1874-) WLA 397 *Chil.*

Thayer Ojeda, Tomás (1877-) C 70; WLA 397 *Chil.*

"Thespis" (*pseud.*) *see* Bunge, Carlos

Thévenin, Leopoldo ("Monsieur Perrichon") HSLU I, pt 4, 13; U 19; UL 192 *Uru.*

Thiel, Bernardo Augusto CA 50 *C.R.*

Thompson, Emmanuel CA 50; IBCR IV, 309 *C.R.*

Thompson, Juan (1808-1870) LA VI, 1122 *Arg.*

Thomson, Augusto ("Augusto D'Halmar") 1880-) BHLA 510, 621; C 22, 66; CG III, 4; LAS 203; NC 310; PLHA 206; SASS 173; WLA 398 *Chil.*

"Tiberio, Oscar" (*pseud.*) A 53, 66 *Arg.*

"Tic Tac" (*pseud.*) *see* Villafañe, Carlos

"Tiempo, César" (*pseud.*) *see* Zeitlin, Israel

Tigerino (or Tijerino), Manuel NL 78; PN 61 *Nicar.*

Tijerina, Juan B. ("Harmodio") (1857-1912) PM 50, 81 *Mex.*

Tijerino, Juan Antonio NL 251 *Nicar.*
Timothee, Pedro Carlos (1864-) QPR (1) 156 *P.R.*
Tinoco, Juan C. V 136 *Venez.*
Tió, Lola Rodríguez y Ponce de León de CT 209 *Cu.*
"Tío, Tom" (*pseud.*) *see* Montalbán, Leonardo
Tió y Rodríguez de Sánchez de Fuentes, Patria (1866-) PA 108; QPR (1) 156; (2) 160 *P.R.*
"Tipo, Lino" (*pseud.*) *see* Colunje, Guillermo (hijo)
Tirado Fuentes, René PM 81 *Mex.*
Tiscareño, Ángel de los Dolores PM 81 *Mex.*
Tiscornia, Eleuterio F. A 66 *Arg.*
"Tisgón, El" (*pseud.*) *see* Guarín, José David
"Tito Salcedo" (*pseud.*) *see* Marcano, Vicente
"Tito Serra" (*pseud.*) *see* Serrato Palma, Orestes
Titu Cussi Yupanqui *see* Castro, Diego de
Tividor, Gabino V 136 *Venez.*
Tobal, Gastón Federico A 66 *Arg.*
Tobar, Carlos R. (1854-1920) CHL 320; CLH 272; E 67, 76; PLE 60 *Ecua.*
Tobar, Miguel de (1782-1861) HLNG II, 342; HPHA II, 38 *Col.*
Tobar, S. Joaquín Co 70 *Col.*
Tobar Donoso, Julio E 68 *Ecua.*
Tobar y Buendía, Pedro de Co 70; HLNG I, 302 *Col.*
Tobar y Freile, Luis F. E 68 *Ecua.*
Tobón, Alfonso Co 70 *Col.*
Tobón T., Marco A. Co 71 *Col.*
Tocornal, Carlos M. C 55 *Chil.*
Todd, Roberto Henry PR 10; QPR (2) 161 *P.R.*
Tognoni, A. Roberto A 66 *Arg.*
Tola, Ángel E 68 *Ecua.*
Tolducal E 68 *Ecua.*
Toledo, Antonio C. (1868-1913) E 68; PE 12; PLE 56 *Ecua.*
Toledo, M. L. Cu 158 *Cu.*
Toledo, Manuel Vicente V 136 *Venez.*
Toledo Ahumada, Juan Francisco C 55 *Chil.*
Tolón, Miguel Teúrbe de *see* Teúrbe de Tolón, Miguel
"Tom Tío" (*pseud.*) *see* Montalbán, Leonardo
Tomás, Vicente A. (1859-1911) Cu 159 *Cu.*
Tomei, Odino H. A 66 *Arg.*
Tondreau, Narciso (1861-) C 40; CLH 222; PCh 87 *Chil.*
Toor, Frances IE 282; TM 576 *Mex.*
Toral Cabañas, Manuel Germano ACe 956 *Mex.*
Tornel y Mendívil, José María HLM 358; TM 354 *Mex.*
Tornero, Enrique C 55, 70 *Chil.*
Tornero, León IBCR IV, 386 *C.R.*
Toro, Alfonso HLM 531; TM 576 *Mex.*
Toro, Carlos (1875-1914) Ig 369; NM 54; TM 140, 355 *Mex.*
Toro, Demetrio B 21 *Bol.*
Toro, E. C 22; NC 500 *Chil.*
Toro, Elías V 136 *Venez.*

Toro, Fermín ("Emiro Casto *or* Kastos") (1807-1873) AEHA 818; BHLA 222, 298; CLH 307; HPHA I, 413; LV 41, 112, 365; V 86, 136, 137; VPF 27 *Venez.*
Toro, Juan Bautista de (-1730) Co 71; HLNG I, 306; LC 93; RHLC 34; SCL 448, 643 *Col.*
Toro, Oliverio TM 355 *Mex.*
Toro, Ulises PR 41 *P.R.*
Toro Castro, Alfonso (1873-) WLA 400 *Mex.*
Toro Cuevas, Emilio del PR 15, 54 *P.R.*
Toro Pereira, Eduardo Co 71 *Col.*
Toro Ramírez, Miguel V 137 *Venez.*
Toro Soler, Ricardo PR 25 *P.R.*
Toro Uribe, Pedro Co 71 *Col.*
Toro y Cuevas, Emilio BDC 95 *Cu.*
Toro y Gómez, Miguel de (1851-) AT II, 1025 *Arg.*
Toro Zambrano y Ureta, Mateo de BHC III, 48 *Chil.*
Torquemada, Juan de (1565?-1624) BHLA 108; HLM 69 *Mex.*
Torrado Martínez, Manuel (1883-) QPR (2) 162 *P.R.*
Torrado y Quiroga, Ramón (-1885) Cu 159 *Cu.*
Torranzos Bardel, Fortunato Par 25 *Para.*
Torre, Carlos de la Cu 159 *Cu.*
Torre, Carlos María de la E 68 *Ecua.*
Torre, Joaquín M. de la Cu 159 *Cu.*
Torre, José María de la (1815?-1873) Cu 159 *Cu.*
Torre, Manuel E. de la Cu 160 *Cu.*
Torre, Miguel Ángel de la Cu 160 *Cu.*
Torre Muñiz, José M. de la (1885-) QPR (1) 158 *P.R.*
Torre y Solá, Enrique de la BDC 95; Cu 160 *Cu.*
Torrealba, Luis de C 41 *Chil.*
Torrealba Arraiz, Rafaela R. V 137 *Venez.*
Torreblanca, M. R. C 22 *Chil.*
Torreforte Arroyo, J. B. *see* Terreforte y Arroyo, Juan P.
Torregrosa, Fernando PA 244; PP 307 *P.R.*
Torregrosa, Luis A. BDC 95; PA 245; PP 309; PR 15 *P.R.*
Torrelio B., Mariano B 21 *Bol.*
Torrendell, Juan A 66; G 390; LAC 118, 155; U 19 *Arg.*
Torrente, Mariano (1792-1856) Cu 160 *Cu.*
Torres, Antonio L. Cu 160 *Cu.*
Torres, Bernardo de BHLA 117; P 34; SCL 391, 446, 643 *Per.*
Torres, Camilo de (1766-1815) BHLA 157; HLNG II, 97, 268; LC 106; RHLC 61 *Col.*
Torres, Carlos Arturo (1867-1911) ALC I, 345; BHLA 486; Co 71; LC 181; PCo 316; RHLC 171, 211 *Col.*
Torres, Celestina Par 25 *Para.*
Torres, Cladera Lorenzo U 20 *Uru.*
Torres, Cristóbal de (1573-1654) Co 71; HLNG I, 130, 170 *Col.*
Torres, Emilio Ig 370; NM 54 *Mex.*
Torres, Eugenia HLM 529; TM 355 *Mex.*
Torres, Francisco Cu 160 *Cu.*
Torres, Francisco de Paula (1808-1885) Co 71; RHLC 159 *Col.*

Torres, Gilberto Ig 370; NM 54 *Mex.*
Torres, Jerónimo (1771-1839) HLNG II, 495 *Col.*
Torres, José Antonio C 22, 70; NC 310 *Chil.*
Torres, José C. PR 54 *P.R.*
Torres, José G. PR 21 *P.R.*
Torres, Juan A 66 *Arg.*
Torres, Luis María (1878-) AT I, 465 *Arg.*
Torres, Luis Vicente E 66 *Ecua.*
Torres, Macario (1854-1885) PM 81 *Mex.*
Torres, Mariano de Jesús PM 81; TM 355 *Mex.*
"Torres, Máximo" (*pseud.*) see Maeso Tognochi, Carlos M.
Torres, Nicanor María PM 81 *Mex.*
Torres, Roberto A 66 *Arg.*
Torres, Teodoro NM 54 *Mex.*
Torres, Teófilo TM 357 *Mex.*
Torres A., Salvador C 55 *Chil.*
Torres Abandero, Leopoldo LV 361; V 137 *Venez.*
Torres Arce, José Antonio (1828-1864) C 55; CLH 216; HC 170 *Chil.*
Torres Arce, José María C 22, 70; NC 310 *Chil.*
Torres Arce, Víctor (1847-1883) C 22, 41, 55; CLH 217; HC 211; NC 311, 500 *Chil.*
Torres Arroyo, Ignacio TM 357 *Mex.*
Torres Berdón, Salvador Ig 371; NM 54 *Mex.*
Torres Bodet, Jaime (1902-) AMP 172; APEH 995, 1193; APMM 201; BHLA 561; CrA 75; G 372; HLM 525; IE 285; LAS 205; NM 4, 54; PM 81; PMM 119; SASS 378; WLA 402 *Mex.*
Torres Bollo, Diego de (1550-) SCL 300, 406, 644 *Per.*
Torres Caicedo, José María (1830-1889) BHLA 410; CLH 303; Co 70, 71, 72; LC 130; RHLC 210 *Col.*
Torres Frías, Domingo A 66 *Arg.*
Torres Frías, María (1883-) A 66 *Arg.*
Torres Guinart, Luis PU 224 *Uru.*
Torres Hernández, Rodrigo APMM 204 *Mex.*
Torres Lanzas, Pedro PR 8 *P.R.*
Torres Méndez, Ramón Co 72 *Col.*
Torres Pinzón, Carlos Arturo Co 72 *Col.*
Torres Quintero, Gregorio Ig 371; NM 54; PM 82 *Mex.*
Torres-Ríoseco, Arturo (1897-) APEH 1002; C 22, 41, 70; CMPC 79; G 326; IE 286; LAS 207; MSAP 206, 326; WLA 402 *Chil.*
Torres Rivera, Enrique PR 7 *P.R.*
Torres Rojas, R. CA 50 *C.R.*
Torres Saldamando, Enrique P 34 *Per.*
Torres Serrato, Mateo TM 611 *Mex.*
Torres Torente, Bernardino (1813-1886) Co 72 *Col.*
Torres Torija, Enrique PM 82 *Mex.*
Torres Torija, Manuel TM 357 *Mex.*
Torres Valderrama, Enrique ("Enrique Rotres V.") (-1902?) Cu 146, 160 *Cu.*
Torres Vargas, Diego de PR 56 *P.R.*
Torres Vargas, Guillermo Co 72 *Col.*

Torres y Feria, Manuel ("Serafín de la Flor") (1833-1892) BDC 95; Cu 58, 160 *Cu.*
Torres y Peña, José Antonio de Co 72; HLNG II, 148; RHLC 54 *Col.*
Torri Máyenz, Julio (1889-) APMM 207; BAMP 77; HLM 518; NM 55; WLA 402 *Mex.*
Torriente Brau, Pablo de la Cu 161 *Cu.*
Torroella, Alfredo BDC 96; Cu 161; G 341; RLC 224; TM 358 *Cu.*
Toruño, Luis F. NL 172 *Nicar.*
Toscano, José María PM 82 *Mex.*
Toscano Refugio, Vda. de NM 55 *Mex.*
Tosta García, Francisco (1852-1921) V 137, 138; VPF 21 *Venez.*
Toussaint y Ritter, Manuel (1895-) APMM 209; HLM 513; IE 287; TM 576 *Mex.*
Tovar, Agustín de J. Ig 372; NM 55 *Mex.*
Tovar, Manuel (1844-1907) P 34 *Per.*
Tovar, Manuel José (1831-1865) B 21 *Bol.*
Tovar, Mariano CA 50 *C.R.*
Tovar, Pantaleón (1828-1876) AMP 242; BHLA 333; CHL 406; CLH 353; HLM 318, 332, 344; HPM 866; Ig 372; NM 55; PM 82; TM 358 *Mex.*
Tovar, Rómulo (1883-) CA 50, 51; CHL 508; EPCR 501; IBCR IV, 153; IE 288 *C.R.*
Tovar Ramírez, Enrique Demetrio (1890-) IE 289; WLA 403 *Per.*
Tovar S., Joaquín Co 72 *Col.*
Toymil, Francisco Cu 161 *Cu.*
Transilvano, Maximiliano BHC I, 3 *Chil.*
Travieso, Juan ARC 64 *Cu.*
Travieso, M. J. PP 45 *P.R.*
Travieso y Quijano, Martín PR 21, 56 *P.R.*
Trebarra, Napoleón NM 55 *Mex.*
Tregui, Antonio José (1864-) WLA 404 *Col.*
Trejo, E. Francisco TM 360 *Mex.*
Trejo, Joaquín PMe II, 247 *Mex.*
Trejo, M. NM 19 *Mex.*
Trejo, Nemesio A 66, 92 *Arg.*
Trejos, Juan de Dios (1853-1912) EPCR 40 *C.R.*
Trejos, Víctor CA 51 *C.R.*
Trelles, Jorge A. Cu 161 *Cu.*
Trelles, José A. see Alonso y Trelles, José
Trelles, Manuel Ricardo (1821-) LA VI, 1083 *Arg.*
Trelles, Rafael (-1880) LA VI, 1083 *Arg.*
Trelles y Govín, Carlos Manuel (1866-) CT 203; Cu 161; IE 292; PR 8, 61; WLA 405 *Cu.*
Tresandi, Lorenzo U 20 *Uru.*
Treserra, José A. Cu 161 *Cu.*
Trespalacios, José María Co 72 *Col.*
Treviño, Alfredo de (1887-) A 66, 92 *Arg.*
Triana, Miguel (1859-1930) Co 72; RHLC 200 *Col.*
Triana Terry, Félix ARC 64; Cu 161 *Cu.*
Trías Dupre, Emilio PU 320; U 20 *Uru.*
Triay, José E. (-1907) BDC 96; Cu 161 *Cu.*
Trillo, Enrique González A 66 *Arg.*
"Trini Sanz" (*pseud.*) see Padilla de Sanz, Trinidad

Trinidad Reyes, José (1797-1855) HL I, 169 *Hond.*
Triñanes, Francisco W. A 66 *Arg.*
Tristán, Flora (1807-1844) BHLA 235 *Per.*
Tristán Fernández, Guillermo CA 51 *C.R.*
"Tristán Maroff" (*pseud.*) *see* Navarro, Gustavo Adolfo
Tristany, Manuel Rogerio U 20 *Uru.*
Triviño, Pedro Ignacio IBCR IV, 102 *C.R.*
Troconis M., Armando V 138 *Venez.*
Troncoso, Fernando TM 360 *Mex.*
Troncoso, José Antonio V 138 *Venez.*
Troncoso, Juan Nepomuceno (1779-1830) ACe 959; HPM 805 *Mex.*
Troncoso, Martín J. A 66 *Arg.*
Troncoso de Oiz, Matilde ("Raquel") (1850-) C 15; Cu 137, 162; NC 493 *Cu.*
Trongé, Eduardo (1893-) A 92 *Arg.*
Trongé, Faustino A 66, 93 *Arg.*
"Trovador cubano, El" (*pseud.*) *see* Poveda y Armenteros, Francisco José
Troyano, Pedro de Co 72 *Col.*
Troyo, Rafael Ángel (1875-1910) CA 51, 52; EPCR 356; IBCR IV, 31, 69 *et passim C.R.*
Trueba, Antonio de Cu 162 *Cu.*
Trugillo, Miguel G. Par 25 *Para.*
Trujillo, Aurora TM 483 *Mex.*
Trujillo, Federico Co 72 *Col.*
Trujillo, José Ignacio (1833-) Co 72 *Col.*
Trujillo de Miranda, Pedro (1875-) Cu 162 *Cu.*
Trujillo Palacios, Luis V 138 *Venez.*
Trujillo y Armas, José (-1911) Cu 162 *Cu.*
Trujillo y Arredondo, Rosa ("Rosa Té") Cu 162; PCu 274; PJC 252 *Cu.*
Trujillo y Marín, Lorenzo BDC 97; Cu 162 *Cu.*
Trujillo y Roldán, Tomás Cu 162 *Cu.*
Trullas y Aulet, Ignacio ("Chantecler") CA 15, 52; IBCR IV, 112 *C.R.*
Truque G., Ricardo CA 52 *C.R.*
Tschudy, Fernando de Cu 162 *Cu.*
Tudela, Ricardo A 66 *Arg.*
Tulio Royo, Jorge Pan 19 *Pan.*
"Tunante, El" (*pseud.*) *see* Gamarra, Abelardo
Turcios, Froilán (Froylán) (1875-) FPA 317, 328; G 347; HL II, 705; WH 188 *Hond.*
Turcios R., Salvador PS 277 *Salv.*
Turena, Leopoldo de C 41 *Chil.*
Turini, Ernesto P. (1884-1920) A 66 *Arg.*
Turla, Ángel (1813-1837) HLC 127; RLC 91 *Cu.*
Turla, Leopoldo (1818-1877) BDC 97; Cu 163; HLC 127; PCu 276; RLC 182, 192 *Cu.*
Turner, Domingo H. Pan 19 *Pan.*
Turolos, Froylán IE 294 *Hond.*

U

Ubago, Juan B. PCu 279; PJC 254 *Cu.*
Uclés, Carlos Alberto (1854-) HL I, 713; II, 291 *Hond.*

Ugarte, Ángel (1856-) HL I, 757 *Hond.*
Ugarte, Enrique A. TM 577 *Mex.*
Ugarte, José ("Jorge Useta") Cu 164; G 373; NM 55; TM 346, 360 *Mex.*
Ugarte, Lucas A. de (1807-1868) BDC 97; Cu 163 *Cu.*
Ugarte, Manuel (1878-) A 66, 72; APAM 122; BHLA 474, 495; C 71; CLH 168; G 319; IE 295; LAC 115, 153; LAND 61; NPA 39; PLHA 133, 263; SAL 14, 281, 335; SASS 65; SD 30; WLA 406 *Arg.*
Ugarte, Ricardo B 21 *Bol.*
Ugarte A., Sinforoso C 56 *Chil.*
Ugarte de Landívar, Zoila E 69; PLE 95 *Ecua.*
Ugarte de Salamanca, Sara (1866-) BT 297 *Bol.*
Ugarteche, Félix de A 73 *Arg.*
Ugo, Judit A 67, 93 *Arg.*
Uhrbach, Carlos Pío (1872-1897) Cu 163; PA 109; RLC 285, 288, 290, 361 *Cu.*
Uhrbach y Campuzano, Federico (1873-) BDC 97; Cu 163; HLC 203; PA 112; PCu 281; RLC 285, 288, 290, 361; SASS 288 *Cu.*
Uhthoff, Enrique Cu 163 *Cu.*
Ujueta Sánchez, Joaquín Co 72 *Col.*
Ulacia, Francisco de Cu 163 *Cu.*
Ulate, Otilio CA 52; EPCR 621 *C.R.*
Ulua, Juan de V 138 *Venez.*
Ulloa, Ambrosio (1859-) Ig 374; NM 55 *Mex.*
Ulloa, Antonio de BHLA 131; SCL 361, 613, 644 *Sp.*
Ulloa, Armando (1901-1927) PCC xxi, 239 *Chil.*
Ulloa, Fernán de V 138 *Venez.*
Ulloa, Francisco Antonio (1783-1816) CHL 271; CLH 230; HLNG II, 95, 215 *Col.*
Ulloa, Gonzalo P 35 *Per.*
Ulloa, I. A. E 69 *Ecua.*
Ulloa, Luis (1869-1936) P 35 *Per.*
Ulloa, Miguel BDC 98; Cu 163; HLM 467; PM 82; TM 505 *Mex.*
Ulloa C., Francisco C 22; NC 311 *Chil.*
Ulloa M., Francisco CA 52 *C.R.*
Ulloa Zamora, María del Rosario CA 52; IBCR IV, 420 *C.R.*
Umaña, Salvador CA 52; EPCR 676 *C.R.*
Umaña Bernal, José (1900-) ALC II, 373; BHLA 585; Co 72 *Col.*
Umaña Espinosa, Rosa NL 176 *Nicar.*
Unánue, José Hipólito (1755-1833) P 35; SCL 561, 572, 644 *Per.*
Uncal, José María Cu 164 *Cu.*
Unda, Gabriel E 69 *Ecua.*
Unda, José Santos PM 82 *Mex.*
Undurraga G. H., Eduardo C 41 *Chil.*
Unghiatti Valle, Juan C 22 *Chil.*
Uquillas, B. Rosendo E 69 *Ecua.*
Uraga, Francisco ACe 962 *Mex.*
Uranga, Julio B. TM 168, 360 *Mex.*
Urbaneja, Alejandro ("Alejandro García Nieto" *or* "Selim-Adbel") LV 132, 346; V 75, 130, 138 *Venez.*
Urbaneja, Diego Bautista V 138 *Venez.*
Urbaneja, Modesto V 138 *Venez.*
Urbaneja, Ricardo V 138 *Venez.*

Urbaneja Achelpohl, Luis Manuel BHLA 521; CHL 379; CLH 327; LV 420; PLHA 214; SASS 534; V 138, 139; VPF 96 *Venez.*

Urbina y Miranda, Gregorio Cu 164 *Cu.*

Urbina y Sánchez, Luis Gonzaga ("El Cronista de Antaño") (1868-) AMP 83; APEH 416, 1186; APMM 210; BHLA 468; CHL 420; CLH 365, 366; FPA 340, 351; G 373; GLO 250; HLM 415; Ig 376; LAND 47; NM 4, 55; PM 82; PMe II, 249; PMM 39; PNM 297; PoM 373; SAL 94 *et passim*; SASS 369; WLA 407 *Mex.*

Urcullu, José de E 69 *Ecua.*

Urcullu, Manuel María B 21 *Bol.*

Urdaneta, Alberto LC 174 *Col.*

Urdaneta, Amenodoro V 139 *Venez.*

Urdaneta, Belarmino V 139 *Venez.*

Urdaneta, Carlos V 139 *Venez.*

Urdaneta, Ildemaro V 129, 139 *Venez.*

Urdaneta, Ismael V 139 *Venez.*

Urdaneta, Luis Co 72 *Col.*

Urdaneta, Nephtalí V 139 *Venez.*

Urdaneta, Rafael V 139, 140 *Venez.*

Urdaneta H., Luis V 140 *Venez.*

Urdemales, Pedro NC 166 *Chil.*

Ureña, Daniel (1876-) CA 52; EPCR 360; IBCR IV, 396 *C.R.*

Ureña, Nicolás ("Nísidas") HPHA I, 309; SD 30 *Dom.*

Ureña de Henríquez, Salomé ("Herminia") (1850-1897) BHLA 436; CHL 493; CLH 433; FPA 227, 232; HPHA I, 310; LD 88; PA 371; PD 207; SD 30 *Dom.*

Ureña de Mendoza, Nicolás (1822-1875) BHLA 225; CHL 492; CLH 432; PD 212 *Dom.*

Uresti, Porfirio TM 205, 360 *Mex.*

Ureta, Alberto J. (1885-) APEH 668, 1188; BAP 23; BHLA 537; IE 297; P 35; PPe 309; WLA 407 *Per.*

Ureta R., F. C 22; NC 500 *Chil.*

Ureta Rodríguez, Juan Francisco C 22, 41, 56; NC 312 *Chil.*

Urgell, Francisco de P. PM 83 *Mex.*

Uriarte, Juan Ramón IE 298 *Mex.*

Uriarte, Ramón (1846-) GPCA III, 563 *Guat.*

Uribe, Antonio José (1873-) Co 72 *Col.*

Uribe, Diego (1867-1921) AC II, 343; ALC I, 375; CHL 347; CLH 298; Co 73; LC 183; PCo 322; RHLC 148; SASS 232 *Col.*

Uribe, Eduardo (1899-) IE 299 *Arg.*

Uribe, José Escobar ("Claudio de Alas") (1886-) A 1; C 1; CG I, 40; GLO 241 *Col.*

Uribe, Juan B. PM 83 *Mex.*

Uribe, Juan de Dios ACe 965; Co 73; LC 176 *Col.*

Uribe, Margarita PM 83 *Mex.*

Uribe Ángel, Manuel (1822-1904) LC 174; RHLC 199 *Col.*

Uribe Echeverri, Carlos Co 73 *Col.*

Uribe Holguín, Alberto Co 73 *Col.*

Uribe Silva, Antonio Co 73 *Col.*

Uribe Uribe, Rafael (1859-1914) Co 73 *Col.*

Uribe Vigueras, Justo C 22 *Chil.*

Uribe Villegas, Gonzalo Co 73 *Col.*

Uriburu, Alberto E. A 67, 93 *Arg.*

Uricoechea, Ezequiel (1834-1880) Co 73; LC 167 *Col.*

Uriel García, José (1891-) WLA 409 *Per.*

Urien, Carlos María (1855-) A 67; AT I, 454 *Arg.*

Uriondo, Osvaldo A 67 *Arg.*

Urioste, Melitón B 21 *Bol.*

Urquidi, José Macedonio (1883-) B 21; BT 303 *Bol.*

Urquidi, Juan F. TM 483 *Mex.*

Urquieta, Antonio NC 478 *Chil.*

Urquieta, Miguel Ángel P 35 *Per.*

Urquinaona, Francisco (1785-) HLNG II, 117 *Col.*

Urquiza, Juan de P 35; SCL 314, 645 *Per.*

Urquizo, Francisco L. NM 55 *Mex.*

Urriola, Ciro L. (1862-1922) Pan 19 *Pan.*

Urriola, José Dolores ("El Mulato") (1834-1883) AP 303; Pan 19 *Pan.*

Urriola, Rufino de (1821-1896) Pan 19 *Pan.*

Urrutia, Francisco José Co 73; E 69; V 140 *Ecua.*

Urrutia, Ignacio de (1730-1790) RLC 31, 43, 45 *Cu.*

Urrutia, Miguel Ángel (1852-) GPCA III, 151; PG 267 *Guat.*

Urrutia de Vergara y Estrada, Manuel PM 83; TM 362 *Mex.*

Urrutia y Guzmán, José María ("Ramoncito") GPCA III, 345; PG 282 *Guat.*

Urteaga, Horacio H. (1877-) IE 299; P 35 *Per.*

Urtecho, José Coronel NL 271 *Nicar.*

Uruchurtu, Alfredo E. (1884-) IE 301 *Mex.*

Urueta, Jesús (1868-1920) G 373; HLMex 229; TM 361 *Mex.*

Urueta, José P. Co 73 *Col.*

Urzáis, Eduardo NM 55 *Mex.*

Urzáis, Fernando (1840-) BDC 98; Cu 164 *Cu.*

Urzúa, Miguel Rafael C 41, 56; CL 528 *Chil.*

Urzúa Cruzat, Leonor C 22, 41, 56 *Chil.*

Urzúa Cruzat, Pedro N. C 22, 41, 56; NC 500 *Chil.*

Urzúa de Calvo, Deyanira C 22, 41, 56 *Chil.*

Urzúa Gana, Teodoro C 56 *Chil.*

Urzúa Rosas, Adolfo C 56 *Chil.*

Urzúa S., F. Javier C 41 *Chil.*

Usatorre, Perfecto F. BDC 98; Cu 164 *Cu.*

"Useta, Jorge" (*pseud.*) *see* Ugarte, José

Usigli, Rodolfo (1905-) AMP 198; TM 363, 577; WLA 411 *Mex.*

Uslar Pietri, Arturo (1906-) BHLA 580; G 393; V 140; WLA 411 *Venez.*

Ustáriz, Francisco Javier CHL 86; CLH 306; HPHA I, 358 *Venez.*

Ustáriz, Luis HPHA I, 358 *Venez.*

Uteza, Antonio BDC 98; Cu 164 *Cu.*

Utrera, Cipriano de SD 30 *Dom.*

Uzcátegui G., Emilio (1899-) E 69; WLA 411 *Ecua.*

V

V., J. M. L. E 69 *Ecua.*
V., N. R. E 69 *Ecua.*
V. M. Y. M. TM 384 *Mex.*
Vaca, María Natalia PE 219 *Ecua.*
Vaca, Telmo N. E 69, 76 *Ecua.*
Vaca Chávez, Fabián (1881-) B 21; BT 305 *Bol.*
Vaca Diez, Antonio B 7, 21 *Bol.*
Vaca Guzmán, Santiago A 67; B 21; LB 600, 603 *Bol.*
Vacarezza, Alberto B. (1896-) A 67, 93 *Arg.*
Vacas Galindo, Enrique E 70 *Ecua.*
Vaccaro, Eduardo A 67 *Arg.*
Vadell, Natalio Abel PU 232 *Uru.*
Vadillo, Basilio NM 55 *Mex.*
Vaïsse, Emilio ("Omer Emeth") (-1935) BHLA 616; C 63, 65, 71; CL 528; N 127; NC 478 *Chil.*
Val, Luis de P 35 *Per.*
Valádez, M. Ig 377; NM 55 *Mex.*
Valarino, Nerio V 140 *Venez.*
Valásquez, Felipe S. A 67 *Arg.*
Valcarce Velasco, Manuel Antonio BHC III, 287 *Chil.*
Valcarcel, César Cu 164 *Cu.*
Valcarcel y Vizcarra, Luis Eduardo (1891-) WLA 412 *Per.*
Valda, Ángel C. B 22 *Bol.*
Valdelomar, Abraham (1888-1919) BAP 25; P 35; SASS 426 *Per.*
Valdemar, Diego Cu 164 *Cu.*
Valdenegro, Eusebio HCLU I, 37; PIU I, 90 *Uru.*
Valderrain, Alejandro PM 83 *Mex.*
Valderrama, A. C 23 *Chil.*
Valderrama, Adolfo (1834-1902) C 23, 41, 56, 71; CHL 256; CL 764; CLH 216; HC 158; NC 313, 482, 500; PCh 61 *Chil.*
Valderrama, Felipe V 140 *Venez.*
Valdés *see also* Valdez
Valdés, Abraham IE 302 *Bol.*
Valdés, Adolfo (1840-1873) Co 73; P 35
Valdés, Antonio CHL 36, 45; CLH 31, 38; Cu 164; SASS 439 *Cu.*
Valdés, Antonio José (1780-1836) Cu 164; RLC 31, 43 *Cu.*
Valdés, Carlos Genaro (1845-1890) Cu 164 *Cu.*
Valdés, Carlos M. PJC 255 *Cu.*
Valdés, Carmelo B. A 67 *Arg.*
Valdés, César C 23; NC 398 *Chil.*
Valdés, Domingo E. Cu 165 *Cu.*
Valdés, Gabriel de la Concepción ("Plácido") (1809-1844) AEHA 831; ARC 33; BHLA 241; CHL 173, 443, 448; CLH 305, 385; Cu 132, 165; FPA 161, 167; G 341; GLO 242; HLC 107; HPHA I, 256; PA 135; PCu 285; RLC 70, 80, 173; SASS 265 *Cu.*
Valdés, Gerónimo de Cu 166 *Cu.*
Valdés, Jacinto BDC 99; Cu 166 *Cu.*
1. Valdés, José ACe 967; PM 83 *Mex.*
2. Valdés, José (189.-) FPA 502, 520
Valdés, José Francisco ACe 968 *Mex.*
Valdés, José Lino Cu 166 *Cu.*
Valdés, José Manuel (1767-1843) P 35 *Per.*

1. Valdés, José María (1770-1803) HLNG II, 69; SCL 543, 645 *Col.*
2. Valdés, José María Cu 166 *Cu.*
Valdés, José Policarpo ("Polidoro") (1807-1852) RLC 87 *Cu.*
Valdés, José Sebastián BDC 99; Cu 166 *Cu.*
Valdés, Juan Evangelista (1863-1918) ARC 64 *Cu.*
Valdés, Juan Nepomuceno ARC 64 *Cu.*
Valdés, Julio César ("Jules Wallas") B 22 *Bol.*
Valdés, Manuel Antonio (1742?-1814) ACe 969; PM 83 *Mex.*
Valdés, Rafael A. (1840-1893) ARC 39 *Cu.*
Valdés, Ramón Francisco (1810-1866) BDC 99; Cu 166; TM 363
Valdés, Ramón M. (-1918) AP 311; Pan 19 *Pan.*
Valdés Carrero, Luis ARC 64 *Cu.*
Valdés Codina, Carlos A. (1876-) Cu 167 *Cu.*
Valdés Codina, Leopoldo (1868-1924) BDC 100; Cu 167 *Cu.*
Valdés Colell, Felipe Cu 167 *Cu.*
Valdés de la Paz, Osvaldo Cu 167; PCu 295; PJC 263 *Cu.*
Valdés de León y Díaz, Lino Cu 167 *Cu.*
Valdés Gallol, Carmela (1918-) PoC 274 *Cu.*
Valdés Herrera, A. Cu 167 *Cu.*
Valdés Jr., Ignacio de J. AP 305; Pan 19 *Pan.*
Valdés Machuca, Ignacio ("Desval") (1800-1851) BDC 100; BHLA 223; CHL 434; CLH 376; Cu 167; RLC 72 *Cu.*
Valdés Marín, Ramón BDC 100 *Cu.*
Valdés Mendoza, Mercedes (1822-1896) Cu 168; PCu 290 *Cu.*
Valdés Miranda, Bruno Cu 168 *Cu.*
Valdés Pita, Manuel Cu 168 *Cu.*
Valdés Quesada, Leopoldo (1879-) QPR (2) 167 *P.R.*
Valdés Rodríguez, Manuel Cu 168 *Cu.*
Valdés Roig, Ciana Cu 168; GLO 245; PJC 206 *Cu.*
Valdés Varela, V. PM 83 *Mex.*
Valdés y Aguirre, Fernando Cu 168; PCu 288 *Cu.*
Valdés y Arce, Octavio (1876-1912) AP 309; Pan 19 *Pan.*
Valdés y Valdés, Miguel Ángel Cu 168 *Cu.*
Valdespino y Díaz, Ignacio (1861-) Ig 377; NM 55 *Mex.*
Valdez *see also* Valdés
Valdez, Anselmo GPCA II, 181 *Cu.*
Valdez, Manuel HPM 480 *Mex.*
Valdez, Rodrigo de (1609-1682) LP 324; P 35 *Per.*
Valdivia, Alberto C 41 *Chil.*
Valdivia, Aniceto ("Conde Kostia") (1859-1927) BDC 100; Cu 87, 168; PA 58, 115; RLC 285, 291 *et passim* *Cu.*
Valdivia, Félix Ramón Cu 168 *Cu.*
Valdivia, Juan Gualberto P 35 *Per.*
Valdivia, Luis de BHC I, 97; II, 49 *et passim*; SCL 280, 645 *Chil.*
Valdivia, Pedro de SCL 146, 645 *Chil.*
Valdivieso de Astudillo, Juana C. E 70 *Ecua.*

Valdivieso Montaño, A. A 140 *Arg.*
Valdivieso y Cisneros, Eladio Co 73 *Col.*
Valdovinos, Arnaldo M. Par 25 *Para.*
Valdovinos, Mucio TM 363 *Mex.*
Valencia, Félix E 70; PLE 100 *Ecua.*
Valencia, Francisco PCo 327 *Col.*
Valencia, Guillermo (1873-) ALC II, 63; APEH 348, 1184; BHLA 463; CHL 539; CLH 472; Co 73, 74, 79; CP 694; FPA 82, 118; G 331; GLO 241; LC 186; MSAP 112, 297; PCo 330; PLHA 118; RHLC 136; SAL 92; SASS 235; WLA 414 *Col.*
Valencia, Juan (-1646) HPM 198; PM 83 *Mex.*
Valencia, Leopoldo TM 364 *Mex.*
Valencia, Manuel María (1818?-1870) HPHA I, 307; SD 30 *Dom.*
Valencia, Miguel Santiago Co 74; PLHA 296 *Col.*
Valencia, Pedro Felipe Co 74; HLNG II, 283 *Col.*
Valencia, Reinaldo Co 74 *Col.*
Valentí, Rubén Ig 378; NM 55; PM 83 *Mex.*
Valenzuela, Bruno de Co 74; HLNG I, 164 *Col.*
Valenzuela, Crisanto HLNG II, 289 *Col.*
Valenzuela, Eloy HLNG II, 338 *Col.*
Valenzuela, Emilio PM 83 *Mex.*
Valenzuela, Jesús E. (1856-1911) AMP 102; G 373; HLM 427; HLMex 217; PM 83; PMe II, 279; PNM 318; SAL 25 *Mex.*
Valenzuela, Mario (1836-1922) AC I, 259; CHL 345; CLH 296; Co 74; LC 158 *Col.*
Valenzuela C., Alberto C 23; NC 318 *Chil.*
Valenzuela de la Torre, Eduardo Co 74 *Col.*
Valenzuela Fonnegra, Eduardo Co 74 *Col.*
Valenzuela Matte, Ramón C 23 *Chil.*
Valenzuela Olivares, Luis Antonio (1859-1906) C 41, 54, 56; PCh 107 *Chil.*
Valenzuela Olivos, Eduardo C 41, 56; PCh 389 *Chil.*
Valenzuela T., Alejandro C 41, 56 *Chil.*
Valera Hurtado, Luis V 140 *Venez.*
Valerino y Quiroga, Lino Cu 169 *Cu.*
Valerio, Juan Francisco ("Narciso Valor y Fé") (-1878) BDC 100; Cu 169 *Cu.*
Valero, María Edilia V 140 *Venez.*
Valero Méndez, Agustín ("Maravelo") PM 55, 83 *Mex.*
Valette, C. de la U 20 *Uru.*
"Valor y Fé, Narciso" (*pseud.*) *see* Valerio, Juan Francisco
"Valromey, Doctor" (*pseud.*) *see* González, Francisco
"Vals, Edmundo del" (*pseud.*) *see* Milla Chapelli, Julio
Valverde, Diego Benedicto TM 364 *Mex.*
Valverde, Fernando de CHL 37; CLH 32 *Per.*
Valverde, Miguel (1853-1920) E 70; PE 246; PLE 54 *Ecua.*
Valverde L., Jenaro CA 53; EPCR 623 *C.R.*
Valverde Téllez, Emeterio TM 577 *Mex.*
Valverde y Bascó, Nicolás (-1924) ARC 65 *Cu.*
Valverde y Maruri, Antonio L. (1867-) Cu 169 *Cu.*

Valladares, Juan R. (1865-) HL II, 645 *Hond.*
Valladares, Paulino WH 188 *Hond.*
Valladares, R. Cu 169 *Cu.*
Valladares, Roberto (1891-1920) CA 53; EPCR 506 *C.R.*
Valladares Márquez, Jorge (1891-) FPA 292, 307; PG 445 *Guat.*
Valladares y Rubio, Antonio ("Charles Carrillo") (1871-) PG 334; WLA 415 *Guat.*
Vallarta, Ignacio L. (1830-1893) HLM 362 *Mex.*
Vallarta y Palma, José Mariano HPM 458 *Mex.*
Valle, Adelina A 67 *Arg.*
Valle, Adrián del ("Palmiro de Lidia") (1872-) A 67; CG III, 379; Cu 89, 169; GLO 246 *Cu.*
Valle, Amado del PM 83 *Mex.*
Valle, Antonio G. U 20 *Uru.*
Valle, Armando del Cu 170 *Cu.*
Valle, Basilio ARC 65 *Cu.*
Valle, Blanca del NL 178 *Nicar.*
Valle, Eduardo del PM 83 *Mex.*
Valle, Félix del P 35 *Per.*
Valle, Guillermo del (1846-1917) Ig 379; NM 55; PM 83 *Mex.*
Valle, Jimena del C 23 *Chil.*
Valle, José Cecilio del (1780-1834) AA II, 43, 337; HL I, 3 *Hond.*
Valle, José G. del PR 10, 48 *P.R.*
Valle, Juan (1838-1865) AMP 262; CHL 396; CLH 344; G 373; HLM 313; HLMex 152; HPM 832; PM 83; PMe II, 283; TM 365 *Mex.*
Valle, Juvencio (1907-) C 41; PCC xxiv, 289 *Chil.*
"Valle, Luis del" (*pseud.*) *see* Varona y Pera, Enrique José
Valle, Luz PG 465 *Guat.*
Valle, Manuel (1861-1913) PG 305 *Guat.*
Valle, Margarita del PCu 297; PJC 261 *Cu.*
Valle, Mariano del TM 365 *Mex.*
Valle, Octaviano TM 611 *Mex.*
Valle, Rafael del (1846-190.) BP 507, 540; FPA 460, 477; PR 28, 41, 54 *P.R.*
Valle, Rafael Heliodoro (1891-1922) APEH 787; BHLA 575; CrA 111; FPA 319, 337; G 347; IE 303; NM 4; PG 454; SASS 129; SD 31; WH 188; WLA 415 *Hond.*
Valle, Ramón (1841-1901) Ig 381; NM 56; PM 84; TM 366 *Mex.*
Valle, Rosa del PM 84 *Mex.*
Valle, Rosamel del (1900-) C 41; PCC xxi, 233 *Chil.*
Valle-Arizpe, Artemio de (1888-) G 374; HLM 515; IE 305; Ig 382; NM 56; TM 577; WLA 416 *Mex.*
Valle Atiles, Francisco del BP 507, 639; PR 10, 28, 48, 54 *P.R.*
Valle de Santiesteban, J. Ig 384; NM 56 *Mex.*
Valle Goicochea, Luis BHLA 610 *Per.*
Valle Moré, José del Cu 170 *Cu.*
Valle Riente, Amado del C 41 *Chil.*
Valle Sárraga, R. del PR 48 *P.R.*
Valle Silva, Luisa del V 140 *Venez.*

Valle y Caviedes, Juan del (1653?-1692) CHL 26; CLH 23; HPHA II, 191; LP 330; P 35; SCL 335, 646 *Per.*
Valle y Talavera, Manuel del NM 56 *Mex.*
Valle y Vélez, Santiago BP 508; PR 28 *P.R.*
Valledor, Manuel F. C 41 *Chil.*
Valledor Sánchez, Gustavo C 41, 56; CHL 262; CLH 222; PCh 141 *Chil.*
Vallejo, Alejandro Co 74 *Col.*
Vallejo, Carlos María de PU 235; U 20 *Uru.*
Vallejo, César V 140 *Venez.*
Vallejo, César A. (1895-) APEH 1134, 1195; BAP 41; BHLA 607; P 36 *Per.*
Vallejo, José Joaquín ("Jotabeche") (1811-1858) BHLA 218; C 11, 17, 23; CHL 240; CLH 200; G 326; GLO 240; HC 69; NC 439, 482; SASS 192 *Chil.*
Vallejo Larrea, Gustavo E 70 *Ecua.*
Vallenilla Lanz, Baltasar V 140 *Venez.*
Vallenilla Lanz, Laureano (1870?-) BHLA 485; V 140, 141 *Venez.*
Valles, Rodolfo Ig 384; NM 56 *Mex.*
Valles B., Juan P 36 *Per.*
Valliera, Juan A 67, 93 *Arg.*
Van Der Biest, Edmundo V 141 *Venez.*
Vando, César del Cu 170 *Cu.*
Vanegas, Alí NL 241 *Nicar.*
Vanegas, Juan D. NL 54 *Nicar.*
Vanini Silva, Blanca C 41 *Chil.*
Vaquero, Francisco (1849-) HL II, 109 *Hond.*
Vaquero, Santos ARC 65 *Cu.*
Varaix, Francisco (1581-1658) HLNG I, 245; RHLC 28 *Col.*
Varallanos, José BAP 91 *Per.*
Varas Calvo, José Miguel (1807-1833) C 23; HC 56 *Chil.*
Varas Espinosa, Manuel (1882-) PCh 259 *Chil.*
Varas M., Carlos NC 484 *Chil.*
Varela, Félix (1788-1853) AA II, 14, 75; ARC 76; Cu 170; G 342; RLC 52, 151, 157 *et passim Cu.*
Varela, Florencio (1807-1848) A 67; BHLA 234; CHL 133; CLH 137; HLA 328; LA VI, 646; PIU I, 157; SPLA 75; U 20 *Arg.*
Varela, Héctor F. E 70 *Ecua.*
Varela, José Pedro ("Cuasimodo") (1845-1879) HSLU III, pt 4, 20; PIU I, 216; U 20 *Uru.*
Varela, Juan Cruz (1794-1839) A 67, 93; AEHA 850; BHLA 208; CHL 121; CLH 104; HLA 238; HPHA II, 415; LA VII, 400; SPLA 53, 148 *Arg.*
Varela, L. Eduardo C 71; NC 484 *Chil.*
Varela, Luis Vicente ("Raúl Waleis") (1845-) A 68, 78, 93; LA VIII, 629 *Arg.*
Varela Zequeira, Eduardo (-1918) BDC 101; Cu 170 *Cu.*
Varela Zequeira, José (1859-) CT 585; Cu 171; PCu 300; RLC 223, 278 *Cu.*
Varela y Morales, Félix (1788-1853) CHL 431; HLC 51 *Cu.*
Vargas, Fulgencio (1875-) G 374; IE 306; PM 84 *Mex.*
Vargas, Ignacio ACe 976 *Mex.*

Vargas, José María V 141 *Venez.*
Vargas, Julio TM 367, 483 *Mex.*
Vargas, L. Serrudo B 22 *Bol.*
Vargas, León CA 53 *C.R.*
Vargas, M. Nemesio (1848-) P 36 *Per.*
Vargas, Pedro Fermín de Co 74 *Col.*
Vargas, Pedro P. PR 41 *P.R.*
Vargas, Teódulo (1844-1911) AC I, 209; Co 74; LC 160 *Col.*
Vargas Bello, Luis C 23 *Chil.*
Vargas Calvo, Guillermo (1881-) CA 53; EPCR 365 *C.R.*
Vargas Coto, Joaquín CA 53; EPCR 679 *C.R.*
Vargas MacDonald, A. TM 16, 367 *Mex.*
Vargas Machucha, Bernardo (1555?-) Co 74; HLNG I, 120 *Col.*
Vargas Márquez, Juan ("Juan del Páramo") C 17 *Chil.*
Vargas Pizarro, L. T. V 141 *Venez.*
Vargas Rodríguez, Alfredo (1897-) QPR (1) 166; (2) 169 *P.R.*
Vargas Tamayo, José Co 75 *Col.*
Vargas Tejada, Luis (1802-1829) CHL 84; CLH 71; Co 75; CoL 268; G 331; HLNG II, 431; HPHA II, 44; LC 113; RHLC 81; SASS 212 *Col.*
Vargas Torres, Luis (-1887) E 70 *Ecua.*
Vargas V., Isidro Co 75 *Col.*
Vargas Vargas, M. T. C 57 *Chil.*
Vargas Vila, José María (1863-1933) AEHA 911; BHLA 475, 518; CHL 541; CLH 474; Co 75, 76, 77; G 331; LAS 205; LC 190; PLHA 268; RHLC 191; SAL 120 *et passim*; SASS 245 *Col.*
Vargas y Gómez, Moisés (1843-1898) C 23; CHL 270; CLH 230; HC 237; NC 318, 398 *Chil.*
"Varmes, Celinda P." (*pseud.*) *see* Silva, Carmen P. de
Varney, León Co 77 *Col.*
Varona, Abelardo S. de Cu 171 *Cu.*
Varona, Adolfo BDC 101; Cu 171 *Cu.*
Varona, Julio D. de (-1889?) Cu 172 *Cu.*
Varona, Ramón Sánchez (1883-) BDC 101; Cu 172; G 342; RLC 368 *Cu.*
Varona Gauchat, J. E. E 68 *Ecua.*
Varona y Pera, Enrique José ("Luis del Valle") (1849-1933) BHLA 374, 448; CHL 480; CLH 419; CT 199; Cu 170, 171; G 342; GLO 246; HLC 61; LH 57; PCu 302; RLC 326 *et passim*; SASS 300 *Cu.*
Varquillas, Francisco V 141 *Venez.*
Varrón, Carlos (-1828) ACe 976 *Mex.*
Vasconcelos, Joaquín (1830-) GPCA II, 69; PG 148 *Guat.*
Vasconcelos, José (1882-) BHLA 487, 498; CHL 429; G 374; GLO 250; HLM 511; IE 307; LAND 121, 134; NM 56; SASS 395; TM 367; WLA 417 *Mex.*
Vasconcelos, Ramón ARC 65 *Cu.*
Vascónez, Francisco E 70 *Ecua.*
Vascónez Cuvi, Victoria E 70 *Ecua.*
Vascónez Tobar, Gabriel E 70 *Ecua.*
Vásquez *see also* Vázquez
Vásquez, Ambrosio C 41 *Chil.*
Vásquez, Andrés Clemente NM 56 *Mex.*
"Vásquez, Daniel" (*pseud.*) *see* Gómez Rojas, Domingo
Vásquez, Donato B 22 *Bol.*

Vásquez, Eugenio 2° C 23 *Chil.*
Vásquez, Francisco SCL 290, 646 *Per.*
Vásquez, Honorato CHL 317; CLH 269 *Ecua.*
Vásquez, Jorge Adalberto PM 84 *Mex.*
Vásquez, Juan Teodoro SCL 391, 646 *Per.*
Vásquez, Miguel Antonio V 141 *Venez.*
Vásquez, Rafael (1899-) ALC II, 401; Co 77; WLA 418 *Col.*
Vásquez, Teodoro Co 77 *Col.*
Vásquez Flórez Co 77 *Col.*
Vásquez Guarda, Efraín C 71; NC 484 *Chil.*
Vásquez Ordenes, Manuel C 23 *Chil.*
Vásquez Santa Ana, Higinio (1890-) IE 310; TM 577; WLA 418 *Mex.*
Vásquez Varela, Alfredo U 20; UL 193 *Uru.*
Vassalo Cabrera, Francisco (1822-1867) PR 54 *P.R.*
Vasseur, Álvaro Armando ("Américo Llano") (1878-) APEH 503; BHLA 466, 487; FPA 528, 540; HSLU II, pt 2, 14; LU 64, 662; LUr 526; PIU II, 307; PLHA 150; PoU 153; U 20; UT 523 *Uru.*
Vasseur, Inés (1853-1878) Cu 173 *Cu.*
"Vate Arrugado, El" (*pseud.*) *see* Roquero y Domínguez, Juan
"Vate Habanero, Un" (*pseud.*) Cu 173 *Cu.*
Vattier, Carlos C 23 *Chil.*
Vaudoyer, Jean Louis Cu 173 *Cu.*
Vaughn, Kenelm PR 21 *P.R.*
Vayo, Estanislao Cu 173 *Cu.*
Vaz Ferreira, Carlos (1873-) HSLU III, pt 4, 41; LU 64, 680; PIU III, 47; UT 527 *Uru.*
Vaz Ferreira, María Eugenia (1873-1924) APEH 902; BHLA 488; CHL 233; FPA 528, 542; HSLU II, pt 7, 40; pt 8, 9; LU 64, 658; LUr 524; PCU 116; PIU II, 239; PLHA 176; PoU 159; U 20; UT 529 *Uru.*
Vázquez *see also* Vásquez
Vázquez, Andrés Clemente (1844-1901) Cu 173 *Cu.*
Vázquez, Arturo H. A 68 *Arg.*
Vázquez, Honorato (1855-1932) E 70; PE 100; PLE 50 *Ecua.*
Vázquez, Ildefonso V 141 *Venez.*
Vázquez, José Cu 173 *Cu.*
Vázquez, José F. TM 611 *Mex.*
1. Vázquez, Juan de Jesús Cu 173 *Cu.*
2. Vázquez, Juan de Jesús HPHA I, 301 *Dom.*
Vázquez, Trina de M. de PD 217; SD 31 *Dom.*
Vázquez Alayón, Manuel (1861-) QPR (1) 167; (2) 169 *P.R.*
Vázquez Cey, Arturo (1888-) A 68, 93; APAM 419; G 319; LAC 145 *Arg.*
Vázquez de Cuberos, Luis Cu 173 *Cu.*
Vázquez de Montiel, María del Carmen ("Concepción Ríos") A 58, 68, 78 *Arg.*
Vázquez Díaz, Manuel (1899-) IE 309 *Per.*
Vázquez Ledesma, Froilán PU 322; U 20 *Uru.*
Vázquez López, Gertrudis Cu 173; PJC 118 *Cu.*
Vázquez M., J. M. AP 313; Pan 19 *Pan.*

Vázquez Sagastume, José HCLU I, 406, 417 *Uru.*
Vázquez y Vega, Prudencio PIU I, 232 *Uru.*
Veas, Humberto C 57 *Chil.*
Vecchio, Carlos del V 141 *Venez.*
Vedia, Enrique de A 68, 93 *Arg.*
Vedia y Mitre, Mariano de (1880-) AT II, 941 *Arg.*
Vega, Alejandro (1864-1903) PCo 346; RHLC 150 *Col.*
Vega, Anselmo Cu 173 *Cu.*
Vega, Bernardo de la HPHA II, 380 *Sp.-Para.*
Vega, Carlos A 68 *Arg.*
Vega, Clemente SD 31 *Dom.*
Vega, Daniel de la (1892-) BHLA 626; C 41, 57, 71; CMPC 110; G 326; PCC xvii, 143; PCh 367 *Chil.*
Vega, Eladio J. PR 41 *P.R.*
Vega, Evelio M. PJC 270 *Cu.*
Vega, Fernando de la (1891-) Co 77; RHLC 212 *Col.*
Vega, Francisco de P. TM 367 *Mex.*
Vega, José de la Co 78 *Col.*
Vega, Rafael Cu 173 *Cu.*
Vega, Ramón TM 613 *Mex.*
"Vega, Raúl de la" (*pseud.*) *see* Diego, Pedro R. de
Vega, Roa de la Cu 173 *Cu.*
"Vega, Santos" (*pseud.*) *see* Rivarola, Enrique E.
Vega, Ventura de la (1807-1865) BHLA 308; HLA 355; HPHA II, 430; LA IV, 1019 *Arg.*
Vega Belgrano, Carlos (1858-) AT II, 677 *Arg.*
Vega Escobar, Hernando Co 78 *Col.*
Vega López, Carlos A 68 *Arg.*
Vega Nevares, Félix (1863-) QPR (1) 168; (2) 170 *P.R.*
Vega y Planas, Luz Cu 173 *Cu.*
Veglia, Pablo (1806-1835) Cu 173 *Cu.*
Veintemilla de Galindo, Dolores (1833-1857) BHLA 321; CHL 317; CLH 269; E 71; PE 64; PLE 34 *Ecua.*
Veintimilla, Marieta de (1859-1907) E 70; PE 220; PLE 54 *Ecua.*
Vejarano, Jorge Ricardo Co 78 *Col.*
Vela, Arqueles (1899-) G 374; Ig 387; NM 56 *Mex.*
Vela, Carlos H. (1885-1912) PG 392 *Guat.*
Vela, Eusebio HLM 187; HPM 220; TM 367 *Mex.*
Vela, Pablo Hanníbal PE 274 *Ecua.*
Vela Jaramillo, J. M. E 71 *Ecua.*
Velado, Calixto (187.-) FPA 501, 510; PS 158 *Salv.*
Velarde, César Augusto ("Brigadier Alfa") E 71 *Ecua.*
Velarde, Everardo AP 307; Pan 19 *Pan.*
Velarde, Fabián Pan 20 *Pan.*
Velarde, Fernando (1825-1881) BHLA 304; CHL 507; CLH 447; GPCA I, 301; HPHA II, 256 *Sp.*
Velarde, Héctor G 383; LAS 202; P 36 *Per.*
Velarde, Mariano B 22 *Bol.*
Velarde, Román Cu 174 *Cu.*
Velarde, Samuel (1848-1902) P 36 *Per.*

Velasco *see also* Velazco
Velasco, Adolfo TM 369 *Mex.*
Velasco, Francisco ACe 977 *Mex.*
Velasco, José del Carmen ARC 65 *Cu.*
Velasco, José Luis E 71; TM 369
Velasco, José María E 71 *Ecua.*
Velasco, Juan de (1727-1792) BHLA 119, 134; CHL 34; CLH 29; E 71; PLE 24; SCL 552, 646 *Ecua.*
Velasco, Leopoldo A 68 *Arg.*
Velasco, Martín de Co 78; HLNG I, 224; SCL 347, 646 *Col.*
Velasco, Zenón J. TM 369 *Mex.*
Velasco Flor, Samuel B 22 *Bol.*
Velasco Reyes, Benjamín C 41 *Chil.*
Velasco y Arellano, José Luis de HPM 454; PM 84 *Mex.*
Velasco y Cisneros, Isabel Cu 174 *Cu.*
Velasco y Pérez, Carlos de (1884-1923) CHL 489; CLH 429; CT 55; Cu 174; GLO 246; SASS 306 *Cu.*
Velasco y Rojas, Matías de, Marqués de Dos Hermanas (1829-1901) Cu 174 *Cu.*
Velasco y Salamó, Fanor (1848-1907) HC 205 *Chil.*
Velásquez *see also* Velázquez
Velásquez, Aurelio PM 84 *Mex.*
Velásquez, Samuel (1865-) Co 78; RHLC 190 *Col.*
Velásquez de Cárdenas y León, Joaquín (1732-1786) ACe 664 *Mex.*
Velásquez García, José ("Julio Vives Guerra") (1874-) E 72; RHLC 190 *Col.*
Velaz Palacios, Matilde A 68 *Arg.*
Velazco *see also* Velasco
Velazco, Ambrosio HCLU I, 433 *Uru.*
Velazco, Enrique A 68 *Arg.*
Velázquez *see also* Velásquez
Velázquez, Alberto (1892?-) FPA 292, 314; PG 412 *Guat.*
Velázquez, Aureliano APMM 219 *Mex.*
Velázquez, Edmundo PCo 348 *Col.*
Velázquez, Juan Luis BAP 103; P 36 *Per.*
Velázquez, N. M. TM 483 *Mex.*
Velázquez, Roberto A. Par 25; PPa 177 *Para.*
Velázquez Bringas, Esperanza (1899-) IE 311; NM 4; SD 31 *Mex.*
Velázquez de León, Mariana ACe 983 *Mex.*
Velázquez Galván, Manuel NM 56 *Mex.*
Vélez, Bernardo Co 78 *Col.*
Vélez, Ismael Ig 388; NM 56 *Mex.*
Vélez, José María A 68 *Arg.*
Vélez, Juan José A 68 *Arg.*
Vélez Ladrón de Guevara, Francisco Antonio Co 78 *Col.*
Vélez Ladrón de Guevara, Miguel (1724-1797) Co 78; HLNG II, 384; LC 99 *Col.*
Vélez Sársfield, Dalmacio (1800-1875) LA VI, 1152; VII, 21 *Arg.*
Vélez Triana, Roberto E 71 *Ecua.*
Vélez y Herrera, Ramón (1809-1886) AEHA 911; BDC 102; BHLA 223; CHL 435; CLH 378; Cu 174; HLC 121; HPHA I, 284; PCu 304; RLC 86 *Cu.*
Veloz, Luis F. PE 209; PLE 86 *Ecua.*
Velujo, Roque TM 370 *Mex.*
Venegas, Caridad G. PCu 308; PJC 265 *Cu.*

Venegas, J. D. PN 169 *Nicar.*
Venegas Urbina, L. Lucio C 23; NC 485 *Chil.*
Venegas y Venegas, José Ángel (1867-) PCh 267 *Chil.*
"Venezolano, Un" (*pseud.*) *see* Yánez, Francisco Javier
Vento y Nin, Rafael Pérez (1875-) CT 147 *Cu.*
Ventura, Tona A 68 *Arg.*
Venturini, Adolfo A 68 *Arg.*
Venturino, Alice Lardé de (1900-) WLA 422 *Salv.*
Vera, Agustín (1889-) Ig 388; NM 56; TM 370 *Mex.*
Vera, Felipe L. PE 82 *Ecua.*
Vera, Fortún de A 68; U 20
Vera, Rafael PR 21 *P.R.*
Vera, Robustiano C 71; NC 485 *Chil.*
Vera y Pintado, Bernardo de (1780-1827) CHL 60; CLH 51; HLA 231; HPHA II, 347; LA IV, 923 *Arg.*
"Veracruz, Alonso de la" (*pseud.*) *see* Gutiérrez, Alonso
Veral, Ángel TM 370 *Mex.*
Veranes, Félix Fernández de RLC 39, 46, 152 *Cu.*
Veras, Filidoro NM 56 *Mex.*
Verbel y Marea, Eva C. (1856-) Co 78; PCo 350 *Col.*
"Verdades, Fray" (*pseud.*) *see* Arcos y Segovia, Luis de
Verdugo Cavada, Ignacio PCh 369 *Chil.*
Verdugo Fálquez, Francisco Ig 389; NM 56 *Mex.*
Vergara, Estanislao HLNG II, 314 *Col.*
Vergara, Luis Aurelio Co 78 *Col.*
Vergara, Marta C 23 *Chil.*
Vergara, Pedro Co 78 *Col.*
Vergara Antúnez, Rodolfo (1849-1914) C 42; HC 250 *Chil.*
Vergara Azcárate, Fernando de (-1761) HLNG I, 316; SCL 454, 647 *Col.*
Vergara Azcárate (Azcaute), José de (1684-1746) Co 78; HLNG I, 316; SCL 454, 647 *Col.*
Vergara Barrios, Francisco Co 78 *Col.*
Vergara Cuara, Tomás E 71 *Ecua.*
Vergara Larraín, Luis C 23 *Chil.*
Vergara Leyton, Ismael C 42; NC 486 *Chil.*
Vergara Robles, Enrique C 23 *Chil.*
Vergara y Caycedo, Felipe de (1745-1818) Co 78, 79; HLNG I, 391; SCL 533, 647 *Col.*
Vergara y Velasco, Francisco Javier Co 79 *Col.*
Vergara y Vergara, Eladio (1821-1888) Co 79; RHLC 176 *Col.*
Vergara y Vergara, José María (1831-1872) AEHA 912; CHL 34, 338, 353; CLH 290; Co 10, 32, 41, 79; HLNG I, xvii; II, 27; HPHA II, 75; LC 142; PCo 352; RHLC 123 *Col.*
Vergés Vidal, Pedro L. SD 31 *Dom.*
Vergez, José F. PM 84 *Mex.*
Vernaza, José Ignacio Co 79 *Col.*
Vernaza, Luis E 71 *Ecua.*
Versón Brunet, Rafael PJC 273 *Cu.*
Vesga y Ávila, José María Co 80 *Col.*

Vetancourt *see also* Betancourt

Vetancourt Aristeguieta, Manuel Norberto (1892-) QPR (1) 169; V 141; WLA 423 *Venez.*

Vetancourt Aristiguieta, I. PB 169 *Bol.*

Veytia, Mariano Fernández de Echeverría y *see* Fernández de Echeverría y Veytia, Mariano

Vial de Ugarte, María C 23 *Chil.*

Vial Guzmán, Wenceslao C 23; NC 335 *Chil.*

Vial Solar, Javier C 42, 57; PCh 113 *Chil.*

Vial y Ureta, Román (1833-1896) C 23, 57; CHL 281; CLH 239; HC 236; NC 399 *Chil.*

Viana, Demetrio Co 80 *Col.*

Viana, Javier de (1872-1907) BHLA 402, 507; CHL 228; CLH 190; LU 64, 671; LUr 507, 538; PIU II, 193; PLHA 227; SASS 478; U 20; UT 537 *Uru.*

Viana, Luis de Cu 174 *Cu.*

Viana R., J. Enrique B 22 *Bol.*

Viancos Calderón, María C 42 *Chil.*

Viaña, José PU 324 *Uru.*

Vicario, Amado R. TM 373 *Mex.*

Vicario, Victoriano (1911-) BHLA 626; PCC xxiv, 293 *Chil.*

Vicarte, Alberto TM 375 *Mex.*

Vicéns Thievent, Lorenzo PU 237 *Uru.*

Vicente Gil, Victoriano de V 141 *Venez.*

"Víctor Gálvez" (*pseud.*) *see* Quesada, Vicente G.

"Víctor Heim" (*pseud.*) *see* Márquez, Antonio José

Victorero, Miguel María A 68 *Arg.*

Victoria, Juan Cheri PD 219; SD 31 *Dom.*

Victoria, Marcos A 68 *Arg.*

Victoria Jaén, Nicolás (1862-) Pan 20 *Pan.*

Victorica, Ricardo A 68 *Arg.*

Vicuña, Alejandro C 57 *Chil.*

Vicuña, Ángel Custodio C 57 *Chil.*

Vicuña Cifuentes, Julio (1865-1936) APEH 722; BHLA 494, 534; C 42, 57, 71; CL 765; CMPC 8; G 326; PCC xi, 31; SASS 146; WLA 423 *Chil.*

Vicuña Mackenna, Benjamín (1831-1886) BHLA 291, 347; C 23, 59; CHL 283; CL 766; G 326; HC 114; NC 335; PLHA 281; SAL 108; SASS 186 *Chil.*

Vicuña Solar, B. C 42 *Chil.*

Vicuña Subercaseaux, Benjamín C 23, 71; LAND 211; NC 336, 486 *Chil.*

Vidal, Antonio Esteban Cu 174 *Cu.*

Vidal, Camilo U 21 *Uru.*

Vidal, Enrique E. (1894-) A 68, 93 *Arg.*

Vidal, Gonzalo Domingo E 71 *Ecua.*

Vidal, José M. U 21 *Uru.*

Vidal de Battini, Berta Elena (1900-) A 68 *Arg.*

Vidal i Núñez, Valentín PM 84 *Mex.*

Vidal Pita, Nicasio Cu 174 *Cu.*

Vidal V., José Co 80 *Col.*

Vidal y Machado, Miguel BDC 102; Cu 175 *Cu.*

Vidales, Luis (1904-) BHLA 589; Co 80; PLHA 167 *Col.*

Vidarte, Santiago (1828-1848) CHL 499; CLH 439; G 385; PP 60; PR 54 *P.R.*

Vidaurre, Manuel Lorenzo (1772-1841) BHLA 191, 195; P 36 *Per.*

Vidaurreta y Álvarez, Antonio (-1899) Cu 175 *Cu.*

Videla, Oscar C 57 *Chil.*

Videnz, Francisco E 71 *Ecua.*

"Vidriera, Licenciado" (*pseud.*) *see* Cruz Ocampo, Luis D.

Vidrio, Tomás L. ("Fray Tomás") NM 56 *Mex.*

Vieco, Julio Co 80 *Col.*

Viedma, Juan de (1830-1869) Cu 175 *Cu.*

Vieites, Moisés A. Cu 175 *Cu.*

Vieitia, José Manuel Cu 175 *Cu.*

Viejaño, César C 52 *Chil.*

"Viejo Pancho, El" (*pseud.*) *see* Alonso y Trelles, José

Viera, Juan BP 508; PR 28 *P.R.*

Viera Gallo, Antonio C 42 *Chil.*

Viesca, José T. PM 84; TM 375 *Mex.*

Viescas, Ramón HPHA II, 91; PE 271 *Ecua.*

Vieta de Álvarez, P. PR 28 *P.R.*

Vieytes, Juan Hipólito SCL 573 *Arg.*

Vigas, Andrés Jorge V 142 *Venez.*

Vigil, Constancio (hijo) A 68 *Arg.*

Vigil, Constancio C. (1876-) UT 547 *Uru.*

Vigil, Francisco de Paula (1792-1875) BHLA 249 *Per.*

Vigil, José María (1829-1909) HLM 403, 490, 497; HLMex 237; NM 4; PM 84; PMe II, 289; TM 376, 484, 578, 620 *Mex.*

Vigil, Manuel Molina GPCA III, 249 *Hond.*

Vigil y Robles, Guillermo (1867-) G 374; IE 313; Ig 390; NM 56 *Mex.*

Vigil y Robles, José (-1913) Ig 391; NM 57; TM 145, 377 *Mex.*

Vignale, Pedro Juan (1903-) A 68, 72; APAM 581 *Arg.*

Vignier, Rafael PJC 278 *Cu.*

Vignola Mansilla, Julio A 69 *Arg.*

Vigues, Pío J. PC 111 *Chil.*

Vila Barraquet, Miguel Cu 175 *Cu.*

Vila Ortiz, Rubén A 69 *Arg.*

Vilar, Ricardo Arturo AP 315; Pan 20 *Pan.*

Vilarés, Tauler ("Violette Lauset") PJC 256 *Cu.*

Vilches, Pablo A. V 142 *Venez.*

Vilches Vernal, Ernesto C 24 *Chil.*

Villa, Adalberto Adán PJC 277 *Cu.*

Villa, Hermanos TM 377 *Mex.*

Villa, José G. (1850-) CT 441; Cu 175 *Cu.*

Villa, Luis Ángel PN 41 *Nicar.*

Villa, Rafael (-1890) BDC 102; Cu 175 *Cu.*

Villa Gordoa, Jesús (1865-) Ig 391; NM 57 *Mex.*

Villa Gordoa, José Ig 392; NM 57 *Mex.*

Villacorta C., J. Antonio (1879-) IE 314 *Guat.*

Villacreses, Luis Alberto E 71 *Ecua.*

Villademoros, Carlos G. HCLU I, 84; PIU I, 92 *Uru.*

Villaespesa, Francisco TM 505 *Mex.*

Villafañe, Benjamín (1819-) LA VI, 614 *Arg.*

Villafañe, Carlos ("Tic Tac") (1882-   ) Co 80; LC 194; PCo 356; RHLC 153; SASS 237 *Col.*
Villafañe, Jorge A 69 *Arg.*
Villafañe, José Gregorio V 142 *Venez.*
Villafañe, José María (1830-1916) Cu 176 *Cu.*
Villafañe, Justo (-1898) ARC 38; Cu 176 *Cu.*
Villafañe, Segundo J. A 69 *Arg.*
Villafuerte, Eliodoro E 71 *Ecua.*
Villagrá, Gaspar de BHLA 63; CHL 18; CLH 15; HLM 104; HPM 208 *Mex.*
Villagrá, R. Segundo C 57 *Chil.*
Villagrán Bustamante, Eugenio PU 326 *Uru.*
Villagrán Bustamante, Héctor HSLU III, pt 4, 46; U 21 *Uru.*
Villalaz, Carlos E. AP 317; Pan 20 *Pan.*
Villalba, Mariano de Jesús E 72 *Ecua.*
Villalba, Rufino A. Par 25 *Para.*
Villalba B., Carlos M. E 72 *Ecua.*
Villalobos, Arias HPM 206 *Mex.*
Villalobos, Asdrúbal (1890?-   ) CA 53; EPCR 626; FPA 123, 158 *C.R.*
Villalobos, Carlos PB 173 *Bol.*
Villalobos, Joaquín HLM 466; PM 84; TM 377 *Mex.*
Villalobos, José Francisco CA 53, 54; IBCR IV, 237 *et passim* *C.R.*
Villalobos, Manuel M. V 142 *Venez.*
Villalobos, Rosendo (1860-   ) B 22; BT 313; CHL 310; CLH 263; FPA 54, 67; LB 609; PB 17; SASS 100 *Bol.*
Villalobos Reyes, J. Ig 392; NM 57 *Mex.*
Villalón, Raúl CA 54; EPCR 682 *C.R.*
Villalón O., Enrique C 57 *Chil.*
Villalpando, Jesús G 374; PNM 329 *Mex.*
Villamar, Luis F. E 72 *Ecua.*
Villamar, Rafael E 72 *Ecua.*
Villamil, Eucario PM 84 *Mex.*
Villamil, Horacio TM 601 *Mex.*
Villamor, Pedro Pablo de Co 80; HLNG I, 299 *Col.*
Villamor y Armendariz, Manuel C. Ig 393; NM 57 *Mex.*
Villanueva, Agustín Ig 394; NM 57 *Mex.*
Villanueva, Carlos A. V 142 *Venez.*
Villanueva, Carlos Elías PLHA 285; V 142 *Venez.*
Villanueva, Felipe G. TM 613 *Mex.*
Villanueva, Francisco Cu 176 *Cu.*
Villanueva, Laureano ("Un Observador") LV 4; V 107, 142 *Venez.*
Villanueva, Mariano Ig 394; NM 57 *Mex.*
Villanueva, Vicente TM 378 *Mex.*
Villanueva Mata, R. V 142 *Venez.*
Villanueva y Francesconi, Mariano Ig 394; NM 57; TM 378, 484 *Mex.*
Villar, Antonio Amado A 69 *Arg.*
Villar, Henrique Co 80 *Col.*
Villar, Lino Cu 176 *Cu.*
Villar, Lorenzo Cu 176 *Cu.*
Villar, Rafael de Cu 176 *Cu.*
Villar, Ubaldo R. Cu 176; PJC 275 *Cu.*
Villar Buceta, María (1898-   ) APEH 951; BHLA 571; Cu 176; G 342; PCu 315; RLC 367 *Cu.*
Villarán, Acisclo (1841-1927) P 36 *Per.*
Villarán, José Luis P 36 *Per.*

Villarán, Manuel Vicente (1876-   ) P 36 *Per.*
Villarán, Matías P 36 *Per.*
Villarino, María de (1905-   ) A 69 *Arg.*
Villaronga, Luis PR 21 *P.R.*
Villaronga Charriez, J. PR 28, 42 *P.R.*
Villarraza, Juan G. BDC 102; Cu 176 *Cu.*
Villarreal, Enrique TM 379 *Mex.*
Villarreal, Francisco Joaquín de BHC III, 121 *Chil.*
Villarroel, Gaspar de (1587-1665) BHC I, 504 *et passim;* BHLA 96, 123; G 345; HPHA II, 82; PLE 10; SCL 435, 439, 648 *Ecua.*
Villarroel Corvalán, Lorenzo PCh 403 *Chil.*
Villarroel Cruzat, Francisco C 42 *Chil.*
Villarroel Fuenzalida, R. C 57 *Chil.*
Villarronda, Guillermo (1912-   ) PoC 281 *Cu.*
Villasante, José de Cu 176 *Cu.*
Villaseñor, Clemente PM 84; TM 379, 380, 484, 578 *Mex.*
Villaseñor, Eduardo NM 57; TM 380 *Mex.*
Villaseñor, J. Ig 395; NM 57 *Mex.*
Villaseñor, José María PM 84 *Mex.*
Villaseñor, José Victoriano ACe 986 *Mex.*
Villaseñor, Mariano TM 381 *Mex.*
Villaseñor, Pablo HPM 826; NM 57; PM 85; TM 381, 578 *Mex.*
Villaseñor, Roberto Ig 395; NM 57 *Mex.*
Villaseñor y Cervantes, José María ACe 984; HLM 245; PM 85; TM 382 *Mex.*
Villaseñor y Cervantes, Juan Ignacio ACe 984 *Mex.*
Villaseñor y Sánchez, José Antonio HLM 209 *Mex.*
Villaseñor y Villaseñor, Alejandro (1864-1912) Ig 395; NM 57 *Mex.*
Villasmil, Daniel V 142 *Venez.*
Villasmil, David V 142 *Venez.*
Villasmil, José Ramón V 142 *Venez.*
Villatoro, Gustavo TM 578 *Mex.*
Villaurrutia, Antonio de (1755-   ) ACe 1011 *Mex.*
Villaurrutia, Jacobo de (1757-   ) ACe 1011; SD 31 *Dom.*
Villaurrutia, Xavier (1903-   ) AMP 178; APEH 1171, 1195; BHLA 562; HLM 526; NM 57; PM 85; PMM 201; TM 485; WLA 427 *Mex.*
Villaverde, Cirilo (1812-1894) BHLA 224; CHL 442; CLH 383; Cu 176; G 342; HLC 179; RLC 70, 130, 138, 310 *Cu.*
Villaverde, Emilio Cu 178 *Cu.*
Villaverde, José R. Cu 178 *Cu.*
Villaverde, Manuel M. Cu 178 *Cu.*
Villavicencio, César D. E 72 *Ecua.*
Villavicencio, Francisco A. E 76 *Ecua.*
Villavicencio, Modesto (1900-   ) IE 315 *Per.*
Villavicencio, Rafael LV 194; V 142, 143 *Venez.*
Villegas, Emilio C. de Cu 178 *Cu.*
Villegas, Guillermo Tell V 143 *Venez.*
Villegas, Rafael (-1927) CA 54; IBCR IV, 75, 159, 290 *C.R.*
Villegas, Silvio Co 80 *Col.*
Villegas Echeverría, José TM 383 *Mex.*
Villegas Soto, Guillermo CA 54 *C.R.*
Villegas y González, Camilo Co 80 *Col.*

Villegas y Hernández, Juan Antonio Cu 178 *Cu.*

Villén, Juan Manuel Cu 178 *Cu.*

Villena Welsh, Federico S. V 143 *Venez.*

Villenave, Carlos Gustavo Ig 397; NM 57; TM 384 *Mex.*

Villergas, Juan Martínez *see* Martínez Villergas, Juan

Villerías y Roelas, José de (1695-1728) HPM 454; PM 85 *Mex.*

Villiers, Balbina de Cu 178 *Cu.*

Villoch, Federico (1867-) Cu 178; PCu 317; RLC 368 *Cu.*

Villoldo y Bertrán, Julio (1881-) CT 53 *Cu.*

Vinageras, Antonio (1833-1905) BDC 102; Cu 178 *Cu.*

Vincenzi Pacheco, Moisés (1895-) CA 54, 55, 56; EPCR 628; IBCR IV, 181 *et passim;* IE 317; WLA 429 *C.R.*

Vinueza R., Carlos E 72 *Ecua.*

Viñolas, Pedro Cu 179 *Cu.*

Viñuela, Mateo Ricardo E 72 *Ecua.*

"Violeta" (*pseud.*) TM 346 *Mex.*

"Violette Lauset" (*pseud.*) *see* Vilarés, Tauler

Víquez, Pío José (1850-1899) CA 56; EPCR 238; FPA 121, 126; GPCA III, 131; IBCR IV, 38 *et passim* *C.R.*

Víquez Segreda, Juan R. CA 56 *C.R.*

Viramonte, Leonardo S. NM 5; PM 85 *Mex.*

Viscarra, Eufronio (1858-) B 22 *Bol.*

Visillac, Félix B. A 69 *Arg.*

Viso, Julián V 143 *Venez.*

Viteri Lafronte, Aníbal E 72 *Ecua.*

Viteri Lafronte, Homero PLE 93 *Ecua.*

Vitier, Medardo (1886-) Cu 179; LAS 203; RLC 353 *Cu.*

Vittini, Manuel C 24 *Chil.*

Vitureira, Santiago PIU III, 230; U 21 *Uru.*

Vivanco, Diego de BHC I, 487 *Chil.*

Vivar, Julián A 69; LA VIII, 585 *Arg.*

Vivar, Víctor L. E 72; PLE 62 *Ecua.*

Vivas Briceño, Clara V 143 *Venez.*

Vivero, Augusto BDC 103 *Cu.*

Vivero, Domingo de P 37 *Per.*

Vivero, Rodrigo HPM 117 *Mex.*

"Vives Guerra, Julio" (*pseud.*) *see* Velásquez García, José

"Vizardi, Ligio" (*pseud.*) *see* Díaz Ordóñez, Virgilio

Vizcaíno, Julio A. E 72 *Ecua.*

Vizcardo y Guzmán, Pablo (1747-1798) BHLA 133 *Per.*

"Vizconde de Lascano Tegui" (*pseud.*) *see* Lascano Tegui, Emilio

Vólferi, Armando A 69 *Arg.*

Volio, Fernando (1902-) CA 56; EPCR 684 *C.R.*

Volio, Julián (1827-) CA 56; EPCR 25 *C.R.*

Votino, Andrés E 72 *Ecua.*

W

"Waleis, Raúl" (*pseud.*) *see* Varela, Luis Vicente

Walker, Alejandro Co 80 *Col.*

Walker Bravo, Maximino (1855-1900) Pan 20 *Pan.*

Walker Martínez, Carlos (1841-1905) C 42, 57; CHL 256; CLH 217; HC 245; PCh 67; SASS 198 *Chil.*

"Wallas, Jules" (*pseud.*) *see* Valdés, Julio César

Wapnir, Salomón A 69; NM 5 *Arg.*

"War, John S." (*pseud.*) *see* Ravignani, Emilio

"Wast, Hugo" (*pseud.*) *see* Martínez Zuviría, Gustavo Adolfo

Weber y Peinado, Antonio BDC 103; Cu 179 *Cu.*

Weigel Muñoz, Ernesto J. (1859-) AT I, 421 *Arg.*

Weinstock, Lia TM 384 *Mex.*

Weisbach, Alberto T. (1883-) A 69, 93 *Arg.*

Welker, Giselda Zanni HSLU III, pt 6, 44 *Uru.*

Welker, Juan C. HSLU III, pt 6, 42; PIU III, 240; U 21 *Uru.*

Wen Maury, José CG III, 688; PCu 319; PJC 150 *Cu.*

Wendehake, José Rafael (1891-) WLA 430 *Venez.*

Wernicke, Berta A 69 *Arg.*

Wheeler, Guillermo J. A 69 *Arg.*

Whilar, Agustín T. (1856-) P 37 *Per.*

Wiesse, Carlos (1859-) P 37 *Per.*

Wiesse, María P 37 *Per.*

Wilde, Eduardo (1844-1913) A 69; LA VIII, 724; SPLA 247 *Arg.*

Wilde, José Antonio A 69 *Arg.*

"Wili, Matilde Elena" (*pseud.*) A 45 *Arg.*

Wilms Montt, Teresa C 24 *Chil.*

Wilson, Jorge C 58 *Chil.*

Williams, Alberto (1862-) AT I, 65 *Arg.*

Williams, Juan PR 21 *P.R.*

"Willy de Blanck" (*pseud.*) *see* Blanck y Menocal, Guillermo de

Winter, Augusto C 42; PCh 395 *Chil.*

Woodgate de Muñoz, Anita Nieva A 69 *Arg.*

Wright, Francisco Agustín (-1853) LA VI, 888 *Arg.*

Wright de Kleinhans, Laureana TM 579 *Mex.*

Wyld Ospina, Carlos (1891-) FPA 292, 302; IE 318; PG 396; WLA 431 *Guat.*

X

"XXX" (*pseud.*) PR 21 *P.R.*

"Xantipo" (*pseud.*) E 72 *Ecua.*

Xarque, Francisco (1609-1691) LA III, 378 *Arg.*

Xavier de Acha, Francisco de HCLU I, 328 *Uru.*

"Xavier de Baza" (*pseud.*) *see* Prado, Eladio

"Xavier de Ximénez" (*pseud.*) *see* Aguilar, Sinforo *or* Sinforoso

"Xavier Icaza" (*pseud.*) *see* Icaza y López Negrete, Xavier, Jr.

Xenes, Nieves (1859-1915) CHL 489; Cu 179; HLC 166; PA 137; PCu 331; RLC 282 *Cu.*

Xerés, Francisco de *see* Jerez, Francisco de

Ximénez, Rafael (1825-1904) HCLU I, 327 *Uru.*

"Ximénez, Xavier de" (*pseud.*) *see* Aguilar, Sinforo *or* Sinforoso

Ximeno y Cruz, Dolores María de Cu 179 *Cu.*

Xuárez *see* Juárez

Xufré del Águila, Melchor (1568-1637) BHC I, 303; CHL 16; CLH 13; SCL 257, 613 *Chil.*

Y

Yan, Mari G 327 *Chil.*

Yanes, Adela A. de Díaz V 143 *Venez.*

Yanes, Emilio Antonio V 143 *Venez.*

Yánez, Francisco Javier ("Un Venezolano") LV 12; V 100, 141, 143 *Venez.*

Yango, José U 21 *Uru.*

Yankas, Lautaro C 24 *Chil.*

Yáñez, Agustín NM 57 *Mex.*

Yáñez, Álvaro ("Jean Emar") BHLA 622 *Chil.*

Yáñez, Manuel R. P 37 *Per.*

Yáñez Silva, N. A 69, 94; C 24, 58 *Chil.*

Yapuguai, Nicolás Par 25 *Para.*

Ycaza *see also* Icaza

Ycaza, Jorge Enrique de Pan 20 *Pan.*

Ycaza, Rosa Borja de (1889-) WLA 432 *Ecua.*

Ycaza de Briceño, María Magdalena de Pan 20 *Pan.*

"Ycpac" (*pseud.*) TM 346 *Mex.*

Ycua Barbat de Muñoz, M. C. U 21 *Uru.*

Yepes, José Ramón (1822-1881) AEHA 912; BHLA 326; CHL 364; CLH 313; FPA 550, 566; LV 136, 275; SASS 507; V 143, 144; VPF 34 *Venez.*

Yepes, Ramón de E 72 *Ecua.*

Yepes Trujillo, Rafael V 144 *Venez.*

Yépez, Domingo E 76 *Ecua.*

Yépez, José Ramón V 144 *Venez.*

Yerovi, Agustín L. (-1903) E 72 *Ecua.*

Yerovi, Leónidas BAP 19; BHLA 551; CHL 306; CLH 260; LP 390; PLHA 157; PPe 301 *Per.*

Yglesias Ogan, Rubén CA 56 *C.R.*

Ylla Moreno, Juan José U 21 *Uru.*

Ynnes González, Eduardo V 144 *Venez.*

Ynsfrán, Pablo Maximiliano (1894-) FPA 402, 427; Par 2, 19, 25; PPa 209; PT 89 *Para.*

"Yolanda" (*pseud.*) *see* Mariño de Riverón, Adelina

Yordán, Manuel N. PR 41 *P.R.*

"Yoyo" (*pseud.*) *see* Quirós Blanco, Teodoro

Ypuche, Pedro Leandro U 21 *Uru.*

Yumet Méndez, José BP 541; PR 41 *P.R.*

"Yumurí, Hija del" (*pseud.*) *see* Cépero, Belén

Yunque, Álvaro A 69; BHLA 637, 640; LAC 136 *Arg.*

Yupanqui, Titu Cussi *see* Castro, Diego de

Z

Z. B. Co 80 *Col.*

Z., O. Cu 179 *Cu.*

Zabala, Alfonso Rómulo (1884-) WLA 434 *Arg.*

Zabala Muñiz, Justino LU 64, 675 *Uru.*

Zabalía, Félix Alberto de A 70, 94 *Arg.*

"Zacintio, Alidauro" . (*pseud.*) *see* Pérez Salazar y Osorio, Ignacio

Zaconeta, José Víctor (1865-) B 22; BT 323 *Bol.*

Zachrisson, Julio Antonio Pan 20 *Pan.*

Zafra, Antonio Enrique de (-1875) BDC 103; Cu 179 *Cu.*

Zahnémen, Raúl de A 70, 94 *Arg.*

Zahonero, José BP 508; Par 25 *Para.*

Zahonet, Félix R. BDC 104; Cu 180 *Cu.*

"Zalacaín" (*pseud.*) C 24 *Chil.*

Zalamea, Jorge G 332; RHLC 173 *C.R.*

Zalazar, José María HLNG II, 211 *Col.*

Zaldumbide, A. E 72 *Ecua.*

Zaldumbide, Gonzalo (1885-) BHLA 486; E 73; G 345; PLE 83; PLHA 265; SAL 243, 244, 245; SASS 339 *Ecua.*

Zaldumbide, Julio (1833-1887) AEHA 913; BHLA 321; CHL 317; CLH 269; FPA 253, 263; HPHA II, 129; PE 175; PLE 34 *Ecua.*

"Zalogón Diza Deñarca Americano" (*pseud.*) TM 346 *Mex.*

Zalles, Luis (1832-1896) B 22 *Bol.*

Zamacois, Eduardo (1873-) BDC 105 *Cu.*

Zamacois, Manuel María TM 386 *Mex.*

Zamacois, Niceto de NM 58; TM 385 *Mex.*

Zamacola, Juan Domingo de SCL 516, 649 *Per.*

Zambrana, Antonio (1846-1922) CA 57; Cu 180; IBCR IV, 16 *et passim*; RLC 71, 137, 139, 227, 229 *Cu.*

Zambrana, Florián (1864-) B 22 *Bol.*

Zambrana, Ramón (1817-1866) CHL 453; CLH 395; Cu 181; HPHA I, 286; PCu 337; RLC 219, 243 *Cu.*

Zambrano, Esperanza PM 85 *Mex.*

Zamora, Alonso de (1660-) Co 80; HLNG I, 278; LC 84; RHLC 15; SCL 213, 375, 649; V 144 *Col.*

Zamora, Antonio G. ("Almanzor") (1868-) Cu 10, 181 *Cu.*

Zamora, B. de C 58 *Chil.*

Zamora, Francisco NL 14 *Nicar.*

Zamora, Hernán CA 57; EPCR 630 *C.R.*

Zamora, José G. PM 85 *Mex.*

Zamora, José Manuel G. Cu 181 *Cu.*

Zamora, José María Co 80 *Col.*

Zamora, José Narciso BDC 105; Cu 181 *Cu.*

Zamora, Luis A. (1879-) G 327; PCh 285 *Chil.*

Zamora, María Amalia (1905-) A 70 *Arg.*

Zamora, Santiago (1670-) HPM 456 *Mex.*

Zamora de Adalid, Laurencio C 24; NC 500 *Chil.*

Zamora Elizondo, Hernán CA 57; IBCR IV, 326 *C.R.*

Zamora y Caballero, Eduardo Cu 181 *Cu.*

Zamorano, Mario CA 57 *C.R.*

Zamudio, Adela ("Soledad") (1854-1928) A 70; B 22; BT 331; FPA 53, 59; LB 612; PB 175 *Bol.*

Zamudio, Everardo F. E. Ig 397; NM 58 *Mex.*

Zamudio-Ballivian, L. (-1918) PB 204 *Bol.*

Zamudio Miguel, Enrique C 42 *Chil.*

Zanelli López, Luisa C 71; CL 767 *Chil.*

Zañartu, Manuel Arístides C 24; NC 350 *Chil.*

Zañartu, Sady C 24; LAS 203 *Chil.*

Zapata, Marcos E 73 *Ecua.*

Zapata, Ramón Co 80 *Col.*

Zapata, Rosaura Ig 398; NM 58 *Mex.*

Zapata Lillo, Francisco C 24, 42 *Chil.*

Zapata Quesada, René A 70; APAM 429 *Arg.*

Zapiola, Eduardo O. A 70; NM 5 *Arg.*

Zapiola, José (1802-1885) C 24; CHL 285; CLH 242; HC 200; NC 487 *Chil.*

Zara, Eliado V 144 *Venez.*

Zaragoza, Antonio (1855-1910) G 374; PM 85; PMe II, 291 *Mex.*

Zaragoza y Escobar, Antonio (1827-1914) Cu 181 *Cu.*

Zarama, Daniel Co 80 *Col.*

Zárate, Agustín de LA III, 295; SCL 76, 328, 649 *Arg.*

Zárate, Eduardo E. (1853-1913) Ig 399; NM 58; PMe II, 299 *Mex.*

Zárate, Fernando de TM 387 *Mex.*

Zárate, Julio HLM 490 *Mex.*

Zárate, Luis G. HPM 477 *Mex.*

Zárate, Miguel TM 387 *Mex.*

Zárate y Ruiz, Francisco Ig 400; NM 58 *Mex.*

Zarco, Francisco (1829-1869) HLM 358, 361; HLMex 189; HPM 837 *Mex.*

Zárraga, Miguel de (1882-) Cu 181 *Cu.*

Zárraga y Heredia, Juana V 144 *Venez.*

Zarranz Beltrán, Félix Cu 181 *Cu.*

Zarrilli, Humberto PIU III, 223; U 21 *Uru.*

Zarzamendi, M. M. Ig 400; NM 58 *Mex.*

Zavala, Álvaro TM 601 *Mex.*

Zavala, Antonio TM 387 *Mex.*

Zavala, Francisco J. PM 85 *Mex.*

Zavala, Jesús APMM 220; PM 52, 85 *Mex.*

Zavala, Lorenzo de (1788-1836) HLM 351; HLMex 141 *Mex.*

Zavala Muniz, Justino HSLU II, pt 6, 8; PIU III, 256 *Uru.*

Zavalía Matienzo, Roberto A 70 *Arg.*

Zayas, Alfredo (1861-) RLC 243, 271, 346, 350 *Cu.*

Zayas, Fernando de Cu 181; PCu 341 *Cu.*

Zayas, José María Cu 182 *Cu.*

Zayas Bazán, Ambrosio de RLC 30 *Cu.*

Zayas Bazán, Laura G. de BDC 106 *Cu.*

Zayas Enríquez, Rafael de (1848-1932) AMP 283; CHL 420; CLH 365; HLM 457, 467; Ig 401; NM 58; PM 85; PMe II, 305; TM 388 *Mex.*

Zayas Guarderas, Pablo E 73 *Ecua.*

Zayas Guarneros, Pablo (1831-1902) HLM 457; Ig 401; NM 58 *Mex.*

Zayas y Alfonso, Alfredo (1861-) CT 377 *Cu.*

Zayat, Antonio V 144 *Venez.*

Zayat, Antoun V 144 *Venez.*

"Zea, Fernando Jules" (*pseud.*) see Alú Fernández, José

Zea, Francisco Antonio (1766-1822) BHLA 156; Co 80; HLNG II, 59 *et passim*; LC 104; RHLC 51; SCL 540, 649; V 144 *Col.*

Zea Uribe, Luis (1872-) Co 80 *Col.*

Zeballos, Estanislao Severo (1854-1923) A 70, 72; G 319; GLO 238 *Arg.*

Zegarra Ballón, Edilberto (1869-) P 37; WLA 435 *Per.*

Zegrí, Armando C 24, 42 *Chil.*

Zeitlin, Israel ("César Tiempo") A 70, 72, 78; G 319; LAC 150 *Arg.*

Zelaa e Hidalgo, José María ACe 988 *Mex.*

Zelaya, Alfonso Guillén WH 188 *Hond.*

Zelaya, Jerónimo (1835-) HL I, 591 *Hond.*

Zelaya, José María (188.-) FPA 358, 377 *Nicar.*

Zelaya, Juan José A 70 *Arg.*

Zelaya, Ramón (1873-) CA 58; EPCR 369; IBCR IV, 162 *C.R.*

Zelaya C., Antonio CA 57, 58 *C.R.*

Zeledón, José María ("Billo") (1875?-) CA 58, 59; EPCR 376; FPA 122, 135; PC 73 *C.R.*

Zell, Rosa Hilda (1910-) PoC 284 *Cu.*

Zéndegui, Gabriel Cu 182; GLO 246 *Cu.*

Zendejas, Josefina PM 85 *Mex.*

Zenea, Juan Clemente ("Adolfo de la Azucena") (1832-1871) AEHA 870; BDC 106; BHLA 330; CHL 468; CLH 409; Cu 15, 182; FPA 162, 176; G 342; GLO 246; HLC 149; HPHA I, 275; PA 140; PCu 343; RLC 191, 212 *et passim*; SAL 137; SASS 276 *Cu.*

Zenner, Wally A 70 *Arg.*

Zeno, Francisco M. (1886-) QPR (1) 174 *P.R.*

Zeno Gandía, Manuel (1855-1930) BP 508, 642; PA 198; PP 120; PR 28, 41, 56 *P.R.*

Zentella, Arcadio (1844-1920) Ig 403; NM 58; PM 85 *Mex.*

Zepeda, Anastasio PM 85 *Mex.*

Zepeda, Jorge Federico G 347; LAS 207; PS 284 *Salv.*

Zepeda Winkfield, Alfonso PM 86 *Mex.*

Zequeira, Trinidad de Cu 182 *Cu.*

Zequeira y Arango, Manuel de (1760-1846) AEHA 913; BDC 108; BHLA 172; CHL 106; CLH 89; Cu 182; G 342; HLC 28; HPHA I, 224; RLC 47, 49 *Cu.*

Zequeira y Caro, Manuel de BDC 108; Cu 183 *Cu.*

Zerbino, Julio B 23 *Bol.*

Zerda, Liborio (1833-) Co 80; LC 174 *Col.*

Zérega-Fombona, Alberto PLHA 268; V 144 *Venez.*

"Zerep" (*pseud.*) see Pérez Cabello, Rafael

Zerpa, Víctor Antonio V 144 *Venez.*

Zeyer, Julio C 24 *Chil.*

Zierold, Pablo TM 485 *Mex.*

Zinny, Antonio A 70, 73; LA VI, 1079; Par 2

"Zöell, R. P." (*pseud.*) see Prellezo, José M.

"Zoraida Díaz de Escobar" (*pseud.*) see Díaz de Ross *or* de Schtronn, Zoraida

Zorrilla, Braulio José PM 86 *Mex.*
Zorrilla, Enrique PA 248; PP 288 *P.R.*
Zorrilla, José LV 30; V 75 *Venez.*
Zorrilla, Manuel Marcos A 70; LA VIII, 591 *Arg.*
Zorrilla de San Martín, Antonio PU 327 *Uru.*
Zorrilla de San Martín, Juan (1855-1931) AB 25; AEHA 875; BHLA 422; CHL 219; CLH 182; FPA 527, 529; G 390; GLO 255; HSLU I, pt 3, 5; LU 64, 660; LUr 473; PIU I, 251; PLHA 73; SA 151; SASS 455; U 21; UL 193; UT 567 *Uru.*
Zouroff, Vera C 24 *Chil.*
Zubieta, Pedro A. Co 80 *Col.*
Zubillaga, Juan Antonio (1870-) HSLU III, pt 4, 47; U 22; UL 194; UT 571; WLA 436 *Uru.*
Zucchi, Amanda A 70 *Arg.*
"Zulema" (*pseud.*) *see* Castell de López Rocha, Adela
Zulen, Dora Mayer de WLA 436 *Per.*
Zulen, Pedro S. SAL 299 *Per.*
Zuleta, Alberto P 37 *Per.*
Zuleta, Eduardo (1864-) Co 80; RHLC 190; V 144 *Col.*
"Zulima" (*pseud.*) *see* López, Lina
Zuloaga, Daniel Co 80 *Col.*
Zuloaga, Eugenio (hijo) V 145 *Venez.*
Zuloaga, Mariano Co 80 *Col.*
Zuloaga, Nicomedes V 145 *Venez.*
Zum Felde, Alberto (1888-) BHLA 492; HSLU III, pt 4, 44; LAS 207; LU 64, 682; PIU III, 321; PU 240; U 22; UT 575; WLA 437 *Uru.*

Zum Felde, Carlos ("Carlos al Campo") HSLU II, pt 2, 14; U 22 *Uru.*
Zumárraga, Juan de CHL 5; CLH 5; HLMex 27; HPHA I, 23 *Mex.*
Zumaya, Manuel HLM 187; HPM 451; TM 388, 613 *Mex.*
Zumbado, Marco A. CA 59; EPCR 686 *C.R.*
Zumeta, César CHL 382; CLH 333; LV 421; PLHA 258; V 145 *Venez.*
Zunino Chacón, M. Teresa C 24, 42 *Chil.*
Zúñiga, Adolfo (1835-) HL I, 357 *Hond.*
Zúñiga, Ana HPM 455 *Mex.*
Zúñiga, Antonio R. A 70 *Arg.*
Zúñiga, Federico PCh 225 *Chil.*
Zúñiga, Horacio PM 86 *Mex.*
Zúñiga, J. I. (1915-) PoC 286 *Cu.*
Zúñiga, José Hilarión ACe 989 *Mex.*
Zúñiga, Pablo Co 80 *Col.*
Zúñiga Montúfar, María CA 59 *C.R.*
Zúñiga Montúfar, Tobías CA 59; EPCR 509 *C.R.*
Zúñiga Portillo, Luis Andrés (1880-) FPA 318, 329; WH 188; WLA 437 *Hond.*
Zúñiga y Tejeda, Arcadio TM 389 *Mex.*
"Zurriaga, Joaquín de" (*pseud.*) *see* Runken, J. E.
Zuviría, Facundo (1793-1861) LA VI, 861 *Arg.*
Zuviría, José María (1830-) A 70; LA VIII, 595 *Arg.*

Key to Symbols for Titles of Books on Spanish American Literature Referred to in This Index

A   Coester, Alfred. A Tentative Bibliography of the Belles-Lettres of the Argentine Republic. Cambridge, Harvard University Press, 1933.

AA   Ghiraldo, Alberto. Antología americana. Madrid, Renacimiento, Volume II, 1923.

AB   James, Concha Romero. An Annotated Bibliography of Latin-American Literature. Pan American Union. Washington.

AC   Isaza, Emiliano. Antología colombiana. Paris, Bouret, 1911. 2 volumes.

ACe   Urbina, Luis G., Pedro Henríquez Ureña and Nicolás Rangel. Antología del centenario. México, Imp. Manuel León Sánchez, 1910. 2 volumes.

AEHA   Sánchez, José Rogerio. Autores españoles e hispano-americanos. Madrid, Perlado, Páez y Ca., 1911.

ALC   García Prada, Carlos. Antología de líricos colombianos. Bogotá, Imprenta Nacional, 1936. 2 volumes.

AMP   Underwood, Edna Worthley. Anthology of Mexican Poets. Portland, Maine, Mosher Press, 1932.

AP   Korsi, Demetrio. Antología de Panamá. Barcelona, Edit. Maucci, 1926.

APA   Puig, Juan de la C. Antología de poetas argentinos. Buenos Aires, Martín Biedma é hijo, 1910.

APAM   Noé, Julio. Antología de la poesía argentina moderna, (1900-1925). Buenos Aires, "Nosotros," 1926.

APEH   Onís y Sánchez, Federico de. Antología de la poesía española e hispano-americana. Madrid, Revista de Filología Española, 1934.

APMM   Antología de poetas modernos de México. México, Tip. Murguía, 1920.

ARC   Trelles, Carlos M. "Bibliografía de autores de la raza de color, de Cuba" in Cuba Contemporánea 43, 1927, pp. 30-78.

AT   Parker, William B. Argentines of Today. New York, Hispanic Society of America, 1920. 2nd edition.

B   Leavitt, Sturgis E. A Tentative Bibliography of Bolivian Literature. Cambridge, Harvard University Press, 1933.

BAMP   Rosenberg, S. L. Millard and Ernest H. Templin. A Brief Anthology of Mexican Prose. Palo Alto, Stanford University Press, 1928.

BAP   Guillén, Alberto. Breve antología peruana. Santiago de Chile, Nascimiento, 1930.

BC   Laverde Amaya, Isidoro. Bibliografía colombiana. Bogotá, Colombia, Imprenta y Librería de Medardo Rivas, 1895.

BDC   Perrier, José Luis. Bibliografía dramática cubana. New York, Phos Press, 1926.

BHC   Medina, José Toribio. Biblioteca hispano-chilena. Santiago de Chile, Imp. de J. T. Medina, 1897-8-9. 3 volumes.

BHLA   Sánchez, Luis Alberto. Breve historia de la literatura americana. Santiago de Chile, Ediciones Ercilla, 1937.

BLN   Biografías de literatos nacionales. Guatemala, Tip. "La Unión," 1889.

BP   Pedreira, Antonio S. Bibliografía puertorriqueña, 1493-1930. Madrid, Hernando, 1932.

BT   Parker, William B. Bolivians of Today. New York, Hispanic Society of America, 1922. 2nd edition.

C   Torres-Ríoseco, Arturo and Raúl Silva-Castro. Ensayo de bibliografía de la literatura chilena. Cambridge, Harvard University Press, 1935.

CA   Doyle, Henry Grattan. A Tentative Bibliography of the Belles-Lettres of the Republics of Central America. Cambridge, Harvard University Press, 1935.

CG   Artigas, Miguel. Catálogo General de la Librería Española e Hispanoamericana. Madrid. Barcelona, Cámaras Oficiales del Libro, 1932. 3 volumes (not finished)

CHL   Coester, Alfred. Historia literaria de la América Española. Madrid, Lib. y Casa Edit. Hernando, 1929.

CL Leavitt, Sturgis E. "Chilean Literature" in Hispanic American Historical Review 5, 1922, pp. 116-43, 274-97, 516-34, 760-76.

CLH Coester, Alfred. Literary History of Spanish America. New York, Macmillan Co., 1916.

CMPC Díaz Arrieta, Hernán. Las cien mejores poesías chilenas. Santiago de Chile, Editorial Zig-Zag, s.a.

Co Leavitt, Sturgis E. and Carlos García-Prada. A Tentative Bibliography of Colombian Literature. Cambridge, Harvard University Press, 1934.

CoL García Samudio, Nicolás. "Columbian Literature" in Bulletin of the Pan American Union 53, 1921, pp. 258-76.

CP Lee, Muna. "Contemporary Spanish-American Poetry" in North American Review 219, 1924, pp. 687-98.

CrA Brenes-Mesén, Roberto. Crítica americana. San José de Costa Rica, Ediciones del Convivio, 1936.

CT Parker, William B. Cubans of Today. New York, Putnam, 1919.

Cu Ford, Jeremiah D. M. and Maxwell I. Raphael. A Bibliography of Cuban Belles-Lettres. Cambridge, Harvard University Press, 1933.

E Rivera, Guillermo. A Tentative Bibliography of the Belles-Lettres of Ecuador. Cambridge, Harvard University Press, 1934.

EPCR Sotela, Rogelio. Escritores y poetas de Costa Rica. San José, Costa Rica, Imp. Lehmann, 1923.

FPA De Vitis, Michael A. Florilegio del parnaso americano. Barcelona, Edit. Maucci, 1927.

G Grismer, Raymond L. A Bibliography of Articles and Essays on the Literatures of Spain and Spanish America. Minneapolis, Perine Book Co., 1935.

GEA Avellaneda, Nicolás. Grandes escritores argentinos. Buenos Aires, El Ateneo, 1927-1928.

GLO Grismer, Raymond L., Joseph E. Lepine and Richard H. Olmsted. A Bibliography of Articles on Spanish Literature. Minneapolis, Burgess Publishing Co., 1933.

GPCA Uriarte, Ramón. Galería poética centro-americana. Guatemala, Tipografía "La Unión," 1888. 3 volumes.

HC Amunátegui Solar, Domingo. Historia de Chile. Santiago, Balcells and Co., 1925.

HCLU Roxlo, Carlos. Historia crítica de la literatura uruguaya. Montevideo, Edit. Barreiro y Ramos, 1912. 2 volumes.

HL Durón, Rómulo E. Honduras literaria. Tegucigalpa, Tipografía Nacional, 1896-1899.

HLA García Velloso, Enrique. Historia de la literatura argentina. Buenos Aires, Ángel Estrada y Cía., s.a.

HLC Salazar y Roig, Salvador. Historia de la literatura cubana. Habana, Imp. Avisador Comercial, 1929.

HLM González Peña, Carlos. Historia de la literatura mexicana. México, 1928.

HLMex Jiménez Rueda, Julio. Historia de la literatura mexicana. México, Ediciones Botas, 1934.

HLNG Vergara y Vergara, José María. Historia de la literatura en Nueva Granada. Bogotá, Edit. Minerva, 1931. 2 volumes.

HPHA Menéndez y Pelayo, Marcelino. Historia de la poesía hispano-americana. Madrid, Librería General de Victoriano Suárez, 1911-1913. 2 volumes.

HPM Pimentel, Francisco. Historia crítica de la poesía en México. México, Secretaría de Fomento, 1892.

HSLU Reyles, Carlos. Historia sintética de la literatura uruguaya. Montevideo, Edit. A. Vila, 1931. 3 volumes.

IBCR Dobles Segreda, Luis. Índice bibliográfico de Costa Rica. San José, Imp. Lehmann, Volume 4. 1930.

IE Velázquez Bringas, Esperanza and Rafael Heliodoro Valle. Índice de escritores. México, Herrero Hermanos Sucesores, 1928.

Ig Iguíniz, Juan B. Bibliografía de novelistas mexicanos. México, 1926.

LA Rojas, Ricardo. La literatura argentina. Buenos Aires, Juan Roldán y Cía., 1924-1925. 8 volumes.

LAC Aita, Antonio. La literatura argentina contemporánea (1900-1930). Buenos Aires, 1931.

LAND García Godoy, Federico. La literatura americana de nuestros días. Madrid, Sociedad Española de Librería, s.a.

LAS Hanke, Lewis. Handbook of Latin-American Studies. Cambridge, Harvard University Press, 1936.

LB Alarcón, Abel. "La literatura boliviana, 1545-1916" in Revue Hispanique 41, 1917, pp. 563-633.

LC   Gómez Restrepo, Antonio. "La literatura colombiana" in Revue Hispanique 43, 1918, pp. 79-204.

LD   García Godoy, Federico. "La literatura dominicana" in Revue Hispanique 37, 1916, pp. 61-104.

LH   Marinello, Juan. Literatura hispanoamericana. México, Ediciones de la Universidad Nacional, 1937.

LP   García Calderón, Ventura. "La literatura peruana, 1535-1914" in Revue Hispanique 31, 1914, pp. 305-91.

LU   Luisi, Luisa. "The Literature of Uruguay" in Bulletin of the Pan American Union 64, July-Dec. 1930, pp. 655-95.

LUr   Barbagaleta, Hugo D. and Ventura García Calderón. "La literatura uruguaya, 1757-1917" in Revue Hispanique 40, 1917, pp. 415-542.

LV   Picón-Febres, Gonzalo. La literatura venezolana en el siglo diez y nueve. Caracas, Imp. "El Cojo," 1906.

MSAP   Craig, G. Dundas. The Modernist Trend in Spanish-American Poetry. Berkeley, University of California Press, 1934.

N   Donoso, Armando. Los nuevos. La joven literatura chilena. Valencia, F. Sempere y Compañía, 1910.

NC   Silva Arriagada, L. Ignacio. La novela en Chile. Santiago de Chile, Imp. "Barcelona," 1910.

NL   Oviedo Reyes, I. Augusto. Nicaragua lírica. Santiago de Chile, Editorial Nascimiento, 1937.

NM   Torres-Ríoseco, Arturo. Bibliografía de la novela mejicana. Cambridge, Harvard University Press, 1933.

NPA   Pedro, Valentín. Nuevo parnaso argentino. Barcelona, Edit. Maucci, s.a.

OA   Donoso, Armando. La otra América. Madrid, Talleres Calpe, 1925.

P   Leavitt, Sturgis E. A Tentative Bibliography of Peruvian Literature. Cambridge, Harvard University Press, 1932.

PA   Bazil, Osvaldo. Parnaso antillano. Barcelona, Edit. Maucci, 1916.

Pan   Doyle, Henry Grattan. A Tentative Bibliography of the Belles-Lettres of Panama. Cambridge, Harvard University Press, 1934.

Par   Raphael, Maxwell I. and J. D. M. Ford. A Tentative Bibliography of Paraguayan Literature. Cambridge, Harvard University Press, 1934.

PB   Blanco Meaño, Luis F. Parnaso boliviano. Barcelona, Edit. Maucci, s.a.

PC   Bolívar Coronado, Rafael. Parnaso costarricense. Barcelona, Edit. Maucci, 1921.

PCC   Solar, Hernán del. Índice de la poesía chilena contemporánea. Santiago de Chile, Ediciones Ercilla, 1937.

PCh   Vera M., Tobías. Parnaso chileno. Barcelona, Edit. Maucci, s.a.

PCo   Caro Grau, Francisco. Parnaso colombiano. Barcelona, Edit. Maucci, 1920.

PCu   Riva Abreu, Valentín. Parnaso cubano. Barcelona, Edit. Maucci, 1926.

PCU   Miranda S., Estela. Algunas poetisas de Chile y Uruguay. Santiago de Chile, Editorial Nascimiento, 1937.

PD   Bazil, Osvaldo. Parnaso dominicano. Barcelona, Edit. Maucci, 1915.

PE   Brissa, José. Parnaso ecuatoriano. Barcelona, Edit. Maucci, s.a.

PG   Porta Mencos, H. Parnaso guatemalteco. Barcelona, Edit. Maucci, 1931.

PIU   Zum Felde, Alberto. Proceso intelectual del Uruguay. Montevideo, Imp. Nacional Colorada, 1930. 3 volumes.

PJC   Báez, Paulino G. Poetas jóvenes cubanos. Barcelona, Edit. Maucci, 1922.

PLHA   Daireaux, Max. Panorama de la littérature hispano-américaine. Paris, Editions KRA, 1930.

PLE   Arias, Augusto. Panorama de la literatura ecuatoriana. Quito, Ecuador, 1936.

PM   Torres-Ríoseco, Arturo and Ralph E. Warner. Bibliografía de la poesía mexicana. Cambridge, Harvard University Press, 1934.

PMe   Esteva, Adalberto A. and José Pablo Rivas. Parnaso mexicano. Barcelona, Edit. Maucci, s.a. 2 volumes.

PMM   Cuesta, Jorge. Antología de la poesía mexicana moderna. México, 1928.

PN   Ortiz, Alberto. Parnaso nicaragüense. Barcelona, Edit. Maucci, s.a.

PNM   Estrada, Genaro. Poetas nuevos de México. México, Porrúa Hermanos, 1916.

PoC   Jiménez, Juan Ramón. La poesía cubana en 1936. La Habana, Institución Hispanocubana de Cultura, 1937.

PoM   Amézaga, Carlos G. Poetas mexicanos. Buenos Aires, P. E. Coní e hijos, 1896.

PoU   Brughetti, Romualdo. 18 Poetas del Uruguay. Montevideo-Buenos Aires, Sociedad Amigos del Libro Rioplatense, 1937.

PP Torres Rivera, Enrique. Parnaso portorriqueño. Barcelona, Edit. Maucci, s.a.

PPa De Vitis, Michael Angelo. Parnaso paraguayo. Barcelona, Edit. Maucci, s.a.

PPe García Calderón, Ventura. Parnaso peruano. Barcelona, Edit. Maucci, s.a.

PR Rivera, Guillermo. A Tentative Bibliography of the Belles-Lettres of Porto Rico. Cambridge, Harvard University Press, 1931.

PS Erazo, Salvador L. Parnaso salvadoreño. Barcelona, Edit. Maucci, s.a.

PT Parker, William B. Paraguayans of Today. New York, Hispanic Society of America, 1921.

PU Artucio Ferreira, Antonia. Parnaso uruguayo (1905-1922). Barcelona, Edit. Maucci, s.a.

QPR (1) Asenjo, Conrado. Quién es Quién en Puerto Rico. San Juan, P. R., Real Hermanos Inc., 1st edit., 1933-1934.

QPR (2) ibid., 2nd edit., 1936-1937.

RHLC Otero Muñoz, Gustavo. Resumen de historia de la literatura colombiana, 1538-1819. Bogotá, Editorial ABC, 1937.

RLC Remos y Rubio, Juan J. Resumen de historia de la literatura cubana. Habana, Tipos Molina y Cía., 1930.

SA García Calderón, Ventura. Semblanzas de América. Madrid, Cervantes, 1920?

SAL Goldberg, Isaac. Studies in Spanish-American Literature. New York, Brentano, 1920.

SASS Holmes, Henry Alfred. Spanish America in Song and Story. New York, Henry Holt and Co., 1932.

SCL Moses, Bernard. Spanish Colonial Literature in South America. New York, Hispanic Society of America, 1922.

SD Waxman, Samuel Montefiore. A Bibliography of the Belles-Lettres of Santo Domingo. Cambridge, Harvard University Press, 1931.

SPLA Morales, Ernesto. El sentimiento popular en la literatura argentina. Buenos Aires, Pedro Garúa, 1926.

TM Monterde, Francisco. Bibliografía del teatro en México. México, Imp. de la Secretaría de Relaciones Exteriores, 1933.

U Coester, Alfred. A Tentative Bibliography of the Belles-Lettres of Uruguayan Literature. Cambridge, Harvard University Press, 1931.

UL Leavitt, Sturgis E. "Uruguayan Literature" in Hispania (Calif.) 5, 1922, pp. 121-32; 186-96.

UT Parker, William B. Uruguayans of Today. New York, Hispanic Society of America, 1921.

V Waxman, Samuel Montefiore. A Bibliography of the Belles-Lettres of Venezuela. Cambridge, Harvard University Press, 1935.

VPF Ratcliff, Dillwyn Fritschel. Venezuelan Prose Fiction. New York, Instituto de las Españas, 1933.

WH Albir, Francisco José. "Writers of Honduras" in Bulletin of the Pan American Union 49, 1919, pp. 187-90.

WLA Martin, Percy A. Who's Who in Latin America. Palo Alto, Calif., Stanford University Press, 1935.

WSAL Wagner, Max Leopold. Die spanisch-amerikanische Literatur. Leipzig-Berlin, B. G. Teubner, 1924.